REFUSING
TO BE ENEMIES

May 9, 2011
Friends' Center

Marina Kaufman Lauster

REFUSING TO BE ENEMIES

Palestinian and Israeli
Nonviolent Resistance to
the Israeli Occupation

MAXINE KAUFMAN-LACUSTA
With a foreword by Ursula Franklin

REFUSING TO BE ENEMIES
Palestinian and Israeli Nonviolent Resistance to the Israeli Occupation

Published by
Ithaca Press
8 Southern Court
South Street
Reading
RG1 4QS
UK

www.ithacapress.co.uk

Ithaca Press is an imprint of Garnet Publishing Limited.

Paperback edition

ISBN: 978-0-86372-380-3

British Library Cataloguing-in-Publication Data
A catalogue record for this book is available from the British Library

Foreword by Ursula Franklin
Jacket design by Garnet Publishing
(photo by Maxine Kaufman-Lacusta)

Printed and bound in Lebanon by International Press:
interpress@int-press.com

CONTENTS

PART III
LOOKING FORWARD

PART IV
ANALYSIS

FOREWORD

Ursula Franklin

This is an important book. Its significance goes well beyond the task of documenting a greatly underestimated facet of the present tragic struggle in Israel/Palestine.

Embedded in the chronicle of remarkable people and events, readers will discover the emerging characteristics of nonviolent responses to strife and injustice in a technological world. Each activity documented in this book is not only an account of a specific event or situation, but also an illustration of an often novel and significant development within global patterns of nonviolent strategies.

To help readers to appreciate both the general and the specific attributes of nonviolent activities is not an easy task, particularly in the binary mindset of the current political discourse with its "yes or no," "in or out," "ally or adversary" modes.

To begin with, there is genius as well as problematique in the very term nonviolence. Resisting force and changing power structures by ways and means that are defined by what they are NOT seems to be vague and indecisive at best. However, nonviolent approaches provide, and have provided, some of the most creative, helpful and lasting social changes, often because the approaches have been situational, site specific, and grown out of practice and have mixed ordinary life skills with extra-ordinary unconventionality.

It has been pointed out frequently[1] that, throughout human history, nonviolent conduct is the normal and expected pattern of social interactions; cooperation and recognition of the needs of others are the given and for this very reason, it is the violent response, the abnormal, that is recorded, analyzed and taught (see also Kuttab later in the book).

What, then, do we mean when we speak of nonviolence? At this point, attention to definitions may be helpful.

In terms of the issues addressed in *Refusing to be Enemies,* "violence" is most usefully defined as "resourcelessness," surprising as it may sound. Yet reliance on one single resource; i.e., the ability to destroy, to inflict harm, is in the final analysis the most telling attribute of violence.

Organized violence—armed force—is frequently the preferred tool of the powerful. It seems so straightforward: nothing more than the translation into daily reality of a threat, "Do as I say, or else ..." when "or else ..." means inflicting destruction, harm and hurt.

While the powerful can command many resources other than force and sophisticated systems of inflicting harm, the oppressed, the powerless, cannot. They may have exhausted the resources within their reach and may therefore fall back on violence from a genuine feeling of being deprived of other resources to address their needs.

Once we recognize violence as resourcelessness—by choice or by perceived necessity—the nature of "nonviolence as resourcefulness" comes into focus. The belief in and the respect for a common human creativity and worth become the resource base from which nonviolent actions can arise. The understanding of nonviolence as resourcefulness thus provides a guide for the mobilization of human and social resources but not a template.

It is my hope that the foregoing thoughts and definitions will illuminate the universal components that link the nonviolent actions documented in this "case book" to past and future nonviolent responses.

Ours is a complex global society, in which unforeseen and unforeseeable instruments of power, control and interaction are emerging at rapid rates. These new power structures are frequently superimposed on traditional arrangements and habits of political and social conduct. Such new developments, often related to modernization and globalization, are altering individual and collective behaviours and a society's sense of belonging and responsibility.

These new features of our interdependent global world are shaping the nature and the conduct of conflicts. On the one hand, the range, force and sophistication of violent actions have increased beyond imagination; on the other hand, the same modern technologies have increased the flow of information, of goods and people, obliterating many physical, legal and emotional boundaries, often the very boundaries that have previously confined the range of organized violence.

New reasons for conflicts, be they military or civilian, commercial or ideological, have arisen as a consequence of the ascendance of technological societies. These conflicts, in turn, are often characterized by very different patterns of conflict resolution and altered notions of territory and boundaries. Yet the ancient notion of "The Enemy" has remained part of the modern world's social and political paraphernalia.

As a category, "the enemy" is significantly different from seemingly related social classifications such as "foreigner," "stranger" or persons "from away." Assigning the designation "enemy" to some people goes well beyond emphasizing a distinction between "them" and "us." The enemy label becomes a coordinate that places and defines the holder within the realm of an existing or implied conflict.

As a class, enemies are deemed to be intrinsically hostile to one party in the conflict, regardless of personal conduct or conviction, merely by virtue of their belonging to a particular group. Kenneth Boulding, in *Conflict and Defense,*[2] defines parties in conflict as "Behavioral Units." Members of such units—nation-states or clans, organizations or churches—are assumed to exhibit the same behaviour with respect to a conflict that impacts them.

Boulding's definition is applicable to principled as well as more casual situations. Thus pacifists expect conflict when they refuse military service; vegetarians may risk social discord when declining to eat meat at a party. Both pacifists and vegetarians choose their respective behavioural units, often in full knowledge of possible conflicts. The designation of "enemy," however, is not self-selected. It is a label bestowed by the opponent.

Moving one's adversaries into the enemy class can be politically helpful. To quote Boulding again, "[A] strong enemy is a great unifying force; in the face of a common threat and the overriding common purpose of victory or survival, the diverse ends and conflicting interests of the population fall into the background and are swallowed up into the single, measurable, overriding end of winning the conflict."

Not only can the presence of "enemies" serve as social glue, their presumed evil intent and unbending hostility can become the justification for otherwise unacceptable actions against them. Once one appreciates the deep social roots of the concept of "The Enemy," it becomes clear that, for individual citizens, refusing to be enemies is a profoundly political act. This act denies the ruling apparatus of all groups involved in a particular conflict the right to label and assign individuals to a particular behavioural unit.

I can not overemphasize the importance of this act. It entails the crucial paradigm shift that can break the stranglehold of violence and open the option of nonviolent action. Nonviolence, after all, is not a bag of tricks to be pulled out if or when violent responses are not possible. Nonviolence is a set of collective insights that, by calling on the human potential of victim and perpetrator alike, opens ways to oppose violence and oppression that are different in kind from the blind tit-for-tat of organized violence.

The events recounted and ideas articulated in this book make it clear that nonviolent strategies are not soft or mushy. Their hard political edge is clear and visible. The goal of the interventions is to decrease suffering and to achieve justice, BUT the changed situations can only be lasting and functional if they assure justice for all. This means that the transformations that specific nonviolent interventions try to achieve must, in the end, yield systemic changes. Those on the ground who constitute the nonviolent movements know this, as they develop their visions of human betterment—to use Boulding's term.

Bertolt Brecht was part of the struggle against the rise of fascism and the rising tide of violence in his time. He wrote in 1935, well before the birth of most of those whose voices this book has captured, on community responses and on the distinction between help and systemic change.

What End Goodness[3]
Bertolt Brecht, translated by Scott Horton

> 1. *To what end goodness*
> *If the good are immediately struck down, or those*
> *To whom they are good*
> *Are struck down?*
>
> *To what end freedom*
> *If the free are forced to live among the unfree?*
>
> *To what end reason*
> *If only stupidity puts the bread on the table*
> *That each of us needs?*

2. *Instead of just being good, make an effort*
   To create the conditions that make goodness possible,
   And better still
   That make it superfluous!

   Instead of just being free, make an effort
   To create the conditions that liberate us all,
   And that make the love of freedom
   Superfluous!

   Instead of just being sensible, make an effort
   To create the conditions that make the stupidity of the individual
   Into a bad deal!

Were he with us today, Brecht would convey his friendship and respect to those whose actions and thoughts this book records. He would be grateful for their courage and creativity as they explore the resource base of nonviolence. He would see, as I do, the bridge across space and time built by all those who, in refusing be enemies, try to build for all a livable world.

As I said at the onset of this foreword, this is an important book. May it be well read.

NOTES

1 Sibley, Mulford Q., ed. 1963. *The Quiet Battle.* Garden City, NY: Anchor Books, Doubleday & Company.
2 Boulding, K. E. 1963. *Conflict and Defense.* New York: Harper and Row.
3 Brecht, Bertolt. 1935. "Was nützt die Güte," in *Gesammelte Werke*, Vol. 4, p. 553.

ACKNOWLEDGEMENTS

I want to express my gratitude and appreciation to the many people who have inspired and supported me in this project. My thanks especially to Ursula Franklin and the contributing authors, as well as the hundred-plus interviewees for this book—including those who, for reasons of space or difficulties with translation, or because their comments somehow fell outside the arbitrary parameters of the present book, were not included: Anton Mura, youth worker at the AEI, Dr Mahmoud Nasr and Dr Abu Hani of Nablus Health Care Committee, Eileen Kuttab of Birzeit University Women's Studies Department, Hava Keller of Women for Women Political Prisoners and Windows, Hisham Jamjoum of ISM, Arabiya Shawamreh and Nada B'dou, Beate Zilversmidt, David Nir, and Edy Kaufman.

This book would not have been written, or probably even conceived of, were it not for the many activists who gave willingly of their time and insights for earlier projects—*Creative Resistance* (1993) and before that, *Curse Not the Darkness*, "the book that never was," for which I interviewed several dozen activists in the mid-eighties. Many of these early interviewees became friends and colleagues, some appear in the present book, and all of them have been an ongoing source of inspiration. Some appear, as well, in *Israeliens et Palestiniens: Les Mille et Une Voix de la Paix,* by Danielle Storper-Perez (Cerf, 1993). My thanks to Danielle for treating me as a colleague and including me in her project, despite my mismatched academic background.

I owe a particular debt of gratitude to several people who believed in my ability to get this book written, and encouraged me even when I doubted myself: Reed Malcolm, who gave me encouragement even while gently rejecting a very early draft manuscript; Kevin Burns, who suggested I approach Ursula Franklin to write a foreword and clued me in to ways to articulate some of my own interpretations of the material; Maia Carter Hallward, whose invitation to participate in her panel on Identity Politics and the Boundaries of Israel and Palestine at the 2007 annual meeting of the Middle East Studies Association (MESA) pushed me to write the paper that provided the basis for my conclusions and epilogue; and activist-academic Denise Nadeau who goaded me to choose a title and encouraged me to join Maia's panel despite my lack of academic credentials in the field. My thanks, too, to the *Palestine-Israel Journal of Politics, Economics and Culture* for allowing me to reproduce in this book a number of ideas and suggestions that were first published in PIJ (Kaufman-Lacusta 2008) in an article based on the MESA paper, and to the Canadian Friends Service Committee for grants towards my travel to Israel and Palestine on two occasions.

Jeff Halper deserves special mention. Besides being an eminently quotable interviewee and speaker, and sharing his analysis and strategic thinking in a contributed chapter, he also helped me enormously in deciding how to arrange the material, and provided invaluable feedback at various stages.

I'd also like to thank Dan Nunn, my editor at Ithaca Press, who provided expert and knowledgeable editorial guidance with a gentle hand that took much of the pain out of the difficult necessity of extensive cuts to the original overly long manuscript. His flexibility and patience have made him a joy to work with.

I'd like to dedicate this book to the memory of my dad, Jack Kaufman, for the example of his sense of social justice and of the need to do more than just talk about it, and to some wonderful people who did not live to be interviewed for it: Yochanan Lorwin of the Alternative Information Center, Mary Khas of the AFSC preschool program in Gaza City, Arna Mer Khamis of Care and Learning in Jenin, Shlomo Elbaz of The East for Peace, and Toma Šik of PINV and WRI and much more.

Last, but definitely not least, I want to thank my loving and supportive husband, Michael, whose suggestions for radical rearrangements, although invariably greeted with stubborn resistance on my part, almost always resulted in significant improvements to the book.

ABOUT THE CONTRIBUTORS

Ghassan Andoni is a long-time nonviolent activist and academic (Physics) at Birzeit University. An active participant in the Beit Sahour tax strike during the First Intifada, he co-founded the Palestinian Center for Rapprochement between People (1988) and the International Solidarity Movement (2001), as well as the Alternative Tourism Group and the Applied Research Institute – Jerusalem. Recent writings include "A Comparative Study of Intifada 1987 and Intifada 2000" in Roane Carey (ed.), *The New Intifada: Resisting Israel's Apartheid* (Verso Books, 2001), and (with Renad Qubbaj, George N. Rishmawi, and Thom Saffold) a chapter on International Solidarity in Stohlman and Aladin, *Live from Palestine: International and Palestinian Direct Action Against the Israeli Occupation* (South End Press, 2003). He was also part of the editorial team for Sandercock, et al., *Peace Under Fire: Israel/Palestine and the International Solidarity Movement* (Verso, 2004).

Ursula Franklin was the first woman professor in the Department of Metallurgy and Materials Science at the University of Toronto (1967) and the first woman to be named University Professor (1984), the highest honour given by that institution (now Emerita). She is a long-time member of Canadian Voice of Women for Peace and is one of Canada's foremost advocates and practitioners of pacifism. Franklin continues to work for peace and social justice, to actively encourage young women to pursue careers in science, and to speak and write on the social impacts of science and technology. She is the author of *The Real World of Technology* (1990, revised 1999), based on her 1989 Massey Lectures on the subject. Her most recent book is *The Ursula Franklin Reader: Pacifism as a Map* (Between the Lines, 2006).

Jeff Halper is coordinator of the Israeli Committee Against House Demolitions (ICAHD) and a professor of Anthropology. He moved to Israel in 1973 from the United States and was employed by the Jerusalem municipality for more than a decade, as a community worker in poor *Mizrahi* Jewish neighbourhoods. He also served as the chairman of the Israeli Committee for Ethiopian Jews. Halper has taught at universities both in Israel and abroad, including Friends World College—teaching at FWC centres in Jerusalem, Costa Rica, and Kenya and directing the Friends World Program at Long Island University, in New York State in 1991–93. He is the author of (*inter alia*) *Obstacles to Peace*, a resource manual of articles and maps on the Israeli/Palestinian conflict published by ICAHD, and *An Israeli in Palestine: Resisting Dispossession, Redeeming Israel* (Pluto Press, 2008).

Ghassan Andoni and Jeff Halper were jointly nominated for the 2006 Nobel Peace Prize by the American Friends Service Committee.

Maxine Kaufman-Lacusta is a Quaker-Jewish activist who lived in Jerusalem for seven years (1988–95), during which time she participated in a variety of anti-occupation and solidarity groups, with a particular concern for the practice and promotion of active nonviolence and joint Israeli-Palestinian endeavours. A founding member of the Action Committee for the Jahalin Tribe (ACJT) and a participant in the Hebron Solidarity Committee, Maxine was also part of a small collective that offered nonviolence training workshops during the early and mid-nineties attended by Jewish, Palestinian, and Druze activists in Israel, as well as one for the ACJT. She served a total of twelve years on the Canadian Friends Service Committee and is currently an associate member for Middle East projects. She stands with Vancouver Women in Black and has published a number of articles on Palestinian and Israeli nonviolent activism and related topics.

Jonathan Kuttab has practiced law in Palestine, Israel, and New York State. His activism spans the realms of human rights, social, and church advocacy, and he has written and lectured extensively. He was a founder of Al Haq (the first human rights organization in the occupied territories), the Mandela Institute for Political Prisoners, the Palestinian Center for the Study of Nonviolence in Jerusalem, and Human Rights Information and Documentation Systems (HURIDOCS), Switzerland, and remains active in many of these, as well as in Nonviolence International and Sabeel-Palestinian Liberation Theology Center. His writing includes co-authorship of *West Bank and the Rule of Law* (ICJ, 1980), and he supervised a team of field workers and researchers who published two book-length reports on the human rights situation in the West Bank: *Punishing a Nation* (LSM/Al Haq, 1988) and *Nation Under Siege* (LSM/Al Haq, 1989).

Starhawk is a committed global justice and peace activist and the author or co-author of ten widely translated books. *Webs of Power: Notes from the Global Uprising*, which won a 2003 Nautilus Award, is a collection of many of her political essays. She made four visits to the occupied territories with the International Solidarity Movement, and essays written on or about those visits can be viewed on the Israel/Palestine page at www.starhawk.org. Starhawk offers training in nonviolent direct action and permaculture, a system of ecological design, internationally, as well as workshops on feminist and earth-based spirituality. On March 16, 2008, she was refused entry to Israel while on her way to Palestine to give a permaculture workshop.

INTRODUCTION

In 1993, while working as a Hebrew-to-English translator in the Jerusalem office of the Alternative Information Center (AIC), I compiled *Creative Resistance*, a short, interview-based book describing examples of nonviolent action by Israeli and joint Israeli-Palestinian groups. *Creative Resistance* was published by the AIC, itself a joint Israeli-Palestinian venture, and its target audience was Israeli and Palestinian peace/justice/ human rights activists. In those days, few activists in either Israel or Palestine used the word "nonviolence" or thought of their actions in such terms. Indeed, many assumed that nonviolence was by definition passive. My not-so-hidden agenda at that time was, on the one hand—in that pre-email era—to encourage greater sharing of information amongst groups and organizations that were engaged in activity that I (though not necessarily they) would define as "active nonviolent resistance" and, on the other hand, to perhaps contribute to an increased acceptance of the concept of nonviolent action on the part of people who were already practicing it, along with an appreciation of its potential and a sense of connection to the world-wide nonviolent resistance movement.

Unlike its predecessor, *Refusing to be Enemies* is not intended primarily for activists. The target audience for *Refusing to be Enemies* is the broader public, much of which is still relatively uninformed on the subject of nonviolent activism in the context of the Israeli-Palestinian conflict and especially regarding its widespread use by Palestinian groups now and in the past. Also new is the present book's elaboration of ways in which Palestinian-Israeli joint activism is pursued as a strategy for nonviolent resistance to the Israeli occupation, and its focus on attitudes towards the dynamics of, and the prospects for the future of, this form of struggle.

The interviews that make up the "meat" of this book took place, with a few exceptions, during three visits to Israel/Palestine, in September/October 2003, December 2005/January 2006, and April 2007.[1] Early on the first trip, I met with my Palestinian editorial partner, Ghassan Andoni, and with George N. Rishmawi, both of the Palestinian

Center for Rapprochement between People (PCR), to formulate a set of interview questions. A week or so later, my Israeli editorial partner, Jeff Halper of the Israeli Committee Against House Demolitions (ICAHD), joined the project and has since given me much invaluable guidance in the shaping and execution of this book. Both Ghassan and Jeff have also contributed—in addition to their interviews and advice—chapters to the Analysis section of this book. Ghassan and George also set up meetings for me with the first of my Palestinian interview subjects.

After just a few days of interviewing, mainly in the West Bank, I was hugely impressed by the number and variety of consciously self-aware nonviolent activists I had met—students and teachers, Muslims and Christians, veteran activists and newcomers to nonviolence, former fighters, those for whom nonviolence was a tactical/strategic choice, and those for whom it was a way of life. Equally heartening was the surprising amount and variety of joint action with Israelis, ranging from the preparation of coexistence and mutual understanding curricula for use in schools in both jurisdictions, through the organization of joint demonstrations and direct actions (removing roadblocks, picking olives, blocking the apartheid wall, etc.), to the tackling of shared environmental concerns together, with the blessing of both Israeli and Palestinian Authority (PA) ministries.

Based on these impressions, I decided that the book should highlight the virtually unknown Palestinian nonviolent movement, rather than give an overview of Palestinian and Israeli nonviolent activism, as had been my original concept. Therefore, in consultation with Ghassan and George, the primary focus of the project was shifted to the immense range and variety of Palestinian nonviolent activism. This meant that, on the whole, I would limit my choice of Israeli interviewees to those who were (or had been) active in the occupied territories or in some other way (such as military refusal), and who had had a direct impact on the struggle to end the occupation and its excesses. As I wrote in my trip diary on September 25, 2003, "[T]he point that we most need to convey with this book has to do with the Palestinians' side of the nonviolence story. The rest of the players are 'supporting cast,' vital as their work may be," and this perspective has informed the project from that point onward.

One outcome of this shift of emphasis was that the subtext of the first interview question ("Why did you get involved in anti-occupation activism? Specifically, what brought you to nonviolence?") was different for the two groups of interviewees. From the Palestinians I was seeking primarily to hear the reasons why they had chosen nonviolence rather than (or after personally rejecting) some other form of struggle, whereas the emphasis of my question to the Israelis was more along the lines of, "How did you come to support the Palestinian nonviolent struggle?" This resulted in very different "flavours" to their respective responses and, I'm afraid, unintentionally deprived some Israeli interviewees (e.g., Amos Gvirtz, a lifelong pacifist and advocate of "principled" [Gandhian] nonviolence) of the opportunity to express their choice of nonviolence in personal terms.

Nonetheless, I hope that "hearing" the many Palestinian and Israeli—Jewish, Muslim, and Christian[2]—voices of the interviewees will contribute to an understanding that what is often misperceived as a clash of cultures and religions is much more a matter of the politics and economics of conflicting nationalisms and land claims in an environment of underlying fears and misunderstandings—a situation where nonviolent activism may well be the only form of resistance that can realistically be expected to bring together members of both nations and of all the local religious communities.[3]

Finally, it is my hope that readers will come away from this book with a heightened sense of the widespread practice of, and support for, nonviolence amongst both Palestinian and Israeli anti-occupation activists, as well as of how the various forms of joint struggle are increasingly bringing together people of diverse beliefs, faiths, and cultures, uniting them in the common purpose of ending the occupation by nonviolent means.

About the Organization of this Book

Refusing to be Enemies is divided into four parts. The first three parts consist primarily of material selected from interviews and public presentations by a total of 115 contributors. My introductory and connecting comments are intended to provide context and indicate the relationships between contributors, so as to paint an overall picture while leaving in-depth analysis to Ghassan Andoni, Jeff Halper, Jonathan

Kuttab, and Starhawk, whose essays—along with my conclusions and epilogue—make up the fourth part of the book.

Part I of the book moves from questions of personal choice to more theoretical considerations regarding nonviolence. In Chapter 1, some two dozen interviewees speak about how they came to choose nonviolence and/or what drew them to anti-occupation activism in general. Chapter 2 begins with descriptions from five interviewees of their activism going back to the era of the First Intifada (1987–93) and before. This is followed by reflections on nonviolence by three local activists and U.S. theoretician Gene Sharp—with emphasis on its relationship to the anti-occupation struggle.

Part II looks at the practice of nonviolence, focusing on strategies employed by nonviolent organizations in the context of resistance to the occupation. It starts with an examination of the choice of nonviolence as an organizational strategy and Palestinian and Israeli activists' descriptions of the groups with which they work and of their activities and strategies (Chapter 3). In Chapter 4, one particular strategy—Palestinian/Israeli joint activism—is explored, beginning with descriptions of joint organizations and strategies and going on to explore attitudes toward, and power dynamics of, this form of activism. In Chapter 5 we take a closer look at three nonviolent campaigns with a significant joint-activism component: the First-Intifada-era tax strike in the town of Beit Sahour, the struggle against Israel's separation barrier/apartheid wall as a focus for joint activism, and the years of nonviolent joint struggle in the village of Bil'in against construction of the wall and a settlement "neighbourhood" on land confiscated for this purpose.

Part III, "Looking Forward," begins with a chapter asking how a more effective nonviolent movement might be built, and in particular, what activists feel needs to change in order for their organizations—and the nonviolent movement as a whole—to more successfully pursue their goals (Chapter 6). In Chapter 7 we take a look at which nonviolent strategies and tactics have been effective thus far, go on to focus on the important strategy of military refusal, and review some important trends in Palestinian nonviolence. In the last two chapters of Part III, interviewees discuss their hopes and thoughts regarding the future of Palestinian nonviolent struggle, and share their visions for the future of the region itself.

Part IV begins with analytic essays by book-project partners and 2006 Nobel Peace Prize nominees Ghassan Andoni and Jeff Halper; by Jonathan Kuttab, a passionately pacifist Palestinian lawyer; and by feminist author and nonviolent activist-theorist-trainer Starhawk. Andoni's piece offers an analysis based on his long experience of nonviolent activism in Palestine, while Halper's chapter postulates six necessary components of an approach to nonviolence that goes beyond the simply tactical—integrating material from the book's interviews so as to give a summary, focus, and analysis to the often free-ranging discussion with the many activists interviewed. Kuttab argues that, even given the Palestinians' right—under international law—to armed struggle, "nonviolence is more effective and suitable for resistance." Finally, in her essay, Starhawk discusses some of the unique challenges faced by the Palestinian nonviolent movement. The book ends with my conclusions on the subject of Palestinian/Israeli joint struggle, including future prospects and some thoughts about additional forms that the Israeli component of this struggle might take, and an epilogue examining the latter in greater depth.

Maxine Kaufman-Lacusta

NOTES

1　I use the words "interview" and "interviewee" here and throughout the book loosely, since twelve "spoke" only through their conference talks and one primarily through written comments. The interview and presentation excerpts have been placed in contexts determined largely by what questions of mine they are responding to, and I have indicated when a given excerpt is from something other than an interview. I have edited the excerpts for clarity and "flow," but not with any intent to alter meaning. Ellipses and rearrangements have generally not been noted, in the name of simplicity (the exception being inclusion of ellipses in excerpts from published material), and I apologize if my editing has unwittingly led to distortion. I sincerely hope it has not. As mentioned, my introductory and connecting comments are intended to clarify context and to indicate relationship among contributions, and so to contribute to an overall picture, while leaving in-depth analysis to Andoni, Halper, Kuttab, and Starhawk in Section IV. Organizational affiliations and positions attributed to interviewees are generally as of time of interview. In a few cases, where more recent information is available, it is noted as well.

2　I must apologize at the outset for the absence in this book of any Druze interviewees. For a sympathetic and thoughtful description of the nonviolent struggle of the Druze of the Golan Heights, please see Kennedy and Awad 1985. *Creative Resistance* contains an account of draft resistance among the Israeli Druze, based on an interview with Druze Initiative Committee spokesman Ghalib.

3　Despite the fact that many, if not most, of the interviewees you will meet in these pages consider themselves non-religious, even the most secular Israelis and Palestinians, when asked, will tend to identify with one of the local religious communities.

PART I

NONVIOLENT ACTION – FROM PERSONAL CHOICE TO POLITICAL STRATEGY

1

WHY NONVIOLENCE? WHY ANTI-OCCUPATION ACTIVISM? PERSONAL RESPONSES

I absolutely believe in nonviolent resistance as the only way to go. I think violence just begets more violence. There's no guarantee that nonviolent resistance is going to achieve anything, but violent resistance achieves the opposite of what you're trying to do. I wasn't just morally opposed to violence; even tactically I think it doesn't work.

Veronika Cohen

This chapter is based primarily on my interviewees' personal responses to two questions: "What brought you to nonviolence?" and "What made you decide to become an anti-occupation activist in the first place?"

Whereas I asked the second question of virtually all the activists I interviewed for this book—hoping to learn something about their personal motivations above and beyond the political impetus for their activism—the first, regarding the choice of nonviolence, was aimed principally at the Palestinian interviewees (all of whom were in some way engaged in nonviolent resistance), as well as those Israelis personally engaged in nonviolent actions of various sorts (as opposed to those in a more indirect support role). I wanted to know what had brought them to choose this—often hazardous, sometimes illegal—approach. The chapter includes, along with a selection of replies to the second question, a varied sampling of responses to the personal, as opposed to the organizational, side of the first. I was surprised to learn, for example, that some of the Palestinians with the strongest ideological—as opposed to simply tactical—commitment to nonviolence were ex-fighters or former supporters of armed struggle.

Many interviewees, particularly Israelis, made no mention of specifically "choosing nonviolence," the nonviolent nature of their actions—which often bring them into direct defiance of the occupation authorities—being taken as a given. None of the Israelis I interviewed advocated the use of violence by themselves or other Israelis, although a few of them felt that Palestinian use of violent means to oppose the occupation was an unfortunate necessity. Indeed, relatively few of those I interviewed, Israeli or Palestinian, condemned *all* violence. While stressing their personal abhorrence of bloodshed and their (and their organizations') choice to act nonviolently, many, especially among the Palestinian interviewees, were careful to make it clear that they recognized the right (under international law) of Palestinians, as of all oppressed peoples, to use whatever means were at their disposal to resist the occupation. Similarly, the bulk of Israeli military refuseniks would be willing to fight if they felt that to do so were truly required for the defence of their country.

Why Nonviolence?

Life-long Proponents of Nonviolence
Nuri el-Okbi
Nuri el-Okbi, a Palestinian Bedouin with Israeli citizenship,[1] has spent decades advocating for the rights of his people. Although not the only Palestinian citizen of Israel represented in this book, because of limitations of space and scope, he and Leena Delasheh of Ta'ayush are the only ones to articulate that point of view explicitly. The el-Okbis, along with most of the Bedouin in southern Israel, were evicted from their tribal lands in the early 1950s and relocated to an area of the northern Negev referred to as the *sayag* (reservation), with the assurance that they could return home in six months, a promise that has yet to be kept. For many years Nuri el-Okbi lived with his wife and children in the mixed Arab-Jewish town of Lod in central Israel and earned his living running an automotive garage. During that time he also founded the Association for the Support and Defence of Bedouin Rights and campaigned tirelessly on behalf of the el-Okbi tribe and other Negev Bedouin. Over the years, el-Okbi has carried out many Gandhi-like nonviolent actions, his latest being to maintain a constant peaceful presence on the tribal lands. When I interviewed him on April 24, 2007, he had been camping there for months, within sight of the tree under which his mother bore him over sixty years previously; he had been detained by the police several times, and had one arm in a cast thanks to rough treatment during his most recent arrest. I asked him why he had chosen this particular method of

pursuing his cause, and he replied, "Because I first of all believe in nonviolence, and I am opposed to *any* violence." He continued:

> One who is right does not need to use violence. Its truth is very strong. Secondly, it's my character. I can't have anything to do with violence. I'm against violence, I call for nonviolence. I say that every drop of blood that is spilt is a sad waste. For many decades we've been suffering, and I believe that no problem can be solved by violence, by force. So I'm trying to find the path through which I can obtain the rights [for the tribe] without causing harm to any human being, to any interest [and] without getting involved in violence. This is very important. I think that human beings are forbidden to use violence.

"It's not that I learned at university that it's forbidden to get involved in violence," concluded el-Okbi, "but I believe that a person who has sense and has a mouth and can speak, that's stronger than using force and violence."

Jean Zaru

Jean Zaru, a Palestinian Quaker from Ramallah in the West Bank, referred explicitly to her choice of nonviolence as being faith-based. She described the concept of *sumud* (steadfastness)—"staying on your land, no matter what, and trying to affirm life in the midst of structures of death and domination"—in terms of "trying to do what God requires of you in these times." "I think that is a nonviolent way of activity," she told me.[2] She added:

> Many Palestinians have chosen the nonviolent struggle out of a faith base, because they feel that all of us are created in God's image and to harm this image—or the dignity of any people—is really doing something wrong. Others find that strategically, with the imbalance of power, using military means is not helpful in our struggle. I don't mean just the imbalance of power between the Israelis and the Palestinians on the level of military equipment and nuclear weapons and so on. It is also the media in the West that have unfortunately played a big part to present the Palestinians struggling for freedom and self-determination as terrorists, and this image should change.

"The structures of violence are silent," Zaru stressed, "and people cannot take pictures of those."

> I think people should wake up and also try to analyze the structures of domination and violence in societies, whether economic, social, political, religious, or environmental. On the religious level, you have fundamentalist movements from the Jewish and Muslim, and the Christian Right of the U.S. that is very exclusive, nationalistic, chauvinistic, against the emancipation of women, and also against any peace solution.

Terming "unacceptable" the "use [of] biblical words to justify oppression and dispossession and the building of settlements and oppression of other groups," she stated, "I would rather like to look at the liberating aspects of faith, of all faith traditions, and see how they can help us, sustain us to really go on working for the reign of God in this world—a reign that does not encourage the structures of injustice and domination and violence." Jean Zaru taught at the Friends Schools in Ramallah for many years, and told me how she had integrated a form of nonviolent resistance into her Home Economics classes in the early years of the occupation—in a desire "to give people hope that they can make a difference, no matter how small." "I taught the girls," she said, "how would you live responsibly to the Palestinian—or to the world— community as a Palestinian young woman" through their choices of what foodstuffs or clothing to purchase, for example—"not buying South African goods, but also not buying Israeli goods. And it is more ecological when you don't buy all the industrialized things. It's helping the simple farmers to survive, buying their products."

In terms of responses to the "long, long occupation and dispossession and very difficult economic situation, the closures, and so on," Zaru described nonviolent resistance as the "the only way of affirming life and dignity," of keeping hope alive.

> Some are tired, and they have withdrawn, either by leaving or by withdrawing into themselves and not being part of resisting these structures. There are some people who try to accommodate. There are some who try to manipulate the system. But all these groups do not bring any transformation to improve the situation. And there are groups who have chosen nonviolent resistance.

Citing the prophetic tradition, "where they spoke so much against evil in society and they wanted it to be changed, and people should have more righteousness and more right relationship with one another," Zaru continued, "So resistance is legitimate, and nonviolent resistance is even better, which is the most important and only choice for me from my faith base."

> I think any faith that values life should really work for nonviolence, because I think violence dehumanizes both societies, the powerful and the powerless. And we have to work together to find the way out of this. Nonviolent resistance is the only way to bring transformation. I wouldn't say that it's easy. I wouldn't say that people will not suffer. I wouldn't say that it might stop the wall. But it starts a discourse that we are not ready to accept this any more. This is not fair and this is not acceptable. And then people would not feel hopeless and useless, that they cannot make a difference and then they stop making a difference in society. So that's why nonviolent resistance is important, rather than complying or accommodating or withdrawing or manipulating.

Amos Gvirtz

Amos Gvirtz is not himself religious, having been born and raised on the secular Kibbutz Shefayim, where he still makes his home. Nonetheless, he is a life-long pacifist who managed to fulfil his compulsory military service obligations in the 1960s by working with developmentally disabled children—despite the official absence of provisions for either male conscientious objection or alternative service in Israel. "I am active because wrong things have been done," Gvirtz told me, "not because I believe I will change something. There is wrong that has been done, so I'll fight it. I'm not sure that I will succeed."

> The way I understand this conflict is that one society came into the living space of another society. This is the essence of the conflict, to my understanding. Therefore my work is directed mainly to face these issues: land confiscation, house demolition, deportations— all of these kinds of activities that Israel is doing—and to the understanding that if this process is not stopped, there is no chance for peace. In recent years, I have become very active [on the issue of] Bedouin inside Israel, because the process of pushing the Palestinians away from their territory was not only in the occupied

territories, it was very active and very intensive inside Israel, and specifically now against the Bedouin.

Gvirtz is involved in a number of activist groups, including the Israeli Committee Against House Demolitions (ICAHD), and views house demolition as a singularly traumatic and damaging aspect of the occupation. From talking with Palestinians, "I can begin to imagine how traumatic it is," he said. "And Israel is building its enemies for generations by these activities."

> But I don't believe I've reached the real deep meaning of it for people, not only to those it happened to, but to neighbours who have seen it. How traumatic it is for children it happened to and for neighbour children who have seen it and are afraid it will happen to them. It is a very traumatic event, and different people react differently to it. But for sure, some percentage of them will retaliate violently. Most of us understand house demolition only rationally, but rational understanding is far, far away from reaching the real meaning of it.

"What is much, much, much less visual and maybe less traumatic, but more essential, is land confiscation," said Gvirtz.

> This is, together with house demolition, the essence of the conflict. You take the territory out from under the feet of the Palestinians; this is the essential issue. The Oslo process,[3] instead of stopping the process of pushing the Palestinians away from their territory, was speeding it up by increasing dramatically the number of settlements—which meant there was massive land confiscation and massive house demolitions, and even deportations. This is why we started the Israeli Committee against House Demolitions.

The real issue in the conflict is not security, as is often claimed, says Gvirtz. "The real issue in our conflict is the land; it is the land and it is the effort to get maximum land with minimum population—continuing the situation as it is, hoping that more and more Palestinians will leave the territories."

> We came into Palestinian territory when there was a foreign ruler that allowed us to do it, and then later we threw out most of the Palestinians from their homes and their land—they became

refugees—so we built Israel on the ruins of the Palestinians. Now we are occupying the rest of their territory with a very oppressive and cruel regime. And yet, for most northern and western people, the Palestinians are the terrorists and we are defending ourselves. Why? The situation is exactly the opposite.

Converts to Nonviolence

Mustafa Shawkat Samha

Several of those I interviewed—particularly amongst the Palestinians—described what might be regarded as something of a "conversion experience" in arriving at their commitment to nonviolence. One of these was Mustafa Shawkat Samha, a twenty-something village activist I met at the Celebrating Nonviolent Resistance conference (held in Bethlehem, December 27–30, 2005). Before his arrest in 2002, said he, "I didn't believe exactly in nonviolence."

> But when they arrested me and some soldiers started to beat me, because I'm handicapped and I cannot protect myself,[4] I discovered that the power of muscles, the power of weapons, is not the only power. We have the power of the mind. We have the power of speech. We have the power of negotiation. We have the most important power, the power of [our] humanity. And I'm sure that those soldiers, who beat me hard, are not happy about their actions toward me, but they're used to doing this. It's the short way to get what they want, to punish. But even while they were beating me, I was talking with them. Like: "Are you really happy with what you are doing? Think about yourself. Think about your humanity."
>
> We, Palestinians and Israelis, are as if we are in a boat in the middle of the sea. So we have the responsibility to protect this boat, to reach the beach. And we cannot reach this beach by hating each other, by killing each other. We can reach this beach if we feel deeply our humanity, if we believe that we have to live together and we both have the same right to be alive.

Samha spoke of nonviolence as being a way that is stronger than violence and one that can "create a new meaning of life for you," whereby you share in the struggle, neither being violent nor passively "standing aside and just watching," a way that encourages "a loud voice from Israel" that proclaims: "Stop killing. We want our rights and they want their rights. Stop killing the others. All of us are human. All of us can live together.

Nobody is a slave for the other, and nobody has the right to kill others." "Because of all these things," says Samha, "I believe in the nonviolence way and I'm working in this way. And if they will they arrest me a million times, I will continue struggling in this way, and I will not change what is in my heart. I cannot hate anybody, even for what they are doing to me."

Sabrin Aimour

Sabrin Aimour is a Bethlehem University student who wears the *hijab* (head covering worn by religious Muslim women), but with a Fatah *keffiyeh* around her neck to show her affiliation in the upcoming student elections. She is a former supporter of Hamas and believed in armed struggle before attending a workshop led by local nonviolence trainer Husam Jubran. She had hoped to learn "something new" during the training, but came away convinced and empowered by the nonviolent approach and is actively recruiting her friends to enrol in future training sessions.

> I was searching for alternatives, but at the same time I believed that violence works in many cases. I came to the training to learn something different, something new. I learned to deal with problems in a different way, to address them in a deeper way, not just to address the surface, but to deeper in understanding the conflict and addressing it. I learned and now I understand that nonviolence is much better than violence and I could help and support people through nonviolence and that to solve problems using nonviolence makes it more efficient and gives me a feeling of security. And it helps me become more powerful in expressing my opinion and not to be afraid, for example, of showing the *keffiyeh* in front of soldiers.

Lucy

Lucy [surname withheld by request] is another young Bethlehem-area woman who is a relative newcomer to nonviolence. I interviewed her at the Wi'am Palestinian Conflict Resolution Center in Bethlehem, where she is now a youth leader:

> I was raised in Bethlehem, and the First Intifada was when I was a teenager. It was a very hard time, and I did not believe in what they called nonviolence. It was a strange idea; I thought it was like a new technique we adopted from the West. During the '67 war,

my grandmother's house was shelled and my grandfather, my aunt, and my uncle had been killed, so I grew up with revenge on my mind.

Lucy described the evolution of her thinking, commenting, "Day by day, I tried to change my mind." As a young person in the 1990s, she sought out organizations that dealt with the conflict in ways that went beyond dialogue (an approach she regarded as ineffectual). She did some support work for the Jahalin Bedouin side-by-side with Israeli activists like Rabbi Jeremy Milgrom, and also worked at the Alternative Information Center (AIC) office in Bethlehem (now relocated to the neighbouring town of Beit Sahour). Her interest in the concept of conflict resolution then led her to the Wi'am Center, where, however, she initially avoided participating in its Palestinian-Israeli cross-cultural activities. "I was against these projects," she told me. "I thought they would not achieve anything, dialogue is not important during this time, what is important is to resist and to get our freedom, to get rid of occupation." It was the increasing militarization of the Second Intifada that ultimately caused Lucy to rethink her position regarding nonviolence.

> I started my life not believing in nonviolent resistance, so how could I change my mind from believing in using arms to achieve what we want to nonviolence to achieve what we want? In the First Intifada, for me, [actions] like throwing stones and carrying the branch of olive trees were symbols of nonviolent resistance. But the Second Intifada is completely different. At a certain point I decided, "No, I have to stop. This is not going to change." Arms lead just to bloodshed and revenge, no more than this. I felt that using arms is not going to achieve anything—just to see more blood, more victims. This was the most important part for me. That's why I promised myself to be an active person in the field of peacemaking: to work hard on that, to educate people to raise their awareness of the effect of nonviolence, especially the methods they use, the skills, and that's what we are doing [at the Wi'am Center].

Nayef Hashlamoun
Several former supporters of armed struggle—including fighters—described circumstances or specific events that brought them to nonviolence. Nayef Hashlamoun, founder of the al-Watan Center for

Civic Education, Conflict Resolution and Nonviolence in Hebron, for example, tells of being involved in military action in South Lebanon. He recalls that the officer in charge of training told him, "Listen, you have to understand what our religion is telling us. You have to know that you haven't the right to kill any people without reason, to kill a tree or to 'kill' even a stone for no reason." After reflecting on this statement, said Hashlamoun, he was unable to sleep that night. "In the morning I took the decision that I have to change my way from the violent way to nonviolence. I left Lebanon to [study journalism in] Jordan. I said I have to fight, but without guns."

Ali Jedda

Ali Jedda worked at the AIC for five years. The son of a Muslim from Chad who had come to Jerusalem on pilgrimage in the early 1900s, Ali grew up in the African Quarter (part of the Muslim Quarter) of the Old City and was a student at the College des Frères when the Israeli occupation began in 1967. "I was looking forward to become a lawyer, to become a doctor, something like that," he told me.[5] But the occupation and consequent financial difficulties had dashed these dreams. Thinking back to those days, he recalled, on top of the disappointment of having to leave school, "first of all, the way the Israeli soldiers behaved to us— stopping us in the streets, harassing us, and sometimes kicking us" and "the way Israeli civilians used to behave when they'd come to the Old City. They used to come in groups to the streets of the Old City, dancing, singing, in a very arrogant way." "I think I lost my dignity," he said, "my personal and my national dignity." He got involved in militant politics and joined the PFLP—Popular Front for the Liberation of Palestine. "And at that time," he told me, "the circle of violence was so wide. I placed [a] bomb at Jaffa Street. Because of that bomb nine Israelis were injured." The attack was meant as a reprisal, he explained, for an Israeli bombing raid on a Jordanian city the day before, which had killed many civilians. "Our main intention at that time was to send a message to the Israeli civilians saying to them, "Look, if you don't protest, if you don't act or react against the brutality of your government, unfortunately at the end of the day, you are going to pay the price. A month later, I was arrested." Jedda spent the next thirteen years in prison, during which time he had a change of heart.

I came to a definite conclusion that my main allies in my fight, in my struggle against the occupation should be the Israelis themselves: the sector of the Israeli society who are totally against the occupation and who are looking forward for a secular democratic state—which is my main idealistic solution—in which both of us can live together in real peace and equality.

Upon his release, Jedda "began working with such people"—at the jointly run Alternative Information Center. A year or two into the First Intifada, he felt "obliged to move once again to the Palestinian side, to be very close to what [was] happening on the Palestinian side."

I was curious as to what brought about Jedda's change of heart. "It's my elementary right as a human being to fight against the occupation," he reminded me, "but today, I say simply I'm not ready to do what I have done in 1968, for two main reasons."

I have today five children, three girls and two boys. If I can't stand that somebody is going to harm my children, I'm not ready to harm children of others. On the political level, my Israeli friends are Israelis who are really serious about peace, and they want to live in peace with the Palestinians. So, if I place a bomb, the bomb can't make a difference between the good Israelis and those monsters—I mean the settlers. So for that [reason], I'm not ready to do it. On the contrary, I'm doing my best now to build a bridge to reach to more and more sectors of the Israeli society and to convince them that the best solution is that we have to fight together in order to achieve that state—the secular democratic state.

Though he doesn't expect to live to see his vision achieved, Jedda hopes that "maybe my sons or grandsons will see it."

I say today simply, I am a candle which is burning itself to give light for others: for my children and for the Israeli children, also. Because both generations—meaning my children and the Israeli children—are [undergoing] a process of psychological destruction, and we have mainly to blame this Israeli occupation. And this is what I think. Whenever they ask me, "how do you look [at] what you have done in 1968," I say to them: "I was a victim. The Israelis who were injured were victims. Both of us are victims of the *occupation*."

Ghassan Andoni

Ghassan Andoni, a cofounder of both the Palestinian Center for Rapprochement (PCR) and the International Solidarity Movement (ISM), recalled "I started my life as a committed nationalist who believed strongly in fighting to liberate Palestinians and return them their rights." First jailed by the Israelis in 1972 while still in high school, Andoni was active in the resistance to the occupation until moving to Baghdad to attend university in 1976. While there, said Andoni, "I was really moved by the scenes of attacks against refugee camps by the Phalangists and the Syrians during the civil war in Lebanon." He continued, "I decided to volunteer and go to Lebanon—to do work that was similar to what ISM volunteers do right now in Palestine."

> I spent three months in Lebanon, and there I had the shock that made me feel that nonviolent resistance or civil-based resistance is the way to fight against oppression and violence. Part of that was that I felt that people who hold guns become captured by the guns, and instead of [them] leading, the guns started leading [them]. I asked so many people the question, "Why are you fighting here?" and I realized that people were fighting because they get used to fighting, and because there is an enemy and then, in order to survive, you need to fight. My concept of fighting was not to survive, but to make things better, more human. Even in Lebanon at that time, I realized that the fighting was pointless. But nobody was questioning it.

"Therefore," he said, "I realized that the gun is leading, not the people, and that made me decide to come back and live in my little town inside the occupied territories, rather than spending the rest of my life in [the] diaspora with the Palestinian liberation organizations or movements." After further study, in Palestine and the UK, Andoni returned in 1984 to teach physics at Birzeit University. With the outbreak of the 1987 Intifada came what he referred to as "the other turning point in my life."

> At that point I realized that civil-based resistance is not only a concept, is not only an idea that is suitable to India, South Africa, the Civil Rights Movement in the States; but I could see the potential in the Palestinian massive resistance—mainly nonviolent—that started in December 1987 and managed, literally in the first few months, to turn the mighty Israeli force to useless. That's why I decided to engage fully in that Intifada. When I cofounded the

Rapprochement group and started working to prepare the society in my town for civil disobedience and started opening channels of communication with Israelis and internationals, we managed actually to contribute to a movement in this little town that attracted the attention of so many people. We managed to build up lots of good models: the tax resistance, throwing back [Israeli] identity cards, boycotting Israeli products, starting underground schools when schools were closed, victory gardens. We started community work that managed to replace the institutions of the occupation. And finally the occupation felt really threatened by a resistance that did not harm or hurt or kill any of its soldiers, but rather forced them to lose control. And that was very frightening to them, and that's why they attacked this little town, Beit Sahour, severely, hoping to crack down on this experience, fearing that this might spread out to other regions and then there would be a total collapse of control.[6]

Andoni's work with PCR and, more recently, with ISM as well, has involved providing leadership and training in nonviolent resistance techniques, since both organizations are committed to this approach.

Promoting Nonviolence through Training and Education
Husam Jubran
Another organization deeply involved with spreading the concepts and practice of nonviolent resistance throughout Palestine is the Holy Land Trust (HLT). I had been impressed by experience-based comments made by HLT's head nonviolence trainer, Husam Jubran, at a workshop entitled "Teaching Nonviolence in an Islamic Context" at the December 2005 Celebrating Nonviolent Resistance conference:

> During the past three years, I conducted more than thirty-five trainings, and more than five hundred people attended the trainings, from extreme right to extreme left. I've had people from Hamas, Jihad Islami, and Al-Aqsa [brigade]. And by the end of each of the trainings, the answer from them was almost the same: "You didn't bring anything new to us. We've practiced this since a long time ago. You only brought us to see it in a different way."

I interviewed Jubran at the HLT office in Bethlehem in January 2006. He told me, "My first activity in nonviolence was during the First Intifada."

In 1987 when the Intifada started, I was about 17 years old, and immediately I found myself in the streets throwing stones at soldiers. At that time, the main idea in my mind was how to say to the Israelis, "We don't want you here," "We want to get rid of you," and "Please leave us alone." And the only way at the moment was to throw stones at soldiers, to put stones in the way to prevent the army from entering the town. Later on we adopted other techniques, like writing on the walls, raising Palestinian flags, boycotting the Israeli goods, general strikes in the morning for all the shops in the city, civil disobedience and giving back our I.D. cards, stopping giving taxes to the Israeli government.

"For all that period," he said, "I didn't realize that everything I did was nonviolent, including the stone-throwing." Jubran sees stone-throwing as nonviolent because "it is symbolic: the meaning is not to hurt the Israeli army." Rather, he says, "this is the way to tell them 'We don't want you here.'"

I don't think that I or anybody in the town hurt an Israeli through throwing stones. The main idea was to hit vehicles, to cause damage to the cars, the jeeps—to break the windshield, for example, or something like that. So the way I saw it, it was more a symbolic gesture of resisting occupation, of saying to injustice, "No!"

After university, Jubran became a tour guide, working in Israel with groups from North America and Europe. His Tourism studies exposed him to "the history of the Holy Land since 3,000 B.C., its religions, archeology, and architecture," through which he gained a deeper sense of the perspectives of "all the parties in the Holy Land."

And also, through my work with internationals and the conversations we had, I started to connect my activities more with nonviolence, and I started to realize—through their questions and asking me about nonviolence—that actually I was a nonviolent activist. At the same time, I developed a political itinerary for tourists, and this gave me the chance to meet different Israeli activists and different Palestinian activists, and gave me the chance to know more about this field; and I decided that I wanted to do more. Later on I managed to get a scholarship, and I did my masters in Conflict Transformation with the focus on nonviolence.

Sami Awad

The director of Holy Land Trust, Sami Awad, credits his uncle Mubarak with inspiring him to become an activist. Mubarak Awad, who founded the Palestinian Center for the Study of Nonviolence (PCSNV) in 1984, was deported by the Israeli authorities in June 1988 for proposing the use of nonviolence to end the Israeli occupation.[7]

> Mubarak Awad is my uncle, whom I always blame for putting me in this mess of being an activist, but he was also my role-model in life as well. Holy Land Trust is an affiliate organization to Nonviolence International [Mubarak Awad's Washington, DC-based organization]. So we've sort of continued carrying the torch that he started in the mid-eighties calling for nonviolent resistance. You know, he is considered a hero now by many [Palestinians], a man who came before his time. Those who rejected him are now very eager to speak to him and learn from him and to see what they can do. He was seen by the Israelis as a very effective threat to them.

Choosing Nonviolence to Bring About Change

Ziad Abbas

Ziad Abbas directs the Ibdaa Cultural Center in Dheisheh refugee camp. Born and raised in Deheishe, he told me how isolated camp residents feel, especially the children "living in this small refugee camp without any rights."

> No one pays attention to us. Even the basic rights of human beings we don't have. When I became a youth, I knew Israelis as jailers and the soldiers who were shooting, so I was dreaming all time to be like Rambo—to have this machine-gun and to kill any Israeli. This was when I was young. But when we grow up and we learn more about the conflict, about the situation, we learned about our rights as human beings, and we learned about the others' rights. So slowly, slowly, you realize the reality as it is.

Conditions in the camp weren't significantly improved by the various Palestinian political factions, he said. "Even after Oslo, nothing changed, so we decided to leave the official framework of political activity and to try to do something for the people that are living inside the camp—for women, for the youth, for children"—and founded "this project which is called Ibdaa Cultural Center." When I asked Abbas why he chose a cultural and educational form of resistance rather than engaging, for example, in armed struggle, he concluded:

> We don't educate people how to use guns! Because we have suffered a lot from violence, we try to solve the problems, the effects on our people and children of the violence. So we are against violence totally, one hundred percent. We hate blood. We don't want to see any blood, no matter if this blood flows from anyone who's Jewish, Israeli, [Palestinian]. We are against seeing blood. But we are fed up with this occupation. I was born a refugee. I don't want to die a refugee.

Muhammad Jaradat

Muhammad Jaradat, though not a refugee himself, has made the plight and rights of Palestinian refugees his life's work. Jaradat is coordinator of the Refugee Campaign Unit at the BADIL ("Alternative") Resource Center for Palestinian Residency and Refugee Rights—where his Austrian-born wife, Ingrid Jaradat Gassner is director. I interviewed him at Badil's office in Bethlehem, where he told me: "The Palestinian struggle has been a form of nonviolence, and we have been exposed to ugly media, which took the exceptions as the norm—where it covered the Palestinians as a violent people."

> Now, I was raised—by political parties or the national movement, as we usually call it—on how to resist the occupation, how to resist the oppression, how to resist the people who make your daily life into a misery; [for example] to go to school and find soldiers in front of you or settlers, since your childhood. You have to learn how to cope with tremendous power with your small power. And this is, I think, the philosophy and the key thing. How to deal with it with our small power, which is great—in my opinion—our moral power, our belief. For me, this is how we build our Palestinian society under occupation. Palestinian society has been built under violent conditions from the occupation, and we succeeded to build it on a civil resistance movement.

Expressing amazement that "people speak about teaching the Palestinians nonviolence and tell them how to be nonviolent," Jaradat declared: "I'm a proud Palestinian, and we have tremendous experience that we should share, and [it should] be recognized as Palestinian experience." Even so, "nonviolent movement" was a phrase he chose to avoid, preferring the term "resistance movement." His objections included, but went beyond, the commonly-expressed desire not to give the impression of delegitimizing other forms of resistance, such as armed struggle. "Nonviolent," he complained, makes it sound as though the Palestinians are on the whole, violent, by contrast. "Resistance," on the other hand, "is a word which includes, not only resisting directly the occupation soldiers and the checkpoints, or in the prisons or interrogations, but also it gives it the social component as you build your society."

Jaradat was a teen in the late 1970s, and credits the voluntary associations that first began to proliferate in those years (generally under the PLO umbrella) with saving him and his peers from aimlessness and a possible life of crime, and enabling them to become "positive elements in society" by involving these young people in useful activities ranging from street-cleaning to helping sick people get to hospital, to teaching children with learning disabilities. "This is also a form of resistance for us," he said. The foundation for Palestinian civil society and the groundwork for the movement of resistance to the Israeli occupation both were laid, he told me, by the "civil society structures" and committees of that era. Regarding his personal choice to eschew armed resistance, Jaradat stressed that, "I do believe in social movements: people are the engine of change, not anything else." And to be that, they require education, as he pointed out:

> You can find hundreds who can carry a gun and shoot with it, but you will not find a good intellectual or activist with a good head, who joins the hand work and the head work. So our great education has been as a resistance movement, and [our great] struggle in Palestinian society [has been] how to advance our education system.

Emphasizing, as well, the importance of education—whether at university or in peer-led study groups in prison—for a successful civil resistance movement, Jaradat remarked that in the 1980s, "I don't think I'm exaggerating if I say that most of the political prisoners were arrested and sentenced to prison based on the fact that they were active in a student group or in a union or in Popular Committees or any kind of civil structure." "Looking back," he mused, "I paid from my life almost five-and-a-half years in prison to build these kinds of organizations: you know, the health committees, agricultural committees."[8]

Why Anti-Occupation Activism?

Deciding to Become an Activist

Galia Golan

University professor Galia Golan was among the early activists in the well-known Israeli peace group, Shalom Achshav (Peace Now). I spoke to her in the fall of 2005 at the University of British Columbia (UBC) in Vancouver, where she had come to give a lecture on the Israeli peace movement. "I don't think I was active in anything, and then I became an active feminist in the early seventies," she told me. Then, when Peace Now was formed, she and her husband "were amongst the first, and that was it."

It really spoke very directly, and I was very, very, very active. The first reason was, in very concrete terms, the settlements. The second was this occupation that was developing—even though we didn't call it an occupation in those years—the radical left did. We didn't in the beginning, but that's what it was. I don't think we fully really grasped the ramifications (I'm talking now about the early seventies), I just knew this was not a good idea. We're not supposed to hold on to the territories! I remember very clearly 1971 when Sadat made his offer, and I remember hearing it and, just a few hours later, Golda's rejection. I remember thinking, "My God! Why don't you think about it? Why don't you consider it? What is wrong with this offer?"

I just don't see how you can not be active when you feel this way, and then you try to find a way to change things. The more you went into the territories—even before the "oppressive" occupation— you'd see what the settlers were doing to expand, harassing their neighbours. And harassing neighbours meant setting fire to a house or breaking the windows. The things at Tel Rumeida [a Palestinian neighbourhood of Hebron] in particular, were really shocking for me: just closing off the street, not letting anybody in except the people who lived there. We went to see Tel Rumeida ourselves. Then we began tours to the place, bringing Israelis, bringing press, bringing Members of Knesset. So, to me it's sort of like an imperative. It's just that if I feel so angry and miserable about what's going on, I have to do something; and the worse it gets, the more active I get.

Although Golan did describe a variety of nonviolent actions pursued by Peace Now over the years and discussed the ongoing debate over civil disobedience within that organization,[9] the question of "choosing nonviolence" for herself did not arise.

Noa Nativ and Leena Delasheh

Similarly Noa Nativ and Leena Delasheh, Jewish-Israeli and Palestinian-Israeli members, respectively, of Ta'ayush (Arabic for "life in common"), a group heavily involved in acts of nonviolent resistance—chose to speak to their Vancouver audience about their motivation for standing together with Palestinians against discrimination and oppression, rather than about nonviolence per se.

Noa Nativ, from a "good Zionist family" (pioneer stock) though not politically engaged, described joining Ta'ayush in response to coming to feel, like Galia Golan had thirty years earlier, that things had gotten so bad that "it seemed like you could not *not* do anything anymore."

> I guess I was born into the occupation, into the state of occupation. And I kind of accepted it as a form of normality—just the way things were. What changed that for me was the events of October 2000, which were a real shock. The deterioration in the situation in our region, the terrible escalation of the violence, the election of Sharon as prime minister, which was totally inconceivable to me—a war criminal being elected—the terrible suicide bombings. Everything just seemed to blow apart, and I couldn't understand how I could be a part of this, how I could see my country doing the things it did in the occupied territories and continue being quiet about it, not doing anything about it. Before, I had this kind of belief that there was probably someone out there that was taking care of things for me, and I didn't have to worry about it. And [now] I just understood that it was my personal responsibility to go and do things, or else I'm dooming myself to living in this reality and being part of the system that perpetuates it.

Nativ shared her feelings with a friend, who invited her to the new Jerusalem branch of Ta'ayush—the first group having been formed one month after the start of the Intifada, in Tel Aviv and nearby Palestinian-Israeli towns.

> I thought I'd integrate just a bit of activism into my life, but it turns out you can't do that. You take down your shields and your walls of detachment and indifference to yourself and the world around you, and you can't keep apart anymore. And it totally took over my life. But the hardest thing about becoming an activist was the mental switch from being a non-activist to being an activist, because now that I began to do something about it, I allowed myself to feel these things, I allowed myself to know—which is what most Israelis don't allow themselves to do.
>
> My grandparents were pioneers. I grew up on the myths, the stories of settling Israel and being such a humane and fair people. And suddenly I saw the implications that Zionism, as it was implemented, had, for all these people around—which I never knew before. And it was very threatening. You know, it's practically an identity crisis to have to re-evaluate all the things you were raised on. I get a whole lot of criticism from people—often I'm called a traitor—for bringing all these new ideas that we're cooperating with Palestinians. But hard as it is, I feel totally privileged to have this knowledge.

Leena Delasheh, from a small Palestinian village in the North of Israel, had recently completed her legal studies at the Hebrew University in Jerusalem, when she and Nativ spoke in Vancouver in the summer of 2002. She described her experience growing up as a Palestinian in Israel, of her feelings of alienation and despair, and now of the hope she's found in this dynamic organization.

> The identity of Israel as a Jewish state deprives me of my right to be a part of my nation, my right to be a Palestinian, my right to live my personal life as part of my group. At school, I've never learned about my history, about my people's history, about my existence. The war of 1948 was never taught to me from the Palestinian angle. The *Nakba* was never mentioned.[10] It's not a word that was relevant or accepted at my school: the Palestinian catastrophe, my catastrophe, my people's catastrophe—the part that is so significant to my definition and my identity—does not exist at the school that I went to.

Despite the fact that she "could see the discrimination and the injustice around me ever since I was a kid," Delasheh had always been active in mixed peace groups.

Then came October 2000. Palestinian-Israelis went out to demonstrate against discrimination and the occupation, and in identification with Palestinians in the occupied territories, and the Israeli police reacted with severe violence. Thirteen young Palestinian citizens were killed by the Israeli police and the [Jewish] Israeli people sat silent and watched, watched crimes being committed in their name and did nothing. They [said they] were "disappointed" in the Palestinians, and they allowed crimes to go on in their name within Israel and in the occupied territories.

Disappointed and desperate herself, Delasheh withdrew from activism until a Jewish friend persuaded her to attend a meeting of the newly formed Ta'ayush.

For me, Ta'ayush gave me back my hope, the hope of a better future, the hope of living together. Ta'ayush was the group that I could struggle in, with a lot of good people, to end the occupation, to end the discrimination, to [struggle for] our right to live normal, and even boring, lives. The only thing that keeps you going is knowing that maybe you could just ease that suffering; maybe you could just do something that could change it.

Dorothy Naor

Dorothy Naor, like Leena Delasheh and Noa Nativ, is a relative newcomer to the ranks of Israelis actively resisting the occupation. Seventy-one when I interviewed her in late 2003, she had only been active since the start of the Al-Aqsa Intifada in October 2000. "When the thirteen Israeli-Palestinians were killed by the police," she told me, "it threw me kind of back to the Kent State days; and the fact that the police would shoot Palestinian-Israeli citizens, when they shot no one else, was very upsetting to me."

I started to ask questions that I'd never asked before, questions about the Jewish state and questions about the history of this country, and questions about the Arabs and why they had to suffer here, even those who served in the army.[11] All these questions kept coming up. As things got worse for the Palestinians, I began going with Ta'ayush and other groups. But basically I always thought that the most important thing is to inform [people at home] and to inform people abroad.

Naor began arranging lectures in the nearby town of Herzliya, bringing in speakers like Jeff Halper and others, including some Palestinians, "who none of these people would have heard [otherwise], and many people came and told me it did change their ideas." She also forwards email messages from New Profile and other "on the ground" organizations, and estimates that she directly reaches between 2,000 and 3,000 people, and many more via re-forwardings and website postings. Although she is choosy about attending the many demonstrations protesting aspects of the occupation, preferring to reach larger numbers via email, one activity that Naor does find time for—on a nearly daily basis—is participation in joint Palestinian-Israeli resistance to the wall and other oppressive measures imposed on her West Bank neighbours in Mas'ha and other nearby villages and at the checkpoints that dot the landscape. She explained her motivations, concluding: "So long as my children and grandchildren and the great grandchildren that I someday will have are going to live here, it cannot remain the kind of country it is now. We have to, the few of us that there are, we have to do whatever we can to bring about change."

Neta Golan
One Israeli who did rise to this challenge is Neta Golan. She recalled how/why she became a "protective presence" in the village of Haris and what brought her to conceive of bringing internationals to stand beside Palestinians in nonviolently challenging the occupation, in what later became the International Solidarity Movement (ISM). Now living in Ramallah with her Palestinian husband and two little girls, Golan had been staying with her future in-laws in Nablus in the first months of the Al-Aqsa Intifada. "My fiancé's brother was working in Haris," she told me, "and he used to call me from there and tell me how the village is besieged."

> People aren't allowed to leave even on foot, it's olive-harvest season and the fruit is rotting on the trees. The settlers and the army have already cut down two hundred trees. The settlers broke the water pipe to the village and the army isn't allowing people to go out and fix it. And the settlers were basically coming every other night and throwing stones and shooting and provoking the village youth, and then when the youth were provoked, the settlers and the army would shoot at the youth.

Golan could hear all this going on in the background when he phoned her from Haris. Her attempts to get the Israeli media interested were unsuccessful. Then she and a friend, Noam, went to Haris to meet with the villagers to ask whether they'd accept the idea of bringing a group from Peace Now "to do an action in Haris and highlight the settler violence that wasn't being discussed at all, to be there when the settlers attacked," in the hope that the presence of Israelis would make the story newsworthy. During the meeting, they heard that youths were trying to remove a road block, and the army and the settlers were there. Aware that the situation was liable to escalate, the two went to the road block and spoke to the soldiers and settlers.

> Noam, being a soldier himself, could really speak to the soldiers and ask them what they were doing there and who gave the orders. Then we went and stood in the middle between the soldiers and settlers and the youths, and because we were standing there, the youths could remove the roadblock without being shot. And that was the first time that I had had that experience. It was a terrifying experience in one way—just the realization that my blood is somehow worth more and because of me these kids weren't shot—I think it really instilled a sort of sense of responsibility, that I have to be there.

Golan returned the following afternoon, in the midst of a confrontation between stone-throwing village kids and soldiers.

> So I came up to the soldiers while they were shooting and asked them, "Why are you shooting live ammunition?" and "What are you here for? What are you protecting? If you weren't here, there'd be nothing to throw stones at." And then I said, "Okay, now I'm going into Haris, to the village, where the kids are." And they were like, "Don't go there, because if you go there, we'll shoot you and you'll complain." And I said, "That's right, I'll complain very much!" And then I went into the village. I wanted to be standing somewhere visible, where the soldiers could see me, but the villagers wouldn't let me. They said it's too dangerous.

So Golan got on her phone and called the army spokesperson and announced: "We're a group [made up] of an Israeli, a Canadian, an Italian, and a Japanese, and we're here in this village, and we just want you to know that some of your soldiers are shooting at us." She left the following day for a speaking engagement in Italy, but on her second day away she received an email saying that a fourteen-year-old that she knew in Haris had been shot in the back and killed. "I felt really terrible," she said, "and when I came back from Italy, I just moved there and stayed for a while."

Golan virtually lived in Haris for the first several months of the Al-Aqsa Intifada, organizing groups of Israelis and internationals to join her solidarity presence there and in nearby villages. Early on, she met and teamed up with Nawaf Souf, the "unelected leader" of Haris, and together they invited Israelis and internationals to take part in the olive harvest. In those early days of the Al-Aqsa Intifada, there was widespread reluctance to work with Israelis.[12] Nonetheless, the people in Haris wanted Israelis to come, and Golan phoned all over the country, "and they came," she told me. "For the Palestinians in Haris, the Israeli peace movement didn't disappear and die like it did for the rest of the Palestinians. But the person that made that possible was Nawaf. He was the one that invited, said 'We're nonviolent,' and told people, 'Yes, we want you to come.'"

> To me, also, the beginning of Ta'ayush was from there. And the beginning of ISM was from there; Nawaf was a cofounder of both these movements. When I met him, he was fresh out of thirteen years in prison, and with no bitterness toward Israelis in general. After [Nawaf's brother] Issa was shot,[13] I remember [Nawaf] telling me that he couldn't think of more blood being spilt—the idea of revenge just seems insane to him. He just doesn't want any more blood. And he was talking about the futility of it. To me, he's just an incredible person in such incredibly terrible circumstances. If you think about those circumstances either really "getting" a person or really making them shine, he's really the case where you can see how somebody grows refined from these kinds of trials.

Huwaida Arraf

Another ISM co-founder, Huwaida Arraf, is the U.S.-born daughter of Palestinian parents. Mentioning that her father, who holds Israeli citizenship, had had the foresight to register her and her siblings as Israeli citizens born abroad, something no longer allowed under Israeli law, she told me, "So anyway, I'm an Israeli citizen." Arraf's Jewish-American husband, Adam Shapiro—deported from Israel/Palestine for his activities with ISM—refuses on moral grounds to apply for citizenship under the Law of Return.[14] "And so," said Arraf, "he's not allowed in the country and I am." She began her activism in Palestine in April 2000 as a program organizer for Seeds of Peace, but resigned early in the Intifada to be a full-time organizer for ISM.[15] She described the early weeks of the Al-Aqsa Intifada as "popular protests [with] some people throwing rocks, but no weapons whatsoever," and the Israeli response as live ammunition from heavily armed soldiers, with a "high level of casualties and reports coming out that most of the people getting injured or killed [had received] bullet wounds to the chest and up, which was like a 'shoot to kill' policy (which was reported by [Ha'aretz journalist] Amira Hass)." Arraf said she saw people losing faith in the effectiveness of nonviolent resistance: "Palestinians were tired and didn't have much hope in this strategy. And so I, who was still one of the ones that was still optimistic, I started thinking about how could we create a resource for Palestinians to carry out a convincing and successful active nonviolent resistance."

> I wanted to be able to present something to people: a viable strategy or resource that could be used that wasn't a factor, perhaps, in the previous years of struggle. And international solidarity was one of those things. Even though documentation and carrying the word out is probably the most important thing you can tell Palestinians that you're doing, I thought it was very important for internationals to get actively involved in the resistance against the occupation here, to form a concrete and a viable resistance. If we can provide that little bit of hope, we can work together—people of all races, ethnicities, and religious backgrounds and Palestinians here—trying to find a way to end the occupation. So for that reason, I've given the last two-and-a-half years of my life to building the International Solidarity Movement, which in numbers and in name has probably grown a lot bigger than I thought it would.[16]

And despite the many obstacles to the building of a massive Palestinian nonviolent resistance movement that still remained, Arraf reiterated her positive stance: "I'm still optimistic, and I'm working with people and groups to try to build a strategy for a powerful people's resistance."

Partnership

Saif Abu Keshek

ISM activist Saif Abu Keshek regards increased international participation in, and publicizing of, the nonviolent resistance in Palestine as a "strategic key in the solution." When I interviewed him during the Bethlehem conference, he spoke of why he himself got involved as a Palestinian coordinator in this organization made up largely of volunteers from outside Israel/Palestine joining Palestinians in acts of nonviolent resistance.

> Why did I join a movement that is practicing nonviolent direct action? I grew up during the First Intifada, and I lived through the "peace process." My parents have been political activists for a long time and still are. All these circumstances influenced my choices. I did see, during the First Intifada, that popular resistance was able to defeat soldiers, was able to defeat guns. Looking at the direction that the Second Intifada took, it was very clear that military resistance is not really a choice. It is not a strategic choice; it is not really able to defeat the Israeli machine. We were losing from all sides in any kind of military confrontation, and I didn't see any positive side to such a situation for the Palestinian cause. I therefore worked a lot in social [service] activities—working with kids, working with people who have been traumatized, working inside society—until I started to know the International Solidarity Movement, and I found a place where I can fit in, where I can contribute, and I can also learn a lot, which is very important to me.

It's not the easiest thing to do, said Abu Keshek, who joined ISM in 2002, but he regards it as the most useful: "I believe in it, strategically and also from the theoretical side. I personally wouldn't do something if I wouldn't believe in it."

Ya'akov Manor

Septuagenarian Ya'akov Manor is no newcomer to nonviolent activism, and is among the most innovative and proactive leaders in the Israeli peace movement. I met this former Peace Now activist during my 2003 trip, when I received an email announcing an olive harvesting convoy to the West Bank. Since early in the Al-Aqsa Intifada, representatives of various Israeli organizations had been making periodic trips to Palestinian villages to serve as a protective presence during the fall olive harvest. I'd been disappointed by an earlier such venture where almost all of the participants turned out to be visitors from the United States rather than members of the Israeli organization that had issued the invitation. But Ya'akov Manor is a man with an impressive ability to inspire other Israelis to follow his lead. That sunny October morning saw three buses from Jerusalem, Tel Aviv, Haifa, and points in between converge on the West Bank village of Yanoun,[17] where they disgorged over a hundred people, from teens to seniors—mostly members of various Israeli activist groups. We spent an uneventful day harvesting olives with village families, sharing lunch under the trees, while hostile settlers occasionally looked on, but kept their distance. Manor, I was told, organizes such convoys virtually every week during the harvest season. I interviewed him in January of 2006. His activism—going back to First Intifada days—is driven, he explained, by his upbringing and his worldview: "I regard the world as one 'courtyard,' and the division of human beings into groups of one sort or another seems to me superfluous and should be done away with," he declared, adding wryly, "I assume this won't happen tomorrow morning."

I wondered out loud what had taken him from the commonplace activities of groups like Peace Now to his unique form of independent organizing that brings together members of a wide variety of organizations—and of no organization at all. Decrying the factionalism of the Israeli left, Manor told me, "People will kill you over a comma here or a period there. They'll nail you to the wall. No one is willing to give ground."

> So I said, "Wait a minute. It's very hard to take all of the groups and to unite them on a common platform, or even in a joint action. So let's create some sort of mechanism that will be able to include them as participants in ad hoc activities, short- or long-term, about which they all could say "Okay, we agree on this. We don't have comprehensive agreement on how the Palestinian state will be, how this or that will be, but we now have an objective."

As to the beginnings of the Olive Harvest Coalition, whose convoy I'd participated in, it seems that someone told Manor that a Palestinian villager had been shot while gathering olives. Manor replied, "Don't worry. We'll start to do it, and everyone will join in." And they did. Whether people agree or not about political details, he told me, "when there is an organized activity that grabs them, they come."

[29]

So that's what motivates me, because I'm the sort of person I am, and the Israeli-Palestinian conflict disturbs me very much. Also because I'm an Israeli and I want a different life here; I want a different future for my children. I want there to be a future for the people who live here, Jews too, not just Palestinians. I always think about my side; I don't care only about the Palestinians. I care about the Palestinians in the common context of our common life.

And, Manor added, "I am today more despairing than I have been in all my history of activism, because the situation is most difficult. *But* we know from many historical processes and incidents amongst the peoples of the world that the most difficult situation has generated the solution, so today I'm also an optimist, even today."

Rabbi Jeremy Milgrom
Rabbi Jeremy Milgrom is another Israeli Jew with a long history of involvement in the nonviolent struggle for Palestinian human rights, both as a participant in organizations such as Rabbis for Human Rights and Palestinians and Israelis for Nonviolence (PINV) and as an independent activist and military refusenik.

I'm interested in fostering a liveable situation, which means that the colonialist domination, the structural domination has to give way to partnership between Jews and Palestinians. That's basically it. On the issue of nonviolence, I'm confronted with the embracing of violence by Israeli society, which has, in my opinion, moved so far away from classic Jewish attitudes which were basically nonviolent; and Israeli society today is at the forefront of the violent reaction against the "enemy," whether it's the terror that Israelis live in or the general challenge that the claim for Palestinian presence on the land represents to Israel. We find ourselves, of course, in a cycle where the occupation has become more and more brutal; and the repression of the Palestinian resistance has gotten to a point where certain concepts, which are really abysmal, such as "collateral damage," have become acceptable to the Israeli public; and all kinds of spin is applied to assassination: various [terms] such as "elimination" and "targeted killing" and "removal" are applied to Palestinian leaders and members of political parties.

Rabbi Milgrom also expressed concern regarding the effect of this kind of thinking on the Jewish religion, which is producing, he says "a very un-Jewish Judaism."

It's totally clear to me that what has happened to Judaism because of Jewish nationalism—because of Zionism—is horrendous. We're not turning the corner; we're not open to another way of existing with the Palestinians. First of all, it means that the Holocaust never becomes the past. It's always dangled as the reason why we have to do this, and therefore the memory of the pain is always a raw nerve, and one doesn't see a decent future happening. The worst in the last six or seven years is the way that the world suddenly said, "Oh, of course we have to join Israel in the fight against Islam." Plus there's this already xenophobic Israeli-Jewish attitude.

On the other hand, he expressed joy at the growing number of young Israelis refusing to serve in the armed forces, commenting that, "It would be wonderful if Israel were confronted by a nonviolent Palestinian resistance, which would take away Israel's excuse of having to defend itself against violence."

The issue of promoting nonviolence will bring one to question some assumptions; for example, that Israel as a state for the Jewish people has a right to exist even if it clearly causes suffering to the Palestinian people. So the question is, what is the basis of that faith in Israel as a Jewish state. Is it a position that's taken because people feel that the world is against us and therefore we have to have a place of refuge and a place where we determine our own fate, that we cannot trust anyone who is not Jewish? If those are the attitudes, then I think that other reactions might still be more appropriate than simply being part of an escalating cycle of distrust that is caused by more weapons and more training and more aggressive responses and everything else. But surely one of the questions that has to be brought to the attention of whoever is supporting the actions of the state is, is this in fact self-defence, or is it an attempt to hold onto territories when there are clear alternatives and now a moderate Palestinian response that speaks of two states, etc.?

But ultimately, I would say that personally, at least for me right now, the notion of nonviolence is more powerful, more all-embracing, than the narrow interests of the Jewish people, which are expressed by most today by the maintenance of Israel as a Jewish state. I think that it's really important that people that advocate and practice and promote nonviolence—people from outside of Israel—engage Israelis on this subject and not accept this notion of "well, what we're doing is self-defence." That is not a sufficient answer. Nor do people have to sit back and hear, "Well, that's fine for Christians to say, but Judaism, you know, allows for violence and self-defence" and all that. I think that this contact, if it's sincere and if it's ongoing, can permit the internal Jewish dialogue that G-d wants of us and, again, bring more Israeli Jews to deal with the prominence of nonviolence in Jewish tradition.

Refusing to Serve

Ironically, perhaps, the closest counterparts to the Palestinian nonviolent resisters—many of whom, as we have seen, while personally eschewing armed struggle against the occupation, do not condemn the use of violence outright—are those Israeli combat soldiers and veterans of combat who employ the fundamental nonviolent technique of noncooperation in declaring their refusal to serve in what they perceive as the illegal imposition of Israeli will on another people, be it in the Lebanon of the 1980s or the occupied territories in the 1980s onward. Although comprising a relatively small fraction of Israeli anti-occupation activists, these refuseniks (as they are commonly referred to) command a great deal of respect amongst both Palestinians and the world-wide community of those who oppose the Israeli occupation and/or militarism generally. Most Israeli refuseniks are "selective refusers," who continue to report for service outside the occupied territories, although a small (but growing) minority extend their refusal to any service at all in the Israeli army so long as the occupation continues, and a minute number are actual pacifists who reject military service altogether, under any circumstances.

Matan Kaminer

Among the refuseniks that I interviewed in 2003 was Matan Kaminer, a third-generation activist and one of the six *Shministim* (twelfth graders/high school seniors) who were eventually sentenced by a military court to a year in addition to time served after having informed the minister of defence in a now-famous letter that they "... refuse to serve the occupation, whether that means to refuse enlisting altogether [or] whether it means to refuse serving in the territories." Matan Kaminer grew up in a political household, "being educated from a small age in my house by my parents and by my grandparents."[18] I met him at the gates of the Tel Hashomer military base not far from Tel Aviv, where he was being held in "open detention" pending the outcome of his trial and that of five of his fellow signers. He had a four-hour pass, so we crossed the road and sat on a weedy slope with our backs to the traffic noise. "I'm part of a growing group of people in Israeli society who are refusing to serve the occupation in one way or another," he told me. "Specifically, I'm refusing to join the army altogether, to enlist. As a young person, all Israeli Jews are required to enlist in the army for two or three years, if you are a woman or a man, respectively." Kaminer explained that the first *Shministim* letter was sent to Prime Minister Sharon in 2001, signed by sixty-two young people facing compulsory enlistment. At the time of our interview, the number of signatories to these letters was estimated at between four and five hundred.

Adam Keller

Like Matan Kaminer, Adam Keller, too, might be said to have imbibed activism with his mother's milk. His mother, Hava Keller, remained active in Women for Women Political Prisoners and other Israel-based peace and justice organizations well into her seventies. Now spokesman for Gush Shalom, and co-editor with his wife, Beate Zilversmidt, of *The Other Israel*, Adam Keller was, like Matan's grandfather, Reuven, a participant in the "illegal" dialogue with the PLO in Romania in 1986. He is a long-time refusenik who moved from selective to total refusal to serve in the Israeli army in the early 1990s. I was a bit surprised, therefore, when he recalled how, as a young conscript in 1974, he was so eager to take up arms that he had energetically protested his exclusion from combat duty (due to poor eyesight), initially refusing to report for a warehouseman's course, saying, "I prefer to go to prison, because I want to be a real soldier." Only after a fatherly officer persuaded him that he might still be in the position of being hit by artillery, thereby becoming "a living torch," did he consent to take the course.

Ten years later, two years into the Lebanon War, and already one of the founders of the Israeli refusenik organization Yesh Gvul, "There was no question whatsoever: I'm also going to refuse. So I did. But there was just one second that I had the thought that at last now the army is giving me what I wanted so much ten years ago, and now when they're giving it to me, I'm going to refuse it and go to prison rather than accept it. But that is part of how a person develops."

Ido Khenin
A time-honoured method of avoiding army service is to feign insanity. In Israel, the "successful" candidate receives the military classification of "Profile 21," the Israeli equivalent of the U.S. army's 4F. Ido Khenin chose that route of refusal.

> I told them that I am crazy, like many other good guys who tell the army they are crazy, although they know in their heart that the army is crazy and Israel is crazy for the occupation and for all the crimes against the Palestinians and against their own citizens. And they said, "Okay, goodbye, we don't need you. We have enough crazy people in the army; we don't need more people that are crazy." And after I got released from the army, I said to myself, "Okay, now you are finished high school; you have to start doing what you believe."[19]

Some jobs—above and beyond the many that require proof of past army service—are closed to a person with Profile 21 on their record, but Khenin is not worried; and for now, has designed his own "civilian service" job, in the absence of a formal program for alternative service to the military, as a volunteer teacher at a kindergarten in a poor neighbourhood in the "mixed" town of Lod in Israel.

> They have no education at home and they grew up in a very hard environment. They are five years old, and they're very cute; crazy but cute. Very wild, but I'm trying to teach them to be good to each other, to be good to people, to be good to everyone. And most of these children when they came were very racist: "Kill the Arabs, kill the Arabs." After a few months with me, they know that they can't say "Kill the Arabs." One day, I remember, one child took a stick and he was like shooting in the air, and then he said "I killed an Arab." But then he saw that I looked at him and he said "I killed a bad guy." It's a little change, but I'm starting. I hope that the children that I teach will grow up—even if there is still occupation—they will grow up to be thinking people, even if they don't agree with me, but they will think and use their minds, not the stick or the rifle.

Yonatan Shapira

Yonatan Shapira was a pilot in the Israeli air force when he, too, decided he'd had enough. He and a few others formed the core of the group of 27 who signed the so-called "Pilots' Letter" in September 2003, denouncing air force actions as war crimes—especially the so-called "targeted assassinations" of Hamas activists, which invariably resulted in the deaths of numerous civilian "bystanders," including young children—and refusing to continue flying such missions. They were dismissed from the air force the following month. The targeted assassinations—*hisulim* in Hebrew—had a profound effect on Shapira, even though he himself, as a rescue helicopter pilot, had not had to carry any out. "At a certain stage I understood that these bombings, which at first I thought maybe were okay, injured civilians, and I regarded this as a kind of terrorist attack (*pigua*): They do a *pigua* against us, we do a *pigua* against them."

I interviewed Shapira on the final evening of a weekend-long conference in Castlegar, BC, in Canada, focused on the issues surrounding the influx of U.S. "refuseniks" during the Vietnam and Iraq wars. One of the speakers at the conference was Daniel Ellsberg, the man who leaked the Pentagon Papers in 1971. Once you know something is wrong, commented Shapira, "there is another stage one needs to go through, of 'What do I need to do?' As Daniel Ellsberg said, you already understand that you are opposed, you want to do something, and you are searching for the most correct thing to do. So that's the process, in short." Shapira and a few friends, after consulting with members of the older refusenik organizations Yesh Gvul and Ometz LeSarev (Courage to Refuse), recruited the other pilots who had signed the letter. And then, he told me, his older brother "began making contact with Palestinians who had been in jail and who also had themselves been fighters. And so began the activism of Israeli refusers and Palestinian former fighters," in a new organization called Combatants for Peace.

Conclusion

Although comprising less than a quarter of the total number of activists I interviewed (or whose conference presentations I received permission to excerpt), the 26 individuals we have just met are a broad sampling of that group. Their responses to my first question ("What brought you to nonviolence?") ranged from a lifelong conviction of its rightness, to conversion-like experiences or more gradual development of a sense that nonviolence was the right approach for them. Some had become convinced of this through nonviolence training or by the example of a strong role model, while others spoke not so much of nonviolence as such but rather of their abhorrence of violence or about nonviolent tactics as being effective means of resisting the occupation.

Accounts of the journey to activism itself were similarly varied, although outrage at the worsening treatment of Palestinians was a common motivation for Israelis. Others included impatience with the factionalism of the Israeli left and concern for the "horrendous" effect of Jewish nationalism on Judaism. Additional factors, too, motivated the Palestinians in this sample: joining a joint Palestinian-Jewish (Israeli) group as a way of contradicting a growing sense of alienation (Leena Delasheh); the desire to help create "a viable strategy or resource" to support Palestinian nonviolence—in the form of international solidarity (Huwaida Arraf); and a sense of both the power of nonviolence and the conviction that participation by internationals in Palestinian nonviolent resistance, and their publicizing of it, was a "strategic key in the solution" (Saif Abu Keshek). The Israeli "refuseniks" in this chapter, although all impelled by their desire to dissociate themselves from the military occupation, are also a varied bunch: one a signatory to the *Shministim* (High School Seniors) Letter who refuses to serve at all in the Israeli military until the occupation is ended (Matan Kaminer); one a long-time activist who went from nearsighted wannabe combat soldier to total refuser (Adam Keller); one who chose to plead "mental unsuitability" rather than serve (Ido Khenin); and one, a pilot, expelled from the air force for signing a letter denouncing its actions as war crimes—now a member of the joint organization of Palestinian and Israeli former fighters, Combatants for Peace (Yonatan Shapira).

The stories told in Chapter 1 will be our most personal "meeting" with these activists (with the possible exception of Chapter 9 on visions for the future). In the remainder of this book, you will encounter most of them again (as well as many more), in a more impersonal mode, as they describe their organizations' strategies and discuss challenges, successes, and prospects for the future of nonviolent struggle. First, though, in Chapter 2 we'll set the scene, as it were, with descriptions of a few key precursors to the present nonviolent initiatives, as well as some recent thinking on the whole question of the application of nonviolence to the Palestinian struggle by seminal thinkers in this field.

NOTES

1 Although *Refusing to be Enemies* is specifically about Palestinian nonviolent resistance to the Israeli military occupation of the territories acquired in the 1967 war and Israeli participation in, and support for, this form of resistance, I am mindful of contributing author and editorial partner Jeff Halper's comment—at the second annual conference on Nonviolent Popular Joint Struggle held in the West Bank village of Bil'in in April of 2007—that "As we concentrate on the occupation, we shouldn't lose sight of the plight of the Palestinian citizens of Israel, who are more and more and more pressured." The Palestinians in Israel comprise 20% of the population, but by law and planning and zoning restrictions are confined to just 3.5% of the land of the country. House demolitions go on inside Israel almost as much as the occupied territories. There are 150,000 Palestinians with Israeli citizenship who live in over 100 unrecognized villages, and they are under siege. According to Stephen Lendman, whose article "'Unrecognized' Palestinians" can be accessed at www.icahd.org/eng/news.asp?menu=5&submenu=1&item=482, these villages are "unrecognized because their inhabitants are considered internal refugees who were forced to flee their original homes during Israel's 1948 'War of Independence' and were prevented from returning when it ended. These villages were delegitimized by Israel's 1965 Planning and Construction Law that established a regulatory framework and national plan for future development. It zoned land for residential, agriculture and industrial use, forbade unlicensed construction, [and] banned it on agricultural land... Palestinian areas are severely constricted leaving no room for expansion. Their land was reclassified as agricultural meaning no new construction is allowed. This meant entire communities became 'unrecognized' and all homes and buildings there declared illegal, even the 95% of them built before the 1965 law passed. They're subject to demolition and inhabitant displacement." (Lendman 2007)
2 For more of Jean Zaru's thinking on nonviolence from her perspective as a Palestinian Quaker woman, see Zaru 2008.
3 "Oslo" refers variously to the Oslo Accords and to related agreements and the implementation "process" that followed the September 2003 Accords. Jeff Halper (2008), *inter alia*, provides a clear description of the main provisions of the 2003 Oslo Accords and the disappointing outcomes of the so-called Oslo peace process.
4 One of his arms is misshapen; I'm not sure what other disability(ies) he may have.
5 In a phone interview on 30 April 2009.
6 See also Chapter 5 on the Beit Sahour tax strike.

7 PCSNV – Founded in 1984 by Mubarak Awad, PCSNV was headed by other local activists after Awad's 1988 deportation. In 1998 Mubarak Awad's nephew Sami Awad moved the PCSNV office to Bethlehem, where it became one of the founding initiatives of HLT. Its work is continued under the name of HLT's Nonviolence Programs (from www.holylandtrust.org).

8 And student organizations, I recalled. One morning in 1991 (while his wife was in hospital having just given birth to their son, Nadim) we at the AIC were greeted with the information that our co-worker Mohammed—this quiet man given to lecturing Israeli soldiers on nonviolence while cooling his heels waiting for this permit or that at Civil Administration headquarters—had been arrested once again and sentenced to a term of administrative detention at the notorious Ketziot prison camp (popularly known as Ansar III) in the Negev, apparently because of past political affiliations in his university days.

9 See Chapter 3.

10 The term *Nakba* ('catastrophe' in Arabic) refers to the creation of between 700,000 and 750,000 Palestinian refugees from the territory of what became the State of Israel in 1948–49, as well as the internal displacement of another *c*.150,000 Palestinians within the state.

11 The Druze citizens of Israel are subject to the draft, many ultimately serving in the Border Guard (a branch of the Israel Police); Bedouin are not drafted, but many volunteer for military service.

12 The issue of so-called "normalization" is treated at length in Chapter 4, in the text of the chapter and in endnotes 1, 12, and 13.

13 In May 2001, Issa Souf, active in Ta'ayush and other joint ventures with Israelis, was rendered paraplegic after being shot in the spine by an Israeli soldier while trying to clear young children from the scene of an encounter between stone-throwing teens and soldiers near his home in Haris.

14 The Law of Return is an Israeli law granting citizenship to anyone who can prove he or she is the child of a Jewish mother and has not voluntarily converted to another religion.

15 I interviewed Huwaida Arraf on 15 October 2003. Huwaida Arraf subsequently studied Human Rights and Humanitarian Law in the United States and now teaches the subject at al-Quds University in East Jerusalem (current as of February 2009). She is also Chair of the Free Gaza Movement.

16 Neta Golan, responding to my request for the total number of ISM participants over the years, replied: "[A]fter our office was raided and database confiscated in 2003 we have done our best not to keep records, my super rough estimate is 8000 internationals." (6 May 2009)

17 See Chapter 7 for more about Yanoun and the role of Israelis and internationals.

18 For more on Matan's grandfather, Reuven Kaminer, see Chapters 2, 4, 6, and 8).

19 See Chapter 5 for Ido Khenin's story of his involvement in the struggle against the wall in Bil'in.

2

NONVIOLENCE IN THE STRUGGLE AGAINST THE OCCUPATION

I was one time driving from Jerusalem to Bethlehem, and I saw an old lady with a child about three or four years old, and she was standing in front of a garbage truck. I was driving by, and then I went back and asked her "What's the matter? What happened with you?" She said, "Israelis, they bring garbage and throw it on my land. I tried to go to court, I tried to go to the [Israeli] authorities, I tried to go to the lawyers, I tried everything. I couldn't stop them, so I decided to stop them myself, to stand in front of the garbage truck and not allow them. And I felt that this is the best I could do, when there would be no help for me." And I said, "Oh, my God! This woman, she's defying everything." And after that, the next week, I put an ad in the Israeli press, in the Palestinian press, in the English—whatever I could, and I say I want to have a workshop how to get rid of occupation. And people said "You are crazy. What do you mean get rid of an occupation?" I said, "Yes, I want to do a workshop how to get rid of occupation." And I thought there would be thirty, forty people to come. We had so many people start coming. I was interested to get rid of occupation from the minds of people that they will not be afraid. And there was a hunger how to get rid of this occupation.

Mubarak Awad (Addressing the Celebrating Nonviolent Resistance conference in Bethlehem, December 27–30, 2005)

Precursors to Current Nonviolent Activism

Although they themselves no longer exist, the initiatives described in this section paved the way for successors in various fields: *New Outlook* magazine for the *Palestine-Israel Journal* (PIJ), First-Intifada-era Popular Committees for present-day Popular Committees against Settlements and the Wall,[1] and the Committee Against the Iron Fist for later joint ventures. Similarly, the initiatives described here by Veronika Cohen are some early examples of responses—whether in the form of short-term actions or long-term campaigns—by Israeli grassroots activists to the need for solidarity with the Palestinian community. Thus, many of the groups described later in this book are descendants—direct or indirect—of these or other early initiatives, and the "illegal" meetings between Israeli leftists and PLO representatives in the mid-1980s, says

Reuven Kaminer, provided "a precursor model" for later negotiations between Israel and the Palestinians.

First-Intifada-Era Activism

Veronika Cohen: Israelis by Choice, and the Beita Committee

I first met Veronika Cohen shortly after moving to Jerusalem in the late 1980s. This music professor turned activist could easily be identified in the largely secular activist crowd by the snood with which she, in common with many other Orthodox Jewish women, covered her hair. Sitting across from me in the small kosher Chinese restaurant in Jerusalem where I interviewed her in January 2006, Cohen was no longer wearing her snood. She had abandoned the head covering, she explained, because it made her look too much like the women of the Israeli settlements in the occupied territories, and she did not wish to be mistaken for a settler. Veronika Cohen was one of the original members of Israelis by Choice, a group formed on an ad hoc basis in 1988 to oppose the deportation of Jerusalem-born Palestinian nonviolence advocate Mubarak Awad from Israel, allegedly because of his having acquired U.S. citizenship while a student in that country. When I asked Cohen how and why she got involved in nonviolent action on behalf of Palestinians, she took me back before the outbreak of the First Intifada.

> It was around 1986. Really, I was at the point where I was so angry at what was happening that I think if I wouldn't have gotten involved in something, I would just burst. Something had to be done. Just reading the newspaper and wanting to scream or cry was not enough. So I was very lucky that one of my friends from the synagogue told me to go to meet someone who was involved in an activity in the neighbouring village of Sur Baher. The villagers had petitioned the court to get back land. The land had been expropriated to build [the "West" Jerusalem neighbourhood of] East Talpiot, and they were advised by their lawyer, after the neighbourhood was built, that they should petition the court to have the land that was not used for the neighbourhood officially returned back to them. They lost their case, and after they lost their case, the army—really as a kind of act of vengeance—began to uproot their vegetable plots which they had been using all this time to support themselves. And the Jewish National Fund planted trees [there], paid for by the money everybody put in the little boxes. So the fight was to get this

land back for the Palestinians to use for their own agricultural purposes. And this was really my first serious political activity; not just going to demonstrations and signing petitions, but actually putting serious work into a project.

The villagers gained the support of then Jerusalem mayor, Teddy Kollek, and the promise of return of some of their land. But then, Cohen said, "in a very insulting fashion, they were told that before they could plant anything, they would have to consult with an Israeli agronomist to find out what is the best crop for them to plant."

After hundreds of years of working the land, they should have this agronomist who was just back from Germany where he had studied, who was going to advise them on what they should be planting. So at that point, they were completely fed up, and as a sort of very aristocratic move at the end of this meeting, they said, "Thank you very much; we decided not to plant anything. We need a football field for our kids, so why don't we put a football field there." Which was a very, very nice move.

Then the [First] Intifada broke out, and there were other things to get involved in. During the Intifada, the first big activity I got involved in had to do with the expulsion of Mubarak Awad. We had formed a group; we called ourselves Israelis by Choice. The idea was, here was somebody who was born in Jerusalem who was not allowed to live here, and we who were not born here are allowed to come and live here. And we had made a decision that if he would lose his court case and would be expelled, then we would make a tear in our I.D. card as a sign of mourning.[2] So the day came, and we went to the trial, and he lost and he was being expelled; and as it turned out, most of the people who had decided together with me to tear their I.D. cards decided at the last minute not to do it. So, we had invited the press to come, and there were hundreds of people, cameras all over the place showed up; and at first, I was the only one who tore my I.D. card. And then when they said, "Are you the only one?" somebody I'd barely known, who was not part of the original group, stepped up and said, "No, she's not alone, and I'm joining her." Then two or three other people joined me, and we all tore our I.D. cards, and this was covered very widely. So a lot of people, a lot of Palestinians, I met said, "Oh, you're the woman who tore her I.D. card."

Cohen's next involvement, in the first year of the 1987 Intifada, was in the Beita Committee. As she explained:

There was a group of teenagers from the nearby settlement of Elon Moreh who went on a hike [to the West Bank village of Beita] to kind of demonstrate that this is their land and they can go anywhere they want. At some point, they sat down to eat and they came under a barrage of stones, and the guard who came with them started shooting and killed one of the Palestinians; and then he had a rock thrown at him and he became unconscious, and then at some point, accidentally, he killed one of the Israeli teenagers.

The villagers, fearing a riot that would endanger both them and the remaining teenagers, invited the Israeli youngsters into the village and hid them inside their houses.

But the army, instead of thanking them for saving the kids lives, basically went on a rampage. They destroyed fifteen houses, they arrested I don't know how many people; in addition to the houses that were destroyed by order, the houses next to them were also damaged. So there were just dozens of houses that had been damaged or destroyed.

"The day we heard about [the incident in Beita], the headline was "Israeli Girl Stoned to Death," Cohen recalled. "By the next morning, people knew that she was actually not stoned to death, she was shot, and she was shot by her own guard. But as it happens, months and even years later, when you mentioned it, nobody remembered that it was [the guard]; they only remembered the initial story, and they didn't remember what actually happened."

The Beita Committee formed itself with the basic goal of awakening the Israeli public to the danger that the settlers were posing. I don't remember who started it, but I got a phone call within a week saying there's this group; if you're interested, come and join. And so the idea was basically we wanted to serve an educational function and say, "Look, the settlers are leading us to the brink of disaster by taking the lead, and the Israeli public sort of blindly follows without questioning, and they're leading us into disaster, and shouldn't we put a stop to it?"

Although, she remarked, "We were obviously not successful," the Beita Committee did raise money to rebuild some of the demolished homes and provided legal representation for the imprisoned villagers, as well as bringing Israeli supporters to witness the trials.

About the second year of the Beita Committee, the settlers called for a day where they had hikes in the territories to kind of prove "this land is our land"—that kind of thing—and five of us women went to demonstrate against them, and a settler tried to run us down. He didn't succeed, so I'm here to tell the tale. It so happens that I saw his license plate, so we knew exactly who it was; and he went to court and he was charged with reckless driving. I think that was the end of it.

I asked Cohen how all this solidarity work influenced the Israeli public. "I think it's very difficult to say," she replied, "I think it influenced their thinking, maybe their lives in some sense. But it's the kind of thing you can never prove." On the other hand, though, she said, "I think we influenced the public climate: Beyond [giving] help, I think that the hope was to make a political impact. And whether one does or doesn't, I think it's very difficult to pinpoint. I have a feeling that we were influential."[3]

Jad Isaac: Victory Gardens and Popular Committees

Palestinian agronomist and researcher Jad Isaac (pronounced Is-haq) has been the general director of ARIJ, the Applied Research Institute – Jerusalem (despite its name, located in Bethlehem) since its founding in 1990. I had heard about him from Veronika Cohen early in the First Intifada, when he was a professor of Agronomy at Bethlehem University. He had, she told me, been jailed for encouraging the local people to grow victory gardens! I asked him about this when I interviewed him in 2003. It was more than just victory gardens, explained Isaac. What he had been involved in was actually the founding of some of the earliest of the Popular Committees, which were emulated throughout occupied Palestine and had made possible the maintenance of some semblance of normal functioning during those difficult days. He elaborated:

> When the First Intifada started, people started having a lot of time at their disposal because until 1991, there were a lot of strike days and closures. It was at that time we decided, a few of us, to take action to help our people. So we started this group in an informal way to encourage people to use their time in a productive manner by going back to the land and trying to raise their own food products,

vegetables, animals, and so on. Neighbourhood committees were established, and each neighbourhood committee [was] allocated a piece of land where all of them would work on a common plot of land to produce for everybody. In addition, everybody who had a piece of land could grow his own. And you started seeing drip irrigation increasing in Beit Sahour. You could see plants growing. You could see people discussing all sorts of things while they were working in the garden, and it became very, very widespread. It moved from Beit Sahour to other parts of the West Bank and Gaza. At the same time, people started utilizing this organizational structure—which is the neighbourhood committees—by having subcommittees: one to be in charge of first aid, one to be for teaching because, you know, the schools were closed.

Schoolteachers in the neighbourhood got together and said, "Okay, we'll start a class." Let's say, Mr. X has a room which he can put at the disposal of the neighbourhood. So this group will be hosting grade one. Another person will have grade two. And if we didn't have enough students, we would combine classes. The children loved it so much because it was a way for them to continue their education, and at the same time, it gave us a feeling of strength. Of course we had a social committee where people decided to do some kind of self-support mechanisms. If somebody lost his job, members of the committee would say, "Okay, we will decide to assist by providing supplies, also by providing in-kind assistance, no questions asked." People were volunteering to do it, and we found that many people even were refusing to take this kind of assistance because they said, "We would like to work."

This became widespread all over the West Bank and Gaza. This was the origin of the Popular Committees. It was considered to be very subversive activity, so we were arrested and I was given a six-month administrative detention, which I spent in Ansar III.[4] They did not charge me officially; I was put there as an administrative detainee—in 1988. They tried to arrest the leadership, but it didn't stop, and the gardens continued to grow.

"When I came out of jail," said Isaac, "I found that the university was simply too much of an ivory tower, so I decided to continue this kind of work, but at a different level. I decided to start doing this through my research and through my development work—and have continued since then."

Michel Warschawski: The Committee Against the Iron Fist,
an Early Joint Initiative

The Popular Committees described by Jad Isaac, which grew to be the backbone of civil society in the villages and refugee camps in the course of the First Intifada, were a strictly Palestinian initiative. On the other hand, Michel Warschawski (aka Mikado), of the joint Palestinian-Israeli activist organization the Alternative Information Center (AIC), described the 1985 founding of the Committee Against the Iron Fist as an attempt to form something new: a joint Palestinian-Israeli political action organization "to keep public protest against the occupation on the agenda" at a time when both the Israeli peace movement and the Palestinian nationalist movement were at a low ebb.[5] The committee was formed, stated Warschawski, with the understanding that it would not be the nucleus for a new movement, nor was it intended to replace either the Israeli peace movement or the Palestinian nationalist movement.

> We knew very well that in the new circumstances, the Israeli peace movement would eventually reawaken as an Israeli peace movement—and not an Israeli-Palestinian one, just as the Palestinian movement would find new ways of struggling as a Palestinian movement and not as an Israeli-Palestinian one. But for the time being, the few forces which remained on the scene could develop a kind of joint project, a movement which would keep public protest against the occupation on the agenda.
>
> We saw our working together itself as having three main objectives: first—to convey the message that cooperation was possible; i.e., being together was in itself an objective. The second objective was to serve each other, so that both sides would benefit from each other's experience by virtue of being active in an Israeli-Palestinian movement. For example, people who were deeply involved in the Israeli peace movement were able to take advantage of their experience of being inside Israeli society and their knowledge of how to approach the Israeli public—from the point of view of language, of where to place emphasis, of how to talk. And the third objective was to learn to think in slightly different terms regarding ways of expressing protest and opposition/resistance to the occupation. For the Israelis, what was different was the common effort itself. For the Palestinians, it was something else. It involved exposure to modes of political expression which were different from the usual very infrequent, massive demonstrations or protest efforts of the Palestinian nationalist movement and its

mainly half-underground activism, which was confrontational with army and police forces. Around these three hubs we built the Committee Against the Iron Fist.

In these three spheres, the success was far beyond anything we had anticipated. First of all, because of the vacuum that existed at the time—especially the media vacuum (though as regards Israel, it was more than just a media vacuum), all of our activities received media coverage. And there were many: demonstrations, protest vigils, almost weekly or even sometimes semi-weekly meetings of the activist Forum. And the media covered all of them, because that's all there was. Peace Now was not active at the time.

The most important success in my eyes was how we learned, in the course of working together, to take into account and to base our activity on, not only an understanding of what was effective for our own constituency, but also what was effective and possible from the point of view of the other. When we wrote a leaflet, we had to know, from the very beginning, not only what I, Mikado, would write to Israeli anti-Zionist activists or Israeli radical activists, but also not to forget that this leaflet was essentially "signed" by people from the Palestinian nationalist movement, and to consider how best they could appeal to the Israeli public. And when they wrote, they had to take into account that they were speaking not only to other Palestinians, but to the Israeli public as well. [...]

In the course of working together on this committee, there quickly developed a "common minimum," if we can call it that, which improved as time went on. That is, participants developed an ability—without giving up their respective uniqueness—to respect, not only the political needs of the other side, but also its fundamental point of view, its ethical boundaries; something which could only be done on a basis of complete trust. There were occasions when we were unable to get together to meet, and I remember several times writing leaflets in the name of the Committee Against the Iron Fist without having been able to get ahold of Faisal Husseini or any other spokesperson for the Palestinian side that day, and knowing that he relied on me, knowing that when I wrote this, I was not only thinking for Mikado, but also for Faisal Husseini, and I knew that the same was true for him.

I will give one example which shows our progress in the Committee Against the Iron Fist and what proceeded from it. In the week of the fifth of June, 1987, we organized the first Israeli-Palestinian march in Jerusalem, marking the anniversary of the occupation. This was a new experience for both sides: for the Jews, demonstrating with Palestinians in the heart of East Jerusalem, and for Arabs, holding a demonstration with Israelis on the one hand,

and a legal demonstration, with police permission, on the other. The fact that we succeeded in reaching an understanding on the part of the Palestinians that it is permissible to demonstrate—it is permissible to make use of the right to demonstrate legally—was one of the tactical achievements of the Committee Against the Iron Fist: if it is not allowed to demonstrate legally, then throw stones, demonstrate as you are able, but if it is permitted, then take advantage of that right. And if the Palestinians have a problem reaching consensus regarding their applying for a permit, let them utilize us Israelis, and we will request permission.

Thus we succeeded in holding the demonstration peacefully. There were a few dozen Israelis and a few hundred Palestinians, 800 or 900 people altogether, marching the length of the demarcation line between East and West Jerusalem peacefully, and the police had to ensure the safety of a Palestinian march, done openly for the first time. There were many restrictions: no shouting of slogans, for example. But the Palestinians knew that either you play the game or not.

And because we were who we were, there was first of all a degree of trust which would be hard to find in the Peace Now-ish crowd. This trust was the outcome of our respect for the Palestinians. Firstly, we told them, "You set the limits, because you are the ones who are demonstrating under occupation." In this case this meant: "If you say that demonstrating without flags is out of the question, and the police say no, and you don't want to demonstrate, fine; if you say okay, we're willing to do without flags on this or that condition, we will be your spokespersons in negotiations with the police, because it's no problem for us and for you it is," not out of obsequiousness towards the Palestinians, but to compensate in some measure for the absence of symmetry in Israeli-Palestinian relations. Secondly, we said, "We will not monitor your behaviour during demonstrations. Each side will monitor itself. I don't see myself as mediating between the police and the demonstrators. If the police say take down a sign, you take down your own sign. We depend on you. We know that this is the agreement which we made with the police, we made it together. It's your responsibility." We have complete trust, and this trust was created in the course of our work.

This was a very good thing. The Palestinians learned a lot from it, and we also learned from this that it is possible and worthwhile to do it. You do pay a price—it's clear that one must compromise on certain things—but we knew the sense of achievement of having close to a thousand people going home and saying, "It's possible, It's possible!" From the point of view of power, it wasn't a demonstration where one looked silly and ridiculous to the police, but rather it was a compelling demonstration of power. And there was the additional achievement of building up momentum, so that many of the Palestinian bodies which had been hesitant about the committee—nationalist factions, trade-unions, and so on—began to take it seriously.

On the Israeli side, however, there was nothing. Several hundred Palestinians and a few dozen Israelis. There was no response on the Israeli side except for the newspapers. But the people did not know what it was about. They thought it was an Arab demonstration, and that didn't interest them. They did not understand that there was an innovation here, something conceptually new. [...]

"The committee did not give birth to the Intifada," Warschawski emphasized, "but there is a clear, unambiguous continuity—both in the people who led the committee on the Palestinian side and in its conceptualization—so that one could say that it was part of the same process."

> It is also possible to say that the conditions and events which made the time ripe for the Intifada did so for the committee as well, at an earlier stage. After the outbreak of the Intifada, the Jews from the committee were occupied with building the Israeli peace movement and the Palestinians were occupied with the Intifada. And essentially all of the Palestinian activists from the Committee Against the Iron Fist—except for Sari Nusseibeh—were either put under administrative detention or expelled during the first year of the Intifada; not coincidentally, but because these were the cadres who made the Intifada. [...]

"It is interesting to note," he concluded, "that the very demonstration which was not permitted in September 1987—identical from the point of view of issues, of its significance for Israeli-Palestinian cooperation, and of the Palestinian forces who backed it—Faisal Husseini and Sari Nusseibeh—was finally held in December of 1989."

> The massive human chain around the walls of the Old City of Jerusalem, [was] organized, on the Israeli side, not by a few radicals, but by Peace Now and by [left Zionist] Ratz Knesset members. In this breakthrough, of which the Committee Against the Iron Fist was essentially a symbol, one sees the power of the Intifada. It also shows that we were not, in espousing joint Israeli-Palestinian

demonstrations, as detached from reality as some of our very good friends thought we were.

Reuven Kaminer: Defying the "Anti-Peace Law"

Reuven Kaminer (Peace Now Jerusalem/Hadash) is another Israeli whom I asked to remember an earlier era of his activism, in the mid-1980s. Kaminer had been one of the "Romanian Four," Israeli leftists who—in an act of civil disobedience—met with representatives of the PLO in Bucharest in 1986, in defiance of a recently enacted Israeli law outlawing such contact (dubbed the "anti-peace law" by its opponents).[6] He recalled:

Somewhere about 1984 or '85, the government of Israel decided to improve on its "anti-terror" laws. It turns out that there was nothing wrong with meeting people from the PLO, per se. The law said there had to be some kind of criminal intent or some sort of proposition of doing something illegal. They found out that people had been talking to the PLO, so they decided there had to be a law against it; and they passed this absolutely ridiculous, idiotic law which said that the mere contact with anybody from the PLO was a criminal act and you could go to jail for four or five years, or something like that. It was never popular in the country for some strange reason. It came out of this atavistic, populist, anti-Palestinianism that said that there should be a law against talking to these people. And since meetings had been going on all along, the crucial decision that people in the peace movement had to decide was whether or not they would continue meeting.

The really unique thing about the meeting between the twenty or so Israeli peace activists from different groups with different orientations, was that it was the first meeting after the law had been passed and was in open defiance of the law. So we met—I think in November 1986—we had a nice meeting and we did it as publicly as possible and as openly as possible, as much under the Klieg lights as possible. I admit that the meeting per se was not one of the most important meetings in the history of Israeli-Palestinian relations; but thanks to the government of Israel, and its prosecution, etc., etc., it became important in the sense that we said that we were going to continue meeting. There were other people who continued meeting at different levels. A lot of people looked for academic coverage, and all kinds of thing—academic conferences with the PLO. But by doing so, we challenged the Israeli government. We had this long court procedure that went on for years, until when our final appeal against the conviction occurred in the Supreme

[49]

Court, the law had already been rescinded. Of course, even if you violate a law and it's later rescinded, that's not a defence per se, but the public aspect was total vindication. So we had had a sentence of six months in jail and a fine, and we had delayed the court sentence all the time the appeal was going on. We never went to jail, so they cancelled, for all practical purposes, everything, and gave us back the money. They didn't actually vindicate us or decide we were not guilty, but it was one of those rare things, almost a total victory against the law—which had become unpopular, and people understood it was just a silly law.

Hillel Schenker and New Outlook: When Enemies Dare to Talk
Hillel Schenker, now Jewish co-managing editor of the *Palestine-Israel Journal of Politics, Economics and Culture*, reminisced about *New Outlook*— "a magazine that got Israelis and Palestinians talking to each other."

When *New Outlook*, the Israeli peace monthly, was founded back in 1957 by a group of Israeli Arabs and Jews, founding editor Simha Flapan came to Martin Buber, whose philosophy of dialogue served as an inspiration for the magazine, with a dilemma. [Flapan] said that "we have established a vehicle to promote dialogue and understanding, but the neighbouring Arabs are not ready to respond to our efforts." This was during the period in the first decade of the State of Israel's existence when Israeli academic participants at international conferences always discovered that intellectuals from neighbouring Arab states were afraid to sit next to them in public, for fear of the flack they might get (and worse) when they returned home. Buber's response was that, "for a dialogue, you don't necessarily need the active participation of the other. You need the other's existence. The actual dialogue will eventually come."

And it did, on the pages of *New Outlook*, and at international conferences, beginning with the Mediterranean Colloquia convened by the idealistic mayor of Florence, Giorgia La Pira, in the late fifties and early sixties. Buber himself, as well as representatives of *New Outlook*, participated in these efforts. In 1978, *New Outlook* convened a path-breaking two-day Israeli-Palestinian dialogue at the picturesque American Colony Hotel in East Jerusalem, which eventually was published in book form under the title *When Enemies Dare to Talk*. And in 1979, it convened an international symposium in Washington, with leading Palestinian intellectual Professor Hisham Sharabi as the keynote Palestinian speaker. At the end of that symposium, Flapan, now considered the father of the New Israeli Historians, said that, "our goal is to eventually establish a joint Israeli-Palestinian publication." At the time, this seemed like a utopian dream. But after having served thirteen years as an editor of *New Outlook*, I now find myself serving as co-managing editor of the *Palestine-Israel Journal* alongside my Palestinian colleagues.[7]

Recent Thinking about Nonviolence

Pragmatic Nonviolence
Gene Sharp
A key theme in recent thinking on nonviolent activism is that of "pragmatic" nonviolent activism, as described in great detail by U.S.-based theoretician Gene Sharp in his classic three-volume work *The Politics of Nonviolent Action* (Sharp 1973). Sharp, who is founder and senior scholar at the Albert Einstein Institution in Boston and has taught at Harvard and the University of Massachusetts, has also authored a number of shorter guides to the practical application of the strategies and tactics of pragmatic nonviolence, including *From Dictatorship to Democracy* (Sharp 1993/2002), which has so far been translated into twenty-one languages and employed by grassroots activists in numerous struggles against repressive governments.

In a 1989 article (Sharp 1989) reproduced in the program brochure of the Celebrating Nonviolent Resistance conference in Bethlehem, December 27–30, 2005, Sharp wrote, *inter alia*, that "Nonviolent struggle is a means of wielding power, a technique that is designed to fight a violent opponent willing and well equipped to wield military force. It is also designed for use against opponents who cannot be defeated by violence ... using psychological, social, economic, and political weapons." He then listed the three classes into which he subdivides his well-known list of 198 nonviolent techniques:

1) [S]ymbolic forms of nonviolent protest (such as vigils, marches, and flying flags); 2) noncooperation (including social boycotts, economic boycotts, labour strikes, and many forms of political noncooperation ranging from repudiation of legitimacy to civil disobedience and mutiny); and 3) nonviolent intervention (ranging from hunger strikes to nonviolent occupations and blockades, the

creation of self-reliant institutions, and the establishment of a rival parallel government).

Sharp's article went on to lay out requirements for effective nonviolent struggle ("including persistence in the face of repression and nonviolent discipline ... [wise] strategy and careful implementation ...") and concluded with the admonition:

> [F]or maximum effectiveness, it is essential that nonviolent struggles be conducted with adherence to the requirements of the technique of nonviolent action, just as is the case with conventional and guerrilla wars. This understanding of nonviolent struggle has great relevance to the Palestinian uprising.

Speaking at the Bethlehem conference, Sharp placed the Palestinian struggle in the context of nonviolence worldwide:

> Pragmatic nonviolent action, which people use because they need some means of struggle, has been the main thrust of the historically significant development of nonviolent struggle for, not decades, but for centuries. There are widespread misconceptions about anything to which the word "nonviolence" is attached. For example, that we must love or we can't really use nonviolent action; that there is really little more that people who have a certain belief need to learn—they already maybe know all they need to know; that it involves a rejection of power. None of these are true. Love can help, but people who hate can also use nonviolent struggle; and they must not be excluded, although they might refine their attitudes, perhaps. Nonviolent struggle is not something for which we have to have a conversion experience. It's based upon being stubborn and difficult. I know all of us have that capacity. Nonviolent struggle did not begin with Gandhi, much less Martin Luther King, important though both of these men have been. It's very old. Nonviolent struggle is something that people have done for ages. The whole assumption that this is something that requires some special development on our part is only half true. We're quite capable of this, but whether we choose to use this in the most effective way is a different question. Nonviolent struggle wields power. It requires courage. It does not, in my humble opinion, require greater courage than the use of violence. In fact, the casualty rates in the uses of nonviolent struggle are significantly lower than if you choose to struggle by violence.

I do not define [nonviolence] as a belief system. It's defined, in my opinion, by what people do; and you can believe in nonviolent means and do something that is catastrophically injurious to your movement, or you can do something that is helpful even though it might be that violence is what you'd prefer to do, but you just can't do it, but you can use the nonviolent struggle.

Sharp congratulated the Palestinian activists in his audience for the great advances made since his previous visit in 1988/89 in both the practice and understanding of nonviolence and, quoting Gandhi, remarked that "Personal nonviolence is not of much use in terms of society. You must learn how to apply this in society and in politics."

The shift in attention and perception and in accurate understanding is really quite remarkable. I heard in the presentations the other day the phrases nonviolent warfare, nonviolent strategic action, mass nonviolent struggle. I saw a poster which, at the bottom of it, said "Wiser than Violence," implying the use of the intellect, as Gandhi emphasized, and political nonviolent struggle. These are not mere changes of words. These are developments of understanding and capacity, and knowledge of nonviolent struggle is power potential. You're capable of doing infinitely more than you usually recognize and give yourself credit for. And this is important.

Referring to the Israeli leadership, he added, "It's not obvious yet, and there are many signs to the contrary, but there is a new understanding of nonviolent struggle that is developing among a significant number of Israelis in significant positions, and we may see more of that in the future." Sharp went on to lay out what he regards as the conditions for success in the use of nonviolence:

Being nonviolent is not good enough to win. After all, in most violent wars, at least one side loses, if not both; so it's not remarkable that nonviolent struggle sometimes fails. Something can be justified but not wise. Something can be nonviolent and not be the thing to do, and even, in my personal opinion, at times not meet the standards of morality. We need to ask whether a planned action is really going to contribute to achieving the goal or not; and if it's not, maybe you shouldn't waste your time and energy and heroism on it. And if it is, then you have to figure out how to ensure that it has that effect. The tools of liberation are not violence. The tools of liberation are people empowering themselves and learning they can act and what their power potential really is.

He assured his Palestinian hosts that he would not presume to tell them what to do. Were he to do so, he added, they should ignore his advice. Indeed, since he was not in their situation and had not visited Palestine in many years, he could only "point in some directions and give some words of caution and just tell [his listeners that] these are the kinds of things you need to take into consideration; these are the tools or weapons or methods of nonviolent struggle, which can be made available." He began by enumerating five basic steps that he sees as prerequisites for a more effective nonviolent struggle in Palestine:

One, we need to understand the situation, your situation, in depth; and that includes consideration of people's insights and capacities. Secondly, we need to understand our opponents in depth, not superficially, not by what they've done in recent years, only: Where do they come from, and what have been their sufferings. And I think this is not yet understood or appreciated among most Palestinians. There may be reasons why [the Israelis] do these ghastly things. That doesn't excuse it, and [such] actions still need to be opposed and overcome. And of course, people see themselves as victims if they're being attacked; the victims of suicide bombings, for example. Those are victims, but that does not mean that their cause is the one that we accept. [Thirdly,] we need to understand nonviolent struggle in depth. We must not only learn from our own experience; we should be wise enough to learn from the experience of other peoples in other countries over decades and sometimes centuries, of how they have struggled for their own liberation against all kinds of forces. [Fourth,] if we accept in principle nonviolent struggle, we must learn how to develop and plan strategies to use our actions most effectively. And I must confess that when I was here the eighties, it was very hard to find Palestinians who understood strategic thinking; I think that has improved significantly since I was here. [Fifth,] we need to thoroughly, as some of the speakers[8] indicated, cast out the violence, because it's counterproductive. Don't throw it away because you're not able to love somebody and therefore you might as well kill them; we need to know that violence is what our opponents want us to use. The opponent prefers violence by the opposition, because they can deal with that. They have means of violent action in control and repression and destruction and killing vastly superior to anything that an oppressed people can possibly muster.

Stressing that the use of violence would, in fact, aid the opponents of the Palestinian cause, Sharp also cautioned his audience against its use "by other people in the name of your cause, because they may be either misguided revolutionaries who naively think that power comes out the barrel of a gun—which is a fascist doctrine, not a socialist or democratic doctrine—or agents, identified or not identified." Inviting the activists in his audience not to rely on "intuition or spontaneity or hunches," but to "study, study, study," so as to be able to join in the ongoing process of "mak[ing] nonviolent struggle more effective in the future than it has ever been," Sharp continued:

> In various parts of the world, the tools of scholars and academics can now be popularized and made available to general populations who want to know how to deal with a particular crisis, and all this can produce what a friend of mine from Tibet, the venerable Sam Dong Rimpoche, [referred to] in English as "wise action." And this is very important: the use of the intellect, which Gandhi firmly insisted upon; wise action, that you think through carefully what you're going to do and then you do it in such a skilled way as you possibly can. And this can produce this expansion of the effectiveness of nonviolent struggle.

Riad Malki
Riad Malki is a long-time advocate of nonviolent means of resistance. As he told those assembled at the Bethlehem conference:

> What we have seen in Palestine in the last decade, and in particular, the last two years, is that the Palestinians have adopted, very clearly, pragmatic nonviolence over principled nonviolence.[9] And whoever sees on television the weekly demonstrations in Bil'in, in Aboud, in Jayyous and many other places in the West Bank where the wall is being constructed, you can see exactly what I mean by the implementation and adoption of the pragmatic nonviolence as an approach for Palestinian resistance.
> What's important here, when we talk about nonviolence, is that nonviolence itself is communication. The Palestinians, when they have adopted nonviolent action, have adopted some acts of nonviolence as a form of communication. When the Israelis reciprocated, they responded with a clear form of political communication, and instead of adopting rational discourse as a form of political

communication, they adopted violence as a selected method of such communication. So, while Palestinians have adopted nonviolence as their form of communication with their enemy, the Israelis immediately responded by adopting violence as their answer to the Palestinian communication. When we talk about communication, of course there are different dimensions of nonviolence as communication. We have the elements of principled nonviolence—conversion, persuasion, symbolic action. There is the element of pragmatic nonviolence—the power of equalization via noncooperation and intervention. And we have also what we have seen in Palestine recently, the mobilization of third parties.[10] This is extremely important, because we always need the mobilization of third parties in order to spread the word, in order to set up a chain of nonviolent actions.

Always first there is a risk of a violent response, and as a result, it is very important for us as Palestinians to maintain nonviolence as a strategy. But what's even more important is that there is asymmetry of the instruments of violence, clear asymmetry. And this asymmetry extends over all levels of confrontation between us and the Israelis. Thirdly is the moral conviction and the political culture that the Palestinians have adopted for a long time.

Malki contrasted the situation during the First Intifada, where over-whelming Palestinian nonviolence neutralized Israeli military superiority, with the current "mixture of activities," and called for "unity of resistance" in commitment to nonviolence.

During the First Intifada, obviously yes, there was a clear centre of gravity that promoted popular participation and popular support, and the result was obvious—that we were able to neutralize the Israeli military superiority in terms of responding to our own asymmetry with them. But in the Second Intifada, the situation really changed; and today what we see is that we have a mixture of activities. On the one hand we see nonviolent activities in different locations in the West Bank, but also we see violent activities. And what happened was that Israel was able to focus on the violence over the nonviolence, and we the Palestinians have not been able to attract the attention of our own community and to bring them to participate fully in the nonviolent activities. As a result, nonviolence did not achieve its objective of becoming the centre of gravity. It was so easy to be attacked; so easy to be isolated within the community itself. So unity is crucial. It is the only standard by which specific weapons, means, and actions can and must be weighed. As long as the unity of resistance is not broken, the resistance can go on—moving from defence into even counter-offence—deepening contradictions in the enemy camp. What counts with a centre of gravity is the popular character of the resistance. Here, as I said, in the Palestinian case, the centre of gravity, the centre of resistance, has not shifted [towards nonviolence], and remained the same, despite the nonviolent action which we have seen recently.

The nonviolent resistance against military forces, as I said, is a highly asymmetric case. It is clear also, that in the general context of nonviolent defence, sporadic violence is wholly counterproductive, in that it lifts the restraints on the enemy's use of violence. This is extremely important. Violent resistance makes violent repression more culturally acceptable, but also more feasible politically. And from a purely strategic point of view, the specific utility of nonviolence, as compared with other means of defence, lies in its dual function: first, giving rise to a wide range of contradictions in the ideological fabric of the enemy camp, and at the same time denying the enemy the justification—the ideological licence—for violence, which a violent response would have provided. So the more the enemy resorts to violent repression, the more he widens the contradictions in his own camp until he either reaches a limit beyond which he cannot go, or else his extreme effort would be wrecked by the weight of opposing forces within itself. Obviously, in the Israeli-Palestinian case, this is still not the situation, because the Israeli camp—in terms of the occupation—has been so solid in terms of its oppression of the Palestinians.

The Escalation of Nonviolence

Amos Gvirtz

"Nonviolence is an attitude," Israeli pacifist kibbutznik Amos Gvirtz told me. Stressing that there is a real difference between "not violence" and "nonviolence," he lamented that although the peace groups in Israel are not violent, most of their members do not come from a nonviolent background and do not necessarily give much thought to the concept. Gvirtz himself, however, has reflected extensively on nonviolence and, in the course of his many years as a nonviolent activist, has also developed an interesting theoretical approach to the subject: "the escalation of nonviolence."

The idea is that, just as there is escalation of violence in conflicts, we have to seek "escalation" in the opposite direction. And for this I make different characterizations of nonviolence possibilities for each side in the conflict. For the Palestinians, I think of what I call "active nonviolence," which was historically done by India in their struggle for freedom, with the leadership of Mahatma Gandhi, or the Civil Rights Movement in the United States, with the leadership of Martin Luther King. I'm giving historical cases of what I mean by active nonviolence: a struggle to achieve something by somebody who is under oppression or under occupation. And for the Israelis, there is something that I call "preventive nonviolence." You come to a [situation with a] very high potential for conflict, and by a nonviolent attitude, you prevent it from happening.

"Historically," said Gvirtz, "preventive nonviolence was done by the Quakers that started Pennsylvania." In the present, when the Israeli peace movement makes demands of the government, this too constitutes "preventive nonviolence."

If we demand an end to the occupation, an end to land confiscation, an end to house demolition, an end to the stealing of water, to stop the settlements—all of these things: the occupation, land confiscation, house demolition, stealing water, building settlements, all of them are done by violent force, by military force, and they cannot be done without it. So when we demand from our government to stop doing things that are unjust, that are done by violence, that provoke violence, our demands are in the [realm] of preventive nonviolence. I will say that every conscientious objector who refuses to be a military tool in the hand of the government or other bodies is doing active preventive nonviolence. In the context of our issue, the soldiers who refuse to serve in the occupied territories are doing active preventive nonviolence. Israelis who are boycotting goods that come from settlements are doing active preventive nonviolence. Israelis who refuse to work there or to be involved in anything that legitimizes the settlements, the occupation—refuse to make a tour there—are doing active preventive nonviolence.

He described, as well, a role for "third parties" or a "third side" in conflicts, pointing out that, "We see in international relations how this works, how a third side can be very effective."

We know about many conflicts or wars where UN forces come to keep a ceasefire in the [role] of a third side who has no enemy in the conflict. We have seen how the United States was serving as third side in achieving peace between Israel and Egypt. They served also as a third side between Israel and the Palestinians without success. A third side is not necessarily objective. Many times a third side is more for one side than for the other side. And we see it very strongly with Israel and the Palestinians. But, again, when the states or the UN are not doing the job, grassroots people can also do it. And I think we have a few examples now in the occupied territories of a third side who has no enemy in the conflict.

The Christian Peacemaker Teams (CPT), International Solidarity Movement (ISM), and the International Women's Peace Service (IWPS), Gvirtz reminded me, come to their nonviolent actions with different attitudes: ISM is clearly pro-Palestinian, whereas CPT and, to some extent, IWPS take a more neutral stance. All three, he said, typically function as a nonviolent "third side," as does the Israeli Committee Against House Demolitions (ICAHD), of which he is a member. On the other hand, though, a given body can perform different roles as circumstances differ.

If we are going to rebuild a demolished home, we are doing active nonviolence. If we are going to pick olives, which was a very successful campaign last year, it is active nonviolence. What's happening in these actions many times is that we come together with Palestinians and foreigners to do actions that come under the category of active nonviolence. But in the action itself, when Israeli forces or settlers come, we immediately—the Israelis and the internationals—become a third side. We give nonviolent defence to the Palestinian with whom we are doing the action.

So you can see that, first of all, nonviolence gives possibilities for Israelis to actively support the Palestinians, whereas we cannot do so when it is a violent struggle. I can think that the Palestinians are right in their fight against Israel. I can think that Israel is wrong—and I do—in what Israel is doing to the Palestinians. I cannot and I will not participate in a violent struggle against Israel. I can participate in and cooperate with a nonviolent struggle. So nonviolence gives a possibility for all of us to work for justice, whereas violent struggle prevents us. And this is one of the strengths—there are many others—of nonviolence.

Now the whole idea is that, just as with violence hate is encouraged and violent attack encourages retaliation, the aim here is that good-will will encourage good-will in the other side—that nonviolence from one side will encourage people from the other side to take more nonviolence, so together we can build trust between the two sides and good-will towards peace and justice between the two sides. This is, in general, the whole idea of the escalation of nonviolence and the theory of different categories of nonviolence.

A thoroughgoing pacifist, Gvirtz is not optimistic about the chances of Israeli peace groups embracing the kind of nonviolent attitude he espouses. "Even movements like Yesh Gvul and Ometz LeSarev—these movements of refuseniks—they don't think in these terms." On the other hand, he does see nonviolence as an effective strategy for the Palestinians.

I believe that for the Palestinians, the nonviolent battlefield is much more effective than the violent battlefield. And this is for very pragmatic reasons. Israel has a very strong army with very strong support from outside—because Israel is a state and has a territory where it can build an army. The Palestinians have no territory, no state, and they cannot build a serious army. And they don't have effective support from outside. So on the violent battlefield, it is totally unequal between the sides. On the nonviolent battlefield, the Palestinians are stronger than the Israelis, to my understanding. Why? Israel is a country that was started very much on the guilt feelings of the northern Christian world towards the Jews. This makes Israel very sensitive to moral pressure, and Israel is very, very dependent on outside countries, specifically the United States, but not only, and public opinion there is very important for Israel.

Most Israelis are afraid to give back the territories because of our security, and every terror attack strengthens this fear for our security. And we know that a terror attack strengthens the right wing in Israel. Remember the elections in ninety-six in Israel, when Peres was running against Netanyahu. Everyone in all the polls showed that Peres was going to win easily. And then the terror attacks in February–March 1996 changed the whole picture, and Netanyahu won the elections. And this was not the only case. Nonviolent struggle would put the picture on the right side of it, very much like the nonviolence in the hands of the black people in the United States did for them. For the white people, black people were criminals and dangerous, and suddenly, again and again they saw how black people were acting nonviolently and were attacked by white people. And those pictures changed the attitude. This is where the Palestinians can gain, not only the hearts of the western and northern people, but also of Israelis.

Building Mass Participation

Michel Warschawski

To Alternative Information Center (AIC) director, Michel Warschawski, "the dividing line between violence and nonviolence is not the crucial line." In his view, the important thing is whether or not an initiative evolves into a mass popular activity. "And then, of necessity, the violent part becomes less central for sure." Despite the fact that he doesn't fit neatly into the category (even my somewhat loosely defined category) of "nonviolent activist," I decided to interview Warschawski—for whom I'd worked at the AIC for four years in the early 1990s—partly because he had been a part of most of the nonviolent initiatives I was aware of during my seven years in Jerusalem and partly because I simply have great respect for his moral sensibility and his thinking on the subject. "There are things," he said, "that I would never accept." "For example?" I asked.

> Killing of civilians. I don't think this is a correct strategy politically, but also a priori from an ethical point of view I reject this. That is, perhaps I sometimes attempt to explain what pushed this young man to go and blow himself up in a supermarket; I think I have a duty to explain this. But I'm not one of those who think that to explain means to justify. To explain is to explain, and to justify is to justify, and these are two [different] things. Having set the boundaries of [actions which] are in my eyes out of bounds politically and ethically, I don't think that I have any a priori preferences [among the rest], but rather they are a function of the situation. Every moment there are methods of struggle that seem to me more correct, more effective, and another moment, *davka*, different methods of struggle, [depending on] whether you are a strong or a weak movement, whether your enemy is on the offensive or you are. These are very meaningful things in determining what is the most effective strategy.
>
> So, to get straight to the point, I do not have a principled opposition to armed struggle. But I also do not have a principled stand in favour of armed struggle. In the end, in my view, any strategy must lead to and must advance and must be effective in bringing about mass mobilization and activism. I don't believe that change that is positive and sustainable is possible if the nation that it affects isn't actually the agent [of that change]. It takes forever until people begin to move; it takes years and sometimes generations. But this must be where the compass points. I unequivocally do not

believe that it is possible to create substantial and positive changes (because it is possible for changes to be bad) solely on the basis of the activism of small groups. With the best intentions and with the most correct ideology, the sum total of the meaning of what I'll call our avant-garde activism is determined by the degree to which it is integrated within an approach that somehow accelerates the struggle.

In this sense, the First Intifada (I don't speak on the subject of the Second Intifada, which in my view is an entirely different matter) is definitely an example of popular struggle. Avant-garde activities did actually have importance, but it turned into what it was, one of the great achievements of the Palestinian struggle for freedom, because it was truly a popular activity in which every citizen, or the majority of the men and the women and the children and the elderly, were partners in this struggle, each in his own way. In my view, the goal essentially needs not so much to be to move from violent activism to nonviolent activism, but from the activism of avant-garde groups to mass popular activism. And mostly—much of the time—they overlap. Generally, popular activism is not armed. What are usually the tools of popular activism? Strike, demonstration, boycott.

Warschawski told me that he totally rejects "and I rejected from day one, the concept of a 'Second Intifada'," despite the fact that he, like many others, may use that term when referring to the period of time following the events of October 2000.

What the First Intifada was and what is called the Second Intifada are two opposite phenomena: the First Intifada was a real—even a model—mass uprising. That is, the occupied Palestinians said "Enough!" They said "No!" and resisted. This was a struggle of decolonization, a struggle where the initiative was Palestinian, and the army, the Israeli occupation reacted to the Intifada. The Second Intifada—despite all, or most, of what has been written about it—was an Israeli initiative of reconquest. It wasn't at the initiative of the Palestinians. Ehud Barak came to take back [lit. re-conquer] the achievements of Oslo, the achievements of Arafat, and the Palestinians are reacting to that. They aren't reacting to the visit of Sharon to the Temple Mount; that was trivial. The offensive was an Israeli offensive, not a Palestinian offensive or a Palestinian uprising. In my eyes the so-called Second Intifada was a reaction, different in its methods, more violent, less populist. But the most important [difference] is in who the initiator was. There is a clear

Israeli plan that was taking form all during '98, '99 of how to take back what [the Palestinians] had gained.

"Thus," concluded Warschawski, "they are two opposite phenomena: it's not one nonviolent uprising and a second, violent, uprising. One was an uprising—one could call it a revolution—and the other a counter-revolution."

Conclusion

Once upon a time, I could recite a litany, like the "begats" from the Bible, for many of the existing Israeli protest groups; now I recall only a few. The Committee in Solidarity with Birzeit University begat the Committee Against the War in Lebanon and the Committee Against the Iron Fist, and the Committee Against the Iron Fist begat Green Line—Israelis and Palestinians for Peace and a host of other First Intifada-era joint initiatives, and these begat ...; the Palestinian civil society initiatives of the 1970s begat the Popular Committees of the First Intifada, and the Popular Committees of the First Intifada begat today's Popular Committees against Settlements and the Wall; and undeniably, *New Outlook* begat PIJ.

Here we have seen examples of Israeli, Palestinian, and joint initiatives, all of which have "descendants" in the present array of nonviolent resistance efforts. These include Israelis by Choice, founded to protest the imminent deportation of Palestinian nonviolence advocate Mubarak Awad (and which "begat" Rapprochement-Jerusalem) and the Beita Committee, an early exercise in Israeli solidarity with Palestinian villagers victimized by the occupation regime; early Popular Committees, whose activities ranged from promotion of victory gardens (i.e., food self-sufficiency) to guerrilla classrooms; and the Committee Against the Iron Fist, which became a real training ground for effectively carrying out joint demonstrations and, like other "radical" organizations of the day, paved the way for such activities by more "moderate" groups, such as Peace Now, that would not otherwise have dared to undertake them. This section ends with an account of the "Romanian Four," who challenged the Israeli government's enforcement of an "anti-peace" law forbidding contact with the PLO and won, and reminiscences about the early days of the now defunct *New Outlook* magazine (which begat PIJ).

We also heard from key thinkers in the area of nonviolence in general. These include Gene Sharp, well-known proponent of "pragmatic nonviolent action," who kindly allowed me to quote at length from my recording of his presentation to the December 2005 Celebrating Nonviolent Resistance conference in Bethlehem; Riad Malki, a former spokesperson for the Popular Front for the Liberation of Palestine, now one of the very few Palestinian activists I met who openly denounces all Palestinian use of violence[11]; Amos Gvirtz, Israeli pacifist and activist who hypothesizes an "escalation of nonviolence"; and, again, Michel Warschawski, a nonviolent activist in practice, if not in theory, with much to say on the subject.

In Part II, we shall explore the nonviolent strategies of several Palestinian, Israeli, and joint organizations, moving from the choice of nonviolence as an organizational strategy to the specific strategic approaches of these groups (in Chapter 3 and the first part of Chapter 4), then looking more closely at some of the discussion around the pros and cons of joint struggle (in the remainder of Chapter 4) and at three significant joint nonviolent campaigns (Chapter 5).

NOTES

1 Referred to as the "separation barrier" by the Israeli authorities, this 723 km barrier, part 8-metre-high concrete wall, part electronically-monitored barbed wire fence plus ditches—punctuated with gates that are more often closed than open—snakes through the West Bank, cutting farmers off from their fields, villages from cities and from each other. It is usually referred to by Palestinians and their Israeli supporters as the "apartheid wall" or simply "the Wall." Even more apt, I think, is the epithet employed by Yehudit Keshet in *Checkpoint Watch* (Keshet 2006): "Annexation Wall."

2 Traditionally, Jews cut or tear a lapel of their clothing when in mourning.

3 For more on Veronika Cohen's work, see her account of the beginnings of the Rapprochement dialogue group and Israeli solidarity with the Beit Sahour tax revolt in Chapter 5.

4 Ansar III is the nickname of Ketziot, an Israeli prison camp in the Negev desert, where many of the prisoners are administrative detainees; i.e., detained under a military order that allows imprisonment without trial for renewable six-month periods at the discretion of a military commander.

5 From an interview originally published in my 1993 booklet, *Creative Resistance: Anecdotes of Nonviolent Action by Israeli-based Groups* (Out of print)—with minor revisions and with deleted sections signified by [...].

6 Kaminer describes this meeting in more detail in his absorbing history of the Israeli Peace movement during the First Intifada (Kaminer 1996).

7 See especially Chapter 4, subsection on Joint Organizations.

8 References to "the conference" in Gene Sharp's talk are all to the Celebrating Nonviolent Resistance conference held in Bethlehem in December of 2005.

9 Pragmatic and principled nonviolence are often referred to, respectively, as Sharpian and Gandhian nonviolence.

10 Third parties: in this case, "internationals" (the International Solidarity Movement [ISM], Christian Peacemaker Teams [CPT], International Women's Peace Service [IWPS], and others), who are neither Israeli nor Palestinian.

11 At time of writing, Malki holds the posts of minister of foreign affairs and minister of communication and justice in the Palestinian Authority.

PART II

STRATEGIES AND APPLICATIONS OF NONVIOLENT ACTION

3
NONVIOLENT STRATEGIES OF
PALESTINIAN AND ISRAELI ORGANIZATIONS

The late Faisal Husseini used to say that if you want to fight Mike Tyson, you're not going to do it in the boxing ring. So we needed to create an arena where Israel was weaker, and that was in the battle for justice and in the nonviolent resistance.

Huwaida Arraf (ISM)

Although I believe that people have to stick to their rights and resist, the way to resist is not to kill. And I believe that killing one person, on either side, is like killing all human beings. I hope that the Palestinians will have realized by now that violent struggle, and particularly killing civilians in Israel, is only destroying the prospects of peace and liberation, and that it only plays into the hands of the extremists in Israel, and vice versa. I hope that now there are now more of them realizing that the only way forward for liberation and for the end of occupation, and statehood and whatever—is only through nonviolent means.

Dr Eyad Sarraj (Gaza Community Mental Health Programme)

I went this way, the anti-violent way, along with Israelis and internationals, and our strategy was to show the world—all the world, but especially Israeli society—that what you hear on your media and what you hear from your government or from your military commanders, is just lies and more lies. There is no people who can rule another people and obtain security and peace and an economy at the expense of the other people.

Nawaf Souf (Haris village leader and activist, ISM and Ta'ayush)

The Choice of Nonviolence as an Organizational Strategy

In this chapter and the two that follow, we will look at organizational strategies and how they play out "on the ground." Before addressing the broader question, "What is your organization's strategy, and how does it fit in to the overall struggle against the occupation?" though, we shall focus on attitudes around the choice of nonviolence as a framework for overall strategy, be it for individual organizations or for the Palestinian resistance movement as a whole.

Nonviolence may be favoured as an organizational/movement strategy for a variety of reasons. Sometimes this is based on the perception, as voiced by Nafez Assaily (Library on Wheels for Nonviolence and Peace, Hebron and East Jerusalem) that "Nonviolence can do what armed struggle failed to do." Or even, as Devorah Brous (Bustan) states, "Nonviolence is the only tool that we have. This is an effective tool to get people to start asking questions. Violence just shuts people down, closes the heart, closes the ears, and just pushes people far away." Or, as Leena Delasheh of Ta'ayush told a Vancouver audience in July 2002, "We can't solve violence with more violence."

> It's a preposterous idea. And in Ta'ayush, we try to bring an alternative. We try to let people know the other side. We try to bring people together. We bring hundreds of Israelis to the occupied territories. We get people to meet, we get people to speak, we get people to see for themselves the situation that brings other people to despair. Because knowledge gives you an alternative, and we try to give people that alternative.

Coupled with most people's preference for peaceful solutions (over and over I heard variations on the theme, "We prefer peaceful means, but the Israelis push us to violence"), a further incentive for Palestinian organizations, in particular, to adopt a nonviolent strategy is, of course, their lack of a state and therefore of a "proper" army in the face of the need to confront the occupation and advocate for the human rights it violates. As Dr Ghassan Hamdan of the Union of Palestinian Medical Relief Committees in Nablus put it:

> We believe if we can have our rights and if we can end the occupation in a peaceful way, it's better than having violence. Another fact: we don't have our army, and we don't have our state, and we don't have the power to face the fourth [most] powerful army in the whole world, the Israeli army. So the most important way to face this army is the nonviolent way. And we try to do that. But, as I mentioned, they are pushing us to have violence.

The sympathies of the international community are, of course, more likely to be on the side of nonviolent resisters than of their violent counterparts. As Israeli anarchist Yonatan Pollak put it:

It's not that I don't think that the Palestinians have a right to shoot at soldiers if they invade their cities; under international conventions that's legitimate. I just think that it's tactically unwise. The international community and international public opinion can relate much more to a child throwing a stone at a tank, even though militarily it's inefficient, mainly because it very visually shows how it is an army versus a population.

And from many Palestinians I heard statements such as: "We've always used nonviolence; it's part of our culture; we just didn't call it by this name," and "Look how much we gained through the nonviolence of the First Intifada and lost through the violence of the second."

Nonviolence: The Best Approach to Resisting the Occupation?
Hanan Ashrawi (MIFTAH)
Scenes of IDF shelling of the population of Gaza City in retaliation for a recent suicide bombing inside Israel dominated the TV screen just behind me as I spoke to Palestinian stateswoman Hanan Ashrawi in the Ramallah office of MIFTAH, The Palestinian Initiative for the Promotion of Global Dialogue and Democracy,[1] not far from the largely demolished Palestinian Authority compound known as the *Muqata'a*. Ashrawi is familiar with Mubarak Awad and his Palestinian Center for the Study of Nonviolence, and she told me that nonviolence itself had been under discussion "for a long time."

> I believe that this conflict in itself and this occupation in itself can only be resolved through political means and nonviolent activism—a sort of intrusive nonviolence—in terms of providing a genuine and workable alternative that could produce results. But unfortunately, the lethal dynamic on the ground is certainly very violent. And this type of mutual exchange of pain and violence and so on has claimed the lives of many and, at the same time has, for a long time, robbed the political and the nonviolent—and the popular—movement of its audience and its momentum, its ability to move. Because whenever we formed any kind of mass popular protest, we'd be met with such violence, with such brutality, that the numbers of regular people would be diminished and we wouldn't be able to move. And, of course, that encourages people on our side to respond in kind.

[71]

It's amazing that you have the vast majority of Palestinians remaining committed to a negotiated settlement, understanding that this situation cannot be resolved violently, and that there are people who are adamant enough and tenacious enough to continue to try—in the midst of this insanity—some kind of sane approach to resolution, and not to dehumanize the other. That's the real issue. That's why you have, on the Israeli side also, some people who are involved consciously in reclaiming the terrain and the legitimacy of a human dialogue and a political agenda that is activist, in a variety of settings and contexts. You have quite a few. But unfortunately, they are not able to break through the violence itself and to create a different dynamic that would delegitimize the violence that is used by the army, by the government, and among us, by the opposition.

Meron Benvenisti

Israeli political analyst/author/columnist Meron Benvenisti expressed a similar point of view, although he cautioned that "there are always very complicated issues of legitimacy, because if you agree to go and start something through political action, then you legitimize the occupation. A lot of dilemmas, moral and political, are involved. So we are not talking about a simple thing, nonviolent action, but a whole forest of issues that must be addressed." Nonetheless, he told me:

> I think that nonviolent action is the only thing that can be useful in this conflict. Violence cannot work. Violence just causes more violence, and [it] really helps the stronger party, and the stronger party is Israel. Israel can always start the sequence when it chooses, so I think that violence is just counterproductive. I don't want to relate to the question of morality, because then I'll have to discuss what is terrorism, what is state terrorism—we're talking about political violence as opposed to nonviolent political action. Then we have to define also the borderlines: there must be a lot of literature on what constitutes violence and what not, because demonstrations can be, on the one hand, a provocation and so on. So if you take the general perception of nonviolence, I think in this situation, that is the only thing that can help, because it neutralizes the rage of the Israelis—of the injured party [i.e., in suicide bombings and the like], which in itself [i.e., the injury] creates more hardships and does not help in solving anything. So, not only do I advocate this, I think this is the only way

Zoughbi Zoughbi (Wi'am)

Zoughbi Zoughbi, director of the Wi'am Palestinian Conflict Resolution Center in Bethlehem, addressed several of the "trees" in the forest referred to above by Meron Benvenisti. To Zoughbi, nonviolence is both the most practical and the most active form of struggle, "from single acts of resistance to mass civil disobedience," for which one endeavours to obtain the solidarity of "the whole world," including the Israeli peace forces. He pointed out that nonviolence has historically been employed by Palestinians in a number of contexts and that a nonviolent approach can unify broad sectors of the population, "across religious backgrounds, political affiliations, social backgrounds, generations, and so on." Outlining the use of nonviolence "in the Arabic and Islamic world" going back to Ottoman times, if not before, Zoughbi cautioned that, "We shouldn't paint a romantic view of nonviolence, that tomorrow it will change the world." "Why I am interested in nonviolence," Zoughbi stated, "is because it is an appeal to the world. That doesn't mean every [nonviolent] struggle was successful; and who says every violent struggle is successful? But at the same time, we are aware of the power imbalance. We talk about good neighbours and not good fences."

Jad Isaac (ARIJ)

The tax strike carried out by virtually the entire population of the Bethlehem-area town of Beit Sahour during the First Intifada is but one example, albeit a particularly impressive one, of recent Palestinian employment of nonviolence. And we have already seen Jad Isaac's account of some of the acts of classic Gandhian nonviolence (e.g., promotion of "victory gardens" to reduce dependency on Israeli produce) that landed this former Bethlehem University professor of Agronomy in an Israeli jail in the late 1980s. Noting that nonviolent struggle has been less widespread in the current Intifada than in the first, Isaac advised:

> I think that we should continue our nonviolent movement and provide Israel and the Israeli public with the security that they are very concerned about: that the creation of a Palestinian state does not mean the destruction of Israel, that it is in the interest of the Israeli people and the Jewish people to have a Palestinian state, that justice and peace are the best security, not fences and not any other thing.

[73]

Ghassan Andoni (PCR/ISM)

One of Isaac's fellow Beit Sahour tax resisters was Ghassan Andoni, who later became intensely involved in the leadership of the International Solidarity Movement (ISM). Long committed to a nonviolent approach, Andoni stated at the December 2005 Celebrating Nonviolent Resistance conference that, "I have a deep conviction that nations that can afford to build popular civil-based resistance would fail themselves if their leadership decides to run the struggle differently." In our 2003 interview, he had made clear the commitment of the Palestinian Center for Rapprochement (PCR) and ISM to what he calls "positive engagement" in the conflict, employing nonviolence. And although some people have questioned ISM's commitment to nonviolence—perhaps based on an early statement which, like those of many other organizations, recognized the Palestinians' right to use any means at their disposal to resist the occupation—Andoni underscored, in explaining the organization's position, the difference between what "we recognize" and "what we encourage."

> ISM does not want to be judgemental of Palestinian resistance groups, because those are people under occupation. And when we recognize their right to fight the occupation, we base that on international law and UN resolutions, which recognize that right. So we said we recognize the right recognized by the international community for people under occupation to fight occupiers. And the second phrase is: "Our way is nonviolence." So this is what we encourage.[2]

Andoni defined positive engagement as a strategy "not based on the idea of condemning, condoling, preaching, or educating" but on action aimed at limiting the ability of the occupier to exert its power over the civilian population, thereby empowering them "in the sense of saying, 'They don't have all the power in the world; we can stop them,' and encouraging more of the average Palestinians to join the struggle—the end result of which will be a reduction in the level of violence." Thus, he declared:

> ISM in the long run saves lives of both Palestinians and Israelis. It is the model of resistance that complements Palestinian resistance and actually presents to the Palestinians another idea, which is civil-based resistance, hoping that Palestinians would finally go in line with this, and this would allow for a more massive Israeli peace

movement to stand in support. And when that happens, I can tell you, peace—a just peace—becomes a realistic option in the Middle East.

As (Israeli) ISM co-founder Neta Golan says: "Creating an option for Palestinian nonviolent resistance to me has two effects. One is challenging the occupation, and the other is that I believe it is completely in the interest of [the Israeli authorities] to have Palestinians resisting violently and resisting through things like suicide bombings. So giving another option also counters that, in my opinion."

Peretz Kidron (Yesh Gvul)

Founded and largely made up of active or retired combat soldiers, Yesh Gvul makes use of the powerful tactic of nonviolent noncooperation "selectively." Veteran refusenik Peretz Kidron emphasized this: "We're not pacifists," declared Kidron, "and I could imagine a situation in which we would say, 'No, this is a time to go into the army and pick up a gun' "— prompting my somewhat bemused response, "But you're choosing a classical nonviolent technique ..." to which he responded:

> Well, by definition, it's civil disobedience. It's not a mutiny, it's not a rebellion, it's focused on a specific issue. It's civil disobedience, which picks out a particular law or a particular set of laws and says, "I will not obey this law, consciously and deliberately, because it's part of a broader policy and it represents and it exemplifies it in a nutshell. It's like Gandhi going down to beach to make his own salt. It was illegal. It wasn't violent—it was making salt—but that was deliberately flouting the law. So here we deliberately flout the law and invite prosecution. That's the way it works. Obviously, we don't want bloodshed. I say there are certain circumstances—I saw this in a leaflet at a Sikh temple that it was part of the Sikh doctrine as well: violence is okay when it's used as a last resort, when there's no other way. So therefore we have no problem with justifying the fact that the Palestinian resistance to the occupation is a violent one. Because the occupation is violent; therefore, resistance has to be violent. There's no way they could fight it by nonviolent means. That's been shown very clearly by the way the Israelis have reacted to the nonviolent protests, which are usually broken up in a very violent way.

Abed el-Karim Dalbeh (the Freedom Centre, Tulkarm)
and Suheil Salman (PARC)

The effects of violent Israeli reactions to Palestinian nonviolence were also alluded to by Abed el-Karim Dalbeh and Suheil Salman, two activists I met on my brief visit to Tulkarm in October of 2003. Although they shared the conviction that, as Salman put it, "Nonviolent actions are more beneficial for Palestinians than anything else," Dalbeh lamented the fact that the violence of the Israeli response to the largely nonviolent resistance of the early months of the Intifada had led to widespread despair in the effectiveness of nonviolence and, consequently, to increased Palestinian violence, whereas the massive nonviolent actions early in the Intifada "brought more attention to our problem and more support for our problem [and more] talk about the occupation."

Salman, an activist in the Tulkarm branch of the Palestinian Agricultural Relief Committees (PARC), pointed out that during the first three months of the current Intifada, when the Palestinians used virtually no arms against the Israelis and "on the Palestinian side there were a hundred martyrs and there were only three Israelis killed, the world was standing with us. We made some mistakes, maybe, but in general, nonviolent action was more effective, and we believe in it and our nation believes in it because we want to be supported by the world."

"As Palestinians, we cannot fight the armed Israelis, because we are not armed. Palestinians have only a few weapons," Salman added, likening Palestinian armed resistance to self-defence against overwhelming odds. He expressed the hope that by using nonviolence, Palestinians can "remove the mask of the Israeli government that [tells] the world that there is an armed struggle between the Palestinians and the Israelis."

Dalbeh, the ISM coordinator in Tulkarm and a member of the Democratic Front for the Liberation of Palestine (DFLP), works for the party-operated Freedom Centre, which deals with human rights violations resulting from the occupation. Though acknowledging the Palestinians' "right to protest the occupation [both] violently and nonviolently," he stated: "I believe that nonviolent action—because our people in the West Bank is not an armed people—gives more benefit for our people because, first of all, most of them can participate. And this is what happened in the beginning of the Intifada."

Riad Malki (Panorama Center, Ramallah)

A strong counter-argument to the contention that there's no way that Palestinians can fight the violence of the occupation by nonviolent means was put forward by the Panorama Center's Riad Malki, a man whose name was familiar to me from my days working at the Alternative Information Center (AIC) in the early 1990s. Although I do not recall having met Malki personally at the time, AIC director Michel Warschawski (Mikado) often mentioned him as one of his Palestinian associates and as a member of the political leadership of the PFLP (Popular Front for the Liberation of Palestine)—a body one was not supposed to "even think about" (much less speak about openly) in those pre-Oslo days. And, although I was quite aware of the fact that—despite its media image as a major proponent (and practitioner) of armed struggle—the PFLP had many adherents who were engaged in essentially nonviolent activities (education and organizational support for agricultural cooperatives, for example, as well as political activity), I was a bit surprised to hear an unambiguous call for exclusive use of nonviolence coming from someone with Malki's political background. When I asked him about this, he responded, "I do believe that there are many former activists who used to belong to the Popular Front for the Liberation of Palestine who have reconsidered their tactics, and they have been the most active in the promotion of nonviolent resistance in Palestine recently," adding that he felt that the Front was the political group that had been most strongly influenced by ideas about nonviolence. Malki also stressed the importance of encouraging groups and organizations to adopt nonviolent thinking.

> As an individual, the impact of my thinking and the influence of my thinking will be very minimal. The idea is to really enlarge that thinking through bringing more people in and starting to think collectively, as groups. Also, work can bring organizations to adopt such thinking to become part of their policy, and then obviously, this might really produce the type of results that one really likes.

Alluding to the imbalance of power between Israel and the Palestinians, Malki elaborated his view of the logic behind the choice of nonviolence as a Palestinian organizational strategy.

Any person that understands very well the balance of powers—or imbalance of powers, the lack of symmetry between the two sides—can immediately understand and can even anticipate what kind of outcome could be if the Palestinians opt for using violence and the armed struggle as a way to solve their own conflict. Because, when you are under occupation and half of your population is in diaspora, dispersed everywhere, restricted in terms of movement and in terms of basic, fundamental rights, and when you know that your occupier is one of the strongest militarily in the world and enjoying a very strong economic base and with military superiority—you cannot, just because you believe your cause is a just one—you cannot with one, two, three, ten, or even a hundred rifles really defeat your enemy. This is a suicidal approach, and for people who have a sense of logic—who can think, and who can interpret matters and analyze between the good and the bad, between making progress and not, between committing suicide and remaining alive, between making achievements and staying where you are or even regressing—obviously one has to understand that the right approach to take is the nonviolent approach, because this will neutralize the superiority of your enemy, give you a certain advantage, and reduce the price that you have to pay in any kind of confrontation that takes place.

And then, from being in a defensive position, immediately you turn the whole situation from defensive to offensive. And the moment you believe in that, then this is really an advantage; it's a superiority—thinking in terms of when you always think that the whole game between the two side lacks equality and symmetry. I believe that when you live in a situation where you see this asymmetry in all facets of life, when you see that the situation is always one of occupied and occupier—that you can't do anything without getting a permit, if and until the Israelis allow you to do so—that forces you all the time to keep thinking and to keep wondering what is the right mechanism to take in order for you to produce symmetry and in order for you to turn your disadvantage into an advantage.

Mass Participation Versus Elitism

Walid Salem (Panorama Center, Jerusalem)

An additional advantage of nonviolence as an organizational strategy is its broadly participatory and non-elitist nature. This was one of the issues addressed by Walid Salem, director of the Panorama Center's Jerusalem office, at a workshop session during the December 2005 conference. In his talk there, as well as in a paper he later shared with me (Salem 2008), Salem contrasted the primarily nonviolent approach of the First Intifada—and the gains this had brought to the Palestinian cause—with the more militarized and elitist nature of the Al-Aqsa Intifada and the consequent erosion of these gains, as well as the suffering the latter has brought to both peoples, including "chaos inside the Palestine society, where armed groups began to rule the streets and undermine the authority of the PA." He described as the two main characteristics of the First Intifada the fact that "it was popular [i.e., community based] and it was participatory." Salem also stressed the importance of nonviolence in protecting the "human security" of both sides by minimizing casualties when compared to militarized forms of struggle. Some of his points (from Salem 2005a unless otherwise indicated) included:

> The Intifada of 1987–1993 forced the Palestinian leadership outside Palestine to accept two new realities. One, the transfer of the [centre of] gravity of the Palestinian struggle against the occupation from outside to inside Palestine: the PLO lost its freedom to attack Israel from those Arab countries bordering Israel (Jordan, Syria and Lebanon). Two, ... the Intifada made it clear that citizens are actors in their own right [including] the recognition by the Palestinian leadership of the importance of nonviolence as an effective instrument in the struggle against occupation. [I]n essence, the First Intifada was participatory, crossing tribal and sectarian cleavages. ... Palestinians living on the West Bank and in the Gaza Strip joined in, men and women, young and old, [from] all sectors of life [and] all areas of the West Bank and the Gaza Strip. Women organized their own Higher Council, while the youth organized themselves through neighbourhood committees, since the Israeli army had closed their schools and universities during the Intifada. ... It began spontaneously, but people rapidly organized themselves in creative ways. Of course, the different factions and political parties, including the Islamists, were participating as well. ... Until 1992 [when the exiled PLO leadership returned], [the Intifada] leadership worked in close cooperation with the people, leaving a wide space for people's initiatives. ...

Salem's paper goes on to describe how—by being non-hierarchical and largely nonviolent—"in various ways, the First Intifada stimulated 'interventionism'"—i.e., grassroots Palestinians got involved, taking responsibility for their own fate, and Israeli groups intervened on behalf of the Palestinians, as did "international civil society," effectively mobilizing public opinion in various parts of the world in support of the Beit Sahour tax strike and other nonviolent initiatives. In addition, the leaflets distributed almost daily during the First Intifada "called upon the people to join the movement of civic resistance activities, and did not call them to use arms ... because armed resistance would provoke devastating retribution by the Israelis."

Salem also cites the process of Palestinian nation- and state-building initiated by the First Intifada—an important component of which involved noncooperation with the occupation through boycott of Israeli institutions while fostering the development of Palestinian institutions and the resultant "emergence of new professional organizations in every field: health, education, research, human rights, etc.—both powerful nonviolent strategies as described by Gene Sharp. Importantly, he stresses that, "the Intifada did not call for the killing of Israelis [inside Israel]..." Enumerating the boycotts, strikes, and the like, which constituted the overwhelming majority of First Intifada actions, he comments that a major benefit of the comparatively low level of Palestinian violence in the First Intifada was the fact that "the First Intifada based on a strategy of nonviolence led to less causalities than the Second Intifada of 2000," backing up his claim with figures from the Israeli Human Rights organization, B'tselem.[3] "Moreover," adds Salem, "no closures were imposed on the West Bank and in Gaza during that Intifada."[4]

He also makes the point that "the First Intifada was aiming at disengagement of Israeli and Palestinian institutions, but not on disengagement at the level of human beings." Salem credits that policy, combined with the basically nonviolent nature of the Palestinian resistance during the First Intifada, with the high degree of "cooperation with Israeli peace organizations in the campaign against occupation," which, in turn, "also helped to reduce violence" (on the part of the Israeli forces). In addition, he describes the creation of an atmosphere where Israel could consider the PLO as a valid partner in negotiations. "The use of nonviolent means in the First Intifada had another advantage. It helped Israel to do some introspection and to rethink its policies towards the Palestinians. The outcome of this process was an Israeli reappraisal of the PLO and the engagement in secret talks in Oslo in 1992, which resulted [in] a declaration of principles [DOP] in 1993."

One of the other changes in the early 1990s referred to by Salem was the return of the exiled PLO leadership, an event that heralded the removal of the initiative from the hands of the people and a return to elitism, with the consequent marginalization of nonviolence. The violent nature of much of the Second Intifada, in Salem's view, compounded this problem. No longer was the broader public participating in the resistance—especially not in its leadership. The violence overshadowed everything else, Palestinians were once again viewed exclusively as terrorists who must end terrorism in order to earn the right to statehood. Thus evolved a situation in which, he remarked at the 2005 conference workshop, "There is a lot of nonviolence taking place during this current Intifada, but all of it is marginalized." Nonetheless—and perhaps ironically—Salem views the failures of the Second Intifada as actually highlighting the benefits of nonviolence, going on to state that, "In a way and through all its failures, the violent Second Intifada proved that nonviolence is the road to choose because it fits with the human security needs of both peoples, and it is based on mutual respect and [sets the stage for] future cooperation." Salem's paper concludes with a call for a new "integrated human security strategy" with "roles for the PA, civil society and individual citizens working together" and for basic changes in the PA itself.

> In other words, a strategy founded on a community-based security system. Moreover, a strategy that excludes both internal and external terrorism, and finally leads to a future demilitarized state. Such a strategy will need first rebuilding the PA upon the lines of working to bring human security to its citizens, and not to continue as it is in its current structures as an obstacle for such society. (Salem 2005a)

S'leiman Abu Muferreh (Mayor of Tequ'a Village)

S'leiman Abu Muferreh, the mayor of Tequ'a village near Bethlehem, has taken a leadership role in local initiatives to organize nonviolent activities "for the whole town" and feels that "this shows that we might have an alternative to military force." Voicing the (commonly held) opinion that Palestinian violence, such as suicide bombings and the like, are a reaction—admittedly an extreme one—to the ongoing violence of the occupation, he stated emphatically, "I don't agree with killing an Israeli kid sleeping at home or an Israeli guy sitting in a coffee shop. I don't think this is the way to get things settled."

> I think waking up the international community and the Israeli community to what's really going on—what's happening to the Palestinians—is more powerful than violence. I think nonviolent activities, through a clear message, very defined goals, and through a strong vision, which clarifies that we are not looking for hurting anyone, we are looking for getting rid of the occupation—which hurts us, which hurts our people, which hurts our land—this is what we are looking for. And we are looking for our Palestinian state according to the international resolutions which give us that right. I think we should continue having such nonviolent activities through ISM [and] any kind of other groups, and really I admire and appreciate the efforts of those people who came from their countries having nothing in mind but to share in making peace and justice.

Abu Muferreh and his friends were planning, he said, "more meetings to think how we can spread the idea of nonviolent activity among our people and sharing it with both sides, the Israelis and the internationals."

Sami Awad (Holy Land Trust)

Spreading the idea of nonviolent activity as widely as possible is a major part of the program of the Holy Land Trust (HLT), the Bethlehem organization headed by Sami Awad.

> The vision of Holy Land Trust as a Palestinian organization is to answer the question of what can we do to strengthen and encourage the Palestinian people. And when we talk about strengthening and encouraging, we talk about two fronts: The first is, what services are we providing the Palestinian people to resist and to end the Israeli occupation of their land? And the second question, which is as important to us, is: What comes after the occupation ends? What kind of state will Palestine be? What kind of government will we have? Will it be a democracy or not? What will the government institutions be like? and things like that. The statement I always make is that as a people, our struggle does not end with the end of occupation, it begins with the end of occupation. That's when you build the nation; that's when you really have to put your efforts to work. And our philosophy to answer both questions is the concept of nonviolence.

With nonviolence, you enable your people to build the capacity to resist the occupation and to show the injustice of the occupation, and to change public opinion in Israel and around the world as to what is really happening here, to show that there are people here who have rights to exist and who have rights to be here and to establish their state. With nonviolence, as well, you empower people to be influential in decision making for the future. So it's not just liberation through armies or generals while the people are ignored—and then you have governmental structures that are just based on these elitists who liberated the land—but you are talking about really having the people run the country in the future.

Husam Jubran (HLT)

Husam Jubran, lead nonviolence trainer at HLT when I spoke to him in January 2006, recalled how he and his fellow activists had laughed at Mubarak Awad when he spoke to them about nonviolence at the beginning of the First Intifada. "We said, 'Who is this guy who's speaking about nonviolence?' I thought nonviolence was associated with surrender, with giving up your rights, with the passive part of nonviolence, not with the active part." But, he observed, "We *were* involved in active nonviolence."

> I simply believe that the Palestinian people, throughout the history of our struggle, adopted techniques that were mostly—about ninety percent—nonviolent techniques. So nonviolence is not something new for us or something different from what we do, but we need to show the people the active part of it. And the moment we do it—and this is what we [at Holy Land Trust] have been doing during the past two years—there are more people saying now "We do that!" And usually when I go and train people, what they say is: "We know everything you speak about. This is something that we do, and we don't have any problem in continuing doing it." And this is mostly what I try to work on right now: just to show the people that nonviolence is part of our history, culture, and religion.

Civil Disobedience: Not for Everybody

Gila Svirsky (Coalition of Women for Peace)

Although Peretz Kidron described Yesh Gvul as embracing civil disobedience (CD) in the form of refusal to serve in the occupied territories—or, in some cases, refusal to serve at all—not all Israeli organizations found CD such a clear-cut choice, whereas in the Palestinian context, this question was all but meaningless, since just about every nonviolent activity—down to victory gardens and attempting to attend school or get to work—was considered illegal by the Israeli authorities and hence was inherently "civil disobedience." Veteran Woman in Black Gila Svirsky is active in a variety of Israeli women's peace and anti-occupation groups. In an article published on the Internet in mid-2003,[5] Svirsky had spoken about nonviolence in the context of the Coalition of Women for Peace, of which she was a cofounder, describing a number of dramatic actions involving CD, as well as a variety of other effective nonviolent tactics. That fall, however, her response to my question regarding her views on civil disobedience/direct action for Israeli and Palestinian organizations made it clear that she had come to favour less radical forms of nonviolence for the former.

> This is really right at the bone of the question of strategy. I personally have many times been arrested, have lain in front of bulldozers ... I have done many, many, many of those things that are risky, on behalf of Palestinians. I do not believe that those things that I've done have advanced the cause of ending the occupation. I am a believer in nonviolence and civil disobedience as an effective strategy, but not by Israelis doing it on the Palestinian side, not at all.

"I'm a believer that Palestinians should be doing it on the Palestinian side," Svirsky said, but not Israelis, even "on the Israeli side."

> I have come to realize that Israelis doing that activity radiates to the Israeli public that we are "on the Palestinian side," that we do not care about Israeli security and Israeli well-being, that all we care about is Palestinian security and well-being. An Israeli who wants to endanger herself by doing any of these actions comes across inside Israel as being "for the enemy."
>
> In the very near future we will be doing olive picking on the Palestinian side, and I'm in favour of that, because there is a time and a place where you have to give solidarity. Without solidarity, there's no strength to the movement. But above all, if we want to persuade Israelis that we must end the occupation, we have to do it in a way that Israelis feel that we're "on their side," and we want to end the occupation for the sake of Israel.

"I'm telling you this," Svirsky said, "because dispositionally, I find that getting arrested and taking my life in my hands and lying in front of a bulldozer is the greatest adrenaline charge in the world. But when I think logically and rationally about what works, what works more is working on the Israeli side to educate Israelis."

Rabbi Arik Ascherman (Rabbis for Human Rights)

The decision to engage in nonviolent acts that involve a certain degree of risk (of arrest or of other unpleasant consequences) can be based on motives as varied as the individuals and organizations that choose that path. Rabbi Arik Ascherman of Rabbis for Human Rights (RHR) spoke of what impelled him to take RHR in that direction.

> First of all, sometimes [civil disobedience] has a function of just helping to publicize an issue; sometimes it is—for myself, as much as for anything else—so I can look myself in the face and say, "I did what I could to stop something." Let's take standing in front of a bulldozer before a house is being demolished: At that point you're probably not going to stop that demolition, but the publicity around that can also create some more international pressure, which may slow down or stop the next phase of demolitions or stop the next demolition altogether.

On the other hand, however, while clearly viewing this and other forms of direct action in the occupied territories that RHR participates in as being greatly appreciated acts of solidarity with Palestinians, Rabbi Ascherman also echoed some of the concerns voiced by Gila Svirsky.

> There was a period—around March, April, May of 2001—where we even did activities such as removing roadblocks and this kind of thing. We stopped, a), because there just weren't enough people that wanted to do it; b), because there were people that felt that even if it was totally nonviolent, very often there was violence afterwards, and Palestinians paid the price. Even if the Palestinians themselves were saying, "We're going in with our eyes wide open," people felt some reticence about that. I think there was a question of whether we were getting too far from the Israeli public; but I actually think we stopped doing that a little bit too quickly.

Galia Golan (Peace Now)
Peace Now's Galia Golan spoke of differing attitudes towards nonviolence and, specifically, civil disobedience, both within her movement and in others.

> We don't use violence, but we're not ideologically nonviolent. And then there's the question of civil disobedience. In Peace Now we've had many discussions about civil disobedience. We did have a division within the movement (not recently, but in the mid-eighties, after Lebanon but before the Intifada, as I recall), where we had a big internal debate over civil disobedience. We never had an ideological division, but we definitely had a tactical division. I don't know, as I say, about the other groups. I don't think any group in Israel, with the exception of New Profile, has ever tackled that issue: New Profile, because they're opposed to militarism. I'm sure—it's the closest I would find to trying to tackle that issue of what violence does in Israeli society.

Nevertheless, remarking, "We're constantly in the territories doing these demonstrations, mainly against settlement-building; we've been doing it for years and getting arrested for years," Golan went on to describe a more daring side of Peace Now than I was, on the whole, familiar with.

> We've had lots and lots [of occasions where] we sit down on the road. We've been doing that from the beginning. In the early eighties, our big thing was, as you know, against the settlements. We used to do much more solidarity things with Palestinians. The first time they started destroying Beit Sahour, we went—years before [the tax strike], even. And other places we would go; for instance, in Hebron, when the settlers from Kiryat Arba were always harassing the neighbours in order to expand, we would go down just to demonstrate with the Palestinians. On many of those occasions, we'd be told to leave—"closed military area"—and we generally didn't until we could work out some sort of arrangement, some sort of compromise. Another time, back in the eighties, at the famous Elon Moreh demonstrations, I stayed home with the baby; my husband and others chained themselves to the bulldozers, and we kept Sharon trapped inside for hours and hours.[6]

Nonviolent Activism within the Wider Struggle

One thing that virtually all of the activists I spoke with had in common was the sense that, whatever their group's particular focus, their specific struggle was part and parcel of the larger one against the occupation as a whole. The organizations and strategies described below—in the Palestinian and Israeli organization portions of this chapter and in the joint organization portion of the next—are a necessarily small sampling of those discussed by the hundred-plus contributors to this book. Nonetheless, I hope they give the reader a sense of the breadth and variety of these groups and strategies and of their important place in the nonviolent struggle for an end to the occupation. More information on these groups, as well as on many that are not represented in these chapters, can be found by accessing the websites listed at the end of this book. Of note is the large proportion of Palestinian groups that have had (and in many cases maintain) some kind of working relationship with Israeli groups and vice versa. This is true of several of the groups described below, as well as many which are not; e.g., Palestinian Land Defence Committees, various local anti-wall committees, the Library on Wheels for Peace and Nonviolence and, of course, the Popular Committees against the Wall and Settlements and many Israeli groups.

Looking at the Palestinian and Israeli organizations represented in this chapter—and throughout this book—I am struck by the fact that, whereas a great number of the Palestinian groups (with the obvious exception of groups constituted specifically to resist the wall or other encroachments by the occupation such as land confiscation) have adopted a primarily educational or social-service strategy, most of the Israeli groups are of a more specifically "activist" nature. If we take into account the concept of *sumud* (steadfastness), I think the reason for this becomes clear. As ISM cofounder Huwaida Arraf points out, ordinary Palestinians' determination not to be forced to leave is an important form of nonviolent resistance to the occupation.

> Palestinians are determined to stay, and that in itself is resistance because with that, you're challenging the grand strategy of the successive Israeli governments. So if a Palestinian father is not marching in the streets, he's trying to figure out a way around the checkpoint so he can feed his children; or a student is studying at home instead of being out there in the street or doing a sit-in or

something somewhere; that is all part of making sure that you can
survive and stay here. And that is a rich part of the resistance that
I think needs to be recognized.

Hence, many of the Palestinian groups that regard themselves as part
of the struggle against the occupation put a lot of their energy into
reinforcing the capacity for *sumud*—by providing education, health care,
legal defence in land claims, and the like. This is one way in which they
contribute to the nonviolent resistance to the occupation.

The Israeli groups that I have included in this chapter, on the
other hand, are on the whole—as befits their role as "supporting actors"
in the Palestinian-led struggle—organizations that concentrate on
actual participation in actions such as demonstrations, home rebuilding,
witnessing and reporting inside the occupied territories. Somewhat
arbitrarily, then, I have not included many of the Israeli organizations
that Amos Gvirtz would classify as practicing "preventive nonviolence"—
the very important human rights group, B'tselem, for example, and
other "non-activist" organizations. For reasons of space, too, I refer the
reader to the Wall and Bil'in sections of Chapter 5 for discussion of
the work and strategies of the principal Palestinian activist organizations
(e.g., the Popular Committees against the Wall and Settlements and other
village-based groups opposing the wall).

Palestinian Organizations

Panorama Center and Holy Land Trust: Towards a Unified
Palestinian Movement for Active Nonviolence

One aspect of the political situation of particular strategic relevance
to organizations opposing the occupation is the fragmented nature of
Palestinian society and the consequent lack of coordination amongst anti-
occupation—and more specifically, nonviolent anti-occupation—groups.
Since 2003, Panorama, the Palestinian Center for the Dissemination of
Democracy & Community Development, and Holy Land Trust have
been partners in a venture aimed at forging a unified Palestinian national
movement for active nonviolence.

At the time of our January 2006 interview, Riad Malki was director
of the Ramallah office of Panorama, an organization with a long history

of involvement in promoting nonviolent resistance in Palestine. He explained that, although Panorama had been unable to find donors to support nonviolent resistance projects in Palestine prior to 2003, they nonetheless had persisted in promoting the concept, alongside existing curricula teaching democracy, citizenship, and human rights—subjects for which funding was more readily available—"and by doing so, we are already building the foundations for something we would like to see in the future." Then the American Friends Service Committee (AFSC) entered the picture, and with the AFSC's involvement on both consultative and funding levels came the opportunity to build on the work of the previous fourteen years and to "set up a structure that could take the lead in introducing and in spreading the whole belief and concepts and principles of nonviolence in Palestine." Said Malki:

> We have organizations like Panorama, like Holy Land Trust, and others, who wholeheartedly believe in the nonviolent approach, so let us work together. Secondly, let us bring the most active and influential human elements together in the West Bank and Gaza, and see if we can really build a movement or a network that is connected.

Leaders of the nonviolence movement in the West Bank and Gaza were identified, "people who are active in their localities, who are implementing their own programs differently," as was the need for increased coordination, with the aim of building "a strong-based network that really brings all activists together and really try to exchange programs, ideas, and experiences and strengthen different programs everywhere."

The Holy Land Trust's Sami Awad had outlined this project for me when I interviewed him in the fall of 2003. In addition to nonviolence trainings and workshops, he described plans for community meetings throughout Palestine that were slated to culminate in a Palestine-wide strategizing conference. He spoke enthusiastically of the "core groups" of young nonviolent activists being trained in various Palestinian cities, young men and women who "are very committed to nonviolence, are committed to liberation, [and] to working with their community as well." Their fifty-hour nonviolence training covered:

> conflict resolution, group dynamics, understanding personalities of a group, working together, strategy in resisting occupation, different

aspects of dealing with media, the role of media in the resistance, how to grow as a group, to bring in new members. And what are the weaknesses of your group—how to determine that, democracy within the group, and so on.

Awad continued, "That's what nonviolence is to us. It's not just weapons to resist the occupation; it is how to build the community for the future, how to resolve internal problems, how to unify the different factions and different ideas that you have in your community, which is a very big problem for us today."

Organizing and strategizing began locally, with meetings and trainings in eleven Palestinian cities, including three in the Gaza strip. In each city the aim was for broad-based representation. Participants in HLT/Panorama-organized meetings included "grassroots organizations, activists, or even people affiliated with political factions or with the Authority; it's a variety," said Awad. In Hebron, for instance, the questions to be discussed at the open community meeting were: "What is nonviolence? What does that mean in relation to armed resistance? What does that mean in relation to negotiations? Can we develop a national popular resistance movement at this time, or not? How does the Palestinian leadership fit into all of this?" In each participating community, too, an elected five-to-ten-member "local committee is now organizing for a series of trainings and workshops that will take place in each area." These committees, then—both on their own and in the company of facilitators from HLT and Panorama—"discuss what a nonviolent resistance strategy should be, in a one-day meeting." The plan was to then bring the various locally developed ideas for nonviolent strategies to the national conference, where the delegates would "discuss together what a national strategy should be." Only at that point would input from experts—Palestinian, international, and Israeli—be invited as well, "to simply cut the rough edges off the strategy that this group will develop." Thus, explained Awad, "It will be a very locally based initiative. And then, with that strategy, we'll go to the people and say, 'This is what you have been wanting; let's do this.'"

Awad expressed optimism regarding the prospects for Hamas participation in this process of nonviolent strategizing, remarking that, "It's not impossible to convince them of the power of nonviolence, but they need to be given the opportunity and time to see that."

We had a meeting, for example, with several political factions, which included the Hamas representative, and we talked about nonviolence. He stood up and said that he wasn't against the activities that we were doing. He actually commended us for the courage in doing these nonviolent activities. He simply said that he does not believe nonviolence will work with the Israeli "enemy." He said that, "they will not understand the language that you are trying to convince them with, and the only way they can be convinced of the injustice they are doing is through the gun." He said that statement, but it was a powerful statement because he did not reject nonviolence. If he is given the opportunity to learn about the power of a popular, united movement, then I am sure that he and others within Hamas will drop their weapons when they learn and see how powerful a nonviolent movement can be. This Hamas person didn't accuse us, like others, of being collaborators, of being CIA agents—we've been accused of this—working for the Mossad, or being people who call for normalization of relations. He just said that he does not believe that the Israeli government or military would understand what we're trying to tell them in this and that they will react to it the same way they react to all forms of Palestinian resistance: with force, and with power, and with destruction. And I told him that that's the expected response, always, from the enemy. Don't expect an enemy to act nonviolently to you when you do nonviolence to them.

Awad also stressed the importance of developing strategy not only for ending the occupation but also for the forging of a national modus vivendi for the fragmented Palestinian society, taking into consideration the varied needs of different communities and localities.

Many people see just the focus on the national strategy, like fighting against the apartheid wall that's being built, boycott campaigns, and so on. What we're ignoring is a lot of the daily struggles that each community [faces] that are unique to that community. So for example, the situation here in Bethlehem, for residents, is not like, for example, the one in Hebron, where in Hebron, they might have daily interactions with settlers. They have to create their own unique forms of dealing with that and resisting that phenomenon. Here in Bethlehem, we don't have those interactions; we have to create our own aspects of dealing with our problems. Now, there are, of course, the national slogans, which we all should carry, like the wall and like boycotting, and like that. So we urge each group to think of what are the local problems that they have to deal with and also how we can connect together as a network with a national strategy.

Holy Land Trust: Taking a Holistic Approach to Nonviolence

Israeli military operations and other problems put the kibosh on the Palestine-wide conference that had been scheduled for February 2004, but HLT has been actively involved in the planning and execution of a number of nonviolence conferences since then, including strategizing conferences held in Ramallah and Gaza in April 2005 as part of the program described above. As well, HLT hosted and cosponsored the international Celebrating Nonviolent Resistance conference in Bethlehem in December of 2005, and nonviolence-related programming is highlighted on HLT'S Arabic-language TV and radio stations and the Internet-based Palestinian News Network (PNN).

Alternative Tourism

The Holy Land Trust's activities range, according to its website, from "working with the Palestinian community through developing nonviolent approaches which aim to end the Israeli occupation and by building a future that is founded on the principles of nonviolence, equality, justice, and peaceful coexistence"—as in the program described above—to those intended for international participants. Alternative Tourism is one option offered by a number of Palestinian organizations for those internationals who wish to learn more about the Palestinian reality than they can as conventional tourists but who are not interested in participating in nonviolent resistance actions with groups like ISM and CPT. Holy Land Trust's Travel and Encounter Program, for example, is designed to acquaint international visitors with the situation in Palestine and to equip them to return home and inform their compatriots. This program begins with two weeks of learning about the situation followed by the possibility of volunteer service locally. "That experience is what changes people's minds and really makes them dedicated to fighting this injustice," says HLT director, Sami Awad. And when the participants return home, he says: "We want you to take what you've learned from here, go to your community, go to your churches, go to your synagogues, go to your mosques, schools—in the U.S., Canada, Europe, wherever you are—and tell of your experiences here. Don't just feel sorry for us, don't cry with us, but become activists." In the years since my 2003 interview with Awad, an annual Home Rebuilding Camp (in partnership with ICAHD) and a Palestine Summer Encounter, incorporating language study and billeting with Palestinian families with volunteer work in the Bethlehem area, have been added to the roster.

Nonviolence Training at the Holy Land Trust: The First Intifada as a Home-Grown Model of Nonviolent Resistance

On the other hand, the nonviolence training sessions given in various regions of Palestine by HLT staff are designed for "local consumption." Describing his approach to nonviolence training, Husam Jubran told me (in January 2006):

> Many people in the West ask me, "You don't use Gandhi in your training? You don't use Martin Luther King?" I tell them, "No, I don't use them." Simply, why, I tell them, "I use the First Intifada." I think it's more effective if you say, "Here are the things that we do." And almost everybody joined the First Intifada, so it's something familiar to them.

"We don't ask people to become principled nonviolence [practitioners]," he explained.

> But we focus mostly on how they could become more pragmatic in their approach: to bring them to the place where their first response will be a nonviolent response. If we bring them to this spot where their first action, the first thing they think about, is nonviolence, then we are succeeding in our work.

"And," he said "we're getting a lot of success."

> During the training, we discuss how we could perform the activity in the right way, and we give them role plays to plan for activities, from A to Z. We lead them to think about every single detail and to be exact in their objective—what they want to do and what's going to happen. If they are ready for confrontation, they should have training [for that]. If they don't want to have confrontation, then that's fine. Who's going to control the people? Who's going to be the decision makers at the spot? Press release, calling media, calling

ambulances, coordinating activities with the PA, bringing water, onions,[7] everything. They have to think about everything. So when people start to think about that, it helps them in the future to organize the activities much better, and also it helps to start to strategize about different activities. They do activities against the wall, they do raising awareness campaigns inside the city.

Besides political issues, said Jubran, "Also there is the social side that activists need to deal with and address: election campaigns, corruption, domestic violence, everything." "So at the moment," he said, "what we mostly do is like spreading the seeds."

The Applied Research Institute of Jerusalem (ARIJ): From Ecological Sustainability to Monitoring Settlement Growth

Jad Isaac, director of the Applied Research Institute of Jerusalem (in Bethlehem), told me that interest in the work of ARIJ was expanding daily. "We have a very active website and around 7,000 hits a day from visitors from all over the world," he said. And as in his days as an organizer of the early popular committees of the First Intifada, nonviolence and joint work with like-minded Israelis remain priorities for Isaac and ARIJ.

> I have not abandoned the nonviolence movement and trying to promote reconciliation through joint work with Israelis, with peace-loving people, trying to make this area a better and safer world for both Israelis and Palestinians. For example, we are trying to work right now to try to look at what would be the best scenarios for managing water in the Jordan Valley around the Dead Sea region. These are the sort of things we are working on with Israelis, directly through research institutions in Israel as well. We're working also in trying to assess the quality of air and the movement of pollutants in this region. Israelis are measuring and we are measuring, and we are trying to together come up with a model for the dispersion of the pollutants and what can be done to reduce it and improve the situation.

I asked Isaac how monitoring the expansion of settlements and bypass roads fit in with his former life as a professor of Agronomy at Bethlehem University. It's all in the realm of sustainable development, said he.

I'm still working with farmers in the area, trying to improve their livelihood through better agricultural practices, through the introduction of organic farming, through better conservation of agri-biodiversity. I'm working in the field of the environment, and I'm following land use in Palestine, whether it is Palestinian urbanization or whether it is settlement expansion. So now I'm continuing the same kind of work, but in more diverse issues.

Explaining that this professional cooperation takes place with the knowledge and blessing of the Israeli and Palestinian Ministries of the Environment and that similar cooperation is being planned in agriculture, also with the blessing of the respective ministries, Isaac went on to outline areas of cooperation between ARIJ and Israeli NGOs as well. Joint activities with Ta'ayush continued even during the 2002 curfew in Bethlehem,[8] he told me, and ARIJ cooperates, as well, with Peace Now and B'tselem on settlement issues and has an arrangement with the Society of St Yves,[9] a legal NGO: "In many cases when we go to fight for a person who has lost his land, etc., and we cannot help him legally, we send him to St Yves, but we do the assessment of the settlements and they follow the legal issues."

Hope Flowers School: Progressive Education and Trust Building

Ibrahim Issa, headmaster of Hope Flowers School (an independent school founded by his late father, Hussein Issa) in the West Bank village of el-Khader, stresses the importance of influencing the young. Although Hope Flowers also has programs to train local adults in nonviolence-related skills in a manner sensitive to Palestinian culture, hoping thereby to allay the mistrust that is often directed at training delivered by foreign organizations, children aged 4–13 are the main focus. Hope Flowers offers them (says www.hopeflowersschool.org) "a progressive education based on Montessori methods and the Palestinian Authority curriculum, with an added intercultural, interfaith, conflict-resolution and democratic emphasis and extra-curricular programs." Since 2004, a trauma-recovery program for children and their families has been added.

One of our goals in Hope Flowers is to create a new Palestinian and Israeli generation who believes in peace, democracy, and respecting the rights of others. So we want this idea to grow with them, because they are the next generation. As I said to you, we work also with adults here, and we are organizing different trainings for people in the field of Peace Education. For example, about three months ago, we organized Compassionate Listening. Compassionate Listening is a pre-step before conflict resolution. So, we are working on different levels, but nonviolence also.

One other program is the Empowerment Training Program— because the situation we live in here is affecting the minds and souls of the people [and] prevents them from being productive, from living their lives they way they want to. This is for school teachers mainly, so that the teachers can transfer the basic concepts of empowerment to the students in their classes. The program initially started with the Hope Flowers School and with international trainers, but from next year it will be the Hope Flowers School and Palestinian trainers, which is very different from the point of view of knowing the details of the Palestinian culture and what fits exactly.

Although in Hussein Issa's day there were Israelis volunteering at Hope Flowers School, as well a student exchanges between Hope Flowers and a school in central Israel, this is no longer possible. Meetings, Ibrahim Issa told me, now have to be carried on in "third countries" or via the Internet. It's dangerous to attempt to organize joint events at the school, they've had no Israeli volunteers since 2000 (the army would send back any Israeli who tried to pass the roadblocks, he says), and obtaining a permit to travel to Jerusalem to plan joint projects with Israeli activists is all but impossible. Ironically, "Jerusalem is 10 km from here; we can't meet in Jerusalem, while we can meet in England, which is 3,000 km from here." Nonetheless, Issa described continuing efforts to maintain connections between Hope Flowers and Israeli schools via the Internet as well as a summer program for youth between the ages of 16 and 25 and, although he thinks it would be difficult to include Israelis, he hopes to have Jewish volunteers participating, including those with dual Israeli-foreign nationality.

Because of the aforementioned difficulties, Israeli participation in acts of nonviolent resistance is also less frequent than in the past (e.g., in the mid-1990s, when hundreds of Israelis joined residents of el-Khader in attempts to block the takeover of village land by "neighbourhoods" of the expanding settlement city of Efrat). Even so, states Issa, "You still find people who nonviolently resist, and there are Israeli peace groups protesting against confiscating of land and house demolition—and the building of the wall."

Sabeel: Liberation Theology in Action

Says Rev. Naim Ateek of the Sabeel Ecumenical Liberation Theology Center in Jerusalem: "Everything that we do, everything that we say, everything that we write is done within the context of nonviolent resistance, because we do not believe that violence is an answer at all. So, this is, again, part of our foundation for the work that Sabeel is doing." Sabeel has done some nonviolent actions on their own, but more often they have joined actions initiated by "other groups within the Israeli-Palestinian nonviolent approach to things." Rev. Ateek characterized Sabeel's principal strategy for building support for opposition to the Israeli occupation as educating and "waking up" their fellow Christian church-goers.

> The goals, I think, are very clear for us: ending the occupation should result in the establishment of a Palestinian state alongside the state of Israel, but it needs to be established on all of the West Bank and all the Gaza Strip—including East Jerusalem—the sharing of Jerusalem. So that's really the objective politically. Our strategy has been trying to wake up the churches, because we believe that Christian churches have so much potential, so much power if they raise their voice. Now, it's not an easy strategy, because traditionally most churches have remained silent in the face of injustice. You always have some prophetic voices every now and then, but most of the leaders want to live comfortably, so bishops and clergy and so on have not really raised their voices that much.
>
> One of things we encourage Friends of Sabeel everywhere [to do] is to get into the church and try to help the members of the church wake up to what's really happening, and to help them also understand that to be involved in politics from a perspective of faith is not something bad or that they shouldn't do. Every month we write a very short piece—maybe a story or a fact of what's really happening there, with a little picture, and then points or ideas of what people should pray for and so on, just a few things—so that it can make a very nice insert in a church weekly bulletin. For example, one time the focus was on uprooting trees, olive trees and so on. If we succeed in educating the church—the parishioners—maybe they will educate others and maybe they will do something about it. That has been a very important focus for us.

Al-Watan Center: An Uphill Battle in a Conservative Town

In 1988, Nayef Hashlamoun (a long-time friend and associate of Mubarak Awad) and some friends opened the al-Watan Center for Civic Education, Conflict Resolution, and Nonviolence in the West Bank city of Hebron. In 1993 they began holding workshops, public seminars, and meetings about nonviolence. Initially they faced considerable obstacles in promoting their activities—from both the Israeli military administration and some members of the local establishment—including the requirement to hold separate sessions for women as dictated by the cultural mores of this ultra-conservative town. And when Marshall Rosenberg led a two-day workshop at al-Watan in 1993 on Nonviolent Communication, Hashlamoun said, some political leaders in the community who participated "thought Rosenberg came here to ask them to stop the Intifada. It was a misunderstanding because they had a negative stereotype about nonviolence."

Although more townspeople now turn out for al-Watan's activities than in the early years, Israeli security forces don't make it easy for them. Many times, said Hashlamoun, "if we have a public seminar or a peace march or something, the Israeli security asks some of the participants [to go] for questioning. For that, the people become afraid to participate and come next time." He told me about how a visit by a group of teens from the al-Watan Center to an Israeli school (arranged with the help of the Israeli branch of Interns for Peace)—"a few years ago, before the closures"—was cancelled at the last minute when the Israeli authorities refused to grant the necessary travel permits. "This gives you an example of how the occupation is," he said sadly. "They don't want even activities for peace, even children. And that was before the closure! Now, of course, you couldn't leave your city, your house sometimes."

Citing frequent participation by Israeli groups like Rabbis for Human Rights, the Mifgash Center for Conflict Transformation, and others, as well as al-Watan's connections with nonviolence centres in the United States, Hashlamoun described a march that members and supporters of the al-Watan Center undertook "in cooperation with some people from the CPT, friends from Japan—like Horikoshi [a Buddhist monk living near East Jerusalem in the West Bank]—and the mayor of Hebron, some Palestinian community leaders, political leaders." This too ended in frustration.

Most of the Old City of Hebron and the downtown are under curfew. We said we have to go on a peace march asking to open the city, because the people there live under curfew, and it's very dangerous for their lives. They want medicine, they want milk, they want food, they want their freedom, they want to be able to see the sun. We went on a peace march downtown until the front-line dividing the city [between Palestinian- and Israeli-held sectors]. There, soldiers with guns, with protective vests, with helmets on their heads, with machineguns stopped us. We told them we wanted to go to visit the families, we want to bring them milk. They said it's not good. Of course, we couldn't pass to downtown, to the Old City, and we went back.

Student Activism at Palestine Polytechnic University

My interview with Nayef Hashlamoun had been set for 9:30 a.m. on September 16 (2003). Chris Brown from CPT accompanied me to our meeting spot. Shortly before his scheduled arrival, however, Hashlamoun phoned Brown to explain that he would be at least half an hour late since a house near his was surrounded by tanks, and he, in his "day job" as a press photographer, was needed on the scene. Ever resourceful, Brown phoned T.M. (name withheld by request), a student activist at the Palestine Polytechnic University (PPU) in Hebron, who turned out to be available for an ad hoc interview.

T.M. told me that he and fellow student activists had recently attended a nonviolence workshop in Beit Sahour, designed to teach them "how to organize [their] thinking about social change: All the tools and the raw materials just exist around you, and you should just organize your thinking and your mind and know how to use these tools and these raw materials in a beneficial way." The student movement at PPU was already involved in nonviolent actions before the workshop, T.M. told me, and its activist-members were interested in learning ways to attain political goals "with your heads, and not military tools or anything—just by using your mind and talking to people and having a good attitude toward the others and being involved in some of the activities here in the city."

Although the student movements in West Bank universities are extensions of the various political movements and factions of the PLO and Islamic groups, T.M. explained that "what really distinguishes [the student movements] is that they aren't involved in any military actions.

If one of the students is involved in a military action, that would be because he is a member of a party or a movement outside the university." Pointing out that "in fact, nonviolent actions have gone on for a long time," he listed some of the kinds of nonviolent actions that he and his friends had been involved in.

> Peaceful demonstrations and protests, and maybe some plays acted here in the city about the situation. Some other nonviolent actions were exhibitions for artists in the city. All of them have a message, and I consider it as nonviolence. We have contacted some people in the West by emailing them, by faxing them, and protesting and giving them the exact picture of the situation. I think that all of this is nonviolent action.

I recalled having taken part (in the summer of 1995), along with another Israeli member of the Jerusalem-based Hebron Solidarity Committee, in an action to re-open the main gate of Hebron University, which had been welded shut and bricked up by the Israeli military—joining members of the Hebron Christian Peacemakers Team (who had been invited by the student organizers of the action). Needless to say, the university gates have had to be unblocked more than once in recent years, and T.M. told me that, "there even were girls from the student body that took down some of the gates," adding: "Knocking down gates of the universities is not a violent act; you are not hurting anyone. So, of course, this is one of the activities. And people have many such activities."

Demonstrations attended by hundreds of students, he said, require only a few organizers or marshals to maintain order.

> [The Israelis] want the situation to blow up, so we will not give them this chance. We are going just peacefully to get inside our buildings, because this is our university and because we were very conscious of the soldiers and [we know that] throwing stones and provoking them will not get us anything and will not be beneficial for us anyway. We have many demonstrations with the students of Hebron University, but at the Polytechnic, the situation was very critical because of the laboratories—so the students were very energetic and active, more than Hebron University.
> You can't give a [nonviolence training session] for all the people how to deal with the occupation when it comes or with the soldiers when they come throwing tear gas and rubber bullets at them. But you can have elements among the people that keep the situation

under control. They tell the people "Okay, we are not fighting, and I'm getting in front or behind the soldiers and I'm not afraid of them." And so the people, when they find such elements that are brave and not fighting, they will follow them. So these elements will be giving the people an example of how you deal with such a situation.

These marshals should not wear distinctive clothing, however: "No, they'll be just like the people, so the people will say 'They're just like us. They are just people and they are not afraid.' So just to stand in front of the soldier or in front of the bulldozer, and you are the stronger side and you are the upper hand in the situation."

The Palestinian Center for Rapprochement: from Dialogue to Leadership of the International Solidarity Movement (ISM)

George N. Rishmawi[10] was still in his teens in 1989 when he was among the founding members of the Palestinian Center for Rapprochement between People (PCR) and took an active part in the centre's dialogue and related activities. I asked George what influence PCR's many years of involvement with dialogue and solidarity activities with Israeli Jews had had on the centre's commitment to nonviolent resistance and, more recently, its decision to invite internationals to take an active part in that struggle (via ISM). Stressing that "we do not consider the First Intifada as a violent Intifada," he pointed out that "it was fertile soil for any kind of resistance," and that, "there were many options that we did not take, because we wanted to take the nonviolent resistance."

From the time of its founding, the PCR took a major leadership role in the Beit Sahour tax strike while simultaneously building a strong, dialogue-based relationship with the Israeli Rapprochement-Jerusalem group. During the mid- and late 1990s, this focus increasingly shifted to work in the local community; and in the early months of the Al-Aqsa Intifada, in the wake of the call by Palestinian NGOs to suspend all joint activities with Israelis—with the exception of joint resistance actions with organizations that publicly maintained a clear anti-occupation stance—the dialogues themselves were suspended.[11] PCR initially dealt with the ban on "normalization" called by PNGO (the umbrella organization of Palestinian NGOs) by inviting Israelis to participate in PCR-led activities such as nonviolent direct actions opposing the occupation as individuals, rather than as organizations. Nonetheless, many of the Jewish dialogue partners (as well as other Jewish-Israeli activists, increasing numbers of whom had joined in such activities as the Christmas Candlelight Procession held annually in Beit Sahour since 1993, for example) felt unsure of their welcome and severed their ties with PCR. More recently PCR has focused much of its energy on building international solidarity for Palestinian nonviolent resistance to the occupation. Former PCR director and ISM cofounder, Ghassan Andoni, explained:

> Dialogue groups and community activities and fighting against settlements (especially Har Homah settlement),[12] were part of the work done by Rapprochement during the years after [the First Intifada], especially during the Oslo period. And Rapprochement started paying more attention to the youth in the community and arranging programs to upgrade their experience, provide them with better opportunities, doing trainings in civil society, human rights, leadership, democracy, and nonviolent resistance. We felt the need for a new generation that would be equipped enough to lead the struggle against the occupation that we thought was inevitable because Oslo wasn't going as we hoped.
>
> When this Intifada started in September 2000, we were moved again to the idea that—even with this level of violence—we need to engage in this conflict and try to engage in it in a nonviolent way and try to see whether we can have civil-based resistance with a base that could be broadened with time and then become an important part of the Palestinian resistance. And that was the main idea behind establishing ISM, the International Solidarity Movement.

Andoni recalled how, from early in the First Intifada, PCR activists acted on their conviction that "an important component of civil-based resistance is attracting activism and sympathy from the enemy side," engaging in extensive dialogue and shared activities with Israeli partners (in this case, Rapprochement-Jerusalem). The Oslo process and the increasingly oppressive conditions that followed in its wake, though, brought Andoni to a different perspective on the respective roles of the Palestinian and Israeli movements, and ultimately, of the role that an international presence could play.

> I'll make a wild statement here. You know, I spent fourteen years of my life in dialogues with Israelis, encouraging dialogues, trying

to bring about more understanding. I did that in the context of the First Intifada [and] during the peace-process time. And at that time, I was thinking—or I at least accepted the assumption—that in order to arrive at peace, you need two peace movements, one Palestinian and one Israeli. At the end of that experience, I realized that this assumption needed to be re-examined. You don't need two peace movements to arrive at peace. You need an active Palestinian resistance supported by an active Israeli peace or anti-occupation movement. If you have those two, peace will become tangible. But if you have two peace movements, peace will run far away.

This is why, he explained, PCR decided early in the current Intifada to become fully involved in building the ISM, which he described above as "the model of resistance that complements Palestinian resistance," providing a living example of civil-based resistance as a way of forging a Palestinian civil-based resistance that would "allow for a more massive Israeli peace movement to stand in support." Therefore, stated Andoni, "right now, we are not trying to build a Palestinian peace movement. We are trying to build Palestinian civil-based resistance."

> ISM has managed to push peace work one step further and turn it into "waging peace" rather than "waving peace": Meaning, "Have the guts for it. Be ready to take risks. Be ready to get hurt—in order to stop oppression on the ground, not by lobbying and not by demonstrating, but by blocking, by actually engaging." I think at a certain point ISM said, "We are willing to take sides. We are with Palestinians against the occupation. Nobody can intimidate us [to abandon] this. We are willing to take risks in order to stand against oppression and against occupation."

By contrast, Andoni was not one of those who placed great store in attempts to influence the international community to pressure Israel to end the occupation. Said he, "My role is to do my best in utilizing the power of Palestinian society to end the occupation. International pressure can assist in that, can reduce the suffering, but cannot do it for us."

Huwaida Arraf went into some detail regarding how she sees the strategic role of the kind of international solidarity embodied by the ISM. The Al-Aqsa Intifada, said Arraf, "was very spontaneous. It had no strategy."

So, I started thinking about how we could create a resource for Palestinians to carry out a convincing and successful active non-violent resistance, and international solidarity was one of those things: internationals actively participating in the Palestinian struggle. I think about twenty percent [of ISM volunteers] are Jewish. About forty percent are American, which is another community that we really have to work on.

Describing ongoing opposition from pro-Israel media, who label statements by returned ISMers as anti-Semitic, "and if they're Jewish, then they're "self-hating Jews," she quipped: "My husband [American-Jewish anti-occupation activist Adam Shapiro] is a self-hating Jew." Arraf went on to enumerate the benefits and goals of ISM's principal strategy.

The first one is that having internationals actively involved reduced the level of violence used against Palestinians. It's very clear that at the beginning of this Intifada, when it was just Palestinians, live ammunition was shot at us, no problem, but when internationals were present, that kind of violence was not [used]—there was more restraint practiced. And so there was more incentive for Palestinians to come out. We wanted to provide that level of protection. Not that an unarmed American can protect a Palestinian, but simply by their presence they could.

ISM's second strategic goal, said Arraf, "was to challenge the misinformation that was out there—that the beginning of the Intifada was all the Palestinians' fault and all Arafat's fault for rejecting Camp David and resorting to violence." The prevailing media message was "See, Palestinians can't live with Jews, and their intent was and had always been to destroy the Jewish state," whereas Arraf and others like her were trying to challenge the mainstream media image of the conflict as "Palestinians vs. Israelis" or "Arabs vs. Jews" and to portray it instead as an issue of freedom vs. occupation.

Palestinians were saying End the Occupation, but that was not what was being reported. So it was very frustrating that the Palestinian voice was not being heard. And internationals, I felt, could give Palestinians that voice. A Swedish national or an Italian or an Englishman participating here and then speaking to their own media could give Palestinians a voice that they didn't have, and I very much thought this Intifada needed to be global; it needed to be an international, global Intifada of people uniting against injustice.

The third thing was the individuals participating here and then going and carrying the message back home could be a powerful means of spreading information—even if we couldn't get through to the mainstream corporate media from the beginning—through people and private channels and personal connections; that we would spread the information of what was happening here and re-educate people about what's happening.

And the fourth, and very important—probably the most important—thing to me is the breaking of the isolation. This occupation very much aims to isolate Palestinians from the international community and from each other. As you've seen and as you know, all entrances and exits out of Palestine—the occupied territories—are controlled by Israel. So Palestinians have a very hard time travelling, and they can only travel with Israeli military permission. And everyone coming in is controlled—it's at Israel's whim who gets in and who gets out. This is an extreme sense of isolation and a feeling you're being killed off. You don't have the weapons to fight like Israel does, and no one is going to see; so you're alone. And the international community is not doing anything to uphold your rights. So international civilians coming in and saying "We see and we hear, and we're going to stand with you" provides a little bit of hope, opens a crack in that window, that I think will give us the opportunity to provide hope that will help in the mobilization of people.

Arraf further elaborated on the implications of this strategy in the broader context of undermining what she calls "the pillars of the occupation."

The first one is the media and the propaganda that Israel puts out that it's doing what it's doing to the Palestinian people for security. And again, it's very much in the Israeli occupation's interest to make it seem like Palestinians or Muslims vs. Jews. And by changing that into an international Intifada against occupation—by having all of the people who come here and participate go back and spread the truth of what's happening—we're creating an alternative information source, and we're starting to form, I think, a big barrier to Israel's propaganda campaign that it's Muslims or Palestinians against Jews.

And another one is American support for Israel. I don't think that anyone contests that Israel could not maintain its occupation without the billions of dollars it gets from America per year. Congress seems hopeless, right now, as far as ever cutting that kind of aid; but if we wake up the American public, I think then we can start to create quite an obstacle for the American Congress' just passing these billions of dollars per year on to Israel. So the first thing is working on the media and awakening the public, and then making sure that that is converted to votes, making sure that that has a political impact. So those are two very big, very strong, pillars of support for the occupation.

Although initially Arraf said that she didn't feel that the ISM had yet tackled the "third pillar" of the occupation—the Israeli military, she remarked, nonetheless:

> Actually, I might take that back, we are doing it, but not very consciously and it's not planned. You know, it's a very racist system that we're working with within the ranks of the Israeli military, within Israeli society, within the international community—[where] the life of an international is more valuable than the life of a Palestinian and soldiers will talk to internationals a little bit more respectfully than they'll talk to a Palestinian. And we raise those questions—we're constantly hitting at the consciences of these soldiers: "Why are you doing this?" And these are the questions we're always asking. And a lot of the soldiers tend to blow us off. But who knows? I always hope and pray that they're going home and thinking about these things. And I have gotten into some meaningful conversations with soldiers that do open up and then say, "I don't want to be here."

Israeli Organizations

As in the case of the Palestinian organizations and strategies, the following sampling of Israeli groups is only a small proportion of those described to me. I believe, however, that they are a fair representation of the broad range of organizations practicing active nonviolence as all or part of their anti-occupation activism. The women of Machsom/Checkpoint Watch, for instance, place themselves literally "on the line" between the Palestinian civilians who must contend with Israeli military checkpoints any time they need to travel any but the shortest distances and the soldiers who man several of the most problematic of these. Other groups engage in activities such as demonstrating against the occupation and publicizing its excesses, participating—both as helping hands and a protective presence—in the olive harvest, attempting to prevent home demolitions/rebuilding demolished homes, organizing convoys of humanitarian or medical aid to the territories, military refusal, and challenging the pervasive militarism of Israeli society.

Machsom (Checkpoint) Watch: Israeli Women Confronting the Occupation with Human Rights Activism, Protest, and Political Savvy

Israeli journalist and author Amira Hass—speaking at the April 2007 Conference on Nonviolent Popular Joint Struggle held in the West Bank village of Bil'in—had high praise for Machsom (Checkpoint) Watch, which she described as "one of the first women's groups to challenge the Israeli male monopoly over the security discourse..." and which, she said, "brought the awareness of Israelis to the checkpoints—in their very meticulous and dogged way of being present there [at the checkpoints], reaching other Israelis, nagging the Israeli military authorities again and again." Once Machsom Watch was able to reach the media, said Hass, Israelis began to understand that, "Oh! there is something wrong with checkpoints."

Maya Rosenfeld, an anthropologist and long-time activist, described the group's beginnings in early 2001, as the idea of four or five women, which quickly spread to "twenty or thirty who started carrying it out." The political definition of our work," said Rosenfeld, "is that we are opposed to the closure policy." After explaining how the meaning of closure had evolved over the years, from the general closure policy (i.e., keeping Palestinians out of Israel proper) of the early 1990s, to an ever-stricter "internal" closure policy, obstructing movement among Palestinian communities within the West Bank, she continued:

> When we started, we identified the checkpoints as the place where the Israeli repressive policy is implemented. And we looked at the checkpoints in general as a place where perhaps activism could take place, a place where we could act. And as time went by, I think that the majority of the women came to the conclusion that the closure policy has nothing to do with the provision of security to the citizens of Israel. It didn't take much time for us to understand

that it's within the larger framework of destroying Palestinian civil life, institutions of the Palestinian Authority, institutions of civil society, etc., etc. And this was made very clear when the closure ceased to be a means of separating the two peoples—what is called a general closure, to prevent Palestinians from entering Israel, which could be a measure understandable under the circumstances—and was directed actually at preventing Palestinians' movement between districts of the Palestinian territory itself. As time went on, we understood the much deeper implications of the closure policy, and our perception of our work changed. For example, on our tags we used to have just "Checkpoint Watch" written, and now we also had "Women for Human Rights."

Within a few months of beginning to monitor checkpoints near Jerusalem, "more and more women" came to understand "that these checkpoints had actually ceased to be points of crossing. They had become points of stopping Palestinians from crossing." This ran counter to the popular perception "that checkpoints are places where Palestinians are being checked and then being allowed to cross."

> The word checkpoint arouses this kind of association, and no matter what you tell people, that's the way they perceive it. They don't understand that checkpoints are there to prevent people from movement—even though the Hebrew says *machsom* (barrier, impediment)." People are used to freedom of movement. It's one of the most basic rights that people can't do without, until they're faced with a situation where they do not have this right. But otherwise, I think they cannot imagine the thought of not being able to cross.

Rosenfeld explained that Machsom Watch had to constantly adapt its strategies in response to qualitative changes in Israel's placement and use of checkpoints. Whereas in its first year-and-a-half of activity, the group was mainly attempting to prevent the abuse of Palestinian labourers caught trying to sneak into Jerusalem for a day's work, a major change occurred with the re-occupation of the West Bank Palestinian towns by Israeli forces in the spring of 2002. Numerous checkpoints were instituted *within* Palestinian territory (as opposed to between Palestinian territory and Israel proper), and Machsom Watch had to learn to cope with the growing phenomenon of "internal closure."

It meant that we actually had to observe what was taking place also deeper into the West Bank, not only in and around Jerusalem. Nowadays, we've got people who go to Beit Furik checkpoint, and we have a Tel Aviv branch and they go to places like Huwarra [the main entry point to Nablus]. We have women going daily to Wadi Naar. We have women in Sawahra all the time. My team that used to go to Bethlehem checkpoint has relocated, and we do our shifts in Halhoul [near Hebron] and we move all around the Bethlehem District. And two more teams also go to two checkpoints in the southern West Bank.

As an Israeli group, Machsom Watch is able to accomplish things Palestinian human rights organizations might not be able to.

They cannot—as we can—take advantage of the fact that we are Israeli citizens. We are not welcome at the checkpoints—on the contrary—but there is not much that can be done about this. We are there, and the fact that we are there has an impact, and the soldiers—we always tell them that they have to be accountable to us as citizens; they don't think so, but still our presence there forces them, in a sense, to communicate in one way or another with us. If we were Palestinian, that would not have been possible.

Now, I believe that the Checkpoint Watch is really a very, very unique kind of activism because it has really merged human rights activism with protest and political understanding and criticism to a level that was not found before among Israeli activists. It's a large group,[13] but it's not an NGO that has paid workers; it's completely voluntary, and the level of commitment is very high. Women commit themselves to at least one shift a week. Each activist has many responsibilities, and it's been going on for ages. It's really kind of confronting the occupation directly where it is most manifest. In terms of civil resistance, I think it's really gone very far in terms of what it offers. Because it's not a one-time demo and it's not a two-time demo. People actually are there to confront the military as civilians and to offer help and assistance to Palestinians, and to have a say about this policy of closure which we oppose.

An important aspect of Machsom Watch's strategy, as with many other such groups, is to make the information its members gather available to Israeli legislators and to the public via reports posted on their website. Says Rosenfeld, "I think that the data that we collect is not similar to anything else, because each day we bring to the forefront what is taking place in all of the checkpoints that were visited that day. It does all these things together, at the same time, and in this respect I really believe it's unique."

Rabbis for Human Rights—of both Palestinians *and* Israelis

When Rabbis for Human Rights first began in 1988, says RHR executive director Rabbi Arik Ascherman, "it was so unusual for rabbis to be concerned with this kind of thing," that a visit from them was sufficient to garner considerable publicity for human rights issues, although this is no longer the case. RHR remains, however, "the only rabbinic organization in this country where rabbis from different strains of Judaism coexist within one organization." Rabbi Ascherman told me that he regards the organization today as having two basic mandates: "to address and redress human rights abuses" and "to introduce into people's intellectual universe an alternative way of understanding Torah"—to counteract the widespread sense that the "very volatile brand of extreme nationalism and extreme particularism" that has become "increasingly in [Israel] the dominant religious ethos" is "the true, authentic Judaism." So, says Rabbi Ascherman, "we try to introduce to people's intellectual universe an equally authentic, equally textually based, equally Jewish-humanistic understanding of the Jewish tradition." This has meant, among other things, a broadening of RHR's areas of activity beyond its early focus almost exclusively on Palestinian human rights.

> Our two main additional areas of activity, I would say, are economic justice for Israelis and educating in the Israeli school system about Judaism—and about Islam—and human rights. In principle, we're always involved in at least one issue that's dealing with the human rights of Jewish Israelis and at least one issue that's dealing with the human rights of non-Jews that are part of our society. We work sometimes with the courts, sometimes in coordination with lawyers, sometimes in public campaigns, sometimes through direct advocacy, sometimes by lobbying in the Knesset, in the government, sometimes by appealing to the international community, and in certain cases through acts of civil disobedience.
>
> We as a human rights organization become involved when the ends are allowed to justify the means. And in all too many cases, Israel has been willing to abrogate human rights in order to strengthen their negotiating position. You want to create facts on

the ground, so you expand settlements or create new settlements. You create a Catch-22 situation that makes it impossible to get permits wherever you don't want a Palestinian presence, and then you demolish the homes that they build without permits. So we could have a debate about whether the idea of redrawing the map [to create a "Palestinian-free zone"][14] is a good one or a bad one, but when you send seven hundred men, women, and children out into the freezing winter, that is a human rights violation.

One major thing that's kind of developed for us since the Second Intifada has been the Olive Tree Campaign,[15] in which we've been involved both in the work to act as human shields to allow Palestinians to harvest olives in places where they can't get to, and replanting trees. It started as a result of the Intifada, replanting trees in places where they'd been uprooted in Intifada-related activities. And this connects to a difficult message we try to get across to the Israeli people that from a Jewish point of view, we believe, on the one hand, we have a right and responsibility to defend ourselves; if people are crossing the border to attack my children, we have a right and responsibility to do what we need to do to stop those people. But even in times of warfare, there are red lines we dare not cross: collective punishment, economic and physical warfare against civilians, and of course, the issue of the olive trees is presented as part of defence policy. When you take a closer look, you find that it's a lot more complicated than that. And so we've been helping people harvest, replant trees. We've moved on from areas that have just been uprooted to areas that are in danger of expropriation and what have you, areas between the Green Line and the separation barrier, etc., etc. We've been helping Palestinians market their olive oil.

"Another thing that is important is our work with Palestinian Muslim, Christian, and Druze clergy," says Rabbi Ascherman. Despite the fact that opinion polls show that a majority of both Israelis and Palestinians favour a negotiated compromise of some sort:

Even a larger majority on both sides believes that there's nobody on the other side that thinks the same way, nobody on the other side to talk to. On both sides, people are so convinced that they are the victims that they don't understand that you can be both the victim and the victimizer. I've heard people say: "We Jews are always bending over backwards to help others, but where are the Sheikhs and Khadis for Human Rights?" So we want to create a little bit of cognitive dissonance, to show that there are sheikhs and khadis and priests who were also willing to condemn violence against Israelis—to try to shake things up a bit. I would say the basic challenge today is that both Israelis and Palestinians are living without hope [and this] creates a situation where the extremists on both sides can play like virtuoso violinists.

"We do, as I said earlier, continue to engage in acts of civil disobedience when we feel there's no other choice," says Rabbi Ascherman, but:

[T]he real work that has to be done if there's going to be change is the grassroots work of going from kibbutz to kibbutz, from synagogue to synagogue, from parliament meeting to parliament meeting. And we haven't done nearly enough of that—of talking to the unconvinced, or even to that kind of "soft" left in this country, that threw up their hands in despair after the outbreak of the Intifada and said "I'm not going to be involved any longer." We've done some of that, but we don't do nearly enough of it. Because on the one hand, I disagree with those who think that it's just about international pressure. That's an important piece of it, but there's going to have to be a change of hearts and minds of Israelis and Palestinians. That doesn't come through getting your picture in the paper, it comes through the much more difficult work of one-on-one or small-group discussions.

Physicians for Human Rights (PHR)

Physicians for Human Rights-Israel (PHR), too, has been active since the days of the First Intifada. Gaza Psychiatrist Eyad Sarraj described the beginnings of the Association of Israeli and Palestinian Physicians for Human Rights (AIPPHR)—in a visit by a delegation of concerned Israeli physicians under the leadership of Dr Ruhama Marton—and how it later became PHR-Israel, an Israeli organization with strong ongoing ties to Palestinian medical and legal service providers.[16] He began with warm praise for "the work of Ruhama Marton, herself, as a founder and really a kind of person who had incubated the idea and really spread the spirit of working for human rights in Israel and beyond. I continue to believe," stated Sarraj, "she is one of the best people working in the field of human rights and peace."

I feel very proud of having known these people for a long time. In fact, in the early days of the First Intifada, when they visited Gaza,

> it was in the wake of the [Rabin] breaking-bones policy. I remember that we had a very good tour of the hospital in Gaza, and many of our Israeli colleagues were shocked to see what was going on. Then later in the day, we had a meeting in my house, and we decided that we had to work together, and within two weeks the Israeli and Palestinian Physicians for Human Rights was established.

After the Palestinian Authority came in, Dr Sarraj explained, AIPPHR was divided into two chapters, one Palestinian and one Israeli. Says he, "Physicians for Human Rights–Israel are doing very important work for peace and against the occupation. They are our strategic partners, and we work very closely with them."

Israeli activists Hannah Knaz and Shabtai Gold, like many of those who work for PHR–Israel, are not themselves physicians. Gold spoke highly of PHR.

> I've worked with several different organizations in the region. Physicians for Human Rights-Israel has the advantage of being involved in [not] only the Palestinian-Israeli conflict, but in human rights in general in the region, focusing on the human rights—particularly the right to healthcare—of all residents of the region (including those who [lack medical coverage] because they are not locals, like refugees, [foreign workers,] and such). I think that this is a very good group, in the sense that we cooperate totally with Palestinian NGOs and get full cooperation from certain Palestinian NGOs. And we also manage to work with local groups.

"Our main aim is," said Knaz, "of course, to stop the occupation because of injustice regarding rights of health needs and health services."

> And we try to help in any way we can, finding cases that need to be transferred to Israel or just supporting or giving education or getting into areas that cannot get to medical assistance because of the occupation, because of the closures and so on. Every Saturday we go out in a joint clinic together with Palestinian medical services.

Coalition of Women for Peace:[17] Political Activism from a Feminist Base

People say, "Why do we need nine different women's peace organizations?" (ten as of 2007). Gila Svirsky's answer to this question is that each group has its own niche; all are important. "One is Women in Black, and all that Women in Black do is a vigil. And then there's Bat Shalom, and that does political work together with Palestinian women. Machsom Watch monitors check points, etc." When the Al-Aqsa Intifada broke out, however, Svirsky and fellow activist Hannah Safran decided "There has to be one, strong, unified, feminist voice talking about peace."

> So Hannah Safran and I, together, called for a meeting of all the old women's peace organizations and women who were not involved and wanted to become involved in this one, unified, feminist voice for peace—we met on November 8, 2000, six weeks after the Intifada broke out, and we decided to establish the Coalition. Amazingly, in record time, we agreed on the nine basic principles. I think this is the fastest that any organization has ever come to political agreement on such a delicate, sensitive point—and we were a very large group of Palestinian-Israeli and Jewish-Israeli women who did come to that agreement. But it was clear we were all driven by a sense of urgency. Basically the statements say that, first of all we must end the occupation; we must evacuate—not dismantle, evacuate—all the settlements; return to the Green Line, and find a just solution for the Palestinian-Israeli conflict—which we do not specify. (It would have taken a lot longer if we had tried to specify.)

"And we felt very strongly, as women, that [there had to be] this organic vision of peace: it's not only about withdrawing our troops, it's also about transforming Israeli society," said Svirsky, so they included in the coalition's principles "points that we felt were important for a feminist analysis of peace: and that includes, first of all, that women should be an integral part of the peace negotiations; secondly, that there has to be justice—economic justice—here in Israeli society."

> And that goes hand-in-hand with ending the occupation: that there has to be freedom, equality, justice, and inclusion for all of Israel's citizens, meaning Palestinian, Ethiopians, etc. So the main principles encompass a broader spectrum than just ending the occupation. It's also about justice.

Regarding the separation wall, Svirsky first set out her personal view and then the contrasting one held by the Coalition.

Strategically it makes more sense to talk about moving the wall to the Green Line, not having no wall. My belief is that there has to be a border between us. I don't mind that it's a wall, so long as the wall is a, so to speak, "user-friendly" wall. I don't like there to be a wall with an open-firing zone on the Palestinian side. Also I'm saying that, not only in principle is it okay for a wall to constitute a border, I'm saying in practice or, again, strategically, the way to convince other Israelis that we must get rid of what is now being built is not by saying, "destroy it," but by saying, "move it." Move it to the Green Line, and then, for my money, there will not be a problem with it.

The Coalition says, "absolutely no wall whatsoever; walls don't make sense." Svirsky described the Coalition's current anti-wall campaign, which included demonstrations—some of them with both Israeli and Palestinian women—participation in the Coalition against the Wall,[18] "bringing a delegation of women members of parliament from the European Parliament to the territories, to show them the wall and to explain what the problems are with this particular wall." Commenting on the difficulty of knowing "what works in terms of ending the occupation," and the high rate of burnout among activists, she stressed that, "What we do has to be effective."

Yesh Gvul: There is a Border / There is a Limit!

Yesh Gvul, the oldest Israeli refusenik organization, is made up primarily of Israeli combat soldiers who have taken a stand of selectively refusing to serve (initially in Lebanon, now in the occupied territories) while remaining an active part of the army. Over the years the group has expanded its mandate to include people who refuse all military service in an army of occupation and even the occasional pacifist. The organization had its beginnings in spontaneous isolated incidents of refusal, and only after several years did it succeed in becoming a full-fledged organization. Peretz Kidron recalled:

In the early months of 1982 or late '81, people were beginning to get together and say, "Listen, this occupation has been running for fifteen years, and it looks as though we have to change strategy." So there was talk then of an organized refusenik movement. And while these discussions were being held, along came the Lebanon War, the whole thing accelerated, and it focused on the immediate issue. So the territories were sort of put on the back burner; it wasn't the main issue, the main issue was to stop the war. That dictated the name: Yesh Gvul [both "There is a border" and "There is a limit!" MKL], meaning "not enough that we have the service in the occupied territories, now you've thrown this Lebanon thing…" That was the last straw, and that gave the whole thing impetus, and that's how it began.

We started with the Yesh Gvul Fund (*Keren Yesh Gvul*) to support the families of people who went to prison, because they're left without an income. You're called up, you lose your civilian income. You're supposed to get an army grant or a grant from the National Insurance, and you don't get that if you go to prison. So money had to be collected to give people something, just to tide families over. And then we began the tradition of the solidarity vigils at the prison, and all these other things. And, of course, the main thing—the political thing—was getting the message out. Because refusal was never an objective in itself: the point was refusal against the Lebanon War and then against the occupation.

The principle we worked on for a long time was "Okay, you go to the army and you refuse specific duties? In that case, we support you." And when some people went to more emphatic or more hard-line positions, we said, "We respect you, but this isn't our thing." [This has changed] partly because the army has moved. There's no part of the army that's not connected with the occupation. In Yesh Gvul we say, "Wherever you draw the line; you have to decide. This is very much a personal, subjective decision, and you have to decide what you're prepared to do." There was the case in the First Intifada where a whole officers' course was drafted in to put down the Intifada; they came into the occupied territories and were told to sign on for equipment, and there were three guys who refused to sign on for clubs. We said, "Fine, that's very good, that's resistance." That's our position; that's Yesh Gvul.

Kidron described the evolution of Yesh Gvul's strategy in terms of "grop[ing] our way: we see that something works, expand it; we see that something doesn't work, we drop it," explaining that in recent years (this interview took place in Vancouver in the summer of 2004), they had begun to concentrate less on political propaganda—such as the refusenik statements collected in the book by that name (Kidron 2004)—after many years of success at getting publicity this way for their cause ("Sgt So and So refused, was sentenced to twenty-eight days in prison; at his trial he said…"), because "the army caught on and they began to lean on the media not to publish this stuff." Leafleting soldiers is one approach they've used for a long time, a new leaflet every few months, but one basic message: "Soldier, think of what you're doing. What's the sense? You're going to protect these settlers. It's only going to drag us into a war; the bloodshed, the waste of resources." Yesh Gvul now also holds seminars about the occupation for young people about to be conscripted: first-person testimony from refuseniks, women from Machsom Watch, human rights lawyers, people explaining the applicability of the Geneva Conventions, etc. "Getting these kids [to understand]: 'This is it. This is the package, and you take it away and you decide what you're going to do with it.'" Kidron attributes the recent upsurge in refusal by graduating high-schoolers at least partly to Yesh Gvul's educational seminars.

> In the past there were one or two *Michtavei Shministin* (High School Seniors' letters) when a group of twenty or forty got together—the first one was in 1970—and writing to say "when we join the army, we will refuse to …." What happened this time is that the time was ripe, and they now have over five hundred signatures on it. I think it's partly due to our efforts to spread the word, to get the kids together. And they come along, they're interested. It's a very hot issue for the seventeen-year-olds who may hear of the seminar. And they come along out of curiosity. I do it with music—it's not "heavy." It's all around the refusal issue, but with a shifting focus as the need arises.

Kidron explained how Yesh Gvul avoided the pitfalls inherent in trying to "work out their ideology," opting instead for a simple and straightforward political program: "Two states for two peoples. End the occupation. Talk to the PLO. End of political program. That's it. There's nothing more, nothing less. We're non-specific beyond the essentials, and I think that's very good."

> There was a wonderful group called Dai LaKibush that got together in the First Intifada—the largest group—a mix: Arab, Jewish. And after a year, they decided they had to work out their ideology, and when they'd finished working out their ideology there was nothing left of the group. They'd simply torn themselves apart over totally unnecessary debates about I-don't-know-what. So we avoided that.

ICAHD: Placing House Demolition in the Context of the Occupation

The Israeli Committee Against House Demolitions (ICAHD), on the other hand, does take political positions beyond its primary focus on house demolitions. A quick look at the icahd.org home page in mid-April 2009 turned up the expected articles on house demolition and closely related subjects like settlement expansion, but also items by ICAHD personnel and activists from other organizations on subjects including violation of medical ethics codes by the Israeli military in Gaza, the plight of Israel's Bedouins, opinion pieces by Jeff Halper on a variety of subjects and, notably more than in the past, coverage of boycott, divestment and sanctions-related issues, including "Who Profits from the Occupation?" the 5 February 2009 announcement of the launch of the website www.whoprofits.org by the Coalition of Women for Peace. In fact, as far back as January 2005, Jeff Halper wrote, in an article calling for selective sanctions ("Sanctions against the Israeli Occupation: It's Time"):

> A campaign of selective sanctions can be effective if the choice of targets is strategic: refusing to sell arms to Israel that would be used to perpetuate the Occupation, especially in attacks on civilian populations, for example, or banning Israeli sports teams from competing in international tournaments, especially potent in the South African case... These and other selected measures could have a great impact upon Israel, as well as the ability to mobilize international opposition to the Occupation.

Halper spoke of this and other aspects of ICAHD's anti-occupation strategy when I interviewed him in Jerusalem in October of 2003. One point he stressed was that, despite extensive efforts to educate the Israeli public (exhibits, conferences, tours, etc.), ICAHD's emphasis is on "international advocacy"—based on the conviction that it's the international community that will, ultimately, force an end to the occupation, and "that it's not going to happen from inside."

> Working with foreign governments, working with hundreds of NGOs all over the world, church groups, Jewish groups, and other groups, and trying to mobilize what we call the international civil society like they did with South Africa. I'm in favour of economic sanctions and political sanctions. It's not against Israel per se; it's

against the Israeli occupation. And once the occupation ends, presumably the sanctions will cease as well.

ICAHD, of which Halper is coordinator, was founded in the late 1990s during Netanyahu's first term as Israeli prime minister, a time when "the whole Oslo peace process collapsed, basically. And the occupation was reasserting itself in different ways; one of those ways was with a dramatic rise in house demolitions."

> One of the things we wanted to do as Israeli activists, was to get more involved in actively resisting the occupation. As we began to reorganize, we wanted to do two things that the Israeli peace movement had not done very well in the past. One was to really participate in activities in the occupied territories: not simply go and hold up a sign and express our solidarity, but to really resist the occupation. And the second thing that we wanted to do more than it had been done before was to engage with the Palestinians.

To accomplish these aims, they chose the related issues of house demolition and land expropriation as their primary foci.

> When we took on the issue of house demolition, I don't think we appreciated the implications and the significance of this issue for the conflict between Israelis and Palestinians—at that time. We could have picked other issues as well, but this is not just another issue. First of all, it's obviously one of the most painful aspects of the occupation for the average Palestinian. We're talking about more than 11,000 houses (2009 figure is over 18,000, not counting the recent devastation in Gaza[19]) that have been demolished since 1967, at the start of the occupation.
>
> You have to understand that a home—anybody's home—is a sacred place. The reason that the fact that people are homeless is such an issue is that it's not just that you don't have a house, you're disoriented. And for a Palestinian family, it's also connected to the issue of the land. This is your patrimony. Especially if you're poor, as many Palestinians are, the only thing you have to give to your sons is land for their sustenance, for building a house on. Obviously there's a national as well as personal meaning to the house and the land. So to lose your house is an extremely deep trauma that's affected hundreds of thousands of Palestinians.
>
> Gaza psychologist Eyad Sarraj has done research showing that the majority of young people that have become suicide bombers

[119]

have either witnessed the humiliation of their father or have had their homes demolished. So house demolition is what we call in anthropology a symbolic wound. It's one of the deepest violations of the essence of the person, the family, and so on. Because it's so painful, it's used extensively. It's also extremely important politically as an issue.

When we go to rebuild a home that's been demolished, that's an illegal act, so it's an act of resistance. It's not only a meaningful political act of resistance; it's not only a way of exposing the way the occupation works; it's not only to expose the lie that it's done to defend ourselves from terrorism. Ninety-some percent of the demolitions—and this is crucial to note—are because Israel wants their land, not because of anything to do with security. Then, when we go out and build with them, it's also an act of acknowledgement that they're here, that we're their neighbours, that they have rights to the country, that we refuse to be enemies, that we have to live together.

"ICAHD really pioneered actually going out into the territories and working with Palestinians and doing these kinds of resistance activities," Halper pointed out, emphasizing that this kind of acknowledgement of the Palestinians' national existence is an important step for Israelis to take. Israel's house demolition policy, on the other hand, "is the epitome of the expression of exclusivity and displacement," and "for any kind of resolution of the conflict, we've got to begin to admit to ourselves that we're not the only people in this country that has national rights, and we've got to find a way to accommodate one to the other."

Ta'ayush: More than Co-existence

Ta'ayush was founded by Palestinian and Jewish citizens of Israel who saw, following the events of October 2000, that the time had come for a new form of struggle and protest—by Palestinian and Jewish citizens of Israel working together—targeting both the continuing Israeli occupation of the West Bank and Gaza Strip and the ongoing discrimination against Palestinian citizens of Israel. "It was just when the Intifada began and so many people were feeling just totally desperate, like everything in the world was just crashing down," Noa Nativ told me.

A big, big trigger was the killing of the thirteen Palestinian-Israelis.[20] It was unbelievable that it could happen! That thirteen citizens were killed! They just got together and said, "We're not going to let this happen again. We're going to be the buffer for this, not to let things deteriorate like that again." It started as a small group, and then suddenly all these people joined. People from Tel Aviv and the villages and towns that are not far away, Kufr Qasem and Jaljulia. And it just grew.

By Leena Delasheh's estimate, some sixty percent of their participants are Israeli Jews, about forty percent Palestinian citizens of Israel, and although at the time we spoke, Ta'ayush didn't have formal nonviolence training for its activists, Noa Nativ emphasized that all their actions are planned in advance to minimize the chances of escalation to violence (by the use of marshals, and the like), and "Every time there's a clash with anyone, we have people just running around and telling everybody to cool things down and not to respond in any way." Added Delasheh:

> Before every activity, we just come and say, "People, you are coming to our activity. We are a nonviolent group. No way is anyone to begin or react to any violence, physical or verbal; nothing." Think of a woman telling a bus full of men, Arab, very macho men, that "People, we are demanding no violence." These people looked at me like, "Who are you?" And then I'd say, "Listen, we are the organizers. We have a great responsibility to get the food in and get the people back home safe, and we demand that it's nonviolent." It's a briefing that happens every time. We say it, we say it, we say it again.

Nativ explained that these briefings are "a real ordeal," since all the information about the activity and the situation—what they expect might happen—has to be conveyed "in three languages all the time, just to make sure that everybody understands. Everything we do is in at least Hebrew and Arabic," and, since Ta'ayush welcomes the participation of internationals in their activities, "often in English too." Ta'ayush members are eager, said Delasheh, "to show people that this story about two peoples being enemies because they have to be enemies is bullshit! It's something that doesn't exist."

> Heck, we're living together. We eat together, and we go and work together, and we help each other—if someone falls, he knows that the other will get him up. And we don't stop; the police are beating us up; we don't stop and say, "Hey, this guy is a Jew, I'm not going

to help him." We just go and help. And I've seen people getting beaten, taking the blows for others. In one case it's a Palestinian for a Jew and in the other it's just the opposite.

In their July 2002 public presentation in Vancouver, Delasheh made a particular point of stressing that, although Ta'ayush is most known for its convoys of Israeli vehicles in which they "bring humanitarian aid—food, medicine, water, clothes, whatever is needed" to West Bank villages suffering from the occupation, "The humanitarian aid is not the main reason we come there. We come there to bring Israelis to the place, to show them what is actually happening, what the occupation is doing, to bring people to protest the occupation, and to bring people together—to meet, to be able to talk, to break [down] the barriers." Another reason for these convoys, said Nativ, "is also not to reach just the Jewish public, but also the Palestinian public, because a lot of the Palestinians in the occupied territories, all they get to see of Israeli society is the settlers and the army, and this is not representative of Israeli society, and we do want to give them also a bit of hope about the people who do want peace in Jewish society." Ta'ayush activities inside Israel include work camps and solidarity vigils in unrecognized Palestinian villages "to raise the public awareness of the conditions in these villages and to bring it into the Israeli discourse" as well as in Arab neighbourhoods in "mixed" towns like Jaffa, Lod, and Ramleh, where evictions and house demolition are still common occurrences.

In an interview a few days later, Delasheh celebrated the flexibility of this group that is mixed, in terms of both nationality and politics.

> Ta'ayush is managing to reach a wider population because of its being a joint [Palestinian-Israeli and Jewish-Israeli] political group and because of its not having this uncompromising set of opinions that you either "take it or leave it." And we have a lot of people who are [also] in other groups. I believe that this flexibility is very unique and adds a lot.

She also spoke warmly of "the unique support that we are giving to each other" in the worsening political climate. Nativ, too, spoke of what an important source of strength Ta'ayush was for its members.

> With our sort of work, you come across so many dead ends, you just have done so much work, and so many times, when it doesn't

work, when it's in your face again, that the group is really a support group, in those situations. Then you're not alone. It makes a big, big difference.

New Profile: Civil-izing Israeli Society

Dorothy Naor, who participates in activities sponsored by a number of groups, including both Ta'ayush and New Profile, told me: "I liked New Profile because it was a whole new idea. The idea of New Profile was to transform Israel from a militaristic society to a civil society. And I like that idea, and the more I listen to it and the more I thought about it, the better I like it, and the more I realize how militaristic Israel really is, in everything." Rela Mazali, one of the founders of New Profile – Movement for the Civil-ization of Israeli Society, spoke to me on October 21, 2003, my final interview of that trip.

> New Profile is a feminist, anti-militarist organization (movement, we call it, actually) that works to demilitarize society in Israel. Why? Because we think that Israeli society is a war society, a war culture that is perpetrating wars, not experiencing wars that are imposed on it from the outside; that the reasons are not external, maybe never were, but definitely haven't been for several decades now; and that it's up to us to become aware of this and to stop it. We think that part of the reason why Israelis haven't done this up until now is that they're caught in these militarized mindsets, behaviour patterns, political structures that are very militarized; and the whole of our education system and our culture are all very deeply militarized in a way that is not always immediately obvious—and we're working to try and change that.

"It's mainly up to Israel to stop the conflict," says Mazali, because Israel controls the greater part of the resources that must be redistributed in order to achieve justice, not only with the Palestinians, but also with *Mizrahi* ("Oriental") Jews and "to some extent, women, who are the largest group marginalized by militarization." She spoke of how militarism functions as a mechanism enabling the dominant sectors of society to retain their power through a process of "other-ing."

> Either you're not a real fighter because you're a woman, so you're an "other"; or you're not a quality soldier because you're not educated enough, so you do more menial jobs and you're another kind of

"other"; or you're the enemy, and that's yet another kind of "other". So a militarized society continuously produces "others" and casts different groups in different roles as different kinds of "others" and keeps them limited, relatively powerless, and controlled; and [it] controls whether the small group of dominant (in our case, Israeli-Jewish, mostly Ashkenazi) men hold a vast amount of our resources and make most of our political and economic decisions. We're trying to undermine that.

Acknowledging the importance of the efforts of the many Israeli groups that work side-by-side with Palestinians, Mazali pointed out that "there's no other group doing what we're doing."

Our work is directed intentionally towards the society that most of us live in, belong to, have grown up in, and were socialized into. That's what we're focusing on. Ever since we started work (in 1998), we have supported [all types of refusers] with information, with networking, helping them come out of their often very painful and acute isolation, giving them moral support, informing them of their rights and their options; if they're interested, and if their families are interested, interacting with their families as well, which is often a major factor in the process, and so on. This doesn't constitute all of our activity, but it's a relatively visible part of our activity, and I know that this part is quite well received and recognized on the other side by Palestinians.

For me, one of the things that's very special about New Profile is that it cuts across age-groups very radically. Our youngest member is around sixteen and our oldest member is over seventy. And we do work together, and we have a relatively large number of young people who are intensely involved with the movement, and that gives me personally—and I think many of us—a lot of hope and energy, and we really need that right now.

Peace Now: Influencing Public Opinion and Political Policy

Historically, Peace Now (Shalom Achshav) has chosen its issues carefully, some might say too carefully, and the veteran Israeli peace group has been accused by those to its left of kowtowing to the centrist-left Labour Party. Galia Golan maintains that this is, in fact, not the case. "We consider ourselves in Peace Now a political movement, where first and foremost we're trying to influence policy, and that means also influencing public opinion, and then it's always a question of how that can best be done." From Peace Now's point of view, says Golan, the so-called disengagement (i.e., the "pullout" of Israeli settlements and military from Gaza in August 2005) brought the issue of the settlements to the centre of public discourse in Israel. The Gaza settlements had been dismantled. The question now became, could settlements in the West Bank also be taken down? "And we felt that was the most important thing, and that's what we've concentrated on."

She described Peace Now's adoption of the slogan "Two states for two peoples" as a sign of the organization's having moved to the left and, she points out, very different from pushing for separation of the "us here and them there" variety. Peace Now began moving towards acceptance of that slogan in 1988, when the principle was accepted by the Palestinians, she told me.

> "Two States for Two Peoples" is a Communist slogan that was the extreme left, and we ultimately picked it up, which is mind-boggling. It certainly wasn't viewed as separation by the Communists! The idea to separate came with Barak and the Labour Party in 2000 and 1999, not Peace Now by any stretch of the imagination. It says, "Create a Palestinian state." It says, "There is a Palestinian people, and there should be two states," but "us here and them there" is not part of our thinking.

Conclusion

In the first section of Chapter 3 we returned to the question of "why nonviolence," this time from the organizational point of view rather than the personal. Activists' views of why the choice of nonviolence was "good for [my] organization" or for the Palestinian resistance movement as a whole encompassed both Gandhian ("ideological") and Sharpian ("pragmatic") factors, and though the latter predominate, there were some surprises (e.g., a number of village activists who speak from the perspective of "this is what we learned at home and it is the right thing" rather than "book learning" or lectures by foreign pundits).

We then moved on to the strategic approaches taken by a number of Palestinian and Israeli organizations engaged in nonviolent resistance, both as uni-national bodies and in conjunction with organizations from "the other side." As mentioned above, space constraints have limited the number of organizations described here—which were chosen from a sample that itself was restricted to those to which I had access and was subject to my arbitrary definition of "nonviolent resistance." Nonetheless, I hope that this glimpse of the variety of such groups and strategies will inspire readers to look further and will, at the very least, serve as a corrective to the prevailing sense that "Palestinians don't *do* nonviolence."

Although a few of the Palestinian interviewees mentioned demonstrations and similar activities (marches, street theatre) as some part of their organizations' strategies (e.g., student activists at PPU, al-Watan Center in Hebron, Sabeel, PCR), the overwhelming need to provide support for *sumud* (steadfastness in refusing to quit the country) is reflected by the concentration on predominantly educational and social-service activities by most of the organizations in the Palestinian sample. Some of these include nonviolence strategizing on a Palestine-wide scale, with grassroots involvement, coupled with training in nonviolence (Panorama, Holy Land Trust); dissemination of information abroad regarding the local situation, and nonviolence-themed radio, TV and Internet programming (Holy Land Trust, Palestinian Center for Rapprochement – PCR); alternative tourism (Holy Land Trust); monitoring and attempted containment of settlement growth (ARIJ); and peace, nonviolence, and democracy-oriented education for children and adults (Hope Flowers School, al-Watan Center, Sabeel). The incorporation of international, and often Israeli, activists in Palestinian resistance activities, as pioneered by PCR and further developed by the International Solidarity Movement, might be considered yet another strategy for supporting *sumud*—in that it functions, in the words of ISM's Huwaida Arraf, as "a resource for Palestinians to carry out a convincing and successful active nonviolent resistance"—aiming to reduce the level of violence against the Palestinian activists, challenging media misinformation by providing first-person accounts by international activists, and spreading this information to their home communities, thereby breaking the prevailing isolation of Palestinians from the rest of the world. Examples of additional activism-oriented Palestinian organizations (Popular Committees against the Wall, and the like) can be found in the latter sections of Chapter 5.

By contrast, the Israeli organizations I have selected all practice some form of active nonviolence. Though I do not wish to downplay the importance of Israeli human rights advocacy organizations like B'tselem, for example, I have decided (see also the introduction to this chapter) to emphasize here Israeli organizations more directly involved in the struggle "on the ground." Strategies described include directly confronting Israeli closure policies and informing the broader public of their ramifications, while actively advocating for the human rights of Palestinians caught in the checkpoint dynamic (Machsom/Checkpoint Watch); confronting human rights abuses while counteracting the "extreme nationalism and extreme particularism" prevalent in the Jewish Israeli religious ethos (Rabbis for Human Rights); conducting clinics and providing medical education in the territories, as well as facilitating essential medical treatment inside Israel when needed (Physicians for Human Rights); a unified, feminist call for an end to the occupation with inclusion of women as an "integral part of the peace negotiations," and a vision of economic justice in Israeli society (Coalition of Women for Peace); various strategies aimed at the mobilization of international civil society to end the occupation (Israeli Committee Against House Demolition); combating the occupation in the territories and racism against Palestinian citizens of Israel inside the state as a unified front of both Jewish and Palestinian Israelis (Ta'ayush); endeavouring to have an impact on Israeli government policies through politically targeted activities (Peace Now); and confronting the militarism of Israeli society, either directly through refusal to collude personally in the occupation by refusing to serve there (Yesh Gvul), or indirectly by providing informational and legal support to would-be refuseniks and by explaining the nature of the military grip on Israel to the population at large (New Profile).

Although none of the organizations described in this chapter are "joint" in the sense of having members from both Israel and Palestine, readers will have noticed that many, on both "sides," are involved in some sort of joint action with their counterparts on the other. The next chapter will zero in, specifically, on the strategy of joint action across national boundaries.

NOTES

1 Ashrawi's Wikipedia entry says, in part, "In 1988 ... she joined the Intifada Political Committee, serving on its Diplomatic Committee until 1993. From 1991 to 1993 she served as the official spokesperson of the Palestinian Delegation to the Middle East peace process and a member of the Leadership/ Guidance Committee and executive committee of the delegation. From 1993 to 1995, with the signing of the Oslo Accords by Yasser Arafat and Yitzhak Rabin, Palestinian self-rule was established, and Ashrawi headed the Preparatory Committee of the Palestinian Independent Commission for Citizens' Rights in Jerusalem. Ashrawi has also served since 1996 as an elected member of the Palestinian Legislative Council, Jerusalem Governorate. In 1996, Ashrawi was appointed the Palestinian Authority Minister of Higher Education and Research, but she resigned the post in 1998 in protest against political corruption, specifically Arafat's handling of peace talks. In 1998, Ashrawi founded MIFTAH—the Palestinian Initiative for the Promotion of Global Dialogue and Democracy, an initiative which works towards respect for Palestinian human rights, democracy and peace."

2 As of April 2009, the ISM's membership criteria are formulated as follows: "To join the ISM in Palestine, you must adhere to the following principles: 1. Belief in freedom for the Palestinian people based on all relevant United Nations Resolutions and international law. 2. Using only nonviolent, direct-action methods, strategies and principles to work towards our goal. The ISM is non-hierarchical. Actions on the ground are coordinated with the larger Palestinian community and moved through a core group of committed activists. The core group is open to all activists, Palestinians or otherwise, who make a commitment to ISM's work and take on coordinating responsibilities. The ISM uses consensus decision making in all of its activities." (www.palsolidarity.org/about)

3 "Numbers of killed in the Second Intifada according to the Israeli Human Rights organization, B'tselem, is 3269 till 30/11/2005, while the killed in the First Intifada is 1420," from footnote in Salem 2005a. For current figures see www.btselem.org.

4 Israeli journalist Amira Hass pointed out (at the April 2007 conference on Joint Nonviolent Popular Struggle in Bil'in) that the policy of installing checkpoints between Israel and the occupied Palestinian territories was instituted in 1991 and not in reaction to suicide bombings or to means of struggle utilized in the Al-Aqsa Intifada. As Hass elaborated in a 2007 article distributed via email ("A regime of ordinances and prohibitions has emptied the roads of the West Bank," *Ha'aretz*, 19 January 2007 [Hebrew, translated by Mark Marshall]): "After the beginning of the implementation of the Oslo Accords in 1994, military positions and checkpoints marked the 'border' between Areas A and B (which were transferred to the civil and police control of the Palestinian Authority) and Area C (which remained under Israeli security and civil control) and the settlements. With the outbreak of the Second Intifada in 2000, the number of checkpoints grew and they were intended to prevent and to reduce the passage of Palestinians into Area C (about 60% of the West Bank) and the nearby settlements. ... That is to say, from 1991 [when the 'general exit permit' for

Palestinians was cancelled and replaced by the requirement that individual Palestinians apply for exit permits] to 1994 the closure policy meant separation between Gaza and the West Bank and monitoring and filtering the entry to Israel. *Afterwards the foundations were laid of potential separation within the West Bank between the Palestinian Areas A that were crisscrossed by Area C. That separation was implemented after 2000*" [emphasis mine, MKL]. For further details regarding the development of Israel's checkpoint-related policies and compelling accounts of the experiences of watchers, see Keshet 2006 (includes historical Foreword by Amira Hass).

5 Quoted at length in Chapter 7. See also citation in note 4.

6 In an entry describing the controversial founding of the Elon Moreh settlement, Wikipedia notes, *inter alia*: "At the time, several hundred Israeli activists of Peace Now besieged the settlement site for nearly twenty-four hours, demanding the settlers' removal, and going away only when then Defence Minister Ezer Weizman arrived by helicopter and assured them the settlers would be removed. The site was dismantled and the group moved to the current location in 1980." (Accessed 4 February 2009)

7 Onions are commonly used as an antidote to teargas.

8 Refers to the frequent curfews imposed during the re-invasions of Palestinian cities by Israeli forces in the spring and fall of 2002. For some moving first-person accounts, see Stohlman and Aladin 2003 and Sandercock, Sainath, et al. 2004, as well as www.electronicintifada.net in the category "Palestine: Diaries: Live from Palestine."

9 Founded in 1991, the Society of St Yves is a Catholic human rights NGO based in East Jerusalem offering free legal and advocacy services.

10 The inclusion of his middle initial is necessary since, George N. tells me, there are some 30 George Rishmawis in Beit Sahour—his first cousin George S. Rishmawi appears briefly in Chapter 5.

11 For a more extensive discussion of this call and the concept of "normalization", see Chapter 4, including endnotes 1, 12, and 13.

12 Har Homah, built in 1997 on land owned primarily by residents of Beit Sahour and the village of Um Tuba on a hill called Jabel Abu Ghneim in Arabic, formed the last link in a chain of settlements encircling Jerusalem, and was strongly resisted both in the Israeli courts and by a coalition of Palestinian and Israeli organizations employing nonviolent means. See www.arij.org for chronology.

13 400 as of January 2007, according to www.machsomwatch.org.

14 "One of [then prime minister] Barak's ideas at the time was to move the Green Line to include major settlements, and without a few pesky cave-dwellers, there's a Palestinian-free zone from the Green Line, through the settlements to Kiryat Arba. And we saw that later on the maps." (Rabbi Arik Ascherman, interview of 12 October 2003)

15 For details of this and other activities of RHR, see www.rhr.israel.net.

16 Links to PHR-Israel's Palestinian partners can be found at www.phr.org.il.

17 The organization's name was originally "The Coalition of Women for a Just Peace." Rumour has it that the "Just" was dropped to accommodate an earlier website URL, though some members stubbornly continue to use the full name.

18 The Coalition against the Wall, Svirsky tells me (email correspondence, 6 May 2009), meets only sporadically and does not maintain a website.

19 "In 1997, nine thousand houses had been demolished since the beginning of the occupation. Today [January 2009] that number is twenty-five thousand—and now in Gaza, maybe another twenty or thirty thousand. We won't know for a while." (Jeff Halper, as quoted in Roth 2009, p. 15)

20 Names, photos, and place and means of death of the 13 Israeli Palestinians killed at demos inside Israel at start of the 2000 Intifada can be found at http://www.adalah.org/features/mahashpressconf/martyrs-en.pdf.

4

JOINT STRUGGLE AND THE ISSUES OF
NORMALIZATION AND POWER

Sabeel has never really said "no" to working with other organizations whenever we've been invited. I think if anyone really looks at the situation—you work with your enemy, in that sense, to make peace. You work with people on both sides, who are committed to nonviolent action, to make peace. Peace is not only what the Palestinians are going to do alone or what the Israelis are going to do alone. For a real genuine peace to take place, you have to have people from both sides working towards peace. So, it is a choice, but it is the right choice, it is the only choice, in one sense. You have to work with other people in order to make peace. Peace cannot really be achieved with only one side. I don't think it can happen.

Rev. Naim Ateek (Sabeel)

What I think can work is joint action. I think joint action is very important, for in itself it breaks some kind of taboos. I think that the decision and instruction to Palestinian NGOs not to work with Israelis was disastrous because this served as an excuse for many Israelis [to say] "They don't want us." And that was a mistake.

Meron Benvenisti (Israeli author and political commentator)

Today we all have one fight, which is ending the occupation. How will I ask people to go to make dialogue with Israeli people when they are dying every day and suffering every day?

Manal el-Tamimi (independent Palestinian activist)

Of course, the Palestinian Center for the Study of Nonviolence always asked people if they wanted Israelis in their activities. We [Palestinians and Israelis for Nonviolence—PINV] never forced Israelis on Palestinians that did not want us there. This was a principle.

Amos Gvirtz (speaking of PINV in the days of the First Intifada and before)

Joint Organizations

How do activists engaged in nonviolent resistance to the occupation—coming from a wide variety of organizations, both Palestinian and Israeli—view joint activism? What do truly joint organizations look like?

What do interviewees see as the pros and cons of working together, whether as individuals in joint organizations or in joint endeavours involving uni-national organizations from both communities? Do they think that activists from the two communities should form joint organizations to engage in this struggle? Should Palestinian and Israeli groups work together—with varying degrees of cooperation, coordination, and joint action—while maintaining their autonomy as organizations? Is joint action effective? And what do they feel about the dynamics at play in joint endeavours (whether joint organizations or less formal formations) and the roles of the two "sides"?

Israeli participation in and/or direct support for Palestinian nonviolent resistance to the occupation has taken many forms. And, as we have seen in many of the personal accounts by Israeli and Palestinian activists alike, as well as in the descriptions of the programs of many of the Palestinian and Israeli organizations, considerable joint nonviolent activism takes place in the context of cooperation between uni-national groups, either through formal coalitions or informal arrangements between Palestinian and Israeli groups. Some examples mentioned or described in this book include the relationship of the Palestinian Center for Rapprochement between People (PCR) in Beit Sahour with Rapprochement-Jerusalem; Physicians for Human Rights (PHR) with a number of Palestinian medical committees; HaMoked with various Palestinian legal NGOs; Rabbis for Human Rights (RHR) with the Jahalin Bedouin; the Arab Educational Institute (AEI), Hope Flowers School, and the al-Watan Center with a variety of Israeli organizations and schools; the Palestinian and Israeli Coalition Against Home Demolition, made up of ICAHD, RHR, the Jerusalem Center for Social and Economic Rights, and other Israeli and Palestinian groups; the Applied Research Institute – Jerusalem (ARIJ) with Israeli research institutes as well as with Ta'ayush and with Israeli organizations that monitor settlement activity, such as Peace Now; and, of course, various Israeli activist groups (Anarchists Against the Wall, Gush Shalom, Ta'ayush, among others) with the Popular Committees against the Wall and Settlements in a number of Palestinian villages—not to mention a shifting array of ad hoc formations (Kaufman-Lacusta 2008). Nonetheless, the number of truly joint organizations is small; groups which, like Combatants for Peace for example, are made up of Palestinian and Israeli individuals (as opposed to coalitions of organizations on both sides, like some of those enumerated above) are a rarity.

Below we shall look at a few of the more-fully joint nonviolent organizations, and then continue with an examination of attitudes towards working together across national lines—especially the involvement of Israeli individuals and organizations in Palestinian-led actions. The second section of the chapter will address the debate over whether this kind of joint work deserves to be stigmatized, as it sometimes is, with the label of "normalization",[1] and the third will consider the dynamics of joint work and activists' views regarding the appropriate role of Israelis—both individuals and organizations—in the shared struggle against the occupation.

Palestinians and Israelis for Nonviolence: a Cross-Border Affiliate of the International Fellowship of Reconciliation (IFOR)

In 1985, a group of Palestinians and Israelis dedicated to practicing and spreading ideas of nonviolence in confronting the occupation—including Mubarak Awad, Amos Gvirtz, and Zoughbi Zoughbi—formed an action and educational group called Palestinians and Israelis for Nonviolence (PINV). PINV later became the local affiliate of the International Fellowship of Reconciliation (IFOR) and the first IFOR branch to straddle a "national" border. As its website states, PINV is made up of "people who believe the conflict in the Middle East and its causes are best addressed through nonviolent activism by the two peoples," unilateral or jointly, as circumstances dictate.

> For several years, a small group of Israelis and Palestinians, who are independently active in other groups, has met to discuss nonviolent strategies and solutions. Occasionally they work together in the name of PINV, in order to engage in actions, lead trainings in nonviolent activism, or to petition Middle East leaders to seek nonviolent solutions.

Although it has become increasingly difficult for the Palestinian and Israeli members of PINV to meet face-to-face, the website contains recent articles on nonviolence by both Israelis and Palestinians. Reminiscing about the early days, Amos Gvirtz told me about a memorable nonviolent action undertaken jointly by PINV and the Palestinian Center for the Study of Nonviolence (PCSN) in 1986, nearly two years before the outbreak of the First Intifada.[2]

The PCSN did many activities of their own with Palestinians, and where it was welcome, they invited us (PINV). There were some very beautiful activities. The first one was, I think, maybe the most beautiful. It was at Kirbat Abu Lahem near Qatana, where Israeli forces had uprooted thousands of olive trees, and we came and replanted. We were Israelis and Palestinians, and I think there were also foreigners, and this was a very good action. First of all, there was good participation, which I believe was more-or-less half-and-half [Palestinians and Israelis]. Second, the atmosphere in the action was very good. And then, when Israeli forces came, we faced them nonviolently. There were instructions that Mubarak [Awad] gave beforehand: before we left Jerusalem, he asked people if anyone felt they could not act nonviolently, to please leave and don't come with us. So this made it clear to people that we were going to do a purely nonviolent action. Israeli forces came and started to uproot trees that we had planted. So [our] people collected what they uprooted, and replanted them. It was ended by agreement that everyone would leave the place and court would decide. So we left, and one hour after we left, the Green Patrol[3] came and uprooted what we had planted; so we learned how they respect agreements with them, and some of us still had to go to trial.

The activists were initially charged with trespassing on state land, but luckily the state prosecutor—afraid of opening a larger can of worms over a jurisdiction dispute—dropped the charges, as Gvirtz explained:

This was a very special case, because before the occupation and after '48 or '49 the lands of Khirbat Abu Lahem were in no-man's land between Israel and the West Bank (which was held by Jordan). Then Israel did something to annex the no-man's land. So when we had our trial, our lawyers said, ". . . [W]e don't accept the authority of the court over that territory." And the judge said to the lawyer of the state after our lawyers made their argument: "Look, suppose I accept they are guilty. They will have to pay a few hundred sheqels. But the [jurisdictional] issue here is so principled and so big, that for such a small thing, it's better we don't discuss it. Give it up." So after two or three sittings of the court, [the state prosecutor] said, "Okay, we withdraw."

The *Palestine-Israel Journal*: a Journalistic Noah's Ark

One reason that truly joint organizations are so rare today is that many such initiatives begun in the Oslo period and before were ultimately abandoned as disenchantment with the Oslo "peace process" grew—and those that weren't abandoned mostly succumbed to the Palestinian Authority's and the Palestinian Non-Governmental Organizations' Network's (PNGO) discouragement of such activities in the early months of the Al-Aqsa Intifada[4] or had to give up their joint activities due to the increasing difficulty of travel between Israel and the Palestinian territories and within the territories themselves. One of the few that has survived is the *Palestine-Israel Journal of Politics, Economics and Culture* (PIJ). Founded in 1994, with the intent of tackling "all of the issues which are the common agenda between Israelis and Palestinians, and step by step to create a forum for dialogue, for ongoing communication and a working relationship, and for raising of ideas and also the understanding of the situation," PIJ can be considered a direct descendant of the Martin Buber-inspired Israeli periodical, *New Outlook* (1957–92) described earlier. *New Outlook* veteran Hillel Schenker, and Zahra Khalidi—respectively, the Israeli co-managing editor of PIJ and its outgoing Palestinian co-managing editor—spoke to me in the fall of 2003 about the resilient journal. For Schenker, PIJ's rigorously egalitarian operation is "like Noah's ark: everybody comes in pairs, two-by-two."

> There are two editors, and we have an Israeli and a Palestinian managing editor. I have been for the last year-and-a-half the Israeli managing editor. And Zahra Khalidi has been my partner for the last year. We also have an international editor. Before every issue, we arrange an Israeli and a Palestinian coordinator who are specialists in the [subject of that issue]. The fact is, the journal really is a living laboratory of dialogue, of getting to know each other, of creating things together, of creating the possibility of working relationships.

As an example of the hurdles placed before a bi-national initiative like PIJ, Schenker described how PIJ is coping with the difficulties of planning what should be a routine event—a conference "that will evaluate the ten years since the beginning of the Oslo process, which are parallel to the ten years of the existence of the *Palestine-Israel Journal.*"

> Because of the tremendous difficulty to get people together, we're going to have simultaneous sessions at Tel Aviv University and in Ramallah connected by a video link. We'll have experts sitting in Tel Aviv, experts sitting in Ramallah, and we will create dialogue and be able to continue the process. So we are, despite everything,

continuing and trying to expand our reach by various means. One of the extraordinary things that we all are experiencing is that, unlike in the First Intifada, now we have email, and we have Internet, and there are means of communication and of organization—digital cameras, cellular phones—so we use all of these means to do our work and also to expand the exposure.

As an indication of support for PIJ among "people who matter and who want to somehow make a difference," he explained that although PIJ doesn't have the funds to pay contributors to the journal, "almost everybody we approach—central people in their fields on the Israeli and Palestinian sides—as long as they have the time, they usually agree. So we continue." Co-editor Zahra Khalidi elaborated on the workings of PIJ.

The process is that the two co-managing editors—that is, the Israeli managing editor and the Palestinian managing editor—and the two coordinators that we choose from the Israeli community and the Palestinian community sit in a joint meeting and we decide on a topic; then we set the core issues within that topic, which creates our Focus Section, and we split them between the Palestinians and the Israelis to deal with in articles that they will write. And also, in each issue we have an interview with a prominent personality, either Israeli or Palestinian or sometimes an international personality. For example, in the last issue (Vol. 10 No. 3 2003), which was on human rights, we had an interview with Desmond Tutu—over the phone, of course—from South Africa. And that was a very interesting contribution, I think. We also have another section, which is called the Round Table, where we have two Israelis and two Palestinians with a specialization that we choose, usually centred on the main political focus of the issue. The other sections are Economics and Culture. In Economics we have sometimes about the Palestinian economic situation, sometimes about the Israeli economic situation; and in Culture, we have contributions from poets, novelists, sometimes artists, etc., Israeli and Palestinian. If we have enough funding for an issue, we have a public event where two prominent figures from the Palestinian and the Israeli communities meet and debate a certain issue.

Khalidi reiterated PIJ's educational role: "We think that our journal offers a forum for people who are ready to debate current issues that are part of the situation. And we think that through this debate, through this forum, that creative suggestions can be made, things can be analyzed, people can be made more aware."

The Jerusalem Link: a True Child of Oslo

Another survivor among the Oslo-fuelled spate of dialogue-centred initiatives is the Jerusalem Link: not "purely" joint, in that it comprises the Jerusalem Center for Women (JCW), a Palestinian non-governmental women's centre in East Jerusalem, and the West Jerusalem Israeli women's group Bat Shalom, but not your average coalition, either. Founded simultaneously early in 1994, the two uni-national groups carry out joint Palestinian-Israeli programs through the Jerusalem Link. A description of the Jerusalem Link on the website of the Jerusalem Center for Women states, *inter alia*:

> The joint initiative between JCW and Bat Shalom marks the first time that Palestinian and Israeli organizations have worked so closely for the advancement of women and human rights in the region, as well as towards resolution of the Palestinian-Israeli conflict. JCW is committed to advancing joint peace initiatives despite changing political realities. We believe that, when seized properly, crises can provide powerful opportunities for positive change. In the wake of rising political frustrations, JCW remains committed to developing relationships with other Israeli peace groups who share our vision for peace building.

I met former JCW director Amneh Badran in a Toronto coffee shop (on the opening evening of the conference sponsored by the North American Friends of Sabeel in October of 2005). She told me that, "The Jerusalem Link defines itself as a joint venture for peace, even though you are speaking about two independent organizations, one in East Jerusalem and one in West Jerusalem." The Link had its origins, she said, well before the establishment of its constituent organizations.

> The two were established in 1994, but it was the result of discussion and meetings and political dialogue between women activists on both sides prior to that, especially in 1989 and 1991. The idea was to institutionalize the process of political dialogue between the two sides, and they were among the first to make public statements speaking about the Palestinian right to self-determination.

Explaining that "Oslo had four dimensions: the political, the security, the economic, and the 'people to people,'" Badran characterized the Jerusalem Link as a "consequence of Oslo."

> It wasn't possible to establish the Jerusalem Link without the Oslo Accords, because up to the Oslo Accords, it wasn't looked at as normal to have joint Palestinian-Israeli peace work. It was each side doing their work, and then one side supports the other. These women came together and found that they needed to institutionalize the processes that they had passed through in terms of activism and in terms of political dialogue, so that they can contribute to women's empowerment and women's participation in peacebuilding. It was very ambitious, and there was the euphoria that peace is coming and women have to be part of that process. Again, it was optimistic, very optimistic. I think the added value of the Jerusalem Link is that it said from the beginning that we cannot speak about peace without defining the peace we speak about. And they made Political Principles to guide their work. They spoke about the two-state solution, about the Palestinian right to self-determination; they recognized Israel. Their first statement said that settlements are impediments to peace. The Jerusalem Link speaks about dismantling all settlements—and the wall. Of course, we don't agree on how we describe it. I would say "apartheid wall"; they [i.e., the Israeli women] would say "separation barrier." I would say "two-state solution, Palestine and Israel," and they would say "two-state solution, Palestine and Israel, and both countries have a right in the land."

Badran, who had been JCW director at the time, described a rocky period in the relationship between the Palestinian and Israeli components of the Jerusalem Link beginning in 1999—and a crisis that peaked in 2000 and lasted some three years, during which the joint board did not meet, and work on revising the Principles was suspended. The Link survived, although in recent years, joint activities have been few and far between.[5]

Action Committee for the Jahalin Tribe: an Oslo-Era Example of Egalitarian Joint Struggle

My personal memories of the Jahalin Bedouin and of their struggle to avoid being forcibly displaced by the expansion of the neighbouring settlement city of Ma'ale Adumim go back to that same heady period immediately following the signing of the Oslo Accords described by

Badran. For the previous couple of years, I had been part of a small group of Israelis and internationals promoting European/North American-style nonviolence training and trying to encourage our colleagues in the Israeli peace and justice movement to prepare themselves—through such training and the use of rapid-response telephone trees—to respond to requests for help from Palestinian (and Palestinian-Israeli) friends, for instance in resisting expulsion or house demolition, by showing up en masse as a nonviolent protective presence. Mikado (Michel Warschawski), my boss at the Alternative Information Center (AIC), had tolerated this eccentricity of mine with more than a little scepticism, so I was quite surprised when I walked into the AIC one morning in October of 2003, to be greeted with, "These are the bulldozers you should be lying down in front of!"

He had just gotten off the phone. It seems that a Jahalin Bedouin man had walked into Orient House, the East Jerusalem offices (since shut down by the Israeli authorities) of the nascent Palestinian Authority, demanding help: Israeli bulldozers were threatening his home in the Jahalin encampment beside Ma'ale Adumim, having already knocked down a couple of sheep pens, and he had only saved his small shack by blocking the bulldozer with his own body. He was sent to the Fatah office, where the call was placed to Mikado: Could he send some people from his joint Palestinian-Israeli centre to see what could be done to help the Jahalin? A number of AIC folks and other interested friends drove the few miles to the Jahalin encampment just outside Jerusalem to find out what was happening. Our group was greeted by S'leiman Mazar'a and a couple of other Jahalin. Mazar'a, at the time the only person from the encampment with a college degree and an office job, spoke English, though little Hebrew. Communicating in English with Mazar'a and in Hebrew with his companions (many Jahalin men had learned Hebrew while working as labourers in Jewish settlements, but few spoke English), we asked, "What would you like us to do? Shall we organize a demonstration, help you block bulldozers?" Mazar'a answered wisely, "Bring more people, and we will talk." And so was born the Action Committee for the Jahalin Tribe (ACJT), a small but vocal group of Jahalin and other Palestinians, Israelis, and internationals who worked with members of the tribe and their lawyer (at that time, Lynda Brayer from the Society of St. Yves) to publicize their plight and campaign for a better deal: writing articles, organizing demonstrations, and taking turns sleeping in a vacant tent with a rented cell phone the size of a WWII army walkie-talkie by our sides to alert the media in case of an eviction attempt. During my 2003 visit, Mazar'a recalled those early days of our joint effort.

> Well, you know, the Jahalin's problems started in about 1993. In that year the Palestinians signed the Oslo Agreements with the Israelis, and [the Israelis] started to expand Ma'ale Adumim; so they asked the Bedouin to move from their places. The Bedouin refused, and they had a lawyer who showed them many activities. People came to us and stood with us and helped us. They taught us how to try to refuse the orders and how to take our rights with nonviolence. So they helped us and stood with us many years. When they heard that the police would attack us in the night, they came and slept with us, they helped bring the media: the television, the radio. Each day you would find them sitting with us.

Despite the efforts of the ACJT, Israeli allies, and their lawyers—which did fend off eviction for over three years—some eighty Jahalin families living beside Ma'ale Adumim were forcibly removed, in February 1997, to an exposed hilltop near the regional garbage landfill on the outskirts of the nearby town of Abu Dis. One of those who had become involved with the Jahalin's struggle in the early nineties was Rabbi Jeremy Milgrom. He, in turn, brought their plight to the attention of Rabbis for Human Rights, who continue to this day to work on their behalf. In April of 2007 Milgrom described having recently completed mapping Jahalin encampments situated on land slated to be on the Israeli side of the separation wall. The hope is that their presence on a contemporary map may help forestall their ultimate "transfer" out of Palestine. But Milgrom is not optimistic: "I hear it now from people everywhere that people are being forced to go to Jordan or beyond; so the transfer is taking place. It's a quiet transfer. I wonder will someone decide that the quiet transfer isn't moving fast enough and we have to do something more dramatic."

Over the years, Rabbis for Human Rights and other Israeli groups have taken up the Jahalin cause, retaining a lawyer, Shlomo Lecker, who has succeeded in obtaining improved conditions for many of the displaced families. And looking back, I see in the work of the ACJT a precursor to the kind of joint struggle now taking place in a number of locations in the West Bank, especially along the route of the wall.

Combatants For Peace: Former Fighters Lay Down Their Arms
Combatants for Peace is the unlikely name of what is possibly the newest truly joint nonviolent organization. Just over two years old when I did these interviews in April and July 2007, they hadn't gone public until after my previous visit (December 2005/January 2006). Although they don't refer to themselves as refuseniks, the Israeli members no longer agree to serve in the Israeli army, and the Palestinians—who are mainly affiliated with PLO factions, the majority being from Fatah, according to Palestinian member Wael Salame—have severed their ties with the military wings of the political factions to which they belong. However, unlike groups such as the *Shministim*/High School Seniors, Yesh Gvul, or Courage to Refuse, the Combatants' refusal to serve is secondary to their primary organizational goal, which is to make dialogue and other joint activism with "the other" possible. As Elik Elhanan explained,[6] "I will not speak with somebody who after talking to me will go prepare an explosive belt or will shoot at soldiers at a checkpoint. In the same manner, I don't expect a Palestinian to talk with somebody who the next day he might meet at a checkpoint or that will impose curfew on his village."

> We started meeting at the end of February 2005, and we have been working ever since. On the Israeli side it was a development of the refusenik movement—people from Courage to Refuse and [signatories to] the different objection letters: from Sayeret Matkal [an elite commando unit in the Israeli army], the Pilots' Letter, etc. We thought that we need to do something more positive. You can refuse once, but it's not very meaningful the second time. And the idea was to meet with people who shared the same experiences we did, that are violent and are willing to [renounce] it and try and promote nonviolent resistance. The question of nonviolent resistance for us is still a very large one; it's not very well defined, but it is something that we'd like to promote, an idea that we'd like to pursue and try and get a better understanding of how we can work together.
>
> For the time being, most of our activity is based around two main axes which are, first of all, getting together those combatants on both sides that are willing to [renounce] violence and try to find another way—in order for them to get acquainted, to meet each other, to hear the stories, to give each side the opportunity to meet the enemy as a person. And second of all, it's to try and inform and maybe start a debate, in both communities.

Combatants for Peace meetings are held in both Hebrew and Arabic. As Elhanan quips, "Since most of the Palestinians spent many years in prison and some of the Israelis have Intelligence background, we have a pool of translators ready."

> In our meetings, we have been concentrating, first of all, on really creating this group: seeing that the basis for dialogue exists and it's really possible for us to communicate. Right now, we're really working on facilitating dialogue, while in the background you have this understanding that violence is unacceptable, any violence.

For the Israelis, at least, finding new members has to be done circumspectly, since counselling refusal to serve is considered "incitement" and carries a seven-year jail term.

> You can influence, you can suggest, but you can't persuade. It's a decision that somebody has to make on his own. We meet constantly with people; we tell them our story, we tell them that we refuse, that we will not go, that we think that going is a crime. We don't tell anyone what to do. We want to work with people who already stopped [using violence]; and basically what we want to suggest, both to Israelis and Palestinians, is the fact that there are people on the other side that we can work with and cooperate with, even the most terrible people that the other side can offer—be it the Palestinian terrorists or the Israeli war criminals. Even among those, you have people you can work with, who have other ideas, progressive ideas; and you can find partners.

Yonatan Shapira, another Israeli member, explained that the official political position of Combatants for Peace, as displayed on the group's website "particularly at the request of the Palestinians in the group" entails a "call for full withdrawal from the territories, an end to the occupation, the evacuation of the settlements, and the establishment of a Palestinian state on the '67 territories with East Jerusalem as its capital, beside the State of Israel, whose capital will be West Jerusalem." In other words, the classic two-state solution.

> That's the basic political position. Along with this, whenever we speak, we stress that we are not politicians, nor are we big experts or scientists. We are principally trying to convince people to join us in refusing, in putting pressure on the Israeli government to end the

occupation, in putting pressure on all sides to end the violence. But, really, as regards perception of the solution and how best to live together, each one has his own ideas, and that's fine. There are many people who think that the best way is to live in one state; there are those who think two are right; there are those who prefer one state, but think that two states are a necessary prior stage—and that's okay. Federation, confederation, all these things. People have many ideas. One needs to remember that we are, after all, a group of former fighters. We don't all have doctorates in Politics.

In addition to meetings for former fighters from both communities, Combatants for Peace send speakers to address groups of Palestinian and Israeli youth in universities and community centres, at home and abroad. They also attempt to reach out to the broader public. Palestinian member Wael Salame explained his role thus:

> I'm working hard with the Israeli partners. I give lectures, I meet many different people from the Israeli side and also from the Palestinian side, to convince them about our idea. Really it's not easy at the beginning. We are working hard, but we hope we will win.

Yonatan Shapira concurred:

> We speak anywhere that we're invited: in parliaments in Europe, at the UN, and in all sorts of places and at all levels; not only grassroots, but also with leaders and members of parliament who come to speak with us. Of course it hasn't exactly worked out to carry on a dialogue with the Israeli government; they don't pay us heed as something particularly relevant, but more as some sort of threat to the continuation of Foreign Ministry propaganda. We're not afraid to say openly that we want there to be pressure on the government to withdraw from the territories, to end the occupation, and to act in accordance with international law.

Attitudes towards Joint Work

Benefits of Israeli Participation
Reducing Violence against Palestinians and Combating Mutual Stereotypes
Despite the dearth of truly joint organizations, participation by Israelis in Palestinian-led actions—whether as individuals or as groups in more

or less formal coalitions—was widely valued by most of those I interviewed. A frequently mentioned reason for this was a sense that the presence of Israelis—even more than that of internationals—tends to result in a reduction in the level of violence against the Palestinian activists. Palestinians arrested alongside Israelis are less likely to be roughed up during the arrest and are often held for a shorter time than otherwise; the presence of Israelis often enables the harvest of olives and other crops in situations where settlers might otherwise block access—or might simply shoot the harvesters. And of course, Israelis who participate in those activities go home with more of a gut feeling for what's happening, for what the Palestinians are being confronted with daily, and bringing home the message of the Palestinian nonviolence they have witnessed is also important. As Nafez Assaily of the Library on Wheels for Nonviolence and Peace put it, "Nonviolence is messages."

> The best people to transfer the message to the Israeli society that the Palestinians are strongly in nonviolence are those Israelis who have contact with the Palestinian community. This will raise a lot of questions—for themselves, for their colleagues, for their government, for their Knesset Members. It is very important.

An additional benefit, also cited by Palestinians and Israelis alike, was how working with Israelis affects Palestinians' perception of members of the occupying society. For example, Elias Rishmawi, reminiscing about the Beit Sahour tax strike during the First Intifada, recalled how the joint work of the Rapprochement Center (PCR) in Beit Sahour and Rapprochement-Jerusalem had shown him that "peaceful coexistence is not an impossibility; on the contrary, it's the people's will on both sides to live together in peace. Some people say side-by-side or others say together. The point is," said Rishmawi, "there is room for living in peace." And Ziad Abbas, my former workmate at the jointly run Alternative Information Center, stated: "This experience helped me a lot, and I learned a lot from this experience. And the way I am looking towards peace and towards the future, I look through this kind of education—that we can live together equal, and that's all. Because I want Palestine to be open for everyone. I just need to get my rights as a human being."

Nayef Hashlamoun of the al-Watan Center in Hebron, Ibrahim Issa of Hope Flowers School in el-Khader, and Fu'ad Giacaman of the Arab Educational Institute (AEI) in Bethlehem—all of whom place great emphasis on the value of education—described to me (see below) their continuing efforts to arrange meetings between Israeli and Palestinian students whenever possible, despite the hurdles they sometimes had to jump to manage this; and Salim Shawamreh, whose family home was demolished four times by the Israeli authorities and rebuilt each time with the help of Israeli and international volunteers with the Israeli Committee Against House Demolitions (ICAHD)—finally as a peace centre—declared: "I think this is giving a clear message to the Israeli occupation government, "We are here together."

> We are here, Palestinians and Israelis and international community. We are giving you a clear message that we refuse to be enemies. We want to live in peace, with real peace—but not the way you are doing: putting the wall, and confiscating the land, and demolishing the homes. We are here, Palestinians and Israelis; we are refusing to be two sides.

As an example of the "added value" of Israeli presence, Liad Kantorowicz described the impact of her and Neta Golan's participation in an ISM action that brought "internationals" (the two are dual citizens of Israel and the U.S. and Canada, respectively) to serve as "human shields" in the Palestinian town of Beit Jala when it was being shelled from Israeli Gilo early in the Al-Aqsa Intifada.

> It's a very small community, so word quickly spread that there were Israelis in town. And, even though we come in as internationals, [our being Israeli] is not something that we try to hide in any way. And basically, every house that we went to and every person that we spoke to—they knew that we were Israelis and we were always introduced as Israelis. And I felt like I was presented with a challenge of proving myself; people would introduce me, "This is Liad and she's an Israeli." So immediately the questions that would follow from everybody that approached us were "How do you feel about actions being taken against Israel?" or "How do you feel about the checkpoints?" and "How do you feel about Israeli participation or lack of participation in the Intifada or in opposition to the Israeli government?" And I guess that the responses that both I and Neta gave to people were satisfactory to the level where they were impressed by us enough and impressed by our understanding of what was happening from the Palestinian side and our willingness to participate in the struggle in opposition to the shelling of Beit

Jala, and generally in the opposition to the occupation and oppression of the Palestinian people, that a decision was made to let other Israelis other than ourselves participate officially.

I think that a part of the reason, too, was that somehow the media leaked the word that there were two Israelis in Beit Jala. And even though to both the Israeli media and the Israeli government, an international presence means something and is a force hindering Israeli forces from shelling the houses, those two Israelis were the focal point, and their safety was at serious risk, and the Palestinian community got to see that and got to see what a difference it made for Israelis to be there and how both Israeli media and several Israeli politicians, including the mayor of Jerusalem and Uzi Landau as well,[7] have picked up and have commented and have brought to Israeli public attention the issue of Israelis staying there. They really understood that in order to make a difference, it really works in everybody's best interest to have Israelis participate. And ever since then, the [Palestinian] community has been very open to accepting Israelis and collaborating with them in actions.

PCR's George N. Rishmawi spoke of how meeting members of Israeli anti-occupation groups personally counteracted common Palestinian stereotypes of Jews/Israelis. He also cited the Israeli participants' increased understanding of Palestinians' need to resist the occupation.

Not many people [in Palestine] know about Jews Against the Occupation or the Jewish Alliance Against the Occupation or Jewish Youth Against the Occupation or Jewish Women Against the Occupation.[8] But they now know about Rabbis for Human Rights, they know about Women in Black, they know about Bat Shalom and Gush Shalom, Ta'ayush, and all these kind of groups, because they meet them, they see them. The Israelis now understand that we need to resist. They know that we, as Palestinians, have given peace talks enough time, and when the peace talks failed us—and also failed the Israelis—then things changed and there has become more need for resistance.

Lamenting the fact that the present situation has forced the AEI and their Israeli colleagues to operate largely "on separate tracks," Fu'ad Giacaman told me about his work with Israeli educators to jointly prepare curricula for use "in some Israeli and some Palestinian schools." "All these educational materials," he said, "are aimed at promoting better understanding through learning, because we do believe that religion can be a truth force, as we do believe that education is a truth force. What is happening at the present time is the misuse of religion, the politicization of religion."

Another Palestinian educator whose efforts to continue joint endeavours with Israelis have been frustrated is Nayef Hashlamoun of the al-Watan Center for Civic Education, Conflict Resolution, and Nonviolence in Hebron. A visit by sixty Hebron teens was planned to the Ben Gurion School in Herzlia, Israel—in the pre-closure days when travel was freer than now—he said. But following extensive preparations, including a visit by al-Watan staff-members with teachers at the Israeli school, permission for this bridge-building event was refused at the last minute.

> We had looked on that activity, not just to build relations between the children, because we knew that if these Palestinian children become friends with Israelis, [it is] not just themselves, also their families. And it's an opportunity next time for this family to invite that family. For that, we said it's a good opportunity, to start with the children. You can see from that how our activities usually face a lot of obstacles.

Ibrahim Issa of Hope Flowers School, too, expressed sorrow at the increased difficulty of pursuing any joint activities. Hope Flowers used to do exchanges with Israeli schools and even had Israeli volunteers teaching courses. Despite the more difficult circumstances, though, the school continues to teach Hebrew, says Issa, "because the language is minimizing fear and preventing stereotypes," and he—like Fu'ad Giacaman of the AEI in Bethlehem—credits students' participation in "third country" meetings and Internet-based programs with allowing them to maintain some contact with their Israeli counterparts.

Radicalizing Israelis
Dorothy and Israel Naor—regular Israeli participants in joint actions in the West Bank—are good examples of Israelis who have been radicalized by this experience (in this case, in their seventies), and do their best to spread the word to other Israelis, as well as to Jews outside Israel. Israel Naor explained:

I definitely feel that field work, which brings us in contact with the Palestinians, is by far a much more effective way, not only to know your neighbour—to get to know the Palestinians and them to get to know us—but also brings us into more-or-less the same atmosphere and the same environment that they're in. It's pretty hard for us to envisage, and to put ourselves into somewhere that resembles the type of living conditions of Palestinians. Most Israelis cannot imagine the Palestinians' living conditions and wouldn't want to be exposed to them, and unfortunately most Israelis don't care. This field work and this exposure has made us feel friends and to become very closely associated with these people, and we of course take it much more to heart than were we sitting at some distance and only working by "remote control."

Neta Golan, too, elaborated on the value of joint action as a way of educating the Israeli participants.

Israelis in general are just terrified of Palestinians. I know, people come sometimes on an action, let's say on a Ta'ayush caravan, and they're terrified of the people that they're coming to help—and they roll up their car windows and whatever. When they finally meet the Palestinians, it changes. But while they're still going through it, it can be "interesting," I would say.

Creating an Option for Nonviolence

Golan would be happier if more frequently "Israelis would be there supporting Palestinian actions, which is something that rarely happens." On the other hand, "when Israelis *are* present, it really obviously makes a difference, especially now," she said, in terms of "creating an option for Palestinian nonviolent resistance."

Everything is important: work within Israel is important and work outside of Israel is important—but the Palestinian resistance, to me, is really important and is kind of the key. In terms of internationals, things have really changed. One thing is that they've changed the laws so that anybody can be deported in a second; it used to be a long legal process to deport somebody. And the other thing is, an Israeli soldier knows that if he kills an Israeli, he'll be held accountable. He knows he can't do that. He knows that if he kills a Palestinian, he won't be held accountable. So he doesn't need to be given the order, "Kill Palestinian kids that throw stones at your tank," but he knows that if he kills them, nobody is going to ask questions. With internationals they didn't know, and they treated us like Israelis for a really long time.[9] And about two weeks after Rachel was murdered,[10] when the army announced the fact that they weren't going to put the driver on trial—a week after that, Brian was shot in the head and a week after that, Tom was shot in the head. Like it was a clear message. So, internationals protecting Palestinians doing nonviolence? It still has some validity, but much less than before. They're more likely to shoot. Israelis, on the other hand, are a whole new ballgame, still.

Conveying a Political Message

Peace Now, which identifies itself primarily as a political—rather than a solidarity—organization, is not generally known for holding joint activities with Palestinians. But, says Reuven Kaminer, an activist with Peace Now-Jerusalem, there's more joint work between Peace Now and Palestinians than people often think, ranging from dialogue groups, through cooperation in the monitoring of settlement activity, to "cooperation with people in the various villages and farms," and bringing Israelis "to see the realities of the occupation, which is a very important thing." Peace Now old-timer Galia Golan reminded me, as well, of the massive "Hands around Jerusalem" demonstration in 1989, where thousands of Israelis and Palestinians literally joined hands to form a human chain encircling the walls of Old City—until violently dispersed by an extremely nervous Israeli police force[11]—and mentioned other joint activities, in most of which cases, however, the association with Palestinian groups is informal. Golan made a point of stating that, "We're not a solidarity movement; we never were a solidarity movement. We have a political purpose; not party political, but trying to influence policy. So when we do things with Palestinians, it's with the purpose in mind of trying to prove there's a partner" (for peace negotiations). In response to my question as to whether Peace Now felt that their work could best be accomplished working in separate national groups, or jointly, such as in coalitions, Golan replied that "it depends on what you're trying to do."

> When we're trying to stop the building of settlements, we never do them jointly with Palestinians. What we're trying to do on the settlements is we're addressing the Israeli public, we're addressing

the Israeli government, and we're saying, "This is just not in our interest, whatsoever. [Settlements] make it impossible to reach an agreement; they're hurting us from every point of view, and so on and so forth." We consider the settlements *our* problem.

Although there have been occasions when, purposely or coincidentally, Peace Now actually has demonstrated along with Palestinians against settlement activity, this is not "policy." And definitely, Professor Golan stressed, "If we're going to demonstrate against a [settlement] ground-breaking, we don't bring Palestinians with us."

> Again, it depends on the point you're trying to make. If you're trying to prove that there is a partner—and that, of course, is something that it's been important to prove in the last few years—then it's very good to do joint demonstrations. But, of course, if we want to get really big numbers [of Israelis], and we want to try to press the government to get out of the territories, or to stop this or do that, we'll usually go internally, to Tel Aviv, even Jerusalem. I think that when you do things together with Palestinians [and when you] do them in separate groups really depends upon what you're trying to do and what audience you're trying to reach, a question of priorities.

Galia Golan concluded our conversation by describing the relationship- and trust-building benefits of joint planning of shared activities.

> If you do joint things, you do the planning together, and actually it's one of the best ways of working with Palestinians. Dialogue as such is good, basically, when there are people who don't know each other and you're trying to get them together, but I've found really one of the best ways that we really reached understanding of the two peoples was when we worked on something together—planning the "Hands around Jerusalem," planning activities, or planning a meeting, because when you're working together, then basically you have the same goal and you begin to forget that you're on different sides, so to speak; the divisions become different, transnational. That's when you really begin to understand each other.

Is Joint Work Always the Right Choice?

Not for Everybody

Some interviewees, while supportive of joint work in principle, were not involved with it themselves. Gila Svirsky, for example, regards working together as a crucial contradiction to Palestinian isolation. "I think working with the Palestinians is critical in terms of their not feeling alone in the world. It may even have an effect on Palestinians' trying to educate their children for coexistence—when they know that there are Israelis who are on their side. There are a lot of important reasons for working with Palestinians." But, she said, "[i]t's not an avenue that I have, myself, given most of my energy to." Svirsky has chosen instead "to emphasize working inside Israel and working on an international level," because in her view, as she has commented elsewhere, "What works more is working on the Israeli side to educate Israelis."

The Right Choice, But Not Right Now

Zoughbi Zoughbi, although personally a veteran member of Palestinians and Israelis for Nonviolence (PINV) and director of Wi'am (a Palestinian organization that has often undertaken joint projects with Israeli groups), expressed mixed feelings when I asked him about working together in the present context.

> Well, there is a possibility, but I believe we are preoccupied with our survival. We are discovering each other, we are in the process of respecting each other; we haven't reached the point of success. Israeli society is moving to the right, not to the left. The peace camp is more fragmented, it's more individualistic, they don't have leverage. At the same time, it's a kind of ray of hope for us to see that more voices among the Israelis should be raised against the occupation. On top of all that, I believe, as a Palestinian who thinks this way, that whatever is my struggle should impact positively on the Zionist side. And the Israeli peace camp should impact my society positively in one way or another.

But, stated Zoughbi, "We can't do it together now; we can work separately, and at the same time take into consideration what is the effect on the other side."

Similarly, when I interviewed independent Nablus activist Manal el-Tamimi in the fall of 2003, she remarked that despite her earlier extensive involvement in dialogue with a number of Israeli organizations and work with Ta'ayush, and despite ongoing contact with individual Israeli friends from Ta'ayush, she hadn't recently worked with Israeli groups—adding: "I believe that this fight is not only my fight; it's the fight of the Israelis against the occupation, because it's something unfair and it's something against humanity, and it's the fight of everybody, it's not only mine. I mean, I'm not making a block between me and Israelis. I'm opening my heart." "Working jointly is good," Tamimi told me, "but joining with goals and targets [as opposed to being physically in the same place]; because I think the Israelis have a big fight to do inside Israel."

One Israeli interviewee who shared the feeling that the time was not right, on the whole, for joint activism was Judith Green—a key participant in the dialogue and solidarity work done by Rapprochement-Jerusalem during the First Intifada who is no longer involved in grassroots activism. Green remarked that, "there are very few areas where I think that the Palestinians can really benefit from Israeli cooperation." And while acknowledging that nonviolent actions such as boycotts, strikes, and other means of noncooperation are legitimate forms of resistance for Palestinians, she nonetheless questioned the value of Israeli participation in these activities: "They don't need us for that, in my opinion. I think that they came to the conclusion themselves at the end of the nineties or so—even before the beginning of this Intifada—that maybe a lot of the cooperative work with the Israeli public was not really bringing the kind of results that they wanted, and they have to find other ways of getting the same results. Maybe the ISM is one of them."

Green applauded Ghassan Andoni and other activists at the PCR in Beit Sahour for their important efforts in working to gain credibility and broader acceptance in Palestine for nonviolent resistance, something she feels has become more difficult since the return of the PLO leadership to the country in the wake of the Oslo Accords, an event that she feels also greatly diminished the role of Israeli activists in Palestinian nonviolence.

> Everything is distorted by the situation to the point that certain kinds of things are just not really possible anymore. There's no kind of normal framework for anything: for health projects, for educational projects, for nothing. So everything's a big strain, and either you have to go to Cyprus or something, or sneak around a bit in the West Bank.

She did, however, acknowledge that there are some activities where an Israeli presence may still be appropriate.

Helping with the olive harvest is something that we used to do a lot, and it was a wonderful activity in a different atmosphere. And now, I still think it's probably one of the best things that are going on, one of the ones I'd give the highest marks to—although the whole atmosphere around that is also, of course, much more challenging, more dangerous. The ante has been upped in everything, but I appreciate that that kind of thing can happen.

Muhammad Jaradat (BADIL Resource Center for Palestinian Residency and Refugee Rights) does not reject joint work with Israelis altogether (see "Solidarity and Joint Work," below), but like Manal el-Tamimi, he sees their primary job as working for change within Israeli society. Characterizing the occupation as but one manifestation of the root problem of Israeli racism, he drew the following parallel from his village childhood.

When we had a bad tree, and it was disturbing the field, the easy way was to cut it down on top of the ground. Then next year it will come up, you know, and then you'll cut it again. So once my father told me, "You are doing ten times the job. Why don't you do it one time?" I asked him what, and he said, "Dig a big hole. Go down to the roots of this bad tree and take it out. It's true you will spend a few hours more working and you will get tired, but next year you will not have a problem with it." So if we want to finish all the misery in this area, our resistance has to work on the foundations of the regime in Israel, of the institutions in Israel, not just the occupation.

The Normalization Debate

In the euphoric immediate aftermath of the signing of the Oslo Accords in September 1993, Israelis became welcome in many places they hadn't been before, and Israeli organizations ranging from those already accustomed to working together with Palestinians—such as Gush Shalom, Israelis by Choice, and the like—all the way to Peace Now, found themselves demonstrating side-by-side with (and sometimes being arrested along with) Palestinians in various West Bank locations. Among the less adventuresome, new dialogue groups sprang up and existing ones thrived, despite the increasingly stringent travel restrictions imposed on Palestinian participants. With the advent of the Al-Aqsa

Intifada in October 2000, however, quite a few Palestinian organizations began avoiding such joint endeavours, seeing them as a form of premature normalization.

In this context, normalization has been extensively debated and discussed. For example, in an article in the *Palestine-Israel Journal of Politics, Economics and Culture*, Palestinian author and director of the Jerusalem office of the Panorama Center for the Dissemination of Democracy and Community, Walid Salem, defined and exhaustively analyzed the concept, examining both pro- and anti-normalization positions, Israeli as well as Palestinian (Salem 2005). I find the following points made in his article to be the most relevant for our purposes here: 1) Palestinians are divided on the issue of normalization between those willing to continue to work with Israeli organizations ("to normalize") "and those who want to postpone normalization until after the establishment of the Palestinian state." 2) Even mainstream PLO groups (e.g., Fatah affiliates) that had been in close relationships (dialogue, joint projects, etc.) before the start of the Al-Aqsa Intifada in 2000 "began to feel that if Palestinians continued to meet with the Israeli movements, this might be viewed as though the situation was satisfactory a d the peace agreements need not be rushed." Finally, 3):

> [S]ince the majority of Palestinians accept normalization with Israel if the occupation ends, it should be emphasized that if the Israeli peace camp strengthens its work against the occupation within Israeli society, it will build trust among Palestinians, which could lead to a willingness to normalize. Another way to change Palestinians' positions is for the Israeli peace camp to show solidarity with them in their suffering from the occupation. This, for instance, is the reason why these Palestinians, although against normalization now, accept and build normal relations with the Israeli Ta'ayush group and other Israeli groups [i.e., "Israeli solidarity groups that honestly and sincerely join the Palestinians in what together they view as a shared struggle for justice and human rights."]

Indeed, although some of those I interviewed felt that the struggle to end the occupation was primarily a Palestinian concern, to which Israeli activists' best contribution would be to stay home and educate their own people—or to work for change within Israel, say in combating racism, which would have an impact on Israel's relations with the Palestinians —virtually every one in my Palestinian "sample" supported at least some degree of coordination/cooperation, and most welcomed Israeli participation in anti-occupation actions, either as individuals, as members of joint organizations, as Israeli organizations in coalition with their Palestinian counterparts, or as Israeli organizations invited to participate by Palestinian host organizations (including local village councils and popular committees). Even so, as Israeli activist Jeff Halper cautions, such endeavours are fraught with "the danger of normalization."

> —especially when liberal elements of the Occupying Power either don't perceive the power differentials or try to minimize the conflict, and latch onto "joint" projects as validating them and dulling the need and urgency of ending the oppression itself. Thus "good relations" are promoted and the source of oppression is downplayed and rendered non-urgent.

The ISM's Huwaida Arraf spoke in the same vein. The sentiment behind the comprehensive ban on joint activities announced in 2000, she told me, was rooted in the post-Oslo period "from 1993, where so much money from the international community was invested in 'people to people' programs and conflict resolution programs and dialoguing" (what Arraf referred to collectively as "Israeli feel-good programs"), which essentially diverted energy from resistance to the occupation.

> They met a Palestinian and they talked to a Palestinian—"He understands me and I understand her"—but in the end, the occupation was just "cemented" really, because the focus was shifted from what Israel was doing on the ground to "let's dialogue and learn to like each other." Palestinians don't have a problem living with Jews and Israelis, so that's not the issue. From the beginning of this Intifada—basically when the Intifada broke out—the Palestinians were saying, "No. No more are we going to be these little chess pieces that are moved around." They didn't want to be part of this thing anymore. The issue has got to be the occupation; that's what the message has to be.

Normalization vs. Resistance

One way organizations such as the Palestinian Center for Rapprochement (PCR) dealt with the problem of normalization was by developing ways that Israelis could go beyond dialogue and join in actively resisting the occupation—a clear contradiction to "normalization." Neta Golan described how Palestinian attitudes towards dialogue groups and similar joint activities moved from enthusiasm to mistrust and how PCR pioneered the shift from dialogue for its own sake to ways of jointly challenging the occupation.

> I was participating in dialogues and I witnessed how—as Palestinians were realizing that the peace process and the dialogue groups were being used as a kind of smoke screen that said "everything's okay," behind which the occupation was reinforcing itself in a very real way—the issue of normalization arose, and people started saying "the world is getting this picture that we're all making up and making friends and having a peace process, and they're ignoring that our land is being stolen, our freedom of movement is being further [curtailed]." When the Intifada started, it was PNGO—an umbrella of Palestinian NGOs—that called to stop the dialogues and any joint actions with Israelis, as a response to that issue of normalization. Rapprochement (PCR), again, was kind of pioneering in that they accepted the boycott of dialogue, but they said, "Okay, but if people are coming to resist with us, then that's not normalization; that's challenging the occupation, so that we will accept."

This was PCR's way of following the spirit, if not the letter, of the ruling by the PNGO network that rejection of normalization required the cutting of ties with virtually all Israeli groups so long as the occupation continued. PCR's liberal interpretation of the PNGO ruling meant that—as George N. Rishmawi (PCR director since August 2005) put it:

> We did not cut all the ties with Israelis; we decided to continue with Israelis, only on a different level. We are willing to risk [challenging the consensus in the Palestinian community] for the sake of direct actions, but not for dialogue or camps or anything like that. Now, that doesn't mean that dialogue is less important or that a [joint youth training] camp was not important, but there is a priority now: being as united as we can with other Palestinians and to go on with our nonviolent resistance. We had Israelis who joined the nonviolent resistance who were initially in the dialogue group. Other new ones came and groups like Rabbis for Human Rights and Gush Shalom. [Our relationship with Israelis has] relaxed and it's changed—from dialogue to direct action. It's time to act. This has caused some people on the Israeli side to drop out. It brought others in, of course.

Thus PCR, and eventually other Palestinian activist groups, have been able to invite Israelis to join in activities whose aim is resistance to the occupation.[12]

Avoiding Normalization in Joint Action
Protecting a Shared Environment
When I asked ARIJ director Jad Isaac whether his work on environmental and agricultural issues with Israeli research institutes (with the blessing of the relevant Palestinian ministries) and his ongoing cooperation with Israeli groups such as Peace Now, B'tselem, and Ta'ayush were considered "normalization," he replied, "No, no. There is nothing called normalization in this process. We have a shared environment; we have to protect it." "If it is a needs-driven project," said Isaac, "I don't think there's anyone who's objecting to that."

The Impact of Joint Action on the Israeli Participants
Liad Kantorowicz spoke of encountering another facet of the normalization debate—the feeling on the part of some Palestinians that "bringing Israelis into the occupied territories makes them feel that 'It's okay, we've done our part and now we can go home' and putting their conscience at ease. Or seeing how it is and saying that it's not that bad." But, said Kantorowicz, what she had observed was the opposite effect.

> I can say for myself, as well as for many activists, that I have seen the reactions on their faces and have spoken with them, that once crossing the Green Line into the occupied territories and seeing how dramatically things change, it's shocking. It's overwhelming, and it has such a tremendous effect on people. You hear things on the news and you see things [on TV], and you really have no visceral understanding of what the situation is on the ground. And once you see it, you get such a more dire sense of urgency to do something, to try to change it. The fact that people's basic means of living are hindered by the occupation; basic things that in cities like Tel Aviv are taken for granted—like going to work, leaving your house, going to school, or sitting down and eating dinner—are completely hindered; having Israelis see that shocks them and startles them to the point that they put a face on it and it makes them feel that they have to act. I've seen people who are not even activists—like some

of my friends who I've taken along with me—who've stumbled upon those situations, and they were just stunned. I think it changed their perspectives tremendously, and so I don't really believe this is normalization.

I think that is something that was much more the case in the years after the Oslo Accords, when there was a feeling of working towards peace and a general feeling on the part of the Israeli left of—how do I say it?—of working to bridge a cultural gap and bringing two peoples together; a feeling of "Look, if you put Israelis and Palestinians side by side, we're sure that they can come to have something in common."

But the situation on the ground has changed; it has gotten a lot more severe, and understanding what makes life in the occupied territories so vastly different than living inside the Green Line and how the lives of Palestinians are so vastly more complex and difficult and burdening than the lives of Israeli Jews is what drives Israelis to act and to return to the West Bank—and even if they don't return to the West Bank, to be a lot more active in what they're doing to end the occupation.

The Importance of Spreading the Word: Palestinians and Israelis Really Can Live Together
The fact that nonviolent actions are being done—whether jointly or separately by Israelis and Palestinians—is not enough by itself, said Palestinian journalist and human rights activist Hisham Sharabati. It is important that word gets out to "show the world that the Palestinians and Israelis can live together."

I always say, when the guns and the cannons are shooting, these are the louder voices and this is what is heard, despite the fact maybe you have other tens of nonviolent activities and Palestinian-Israeli joint activities that nobody hears about; because the media like the excitement, they like the clash, the action, and in many cases the nonviolent activities are not "action" for the media. Whether it is joint groups or not, I believe that working together is important. First thing, we should show the world that this Palestinian-Israeli conflict is solvable and that the Palestinians and the Israelis can live together and can work together. It's not a conflict of extreme Islam against the Jews because they are Jews—because on the other hand, we see Jews and Palestinians, who are mainly but not only Muslims, working together side by side, and they respect each other. In many cases you find the Palestinians and the Israelis respect each other much more than they respect their own political leaders. I think it is important for both the Palestinian people and the Israeli people to pass this message to the world, because part of the propaganda in the world, part of the official propaganda of the Israeli government and the extreme right in Israel is that this is a war against terror. Many of the mass media in the West cover it as the war only of Hamas and Islamic Jihad, and Israel is only reacting to them, whereas actually the Palestinians are the victims of such practices of the occupation government in Israel.

Working Together to Create Something

"We're not going to stop the *Palestinian-Israel Journal*, because we are not a 'joint Palestinian-Israeli project'; we are one organism working together to create something." So said Ziad Abu Zayyad, PIJ's Palestinian co-founding editor, in reaction to the Palestinian Authority's directive regarding normalization,[13] Hillel Schenker recalled.

> And throughout the Intifada, particularly in the difficult period of the first year, when there was this tremendous sense of disappointment and frustration on the Israeli side, because of the break-down of Camp David and Taba and the election of Sharon, and the suicide bombers, the *Palestinian-Israel Journal* was practically the only place where Israelis and Palestinians on an ongoing basis were meeting regularly to work together, to continue to try to produce something which was fulfilling the mandate it had set for itself, and which, in a sense, served as a beacon to both Israelis and Palestinians—"Look, there are still channels of communication; there are still possibilities."

This is a sentiment reinforced by Zahra Khalidi, a Palestinian co-managing editor of the PIJ:

> We are a cooperative effort. We produce a quarterly journal, and its nature is semi-academic. We try to appeal to a wide range of specializations and not just to academics. We're talking to the other people who are interested, like journalists and people who are interested in the Middle East for various reasons. We think that this joint effort is very relevant because it creates a paradigm, and example, for possible joint, cooperative efforts in other fields; because there is so little contact on a grassroots level between people in the area. And we can see, through our working out the focus topics that we want to deal with in each journal and the other

topics, that actually cooperation can work between Palestinians and Israelis.

Restoring Palestinians' Hope

Rabbi Arik Ascherman of Rabbis for Human Rights (RHR) affirmed the importance of Israeli participation, particularly in activities that go beyond simple "presence": "[Early] in this Intifada, when there was a lot of sentiment on the Palestinian street not to work with Israelis, I know for a fact that we succeeded in restoring the hope of some Palestinians—even at some very high levels—that there are some Israelis that you can talk with." In fact, Ascherman has attempted on a number of occasions to block bulldozers threatening to demolish Palestinian homes, and has been arrested and tried for his actions. He acknowledges this kind of action is unlikely to prevent the demolition. It may, however, generate publicity and help create the sort of pressure that might slow or even stop the next wave of demolitions. He also said of this and other actions, such as home-rebuilding, undertaken by RHR side-by-side with Palestinians in the occupied territories:

> It's also an act of solidarity with Palestinians. I don't know how many times I've gone to help rebuild a home that's been demolished, and the parents have come and said, "We want you to meet our children. Our ten-year-old has just seen his home demolished in front of his eyes; he's just seen his parents humiliated in front of his eyes. What do we say to our ten-year-old child when he says, 'I want to grow up and be a terrorist'? We want him to know that not every Israeli comes with guns to demolish our homes; that there are Israelis who are willing to stand shoulder-to-shoulder with us to rebuild our homes."

The Importance of Political Commitment

Although the simple act by an Israeli organization of standing "shoulder-to-shoulder" with Palestinians, be it to rebuild a demolished home or to otherwise resist the occupation, is often warmly welcomed and recognized as something other than normalization, an Israeli group's political stance can sometimes be a stumbling block for sustained joint activity. Now pursuing graduate studies in the UK, former Jerusalem Women's Center

Director Amneh Badran applies strict criteria in choosing which Israeli organizations she would regard as genuine allies. Characterizing even Gush Shalom's Uri Avnery as "a compromise person, a Zionist leftist," she singled out a select few groups as being worthy of the sobriquet the "Israeli left of the left," her gold standard being Zochrot, interestingly, a group that works *inside* Israel raising awareness of the 400+ Palestinian villages that were destroyed during and after the 1948 *Nakba* and generally "involve[ing] the Jewish public in remembering and talking about the *Nakba*."

> You know, I've worked with Israeli groups and I'm now studying Israeli groups. Israeli peace groups, the majority, are seeking a compromise based on self-interest, and they are not seeking a solution based on principles. Uri Avnery is left of Peace Now, but he's also a compromise person. He's more critical than Peace Now, but he's a Zionist leftist. He wanted to develop Gush Shalom to be a more peaceful organization than Peace Now—more peaceful in terms of being more critical—and to have more progressive positions, but still it is within the compromise. The "left of the left" will be people like Zochrot, people like AIC, and ICAHD to some extent. And New Profile: even though they do not have political positions as a platform, still they are pressing a core issue, which is militarism in Israeli society and Israeli politics.

Rev. Na'im Ateek (Sabeel), too, regards ICAHD as a worthy partner, with a commitment to political as well as human rights.

> We recognize that some Israeli groups are very much committed to nonviolent direct action, so it is much easier for us to really support them in any way we can and to be with them whenever we can. We have not really been very close to the Rabbis for Human Rights, but we like some of the work they are doing. We have also invited some of them to speak at some of Sabeel's functions or programs, like Arik Ascherman, who has been with us on a few occasions. I feel that they have a great commitment to human rights [but] many times I'm not really sure where they stand on political rights. There are some rabbis who express commitment on the human rights issues, but they still hold—underneath it all, in their psyche, in their theology—that the land really somehow belongs to the Jews more than it belongs to the Palestinians. So they're really working for human rights issues rather than the whole idea of sharing the land—that the land belongs to Palestinians as much as

it belongs to Jews. You see? I think it is limited so long as they don't really accept the political rights of the Palestinians. But I commend them for what they are doing, although I don't think they go far enough theologically.

Challenging the Israeli Policy of Separation

At the Second Annual Bil'in Conference on Nonviolent Popular Joint Struggle in April 2007, Israeli Journalist and author Amira Hass spoke of how joint struggle is often perceived as normalization, whereas in her view such actions, on the contrary, constitute a significant challenge to the Israeli occupation authorities' goal of keeping Israelis and Palestinians apart.

> I hear it amongst Palestinians—that joint struggle by Palestinians and Israelis is like "normalization." Joint struggle suffered a severe blow in the Oslo years, when the promotion of meetings between Israelis and Palestinians was turned into a business, a business which also bought political silence and political cooperation in a situation that was actually one of neo-occupation. This is why it is so difficult to convince people today that common struggle—joint struggle by Israelis and Palestinians—is the only way to destroy the [occupation] system.
>
> We have to look at the real goal of these policies—of the wall—but the wall is not the only one. The wall is perhaps the culmination of an Israeli policy of the last sixteen years, the policy of separation. The means by which Israel is achieving this goal is the revocation of Palestinian freedom of movement. Separation was initially imposed between Palestinians and Palestinians, between Gazans and the West Bank. This began in '91: not with the disengagement of 2005, but in 1991. It was continued by all Israeli governments: Likud, or Labour, Labour and Meretz, Labour and Shas, Shas and Likud—it didn't matter. It was cross-governmental.
>
> The other [form of] separation is between Israelis and Palestinians. Israel has encouraged Israelis to meet with Palestinians as if we were two symmetric, or equal, parties, as if the occupation did not exist; but Israel does not want Israelis to meet with Palestinians on a human, equal basis, when the platform is opposition to the occupation.
>
> Another Israeli goal is to separate Palestinians in the West Bank from each other and Palestinians in the occupied territories from Palestinians in Israel proper.

So even though we have not seen immediate, real structural change and have not succeeded in halting this occupation "right now," and even though we all know that it is still a long time before we will see a change, what this form of struggle—joint struggle by Israelis and Palestinians—does is challenge the primary Israeli goal, that of separation. All the Israeli groups which are active with Palestinians against the occupation are, first and foremost, defying Israel's—unfortunately successful—attempts to create an unbridgeable distance between the two peoples. And this is, I believe, the main success of such activities.

The Primacy of Struggle Against the Occupation

Bil'in activist Mohammed Khatib, addressing the same conference, described the "special relationship" that had developed between the people of his village and their Israeli "partners in struggle" over the past two-plus years, although "In the beginning," he said, "there was great opposition within the village. Even now there is a segment of the population who still criticize us because of this connection between Israelis and Palestinians."

> However, with time, when we Palestinians see the Israelis who participate with us—we see them being wounded like us. This experience "on the ground" strengthened the connection between the Palestinians and the Israelis and made of the Palestinian a man who believed more in the role of the Israeli. It made it possible for us Palestinians to open our homes and relationships and our personal lives to accept them amongst us as partners in struggle. We view this Israeli not as coming to beautify the face of the occupation: he comes to be a partner and to share with us in the popular struggle against the occupation because he is against the occupation. In this sense, the relationship between us and the Israelis became stronger day after day, and the opposition to the Israelis began to diminish.

Khatib concluded by emphasizing what many others had indicated—that in order to avoid the pitfall of being perceived as normalization, it is important that "the Israeli participation is built on and rooted in the struggle against the occupation."

Dynamics of Power between Palestinian and Israeli Activists

Seeking a Modus Vivendi

The issue of Israeli participation in joint activities with Palestinians cannot, of course, be contemplated in isolation, but must be considered within a context that goes beyond the simple question of whether such activities serve a useful purpose (political, practical, or both) or not, or even whether or not they are tarred with the brush of "normalization." As Amneh Badran explains, for example, the Jerusalem Link's Palestinian and Israeli constituent organizations spent a great deal of time and effort working out a modus vivendi allowing them to continue joint activities at a time when the impact of the deteriorating "Oslo peace process" was causing increasing discomfort for both sides in their endeavour to revise the Link's Political Principles to reflect changing realities. One point of contention was the Palestinian right of return.[14] This had not been part of their official statement of principles, and as time went on, the Palestinian members felt increasingly strongly that it should be included because, said Badran, "The peace process was not moving forward. It was, rather, moving backward."

> So in August 1999, the two boards came together and they made an agreement for a new version of [the organization's] Principles, which includes the right of return. But once the Israeli side went back to the [general membership] of Bat Shalom, they refused to accept it. And then the Palestinians ended up having one version of the Principles and the Israelis had another version of the Principles.[15]
>
> In our work, trust is a cornerstone. I think both sides thought we have to focus on what we agree on; not to disregard what we disagree on, to keep working on what we disagree on, but let's not say "either this or that." So, in that sense, it was very much what allowed both to survive together. We spoke about international law; we spoke about values, but we didn't achieve much in terms of recognition of justice and equality when it comes to the issue of the right of return. It was very clear that we speak about equality all the day, and we speak about justice all the day, but the Israelis are not accepting the right of return.

With the outbreak of the Al-Aqsa Intifada, things became more difficult.

> At the beginning of the Second Intifada, Bat Shalom [the Israeli sister organization in the Jerusalem Link] was one of the organizations

that accepted Barak's bluff.[16] As well, it was one of the organizations that blamed the Palestinians. For the Palestinians it was a big shock. I was there. I wasn't yet the director, but it was like, "Oh my goodness! All this missile launching, all this killing!" So by the first six weeks, the Palestinians sent a letter to Bat Shalom and said, "We are freezing relations; we are freezing the Jerusalem Link; this is not the partner we expect to have." They didn't cut off relations, but trust was totally zero. At that point there was a lot of anger, and the Palestinians wanted to re-evaluate and see where to go from here.

In the three years that elapsed before the joint board was able to meet again to resume work on the Principles, the Jerusalem Link managed to continue their joint work in the absence of real agreement.

All that previous work of political dialogue and encounter stopped. We started to do joint advocacy work for a just peace, and if we would go on delegations, I would say my position and [the Israeli delegate] would say her position; we would say what we agree on and what we disagree on. There was the work with media, and each would work on their own society. Sometimes we did some vigils, demonstrations, things like that, but we focused also on giving support to those in need in the Intifada, especially in the Jerusalem area. This empowerment, and especially this humanitarian counselling, became part of our emergency program. So we looked at the needs of our society, in Jerusalem in particular. We didn't claim that an organization of our size could work in the entire West Bank, and we said there are only a few [Palestinians] who are left in Jerusalem, and we should strengthen our existence in Jerusalem, and we should enhance our work in support of women in Jerusalem. So this was the case.

Nonetheless, Badran left the centre to pursue her graduate studies in the UK, and in October 2005 told me, "Still we don't have an agreement: we don't have agreement over issues of the right of return; we don't have agreement over the right of the Zionist project in Palestine; we don't have agreement over the issue of boycott [of Israel]. I left the centre with these issues on the table."

Avoiding Reproduction of the Oppressive Relationship

An important question faced both by joint organizations and coalitions is that of the appropriate roles to be played by members of the two nationalities, as well as the dynamics of their interactions within these formations—especially given the inherent power imbalance and other features of the existing oppressor–oppressed relationship between the two peoples. A number of those whom I interviewed were particularly sensitive to these issues, and a few expressed strong misgivings concerning what they regarded as indications of impingement by the existing political/structural power imbalance on the relationship dynamic between Israeli and Palestinian members of joint anti-occupation and anti-wall groups and initiatives. I first encountered this concern early in my 2003 trip, when I interviewed Kathy Kamphoefner, a Quaker anthropologist from Ohio who was then serving with the Christian Peacemaker Team (CPT) in Hebron, having spent varying periods of time with the team over the preceding eight years. Although Kamphoefner's perspective altered significantly in light of the developments of the subsequent two years, her initial unease alerted me to an issue with major relevance to the overall question of "joint struggle."

Most of the local activists to whom I broached the topic, whether Palestinian or Israeli, regarded it as the responsibility of members of the dominant and/or oppressor societies—i.e., Israelis and, in some cases, internationals—to be sensitive to the danger of unwittingly reproducing this oppressive relationship in their own interactions and to take appropriate measures to avoid this, and a number of them had specific suggestions or guidelines on how to do so. A few, like Muhammad Jaradat, for example, felt that Israeli activists' primary, if not sole, role was to tackle—in his words—"the foundations of the regime in Israel, of the institutions in Israel, not just the occupation."

When I first interviewed Kathy Kamphoefner, in 2003, she had begun by contrasting the direct Israeli—especially sabra—communication style (which she described with the Arabic term *dughri*, used also by Israelis) with the Palestinians' more circuitous *musayara* approach. Affirming the importance of Israeli-Palestinian cooperation, Kamphoefner described some of the consequences of this difference in communication styles which, she explained, she has "seen played out very concretely in meetings between Israelis and Palestinians who want to cooperate."

> For one thing, the *dughri* style feeds a tendency towards dominance. And that's already a problem, since [the Palestinians] are already dominated by the Israeli government. On the other side, the *musayara*

kind of style is respectful to a very high degree and much more indirect. In any case, you add to that the [power imbalance] between the two sides, Palestinians don't trust, after having been occupied for so long. And Israelis sometimes have been inculcated with a negative stereotype of Arabs—in the extreme, the stereotype of terrorists and so on—and that takes some overcoming, I think. Progressive people, of course, know better on an intellectual level, but I think the mistrust still comes up in many situations. So, the cultural differences are really aggravated by a kind of mistrust on top of the pretty large cultural differences.

Related to this, and to the smooth-going-along sort of laid-back kind of style that's more typical of Palestinians, is the sense of time being more fluid and of it not being important to be so precise and certainly not of "time is money." It's not a linear culture, anyway. If you read things written in Arabic, it's written holistically, sometimes almost circularly. You make a point and then you come back to it, then you tell another story about it and then you come back to it; and the sense of time is that way too, it's more circular than linear. I've literally sat in meetings and had Israelis, in a very linear style, going down an agenda and spelling out, "Now who's going to do what?" and "When will you do it?" and "What time will this happen?" and "What will happen on that day?" And Palestinians don't think that way. When Palestinians in those meetings have said, "Okay, we'll take care of that" as an organization, the Israelis are still wanting to know, "Who's going to do it?" and "What's their phone number?" And they want to follow up. And, although that's normal operating procedure for Western-based cultures, for Palestinians it's like, "Why do you need that?" or potentially even insulting, like "Well, don't you trust us? We said we're going to do it." And it's true that, when it comes down to whatever the action being planned is, it happens. They *do* do it. Sometimes they do it what we would say is too last-minute, but they do usually come through. It breaks down once in a while, but all organizations do, Israeli ones as well. So [for Palestinians] it's usually, "My word is my bond."

By 2006, however, Kamphoefner—now (along with her husband, Paul Pierce) a Quaker International Affairs Representative (QIAR) in Jerusalem[17]—had begun to detect some improvement in the situation. Noting that the dynamic between Israeli and Palestinian activists had indeed changed, "depending on where you're speaking about," she cited the example of "Bil'in, where there's weekly demonstrations against the wall expansion."

There seems to be a lot more cooperation, and I think that the shift that's making sense to people is to a relationship that is actively involved in resisting the occupation. A lot of the military refusers are regularly there, Ta'ayush is very active, some folks from Gush Shalom, and the Anarchists Against the Wall. They're very faithful in their participation in those resistance activities.

Recalling an earlier period—when the Bil'in actions had, she said, come to be dominated by Israelis with the result that most villagers had quit participating, leaving small demonstrations peopled by mainly internationals and Israelis—Kamphoefner commented that, by contrast:

> Now, with this new, inventive strategy of placing the [house trailer] and then building a small house next to [the under-construction settlement neighbourhood of] Modi'in Ilit,[18] I think we're seeing a re-energization of the efforts and a lot more people excited and getting involved again. So that's the main difference, I think. It is, of course, increasingly difficult for Israelis to come to the West Bank because of the wall being much more extensive, and at checkpoints they tend to get harassed more for having gone into the territories. So they've had to get more creative about how they would get there, including walking considerable distances in. But they did that, much to their credit and very, very important in terms of solidarity of those efforts. The last time we went, [the Israeli military] had invaded the village at four o'clock in the morning and began tear-gassing everything, even the mosque, to try to pre-empt any possible demonstrations for that day. They tear-gassed from one end to the other, and the whole day, the village was blockaded. That day several hundred Israeli activists marched in over the hills. So that was a really important contribution to the effort.

Complementary—but Different—Roles

Sami Awad of the Holy Land Trust (like Ghasan Andoni of PCR and ISM) made clear his views on the different but complementary roles of Palestinians and others (Israeli or international) in the struggle—and like Muhammad Jaradat, for example—stressed the importance of Israelis' focusing on change within their own society.

> We believe that it is the Palestinians who will liberate themselves at the end. We do agree with and support international and Israeli

peace forces who come in solidarity for the Palestinians, but it is the Palestinians who have to lead these initiatives. That's why we are dedicated to work directly with the Palestinian people in this. We have good communication with Israeli groups. What I personally believe in is that it is really up to the Palestinians to do the work themselves, and there is a role for internationals and there is a role for Israelis, but we have to rebuild the Palestinian movement at this time, and then bring in the Israeli and international partners to it. When talking to Israeli friends about this, I always tell them: "It is so wonderful for you to come and join us in an activity that we're doing: you feel good about it, we feel good about it, we achieve something, and so on. The question is, what do you do when you go back home? When you go back to Tel Aviv or to Haifa or to the kibbutz where you came from, do you run to your home and lock the door and turn on the TV and say, 'I hope the TV didn't get a close-up of me, because I don't want my neighbours to know what I did. I don't want to get in trouble'? Or do you go home to your apartment building and knock at your neighbour's door, and say, 'Hey, guess what I did today. I just removed a road-block that our military illegally put between two Palestinian villages'?" That's what we want to see in the movement.

The idea is that we need to help develop an Israeli nonviolent movement to oppose the policies of the current Israeli government that are not just destroying the Palestinians, but are destroying Israeli society as well. It's easy for Israelis to come and join us in these activities, and even most of the time, Israelis who come and participate with us are recognized by soldiers and border police as Israelis—by their language or by their identity cards and so on—and you can get sort of a break, not always very violently reacted to and so on. And I've seen that happen. You know, we'll be in a demonstration, and an Israeli activist will say, "But I'm an Israeli, don't come close to me!" to a border policeman or a soldier, and the soldier doesn't know how to react to that. So that's good protection for us and we can achieve something. But really we need to focus within Israeli society and how we can build a movement in Israel, maybe not to resist, but to oppose the policies of the current Israeli government. That's what I see the role of Israelis as.

Solidarity or Joint Work?

Muhammad Jaradat rejected outright the concept of "solidarity" as an appropriate role for Israelis—while applauding "joint work."

As a Palestinian, I always felt that what I'm doing is not only for the Palestinians; it's also for the Israelis. But I'm doing it in my community, in my society, because I know how to deal with it. I don't need the Israelis to be in my solidarity, because the occupation is destroying them more than me. No, my dear [Israeli] friend, you are in solidarity with yourself, and better you struggle to change your system and your machine of aggression, because you will live more healthy and you will be in a better society than you have now. So work in your own ground! I'm a Palestinian; I should work in the Palestinian community, and this is my heavy duty and my heavy task, and my worry twenty-four hours [a day]. You, Israeli Jew, it is your duty in the neighbourhoods of Israeli towns and cities and villages.

"And then," he continued, "and then we can find a common ground to stand, we can strategize together, we can build a vision together, we can build a struggle together. But not 'you are in my solidarity,' because you have to do *your* job. You can be Americans with me in solidarity, or internationals, but not Israelis."

Here Jaradat made an important distinction—differentiating between his conception of "solidarity" and joint work, the latter exemplified by BADIL's cooperation with the Israeli organization Zochrot and discussions between BADIL and Israeli groups seeking restitution for Jews who had to leave property and other assets behind when they emigrated from Arab countries to Israel. He also cited BADIL's relationship with the antimilitarist organization New Profile as an example of his preferred model for working with Israelis.

And here, you know, there is a difference between solidarity and joint work. Joint work, each one with his or her foot in their own community, working—Palestinians in their community, Israelis in their community—and then there can be coordination, can be building a strategy together. You know, Israeli society is a militarized society. New Profile is doing a great job. They are in their society, they are working in exactly the right place, and we have meetings with them. They don't tell us how to work, and we don't tell them how to work. We share values—not necessarily all the values—but we share certain values that are important for us and for them. If we do not have a strong Israeli community of resistance to the militarized society, to the racist regime in Israel, we will not make a big change.

Muhammad Jaradat's views on the need for Israelis to concentrate on influencing Israeli society are not without echoes in the Israeli activist community. As Jaradat mentioned, New Profile focuses on this in particular. And one need only visit their website and those of ICAHD, Ta'ayush, and Zochrot, among others, to get an idea of the variety of such activities these groups organize or take part in. And of course, there are also the refuseniks who—in addition to their significant noncooperation with the occupation regime—do major educational work with Israeli youth, as well as folks like Ido Khnein and Ya'akov Manor, for instance, who, while being fully committed to promoting the participation of Israelis in the struggle in the West Bank, are clear about the need, as Manor puts it, for "some sort of change within Israeli society—within the way Israelis think." "The majority are not with us," says Manor, "but if there is not a change within Israeli society—if we don't work on Israeli society and try to influence them from within—nothing will happen."

In light of Jaradat's clearly reasoned but—I thought—somewhat harsh dismissal of much Israeli work with Palestinians inside the occupied territories, I found reassurance in the balance of Manor's approach, as well as in the declaration by Saif Abu Keshek (a Palestinian coordinator with ISM) that, "I see the importance of the continuous [Israeli] movements that are working in terms of nonviolent direct action that are entering the territories [as] equal [to that of] the movements that are working inside Israeli society on the level of education and social [action] work." Abu Keshek expressed his support for Israeli participation in Palestinian nonviolent actions in the context of his conviction that the future held one state for both Palestinians and Israelis.

> It is very important. I personally believe in a one-state solution; I don't think a two-state solution is achievable. For this reason, the moment I see an Israeli standing side-by-side with me against the Israeli occupation, it is the moment that I start to believe that yes, I am able to live with this person. I'm able to have a joint life. I'm able to live as neighbours with this person. You know? I'm able to share my life with this person. I don't have a problem anymore.

Redressing the Power Imbalance

Several of those I interviewed echoed the concerns voiced by the three quoted above, stressing the vulnerability of the dynamics of joint

Israeli-Palestinian (or Palestinian-Israeli) action—whether within a single organization, a coalition, or in separate groups working in coordination—to the influence of the region's prevailing power imbalance and, as well, how they can be complicated by (often subtle and not-discussed, perhaps not consciously perceived) cultural differences among participants. It was encouraging to discover, therefore, how many interviewees demonstrated an awareness of the potential problems these factors might lead to and described specific measures they are taking—both as individuals and as organizations—in order to avoid or at least minimize these difficulties. Clarity regarding the respective roles of Israelis and Palestinians in the planning and execution of joint actions (i.e., an understanding of and respect for the fact that the Palestinians, as hosts, were the appropriate initiators/leaders) coupled with sensitivity to the feelings and needs of local Palestinian communities, were central aspects of most of these.

Palestinians are the Hosts, Israelis and Internationals are the Guests
Neta Golan brings an interesting perspective to this question of Israeli-Palestinian dynamics, as both an Israeli and an international (holding dual Israeli and Canadian citizenship) and as part of the policy-setting "core group" of the Palestinian-led ISM. While sharing the concerns and criticisms voiced by Kathy Kamphoefner and a number of other interviewees, she described specific ways in which she as an individual, and her organization as well, endeavour to avoid the worst of these pitfalls.

> I can say that I'm very aware of the problem; therefore, I've always tried not to be that way, not to come and think I know what needs to be done and what needs to happen, but to take the Palestinians' lead and support whatever they want to do. That's why ISM, despite the fact that we're a non-hierarchical organization, say that we are Palestinian-led. So I hope that I'm not that way, but just because I am Israeli and coming from a culture that's very up-front and outspoken, and Palestinians can often be a lot more polite, I know I have made that mistake. I think ISM and Ta'ayush are very aware of this [danger of "reproducing the occupation"], but there's still a tendency for Israelis and for internationals to come anywhere—even to be activists—with a colonial attitude, like "We're going to tell you how it's to be done, and what needs to be done."
>
> One of the things we do in order to try to avoid being colonial activists is that we don't assume that people want to work with

[ISM]; and we don't assume that people want to work with Israelis, that we or Israelis have a right to be in a place. I mean, we're guests! We're invited by a local community, and *we* cannot invite Israelis. So when there's an action where the local community is interested in inviting Israelis, the invitation comes from *them*. Some Israeli groups in the beginning were very upset about that, that we would sometimes do things without Israelis. I haven't heard complaints about it for a while.

Sometimes communities would say, "No Israelis at all." That was very rare; that almost never happened. But sometimes people would say only individuals, not groups. It changes, also, depending on what's going on. Here in Nablus right now, or last time we asked, they thought it wasn't a good idea to bring Israelis. But the villages around Nablus want Israelis. Anyway, it's their choice. I think that the [Israelis] who had complaints about it wanted it to be "work with everyone or don't work with any." To me, that's sort of like saying "This is my home."

Palestinians Lead, Israelis Follow

For Ghassan Andoni, too, the principle of Palestinian leadership in joint activities is fundamental. Andoni clearly defined the roles that he envisions for Palestinians and Israelis, respectively, in the overall struggle against the occupation when he stated: "You don't need two peace movements to arrive at peace. You need an active Palestinian resistance supported by an active Israeli peace or anti-occupation movement." Andoni addressed the participation by Israelis in nonviolent actions supportive of the Palestinian resistance itself by summing up PCR's and ISM's policy on this matter as follows: "In general we encourage the participation of Israeli groups in civil-based resistance in the occupied territories. That's one of the main lines that we would like to encourage, but we don't force it on Palestinians." Outlining ISM's rules regarding Israeli participation, he laid particular stress upon the importance of consultation with the local communities hosting each action. Of particular note is the distinction made between individual Israelis, who are welcome to participate within the organizational framework of ISM, and Israeli groups or organizations.

In terms of membership, individual Israelis, similar to others, are accepted as members of ISM, because we accept people without checking their colour, race, nationality, etc. So ISM is open to the participation of Israelis, as long as they recognize our rules and objectives. There's no discrimination there against Israelis. But ISM, because of its international identity, does not act as a host, but as a guest. So we don't invite Israelis to join, we consult with local communities. If the local community is willing to invite Israeli groups to join activities, we would welcome it and encourage it. If the local community has problems with that, and that could disturb its unity and create problems inside it, then we give priority to Palestinian communities' unity and functioning over the participation of Israeli groups. You know, we address the community, and if there is a request from an Israeli group to participate, if the community approves that, then the community issues the invitation. There are things you need to take into consideration. One: you cannot invite Israeli groups into cities and refugee camps, where people are more suspicious and worried, because in cities and refugee camps there is a lot of army activity, and sometimes even disguised special units;[19] there is an active core of resistance there and, therefore, people have the right to be cautious. So even when we introduce ISM into those places, we need to be cautious, well-connected, be sure that people understand fully and recognize fully ISM. In villages things are different. In villages, people are more open to work with Israeli groups. So you have to take into the consideration the complications at different places. So far, there is an increasing level of inviting Israelis.

Israelis and Internationals Welcome—Sometimes!
Nonviolence trainer Husam Jubran[20] told me he generally preferred exclusively Palestinian activities, one reason being that "the presence of Israelis or internationals could give the wrong idea about nonviolence: people will again associate it with something coming from the West or from Israel, and they will become suspicious." This was not a hard-and-fast rule, however.

That doesn't mean that we don't need international or Israeli intervention at all. The presence of Israelis and internationals in Budrus and Bil'in and all the demonstrations that took place in different villages to say "no" to the wall was crucial. It was important to have them there for many reasons. It attracted the media, they managed to reach different segments in the Israeli society; there are a lot of benefits to having them there. But again, the most important thing is that decision making should be in Palestinian hands. The second thing: Palestinians should be in the first line. Internationals and Israelis should be in the second line. In some cases, we see Israelis and internationals taking the initiative, and I don't think this is right, because many people will say "Look, Palestinians are doing nothing, and internationals and Israelis are doing all the work." So those are the two important things for me: Palestinians to be in the first line and Palestinians to be in charge of making all the decisions, in consultation with Israelis and internationals.

Israelis Must be Junior Partners

The Israeli Committee Against House Demolitions (ICAHD) can be described as a group that fulfils both of the functions set out above by Sami Awad,[21] since participation in its activities both involves members in direct help for Palestinians and at the same time equips them with the direct experience necessary for correcting Israeli misconceptions and building a stronger, better-informed Israeli opposition movement. ICAHD's Jeff Halper explained how the recognition that "the Israelis have to be the junior partner when on [Palestinian] territory" transformed the power dynamic between them and increased ICAHD's credibility within the Palestinian community.

> We have to get used to the fact that the Palestinians are not merely the victims of our occupation, that they are people; and that in terms of whatever Palestinian state or entity or whatever is going to emerge, we have to get used to the idea that we are guests in their country. We have to be a partner in resisting the occupation, but the Israelis have to be the junior partner when we're in their territory, when we're in their country, especially working on issues of concern to them in terms of the occupation. So as Israelis, we're resisting the occupation, but we're doing so, not only together with Palestinians, but while we're in their country, we are under their supervision. They have the right to say, "No, this isn't a good idea" or "Let's do it this way and not that way." Because even though we're the peace movement in Israel, even though we're the "good guys"—we're the occupiers. I don't go around worrying that someone's going to demolish my house. I can go to a movie. I can talk in a loud voice. I can think out loud, because I don't have to pay any price. And I'm not part of all the conflicts, considerations, and deliberations that the Palestinians have to go through in terms of what's effective, what's possible, how is the army going to react, all the factions within their own society. They have a lot of considerations that I have to respect; I can't come in and tell them what to do.

Because ICAHD realized this, said Halper, "That changed the power relationship between us."

> One of the things we did, back then, was to ask the Palestinians, "What do you think would be the best way for us to engage with you? What are the issues that you think that we should deal with?" Because the Israeli peace movement often decided, itself, what the issue was; then we'd go demonstrate and even not inform the Palestinians, or we'd invite some token Palestinian to say a few words.
>
> We also decided that we would never do an activity that wasn't coordinated with the Palestinians, because this was part of the power issue. If we would say, "You know what, there's a house being demolished, and we're going to come and we're going to rebuild the house," that would be replicating the occupation; we're replicating those power relationships. So we decided we'd work through Palestinian partner organizations. Everything we do is coordinated with the Palestinians, and that's given us a lot of credibility over the years for being a partner with the Palestinians but trying to avoid this feeling sometimes among the Palestinian that Israelis—it doesn't matter if they're occupation forces or peace forces—"they're coming in and telling us what to do, and they're being patronizing," and so on. So I think that that's a key: not only the political issues that we took on and the resistance we took on, but I think our decision on how to work with Palestinians has played a key role in our ability to succeed and to develop the relationships that we have developed.

Rabbi Arik Ascherman of Rabbis for Human Rights—a group that, like ICAHD, has actively resisted the demolition of Palestinian homes, sometimes putting their own bodies in the way of the wreckers' bulldozers—echoed Halper's image of Israeli activists as "junior partners," adding, regarding the Palestinian home-owners, "They're the bosses, not us."

> I think one of the differences in the way we relate to Palestinians as opposed to the way some other groups do is that we don't just come into a village and say, "We're going to do this, this, and this…" We have a real partnership; things are done in coordination—we're even the junior partners. We aren't perfect, but we try not to do any kind of activity not in coordination with some Palestinian partner. There've even been cases where we've been in an area where a home is about to be demolished, have ourselves been ready to resist to the end, and the family says, "Enough is enough." In the beginning of this Intifada, when many people were saying, "Don't come now,"

we didn't come until we found people that were inviting us and wanted us there, and that's absolutely the way we work.

Palestinians May Face Consequences of Israelis' Actions

Yonatan Pollak of Israeli Anarchists Against the Wall expressed a similar attitude.

> Whatever I do—and the people I work with do—we always try to do with the direction of Palestinians, with Palestinian coordinators, and with others consulting. We always have to remember that most of the repercussions will be on the Palestinians, not on us. So, for instance, if we want to take down a fence and the Palestinians don't, we look for another village. If we don't find one that wants to do that, we don't do it. It's a bit harder working that way, because emotionally you're very much involved in the struggle, in the process, and "I will take down the fence because I want to take down the fence!" But in reality, you have to consider other things, and it's annoying, but that's the way it is.

Other Factors to be Considered

Adam Keller of Gush Shalom has had extensive experience working with Palestinians, both in nonviolent actions and on a quasi-diplomatic level. He pointed out a number of additional factors that one needs to be aware of in embarking on joint endeavours.

> The basic problem with Israel-Palestinian cooperation is that each one of us is a member of a society that is in conflict with the other society. And each one of us has always to look over his shoulder and to think how his or her own society will regard what we have just said and what we have just done. And an Israeli, even the most radical, needs to think how Israeli society will react to what I say about suicide bombings. The Palestinian, even the most "radically moderate," needs to think how the Palestinian society will think about what I say about the right of return and what I say about the occupation—and whether nothing that I said will make me be accused of being too soft on the occupation or that I am cooperating with "hidden Zionists," or with open Zionists. And especially when there is something that is firing up the atmosphere on one or both sides, then very often both sides feel the need to accommodate themselves in opposite ways.

So, using an architectural analogy, a joint Israeli-Palestinian organization cannot be a skyscraper. It could be a hut. It works quite well on an ad hoc basis—that you get a call from a particular village and you get told that "We in this village have a problem that our land has been confiscated" or "The settlers don't let us harvest our olives" or this or that, and "Can you come and help us? Can you come and make a demonstration with us? Can you come and help us with the olive harvest?" or with removing the road block, or whatever. And then the routine is that we try to find out how much of the village the person with whom we talked represents. Does he speak for the whole village, or does he speak for his own family or a particular faction? It is important to try, if possible, not to be involved in factional fighting inside the village. Like, if you are brought in by Fatah people, then the Hamas people don't like it. Or it could also be not political: you are brought in by one *hamula* (extended family; clan) in the village and the other *hamula* doesn't like it that you are coming. So we try, if possible, to have the official authority, like the village headman, or the mayor if it is a big enough town, to be involved. But it's not always possible to find this out, and sometimes when somebody makes an urgent call, you still come.

This works out quite well. Gush Shalom has had a lot of experiences like this, and it sometimes continues for years, like with the olive harvest. We get requests from people [we worked with] the previous year, and they ask us if we can come also this year. By the way, this also could create a problem. This week we had an organizing meeting of what you could call the Olive Coalition. And there was a problem pointed out that very often when you very much concentrate on a particular village, you create rivalries and jealousies, and people from the other villages around are asking why you are not coming to them: "Our problems are not less then theirs" or "... are more than theirs."

The Importance of Clear Communication

Besides differing Israeli and Palestinian styles of communication and the other culturally mediated complications mentioned above, sometimes the source of miscommunication is something as simple and mundane as the same neglect to confirm that both parties have the same expectations that plagues many a relationship between groups (and individuals!) who may make assumptions based on their (mis)perception that they know the other better than they actually do. My fall 2003 conversations with

Hanan B'leidi (Tulkarm district Women against the Wall) and Gila Svirsky (Bat Shalom, and the [Israeli] Coalition of Women for a Just Peace) illustrate this sort of dynamic, I believe. I started by asking B'leidi (with Abed el-Karim Dalbeh translating) her impression of the "joint" demonstration that had been held a few weeks before (September 6, 2003) at the main gate in the wall separating Tulkarm from Israeli territory, explaining that I had heard two very different interpretations of what had transpired.

> One says it was very successful, that Israeli and Palestinian and international women were able to come together to demonstrate together against the wall. And other people who were there said that they felt that the Israelis were too weak, that instead of just sitting down and blocking the gate so it couldn't be closed, they agreed to move back, allowing the soldiers to close the gate and to teargas the women on the Palestinian side of it.

B'leidi told me, "I am of that second opinion, that the Israelis were very weak and they did what the soldiers told them to do." When the Israeli soldiers started shooting into the air and throwing teargas at the demonstrators on the Palestinian side of the wall, she said, the Palestinian women had expected the Israeli women to join them in solidarity, "but they didn't do that."

> And we are a little upset about that action, and as I told you, after about two hours a group of Israelis—not the whole group on the other side; only about twenty people—were allowed to come, and just for a short period of time, just to come and to talk and to return back. And that's what happened. They allowed the Israelis to come because of the negotiation of internationals and Palestinians [including B'leidi herself, said Dalbeh in an aside to me] to persuade the soldiers that we need our friends from the other side, and you must bring them. It was not the Israelis who negotiated with the soldiers.

I must admit I was pleasantly surprised at B'leidi's accepting (and realistic) attitude when she stated, "In general, this is our problem, not the Israelis' problem. And we are going to arrange some activities with Israelis or internationals who believe in our rights and can help us," adding:

We said to them, after that action, that they must be stronger, and we hope they will be. But we feel if they are not, it is not their problem, and we will continue to participate and arrange activities with them—and with anyone, whether they are stronger or not, because we feel it is our problem and we need whatever help from others that they can give; we cannot force them.

I met with Gila Svirsky a few days after my visit to Tulkarm. I told her that Hanan B'leidi and I had had an interesting discussion about the September 6 demonstration. Although I hadn't been there, I told Svirsky, I had heard from a couple of people, particularly internationals, who had told me that they had heard the organizers announce that, "Since this is a nonviolent action, we have to do what the army says." So when the Israelis and internationals on the Israeli side of the gate were ordered to withdraw, they did so, instead of sitting down on the spot or otherwise demonstrating unwillingness to be separated from the Palestinian women. This meant that the Palestinians, once isolated, were targeted with teargas. My informants felt that there had been a sort of capitulation by the Israeli women in the name of "nonviolence." The question is, I asked Svirsky, was this a misunderstanding of what constitutes nonviolent resistance or was what I heard based on a misunderstanding or a mistranslation?

I'm speaking of right at the beginning, when the army said for the Israeli women to back off and they did, and this gave the army an opportunity to close the gate and teargas the Palestinians. When I spoke to Hanan in Tulkarm, I said, "I've heard two versions of this action. I've heard that it was really very successful and wonderful, and I've heard another version..."

Gila Svirsky, whom I've known as a fellow activist since the late 1980s, and whom I know to have a good understanding of nonviolence theory as well as practice, replied with some valuable advice: "It's very, very important to decide in advance what a particular action is going to be. You and I know that from our training."[22]

It was decided in advance that this action was not going to be resistance; it was not going to be civil disobedience. It was announced on the buses and in the general meeting we held before: "This is not the opportunity to get arrested." The goal of this action was not demonstrating something important to the Palestinians.

The goal of this action was to draw international attention to what we were doing as a form of sisterhood, of Palestinians and Israelis and internationals who were working to end the wall. That sisterhood image would have been compromised by an image of adventurism. Now, clearly it was the case that [in planning the September 6 action, the representatives of the Israeli Coalition of Women for a Just Peace and the Palestinian women, respectively] did not make that perfectly clear between the two of them, and that is a problem, and it certainly should be discussed among us that, in the future, [the aim of each action] should be made clear.

Healthy Dynamics

The difficulties discussed above were by no means universal, however. For instance, Jamal Dar'awi, in telling me about his Bethlehem-area Popular Committee against Settlements, and describing its interactions with Israeli groups, mentioned the development of mutual respect with Ta'ayush, whose members have responded to cell-phone calls reporting the detention of Palestinian demonstrators by coming to where they are being held and staying until they have been released. His was one of innumerable such examples of a positive dynamic between Palestinian nonviolent organizations and the Israelis who support their struggle in a variety of ways.

Similarly, Zahra Khalidi of the *Palestine-Israel Journal* (PIJ) saw the interactions between Israeli and Palestinian employees of the journal in a positive light, reassuring me that, contrary to concerns regarding Israelis' unintentional imposition of their ideas because—for example—of their generally more direct style of communication, at PIJ:

> There's actually a much more democratic way of going about things. There's no dictation; there's a full discussion of the issues that are in contention, and we usually come to some kind of a compromise. Sometimes there are rough patches, but we've managed to smooth them over very efficiently, in a very amicable way, because we take it all very calmly. It's mainly over terms used or over the concepts one or the other rejects. But we have a discussion with the editors and the editorial staff, and we usually come to some kind of a compromise where we're able to accommodate both sides' opinions, or balance them out in a way.

ISM coordinator Saif Abu Keshek (interviewed December 2005) was also quite comfortable working with Israelis and, in fact, tended to see the cultural similarities between Israelis and Palestinians as more important than the differences, at least in the context of anti-occupation activism. Thus, when I asked him if he felt there was an unhealthy dynamic of Israeli domination in joint endeavours, he responded unambiguously that, "No. I don't think this is true."

> I think we do have two very similar cultures. Though Israel is more open to Europe, we do have very similar common ways of thinking and looking at things. And the Israelis that I have met do care about this specific situation. They make an effort to understand the Palestinian culture, how the Palestinians function, how the Palestinians move; and the Palestinians also make an effort to do the same for the Israelis. I think this is actually a very healthful dynamic and it's very important for the continuation of this movement. If we expect that these people will one day be able to live together, or at least have some kind of joint, common parts of life together, these dynamics are very important.

Mas'ha activists Nazih Shalabi and Tayseer Arabasi had expressed similar sentiments to these when I spoke to them in 2003, as had the village activists from Bil'in and elsewhere whom I spoke to in January 2006. Perhaps, then, the combination of mutual respect and commitment to a common goal can trump cultural factors, and—just maybe—individual differences in personality may play an important role as well. For example, Lucy, a bright and energetic young youth worker at the Wi'am Center in Bethlehem, recalled the first joint Israeli-Palestinian activity she participated in. She had been so determined to take part in this dialogue/discussion between Wi'am (the Bethlehem organization where she is now a staff member) and Jewish-Israelis from the Peres Center that she decided to go despite the risks for her of travelling inside Israel without a permit.

> We went to Nazareth, and in the beginning it was very stressful for me. The Israeli facilitator wanted to impose things on us, and I stood up and I told her, "Listen, we are here to talk, and if you don't believe in dialogue, then let's go back home; we're in the wrong place." We were supposed to talk in that program about three pending issues: refugees, Jerusalem, and water. And when we

were there, they decided this was a hard topic, so we have to change it. The Palestinian group decided, "Oh no, we are here to discuss these things." So we sat together and we tried to find a way: if we have to go back, or shall we continue, and what will we talk about. I don't know where I got this idea, [but I said] "Okay, guys, let's talk about our daily life." They said, "Yeah, but what do we have to say?" I said, "Topics you can talk about: Okay, in the morning, you want to wash your face, you won't find water, especially during summer time. So we will talk about water issues. Okay, I still have a dream: the key of my uncle's house [in a Palestinian village inside Israel's pre-1967 borders] is in my hand, and I have a dream that one day my uncle will come from Jordan or Iraq or Syria—from the refugee camp. And the other part is Jerusalem: Easter is coming, and we have to worship in Jerusalem.[23] Jerusalem is the heart of the three religions."

Lucy's group accepted this way of speaking about the issues that impinged on their lives, and the dialogue went ahead.

Nawaf Souf, in his capacity as a local activist leader and organizer in the few years since his release from prison,[24] has had considerable experience working with both international (particularly ISM and IWPS) and Israeli organizations. The latter include Physicians for Human Rights (PHR), with whom his group in the village of Haris has coordinated to hold local clinics, and Rabbis for Human Rights (RHR), with whom they have planted olive saplings to replace trees uprooted by marauders from some of the settlements that encircle the village. Of the Israeli groups he works with, Souf has the closest ties with Ta'ayush. In fact, his role in that body is an (admittedly rare) example of Palestinian leadership in the activities of what is essentially an Israeli (albeit both Palestinian- and Jewish-Israeli) organization.

Ta'ayush was established inside Israel, within the Green Line. There were good people from among the Arabs and Jewish inside Israel—really the most respected people. When the Intifada started here, they came to me here, sat and discussed this matter, and we began [to work together]. Ta'ayush in the territories began here in our area, in the area of Salfit. Thank God, [in] all the actions that Ta'ayush [did] and that I organized on our side—Ta'ayush passed from victory to greater victory. For example, in the beginning, they came to Haris and other places with food and things like that. We went to Yasouf, we went to Huwarra, and there was a demonstration there against the wishes of the army. I organized an action for them to go to Palestinian President Arafat in his office, when he was [under siege there] and this was a big group, close to five hundred people. We went to Qalandiya checkpoint. The Ta'ayush people weren't allowed to cross with their own vehicles, they crossed Qalandiya on foot, and from there we brought them in [minibuses] to Arafat's office. And after the meeting with the president—he spoke and some of the representatives of Ta'ayush spoke—we went somewhere else and had another meeting in Ramallah, in the Ministry of Education and Culture, with professors at Palestinian universities and with member of the Legislative Council and with many people.

Nawaf Souf's warm feelings for Ta'ayush are evident as he recalls that after his brother Issa was shot by Israeli forces: "That same night, despite the fact that there had been an attack that night—I don't remember where, in Tel Aviv or somewhere—[Ta'ayush people] went beside the Ministry of Defence in Tel Aviv and had a demonstration there: "Why did you shoot Issa Souf," etc., etc., etc. After that, several of them came to us to try to help, to stand with us, to support us to get through this black period in our lives."

AIC's Michel Warschawski covered a number of these points in summing up his view of the proper role for Israelis in the anti-occupation struggle.

The place of the Israeli activists in the context of the general struggle is not and cannot be and should not be symmetrical with that of the Palestinians. The Palestinians are those who are conducting their struggle in their own way—or own *ways*; they don't have [only] one way—and the essence of our role is, from within the place we are in inside Israeli society, to aid them to the maximum in the success of their struggle, including by explaining this struggle (why, and why this way) and also, on occasion, by explaining the disputes that occur [i.e., within the Palestinian ranks], so that there will be better acquaintance with the true, living Palestinian reality, and not the fantasized one. Really to place ourselves, in a fundamental way, as a kind of helping force.

Conclusion

The five fully (or almost fully) joint nonviolent action organizations active today, or in the recent past, reviewed in this chapter all date from the era of the Oslo Accords or later, with the exception of Palestinians and Israelis for Nonviolence (PINV). Founded in the mid-1980s with a flurry of nonviolent resistance actions, the "on the ground" activism of PINV's pacifist membership is now confined to uni-national frameworks and to such virtual activism as writing about nonviolence on the PINV website and making written appeals to politicians.

The Jerusalem Link—despite its constituent Israeli and Palestinian sister organizations having been founded, following the Oslo Accords, with the express intention of working together—has struggled, especially since 2000, to find a modus vivendi that will allow them to continue joint activities despite their inability to agree on basic political questions.

The *Palestine-Israel Journal* (PIJ), on the other hand, is one of the few joint initiatives of the Oslo era (1994) still intact and thriving. Its Palestinian co-founding editor goes so far as to reject the term "joint," and describes PIJ instead as "one organism working together to create something." Perhaps the journal's resilience has something to do with its commitment to promoting dialogue between the two sides and with the fact that its very structure and way of operating reflects this commitment—with all posts, from managing editor through to its 22-member editorial board, being equally divided between Palestinians and Israelis, from a variety of political backgrounds. As its website proclaims, "... the *Palestine-Israel Journal* testifies to the fact that it is possible to work together in a spirit of mutual respect, cooperation and recognition, even on the most conflicting and sensitive issues."

Another "survivor" of the Oslo period, in spirit if not in fact, is the Action Committee for the Jahalin Tribe (ACJT). Although politicians from both sides participated in ACJT demonstrations, the committee's activities were not dependent on them, but were more an expression of practical, neighbourly concern and growing friendship. Probably the least "political" of the groups described in this book, ACJT no longer exists as such, but its legacy lives on in the form of continuing support for the tribe by former members and organizations such as Rabbis for Human Rights, which became involved via ACJT connections.

Combatants for Peace, founded less than five years ago (at time of writing), is a unique group of Israeli former military and Palestinian ex-fighters whose renunciation of violence is not an end in itself but is a means to achieve their primary goal of facilitating dialogue and joint activism in order to bring an end to the occupation. Although the group's official position is that of a two-state solution, "each one has his own ideas" regarding the ideal solution, and, says combatant Yonatan Shapira, "that's fine."

Attitudes towards joint activism were overwhelmingly positive amongst those I interviewed, emphasizing benefits to Palestinians of the presence of Israelis: reduction of the level of violence and "creating an option for Palestinian nonviolent resistance"; contradicting Palestinians' sense of isolation while conveying to the Israeli people back home firsthand accounts of the situation as well as Palestinians' message of "refusing to be enemies" and the sense that "there is a partner for peace"; increasing the Israelis' awareness of the Palestinians' need to resist the occupation; as well as mutually beneficial promotion of understanding of each other through joint actions and planning, and the smashing of stereotypes of "the other side." The only negative responses I received were from a few who felt that joint work, though important, was not for them (Gila Svirsky) or not appropriate at this particular time (Zoughbi Zoughbi, Manal el-Tamimi, Judith Green), and one (Muhammad Jaradat) who exhorted Israelis to concentrate their energies on eradicating the roots of the occupation in the inherent racism of Israeli society.

All of my interviewees were wary of the dangers of normalization; i.e., no one thought it was a good idea to promote good relations at the expense of downplaying the urgency of ending the oppression of the occupation. The various individuals and organizations, understandably, drew their lines differently, but on the whole they agreed with Mohammed Khatib of Bil'in regarding the imperative that "Israeli participation is built on and rooted in the struggle against the occupation."

An important aspect of the question of the power dynamics between Palestinians and Israelis—whether between activists in joint organizations or between organizations working together in a joint activity—is that of avoiding reproduction of the oppressive relationship inherent in the occupation itself. Ways of achieving this include striving for clarity of communication (including awareness of different culturally conditioned conversational styles) and scrupulous attention to differentiation of roles, making sure all joint actions are led by Palestinians, with Israelis in a supporting, clearly secondary, position. Finally, I believe that the ideal role for Israelis, as perceived by both the Palestinian and Israeli activists I interviewed, was well summed up by Mikado, in his statement that "The place of the Israeli activists ... is not and cannot be and should not be symmetrical with that of the Palestinians. The Palestinians are those who are conducting their struggle in their own ... ways ... and the essence of our role is ... to aid them to the maximum in the success of their struggle, including by explaining this struggle ... so that there will be better acquaintance with the true, living Palestinian reality, and not the fantasized one. Really to place ourselves, in a fundamental way, as a kind of helping force."

Bearing these issues very much in mind, we will now take a closer look at three specific examples of joint nonviolent action campaigns: the Beit Sahour tax strike, resistance to the separation barrier also known as the apartheid wall, and the joint struggle in the village of Bil'in.

NOTES

1 Normalization is a derogatory term denoting a relationship between Israelis and Palestinians (usually organizations) carried on as if all were normal between Israel and Palestine, even as the oppression continues. Israeli activist Liad Kantorowicz describes it as "overlooking the real issues and just saying, 'Well, we're just people' in [a] very blanket sort of statement." The concept of normalization will be expanded on in the second subsection of this chapter—see also notes 12 and 13.

2 Founded in 1984 by Mubarak Awad, the PCSN was headed by other local activists after Awad's 1988 deportation. In 1998, Mubarak Awad's nephew Sami Awad moved the PCSN office to Bethlehem, where it became one of the founding initiatives of the Holy Land Trust (HLT), where its work is continued under the name of HLT's Nonviolence Programs (from www.holylandtrust.org).

3 The Green Patrol is a paramilitary unit of the Israel Lands Authority notorious especially for its ongoing harassment of Bedouin citizens of Israel living in "unrecognized villages" (see Chapter 1, Endnote 1)—destroying their crops, demolishing their homes and confiscating their livestock.

4 See "The Normalization Debate" section of this chapter and notes 12 and 13 below.

5 A November 2009 visit to the recently redesigned JCW website found no functioning link to the Jerusalem Link nor any mention of it in the description of the JCW's founding, as an outcome of meetings held in 1989 ("in Brussels between prominent Israeli and Palestinian women peace activists").

The link to the Bat Shalom site was also inactive. Although the inactive links may be the outcome of a new site, still being developed, the deletion of previously existing references to the Jerusalem Link and its activities appears to be intentional. The website of Bat Shalom (the Israeli half of the Jerusalem Link), by contrast, does include information about the Jerusalem Link, as well as about some joint activities undertaken with Palestinian women (organization not named) as recently as International Women's Day 2007. Events done explicitly under the umbrella of the Jerusalem Link, however, seem—even according to this site—to have ended with a joint declaration on the occasion of International Women's Day 2003 ("PRESSURE ISRAEL TO END THE OCCUPATION [and] ENSURE INTERNATIONAL PROTECTION FOR PALESTINIAN CIVILIANS" listed, ironically, under "Current Activities"). The link to the Jerusalem Center for Women from the Bat Shalom site is active.

6　Elik Elhanan comes from a family of political activists. His late grandfather Mattityahu (Matti) Peled was known internationally as an outspoken critic of Israeli occupation policies and a staunch supporter of the two-state solution. His mother, Nurit Peled-Elhanan, is an educator and speaker who in 2001 was awarded the Sakharov Prize by the European Parliament for her advocacy for peace in the occupied territories. Her daughter, Smadar—Elik's sister—was killed in a suicide bombing in 1997.

7　Uzi Landau was the Minister of Internal Security under Ariel Sharon (March 2001–February 2003).

8　North American Jewish anti-occupation organizations.

9　Neta Golan is an "international" in the sense that she has Canadian, as well as Israeli, citizenship.

10　Rachel Corrie, a 23-year-old volunteer from Olympia, WA, was the first of two (so far) international participants in the ISM to be killed "in action." See especially www.rachelcorriefoundation.org. Twenty-two-year-old Tom Hurndell of the UK was the second. Brian Avery, a 24-year-old ISMer, was seriously wounded. All of this took place within a three-week period in early 2003 (Hurndell remained in a coma until his death in January 2004). To my knowledge, no Israelis have been killed during solidarity actions, although several have been severely wounded. Scores of Palestinians have been killed in the course of nonviolent protests, and many more seriously injured.

11　Note of historical interest (or not): In the photo depicting the mob scene that ensued—in the bottom panel of the cover of the January/February 1990 issue of *New Outlook Middle East Monthly*—I can be seen simultaneously fleeing the tear gas and trying to protect my cameras and tape recorder from the green-tinted water being sprayed on us from police fire hoses.

12　On 22 October 2000, the General Assembly of the Palestinian Non-Governmental Organizations (PNGO) issued an announcement calling on "all Palestinian NGOs to stop all joint programs and activities with Israeli organizations, especially projects conducted in the framework of the 'People to People' program, the Peres Institute for Peace, and the 'Joint Projects Program' funded by the American Agency for International Development (USAID), as well as any other project aiming at normalization with Israel." It is noteworthy that this prohibition includes the following specific exclusion: "These decisions do not apply to cooperation with solidarity projects launched by Israeli human rights organizations and to cooperation with Israeli institutions which support the Palestinian right to freedom and statehood and a comprehensive, just and durable peace that meets Palestinian national rights." This announcement is reproduced in full in a press release from BADIL Resource Center for Palestinian Residency and Refugee Rights entitled "Palestinian NGO Network Conditions Cooperation with Israeli Organizations" and accessible at http://www.badil.org/en/press-releases/53-press-releases-2000/191-press134-00. The statement can also be accessed, in the context of the full PNGO Annual Report for 2000, at http://www.pngo.net/data/files/reports/annual/report2000.pdf. This emphasis on the requirement that any cooperation with Israeli organizations or institutions be based on the premise that (as Huwaida Arraf stated above), "The issue has got to be the occupation; that's what the message has to be"—and the importance of such cooperation—has frequently been reiterated. A recent example of a related sentiment can be found in Omar Barghouti's October 21, 2008 article on *CounterPunch*, "Countering the Critics: The Boycott and Palestinian Groups," where he remarks, *inter alia,* that "the only true fighters for peace in Israel are those who support our three fundamental rights: the right of return for Palestinian refugees; full equality for the Palestinian citizens of Israel; and ending the occupation and colonial rule. Those are our true partners." (http://www.counterpunch.org/barghouti10212008.html)

13   The Palestinian Authority, too, spoke out against joint activities at that time: "When the Second Intifada broke out, there was a moment when the [Palestinian] minister responsible at the time for the People to People activities, Hassan Asfour, issued a directive that all joint Israeli-Palestinian projects should stop, 'because we're not getting anywhere; look at what's happening.'" (Hillel Schenker, PIJ)

14   The term "right of return" refers to the right of Palestinian refugees and their descendants to return to Israel and/or territory under Israeli control. Most Palestinians I've discussed this with say that the most important aspect of this would be official recognition by Israel of this right and of Israel's responsibility for their becoming refugees in the first place. Actual return is secondary and in fact in a survey conducted by Dr Khalil Shikaki of the Palestinian Center for Policy and Survey Research in 2003, in which more than 4,000 Palestinian refugees were asked if they were to exercise a right of return, where would they choose to live, only about one percent cited both residency and citizenship in the State of Israel. Dr Shikaki is quoted in a transcript of an interview on the NPR program *All Things Considered* (July 13, 2003) as stating: "The overwhelming majority wanted to live in a Palestinian state; only a small minority wanted to live in the state of Israel. That minority that wanted to have the state of Israel as the place of permanent residency was only 10 percent. But even in those 10 percent, only 10 percent of them wanted to have Israeli citizenship or Israeli passports. Ninety percent of those who wanted to have Israel as a permanent place of residence said that they would rather have a Palestinian citizenship and a Palestinian passport." (www.npr.org/programs/atc/transcripts/22003/jul/030714/shikaki.html)

15   The Palestinian version (i.e., that of the Jerusalem Center for Women) of the Jerusalem Link Principles reads: "Israel accepts its moral, legal, political and economic responsibility for the plight of Palestinian refugees and thus must

accept the right of return according to relevant UN resolutions." The Israeli version (i.e., that of Bat Shalom) reads: "Israel's recognition of its responsibility in the creation of the Palestinian refugees in 1948 is a pre-requisite to finding a just and lasting resolution of the refugee problem in accordance with relevant UN resolutions." (from www.batshalom.org, Jerusalem Link Declaration of Principles, as revised 2001)

16 This reference is to what was touted as "Barak's generous offer" to Arafat and the Palestinians in June 2000. For Israeli critiques see Reinhart 2002, Halper 2008, and www.gush-shalom.org.

17 Kathy Kamphoefner and husband, Paul Pierce, served as Quaker International Affairs Representatives (QIARs) in Jerusalem from November 2003 to September 2007, but were still with CPT in Hebron when I interviewed Kathy the first time. Our second interview—in January 2006—took place in the QIAR office in East Jerusalem.

18 For more extensive coverage of the impressive joint activism in Bil'in, including the Conference referenced here as well as preceding and subsequent conferences in Bil'in, see Chapter 5, www.bilin-village.org, and www.awalls.org.

19 Andoni is referring here to the so-called *mista'aravim*—members of special Israeli army units disguised as Arabs, used in assassinations and as agents provocateurs.

20 Though at the time of the interview, he was working for Holy Land Trust, Jubran has since set up as an independent nonviolence trainer.

21 ICAHD, along with groups such as Ta'ayush, Gush Shalom, RHR, PHR, Anarchists Against the Wall, and others.

22 Gila Svirsky and I participated together in a training session for nonviolence trainers given by a couple from the Netherlands in Jerusalem in 1992.

23 Even then, access to Jerusalem for Palestinians from the rest of the West Bank was severely restricted.

24 Where he spent thirteen years (1986–1999) for his activities as a part of a "Fatah cell."

5

THREE NONVIOLENT CAMPAIGNS: A CLOSER LOOK

In the 1988 Intifada we jointly—Palestinians and Israelis—did a lot of activities that proved that we are ready for coexistence and can work together against the occupation with nonviolence. That was a very significant change, both in the Israeli-Palestinian conflict and in the Middle East at large. I would say that, with the direction we took in 1988, especially in resisting the Israeli military tax system, we created a lot of changes on the ground in terms of the nonviolent resistance, and we imposed important changes on the Israeli policy makers to the point that the movement became important in not reacting but acting in a very strong way, in nonviolence, that was so influential on all those concerned: Palestinians, Israelis, the Palestinian Authority, the Israeli authorities, the international community. I think that everybody was at some point influenced by this movement.

Elias Rishmawi (Beit Sahour tax strike activist)

We in Beit Sahour have succeeded in building a model during the First Intifada, and in the Second Intifada we have Bil'in. So this link between the people of Beit Sahour and the people of Bil'in through resisting the occupation through nonviolent means is already there.

George S. Rishmawi (of the Siraj Center in Beit Sahour speaking at the Second Annual Bil'in Conference on Nonviolent Popular Joint Struggle, April 2007)

This is really crucial, the work that's being done here, because this is the resistance on the ground. Without this, all our other work doesn't mean very much. This is where the issue is kept all the time in the public eye, and it's a place where Israelis and Palestinians can work together jointly for peace, together with international civil society.

Jeff Halper (Israeli Committee Against House Demolitions, speaking at the April 2007 Bil'in conference)

At one of our demonstrations, [Sheikh] Hassan Yousef—he's one of the Hamas leaders— and also [a leader] from Jihad Islami were here. And when [a reporter] from Ha'aretz newspaper asked them about their opinion about what's going on, they said, "If we will see this way of resistance will shorten the time of the occupation, we will be the first people who will follow it." So we decided to succeed in this struggle.[1]

Mohammed Khatib (Bil'in Popular Committee Against the Wall and Settlements)

Introduction: From Solidarity to Joint Struggle

In the preceding chapters we have seen how a number of Israeli organizations that began as "solidarity groups" delivering practical assistance in close coordination with Palestinian organizations and village committees (the PHR model) were, by 2005/6, beginning to become part of long-term formations dedicated to joint or common struggle—though mostly without becoming joint organizations, as such—until, in the struggle against the "apartheid wall" in general, and in villages such as Bil'in, specifically, we see what AIC's Michel Warschawski has described (2006) as "a real joint Palestinian-Israeli struggle, built on trust, mutual respect and true cooperation on the ground" (Kaufman-Lacusta 2008).

In this chapter, we shall take a closer look at two campaigns that stand out among the many instances of nonviolent resistance in both the First Intifada and the Second Intifada, offering what might be called examples of "best practices" in terms of participation by Israelis in Palestinian nonviolent struggle: the Beit Sahour tax strike and the building of an Israeli support network via the PCR/Rapprochement-Jerusalem dialogue (a classic example of First Intifada-era solidarity at its best),[2] and the ongoing joint struggle in Bil'in[3] by villagers and their Israeli and international allies, against the expropriation of village land for the separation barrier and a settlement "neighbourhood." In addition, we'll take a brief look at the broader struggle against the wall.

The Beit Sahour Tax Strike

Elias Rishmawi

No longer politically active when I interviewed him in 2003 and 2006, Elias Rishmawi had been one of the major players in the Beit Sahour tax strike and in related activities of the First Intifada years. A pharmacist whose inventory was confiscated as a penalty for his refusal to pay value-added and other taxes imposed by the Civil Administration,[4] Rishmawi, like many Beit Sahour residents, also saw his family home stripped of most of its furnishings and spent several months in jail for his tax resistance. The tax strike began, he told me, in early 1988, with a leaflet distributed by the Unified National Leadership[5] of the Intifada.

The leaflet called upon Palestinians to withhold taxes of all kinds from the occupation authorities, contending that instead of using these funds for the benefit of the people—as required by the Fourth Geneva Convention—the Israelis were using the money to finance the occupation, including the purchase of tanks and ammunition used largely against young people armed only with stones, if at all. Ultimately, Beit Sahour was the only community where the tax strike was maintained for any length of time, and the town thus became famous for its steadfastness. Rishmawi explained how the Israeli imposition of a militarized tax system made the strike so important.

> What happened with the military tax system was that they cancelled the civil tax courts and civil courts of appeal and substituted for them military tax courts and military courts of appeal. Of course they gave the tax collectors the right to act as soldiers, which gave them the right to detain people, to imprison people without a court order, do break-ins, intimidate people, confiscate property, etc. And working from this framework, Israel managed to contain any economic development in the occupied territory.
>
> When you are taken to a military court with a military judge, with a military prosecutor, then the laws that are applied are the military orders and not the civil tax laws. Hence, they would assume that you made this or that mistake in reference to the military order, not in reference to the civil tax law. And then people are subject to severe fines and penalties, to the point that people start thinking: "Why should we invest if we are going to suffer those penalties and economic hardships? It's a lot of tension, besides losing our income. It's a lot of tension; why should I do that?" You have to be afraid all the time that they may raid your place, take your books, and possibly they will find something here or there that they think is not according to military law. Then you have to prove the opposite, and then the argument is put before the military court, and in the meantime you are in prison; you have to stay in prison until the whole damn thing is over.
>
> In fact, Israel managed to deter most of the economic sectors in the Palestinian occupied territories. And what happened after that, which was worse, was that when people [i.e., local people with money] found there was no chance for investment, they simply moved away and 'transferred' themselves, and went outside to invest. We suffered most by having the cream of our people leave the country, the highly educated and the well-to-do families.

Despite the hardships he endured during the long strike, when I asked Elias Rishmawi about the tax strike, what he most vividly recalled of those days were the joys of his town's steadfast and creative resistance to the suppression of the strike and the friendship and solidarity of the Israeli members of the Rapprochement dialogue group.

> This brings me back to the great days of the late eighties, when things were really different and people were deciding for themselves what to do and taking their strategic decisions related to resistance and their daily life as well. I would say, in that sense, that tax boycott was a major element in the nonviolent resistance to the Israeli occupation in the occupied Palestinian territory. We started, I believe, in February 1988. Most of the people were in compliance with the leaflet that called upon us to stop submitting the monthly tax reports; and the Israeli occupation authorities tried to enforce [payment of taxes] by force, by army, by prison, by collective punishment. In Beit Sahour they failed, actually, and people continued with the resistance. By June 1988 they started to harass people in the town. The military tax collectors came in supported by huge armed forces, and they started to stop people in the streets, harass them and confiscate their cars, and so on.
>
> The people in Beit Sahour responded by gathering in the municipality [i.e., municipal government offices] the next morning and "throwing back" their I.D.s in the famous incident where the deputy mayor of Beit Sahour, who was then the acting mayor, took the I.D.s and sent them to the military governor of Bethlehem, who got crazy! It was more than he could tolerate. I think he had never been used to seeing Palestinians disciplined and acting in nonviolence to such an extent. That night they imposed a curfew on Beit Sahour and put many people they believed to have influence on the resistance in prison. And after two weeks they lifted the curfew and became very cautious in tackling the tax issue in Beit Sahour—until a few months later they again started the harassment and tried to break down the town's stand of not paying taxes. Again the game started between the people and the Israeli military authorities, where again they started harassing people, confiscating their property or their cars and put them in prison for short terms, until it was so clear that something was going to happen.
>
> On the nineteenth of September, 1989, Beit Sahour was besieged and all entrances were closed. The military forces came in, and tax collectors started to move in the streets during the day, stopping people. They had lists and were looking for the names, houses—they went into properties, confiscated and attacked over

200 businesses and houses, and during forty-five days of continuous curfew, they managed to break down the whole economic infrastructure of Beit Sahour. They confiscated everything, everything that you can think of, from small machinery and tools for production to washing machines, TVs, etc., etc. and pharmaceuticals—my pharmacy was completely cleaned out. But nevertheless, the tax resistance continued. By then we were in a good position: we had nothing to lose, and the Israeli military authorities had nothing more to confiscate. They put people in prison—I think there were more than forty or fifty Beit Sahourians that were put in prison for administrative detention for different periods of time, from three months up to six months—and the Beit Sahourians said, "We will not open our shops until our people are out of prison."

The fact is, the shops stayed closed afterwards, because people realized that with closed shops they are not under the obligation of submitting tax reports, and then they can work at home and support their daily living. And we started parallel businesses—an alternative structure. Most of the people who had their production tools confiscated started again to do some small work from their houses, and grocers were doing their sales from their houses after the groceries were cleaned out of goods.

In 1992 together with my lawyer, Avigdor Feldman, who is an Israeli civil liberties lawyer and one of the best lawyers I have ever known, I brought the whole tax issue in the occupied territories before the Israeli Supreme [Court]. And in this test case there were about 120 merchants and business people representing diverse sectors of society from different towns and villages in the occupied territory: from Jenin, Nablus, and Tulkarm in the North; Ramallah, Jerusalem, Bethlehem, Hebron, and Beit Sahour, of course. Shortly after the case was accepted by one Supreme Court judge—which was a precedent, and a precedent that we applauded—Rabin (who was, I think, defence minister then) issued for the first time during the occupation the budget of the occupied territory, which was then considered to be classified material.

In accordance with international law, Israel was supposed to bring all the money it collected in the occupied territories back to the occupied territories—to be spent on the local people. But we found out that Israel was profiting dramatically from occupying the Palestinian land—from direct taxes, indirect taxes, taxes on the workers inside Israel, taxes on imports, taxes on people leaving the country, using Palestinian land, using Palestinian resources, water resources. Some professors in the local universities had made a calculation in around 1988 or '89, and they found out that the sum of all this money was around 1.3 or 1.4 billion dollars a year. Now, when we forced the late Israeli prime minister, Rabin, to disclose the budget for the first time in thirty-something years of occupation—through the injunction that I, together with around 120 merchants in the Palestinian territory brought to the Israeli High Court of Justice[6]—he disclosed a [yearly] budget of $273,000,000. For God's sake, where did the billion go? Of course, our economists brought up the figures after the budget was disclosed, and as such, this was a clear violation of the Geneva Convention and the Hague Regulations. Israel—an occupying power—should use the money for the benefit of the people, but should not make money from this.

The moment that the Supreme Court accepted the case, this was by itself a kind of de facto protection for us against any more harassment. So at some point, we managed to freeze the whole issue and come to an agreement with the tax authorities that we will start to pay taxes afterwards, and not retroactively. Of course after cutting the deal, they started to harass us again and tried to force us to pay [back taxes], but nevertheless, we did not. And that was the case until the Palestinian Authority came in and took over taxes and other areas.

Post-Oslo, however, when the PLO leadership were allowed to return to the territories and assumed leadership of the Intifada, their lack of support for the tax boycott, said Rishmawi, only exacerbated the difficulty of sustaining it.

At the same time we found ourselves trying to face, with nonviolent tax resistance, the Israeli occupation and from the other side the non-acceptance by the PLO leadership of this [strategy]. This confused many people, and I think that this was one of the main reasons that the tax resistance—or civil disobedience on a large scale, because this was the ultimate goal—failed in the occupied Palestinian territories.

In Beit Sahour people are so close to each other—relatives, neighbours—and it is very homogenous. The people of Beit Sahour are known to be highly educated and to be highly entrepreneurial to the point that we were considered to be the Japan of the West Bank. In my opinion, the perfect place was Beit Sahour, and all the elements of success existed in this society, regardless of the huge pressure that was applied by the Israeli military occupation. And Beit Sahour managed to bring the whole issue to international awareness, and at some point we exposed the whole system of occupation, the whole system of tax collection, tax enforcement, and other things related to the subject before the international community. And not only that, but also our counterparts in the peace movements in Israel geared up interest in the tax resistance—at some point this was the focus of interest everywhere. This supported us in going on with this kind of resistance.

I think all you need is a trigger or a reason to do it. At some point, we found we were so efficient in doing it and gearing up support inside Israel and inside the international community, regardless of the stand of the PLO leadership. It became more a personal thing, actually. And for us, the nonviolent resistance proved our dignity; and the moment it was considered a part of our dignity and our national aspiration, I think that placed it in a key role in unifying people around it. At the same time, I must say that the Israeli occupation authorities have helped indirectly. There were some people who were trying to pay taxes, not only in Beit Sahour but in other places. Instead of having their process of paying taxes being easy, they were more harassed by the Israeli tax authorities than people who did not pay. The more you start paying, the more you'll be more harassed. This also played a positive role in persuading people that even if you pay, you will not escape the harassment.

The uniqueness of our nonviolent resistance against the Israeli military tax system was that we used the Israeli judicial system, so that the resistance was from within. This is what makes it unique, in that we used their previous decisions in the High Court of Justice to accuse them of not implementing their own [decisions]. Hence it was a very strong case, I would say. It turns out that this kind of resistance was very efficient and very effective in terms of driving the occupation forces crazy and driving them to really losing control of the occupied territories. We believe our contribution to the conflict was proving that we could do it with nonviolence.

Rapprochement

Elias Rishmawi was among the founding members of the Beit Sahour Rapprochement dialogue group which went on to found the Palestinian Center for Rapprochement between People (PCR). The dialogue was begun early in the Intifada, he said, in an effort to add a "human dimension" to the struggle.

And face-to-face human contact was a very important element that we achieved when we decided on starting a dialogue with our Israeli counterparts. That was a breakthrough in a lot of taboos on the Palestinian side and the Israeli side as well; and as time went by, we were so close that people started to look at things differently.

Ghassan Andoni, another founding member of the PCR, also stressed the role of dialogue—particularly when linked to civil-based resistance. "We felt that an important component of civil-based resistance is attracting activism and sympathy from the enemy side," he said, telling me how the dialogue idea had come up in discussions with the Israeli lawyer who defended the tax strikers while they were in prison.

> Then he suggested the names of friends that he knew, and then he introduced us to the friends, and it happened to be that the friends were the right persons. We said, "Why not?" and arranged for the first meeting. Then we started a series of meetings to build a certain level of trust and confidence, and then moved immediately towards actions. I think from the beginning the Rapprochement group decided that communication and dialogues and peace work should always be linked with civil-based resistance as two necessary components to reach a just peace. So the idea was not only to increase the level of understanding and fight against stereotypes, but as well, together to fight against occupation.

Rapprochement-Jerusalem member Veronika Cohen described how she came to be involved, after receiving a phone call from fellow activist Hillel Bardin "saying there was a group of people from Beit Sahour who would like to meet with Israelis."

> Hillel went to meet with them and came back and said, "This is just the kind of thing you would probably enjoy doing." And so he set up the next meeting, in Jerusalem, and they came into Jerusalem. By the time they came to Jerusalem, Hillel had been arrested. He was a [reserve] soldier in Ramallah, and he had wanted to organize a dialogue with Hanan Ashrawi, and since he did that while he was in uniform, he was arrested for it. So by the time the dialogue [with the Beit Sahourians] took place, he wasn't there; I was there. And we realized that these people were just incredible to talk to, and that there was so much we didn't know about each other, and that talking was really an important activity. And that's how the dialogue in Beit Sahour got started.
>
> That year we met every other week, once in Jerusalem and once in Beit Sahour for a whole year, and it was done in secret. Nobody knew about it until the end of the year; and at the end of the year, some of the [Beit Sahour] people got arrested. At that point, we decided to go public and tell the press that here these people are so committed to nonviolence, and yet they are arrested

and put into administrative detention. I don't think they ever found out why they were arrested. Some of them sat for three, some for six months. In administrative detention they don't have to give a reason. Ghassan [Andoni] was arrested; almost everybody at some point was arrested. So we went to the press and said, "Look, Israelis are arresting people who are committed to nonviolence. Is this really what you want to do?"

This is how the dialogue group became known. Up to then, only the people who participated knew about it. It was sort of word-of-mouth, and the people who came to the first dialogue (mainly people from Israelis by Choice or people from our synagogue), almost everybody wanted to stay with it. They just found it something very meaningful, very important for them. In one form or another, it went on until the beginning of this [Al-Aqsa] Intifada.

Judith Green, like Veronika Cohen and a handful of other modern Orthodox Jews from West Jerusalem, was part of the Israelis by Choice group that responded to the invitation from Beit Sahour tax strikers early in the First Intifada to engage in dialogue—an experience that culminated in months of solidarity work during the protracted strike and developed into something that went far beyond mere dialogue. The dialogue partners in West Jerusalem and Beit Sahour adopted the paired names of Rapprochement-Jerusalem and the Palestinian Center for Rapprochement between People (PCR), respectively. The latter, as we have seen in Chapter 3, has since become an organization in its own right, promoting nonviolence locally as well as providing journalistic coverage of the situation throughout the territories (the International Middle East Media Center—IMEMC), and, beginning in the early months of the Al-Aqsa Intifada, also much of the Palestinian leadership for the International Solidarity Movement (ISM). The Israeli Rapprochement group, however, has become, in Judith Green's words, "sort of paralyzed, because we could not agree among us on what it is we can contribute now."

We started at the very beginning of the First Intifada, in 1988, just sitting in homes in Beit Sahour and in Jerusalem, a small group of people—about maybe ten people on each side—to discuss what was going on. Sort of just to find out what the Palestinians are doing, what's the message of the action, and how are Israelis responding; and just to open some kind of communication on an interpersonal level about what was happening, without being dependent on the news [media]. That was in 1988, when it was very easy to move around. There were no roadblocks and borders and all of that. A lot of things were a lot simpler. It just, I think, is a kind of luck. I mean, people who study dialogue groups can have theories about it, but there's a certain personal chemistry that's important in any dialogue group; and I think the group shaped itself over a couple of months into one that just felt very comfortable with each other, that communicated well, that were sort of on the same level, we'll say, of political sophistication. And it gelled. As a group, we enjoyed being with each other and talking and exchanging impressions, so very quickly it became a 'once-every-two-weeks for about two-to-four hours' meeting.

Soon, after we had met for about three months, we started thinking about public activities that would carry some of the messages that we had for each other into the community sphere, as I think particularly the Palestinians, then, were concerned that whatever they did not be seen as elitist, or secret, certainly, or factional. They were, from the beginning—this is in Beit Sahour, of course—very aware of the importance of expressing the community's needs and not having the particular dialogue group or action group be expressing the needs of the individuals who were in the group, and we really were impressed by that and thought it was also correct and hopeful for the future. Because all of these groups are small in terms of the activists that are in them, but we wanted them to have some public effect on a grassroots level. We weren't really thinking so much of political effect yet, but of public discussion, message, and so forth.

In our particular organization, in Rapprochement [-Jerusalem]—and I think our partners understood this—we didn't want to be seen as anti-Zionist or far-left. A lot of us came from the religious community, from the Orthodox community, from a certain synagogue, and we made real attempts to bring people to speak in synagogues and in front of religious audiences. We also had a separate dialogue group with settlers at the time, who were mainly from Gush Etzion, the Efrat area. So we tried. Also, on the Palestinian side, they were really very interested in bringing in all the political factions in Palestine into their own inner dialogue on their own side and to include them in the work that was being done with Israelis. This wasn't always true of the nonviolent work that was done in Palestine then, or now. So, both they and we wanted the work that we did to speak to a kind of consensus. In other words, we didn't want to be seen as either radical or secretive or factional. And it was really the case, because we were just, on the Israeli side, a kind of random bunch of people. We weren't from a certain movement, or political party, or anything like that; it was a—what do you call it? Word-of-mouth?—a very grapevine kind of activity.

The kinds of activities—like spending the Shabbat in Beit Sahour—had a kind of religious aspect, and it was very nice. We wanted, through that kind of thing, to appeal to a certain kind of community, to have family activities. All the activities had a message that could be considered political, or directly connected to the occupation and the experiences of the Palestinians; but we wanted them to also have a human side, to be appealing enough that you could arouse the empathy of people who might not otherwise have taken part. And when we did educational activities, like panel discussions, we tried to bring in people from the Israeli and Palestinian sides who were from other groups and other approaches: lawyers, teachers, social workers, and so forth. That was always the approach. We did some kind of supportive things in the tax strike period, and in prisons. There was a certain amount of civil disobedience and some slightly provocative behaviour. But I don't think that we saw that as a goal in itself.

It seems to me that there are times, and this is one of them, where I can't find a constructive activity to do, other than occasionally calling up my Palestinian friends and talking to them, you know; and that level of personal supportiveness or continuity is important to me: to have contact with people. But somehow, within Rapprochement, we've sort of [been] paralyzed on the Israeli side. We could not agree among us on what it is we can contribute now, because we want to stick to our original mandate. If we want to remain who we were then, then I think we've come to the conclusion that we can't really function; we can't do the kinds of work now that we did then, and maybe there will be another time that we can. We can't physically get people together. We can't coordinate. We can't really plan things together in an egalitarian way, the way we used to. We're not interested in being a Palestinian support group, and that's what I think a lot of the left-wing activity is now.

Outsmarting the Israeli Army: My Memories
of a Solidarity Weekend in Beit Sahour

I was living in Jerusalem in the days of the Beit Sahour tax strike and was able to participate in some of the Rapprochement-Jerusalem activities. These included solidarity visits to the Beit Sahour dialogue partners, which could sometimes mean sneaking into town while it was under curfew. For example, just before sunset one Friday evening in the spring of 1989—at the height of the tax strike—entire families of Israelis, from babies in strollers to elderly grandparents, disembarked from rented buses on the outskirts of Beit Sahour (after arriving by a roundabout route in order to evade the gaze of the Israeli military) and clambered over stone walls to gain access to the town (in the process, startling some Bedouin shepherds, who may well have thought we were the "nucleus" of a new Israeli settlement) to spend Shabbat with our Palestinian dialogue partners. The weekend began with a kosher Shabbat dinner brought along by the mostly observant Jewish group and concluded only the following day, after the Israeli army, which had found out where we were via a Saturday morning TV report, confronted the group in the main street of Beit Sahour, blocking our way to an appointment with the town's mayor.

There were, of course, many other instances when a small group of Jewish dialoguers would go to the besieged town just to be with their friends when there was a curfew, sometimes bringing food and often simply moral support; sometimes bringing other Israelis, as well as internationals, into homes where most of the furniture and appliances had been confiscated—giving these visitors a rare glimpse of life under curfew. The relationship that developed between Rapprochement-Jerusalem and the PCR group in those First Intifada years was truly something far beyond mere dialogue.

The Wall as a Focus for Joint Activism

Long-term relationships like that which developed between the Palestinians of Beit Sahour and the Israelis of the Jerusalem Rapprochement group in the context of the Beit Sahour tax strike were a rarity in the days of the First Intifada; shifting ad hoc formations were much more typical. And, as we've seen, the spate of joint endeavours that blossomed in the wake of the signing of the Oslo Accords in late 1993 concentrated primarily on promoting mutual understanding through dialogue and other "people to people" activities rather than on anti-occupation activism. Ironically, perhaps, the hated security barrier (aka apartheid wall) has been the catalyst in forging a new brand of joint activism, providing a focal point for the transition from solidarity to truly joint struggle.

Beginnings of Joint Resistance to the Wall: The Mas'ha Peace Camp

Despite the mixed—even if largely positive—attitudes surrounding participation by Israelis in Palestinian-led nonviolent actions, and in spite of the normalization debate and the sometimes problematic dynamics involved in such activities—a sampling of which we've seen in the previous chapter—the many joint campaigns that have developed around opposition to the wall, beginning not long after commencement of its construction in mid-2002, have garnered near-universal approval from the activist community, nonviolent and otherwise. As I write from the perspective of 2009, joint Palestinian/Israeli (and often also international) ventures in nonviolent resistance to the encroachments of the Israeli separation barrier/apartheid wall have become widespread, with the joint struggle focused on the Ramallah-district village of Bil'in providing an outstanding example. Although Jayyous was the first Palestinian village to carry out regular, large-scale protests against the construction of the wall, as early as September 2002, the summer 2003 peace camp in Mas'ha was one of the earliest concerted efforts of this kind. When Israeli participant Dorothy Naor spoke to me that fall, she enthusiastically described the encampment at this small village not far from the settlement city of Ariel, where land was being gobbled up by the wall, as a camp where "Israelis and internationals and Palestinians work together against the occupation, against the wall, sit, talk to one another."

> The camp was a twenty-four-hour-a-day thing for four months. Nazih [Shalabi, qv below] stayed the whole time. He was one of the organizers. From the Palestinian side he was *the* organizer, and losing the family trees was not easy for him. Mas'ha lost over ninety percent of its agricultural land: from 6,000 dunam, it went down to 500 dunam. This is stealing Palestinian land. This is why Hani, whose house is going to be walled in from all sides, was today offered a blank cheque to fill in whatever sum he wanted. And he said his house isn't worth anything, but he will not sell Palestinian land. And when the Norwegian TV crew today asked Rayad what he wanted to do in the future, he said he has no future. But will he leave? No. He says, "This is what the Israelis would like. They'd like the Palestinians to get up and leave and disappear." But most won't do it. On the other hand, quite a few have left—those who have the means. They might have come back, had there been peace, but I don't know when it's going to happen.

I met Nazih Shalabi at a planning meeting in Mas'ha. He explained that Palestinians, internationals, and "peace-loving" Israelis had set up a tent together to protest the wall. "In the end this grew and there was cooperative work between Palestinians, Israelis, and internationals—opposition to the occupation without violence. We don't believe in violence. We believe in negotiations to resolve all the problems." Shalabi told me that he feels it is important to recruit as many Israelis and internationals as possible to join in anti-wall and anti-occupation efforts: "Three or four thousand people came here to me. And we ate, drank, slept—did everything together. This was shared work, all of it. This gives a good example, that not only violence solves problems. If we want to go for peace, we can." Fellow Mas'ha activist Tayseer Arabasi described how camping together, the Palestinian and Israeli activists "weren't afraid of anything but the soldiers."

> The most important thing that I felt was that we were on the mountain under the trees at night—we weren't afraid of anything—Palestinians and Israelis [together], weren't afraid of anything but the soldiers. This is also interesting—that you're not afraid of the name "Israeli." It may be that you are afraid of a small segment of that name, that is the soldiers. So together we were afraid of the soldiers; together we felt that we were afraid if soldiers or settlers were to come, what would we do? This means that the Palestinians and the Israelis—true, they're two peoples—in the end they're human beings, comrades/friends, afraid of the same thing: the occupation and the soldiers.

In October of 2003, when I interviewed the Mas'ha activists, the Palestinian-Israeli-international peace camps held there earlier that year had not yet spawned the movement that has since grown up around Bil'in and other Ramallah-area villages, yet I was impressed by their creativity and by Shalabi's optimistic—while realistic—steadfastness.

> Look, we are few, so far. It will take time to do what we're doing: to convince as many people as possible takes time. We felt this when we were in the camp. A few media came, only a few. They didn't talk much about [the camp], and today the way to convince people is via the media. So we're doing our own media work, and we have everything on other peace websites.[7]

Wall Tours

Another way of spreading information about the wall and the evils of the occupation generally, which seems to be successfully reaching a larger segment of the Israeli public, is the wall tours described to me by Elana Wesley—a Jaffa activist who, like Dorothy Naor, distributes a huge volume of information via email to a long list of interested folks around the world on a daily basis. These tours, says Wesley, are being conducted by the Coalition of Women for Peace and other organizations and attract Israelis who, though interested in broadening their understanding of the situation, are not yet at the point of actively participating in the more hands-on activities of groups like Ta'ayush, ICAHD, or Machsom Watch.

> I know about tours by the Coalition of Women for Peace and by ICAHD, and there may be one or two more Israeli groups in addition to the Palestinian groups[8] that are doing this. They tour the wall, and there are also meetings with Palestinian families. If they meet with Palestinian families, wherever they happen to be, they'll hear the story of what happened in that particular place. And they're somehow reaching people. I guess people don't feel so threatened by it. So some people who would not come and participate in some protest action or activist action of some other kind are coming on these trips, and they've gotten to several thousand people.

Bil'in as a Rallying Point for Anti-Wall Activism

For those Israelis (and internationals, of course) who do wish to participate directly in the struggle against the wall, the now four years plus (since early 2005) of weekly nonviolent demonstrations in Bil'in (organized by the Bil'in Popular Committee against the Wall and Settlements in consultation with a small group of Israeli activists, primarily Anarchists Against the Wall) have provided both a focus and a training ground, a place for learning firsthand about the issues confronting the villages impacted by the wall and for personally experiencing the roadblocks, teargas, and rubber bullets that are but the tip of the iceberg of the oppression suffered by the villagers. As Iyad Burnat of the Bil'in Popular Committee pointed out in January 2006 (after the first year of weekly actions), "All the world is now talking about Bil'in, and they know that this barrier is not a security barrier." Effective use of the Internet (websites and email) and other media is paired with bringing growing numbers of both Israelis and internationals to see the situation created by the wall with their own eyes—a successful combination. Burnat added that more and more Israelis are coming to Bil'in.

> In the beginning there were ten Israelis who came to demonstrate with us. At one of the major [recent] demonstrations here in the village there were four hundred Israelis. Every week we bring a group of Israelis in by bus, new ones, and they come and look at the land, at the barrier, and they can't believe it. Because they heard inside [of Israel] that it's a security barrier, and then they see it with their own eyes and can't believe [what they see]."

One of the Israelis most involved in the Bil'in struggle is Yonatan Pollak. He and the other young people who make up the small band of activists called Israeli Anarchists Against the Wall have formed the "hard core" of Israeli participants in the campaign against the wall ever since the days of the Mash'a peace camp and have provided a reliable—and highly visible—Israeli presence at the weekly nonviolent demonstrations in Bil'in since the beginning of this ongoing campaign. When I interviewed him in the fall of 2003, the Bil'in campaign had yet to begin, but Pollak and his friends had already been active in actions against the wall for some time. He recounted an instance where the visible presence of Israelis had contributed to restraint on the part of the soldiers—when villagers and others pulled down a section of barbed-wire fencing (part of the "wall" in that area) that cut the village off from 10,000 dunam (about 2,500 acres) of its agricultural land.

> What we did there was, together with people from that village and international activists, we took down the fence, physically. We were not throwing stones—I don't think there was stone-throwing that day—but it was very evident that we were on the Palestinian side of the fence and that we were acting with the Palestinians to help them get to their fields. So we were on one side; the soldiers were on the other side. We had signs in Hebrew and we shouted slogans in Hebrew, and they all knew that Israelis were there. There were rubber bullets and there was tear gas, but there was no live ammunition, and no one was seriously injured.[9]

The Wall and the Law—Some Victories, Large and Small

A major victory in the struggle against the wall, which we must not forget, is the July 9, 2004, advisory ruling by the International Court of Justice in the Hague that the construction of the so-called separation barrier by Israel in the West Bank and in and around East Jerusalem is in contravention to international law (specifically the Fourth Geneva Convention) and that Israel must dismantle it and pay compensation for damage caused by its construction.[10] Several of those I interviewed credited the widespread popular resistance to the wall and the publicity garnered by this nonviolent campaign worldwide with making this decision possible. Although the Israeli government has thus far declined to implement the ICJ ruling, there have been a number of small victories in the grassroots struggle against the wall.

One such victory occurred at the Abu Dis campus of al-Quds University near Jerusalem. Nasir Samara, an al-Quds student I met in Bil'in on January 1, 2006, described a creative campaign that had taken place a couple of years earlier, when students and faculty literally camped in the path of the advancing wall—which threatened to cut them off from their playing field—and succeeded in a legal petition to have the wall's route revised to leave university and playing field on the same side.

> The student council decided we want to make a camp here, a tent, and we would sleep here and never leave it until they move the wall back or don't build it [at all]. So every night we had a new course, singing, or folklore [i.e., Palestinian cultural performances]. We made a stage, and we continued for a month. Each student stayed there at least five or six nights and slept in the tent with the internationals who supported them. The lawyer of the university went to the High Court in Israel; they moved back and they built the wall at the border of the playing field. And if you go there now, you will find it at the end of the football field.

A success with even more far-reaching implications—achieved, in this case, by non-activists—was described by Rotem Mor, a young refusenik who works for the American Friends Service Committee in Jerusalem. This involved joint work and resistance by residents of Mevasseret Tzion (the Jerusalem-area Israeli town where Mor's parents live) and Palestinians from the village of Beit Suriq—only a five-minute drive away, in the West Bank. Mor described their action as offering a successful model, "similar in many ways to what we do in Bil'in and other places," but also different in that "who was doing the resistance were not activists like me or like Iyad or other Palestinian activists, but the people living there."

And their statement was, "We haven't had any problems in this area. The wall will not bring us security, because there is not a problem right now. And we are scared of the wall." So basically, the Jewish residents of the Mevasseret, where I was, set up a council and the people in Beit Suriq set up a council, and we did many activities together. We did a kite event, we did demonstrations against the wall, we had Israelis come and do a tour of the village; and eventually we were able to push the wall back in our region and—not just in our region—in the whole of the West Bank through a petition to the Supreme Court.

What happened in this case was that neighbours from the neighbouring Israeli community said, "We support the Palestinians in their claim. We want the wall to be as far away from their community as possible, because that's a prerequisite for our security." And because the Israelis said this, the Supreme Court couldn't just say that it's just Palestinians crying about their rights, and what they really want to do is to hurt us. Because the Israelis were saying, "No, this is not true." So the case got a hearing, and eventually, after six months of work, the Supreme Court declared that the building of the wall in our region—and that meant in other regions as well—was illegal, and the army had to go back and re-plan the whole wall, so it will hurt Palestinians much less.

This is a famous Israeli case, and it basically originated from two small communities of Israelis and Palestinians who decided that they didn't want the wall the way it was. And I think that the message of this really is that if we want to resist the wall—if we want to resist the war on terror, or the clash of civilizations—the only way that I've found is effective is through working together. The second you're working together, you're saying "There is no clash of civilizations, but there is injustice: let's speak about this injustice."

Budrus: Keeping the Wall off Village Land

Yet another successful model of nonviolent resistance to the wall is that of the village of Budrus. This is described at length in an article published on *The Electronic Intifada*, in June of 2007 (Audeh 2007). Located but three kilometres from the Green Line, Budrus lost eighty percent of its land to Israeli confiscations in 1948. Yet, says the author,

"Despite the provocation of [an army] base on village lands, not a single shot was ever fired by the villagers, and not a single suicide bomber ever emerged from the village." Following the 2004 advent of bulldozers preparing the way for the wall, the people of Budrus mobilized to save their olive trees and their land, and, repeatedly, "brought the bulldozers to a standstill." Although they paid a high price in terms of arrests and injuries, the people of Budrus were able to change the course of the wall, thereby preserving ninety-five percent of the land slated for confiscation—both from Budrus and neighbouring villages. Audeh's article (based on conversations with one of the coordinators of the popular resistance committee formed to confront the wall, Abd al-Nasser Marrar) describes a struggle with a number of noteworthy features. These include blocking the bulldozers by a mass turnout of villagers (all sectors and factions) on any day they appear, avoidance of confrontations with soldiers, and the very high level of participation by women (for information on *Budrus*, a powerful new film documenting this struggle, see www.justvision.org). Marrar states:

> In every march in Budrus, about 99 percent of the residents participate. Moreover, we did not have a specific day of the week for our actions. It was a daily thing. Any day the bulldozers appeared, we had some type of action to oppose them. This meant that people's lives came to a standstill; employees lost work time, housework didn't get done. This was an unusual characteristic, the daily activities.

Photos taken at demonstrations, says Marrar, show women blocking the bulldozers. "And this happened more than once in Budrus, and they succeeded in getting to the bulldozers before the men did. They were lying down in front of the bulldozers. I haven't seen similar participation by women in any other location." Describing one of the early campaigns, he says:

> The families got to the property and found the army there. People sat under their trees, even though they were beaten with sticks. The bulldozers couldn't move that day. This went on for a week. The courts stopped activity on the wall for two weeks. These two weeks changed the course of the wall, [bringing it closer] to the 1948 line. They started to work on the western side. So the same thing happened; the lands they were threatening to take were all olive tree groves, like the northern side. About 300 people were injured with

rubber bullets or tear gas inhalation in the protests; about 30 were jailed. Often the soldiers got out of our way during the marches; they saw that force was not necessary when they face 100 kids who have neither sticks nor stones.

The bravery and persistence of demonstrators—both villagers and, often, Israelis and internationals as well—resisting the wall is reflected in reports of actions from villages all along its length. Budrus is but one outstanding example. Another is the now four-year-long nonviolent struggle of the village of Bil'in.

Resisting Together in Bil'in

With the overall struggle against the wall, its hard-won victories and disappointing setbacks, as the backdrop, we will now move on to look more closely at one of the major campaigns in that battle—one which exemplifies joint struggle by Palestinians and their invited Israeli partners, and support by internationals, with over four years of weekly nonviolent demonstrations (since March 2005), four international conferences, widespread media coverage, and at least two full-length films: the persistent resistance of the village of Bil'in.

In April of 2007, I spent several days in the Ramallah-area village of Bil'in, where I had come to attend the Second Annual Bil'in Conference on Nonviolent Popular Joint Struggle,[11] and to conduct a few more interviews for this book. By that time, Bil'in residents and their Israeli and international supporters had been holding weekly nonviolent demonstrations protesting the confiscation of over half of the agricultural landholdings of the village for the construction of an Israeli settlement "neighbourhood" and a section of the separation barrier (a trench-protected, gated fence on this part of its route) for just over two years, since March 2005. I had been in Bil'in twice previously, in January 2006, once to interview local activists and once to participate in a Friday afternoon demonstration. Participants in the April 2007 conference, as well as people I spoke to during the demonstration at its end and in the course of my 2006 and 2007 interviews, in Bil'in and elsewhere, spoke about the joint nonviolent struggle in Bil'in from a variety of perspectives and voiced differing ideas of its future prospects, but all who were familiar with it (among proponents of the Palestinian cause, of course) viewed the example of Bil'in as a powerful and positive model, including some who did not otherwise support either nonviolence or joint efforts by Israelis and Palestinians.

The Centre for Joint Struggle

> Our struggle is against the occupation and everything that represents the occupation, whether it's a settler or a soldier ... We will not cause physical harm; we struggle with our brains, not our hands. ... And we hope that our struggle will spread to other places, and ... this building that you see here—this small house—is the first we've built, and we have named it the Centre for Joint Struggle. And we hope that from this small house a great revolution will go forth, and that there will be a large movement for joint Palestinian-Israeli, and also international, work, and that all of us together will work for peace, for an end to the occupation, for the rights of every one of us.

These words, spoken by Mohammed Khatib, a leading member of the Bil'in Popular Committee against the Wall and Settlements (henceforth, Popular Committee), greeted me as I approached the demonstration site in this small Palestinian village a few minutes' drive from Ramallah in the West Bank, on my first visit there, on January 1, 2006. I had heard about Bil'in from Palestinian activists at the Celebrating Nonviolent Resistance Conference in Bethlehem the previous week. Whereas people from a number of the West Bank villages impacted by the wall had attended the Bethlehem conference and several had spoken, the Bil'in activists had not. Too busy at home, I was told, but "you should come on Friday after the conference and join the weekly demonstration there." I didn't make it to Bil'in that Friday, but I did manage to join in a demonstration outside the Centre for Joint Struggle the following Sunday. This demonstration was sponsored by Gush Shalom (the Israeli Peace Bloc) and was attended by many Israelis, from that organization and others, whom I remembered from my activist days in Jerusalem in the 1990s. It took place only coincidentally on western New Year's Day (and equally coincidentally the anniversary of the Fatah movement), and actually marked the eighth and final day of the Jewish holiday of Hanukah.[12] Explaining the symbolism of having the demonstration during this holiday, Gush leader Uri Avnery referred to the people of Bil'in as "the Maccabees of these days" and the occupation as Antiochus, and in full view of a settlement "neighbourhood" of the settlement of Modi'in Ilite (Upper Mod'in), under construction on land confiscated from Bil'in, eight torches symbolizing the eight Hanukah candles were lit by Israeli activists—each of whom made a short dedication: "I light this torch for the fighters against occupation and oppression, in the spirit of the Maccabees, who were the sons of this soil!" ... "I light this candle for peace between the two peoples, sons of this country!"[13]

Khatib, a prominent figure in the village's ongoing struggle against the Israeli "separation barrier," who was addressing the assembled Israeli and Palestinian activists when I arrived, continued with his fascinating account how the Centre for Joint Struggle had been built. After deciding to place a "Palestinian outpost" on land that had been confiscated from Bil'in for construction for the wall and a settlement "neighbourhood," Khatib explained, the villagers had brought in a mobile home ("caravan") such as are used by Israeli settlers in establishing their outposts. Within thirty-six hours, the caravan was removed by men from the Civil Administration. The villagers brought another.

> It was rainy, so they didn't see us and didn't discover that we were here until noontime. Then [people] from the Civil Administration came, but it was getting late and they were unable to take the second caravan. So they said, "Prepare yourselves for tomorrow. At 7:30 in the morning, we're coming to take your caravan." We said to them, "If that's so—that you took the first one and you're coming to take the second one—then stand back a little and look at those high-rise buildings [under construction in the settlement across the road]. Why aren't you dealing with them, even though you know—according to an article in *Ha'aretz*[14]—that they are illegal according to Israeli law?" And they said, "That's because those are buildings. It takes a process to stop them. It would take days until they stop [construction]." And we said to them, "If we had a building like that?" And they said, "You'll succeed in building it? So build it, and we'll deal with you the same way we deal with them."

The villagers had then asked, "What is a building from your point of view?" And the Civil Administration men replied, "It's ten metres [square]; it'll have a roof, windows—that's a building."

> We said, "Okay." We knew they would be coming in the morning.
> We decided, along with our Israeli partners who were at the place
> and with the internationals who were [here], that all of us must
> now build a house by 8:00 in the morning. True, it was difficult,
> but it wasn't impossible. In our struggle, we believe that there are
> difficult things, but impossible things, there are not. We always
> can do things even if they're difficult.

With some difficulty the villagers and their friends—including a
sympathetic settler with a car—had hauled building materials through
the mud to the site beside the barrier, working through the rainy
December night to construct a small cinderblock room, complete with
corrugated tin roof and a window cannibalized (with permission) from
a house in the village. Supporters from Israel and abroad now often
spent the night in or just outside the Centre, said Khatib.

After the speeches and "candle" lighting, and a medley of satirical
songs by the Israeli Raging Grannies (*Savta-ot Zo'amot*), I spoke to
a number of village activists and Israeli supporters who explained
the background of their campaign—the fencing off and subsequent
confiscation of fifty-five percent of the agricultural holdings of Bil'in
for construction of a Jewish settlement "neighbourhood"[15] and the
"separation barrier," allegedly for reasons of security; their discovery of
the illegality (under Israeli law!) of this settlement, and the months
of weekly nonviolent joint demonstrations and other actions—the
highpoint being the erection of the Centre for Joint Struggle. The
concept of a "Palestinian settlement outpost" built on land reclaimed for
that purpose years after its confiscation by the occupation authorities
excited my imagination, so I asked one of the Bil'in activists if I could
stay there that night. "You are welcome," he told me, "but first join us
around the campfire."

I joined the shifting group seated around the fire—supporters
coming and going, journalists conducting interviews, villagers passing
the time of day. Of course, since the very existence of the Centre for
Joint Struggle signified a major achievement in this campaign, it and the
ongoing campaign being pursued jointly with Israeli and international
partners were high on the list of subjects that folks in Bil'in, Palestinian
villagers and Israeli supporters alike, were talking about at the time.
One of these was Nasir Samara (the English-speaking student who told
me about the successful campaign by students and faculty of Abu Dis

University to rescue their playing field from the wall). Particularly thrilled about the Centre for Joint Struggle—built on village land that had been confiscated three years previously—he enthused, "Before, when we started resisting the wall, the army didn't allow us to come close to this area. Now we are living here. Living here!"

> We and the internationals and Israelis, we feel that we are really one family, you know. If you are sleeping here in the night, maybe the blanket that you cover yourself with will fall off, and you will find me or another one who will cover you with the blanket. They are staying awake all night to keep the fire burning in order to get some warmth, not just for [themselves], for you if you are asleep. So really I feel that we are just one family.

Speaking about the participation of Israelis and internationals in the weekly demonstrations, Samara told me:

> It's good to know that it's encouraged by people outside; all of them trying to support us and help us by sending more volunteers, more activists, Israelis and internationals. Others come here more and more. You can participate in a demonstration; you'll find a hundred Israeli Anarchists and internationals. Every Friday you will find more, and very famous persons from all over the world come here. Israeli Knesset members, both Arab and [Jewish] came to this village, and internationals; Kofi Anan's deputy for human rights came here; the parents of Rachel Corrie came here. We have a message to the world that we can build our future home in a nonviolent way. We can resist the wall and stop it by these demonstrations.

One of the Israeli supporters I met that evening was Ido Khenin, a young refusenik who credits his family background for his political awareness and his dedicated participation in the Bil'in struggle. With Communist parents and a set of grandparents who are Holocaust survivors, says he, "I have lots of political education against fascism, against racism, against things like the occupation, and pro-man and pro-peace and all the good things that we're trying to build now in Bil'in."

> I first came to Bil'in in March 2005 and I joined a few of my friends, like Yonatan Pollak and lots of good people from Tel Aviv who are in the group of Anarchists Against the Wall. Although I'm a Communist, I joined the Anarchists because they're doing a really

good job here with the Popular Committee, and I joined them and we went to a demonstration in Safa, the next village to Bil'in. After this demonstration, we went with Eyad [Bornat] to his house and we ate and we saw his children and talked and had fun. After that, he told me that they are starting a wave of demonstrations in Bil'in, and he told me to come, if I want, to a demonstration three days from this date with the children from the village. And after that, we heard that another week from then there was another demonstration. These demonstrations are against this wall that is taking the land from Bil'in and against the settlements that are also taking the land and food of the people. Now this fence takes half of the land of the people of Bil'in, and that means half of the food, half of the money, and half of the future of the people of Bil'in.

I see myself now and I see what a good life I have here with the people of Bil'in. First of all it's friendship and it's fun to be here, and it's good for me to be here. And of course, I feel that we are doing together the most important thing, which is peace. And in all the books of all the religions of the people who live here—in the Old Testament, in the New Testament, in the Qur'an—if you open them, you will see that the most important thing is Salaam, Shalom, Peace.

Ido Khenin and I spoke while sitting in front of the Centre for Joint Struggle on the morning of January 2, 2006. While I and a Greek woman from the ISM had spent the night inside the small building, the male supporters and villagers had slept on the ground outside, beside the embers of the campfire—and had received a visit from an Israeli military patrol. "The people here are really brave," said Khenin.

Last night three soldiers came. We hosted them and we gave them tea to drink and we sat with them and talked. I was with two friends [from Bil'in], Haitham and Nasir. They are so brave, because soldiers like those soldiers killed their friends, and shot at them, and took them to prison. Haitham was in prison for two years, and he saw his friends die before his eyes because of soldiers like this, but he is such a good man and such a great man that he put it all aside and when the soldiers came, he was nice to them. I saw that it was hard for him to talk, because he was shaking, but he didn't shout at them and he didn't tell them "go away" and he didn't take something and hit them. I don't know if I could do that if I were him.

I really hope that my friends will keep being so brave and that they won't give up to those soldiers, and will keep being brave against the occupation and against violence—although we are Israelis and although these bastards represent us. I hope that they will know always that we are with them, and we're trying to make change from inside Israel. And I hope in the end that the change will come from Israel, because Israel is the strongest here, and Israel has the United States behind it, "the evil empire."

"Until the wall will fall," Khenin concluded, "we will be here and we will struggle together, Israelis and Palestinians."

I wanted especially to hear firsthand accounts of the impressive array of varied nonviolent actions that had been carried out in Bil'in, but I was also curious about the activists' attitudes to nonviolence in general. After all, unlike many of the Palestinians I had interviewed on this subject—notably those involved in the Beit Sahour tax strike and dialogue—the people I spoke with in Bil'in were, by and large, farmer-herders, rather than college-educated professionals. I therefore found their responses both exciting and encouraging and, yes, a bit surprising, given their relative isolation and lack of formal "higher" education.

I interviewed Iyad Burnat (head of the Bil'in Popular Committee), also on the morning after the Gush Shalom demonstration. He spoke to me in Hebrew, as did most of the male villagers I met, his friend Haitham Khatib translating between Hebrew and Arabic in the few instances when this was needed. Burnat reaffirmed Bil'in's commitment to nonviolence.

> We believe in the way we are following, the nonviolent way against the barrier and against the occupation. So we decided to continue in this way, the nonviolent way, to get back our land and to advance toward peace without violence—like tying ourselves to olive trees, putting ourselves in barrels on the barrier; ourselves, along with our Israeli friends who have been standing with us from the start, and internationals. We carried out many ideas at six in the morning. We would come to the route of the barrier before the arrival of the army and so on, and would tie ourselves to the olive trees, keeping the bulldozers [from moving] for hours, tie ourselves to the corners of the fence sometimes. We carried out many, many ideas, including a cage—[to symbolize] that the barrier makes all Palestine into a prison—with a goat, and women and internationals and Israelis and other people from the village.

Pointing out that the route of the barrier where it cuts through Bil'in's land is seven kilometres from the Green Line, and that in some places it strays as far as twenty kilometres into the West Bank, Burnat rejected claims of its function as a "security barrier."

> We believe that this is not a security barrier, it is a barrier for stealing land. For one thing, to build settlements here on our land, to uproot the olive trees, to steal them, to take the land, so they [can] bring more Israeli people to live here. This is something that pains us. The landholdings of the village of Bil'in are 4,000 dunam (1,000 acres), and of these they took 2,300. That's more than half. They have taken some sixty percent of our land and they just say that this is for security. What is security? To kill people is security? To take their land, and so on and so forth? So we eventually decided that we want our land back, because this is not just. We just want to tell the world that we want peace, real peace, a peace that makes two states for two peoples that will live in peace. The barrier will not make peace between the two peoples.

"All the world is now talking about Bil'in, and they know that this barrier is not a security barrier," he went on, pointing out that Israelis, too, have become aware of this and are joining the weekly demonstrations in increasing numbers.

> [The Israeli authorities] know that this is our land. What can they do? We are demonstrating without violence, and they know that this is our land, and we know it too. What can they do? What did the court decide they could do? Nothing. But in the end, we succeeded to bring the media here to the village of Bil'in, and we have attracted more people here—who will speak about Bil'in—both from America and the whole world. We succeeded in this, because truth/justice/the law is on our side. We believe in peace and in a nonviolent way, and this is something good. All the world is watching this and see that it is something good and say that it is something good.

"But," I asked, "what if (as I have often heard) someone comes and says: 'For all the years, the Palestinians have resisted the occupation in a mainly nonviolent way, yes? And the Israelis have only responded to us with violence, so we're fed up. We have the right under international law to defend ourselves however possible and that includes violence'—What do you say?"

We say that we are continuing in a nonviolent way. We know that the army always starts the violence, and the whole world knows this. [The broadcasters] say to people in their news broadcasts that we start the violence and so on. So from the beginning, we've photographed our demonstrations, and there are also pictures [and videos]. And sometimes in court the soldiers were shown to be lying—when they said that people had thrown stones[16] and so on. We sent the pictures to the court, and they were shown to be lying by the [Israeli] court. By these pictures we are able to show the world that listens to the Israeli media—which is picked up all over the world—[where] they sometimes hear that Palestinians are terrorists, and so on. We have the pictures of who is the terrorist, who starts the violence, who hits old people and small children. We have all of this [on film]. The soldiers sometimes travel to the village at night, they turn the homes in the village upside-down, and there are also pictures of that, and they know it. But we want to show the world: the people in the world, not the governments.

The governments all know that the Hague Court said to dismantle the barrier, right? But nobody did anything. So we want to show the [people of all the] nations, the people who don't know this, that there is an army here that behaves violently against nonviolent demonstrations: that they start [the violence] all the time, that they enter the village; they detain even young children, they throw [tear] gas inside homes. They once threw a gas grenade at a wedding in the village, where there were children and women.

Media coverage of the weekly demonstrations has been good, says Burnat, "they showed it on television, including Israeli, and now, *insha'allah*, we will succeed at last and all this will go away."

Haitham Khatib, also a member of the Bil'in Popular Committee, shared his feelings about nonviolent struggle as well.

I'm speaking personally. I think the nonviolent way is the right way that we are doing now. Why? You can see that the other side is ruling and is very strong and can rule and can steal and is able to do everything. We've believed in the nonviolent way for a long time, and a bridge needs to be built so that all the world will know that we are a weak nation whose land is being stolen, and who is unable to do anything [about it]. We hope that the bridge that we want to build will be very strong for the sake of peace, let us say, for the two peoples, for our children in the future. We are thinking of our children's future. We have lived through very difficult times, and we don't want our children to live this kind of life.

He spoke of widespread support for Bil'in's nonviolent approach.

> [People from] many movements have come, first to look and after that to participate, because this is the correct way. This is the correct way that should have been [followed] long ago—for making peace. We are working to make peace together. All kinds. There are [Palestinian] movements, and there's ISM—internationals—movements from Israel; for example, Gush Shalom, the Anarchists, many movements. We've done this together.
>
> I think that most of the Israeli people don't know what's happening. The land thefts are as if by the Mafia. Contractors and companies steal the land and afterwards the army comes to protect the people who live around there, to protect the security of the State of Israel. I think it's protecting the thieves; what it comes to is that it's protecting the thieves.

To Haitham Khatib, too, I put my question about how he would respond to those who say, "We've done nonviolent things for many years, and the Israelis only respond with violence, so we too have the right to respond with violence." Like Iyad Burnat, he counselled persistence in the way of nonviolence.

> I say to them, "We started on this way, and we will continue." The soldiers have arrested twenty-two of the young men who were in demonstrations. They have wounded more than 250 youths and women, internationals, and Israelis. A bullet leaving the gun can wound anyone in the demonstration. It cannot tell whether it is an Israeli or a Palestinian or an international, or whether it is a woman or a child. For a long time we have suffered, but we believe in this way, and we will continue. Whatever they do to us, we will continue—again and again and again, until we arrive. With God's help, we will arrive in the end and we'll make the peace that we are hoping to make.

"We've sat with the soldiers," said Khatib, "and spoken with them. And they said, 'We don't know much about this. We have orders to guard, to protect the security here.' That's what they say. I'm speaking about my village: they stole more than half of the land of my village. That is, eventually we'll be out of land. Where will we go in the end? We are now in jail. We're exactly in jail. That's it." He, too, described the late-night visit by soldiers in their hummer, which Ido Khenin had alluded to earlier.

First they brought their hummer here and lit the headlights on the jeep; they were bothering us with this light, not letting us sleep and not turning out the jeep's light; they did this on purpose. [We talked about] all the things about the theft of land, and they don't know anything [about this], so we told them. And they're working for their government, protecting the mafia which we spoke about, and in the end they're the patsies [he used the Hebrew term *frierim*]. The soldiers earn little money for their guard duty, and the companies take billions. They began to be convinced; they almost began to be convinced, and they said "You're right, this is your land."

After we spoke, they moved the lights, and we felt they'd changed a little. This is because of the way we have chosen. We feel that we are progressing. We're progressing; eventually we will arrive. This small example gave us hope; every small thing we do gives us hope for progressing a little.

Haitham Khatib also told me that religious Jews from the nearby settlement of Kiryat Sefer have told him that they were not aware that their settlement was built on confiscated land. "We told them that these apartments were built without permits and the land was stolen. And these religious people told us, 'We didn't know about this, and if we had known, we wouldn't be living here.'"

The previous night, while I sat with Nasir Samara and the others around the campfire in front of the Centre for Joint Struggle after the Gush Shalom demonstration, there had been a steady stream of Israeli supporters coming and going, mainly "regulars" dropping by for a visit like neighbours or relatives from out of town. One less-typical visitor was a young religious woman from a settlement a few kilometres down the road, who had hitched a ride to Bil'in with another Israeli out of curiosity. Joining the group around the campfire, she had tea and—after being assured that it was kosher—a cookie. She had heard about Bil'in and had come to see for herself. Wajee Burnat assured her that she and her friends would be welcome to visit inside the village. He and she, observant Muslim and Orthodox Jew, agreed that "a human being is not born to be closed; he has to think [Wajee Burnat]," and "G-d wants us to think what's good for us, what's correct. What G-d wants, that's what we want to do [settler woman]." As she left, they wished each other a good week, and she promised to return with more people—"It's most important that here will be even more people." I'm told that she's far from the only settler neighbour who has come to see for themselves, some even becoming friends and supporters (like the driver that helped haul building materials for the Centre for Joint Struggle).

Wajee Burnat told me of his life-long commitment to nonviolence. "What do I gain if I do violence?" he asked. "I lose more and they lose more, so in the end, both of us lose."

> So I decided to be this way, without violence, without any [weapon]. I never got it into my head that the occupation will come to my house some time with a bouquet of flowers and tell me "good morning," and so on. This too, it's no surprise for me. And I never have been and never will be violent. I don't believe in violence. Violence just brings violence and hatred, it doesn't bring peace. And the "big ones" never think about peace, never. Peace comes from the private people [i.e., private citizens as opposed to politicians].

A Friday Demonstration

My second visit to Bil'in was a couple of weeks later (January 13, 2006). I wanted to participate personally in one of the weekly Friday demonstrations. Although that demonstration was a small one and relatively uneventful, this excerpt from an email message from Zalman Amit gives a taste of the larger demo of the following Friday.[17]

> People were shouting slogans, waving flags and singing in Arabic, Hebrew and even in Spanish. All along the sides of the road villagers were lined up offering drinks of water, *pitot*, cookies or what have you. After a while one could begin to see "the fence" on the horizon with a thick and solid row of soldiers and Police Border Patrol lining it. Throughout all this I was trying to keep my place in the human flow and at the same time take photographs. Changing films on the go in the middle of a thick crowd is not simple but I managed. Anticipating the end of the march near the fence I stepped out of the line to take a photo when a stun grenade exploded not more than two feet from my legs. For the next 30 minutes, aside from the loud ringing in my ears I could not hear a thing. The tear gas canisters were next and thick clouds of gas were enveloping us rather quickly. I was ready with my onion and handkerchief and altogether, in the open air, at least initially, it wasn't too bad, as long as you did not rub your eyes which only made things a lot worse.
> As usual the army was ready, loads of soldiers and Border Patrolmen appeared on the horizon and charged the crowd, some

with broad smiles on their faces, others perhaps a bit ashamed of what they were doing. To my right I saw some demonstrators carrying the unconscious body of one demonstrator, the first serious injury. To my left I saw two soldiers dragging a young woman on the rocky ground and I shuddered to think what the skin on her back will look like later in the day. Being right in the middle of the crowd, I can safely say that at that point there were absolutely no provocations that required the action the soldiers took or any other action for that matter. The gas, the stun grenades and the physical action of the soldiers were totally unwarranted. ...

To my surprise, dozens of young demonstrators grabbed stones and instead of throwing them at the soldiers they simply began to bang the stones against the fence. They did so in an African rhythm and it was actually an interesting, loud and quick beat. The soldiers were obviously surprised and clearly didn't know how to react. The demonstrators took advantage of this and about 100 of them managed to cross the fence line at a spot where the fence was not yet completed and this way they succeeded in raising their flags and slogans on the stolen land where a few weeks before the people of Bil'in managed, in one night, to erect the "Bil'in Outpost" [i.e., the Centre for Joint Struggle].

The Second International Conference in Bil'in

I was quite excited when I heard that an international conference on nonviolent joint struggle was being planned for February (2006) in Bil'in—and equally disappointed that I wouldn't be able to attend, since I would be returning to Canada before it was scheduled to take place. Having missed the February 2006 conference, though, I jumped all the more eagerly at the chance to participate when I heard that a second such conference was to be held in April 2007. The Second Annual Conference on Nonviolent Popular Joint Struggle followed more than two years of weekly nonviolent demonstrations and the production of two feature-length films about Bil'in's struggle to reclaim its land.[18] The conference addressed a broad range of subjects, including impediments to and prospects for Palestinian economic development, media issues, and of course Bil'in's story. Israel's flagrant violations of international law and its apparent impunity to international censure were cited by several speakers, as well as by conference participants speaking from the floor—condemning the international community for their inaction on these issues while imposing a destructive "siege" and boycott on the

Palestinian people for the "crime" of electing a Hamas-led government, and urging them to end this policy and to come out in support of the new National Unity Government, a move that might well have prevented its subsequent dissolution in renewed Hamas–Fatah hostilities. Mohammad Nazzal of the Bil'in Popular Committee reported on a conference held the previous month in Bil'in to establish "a movement against the occupation to be supported by the nations of the world," with emphasis on encouragement of international BDS (boycott, divestment, and sanctions) and other expressions of solidarity. Welcoming conference participants on behalf of the Bil'in Popular Committee, Basil Mansur reviewed the thirty-year history of land confiscations affecting Bil'in, stressing that although "the main justification for the Israelis for building the wall is to protect the settlers, in Bil'in it was meant for establishing new settlements, because there were no settlements here that they can claim that they are building a wall to protect them." He also presented an overview of the current resistance, emphasizing the role of Israeli and international supporters.

Further details about the April 2007 conference and the ongoing weekly demonstrations (with photos and video clips, including of several of the conference talks) can be accessed at www.bilin-village.org. Here, though, I want to share a few of the many comments by conference speakers and others on two recurring themes—ones that I feel are most relevant to this book: the joint nonviolent struggle (with ongoing Israeli participation forming an important part of the campaign) and the idea of the "reproduction" or "generalization" of the "Bil'in model" beyond the borders of this small village.

The joint nonviolent struggle was praised by European Parliament Vice President Louisa Morgantini from Italy, Irish Nobel Laureate Mairead Corrigan Maguire, representatives of French peace organizations (including Jewish Women for Peace, an affiliate of European Jews for a Just Peace, and representatives of Juifs Francais pour la Paix), the Green Alliance (Denmark), the international secretary of the Union of Metal Workers in Italy—and representatives of other organizations, as well as individuals such as a representative of Palestinian President Abbas, and many local activists. Stephane Hessel, a retired French diplomat, spoke from the perspective of one who had been part of the WWII French resistance, praising the "courageous Palestinians, courageous Israelis—our comrades and friends." French parliamentarian Jean-Claude Lefort (whose subject was the double standard that penalizes the occupied with siege and boycott while never imposing upon Israel the condition that it should recognize the borders of 1967) also emphasized the joint nature of the ongoing struggle: "Week after week, they meet here and they demonstrate peacefully—Palestinians and Israelis—for rejection of these tremendous injustices and to keep the land alive and green." Dr Mustafa Barghouthi, minister of communication in the newly formed (and short-lived) National Unity Government[19] and an outspoken advocate of nonviolent civil resistance to the occupation, thanked "the people of Bil'in for their wonderful performance in presenting to the whole Palestinian people and the world an example of a resilient, militant, nonviolent form of struggle that the Israelis could not break over a period of two years' time" and called for the generalization of this form of resistance.

> This is something that gives us a lot of courage; this is something that gives us a lot of hope. And I think it is not a secret if I tell you that we are determined to create many similar spots to Bil'in all over the occupied territories, and I believe if we reach a point of creating seventy spots like this all over the occupied territories— where every Friday people get out and march peacefully, in a nonviolent manner against the occupation and against apartheid—I think this occupation cannot continue. And if we do that, we can make a difference.

Referring to other locations where nonviolent campaigns had begun (Jenin, Hebron "and most especially the people in the south of Bethlehem, who have been demonstrating also every week during the last two months, copying the very good example of Bil'in"), Barghouthi declared, "In my opinion, this is the biggest success of Bil'in, that it could replicate itself in many other places, so that this would become a massive, popular, nonviolent struggle all over the occupied territories."

Like Barghouthi, Eyad Morrar—veteran of the successful nonviolent struggle by the village of Budrus to change the route of the wall in 2003/04[20]—stressed the primary importance of involving the Palestinian masses in the struggle.

> How do we encourage the Palestinian women to be a part of the resistance? How could every political organization be a part of this? We have to set the example of this. Then solidarity people will be proud to say that they came, and then we will succeed in defeating

the wall just like we did in Budrus and the rest of the locations. This will generalize the concept and the experience.

Importantly, Palestinian speakers repeatedly affirmed, as had Mohammed Khatib, that this kind of joint work should not be considered to be "normalization." One of these was Feryal Abu-Heikal, headmistress of the Kortoba School in Tel Rumeida, Hebron, who spoke of being accused of normalization when she worked with some Israelis on a project to help local women.

> If I am misunderstood, I can't do the work that I've done here. I therefore hope that we will be able to convey to the people that these Israelis that we're working with are not people who come in order to beautify the face of the occupation, but that they come in order to strengthen the people who are here "on the ground" so they won't lose their homes.

Bil'in and Beyond

Elana Wesley—an Israeli woman with decades of activist experience, whom I interviewed in her Jaffa home shortly after my January 2006 visits to Bil'in—spoke about obstacles to effective/responsible use of Palestinian power, in Bil'in and elsewhere.

> The problem is, even if you do theoretically have that power, you have to be free enough of your daily worries and cares—like how to get through the day and stay alive and have food for your family and not have more heartbreak than you can take, and not have to look forward to trying to get through checkpoints and just the uncertainty of the day—in order to be able to use the resources that theoretically are at your disposal.

On the other hand, one might argue that Bil'in and other foci of vigorous and creative nonviolence are the visible tip of a veritable iceberg of such use of power, ranging from *sumud* to direct nonviolent confrontation aimed at the wall and other manifestations of the occupation. Said Wesley:

> Take a look at what Bil'in has managed to come up with, considering what their daily lives are like: every week, a new, original idea for the weekly protest that they've already been doing for, what? thirty weeks or more [at the time of our January 2006 interview]. Their

latest idea [the Centre for Joint Struggle] was extra special, and who knows what they'll come up with next week? And they get arrested, the same guys who make up these ideas, and they get manhandled and beaten, at least the regular shtick of anybody that gets arrested. So they know what they're in for. They are utilizing to a maximum, I think, the possibilities that they do have.

Yonatan Shapira (Combatants for Peace, interviewed in Castlegar, BC, Canada, 7 July 2007), praised the organizers and activists in Bil'in as the "vanguard of the nonviolent activism."

> In my opinion, the people who are organizing the activism in Bil'in, doing the weekly demonstrations there and all the rest of the activism—of course the Palestinians (these are their lands), and the Anarchists, and the Coalition against the Wall, and all of these groups—they are the vanguard of the nonviolent activism today in Palestine and Israel. And I personally admire these guys who go there every week. And also people from our group go there and participate with them. I think this is one of the most important things and also one of the most important symbols that will be remembered in the future as places that were the centre of the struggle. This is a common struggle. It's no longer Israelis struggling alone and Palestinians alone. Now we are struggling together as a bloc.

Mikado (Michel Warschawski of the Alternative Information Center) had been slated to speak at the April 2007 conference, but was called away and was unable to attend. I caught up with him in Jerusalem on 25 April. He too had high praise for the Bil'in struggle. A year earlier he had written, *inter alia*, that—

> [T]he struggle in Bil'in has become the most emblematic symbol of resistance against the Israeli Occupation, and the Wall in particular. One can identify several reasons for this. First, unlike in many other mobilizations against the Wall and land confiscations, the struggle in Bil'in has been continuous: for more than a year and a half, hundreds of activists have been permanently mobilized in a variety of protest actions, with at least one demonstration per week. Second, it has been a consistently inventive, non-violent mobilization, able to unmask the Israeli military's provocative violence, and its permanent lies aimed at justifying the use of violence against nonviolent demonstrators. Third, the struggle in Bil'in has been

real joint Palestinian-Israeli struggle, built on trust, mutual respect and true cooperation on the ground. Fourth, it opened a space to a longstanding international involvement and the continuous active presence of dozens of activists coming from all over the world." (Warschawski 2006)

Now (April 2007) he had this to say:

> In my opinion there is a huge amount to learn from Bil'in. We've accumulated two years of experience of what's successful, what's less good. It is an example of the younger generation truly directing the struggle. It's not the veteran politicians; this is really another generation, and so it should be. It is the role of our generation to step aside a bit—not to leave the struggle, but to let the generation that's directing the struggle direct it in its own way: things that I am perhaps incapable of understanding, including the nonviolence.

He expressed a bemused admiration for this "new generation of activists" who are willing to place themselves in a totally passive state (e.g., tied to a tree) and to take a beating without fighting back.

> I'm willing to take a beating—I've done so more than once in my life—when I'm free to fight back. And then that gives you a kind of courage; gives me courage. But to be [passive] like this and to take a beating requires a courage that I don't have. I don't have it, or I don't have the training for this. I don't know. I assume it's both. I'm not accustomed to this. I don't have this culture. So I'm full of admiration, and I don't under any circumstances come to judge that this is good or not good compared to [another] way. In general it's a way that succeeds and it answers the political needs and, I would say, culture of the new generation of activists. And they need to direct their struggle in their way. The role of what's left of the old generation is to be there, to give them a shoulder to lean on, to give them advice *if* they ask for advice and *if* we have something to say, which the majority don't.

On a more sombre note Warschawski commented that, whereas on the one hand, Bil'in had become symbolic of "(A) resistance, (B) the popular resistance, and (C) the joint, popular, Israeli-Palestinian-plus-international struggle," on the other, "we're not advancing."

> A symbol isn't sufficient for advancement. If I compare today with a year ago, we're in the same situation, with just one exception: then,

exactly a year ago, the struggle was to prevent the erection of the barrier; now the barrier exists. So this has turned into a protest. We go to Bil'in, once with this gimmick, once with another gimmick, but all-in-all march the kilometre-and-a-half to the barrier, yell at the soldiers, the younger ones take a beating, inhale teargas, and go home.

"If this is not part of some strategy or other that's supposed to lead to something else ...," he warned, there is a distinct possibility that this campaign might degenerate "into a cult where we go every Friday—I, regretfully, not every Friday."

More optimistic voices were heard, though, especially at the April 2007 conference, where a typical comment was that of Nobel laureate Mairead Corrigan Maguire: "I fully support and encourage you to continue in peaceful organizing to protest and resist and continue to build your nonviolent grassroots people's movement, which will be the cornerstone of a new Palestine/Israel and a new Middle East." Later in her talk, Maguire declared:

> This movement of nonviolent people united in working for justice and equality and irrespective of nationality or religion, unarmed and willing to take risks protecting civilians in danger is one of the most helpful and inspiring and hopeful movements of our time. I myself am very hopeful for the future of the Middle East. From where do I get my hope? From the people of this place and those Israeli and Palestinian peace activists who believe passionately that, given justice and equality for all its citizens, peace and human security is possible in this holy land. I take hope, too, from the courage of the young Israeli reservists who, following their conscience, have refused military duty in the territories.

And, said Israeli activist Rachel Benshitrit, "It's a very lovely thing that out of the difficulty and this dark period and the bad things that are coming out, this is one of the good things that have sprouted."

> Bil'in is a spot where there is a very special struggle, in that it has already continued for a long time with persistence and all that. And yes, this can bring some optimism that perhaps, yes, we will be able to break through this separation and to say that it *is* possible to talk to each other, and it *is* possible to live with one another. And we hope there will be—indeed there are [similar struggles being carried out]—in other places along the barrier.

When I quoted what Mikado had said about not having moved forward in the year following the exciting conference the previous year, Benshitrit countered:

> First of all, just the fact that this has continued until now is already an achievement. Let's say it this way: the normal expectation was that nothing would succeed and the barrier would be built in any case, and the lands would be stolen in any case, and we would not succeed in anything. But there were successes in the High Court of Justice—where I think that some of the considerations that influenced the court's decisions [had to do with] the public struggle that is going on. And despite that it's pretty few people and still hasn't captured the [wide] distribution and the resonance that Mikado would wish—the very fact that Israelis and Palestinians proved that they were able to cooperate in such a lovely way is also an effect in itself. And this has aroused a lot of mutual trust between people. Let's put it this way: Maybe there hasn't yet been enough weight to make the [necessary] change to break through the wall, but it still can gather momentum, and I hope that it has the potential and that in time that is what will happen. Because it hasn't yet died down. It's still alive.
>
> In Bil'in this really continued. I've heard of other places; South of Jerusalem, near Bethlehem, all sorts of villages are beginning to organize for themselves joint actions and things like that. I hope that this maybe will actually break through the wall of silencing [caused by] this deception that the authorities and media are trying to sell us that the security situation and all that [are the reason for the wall].

A Bit of History

The small West Bank agricultural village of Bil'in, situated 4 km east of the Green Line, lost 1,980 of its original 4,085-dunam (approximately 1,000-acre) landholdings to state confiscation between 1982 and 1991. Then, in early 2005, it was subjected to the expropriation of an additional 260 dunam—expressly for construction of the wall—states a November 7, 2009 dispatch from Iyad Burnat on behalf of the Friends of Freedom and Justice–Bil'in.[21] This, despite the summer 2004 advisory opinion of the ICJ regarding the illegality of the so-called "separation barrier" mentioned earlier in this chapter. Burnat's dispatch continues, giving a brief history of the village's resistance to the wall and noting that:

Bil'in has become a symbol for popular resistance. Almost five years later, Bil'in continues to have weekly Friday protests. Bil'in has held annual conferences on popular resistance since 2006, providing a forum for activists, intellectuals, and leaders to discuss strategies for the non-violent struggle against the Occupation.

Since March 2005, when Bil'in's weekly nonviolent demonstrations began, seventy-five Bil'in residents have been arrested for participating in and/or organizing the protests, hundreds have been injured, some severely, and one beloved organizer, Bassem Abu Rahmeh, was shot in the chest with a high-velocity tear gas canister during the April 17, 2009 demonstration and subsequently died in hospital.[22]

In the fall of 2005 Bil'in augmented its grassroots resistance by initiating legal proceedings in the Israeli Supreme Court (sitting as the High Court of Justice), with the support of a legal team headed by Tel Aviv attorney Michael Sfard. Finally, two years later, on September 4, 2007, the High Court handed down a ruling "that due to illegal construction in part of Modi'in Illit, unfinished housing could not be completed and that the route of the Wall be moved several hundred meters west, returning 25% of Bil'in's lands to the village." (Figures and quotes in the preceding four paragraphs are from Burnat's dispatch of November 7, 2009, unless otherwise noted.)

The Israeli Supreme Court Rules in Bil'in's Favour—But . . .

Despite the partial nature of the September 4 ruling—and the fact that the very next day the High Court rejected Bil'in's petition to halt construction on the remainder of its confiscated land—Mohammed Khatib reiterated Bil'in's determination to persist in its nonviolent resistance despite such disappointments.

> [W]hen the Israeli army started bulldozing our land and uprooting olive trees to build the wall, we went to our fields to protest. We learned from other West Bank villages that nonviolently resisted the wall, and we studied Gandhi, King and Mandela. We developed creative activities for our weekly protests. . . . [held] international conferences on nonviolent resistance . . . . Our achievements are due to our persistence, the worldwide media attention we attracted, and the support we gained from committed Israeli activists. ...

"We will continue to challenge these expanding settlements because they threaten the futures of Bil'in and the Palestinian people," Khatib concluded, "And we will put our experience at the service of other communities struggling against the wall and settlements. From Bil'in, we call on Israeli and international activists to join us as we renew our joint struggle for freedom" (Khatib 2007).

Postscript (Summer/Fall 2009)

In June 2009, Mohammed Khatib made a cross-country speaking tour of Canada, culminating in appearances before the Quebec Superior Court in Montreal. Travelling with Khatib was Emily Schaeffer, a member of Michael Sfard's legal team, which has been representing Bil'in pro bono in its court challenges to construction of the wall and settlement housing on its land. In July of 2008 Sfard's law firm had launched a suit on Bil'in's behalf in that court, against Green Park and Green Mount, two of the construction companies building the neighbourhood of Matityahu East in the settlement of Modi'in Ilit on land confiscated from Bil'in. These companies are registered in the Canadian province of Quebec, even though their actual Canadian presence seems to be limited primarily to a postal address and a single director in Montreal. Thus, on June 23, 2009, Justice Louis-Paul Cullen heard arguments regarding the question of Canadian jurisdiction in this case. Had Justice Cullen decided to allow the suit to go ahead, this would have marked the first time that Canada's War Crimes and Crimes Against Humanity Act of 2000—which, like the fourth Geneva Convention, prohibits the transfer of parts of the civilian population of an occupying power into territory it occupies—had been employed in a civil case.[23] Unfortunately, though, on September 18, he dismissed the suit, maintaining that the case should be heard by the Israeli High Court of Justice. On October 19, Mark Arnold of Sfard's legal team entered an appeal of the dismissal, on the grounds (among others) that the defendants "are registered and domiciled in Quebec," and that the Israeli High Court hears only petitions against the State of Israel and, in any case, "had repeatedly refused to rule on questions involving the legality of the settlements. . ." (Izenberg 2009a).

When I spoke to Mohammed Khatib on 26 August 2009 to get an update on Bil'in's situation, there had still not been an acceptable proposal from the state in response to the Israeli High Court's September 2007 decision,[24] even though, as he pointed out, the High Court had called for the return to Bil'in of just a part of the village's expropriated land ("700 of the 1,700 dunams, or 170 hectares, that were set to be located on the 'Israeli side' of the barrier in the original proposal," according to a 26 April 2009 *Jerusalem Post* article [Izenberg 2009]).

Our brief phone interview took place just a few days after Khatib's release on bail after two weeks' imprisonment. He had been detained during a recent spate of attacks on Bil'in by the Israeli military and the arrest of a score of activists, fourteen of whom were still in custody at the time of our interview.[25]

> They said that I am one of the organizers and that I was organizing the demonstrations, and they tried to say that I am telling the kids and the others to break the law and to throw stones, and also they said that I throw stones. But we brought our passports and we showed that we were in New Caledonia at the time.

The stone-throwing charge was dropped, and when I spoke with him, Khatib was awaiting trial for the remaining charges, one condition of his bail being that he was not allowed to be in Bil'in on Fridays, the day of the weekly nonviolent demonstrations at the wall. Nonetheless, he spoke optimistically of prospects for the future of the struggle against the wall and the occupation in general.

> We hope that this struggle will succeed. We are sure that we will succeed to change the route of the wall. It will take time to fight this apartheid system and this occupation system that is so strong, but we hope that by this struggle—by this nonviolent struggle and joint struggle—that we can achieve our goal.

Adding, "We are satisfied that this struggle is also not only in Bil'in. It starts to spread and. . . to be in other villages and other places." This is the reason, said Khatib, that Israel has stepped up the intensity of its efforts to suppress such activity: "they want to stop it before it becomes more powerful and more strong in other places."

Finally, when I asked him what Israelis and internationals could do to help the people of Bil'in, besides participating in demonstrations and other acts of nonviolent resistance side-by-side with them, he stated emphatically that the "most powerful thing" they could do would be to participate in "the BDS campaign of boycott, divestment, and sanctions against Israel."

In response to the arrests of nonviolent organizers and demonstrators in Bil'in and other villages and increased violence by the Israeli forces at demonstrations in recent months, Mohammed Khatib wrote (in "Palestine's Peaceful Struggle," published on the website of the prestigious U.S. news magazine, *The Nation*, on 11 September 2009 (Khatib 2009):

> Why has the Israeli government decided now to increase the suppression of demonstrations and to break the spirit of protest leaders? Maybe because they realize that the nonviolent struggle is spreading, that more and more villages have created popular committees that are organizing demonstrations. Perhaps the crackdown is a result of their concern and the growing international movement for the boycott of companies and businessmen ... who are involved in Israel's land grab. Or maybe they fear that the new American government could learn through our demonstrations that Israel's wall is a means to annex land for the growing settlements, and that nonviolent Palestinian protests are being brutally suppressed.

The conclusion of Khatib's *Nation* article provides a suitable closing for this chapter, as well. Says he:

> Israel's actions suggest that it is intimidated by people struggling for their rights in a nonviolent manner. The Israeli government seems to believe that Palestinians who struggle while partnering with Israeli activists endanger Israel's occupation and that tearing down human walls is a dangerous act. Perhaps what the state of Israel fears most of all is the hope that people can live together based on justice and equality for all.

Conclusion

An early idea for the title of this book was *From Beit Sahour to Bil'in*—as these two struggles seemed, in Jeff Halper's words, to "book end" the development of nonviolent joint struggle as recounted by the activists I interviewed. Although I ended up choosing (after an informal poll of friends and colleagues) a more general title, the sense of this development has remained in the background of my thoughts and undoubtedly has played a role in shaping the book. This chapter follows a trajectory from solidarity to joint struggle and from Beit Sahour to Bil'in (via the wall).

Elias Rishmawi describes the Beit Sahour tax strike in which he played an important part, as did solidarity with Israeli partners sought out early in this struggle. Although a boycott of Israeli taxes was called for by the Unified National Leadership of the Intifada in February of 1988, ultimately Beit Sahour was alone in persisting in its tax resistance, and did so despite months of virtual siege and years of arrests, confiscation of property, and general harassment. Only after the return to the occupied territories of an unsupportive PLO leadership in 1994 was the tax strike fully discontinued.

Highlights of those years, according to Rishmawi, included the Beit Sahourians' success in exposing "the whole system of occupation ... of tax collection, tax enforcement, and other things related to the subject before the international community"; their use of the Israeli court system to challenge the actions of the occupation authorities; and "proving that we could do it with nonviolence." An important aspect of the Beit Sahour tax resisters' nonviolent strategy was the relationship they cultivated with a number of mainly modern-Orthodox Jews they had met through their Israeli lawyer, with "the idea ... not only to increase the level of understanding and fight against stereotypes, but as well, together to fight against occupation" (Ghassan Andoni). Activities of this group became a major source of support for the strikers, and ranged from publicizing their situation inside Israel to solidarity visits, panel discussions, and what Judith Green referred to as "a certain amount of civil disobedience and some slightly provocative behaviour" and other activities, all of which "could be considered political ...," but with "a human side." The dialogue relationship persisted until 2000, when it succumbed to the pressures of the Al-Aqsa Intifada period.

Palestinian resistance to the wall began as early as September 2002, in the village of Jayyous. The four-month-long peace camp in Mas'ha the following summer was an early instance of nonviolent resistance to the wall incorporating Israeli and international activists. Since then, nonviolent protests have spread to myriad villages, many of them welcoming Israelis and/or internationals—and the wall has become a convenient focal point for joint actions. Information about the wall and the struggle against it must frequently bypass indifferent mainstream media, and reaches the public largely via such means as the Internet, activist-made films (e.g., *Bil'in Habibti*), reports by returning Israeli and international activists, and guided tours along its route by both Palestinian and Israeli organizations.

In addition to demonstrations against the wall (in some places weekly over a period of years, in others daily for months), there have been legal appeals, both in Israel and abroad, with the advisory ruling by the International Court of Justice in the Hague (July 9, 2004)—that the wall contravenes international law and must be dismantled—deemed a major victory. Other successes have included Palestinian university students and faculty of Abu Dis University holding classes and cultural events in a tent in the path of the wall—thereby avoiding being cut off from their playing field by its construction; villagers, especially women, in large numbers blocking bulldozers and preventing their work in Budrus—leading to a major rerouting of the wall; and Palestinians in Beit Suriq and their Jewish-Israeli neighbours in Mivasseret Tzion jointly petitioning the Israeli Supreme Court to stop the construction of the wall between them—and succeeding in "pushing back the wall ... in the whole of the West Bank."

During my three visits to Bil'in—two in January 2006 (for a joint demonstration with Gush Shalom and for a Friday demonstration at the separation barrier) and one in April 2007 (for the Second Annual Conference on Nonviolent Popular Joint Struggle)—villagers spoke of their commitment to nonviolently regaining the nearly sixty percent of their farmland that had been expropriated to build the wall and an Israeli settlement "neighbourhood." Israelis I met in Bil'in were also devoted to this goal. At the conference many speakers—Palestinians, Israelis, and internationals alike—affirmed their support for the ongoing participation of Israelis in the weekly demonstrations in Bil'in and lauded the spread of this form of resistance throughout the occupied territories—as did those I interviewed about it afterwards.

After four years of weekly demonstrations and other acts of non-violent resistance (such as the overnight construction of the Palestinian "outpost," the Centre for Joint Struggle, on confiscated Bil'in land) and despite an Israeli Supreme Court ruling in Bil'in's favour in September 2007, as of November 2009 a satisfactory rerouting plan acceptable to the court has yet to be offered, while the Israeli forces have stepped up the intensity of their repressive actions, leading to the death of one demonstrator in April and increased injuries, both at the continuing demonstrations and in the course of recent incursions into the village. A positive decision re jurisdiction in a lawsuit against two Quebec-registered construction companies active on Bil'in land, heard in June 2009 in a Canadian court, would have constituted "an important legal precedent about corporate accountability for violations of international law," stated Emily Schaeffer, one of Bil'in's Israeli lawyers.[26] The September 18 dismissal of this suit is being appealed.

In Part III, Looking Forward, we shall begin by reviewing some of the many challenges faced by nonviolent activists in both societies and some ways of confronting these in order to build a more effective movement (Chapter 6).

NOTES

1 Wanting to hear for myself what a Hamas person would say about the nonviolent joint struggle in Bil'in, I was pleased when Husam Jubran was able to arrange an interview for me with Nur ed-Din Dannoun, the Hamas representative in Bethlehem. With Jubran interpreting (23 April 2007), Dannoun acknowledged the effectiveness of this approach "in certain circumstances." Though he, not surprisingly, maintained that armed struggle must not be abandoned, he said, in response to my question as to his views regarding the joint nonviolent struggle against the wall in Bil'in and elsewhere: "This thing is part of the whole resistance. There are different ways to resist the occupation; part of it is the peaceful and nonviolent resistance, and also the armed struggle. And one way or another, peaceful or nonviolent resistance is effective, especially against the wall; and I see that even the Israelis or the occupation [authorities] try to silence such activities because they know it's very powerful and effective."

2 Looking back, I would even suggest that the relationship between the Israelis who became the core for Rapprochement-Jerusalem and the Palestinians who went on to found PCR (the Palestinian Center for Rapprochement between People in Beit Sahour) could be characterized as being an early instance of joint struggle as defined by Mikado. Even if we apply, in addition to Mikado's, Muhammad Jaradat's criterion—wherein the latter presupposes a significant degree of participants' involvement in their own respective societies—I think a case can be made for defining the work of the Israeli members of Rapprochement-Jerusalem (or of a significant proportion of them) as joint struggle rather than simply solidarity.

3 Although the joint nonviolent struggle in Bil'in is the longest-lasting (four years at time of writing) and most well-publicized of such campaigns, it must be

noted that the anti-wall struggle began in Jayous in 2002, and the first ongoing joint effort took place in Mas'ha in the summer of 2003. As well, the campaign in Bil'in is informed by the earlier experience of Budrus and Biddu, and that even now, in villages such as el-Khader and Ni'ilin, analogous campaigns are developing. Coverage of various ongoing campaigns can often be found on YouTube, as well as links from www.bilin-village.org, www.palsolidarity.org, www.awalls.org, and other sites listed in the glossary.

4 Beginning in November 1981, the Israeli occupation authorities adopted the misleading name, Civil Administration, to denote the military apparatus by which the occupied territories were governed—by a combination of Jordanian law and an increasingly large body of military orders. According to the Jerusalem Media and Communication Center, over 2,300 such orders (over 1,300 in the West Bank, over 1,000 in Gaza) were issued between 1967 and 1992. *Special Reports from Palestine – Israeli Military Orders in the Occupied Palestinian West Bank: 1967-1992* (JMCC, 241pp, 2nd edition, 1995)—accessed 20 February 2009 at www.jmcc.org/research/special/military.html.

5 The First Intifada was directed by an indigenous underground leadership referred to as the Unified National Leadership of the Intifada. These anonymous leaders periodically issued leaflets (typically distributed by young boys with their faces masked) calling on the population to undertake specific actions in resistance to the occupation, to commemorate specific events, etc. Various estimates place the non-violent content of the actions called for in these leaflets between 85% and 95%.

6 When the Israeli Supreme Court is called upon to rule on the legality of decisions or actions of State authorities—as a court of first instance (as opposed to an appellate court vis a vis decisions of lower courts)—it is referred to as sitting as the High Court of Justice (often referred to by the Hebrew acronym, *bagatz*).

7 For example, see www.awalls.org, "About AATW" for a brief timeline from Mas'ha to Bil'in. More recently, the village of Ni'ilin has also been conducting weekly nonviolent demonstrations against the wall with AATW participation.

8 Palestinian organizations that sponsor tours that include the wall and visits and/or home stays with Palestinian families include Holy Land Trust and the Alternative Tourism Group.

9 Pollak himself (hit in the head by a teargas canister fired at him in Bil'in in April of 2005) was among the several Israeli demonstrators to have been seriously injured subsequent to our 2003 interview.

10 The full text of the ruling can be found at www.icj-cij.org. To access a PDF in French and English of the Advisory Opinion of 9 July 2004 on "Legal Consequences of the Construction of a Wall in the Occupied Palestinian Territory," search for "Israeli" and scroll down the list that appears.

11 The Fourth Bil'in International Conference on Popular Nonviolent Resistance was held April 22–24, 2009, dedicated to the name of Bassem Abu Rahmeh, the Bil'in activist killed by a high-velocity teargas canister fired from close range just one week before. See www.bilin-village.org for extensive coverage of this and past conferences. The trend towards generalization of the struggle is reflected in the note on the website, regarding the 2008 conference, which states: "This year, a day of the conference was dedicated to visit other towns and villages who are also facing the expansion of colonization and occupation on a daily basis. In addition, Hani Amer (from Mas'ha village) and Feryal Abu Haikal (from Tel

Rumeida) were also present at the conference to explain the situation in their respective town and village."

12 Hanukah marks the rededication of the Jewish temple in Jerusalem after a military victory against the forces of the Greek-backed occupier, Antiochus IV of Syria, in 165 BCE. The leaders of the revolt, the Maccabees, were said to have come from the biblical-era town of Modi'in, somewhere in that area.

13 Since my recording of the torch-lighting dedications was not totally intelligible, I found the text in an account of that day at http://desertpeace.wordpress.com/2006/01/page/3/.

14 Writing in *Ha'aretz* in December 2005, Akiva Eldar states in part that: "Two weeks ago it was first published here that adjacent to Bil'in, in the Jewish settlement of Matityahu East, a new neighborhood of Upper Mod'in, hundreds of apartments are going up without a permit. The lawyer for the inhabitants of Bil'in, attorney Michael Sfard, sent the state prosecutor's office a copy of a letter that Gilad Rogel, the lawyer for the Upper Mod'in local council, wrote to the council's engineer. Rogel warned that entrepreneurs are building 'entire buildings without a permit, and all this with your full knowledge and with planning and legal irresponsibility that I cannot find words to describe.' In a report that he sent to the interior ministry, the council's internal comptroller, Shmuel Heisler, wrote that the construction in the new project was being carried out contrary to the approved urban construction plan and deviates from it 'extensively.' The justice ministry has confirmed that 'apparently illegal construction is underway in the jurisdiction of the locale Upper Mod'in...'" (Akiva Eldar, "There's a system for turning Palestinian property into Israel's state land," 27 December 2005, currently accessible at http://www.haaretz.com/hasen/pages/ShArt.jhtml?itemNo=662729)

15 Since construction of new settlements was prohibited under the provisions of the Oslo Accords, "neighbourhoods" of existing settlements—often a kilometre or more from the rest of the settlement—have sprung up all over the West Bank.

16 Although stones do sometimes get thrown at demonstrations in Bil'in, the organizers ask the young men of the village to delay such activity until after the end of the "official" nonviolent demonstration. In fact, on at least one occasion when stone-throwing took place during the main demonstration, it was found that the perpetrators were agents provocateurs from the "special" *mista'aravim* units of the Israeli forces.

17 Account used with permission of its author; see also the account of the January 20 demonstration in Shulman 2007, pp. 202–07. Israeli-born Zalman Amit is professor emeritus at the Center for Studies in Behavioural Neurobiology in Concordia University, Montreal and now divides his time between Canada and Israel. His writings have appeared on Counterpunch.org, *inter alia*.

18 One of these, *Bil'in Habibti* by activist-film-maker Shai Carmeli-Pollak (brother of Yonatan Pollak), was awarded a first prize for best documentary at the 2006 Jerusalem Film Festival (available from www.claudiusfilms.com).

19 The Palestinian National Unity Government, for which Dr Barghouthi expressed such high hopes, was formed on 17 March, 2007 and came to an untimely end just three months later, on June 15.

20 Of particular interest are these articles on Budrus's nonviolent struggle on the Electronic Intifada: Audeh 2007, excerpted in the Wall section of this chapter,

and "Peacefully Confronting the Wall in Budrus" by Iltezam Morrar, 16 July 2004. http://electronicintifada.net/v2/article2924.shtml

21 "Support Bil'in's Struggle," accessible at http://www.bilin-ffj.org/index.php?option= com_content&task=view&id=212 &Itemid=1

22 "An Israeli attorney and a Bil'in resident both suffered permanent brain damage from rubber-coated steel bullets shot from close range. Another Palestinian lost sight in one eye" (Khatib 2007). IMEMC and Ma'an news Internet dispatches from 17 and 22 April, 2009 reported that Bil'in sustained its first demonstration-related death when 30-year-old Bassem Abu Rahmeh died after being shot in the chest with a high-velocity tear-gas canister while pleading with soldiers to stop shooting because children were present. Film footage taken by fellow-demonstrators shows Abu Rahmeh appealing to the soldiers to allow for removal of several goats from harm's way, and then calling the soldiers' attention to what he thought was an injured Israeli demonstrator, just before being shot.

23 "Palestinians take construction firms to court in Quebec: They're building condos on our land, villagers say," by Sue Montgomery, *The [Montreal] Gazette*, June 21, 2009, accessed September 13, 2009 at www.montrealgazette.com/news/Palestinians +take+construction+firms+court+Quebec/1718011/story.html.

24 "To date [November 7, 2009], the high court ruling has not been implemented and settlement construction continues" (Burnat 2009).

25 Night raids and arrests targeting protesters and the leadership of Bil'in's Popular Committee began on 23 June 2009, concurrently with the preliminary hearings of Bil'in's Canadian lawsuit—and some of the 27 Bil'in residents arrested (16 of whom remain in custody as of 7 November) report having been questioned about the Canadian lawsuit during their interrogation. After overwhelming international support and outcry the raids appear to have ended (the last took place on 30 September 2009) and the village continues to hold weekly demonstrations (based on information from Burnat 2009).

26 "Bil'in village continues battle against Israeli settlements in Quebec courts," June 27, 2009, accessed July 14, 2009 at www.tadamon.ca/post/3967#more-3967.

Part III

—

Looking Forward

6

TOWARDS A MORE EFFECTIVE NONVIOLENT MOVEMENT

The disasters and failures of the use of violence are becoming clear in most parts of the world. We know what extreme violence can do, and we know how relatively impotent resistance violence can be and how counterproductive. And that really must not be tolerated. So people are now beginning to look—is there something else? And whereas the Palestinian people have had great experiences and applications of nonviolent struggle, now people are beginning to raise the question: How can we develop strategies to make our resistance most effective?

Gene Sharp (Nonviolence theoretician, addressing the Celebrating Nonviolent Resistance conference, Bethlehem, December 2005)

The Israeli military activity in the land makes our work harder. If they stop the military activity in the occupied territories, I think more than ninety-eight percent of the Palestinian population are agreeing with us. The ball is now in the hand of the Israelis and the USA. If they want to bring peace to this area, they can bring it immediately. But they don't want. They don't want.

Wael Salame (Palestinian member of Combatants for Peace)

In spite of all the effort we are making, I do confess that we are still not doing sufficient work to convey our message to the world, and we should be stronger in conveying that message.

Jamal Dar'awi (Popular Committee against Settlements—Bethlehem area)

Combating Marginalization of the Nonviolent Movement

With all the will and the abundance of creative ideas displayed by so many activists, why has the nonviolent resistance movement not been more successful in bringing about major changes in the existing situation? Is the widely perceived marginalization of nonviolence a major barrier to success? Walid Salem, you may recall, has contrasted the First Intifada—a popular, participatory struggle carried out principally by nonviolent means—with the Al-Aqsa Intifada, which he described as characterized by a return to elitism and the escalation of violence, one of the results of which has been the marginalization of Palestinian nonviolence. When asked in early 2007 whether he felt nonviolence had become any less marginal, given the escalating actions in Bil'in and elsewhere in recent months, Salem reiterated his position that Palestinian nonviolence would remain a marginal phenomenon until such time as "a strategy of a sustainable and comprehensive non-violence campaign" was adopted (email correspondence, January 27, 2007). By contrast, nonviolence trainer Husam Jubran (writing in mid-February of 2007, during widespread interfactional fighting in Palestine) expressed a more optimistic view, stating that "If the internal fighting had not erupted, I believe by now we could have seen strong and widespread nonviolent activities."

> To be clear here, I am not trying to put blame on internal fighting for this setback. I think the main reason is the inability of civil society to address the internal fighting. The lack of involvement from the civil society and other political factions and their failure to use nonviolent techniques to stop the fighting would be, in my opinion, a major factor in roles and perceptions of nonviolence. Therefore, I think there is a need to have a debate about the role of civil society instead of blaming the political factions. (Email correspondence February 15, 2007)

Whatever the causes postulated or remedies suggested, though, it was clear—in 2007 as in 2003 and 2005/6—that a sense of marginalization was a common perception amongst both Palestinian and Israeli nonviolent activists and their supporters. The December 2005 Celebrating Nonviolent Resistance conference, in itself, signalled a significant advance in the struggle to rectify this situation—at least as far as the Palestinian community was concerned. This high-profile conference, which brought together grassroots activists and nonviolence theorists and educators—academic and otherwise—from the Palestinian territories and elsewhere (including inside Israel), as well as a number of local political figures, provided a rich variety of opportunities for sharing and for learning from one another's experience and thinking.

In his presentation to the conference plenary, one activist-turned-theorist/educator (and now government minister), Riad Malki of Panorama's Ramallah office, began his outline of specific suggestions for increasing the effectiveness of the Palestinian nonviolent movement by addressing the issue of marginalization, stressing the need for nonviolence to "be adopted as a holistic approach to resistance" and to "become the mainstream development within the Palestinian resistance movement."

First, nonviolence should be adopted as a holistic approach to resistance. It will produce negative results if only one group adopts nonviolent methods while other groups—at the same time, under the same circumstances, and in the same location—adopt violent methods of resistance. We cannot combine [both approaches], because combining them weakens our ability to protect ourselves and to achieve the objectives that we would like to achieve. This nonviolent action should not represent marginalized thinking by any active group. Instead, it should represent the mainstream thinking. Any marginalization of nonviolent groups within the society weakens such groups and encourages the enemy to adopt stronger measures. We are still a nascent movement of nonviolence (despite the fact that in 1936 we saw a nonviolent action of six months of [general] strike, and we have seen it in the First Intifada), and right now we are witnessing a real development of a nonviolent movement in Palestine, and this has to be strengthened, this has to be empowered, and this has to become the mainstream development within the Palestinian resistance movement.

We have to encourage the participation of all strata of society in this activity. They have to adopt this and see it as a mechanism for liberation and for resistance, and also as a means of empowerment to achieve their own objectives. It should take the enemy by surprise by adopting new, original methods, unexpected methods to limit the superiority of the enemy and to neutralize its military advantages. Whoever has witnessed the creativity of the Palestinian nonviolent resistance movement in the last two, three, four months has to acknowledge the creativity of the thinking in adopting new methods that surprised not only the Israeli soldiers who stood facing such a situation and not knowing what to do, but that also surprised most of the observers who were watching the development of the nonviolent movement in Palestine.

And finally, it [i.e., the Palestinian resistance movement] should adopt nonviolence as strategy and not as a seasonal reaction to Israeli actions. If we want to build a nonviolent Palestinian movement here, we cannot use nonviolence only as an activity of two hours a week. It should not be only an activity on Friday afternoon, at the end of which we go back to our daily lives as if nothing really has happened. I think it is really very important to allow this concept, this thinking, to penetrate the life of each of us and to become our own way of resisting the occupation, but also our own way of maintaining our survival in the Palestinian territory until, of course, ending the occupation and liberation.

Marginalization was one of the issues about which Ghassan Andoni (in his role as my principal Palestinian partner in designing this book project) was particularly interested in hearing our interviewees' responses. Were their organizations influential in and supported by their communities, or were they as marginal as, for instance, depicted above? And what about their reception by the "other" community? This line of questioning elicited a variety of responses from both Palestinians and Israelis, but on the whole, a sense of endorsement by the mainstream was rare. Support by specific segments of the community (or communities) was more commonly reported; for example, the comment by Hillel Schenker (Israeli co-managing editor of the *Palestine-Israel Journal*) that despite PIJ's inability to pay contributors, "almost everybody we approach—central people in their fields on the Israeli and Palestinian sides—as long as they have the time, they usually agree."

When it was a question of broadly based support, however, few of those who believed their organization or their approach (i.e., nonviolent resistance to the occupation) to be perceived in a positive light by their community were Israeli. In fact, almost every one of the Israelis who spoke of enjoying community support was referring to the Palestinian and not the Israeli public (e.g., both Rela Mazali of New Profile and Peretz Kidron of Yesh Gvul referred to the fact that their work with refuseniks is well-received by Palestinians, although both organizations feel quite marginal within Israeli society). This is perhaps to be expected, since the political views of most of the Israeli organizations that participate in acts of nonviolent resistance are well to the left of the mainstream. (Israeli) Combatants for Peace activist Elik Elhanan expanded on this point.

> As I see it, the huge problem is that today the discourse in Israel is extremely limited and extremely narrow. People's opinions are very cowardly; nobody has the guts to say anything. The Zionist left has left the street, and they base everything they know and everything they project and all of their ideas on the same methods that everybody else uses; that is, public opinion polls and media consultants and so on.

Making it clear that this particular criticism didn't apply to "people like [Gush Shalom spokesman and co-editor of *The Other Israel*] Adam Keller" and others of this ilk, Elhanan expressed regret at what he perceived as the limited influence of this "marginal left" on the broader society.

> With all the great respect I have for those people—and this is where I place myself—I don't really think that we can create the critical mass to change things. I *do* think we can create the critical mass to show Shalom Achshav (Peace Now) and Meretz [the major left-Zionist party at the time] that maybe talking nonsense and not saying anything for six years is *not* the way to promote peace, but really that being active clearly and loudly in the street is the way to do peace. Meretz and Shalom Achshav can fill Rabin Square,[1] but for the time being they're afraid, and they won't say anything. You go to demonstrations and you see this absurd situation, where we stand, and they stand apart so they won't be associated.

This brought to mind something another Israeli "marginal leftist," Shabtai Levi, had told me at the Bil'in conference earlier that same week: "I think that if there were even closer cooperation and there weren't this factionalism, perhaps it would be possible to do something. Perhaps. I think that the critical problem of the [Israeli] left is to unify the lines."

The Movement's Impact on Israeli Society

Of the forty-odd Israelis I interviewed, Reuven Kaminer (Peace Now/Hadash) was among the very few who felt that—despite the influence of the settler movement on the Likud and, through it, on the Israeli government—great strides had been made towards persuading the Israeli public of the validity of the Palestinian cause. Said Kaminer:

> The amazing thing is that on certain key issues, the Israeli body politic does support the idea of a Palestinian state, they support the idea of negotiations, etc., etc. The important developments are some of the declarations, like the very important statement by Avraham Burg, who is a key personality.[2] And I'd like to add also that it seems that one of the cumulative strengths and achievements of the Israeli peace movement is that an awful lot of people in the middle who haven't taken a position are beginning to understand how horrible the occupation is. I was speaking recently in the

States, and there's always people who will argue with you. Many of the pro-Israeli people would start off by saying, "I'm against the occupation as much as you are, but ..., " etc. I think that the message is sort of getting through. It doesn't get through to the hard core of Israeli support—the settler sympathizers, who can't even conceive of making that sentence—but I would say that an awful lot of pro-Israelis who are trying to defend the Israeli position understand that they have to dissociate themselves from what's going on in the territories.

Gila Svirsky (Coalition of Women for Peace/Bat Shalom) is another Israeli activist who expressed a sense that these organizations and related ones "are being effective, not just on the margins."

This whole country, now, agrees that the occupation must end. They haven't heard that from Sharon or from Shamir. They've heard it from other elements, such as the Coalition, who have posed the alternative to the current occupation; the alternative is a two-state solution. So now, seventy or eighty percent of Israel feels a two-state solution is inevitable, and two-thirds of Israelis believe that a two-state solution is the way to go. So I think we have had tremendous success over the years, because we see that public opinion has swelled on the issue of a two-state solution and on the issue of Jerusalem as a shared capital (although they talk about dividing Jerusalem and I talk about sharing Jerusalem).

Most of the Israeli activists I spoke to, however, reported feeling marginalized in their own society, not so much because they espoused nonviolence, but because their political stance was not accepted by most other Israelis. As anarchist Yonatan Pollak put it:

I think in Israeli society there is virtually no support for what we're doing. But that's to be expected, since I oppose everything at the basis of the Israeli experience. On the Palestinian side, I think there's more support; I wouldn't say it's complete. I don't intend to sell some utopic reality, that everything's great, and the Palestinians are willing to accept a radical change in the power structure. We have a lot of work [to do] on both sides. But I think there's more willingness on the Palestinian side, probably because they're the suffering side.

Indeed, many Israeli interviewees found themselves in the same position as Devorah Brous, who said of her organization, Bustan—which works primarily with the disenfranchised Bedouin in the many "unrecognized villages" inside Israel[3]—that despite efforts "to expand the discourse, expand the circle of activists that are involved, [it is] pretty much the same ten, fifteen that are always out there getting arrested or the same couple of hundred that are going to every demonstration and every action."

Humanitarian and Educational Activities More Widely Accepted—In Both Societies

Human rights groups were regarded somewhat more positively by the Israeli public—and establishment—than were outright activist organizations (Rabbis for Human Rights [RHR], for example, has received official recognition for its work: the 1993 Speaker of the Knesset's Prize for contributions to Israeli society), and RHR's Rabbi Arik Ascherman cited a 2003 Israeli study of public acceptance for the human rights organizations working in the occupied territories that reflected a "generally positive view" of these groups, despite the perception that they were "only interested in Palestinians."[4] Said Ascherman, "The most popular were Physicians for Human Rights. They had sixty-five or seventy-five percent recognition, almost all of it positive," whereas the more activism-oriented RHR was "one of the less popular organizations," with only about fifty-one percent recognition, less than two-thirds of which (thirty-two percent of the sample population) was positive.

Rabbi Ascherman (in an interview held in October 2003) told me that in the preceding year, Israelis had become increasingly reluctant to participate in most activities in the occupied territories, that they were "feeling a little bit hopeless and therefore being more choosey in what activities they're going to get involved in." Participation in the West Bank olive harvest (which has become an annual tradition with growing support since it's tentative beginnings in 2000), however, was an exception: "The olive harvest is one of the most successful in terms of people's willingness to come and do that—and the media gets interested. I guess it's because they see it's something very concrete. We're helping people harvest, and it's very concrete and practical."

Amongst Palestinian organizations, too, those boasting a high level of community support were often groups perceived to be helping people directly, quite aside from any specifically political or "nonviolent" content to their activities or educational philosophy. Not surprisingly, Project Hope (which works with traumatized children) and the Union of Palestinian Medical Relief Committees (which does medical work) reported wholehearted acceptance within Palestinian society. Similarly, organizations with an educational and/or service component were generally well-supported.

Ibrahim Issa (Hope Flowers School—El-Khader, West Bank) was among those reporting "strong grassroots support." Hope Flowers, a peace-oriented Muslim elementary school, also offers programs where adults from the community can learn nonviolence-related skills including Compassionate Listening and has, for the past few years, "been moving towards community-based organization."

> Most of the people who send their children here are [doing so] because they choose to provide their children with peace education. But also we have very strong grassroots support in our community. For example, we have a Palestinian volunteer program. Also, we have an international volunteer program to promote intercultural understanding. All this emphasizes the position of the Hope Flowers in the local community.

On the other hand, when speaking about local acceptance for the nonviolent movement itself, Issa was less sanguine, stating that, "A lot of Palestinians think nonviolence is some kind of collaboration with Israel."

Rev. Naim Ateek, Palestinian Anglican liberation theologian and author, described the programs delivered by his Sabeel Center as being "very well-received, well-attended" by their mainly "grassroots" participants, despite a degree of resistance from the church hierarchy.

> The church hierarchy has always stood for nonviolence, the ending of the occupation nonviolently, and they've always been against the violence; but sometimes we feel that they don't really perceive Sabeel very positively, for their own reasons. But others do. Sabeel is not affiliated with any one denomination, so we work ecumenically, and trying to reach the grass roots is really our interest—to work with them, from all the different churches, that's really where we are, and thank God that's really happening continuously. The reception of the programs by the people, whether in the Galilee or in the Jerusalem area, has been very, very encouraging.

Holy Land Trust (HLT), another service-oriented organization, places particular stress on providing education about and training in nonviolence for all sectors of the public, Muslims and Christians from a wide range of political backgrounds. HLT's director, Sami Awad, expressed his conviction that "the majority of Palestinians understand what nonviolence is"—that they are aware that it is more than simply not being violent.

> The two terms we use most are popular resistance and political defiance—as concepts of what nonviolence is. So when you talk to people about popular resistance, they understand it and they support it and they're for it and they want to be active in it and so on. It's incredible the interest people have in learning about what nonviolence is. We actually get more demand for work than we can offer: trainings, workshops, and so on. People are really looking for something. And that's really positive, because, you know, people living under occupation for so long—thirty-six years now [at the time of interview in September 2003], and especially the last three years of Intifada—they're not losing hope. The worst thing that can happen to a people is to lose hope. You know, if we do anything with our trainings and workshops or activities, it is just to keep that light of hope lit in people, just to keep it burning, just to keep that fire burning. That's the service we can provide for people here. Because once you lose hope, that's it. You have no reason to live, to look forward to tomorrow; and that can be a disaster for everyone, for Palestinians and Israelis.

Increased Acceptance of Nonviolence within Palestinian Society

Even as early as 2003, activists from a variety of Palestinian organizations told me they felt that the level of acceptance for the concept of nonviolent resistance was growing, a trend I found to be even more pronounced in 2005/6. Tequ'a mayor S'leiman Abu Muferreh described support for nonviolence in his village as "not that huge, but it's increasing, I think, every day, for different reasons." Said he, "The main thing in mind to the Palestinians is not the violence itself, the main thing in their mind is to have their rights, to get free. But how? Sure it should be, and every rational person should choose, the less costly, the less bloody, the less violent." Palestine Polytechnic College student leader T.M. also felt supported in his advocacy for nonviolence—by "maybe fifty percent of the people." "There are many people who believe in nonviolence," he told me, and even those who aren't convinced of the effectiveness of nonviolent action, "find it a good way to express their opinion and to express their anger and to protest, because this is the only way to have if you are not organized or militarized, or if you find that military action is not useful in this conflict. So they find it is the only way, in most cases." And in Mas'ha—where a summer 2003 tent camp incorporating Israeli and international supporters in the village's nonviolent struggle against the wall was an early instance of the form of joint action seen in Bil'in and elsewhere today on a much larger scale—organizer Nazih Shalabi spoke of having "lots of support, and this is growing from one day to the next."

But even for Palestinian organizations, acceptance by the community at large was often hard-won and/or partial. Ghassan Andoni was the executive director of the Palestinian Center for Rapprochement (PCR) in Beit Sahour at the time of our interview (September 2003). He contrasted post-2000 attitudes towards PCR's work—especially regarding its leadership role in the International Solidarity Movement (ISM)—with the situation during the First Intifada, when the entire town had participated in the protracted tax strike against the occupation authorities.

> When we started the work during the 1987 Intifada, Rapprochement's experience was different because the resistance was actually conducted by the community. It wasn't the work of a [particular] group. And that's why we moved with the full community towards our goal. During this [current] crisis, I should admit that at the beginning, we were swimming against the tide. The tide was "fight!"—militancy— and at the beginning, Palestinians in general were questioning: "Why are you doing this [nonviolence]? Why are you inviting those internationals here? Who are they?" The change [since the First Intifada] is actually the deep level of frustration; a new, angry generation taking over. That's why the whole idea of peace and nonviolence was really very much questioned, and there was a high level of patriotism and heroic attitudes glorifying fighting. People had become more frustrated and lost faith and actually lost trust because of the way Oslo went, and so on.
>
> But with time, and because ISM decided to complement [the existing resistance movement] and integrate [with it] and decided to do everything by direct nonviolent action—it wasn't protesting or waving flags; it was actually trying to dismantle the ability of the occupier to occupy; removing roadblocks, blocking tanks with your body, stopping the demolition of homes (which is a collective

punishment)—when Palestinians saw this happening, they started realizing that those people have guts. They are not motivated by money, nor is this a personal agenda; those people are willing to take risks, and willingness to take risks is the first step towards being recognized.

During the Oslo period there were so many groups and organizations—fund-oriented, getting money, [and] doing nothing but media stunts in order to get more money—and people realized that "Somebody's taking advantage of my suffering. Somebody's putting more money in his pocket and pretending that it's helping me," which was not acceptable. The minute they realized that ISM is ready to take risks, we started seeing a change in the popular perception that, "Well, what you do is nice, but that's for you, it's not for me. You can do it because many of your activists are blond with green eyes, and Israelis will not shoot them. But if I do it, they will shoot me in the head and I will be dead." With time we started seeing more appreciation, but not yet a level of participation.

When ISM bled, with the killing of Rachel [Corrie], the Palestinian community—in Gaza *and* the West Bank—recognized ISM as part of the resistance movement. In this area, unfortunately, you need to bleed to be recognized. People trust fighters, they don't trust politicians. And from that time on, we started seeing not only sympathy but a wider level of participation, which broadened the community base of the work of ISM.

Israeli Violence and Palestinian Despair

Ironically but understandably, for many mainstream Palestinians and Israelis, the very fact that they are, indeed, "bleeding" is one of the factors fuelling the sentiment that "nonviolence can't work." Hanan Ashrawi touched on this major obstacle faced by those who strive for a nonviolent solution to the conflict when she characterized Israeli violence against the Palestinian populace, on the one hand, and the reciprocal "targeting of innocents" by Palestinian extremists, on the other, as a "mutual exchange of pain and violence [that] has claimed the lives of many and, at the same time has, for a long time, robbed the political and the nonviolent—and the popular—movement of its audience and its momentum, its ability to move."

When a local grocer told Hebron journalist and nonviolent activist Hisham Sharabati that people in his neighbourhood were joining in the boycott of Israeli products, Sharabati found this encouraging.

Backing for a fully nonviolent approach to resistance, however, was less widespread.

> Many people believe that nonviolent resistance does not contradict armed struggle. Many people believe that both can go together. There are many Palestinians who believe in completely nonviolent resistance, but they are not a high percentage in our community, to tell the truth. Part of how the people actually determine what is good and what is bad (It's not determined only by your morals and what you read in books, and not only the political beliefs) sometimes is the methods the other side uses. The people speak about the Israeli occupation—how they assassinate people, continue confiscating land, and all this stuff—and it's pushing them to a bad situation. Sometimes people cannot control themselves anymore. The woman who committed the suicide bombing two days ago [October 4, 2003] had her brother and her cousin, who was her fiancé, assassinated by the Israelis. She was a woman with a promising future; she was training to be a lawyer, good looking, and things like that. What pushes a person like this to put an end to her own life? When you push the people to the bottom, you don't expect reasonable responses. I don't believe in unreasonable responses, but in Arabic there is a saying, "Patience has limits."

Fu'ad Giacaman of the Arab Educational Institute (AEI) spoke of AEI's recent involvement in a Bethlehem-area Right to Education Campaign with "the support of local institutions, and the Ministry of Education, and the PNA Governate, and very, very supportive comments and solidarity from abroad," but he too commented on the deleterious effect of Israeli violence on Palestinians' commitment to nonviolence.

> As you know, Palestinians are believers, Christians and Muslims, and a true believer does believe in peace and justice and human values. But any believer who suffers on a daily basis, who is always being exposed to so many repressive actions and to violence, and to reaction to the violence—to demolition of houses, assassinations, killings, imprisonment—all these affect his or her belief. So their support depends on political circumstances. We see the people sometimes very supportive—with thousands, or with hundreds—and sometimes very few, because belief and faith need actions, which either encourage them or sometimes disrupt them. The more we see on the ground actions from both sides coming to recognize [each other's] rights, you see the people in favour of peace and nonviolence.

But so many times people are frustrated and hopeless, and so they keep away from nonviolence because sometimes they cannot endure it as human beings.

Suheil Salman, an activist with the Palestinian Agricultural Relief Committee (PARC) in Tulkarm reiterated a theme that I heard over and over.

> In Tulkarm and in all of Palestine, Palestinians in general support nonviolence. But who brings violence to this area are those responsible for the Israeli government. You see the violence came from the Israeli side. When the ceasefire was established, who began the violence again? They started continuous killing of people with bombs, with tanks, by destroying houses. What is the difference between one person who goes and explodes himself in a bus or in a building or in a restaurant or something—what's the difference between that and an Israeli airplane or Apache helicopter that came and destroyed a building or a car in the street? Why is one terrorism and the other one self-defence?

ISM's Huwaida Arraf (who is a Palestinian-American citizen of Israel) had some sobering comments regarding the pervasive desperation of the Palestinian public as reflected in widespread support for violent forms of resistance.

> All the statistics that come out that say seventy to eighty percent of the Palestinian people support the suicide bombing lead you to believe that the Palestinian community is a very violent community, that they love killing and they teach kids this and glorify it. And it's so opposite of the truth, but what [Palestinians] have been led to accept is that we have no other way of fighting. People truly believe that those soldiers and the Israeli government have no respect for Palestinian human life, want them gone, and will continue to kill them off and will demolish our homes and kill our children. "So what can we do to survive? We're going to attack in return." That's why you don't see the big voice against the strategy of suicide bombing. If you show them a way that can work, then you will have support.
> [Palestinians] don't believe that without [suicide bombings] things would get any better, and sadly, they have indications. There have been months that have gone by without a Palestinian attack on Israel or Israelis anywhere, not even soldiers, but there were

killings of Palestinians and home demolitions. Last year, almost two months went by when no Israeli was attacked, again, not even a soldier. In that time—six weeks it actually was—seventy-two Palestinians were killed. And so people turn around and say "We stop, we don't attack them, and they continue to do it. We don't have tanks and we don't have the explosives that they've put in buildings. We don't have the tanks that they fire at our schools. We don't have the helicopters and the missiles that they shoot down at our cities." And people are willing to turn themselves into bombs. It's a horrible phenomenon, but it's one that's easy to understand.

The Conservatism of Palestinian Society

The conservatism of much of Palestinian society is another factor slowing its acceptance of nonviolence. On the one hand, Nafez Assaily (Library on Wheels for Nonviolence and Peace, Hebron and East Jerusalem) described a growing openness to nonviolence: "In the eighties, we were accused of being CIA agents or Jordanian agents, because nonviolence was very difficult. Now, when we speak about nonviolence, you will find a lot of intellectuals, a lot of people, who claim nonviolence." On the other hand, however, when I asked him how much support there was for nonviolence in the local community, he replied, "Well, it depends."

> Whenever we have a lecture here, many people come. They say, "Okay, your talk changed something in our life, your talk ta-ta-ta-ta-ta-ta," but whenever we have an action, nobody appears. At least we showed them something, and when they are ready, they have [something they can] do. We, the Palestinians, are very slow to absorb ideas. It takes a long time.

Nayef Hashlamoun, founder of the al-Watan Center for Civic Education, Conflict Resolution and Nonviolence in Hebron, also cited the conservative politics and cultural milieu of his city, Hebron, as an impediment to his work, along with negative stereotypes about nonviolence. But trust in him and his organization has allowed them to make headway, even if slowly.

> Most of the people believe in violence against the occupation, because the occupation came by force and they think it must leave

by force. Some of them misunderstand what we do [i.e., education about nonviolence] and think that this is part of cooperation with the occupation. And some of them asked us, "You are talking about peace with Israelis, and look what we have: we have massacres, we have curfews, we have confiscated land or demolished housing..." Of course, it's not easy, especially if they are a victim's family. We say to them that a human is a human, and not all Israelis are the same. And also we say to them that all religions are asking for peace; not all Jews mean Zionism, and not all Muslims mean terrorists or something like that. And we try to quote suras from the Qur'an, from the Prophet Mohammed's speech. It's not easy, but because they trust us, it becomes easier for them to understand us.

For us in the Hebron area it is more difficult than in other places, for many reasons. First of all, because Hebron area is not open like Bethlehem or Jerusalem or Ramallah. We have very few international people here. This is one reason. Another reason is that most of the people here are Muslims. They have a negative stereotype of the West. They think that everything that comes form the West is bad—because colonialism comes from the West, and also because in Hebron we had bad luck during the occupation.

Referring to the 400-plus settlers in Hebron as "criminals from Brooklyn" who "don't want to understand or to live with the people," Hashlamoun pointed out that, "Before 1929 there were many Jewish families."

They were living in the same buildings with the Muslims. They were Palestinians, Palestinian Jews. And they were in business together—stores for a Jew and a Muslim together. And they were like brothers in the city. For that reason, the relatives from those families come to visit the Hebron Municipality and Palestinian families, and they say, "We refuse to come back and to live with the settlers; we are not settlers, and we do not agree with what the settlers are doing in Hebron. The Palestinians are our people; we feel that we are friends and brothers, and we lived in peace, and we can live with them in peace, of course."

But the settlers, as I told you, they don't want peace with the people. There are other reasons that our people feel that peace education or nonviolence is not valid to deal with these settlers: from time to time they shoot at people, they beat people. It doesn't matter: men, women, elderly people, children. Also the mentality: the head of the Hebronite is too strong [i.e., obstinate]. All of these points look like rocks in our way [i.e., obstacles] to nonviolent actions or education or activities.

[257]

Despite this, many Hebronites—sometimes hundreds at a time—do join in al-Watan Center programs, although Israeli security harassment of participants is sometimes a problem. Says Hashlamoun, "We help and assist the victims' families and try to support them. We try to stand behind them. For that, also, they know us and love what we do, and they give us their emotions and good wishes and love and support to us. If we have a peace march or any action, they come."

Wi'am director Zoughbi Zoughbi's comments struck me as reflecting a particularly realistic view of Palestinian ambivalence towards nonviolence.

> As you say between two Israelis there are three opinions, between three Palestinians there are five opinions. We have support, but some people say, "This won't work"; some people say, "You are crazy, you are wasting your time." I believe that people at this moment are hopeless. The Palestinians are hitting bottom. There should be a jump-start, a way to have hope, maybe to inject hope in people. I don't know how. Because you need to see progress, and what we see is a lot of [retrogression]. The Israeli right-wing government is doing a lot of illegal things—building settlements, building a wall—so people say nonviolence won't work. The question is, would violence work?

Of his own organization, Zoughbi said, "We don't have an answer, but we have possibilities, and this land is a land of potentials, so therefore there is some support."

> But we are not really talking about nonviolence all the time. We don't preach, we act. Others who join us, join us. So, we are not a centre of nonviolence; we are not a centre of big names. We try with humble steps to do humble actions with love. That doesn't mean solving the bigger problem. We try to work with others; we try to do things together. The situation is difficult, as you know. This is the least to say. I don't know what to say. You plant the seeds. Things grow sooner or later.

Marginalization Greater in Israel
In Israel the nonviolent movement seems to be even more thoroughly marginalized than its Palestinian sister movement, although, as mentioned above, for different reasons. "We don't even get support within our own

families. Even our own kids don't support us," complained Israel Naor, when I asked him how his activities and those of his wife, Dorothy, were received. And Dorothy Naor—although she finds the people (mainly abroad) to whom she sends voluminous quantities of email about the situation largely supportive—lamented that, "Israel and I sometimes feel we live on a different planet from the rest of society, because of our experiences, the things that we see, the things that we know."

> You know, when a soldier tells you at a checkpoint that his humanitarianism consists of the fact that he doesn't beat the Palestinians, *we* hear it and other people don't; and you go and try to tell them, and they don't believe you. So I've stopped trying to tell people. I've stopped trying to argue with most Israelis I know. I don't have much to talk to them about; it's rather sad. I have one argument that works to a degree, and that is when I tell people, "Israel was supposed to solve the problems for Jews and has turned out to be just the opposite. Not only is it unsafe for Jews here, it's also become a problem for Jews in many places abroad."

Young refusenik Matan Kaminer characterized refusal as still "marginal in Israeli society." The refusenik movement is growing, he said "but we're not a lot."

> We're, say five hundred out of sixty or seventy thousand soldiers on active duty, which is not much.[5] But it's interesting how the way people disagree with us differs from person to person. There are basically three approaches. There're the people who disagree with us ideologically and who think the Palestinians shouldn't have a state and the occupation should continue and that there's nobody to talk to on the other side, and so on. There are the people who disagree with us on political grounds, who say it's an illegitimate move to refuse enlisting and you shouldn't withdraw yourself from the consensus on the Zionist left. There's a third approach, which isn't very well represented in the press, so you don't hear about it much probably in Canada, but it's extremely well represented amongst the people that I meet here, which is, "Why bother?" It's pretty damn easy to get out of the army, to dodge the draft in one way or another. You act crazy, you get a psychiatric discharge. You just don't come, then you sit awhile in jail and they release you. And so on. Declaring your conscientious objection to serving in the military is the hardest way of getting out of the military in Israel.

Lots of people aren't very political and they don't have very strong opinions this way or the other on the conflict, or, even if they do, they find it really, really hard to believe that we, of our own will, make life so hard on ourselves. On the one hand, I think this is an encouraging reaction; on the other hand, I think it's discouraging. It's discouraging because people basically don't see collective action, or political action, or action for change as something that's relevant. People don't understand our state of mind which makes us do something which isn't in our personal interests, but is in the national interest, or in a common interest, or a collective interest. It's really hard for them to understand that we would be doing this. They keep asking, "But, what's in it for you? What's in it for you? I don't get it." That's discouraging, because I think that's a symptom in modern Western society generally, but in Israel specifically, of apathy, of people not believing in the political process. A lot of people just want to get the hell out of here when they grow up, and they don't see this as a place they want to sacrifice for, or anything like that, which, as I say, is discouraging.

Uri Ya'akobi, like Kaminer both a youthful refusenik and a third-generation activist, told me he saw no real support for ideological refusal, whether rooted in leftist sympathy or pacifism.

None. Not really. You know, when I was in jail, most of the soldiers were happy to accept people who said, "I don't want to go to the army." But they would not accept me; they would not accept conscientious objectors. They would not accept people who would say, "I don't want to go to the army because of what the army does." They will accept easily people who say, "Well, I'm lazy; I don't want to go to the army." But they won't accept anyone who says, "I don't want to go to the army because of being a pacifist." So at this point there's not any support for the left wing, basically. You know, a lot of people in Israel don't go to the army, but they still think we should kill all the Arabs. They don't see the connection.

One refusenik reporting a degree of acceptance by his own community was Yesh Gvul activist Peretz Kidron, who estimated support for the refusal movement at between one-fifth and one-fourth or more of the Israeli public (speaking in June 2004).

[This] means, in effect, that we have the support of all the left wing, all the Meretz voters, and possibly even a chunk of the Labour Party.

And that's very interesting, because for instance, [Meretz leader] Yossi Sarid used to attack us bitterly—he and his whole gang. And an interesting thing happened. They've shut up. They don't support refusal, [but] they don't talk about the issue. There was a rally a couple of years ago [in 2002], just after the Courage to Refuse letter was published, and a there was a series of speakers. Yossi Sarid made his speech; no mention of refusal. This one [and that one] made his speech. Finally, up gets Roman Bronfman: he's a Russian, came from the right, he's a Liberal [part of the right-of-centre Likud]. He stood up and he said, "Greetings! We support the refuseniks." And Yossi Sarid went crazy, but he couldn't say a word because the audience was wildly cheering. Yossi Sarid realized that his own rank and file were solidly behind the refuseniks.

The Impact of Suicide Bombings

Despite this apparent increase in support for the refuseniks, however, Kidron bemoaned the marginalized state of the Israeli peace movement as a whole, especially in the wake of the escalation in suicide bombings beginning in early 1996.

> We have a very active peace movement; people are really dedicated and devoted and give their time and take tear gas and beatings and a lot of shit to push ahead with this, but we're still marginal. The settlers [used to be] marginalized. In the mid-nineties, they used to drive around with a sticker, "*YESHA zeh kan!*" (YESHA –acronym for Judea, Samaria, and Gaza—is here!).[6] And we always argued it's not; there is a clear distinction. And there was a lot of resentment among the general public: "A lot of money is going into the settlements, and who the hell needs them, and they're fanatics..." There was a lot of hostility towards these people. And they felt themselves persecuted at that time, which in a sense, they were. They were totally marginalized. And if at that time, for instance, if after the Goldstein massacre Rabin had kept up the courage and moved Levinger and his gang out of Hebron, there would have been public support for it.[7, 8]
>
> Then, along came the Palestinians, bless them, with the suicide bombings; and they proved the point that the settlers made, because then, "*YESHA zeh be'emet kan*" (Judea, Samaria, and Gaza are *really* here). So you have the Palestinians carrying out, in fact, what the settlers had said. And you had a lot of people saying, "Well, if I'm going to be bombed irrespective of whether I live in [the settlement city of] Ariel or Tel Aviv, they obviously want to throw us into the sea."

[The Palestinians] really fell into the trap of playing along the lines of the Israeli propaganda, and the fact was that they couldn't impose the kind of internal discipline and make the kind of selection that Yesh Gvul makes in saying that there's a distinction between the legitimate defence of the State of Israel and the non-legitimate defence of the settlements and the occupation, which would have sent a very clear political message and would have had a whole different impact on Israeli public opinion. As it was, what came through was the combination of brainwashing by Barak and his gang and the right wing, and what the Palestinians were doing in practice, and people said, "Well, it's clear. They don't want to make peace; they want to kill us; they want to throw us into the sea; they want to blow us all up."

Along these lines, Judith Green, an early participant in both Israelis by Choice and Rapprochement-Jerusalem who is no longer involved in grassroots activism, went so far as to suggest that Palestinian nonviolence was totally overshadowed—in the eyes of mainstream Israelis—by the coexisting violence.

I really feel strongly that their nonviolent organizations, activities— whatever they plan—the importance of them is on the Palestinian side and not on the Israeli side. They're not going to impress Israelis with their nonviolent activities, I can tell you. I don't live in a very left-wing world entirely, because of being an Orthodox Jew and having a lot of family connections that aren't left-wing. And it's all a hopeless cause. At the same time that there's so much violence going on and anticipated violence and suspected violence, but on a really life-and-death level, Israelis are not going to be impressed by some nonviolent demonstration or activity that Palestinians are doing into believing that really expresses something essential about the Palestinian resistance. They're just not. There's no point even in thinking in that direction, in my opinion.

Perception of Some Israeli Activism as Subversive

In Jeff Halper's view, by contrast, support for organizations such as ICAHD is so meagre within Israel, not because of anything the Palestinians do or don't do, but because these organizations challenge basic Zionist assumptions, thereby becoming "too threatening to Israelis."

We don't have much support in the Israeli public. As a matter of fact, we have an argument within our own committee if it's even worth while talking to the Israeli public. ICAHD pioneered actually going out into the territories and working with Palestinians and doing these kinds of resistance activities; but still, the people that are willing to come are the really convinced already (which isn't bad, because they need much more to deepen their experience and to know and to be reinforced). But I don't think we've succeeded yet to really reach the masses of the Israeli public. And I think one of the reasons is that this is much too threatening to Israelis. In other words, this isn't just a political policy that you can be for or against; this brings up the whole moral basis of Zionism, this whole issue of an exclusive claim to the land, the issue of our responsibility towards refugees.

[What's needed is] a fundamental restructuring of both the society and the whole land, something like happened in South Africa. It really means a restructuring of land ownership and the fundamental configuration of the entire country. But it means, no less, a fundamental reconstruction of Zionism, or even going beyond Zionism and reconstructing the entire national meaning of Israel. And people are obviously unwilling to do that or are afraid of that or feel threatened. They haven't conceptualized it, but they know "there is something fundamentally wrong, and therefore I'd rather just deny it and keep it out and not know." So we're, in a way, very subversive to Israeli society because through us, they can really see what's going on; and that makes us much more threatening than another peace group where you can go out for an hour and hold up a sign and go home and you don't see very much. (See also Halper 2008)

The relatively marginalized position of nonviolent resistance to the occupation in both Israeli and Palestinian society—albeit to differing degrees and for different reasons—is a major impediment to the movement's effectiveness, as we have seen above. In the remainder of this chapter we will explore other factors that Palestinian and Israeli activists regard as needing to change in order to maximize the success of their work and that of the nonviolent movement as a whole—and some of their ideas for effecting the required changes.

External Impediments to Effective Nonviolent Organizing

Responses to the question "What needs to change in order for your organization or the nonviolent movement to be more effective in pursuing its goals?" made it clear to me that, while it is true that many activists recognized the need for change in a number of basic areas of their own work, behind this recognition of improvements that activists themselves might work towards, there lurked a strong sense of the presence of major, externally imposed, impediments to such change. For instance, many Palestinians pointed to a lack of will on the part of the Israeli authorities. Abdel Hadi Hantash, for example, cited the absence of an "Israeli personality there to say that 'we want to stop the [occupation]; we want to give the Palestinian people their rights, and we want to live together.'" Stated Hantash, "Rabin tried to make a solution with the Palestinian people—and they [i.e., Israeli extremists] killed him. This is the violence. This is the terrorism: from the Israeli side, not the Palestinian side."

Israel's "Colonialist" Characteristics

Israeli journalist and author Amira Hass went even further, stating (as part of her response to a question put to her following her presentation at the April 2007 conference in Bil'in):

> Let me say the Oslo years proved that Israel was not ready to give up its colonialist characteristics. I think that those historians who say that Israel has no colonialist characteristics have to answer why, when the Palestinians presented us with a golden opportunity to achieve a two-state solution, we did the opposite [of what was required]. Why, since '93—actually since '91, in nearly a decade of peace talks—Israel has done its utmost in order to appropriate more and more land, to colonize more and more land, and to settle more and more colonists in the occupied territories. You know, it is often said very patronizingly that Palestinians never miss an opportunity to miss an opportunity for peace. But I think it's the opposite: that we [Israelis] are the ones who missed our opportunity—in '93, '94—to show the world that we can disconnect ourselves from the colonialist past and colonialist characteristics and start to work on a different future, which is not based on ethnic superiority.

Hass added, pointing a finger at the broader Jewish-Israeli public, "I believe that the main reason that this occupation has been allowed to continue unhindered and has spawned a proliferation of new manifestations is that Israeli Jews have an interest—they have benefited from this occupation."

In a way, during the Oslo years—and with the Palestinian leader Yasser Arafat—Israel was given more license than ever to offer Israeli Jews benefits deriving from the occupation and from the colonization of the land. And as long as Israelis do not feel or do not sense that occupation does not pay, they will continue to support occupation. It is difficult to convince them, and (this is a very sorrowful conclusion of my sixteen years of writing) appealing to the conscience and appealing to morals and appealing to sense of history is not enough. Israelis have to feel that occupation does not pay, and so far it has paid.

Difficulties Caused by Travel Restrictions

Palestinian educator Ibrahim Issa condemned the erection of ever-higher barriers (both physical and administrative) to contact between Palestinian and Israeli activists, including the increasing difficulty of obtaining permits to enter Israel. "They say, either for commerce or for medical reasons; but I don't want to go for either of these, I want to go for peace activities. I want to arrange something together with Israelis, and they refuse that." Israeli-imposed impediments to mass nonviolence were emphasized by Huwaida Arraf, as well.

> I was just speaking to someone who was very hopeless [who said]: "I just don't think we can do it. What can we do? They continue killing us, we continue killing them." One thing that people don't recognize when they say, "Oh, there should be this massive Palestinian nonviolent movement" and "Where is the Palestinian Gandhi?": they don't look at the [U.S.] Civil Rights Movement or even the India liberation movement. You had people who were able to get together and to work together. You had people in the Civil Rights Movement who were trained to carry out certain acts. You train, you meet, you strategize. Palestinians can't even do that.
>
> When every element of your life is controlled by the occupation, it's very difficult to try to figure out if you're going to get to the neighbouring village one day, much less to figure out how you're going to get thirty kilometres up the road to meet with your colleagues who are also thinking the way you do and are also working in their own communities. So there are lots of obstacles, big and small, working against a huge, massive, Palestinian nonviolent resistance movement.

Echoing Arraf's words, Hanan Ashrawi pointed out: "You may lead theoretically, but you cannot bring people out into the streets when they're in prison, they're under curfew. So, the thing is, to be able to get people to move massively, you need to be able to have the ability." While acknowledging the dearth of nonviolent leadership in Palestine, Ashrawi emphasized that effective leadership requires both a suitable candidate and the proper conditions: "Leaders are not people who choose themselves, or appoint themselves as leaders. They have to get the credibility, to get the respect, the persuasion—they have to be able to persuade, and you persuade by living, by embodying what you talk about."

Lack of Vision and Leadership from the Palestinian Authority

Sami Awad (Holy Land Trust) cited constraints on the official Palestinian Authority (PA) leadership as a major factor hampering the effectiveness of the Palestinian anti-occupation movement.

> The problem is not with the local population accepting nonviolence or not. It is with the local population not seeing the vision of where we want to go, not seeing the strategy, not seeing where the Palestinian Authority wants to take us. Either due to internal difficulties and problems or to external pressures, we're not seeing this leadership evolve within the Authority. The Authority has reached the point now where there's so much pressure on it that it's really not able to raise its head just to try to look towards the horizon and see. And that's the problem with our leadership. Just like I was saying earlier about the movement itself, the Authority is always reacting: reacting to different statements, reacting to different Israeli attacks and incursions, U.S. vetoes, international policies and campaigns and things like that. It's not leading and initiating or being proactive in these things. There's always this pressure on the authority that's preventing it from that. And that pressure also prevents it from presenting a vision to the Palestinian people.

Problems Caused by the Mainstream Media

Many regarded the media as contributing more to the problem than to its solution. Ibrahim Issa perceived the media on both sides as "stimulating the hatred and stimulating the violence," and Abdel Hadi Hantash called upon the American public to "see what is happening on the ground; to see the situation here and to compare between the violence and nonviolence and who is doing the violence, the Palestinian people or the Israeli government," since they would not get this information from the American media, which he described as "colonized" by the Israeli government.

Speaking on the Media panel at the April 2007 conference on Joint Nonviolent Popular Struggle in Bil'in, Dr Mustafa Barghouthi—at the time, minister of communications in the short-lived Palestinian National Unity Government—spoke about the "domination of the Israeli narrative in the media worldwide."

> It's not just about the kind of information you can get; it is more than that. It's about the kind of questions you will get from the journalists. It's about the whole paradigm that is present in people's heads when they deal with the Palestinian question. Robert Novak, the American journalist, told me recently that fifty percent of American people think that Palestinians are the ones who are occupying Israel. I don't think it's news to you that many people in the West think, when you say the word "Palestinian," that it is a synonym to "terrorist." This is what I'm talking about, this predominance of the wrong narrative.
>
> This is something we have to struggle against—not with just demonstrations, which is great; not just to have activities, which is great—but also we have to get into the media and show exactly what is happening in Palestine. And our goal, our message, our duty is nothing but showing the truth. We do not need to show anything more than the truth. We don't need to make this truth better than it is; we do not need propaganda; we do not need to do any cosmetics to our situation. All we need is to present the truth as it is; because in my opinion, the truth is quite sufficient to make everybody understand and believe that Palestinians must get their rights.

Barghouthi elaborated further during the question-and-answer session, giving examples of how the dominant Israeli narrative had influenced even the Palestinian political forces ("[In] media interviews they started competing with each other [over] who liberated Gaza: was it Fatah who liberated Gaza, or Hamas who liberated Gaza, or was it the Left who liberated Gaza?" when, "as a matter of fact, Gaza was never liberated") and of how it determines the questions asked by journalists.

The truth here gets lost, because Gaza is now under occupation, but a different form—under electronic occupation. The planes scan the sky of Gaza around the clock. Every person who walks in the street, they can see his face. All the borders to Gaza are closed. You cannot get in or out without Israeli permission. At the Rafah crossing there is no Israeli army; there are European observers. The European Union is the one that pays their salaries, but these European observers work for Israel because it is Israel who decides whether the European observers will allow Palestinians to get in or out. The sea is monitored by Israel, and Palestinian fisherman since June cannot go inside the sea and fish properly; that's why the amount of fish they collected since June went down from 850 tonnes a month to fifty. This is the reality. Israel still occupies Gaza, but the narrative that is dominant is that Israel has left Gaza. And people forget Gaza is only five percent of the occupied territories. Also people forget that Israel took out the 8,000 settlers from Gaza, but 8,000 settlers are only a small minority in comparison to 460,000 or 480,000 settlers in the West Bank [i.e., including East Jerusalem]. And people forget that Israel took the settlers out of Gaza for a very simple fact, which was that there is no more water in Gaza that is proper for human consumption. All these facts get hidden, and you keep getting the same question: "Why, after Israel's withdrawal, are there still missiles coming to Israel?" Nobody remembers that the Palestinian forces—all of them—have agreed to stop shooting all these missiles—these pipes—completely if Israel just accepts to stop the violence against Palestinians.

Israeli criticism of the media was similarly abundant. Amira Hass has written about the impact of the occupation in Gaza and the West Bank for many years, often in her capacity as a staff reporter for the Israeli daily *Ha'aretz*. Her primary focus is on the "policy of robbery of freedom of movement [which] has been constant since 1991, Intifada or not, peace talks or not." But, she told the April 2007 Bil'in conference, this "robbery of space and robbery of time of Palestinians" gets little media attention, since "the Palestinian *versions* (not just one version) of armed struggle have monopolized [media attention]," usurping the place of the many other methods of resistance. "And this is a big problem, because the media love blood; and when we don't talk about that..."

Rachel Benshitrit, a participant in demonstrations and other non-violent joint activities in Bil'in, was also critical of media coverage for such events. Although she did have good words for the lone TV feature on the subject of the struggle over land in Bil'in, she complained:

> I know what happens there and I know who commits the violence, who it is that starts all the "measures," as they're called, all the aggression. And then on the news, if I hear anything at all, I hear that two Israeli soldiers were wounded. You don't hear at all about how many demonstrators were hurt, and you don't hear that this is ongoing, and you don't hear at all about all the beauty of this activity, of this struggle; you don't hear what this struggle is about.

On the one occasion Benshitrit could think of when Israeli television had presented an in-depth look at what was going on in Bil'in,[9] however, she noted that it was made clear that, rather than being a matter of security, the routing of the barrier through Bil'in lands was really about the interests of real estate developers, and "that we Israelis feel that we are partners with the Bil'in folks in a struggle against the capitalists/developers and not so much in a nationalist context."

Referring to meagre Israeli coverage of the growing refusenik movement, as compared to "quite satisfactory" coverage by the international and Palestinian media, Matan Kaminer remarked that, "In Israel, not only are we marginalized by the media, but the media has a particular spin on the whole refusal issue." He gave the example of the Pilots' Letter that was much in the news during my 2003 visit.

> That did get a lot of media coverage, but the whole thing was very systematically spun to one angle of the story, which is the legitimacy issue. This is extremely vital to a certain sector of the media and to public opinion, but I think for not so innocent motives. There is this wonderful deep philosophical discussion that keeps coming up about refusal in democratic society, and whether it's legitimate or illegitimate in some situations that we haven't reached yet, and so forth and so on. I think the basic idea behind this is *not* to talk about the occupation, *not* to talk about the reason why we're refusing. They have all sorts of arguments against us. Their favourite one in the recent past is that if refusal on the left is acceptable, then why isn't refusal on the right acceptable? We have answers to that; we're very well versed in all these arguments. But basically, I think the point behind the arguments is not to talk about why we're refusing, it's to get out of talking about the occupation, about why there's terror, and about why we can't get the hell out of the settlements today or tomorrow. As one of the pilots said, "The media kept talking about the legitimacy of our appearing in our pilot's uniforms instead of talking about the legitimacy of bombing civilian populations." Okay, they shouldn't

have used their uniforms, but what the hell does that matter? We have life-and-death issues here on our hands.

Neta Golan, too, was mistrustful of the media, especially as regards the attention she received when living in Haris.

> I know why I got all this publicity was so [the foreign press] could talk about the occupation without being called anti-Semitic. So on the one hand, it gave me a chance to talk about the occupation; on the other hand, it fed into this image that people have of the "good Israeli," the "good Jew." Here are these "good Jews" who want to help the Palestinians, and then there's the violent Palestinians.

Societal and Cultural Constraints on Nonviolent Activism
Elias Rishmawi, a leader of the Beit Sahour tax strike during the First Intifada, spoke sadly of the current situation, when I interviewed him in 2003,[10] touching on a number of impediments to the development of a viable nonviolent movement.

> There are lots of constraints and restrictions on both sides in doing anything, I would say. But in my opinion enough is enough, and at some point a new voice has to start coming up in both societies, in Israel and Palestine. We have to do something to stop this violence from going on and on, to stop this killing, this crazy killing. It seems that there are no social leaderships these days, contrary to '88 and '89, and only the political leaderships on the Israeli and the Palestinian sides are the active power. Something is negatively happening in both societies: nobody is thinking about nonviolence; I don't know why. Perhaps there are people who are thinking about nonviolence; they're just not talking about it. The only thing they're thinking about, especially on the Israeli side, is to make separation. I think that the political machine has influenced us negatively to the point that somebody else is thinking for us, and that's too bad. That's really too bad. Both sides are suffering, they're deeply suffering, and I think the politicians are destroying our lives and destroying the possibilities for living, each in his own way.
>
> In my opinion the nonviolent resistance has not been given a chance in this round of the confrontation, and this is what makes people flee from being part of what's happening. There is no leadership to carry on this slogan and to work for its implementation.

When soldiers of the Israeli army are shooting and Palestinians are retaliating, or vice versa—however each side explains it his way—sometimes you fall into the trap of who's right and who's wrong: Palestinian says, "We are right;" Israeli says, "We are right." But at the end of the day, people are getting killed—no matter who's right and no matter whom you are defending or protecting. At the end of the day, innocent people are killed, and it is not justified. [Whether] you are killed by an F16 or an M16 or a tank or a rocket or whatever it is, it's the same; it's the same.

At the 2005 Celebrating Nonviolent Resistance conference, Mohammed Abu-Nimer devoted the greater part of his plenary address to describing the "gap between what the idea of Islam is and the reality as experienced by Muslims" and the impact of this gap on the nonviolent movement. While acknowledging the malign influence of Zionism, colonialism, imperialism, and globalization on the Muslim world, he directed the attention of his largely Palestinian audience to factors within their own culture ("the internal component of our reality") that might be playing a part in this process.

Firstly, I think we are ruled by a government that loves bureaucracy, and they recruit governing officials, governing officers who in general tend to be incompetent, because the emphasis is on loyalty rather than performance. Secondly, there is cooptation of religious leaders. Even in the Palestinian context, our religious leaders in general are co-opted by the Authority rather than separate from the Authority, rather than—as somebody said yesterday—"speaking truth to power." And maybe that gap allows the so-called Islamic fundamentalists to succeed in providing an alternative, too. Corruption and law: I don't need to say much about that. I want to say more on the patriarchal system.

Culturally and socially we have a patriarchal system that is based on men; not only men, but an authoritarian system. It's not egalitarian. And to bring in a nonviolent peacebuilding component, you have to believe in equality as a basis for your system. This patriarchal system comes from the very core Arab tribal system and Bedouin traditions that have existed in the Arab world for at least the last fifteen hundred or two thousand years. And Islamic values could not change that. In fact, they took Islamic values, and adapted them to the patriarchal system. So today, a patriarchal system looks at the Qur'an and sees patriarchy rather than equality. We love authority! We obey authority. That's how we are raised. We are not raised to examine, to challenge authority. We seek the authority—whether it's in the land or in the mayor or in the leader, we seek it. Culturally, we seek it in every sense. Those aspects of the culture are contrary to, or obstructive of, genuine applications of nonviolent resistance. If you're engaged in nonviolent resistance, you have, at the very least, to challenge these aspects. This means expanding your resistance so that it relates to everything violent in your environment.

Finally, Abu-Nimer criticized the avoidance of "social self-examination," of being "able to critically examine our own tradition, our own world, our own culture, not because we don't want to, but because we think about this as damaging our self-respect"—a fault he found especially noticeable in the educational system. "In nonviolence and peacebuilding," declared Abu-Nimer, "this capacity to criticize your own actions and environment is the core: the ability to challenge your own assumptions and then being able to look at the other critically."

Internal Factors Limiting the Effectiveness of the Nonviolent Movement

Lack of a Coherent Strategy for Resistance

From her perspective as one of the founders of the International Solidarity Movement, Huwaida Arraf described the absence of a coherent Palestinian strategy for resistance and the effect of this lack on the nonviolence movement.

> I think in general, everyone working against the occupation—from inside Israel or inside the occupied territories, and outside—needs to have more discussion and strategy. Right now I'm at a point of recognizing that I have helped build this resource [i.e., international solidarity with Palestinian nonviolence] to be put to use by the Palestinians struggling against the occupation, a tool in the hands of the people here to resist the occupation more effectively. But there's also being realistic and recognizing the state of Palestinian politics and Palestinian society today: There's no strategy for the resistance; there's no strategy for getting to where we need to go for our independence. We don't have a strategy for achieving it.
>
> The Palestinian leadership thinks that strategy needs to be negotiations. I'm not opposed to negotiations, but I recognize that

the Israeli government is led by the Zionist ideology, and we cannot expect that Israel is just going to give us this land because it's right, because it's just, because we're human beings. That's not going to happen. The Israeli government—the Zionists in this area—have had a long-term strategy, and they're implementing it very slowly, and the Palestinian community does not have a strategy for reaching their independence. So, whereas I'm not opposed to negotiation, I don't think we can negotiate in the absence of a very strong backing: an active resistance and a nonviolent resistance.

"But," said Arraf, "the Palestinian community has been so divided and traumatized, that kind of leadership doesn't exist today." And she spoke of a pervasive resignation to the ongoing violence, as reflected by statements like: "We just have to keep fighting in this way, because the level of force Israel is using can only be confronted by a level of force."

If you look at Hamas or one of the groups that actively strategize and carry out the attacks inside Israel, they can probably point to the thousands of Israelis that have left the country because they've created a situation that's not just *as* bad [as in Palestine], but *is* bad inside Israel, and [to] the Israeli economy that has been decimated. So you can say that, in a sense, they're more strategic than the Palestinian Authority. I think that, if you weigh the pros and cons, that [violent] strategy is a losing strategy; it defies all the moral judgement I have. But they can argue for that kind of strategy, because they'll show you how nothing else has worked. This is what we're up against now.

We have the International Solidarity Movement, but that's turned into trying to lessen the atrocities committed by the Israeli military against the Palestinian people by witnessing what's going on and trying to get in the way sometimes, and I don't want it to be that. I don't want to be just responding to the Israel strategy and just responding to the violence and the initiatives of the Israeli military and government. I want the Palestinian community—the anti-occupation forces—to be hitting at the occupation, and I have to say that that's not happening now. The reason is, I believe, that my community, the Palestinian community as a whole, is lacking that leadership.

Coordination, Leadership, and Strategy: the "Big Three"

Palestinians and Israelis alike frequently cited the need for better coordination among organizations involved in nonviolent resistance, in

addition to more effective leadership and a clearly articulated strategy—
as witness the comments of Nafez Assaily, Rev. Naim Ateek, and Meron
Benvenisti, as well as First Intifada activists Elias Rishmawi and Judith
Green. Assaily, for instance, called for "a clear strategy of nonviolence for
all those who believe strongly in nonviolence as a strategy for liberation,
a clear strategy of what we have to do next with nonviolence. Also,"
he added, "what we need is leadership for nonviolence." Assaily's concept
of the "leadership for nonviolence" includes a president who "takes off
his tie" and "goes down in the streets to open blockades" side-by-side
with the people. "This is the kind of leadership we need."

To be more effective, stated Rev. Naim Ateek, "I think there is a great
need for better organization and coordination, working more closely."

> But I think, again, part of the difficulty is that every group has
> its own agenda. I think, personally, that we can do so much more
> if there is more coordination on both sides, and within the same
> country. I think Palestinians could do so much more within Palestine
> if we were able to see the emergence of a stronger nonviolent
> movement. Part of my difficulty, part of my disappointment,
> actually, is that we really have not been able to see the emergence of
> a very strong movement of nonviolence. [There is] lots going on
> in different places, but not a movement like in the [U.S.] Civil
> Rights Movement. I can understand some of the difficulties for that,
> because Israel, I think intentionally, wanted to crush the emergence
> of such a movement, and to some extent, they have. I mean, the
> fact that they will allow themselves to get a bulldozer to walk over
> people—like in the case of Rachel [Corrie]—this was an intentional
> strategy to kill any movement from taking place.

Lack of coordination plagues nonviolent groups inside Israel as well as in
the occupied territories, said Rev. Ateek: "There are many small groups
that are doing good things, but not a movement."

> So, whether this means that we have not really found a Martin
> Luther King or a Mandela or whatever—inside Israel or on the
> West Bank—to really bring this into being, and that we need to have
> that kind of a figure in order to really see it, or because we have not
> had better organization or better coordination, is something to be
> looked at more carefully.

One solution, he mused, might be to encourage the development of a
strong nonviolent movement in the United States, far from "the struggle

and the problems we're facing" and where there is more freedom. "Then it will spill over and affect the movement back home. This is something to really think through, if possible."

Israeli historian and political commentator Meron Benvenisti agreed that "If you're talking about a mass movement, I don't think it can work if you have [a variety of small groups] and they're not organized." What is needed, he said, "is one public figure that will somehow capture the imagination of people, a person of the top league who is ready to openly say, and some of them do say this: 'Violence would lead us nowhere. I'll declare a new policy or a new strategy of nonviolence.'" Benvenisti also stressed the need for the movement to be proactive—rather than "to react to this thing, that thing"—and to develop a coherent nonviolent theory.

West Jerusalemite Judith Green, an "old-timer" with memories of the Beit Sahour tax strike, also underscored the need for greater coordination.

> If you're talking about changing—not just acting out what you think is the proper way to behave—if you're trying to use nonviolence as a tool, it can't be just a little pocket here and there. In Beit Sahour they had the tax resistance. It never spread to all of Palestine. Even then, we were never able to set up an umbrella organization of dialogue groups or something like that. We found total noncooperation between geographical units in Palestine. It's been a problem in Palestine all along: there's a lot of local autonomy, which maybe is a nice thing, but there's very little overall strategy. If they can now develop a strategy that isn't just based mainly in the Bethlehem area, of nonviolent groups and mediation groups and all of that—which are all wonderful things—if they want it to have a political effect, it has to be a strategy for all of Palestine. I assume that's what their vision is too, and that they're trying to [achieve it]; but without that, it's kind of hopeless.

"A new Israeli-Palestinian coalition, a people's coalition that rejects violence and that wants to start something," was the vision described by Elias Rishmawi (who had been, in addition to his activism during the Beit Sahour tax strike, a key participant in the Rapprochement dialogue group during the First Intifada). "This coalition should have Palestinian and Israeli leadership who will start talking openly, loudly, and trying to bring up masses from Israel and Palestine who are interested in this." Said Rishmawi, "I wish somebody would do that."

Awakening Compassion

For Veronika Cohen—another core member of the First-Intifada-era Jerusalem/Beit Sahour dialogue group and of other Palestinian-Israeli dialogue groups of the day (e.g., with Nablus and with Dheisheh refugee camp) and co-organizer (with Hillel Bardin) of many of the solidarity activities undertaken by the Israeli dialoguers—the chief need is a way to "awaken compassion" and to more effectively convey to the Israeli public the message of shared Israeli-Palestinian destiny.

> When we started the dialogue, we somehow assumed that the Israeli public was ignorant of the Palestinians, that they were assuming that every Palestinian was a terrorist and every Palestinian would secretly like to murder Jews; and we thought that really our most important mission was to get them to meet Palestinians and realize they're not the bloodthirsty monsters that they think they are. But today I think that that's not enough. I think that the average Israeli knows that, and knowing that is not enough to make him sympathetic or empathetic or make him care about their suffering. So it's not enough that they know that the Palestinians don't want to kill us. One has to do a lot more to awaken compassion. Our message always was that we are linked, our fates are linked, and what's bad for them is bad for us, too. And I think that until Israelis understand that, we're not going to get very far. That was and still is the main message: to make us, to make Israelis, understand that we're in the same boat, and either we all sink or we all float, and it will be done together.

Improved Communication

Despite the problematic nature of the mainstream media, it was recognized that better use could be made of various media in the service of truth and peace. As (Palestinian) Combatants for Peace member Wael Salame put it, "Just to let the people know the truth, and that's it. Maybe in many different ways: on the TV, in the movies, in lectures, on the Internet."

> We in the Combatants for Peace have to prove ourselves as fighting for peace. And we need help or support from the other organizations that are interested in peace in the whole world, not especially in Palestine or in having a solution of the conflict between Israel and the Arab countries. No. For the whole world. Also, we are ready to help and to be there, and we are choosing a nonviolent way.

Overcoming Impediments—Working Towards Solutions

Developing a National Strategy for Nonviolent Resistance

Sami Awad of Holy Land Trust and Ibrahim Issa of Hope Flowers School both address these issues in a holistic manner, aiming to build Palestine-wide coordination and, in Issa's case, concentrating on developing a model suitable to Palestinian culture, as well as a component of media-based communication aimed at both the Palestinian and Israeli public. Like many of the other Palestinians I interviewed (Nafez Assaily, Ibrahim Issa, Rev. Naim Ateek, among others), Awad stressed the need for a specifically Palestinian strategy of nonviolence.

> We don't have a strategy now. All Palestinian organizations, working together or separately—what we currently have is sporadic activities that take place. So for example, a road is blocked; we go and remove it. The wall is being built; we go and protest it. The Israeli army imposes curfew; we defy the curfew and go on the streets. Now these are all very dangerous and very courageous activities, but they're all just reacting to what the Israeli military's doing. A strategy means we set up the plan of action of what we want and be proactive in this matter.[11]

Better Communication and Coordination for "The Work of Nonviolence"

Although bemoaning the scarcity of "people who have a nonviolent vision and work towards it whatever the price," Ibrahim Issa also spoke of his dreams for the future unity of nonviolent organizations in Palestine as well as some creative ways of disseminating ideas of nonviolence on both sides of the Green Line. Issa emphasized the importance of training Palestinians "to do the work of nonviolence" and made the point that "ceasefire is a first step—the next step, which is very, very important, is reconciliation; and without reconciliation, there will be no peace." When I said that I had been impressed with the large number and variety of Palestinian nonviolent organizations I had encountered in my few weeks of interviewing, though, he reiterated his misgivings at their lamentable lack of coordination.

> Very few of them are working together or planning together. This makes the Palestinian nonviolence, in my opinion, very weak.

What we need here is a network of nonviolent organizations or, actually, joint activities among the Palestinian nonviolent groups. Also, we need to spread information to the Palestinians. Because one of the problems facing Palestinian nonviolence is among Palestinian society itself: a lot of Palestinians think nonviolence is some kind of collaboration with Israel. So, in my opinion, also as someone engaged in nonviolence, I think that the Palestinian organizations have failed to bring the ideas of nonviolence to Palestinian society. What we need is coordination of all these groups together. We shouldn't form one organization; that's not what I'm saying. It's most important to keep openness with the people and to keep coordination with the other groups. I believe that not one of these groups is complete, but we all share completeness: What we don't have here in Hope Flowers, maybe other organizations have. And what other organizations don't have, we have it here in this group. We need coordination, and we need also to spread information among the people here and to teach them what nonviolence means.

As had Husam Jubran, Issa stressed the importance of a home-grown model of nonviolence.

The nonviolent philosophy is very much related to culture. We shouldn't think that the Indian model will be applicable in Palestine. What we need is to find a model of nonviolence to match the Palestinian culture and to fit into Palestinian society, which is much more effective. One of the gaps that exists in nonviolence is that a lot of the people involved in nonviolence are from international organizations, and a lot of [local] people are suspicious of these organizations. So in order to be effective, let the Palestinians do the job of nonviolence; that will increase the trust. For this [reason], we choose to work with our programs to train Palestinians to do the nonviolence, not waiting for Americans or Europeans to do the nonviolence work. And the Palestinians know more about the little details of their culture than others, even [those who] are very much aware of the culture.

Israeli psychotherapist/activist Yitzhak Mendelsohn also addressed the deficit in coordination. In addition, he advocated the use of mediators and spoke, as well, of the need to re-examine how power is used by Palestinians as well as by Israelis.

There are many, many initiatives between Palestinians and Israelis. There are many initiatives between Palestinian citizens of

Israel and Israeli [Jew]s. And there may be true communal work, as happened in Ireland. Some critical mass could be created by putting together initiatives in terms of [those] against extremism, of recovering independence in the way the people respond, taking a lot of risks from both sides. But it's impossible to solve the conflict without mediators.

With the help of clever mediators who understand the dynamics of the relationship between the sides, maintained Mendelsohn:

> It's possible to help the Palestinians to review the way they're using their strength, the way their society is dividing them, and the myths that are created in them. Some communal work should be started in terms of taking responsibility for the well-being of the small places, by understanding that this is not anymore something that is unilaterally created, even if the story of the conflict and the story of what's happening started with a huge asymmetry.
>
> Every conflict and every people who try to liberate themselves comes to a place where he is stronger and has the power to create damage to the other side. And I hope that maybe some international mediators can come and try to also help Palestinians to see that they can use their power in a different way. They have to try to bridge between Israeli communities and Palestinian communities, try to share projects of all types of nonviolence, strengthened by the idea that we want to use the power that we have in a different way.

Complimentary Roles for Palestinian and Israeli Movements

Like Ghassan Andoni ("You need an active Palestinian resistance supported by an active Israeli peace movement or anti-occupation movement. If you have those two, peace will become tangible. But if you have two peace movements, peace will run far away"), and Amos Gvirtz, who delineated distinct roles for the Palestinians ("direct nonviolence") and Israelis ("preventive nonviolence")—as well as a separate role for third parties—Zoughbi Zoughbi articulated a need for interlocking roles in building an effective nonviolent movement.

> I feel that nonviolence will not work unless there are three dimensions of struggle cooperating with each other: the Palestinians continuing their struggle, the [Israeli] pro-peace camp/protest camp to continue their struggle to get rid of the occupation, the third party in the whole world assuming collective responsibility. Like

[279]

what happened in the struggle of South Africa, the issue of boycott and divestment in South Africa.

"Although," he added, "that struggle hasn't been finished; it could be that political apartheid has been finished, but not economic apartheid." Zoughbi expressed appreciation for the work of the Israeli peace movement, as well as his hope "that they will have more voices. I hope the Palestinians will also respond more to such initiatives, because this is how we build quantity that leads to qualitative change."

Working Within Israeli Society

Daphna Banai is the founder of the Tel Aviv branch of the Israeli women's organization Machsom Watch. I met her when she joined the group socializing around the campfire in front of the Centre for Joint Struggle in Bil'in on the evening of January 1, 2006. Deploring the apathy of most Israelis, Banai called on her fellow activists "to do the work inside Israel."

> We support the Palestinian struggle for liberation; and if it's not violent, then even more. It saddens me to see that it's small, because I think that being small, it's hard for it to garner results. If only it were possible to recruit people to the nonviolent struggle. You know, I know so many Israelis who have said, "Why do they do terrorist attacks?" and the like. But on the day that there is a nonviolent struggle, they don't show up to help. Why? Because they don't care. This business of opposition to terrorism and "I'm not active because of terrorism" is an excuse: "I'm not active because I don't care." This apathy is quite revolting.

Even so, Banai felt that the public's level of awareness was improving, though much remained to be done.

> I think that gradually, by means of some television programs, greater awareness of the injustice has developed a little—of the injustice that the [separation] barrier imposes. That doesn't mean that the nation of Israel is rising up in opposition to the barrier, but more people are aware that the barrier is annexing land and causing injury. I think that it is necessary to do the work inside Israel—by informational work and distributing flyers—and to create pressure from inside.

ISM, too, "could probably be doing more in Israeli society," according to Huwaida Arraf.

> Right now, Israeli society is, I think, blinded by the misinformation that Palestinians are intent on using terror to get rid of them and that it's, again, that the Jewish people are fighting for their survival. This misinformation is put out there by the proponents of the occupation. I think the forces that are propagating this kind of information have been doing a more effective job in Israeli society than we have, and we haven't invested too much effort in going out into Israeli society; we work almost exclusively in the occupied territories—in the West Bank and Gaza—with the Palestinian community, in strengthening and supporting the Palestinian non-violent resistance.

Attracting Diverse Communities

Feminist Yvonne Deutch had some words of criticism aimed specifically at the women's peace movement and the feminist movement in Israel, for their lack of inclusiveness, as reflected in their mainly Ashkenazi (European Jewish) makeup. But, said the long-time activist, "What is important is creating a political culture and, by the very substance of our work, organizing to create change. I'm interested also that it won't be only Ashkenazi people." Matan Kaminer, too, spoke of seeking ways to expand the movement's base, in his case by involving apolitical Israeli youth.

> These are people who aren't militarists. They see the army as the ridiculous institution that it is, and they may not have anything specifically against the Palestinians, they just want to live their own lives and not blow up. That's an attitude that could go in the right direction if we find the right way to make these people active. Outright refusal requires more sacrifice on a personal basis than these people might be willing to make. But refusal is a good way to get the message out to these people. The next step would be widening protests and widening the movement against occupation to other venues which don't require so much personal sacrifice.

Kaminer gave an example of a project that he and a fellow refusenik were planning, "Rock Against Occupation," hoping to attract large numbers of young people to hear the artists' anti-occupation message. "That's creating space for rejuvenation of the peace movement."

A Return to First Intifada Tactics

Kaminer also spoke regretfully of the more "militarized" character of the Al-Aqsa Intifada, and expressed hope for a return to "more First Intifada tactics" on the part of Palestinians. Describing what he regards as the requirements for an end to bloodshed (withdrawal...) and the importance of conveying to the Israelis that the Palestinians are potential partners and to the Palestinian that not all Israelis support the occupation, he stipulated that, "This entails a change in the Palestinian behaviour as well."

> I think that nonviolent, or at least non-lethal resistance on the Palestinian side will be very important. I'm talking about more of the means of the First Intifada and less of the Second Intifada: stopping bombing people in buses and discos, and going back to mass demonstrations, and general strikes, and all that, which has its own problems, as I'm aware: it's not so easy to conduct a mass demonstration when you get shot at.

Also harking back to the days of the First Intifada, former PIJ co-editor Zahra Khalidi expressed her desire to "see the Israeli people move like they did ten or twelve years ago and were really able to push their government into taking many steps forward." Jad Isaac and Ziad Abbas, respectively, appealed to the Israeli peace movement to "wake up and take the lead" and to "really be activist and change public opinion from inside," whereas Zoughbi Zoughbi called for both a more assertive Israeli peace movement and efforts by activists on both side to proactively mobilize their own societies. Said Zoughbi: "As a Palestinian, I believe the Israeli left wing needs to be much more assertive. The right wing is aggressive. You cannot really be successful if you are not assertive, if you don't go to the grass roots, if you cannot mobilize people." That said, though, Zoughbi named some organizations whose work he greatly appreciated: "Ta'ayush, of the Alternative Information Centre, the Peace Bloc (Gush Shalom), and many women's groups and political groups, and," said he, "I look at them as good examples for future cooperation. I look at them that they might give us inspiration." Acknowledging that "The Israeli peace camp is probably frustrated with us, too," and assuring me that, "I wouldn't like to condescend or patronize. I know what I should do, but I wouldn't tell others what to do," he went on:

I feel that everyone should work in his or her own society, taking into consideration how to link to others in a more positive, peaceful way. Because what is needed is a more proactive approach and not a reactive approach. It is needed more to do something rather than just sit and talk. How to mobilize masses—in our society or in their society. We appreciate the voices of the peace camp in Israel; despite the fact that it was outlawed to meet with us, they came to meet. So it is the issue of how really to get out of the silence, in all societies.

Involving the Mainstream

Several activists called for a basic change in attitude on the part of the Israeli movement: a more positive approach ("less 'anti' energy"— Devorah Brous); increased willingness to take part in nonviolent actions inside Israel (Nijmie); greater readiness to sacrifice (Yossi Wolfson, Ghassan Andoni)—perhaps as a by-product of the increased empathy and understanding gained through more firsthand exposure to the conditions of Palestinian life in the occupied territories (Neta Golan, Yonatan Pollak). Brous—whose organization, Bustan, works mainly within the borders of Israel, asked:

> So how do we get deeper inside Israeli society, or how [do we get] mainstream Americans and Europeans to get involved and to believe that they have a critical piece in helping to dissipate the tensions in this region? I think the core actions can't just be protest after protest. I think that this energy of being "anti"—anti-occupation—it's not enough. First of all, you can't define the occupation as just what's happening beyond '67,[12] and that's one of the major messages that we're trying to bring to light. Secondly, "anti" energy, and all the time coming from this place where you're challenging, is exhausting. A lot of people are burned out, and it's ineffective, because the people and the mechanisms—the apparatus of the occupation or the policy makers—are not open-eared, wide-eyed, and waiting to hear the message of the protestors. They're much more effective at bringing an even louder "anti" message: dropping a bomb is an act that can take less than half an hour, and so all of our coordination and all of our mobilization to bring five hundred people to cross a checkpoint with food parcels for a village under siege in conjunction with a coalition of Israeli and Palestinian organizations and protesting the policies of the occupation can't possibly be on a par with the apparatus of the occupation, which is using this whole idea of being "anti."

Just as many have pointed out that the Palestinians are not in a position to "outviolence" the Israeli military forces and well-armed settler militants, Brous stressed that the Palestinians and Israeli peace/justice forces cannot "out-'anti'" them either: "We can't use their tactics and expect to beat them at their own game. We need to come up with our own. I do think that it's critical for us to be getting more creative, because we're all banging our heads against the wall, and our heads are scarred and bloody and sore."

Promoting Increased Participation in NVDA and Noncooperation inside Israel

As an international working with both Israeli and Palestinian groups, International Women's Peace Service (IWPS) volunteer Nijmie called for more nonviolent direct action inside the borders of Israel.

It has been done, but there are still a lot of people who don't think it's really useful. [We need] more people generating more ideas and learning what it takes, and that whole mode of thinking. Many [Israelis] say, "Oh well, it's not working. Nobody understands that kind of thing." It seems like some of the anarchist groups and some of the younger activists in Israel, and some of the GLBTQ (gay, lesbian, bisexual, trans-sexual, queer) groups like Black Laundry, and groups like that are actually in a similar line of thinking, more so than groups like Gush Shalom or like Ta'ayush or like Rabbis for Human Rights, or any of the other groups that are kind of like—yeah, they're against the occupation, they're humanitarian, they're this and that, but they wouldn't necessarily be in favour of doing direct actions inside Israel. Rabbis for Human Rights, for example, won't necessarily defy military authority in the West Bank. They'll try to support people up to a certain degree, but then if the military tells them to do something, they'll do it. So it's just sort of like when people take positions on how they're going to actually oppose this stuff, I think that it needs to go farther than "Yah, we feel bad for the Palestinians. We'll help the Palestinians. We'll bring humanitarian aid to the Palestinians. We'll be in a demonstration as long as the Israeli army doesn't tell us to go away." It's the whole thing about whose authority are you really respecting, and what's the underlying message in what you're doing: if you'll do something up to a certain point, but you're really not taking a particular stand on military authority in the West Bank or on any kind of control over other people's lives.

Yossi Wolfson is both a lawyer with the Israeli human rights organization HaMoked: Center for the Defence of the Individual, and an activist with a variety of groups, including the gay rights group Black Laundry and the animal rights group Anonymous. Although Wolfson acknowledges the recent growth of nonviolent direct action (NVDA) in the region, he qualifies his assessment of the accomplishments of NVDA, and describes what he feels are the conditions for its long-term success in terms reminiscent of Ghassan Andoni's dictum that "You don't need two peace movements to arrive at peace. You need an active Palestinian resistance supported by an active Israeli peace or anti-occupation movement."

> I don't see the possibility that [NVDA] will stop the occupation or hinder things on a very large scale unless there is a very big popular group like, on the Palestinian side, a noncooperation movement on a very big scale, [in which case] it has a very good chance to succeed. And if Israelis started on a much bigger scale, it would have a chance, too, to succeed. But that means a very big personal price. People who usually do it are people who have a lot of time to give and who are ready to endanger themselves. And there are very, very few instances of large-scale nonviolent direct action. For example, there was one time (during a demonstration in Ramallah) when people just went into the streets and the Israeli army did not know what to do. There was curfew, of course, and they were breaking it, and the army didn't know what to do. A very big action and very successful. It's very difficult to keep up such actions for a long time.
>
> I think the Israeli army knows its limits: the curfews that are not always enforced, for example. Many times there is a formal curfew, but people go out and do whatever they like in those parts of the city where the army is not in the streets. So there are some kinds of limits to the use of force. And nonviolent noncooperation seems to be a very effective method, but it has its limits. As I said, people need to be ready to sacrifice.

Israelis Must Go Out and Experience Palestinian Reality

In a similar vein, Ghassan Andoni (e.g., in his earlier discussion of strategy) voiced the need for peace activists to "wage peace" by having guts and being "ready to take risks... ready to get hurt—in order to stop oppression on the ground, not by lobbying and not by demonstrating, but by blocking, by actually engaging." And ISM cofounder Neta

Golan and anarchist Yonatan Pollak—speaking largely from personal experience—suggest one way that Israelis might develop this kind of self-sacrificing sensibility. Golan, an Israeli woman who virtually moved in to the village of Haris—as a "protective presence"—after hearing her future brother-in-law's accounts of settler abuse of West Bank villagers, threw out a challenge.

> I did what I believe needs to be done, which is go out, join Palestinians in nonviolent direct action; and I think more Israelis need to do that. Another thing in terms of doing what I think needs to be done: Israelis are sending their kids [to the army] and risking their kids' lives and going themselves and risking their lives, all for the sake of the occupation and for God knows what. People send their children to kill and be killed without even thinking about it; it's just an obvious thing to people that go. But those of us that want peace, that want a sane world for our children, we wouldn't even consider taking those kinds of risks—usually. Or making those kinds of sacrifices. And I think that needs to happen. I mean doing more than what's comfortable. I realize now, being a mother, that it's much more difficult for most people to have this responsibility. But I hope I still find ways.

Yonatan Pollak and his fellow Israeli Anarchists Against the Wall haven't quite taken up residence in Bil'in, but since early 2005, many of them have spent virtually every Thursday afternoon and Friday supporting the villagers in demonstrating against the wall and settlement neighbourhood being built on land confiscated from Bil'in. Based on his past experience of solidarity actions in Hebron and elsewhere, Pollak told me in October 2003 that "more people need to see what's going on, actually see with their own eyes."

> You can read and hear and talk to people endlessly, but until you've slept in a house occupied by the army [and under] curfew for the last three years, you don't know what it is. You can't understand the fear and hostility that it creates. And once you have, even for one night, I think a person can have a much more thorough understanding of this conflict, because history and political analysis all these intellectual levels are important—and we should study history, we should know what happened—but what's more important is what's happening now; and the suffering of people is wrong, regardless of what happened in history. It doesn't matter if

the Palestinians started it. It has no relevance. I think they didn't, but that's another story.

Long-Term Planning and a Program Based on Human Rights Law

Others cited more specific foci for strengthening the movement. For many, as we have seen, the separation wall provided such a focus. Jeff Halper, though, proposed looking beyond immediate issues and planning for the long-term.[13] In addition to the need for better coordination, Halper stressed the importance of having "a program to sell," one focused not on a specific political solution but on human rights and international law.

> One of the problems is that events on the ground happen so fast that you're just organizing about one thing, and it all-of-a-sudden becomes irrelevant and you're in a whole different situation. That, to some degree, I think, is happening with the wall. It's very important to organize against the wall, but at the same time, events are moving much faster than that. The problem we have in the Israeli peace movement—and I think a problem facing the Palestinians—is that we don't have a program to sell. We still have to say "End the Occupation," but you have to bring into the discussion human rights and international law (the Fourth Geneva Convention), because whatever the actual solution will be, that gives us certain guidelines.

After elaborating on the need to address issues of human rights and international law in the struggle against the occupation, Halper made the further point that this approach was of particular significance for Jews.

> I think that the source of persecution against the Jews is that over the centuries the Jews were outside: they were outside of ecclesiastical law, they were outside of tribal law, they were outside of civil law in many cases. Only through human rights and international law are Jews included. And here's a real divergence between Jewish interests and Israeli interests. For Israel, it's very convenient in the short term to step out of international law and say "it doesn't apply to us." "The Fourth Geneva Convention doesn't apply," and so on, and to have America as an ally and put the whole thing on a power basis. For Jews, now that we're finally "in"—we're in the human

family; human rights are universal—for Jews to then step outside of that again, I think it's something very perilous. Do [American Jews] want to step out again and say, "We're special. Human rights don't apply to us. Israel's outside of accountability"? So on all kinds of levels, I really think the human rights/international law paradigm really has to become a basic part of our vocabulary.

Meron Benvenisti—whose warnings that the time for an achievable two-state solution had passed date back to the early 1980s—also proposed a rights-based reframing of the struggle.

What I suggest now is to stop thinking about a two-state solution and [to begin] thinking about the whole Israeli-Palestinian issue as a question of civil rights and human rights, taking the present bi-national situation and trying to work from within that. Because I think that what Beilin[14] and the others are doing is postponing everything to the future without addressing themselves to the present. So that's why I'm now advocating a struggle that is totally based on political action. I don't think that a partition of Palestine is viable, is now possible to achieve. They go through the motions of saying, "we'll evacuate 400,000 settlers." It will never happen. In the meantime, you think you've done your duty to your conscience by coming up with a plan.

Rejecting the Victim Role, Organizing Women and Other Sectors

"I think we need a real, effective public dialogue and debate on the issues," Hanan Ashrawi told me, stressing the need for Palestinians to step out of the "victim" role, as well as to return to sector-based organizing.

When people react through pain and they speak through victimization, it's not necessarily a rational moment. So you need to try to minimize the pain of the moment, and you need to create some distance, so people don't say "revenge is the mode," or "my pain drives me," or [express] the sense of victimization that says "I can do unto others what was done unto me." To break that mode, it takes a lot of doing and a lot of creative ideas. And, of course, you have to show how adopting the same tactics, the same methods that were used against you doesn't work; on the contrary, it only creates more victims.

I think that it's important that we work the way we started, with sectors. For example, women can be a force for change, and we need to pull together, work together through existing grassroots organizations, think tanks, women's groups, and so on—to be able to move on. Also, remember, we had the march of the intellectuals, the authors, and academics, and so on. Sectors can mobilize, move, and then bring together others. Women can be a force for change within society as a whole. It has to be done systematically and incrementally, also.

Proactively Improving Media Coverage

Not surprisingly, quite a few of the activists I interviewed—in particular the Palestinians among them—had suggestions for both Palestinian and Israeli movements on how to improve their relationship with the media and to thus be better able to disseminate their views and accounts of "the true situation," and some proposed specific ways of virtually "becoming" the media (my words). Refusenik Matan Kaminer told me, apropos his critique of the Israeli peace movement's relationship with the media, "If I could change one thing, that would be the thing I would change."

> I would get the media to start covering us in a way that would be meaningful, in a way that would connect the whole thing to the reason why it exists, which is the occupation. It's hard. It's really hard. That's maybe one of the downsides of refusal as a public phenomenon and as a way of organizing politically. I think what we need to do is we need to keep linking it, by talking to Palestinians, by being in touch, by publicizing our approach as a nonviolent approach, which is relevant to the other side as well, which is being carried out on the other side by lots and lots of people who also aren't covered by the Israeli media, and so on. That's the way things need to go, but it's difficult, because the army doesn't want Israelis entering the territories for a reason, because they don't want Israelis talking to Palestinians. That's the interest of the establishment: not having that meeting of minds and of people between the two sides, keeping fear alive by demonizing the other side, which is hard to do when you know people on the other side. So, getting to know people, that's one way, that's the important way.

Hebron student organizer T.M. suggested that perhaps Israeli peace groups should themselves "have media agencies or more organizations or institutions concentrating on media in their community, because they are very weak in this field, they are very, very weak." And in fact, some Palestinians have thought of ways to get the word out to the Palestinian and Israeli public themselves, bypassing the mainstream media.[15] S'leiman Abu Muferreh, mayor of a small Palestinian village not far from Bethlehem, told me how he and his friends have been personally spreading the word about their nonviolent activities opposing the wall, and Hope Flowers School principal Ibrahim Issa was of the opinion that a Hebrew-language Palestinian TV channel would answer a real need.

> I can see that the Israeli politicians [and] the Israeli population knows very little about what's going on. And I think that the government doesn't provide them with the real information of what's really going on. And we faced that during the occupation of Bethlehem. In one day twenty-one people were killed in Bethlehem, and I know personal stories; they were mothers, wives, parents, fathers, grandfathers, and when I listened to the Israeli media that day, they said that they are [armed] resisters. I knew from the hospital that these people were civilians. At that time I really recognized how much the Israeli government is preventing its people from getting information. So what we need is a Palestinian channel speaking in Hebrew, and this should be directed to Israeli society to inform them of what's going on here. This is one of the nonviolent concepts that I hope that the Palestinians will one day invest in, instead of financing [violent] resistance groups here. So what we need is a channel or way to transform [i.e., transfer information about] our conflict to Israeli society and to do it in a human way. It's still very much needed to promote the nonviolent philosophy. I think if the Palestinians also intensify their efforts to communicate with the Israelis nonviolently and just spread information to them in the sense of "we want you to know," I think we will sooner or later win this struggle against occupying the hills or confiscating the land.

In April of 2007, speaking in Bil'in, Dr Mustafa Barghouthi cited the need to combat "the dehumanization and delegitimization of the Palestinians" practiced by the media since the start of the 2000 Intifada and stated that "we have a duty as Palestinians to give the world the right narrative about Palestine." The then Palestinian Authority minister of communications expressed the conviction that the Palestinian National Unity Government formed the previous month must act "to give the world a unified Palestinian message and also a unified Palestinian narrative." This, said he, "would be very, very instrumental in the future." Although the disbanding of the unity government in mid-June of the same year amidst renewed fighting between Hamas and Fatah perhaps marked the demise of hopes for a unified "official" Palestinian message in the foreseeable future, another of Dr Barghouthi's suggestions for having an impact on the media may have more immediate practicality. Like Jeff Halper's call for an international campaign against Israeli apartheid,[16] this would depend on the participation, along with members of Palestinian civil society, of Israeli and other international supporters. Offering briefing materials to all who might request them, Dr Barghouthi declared:

> What we need is to organize. Yesterday I was receiving people from Reuters and different media, and they told me, "Whenever we put something that is questionable for Israelis, we receive hundreds of calls, and if it is too harsh, maybe thousands of calls. When we put something that is dissatisfactory to Palestinians, we get no calls." So the journalists, the correspondents, gradually develop a system of self-censorship, and they start being in a way biased, because they don't want to keep receiving these protests and they don't want to lose their jobs. In my opinion, the best way of balancing what the Israeli lobby has created is to get organized and to have this strong solidarity movement organized in a network that could be influential and could interact.

ISM coordinator Saif Abu Keshek, speaking at the December 2005 conference in Bethlehem, had also advocated a do-it-yourself approach to media work.

> We are trying to work on the media. We try to make documentary films, we do write reports, we write articles, but also we have to understand the global situation that we are facing. I mean there is always a blackout—not only on the nonviolent resistance in Palestine, but on the daily life under occupation, on the daily life that people are facing. These are the other things that they don't see outside. I've been travelling around. I looked at maybe 6,000 journalists who are covering the Gaza pullout, and there were only 7,000 settlers, almost a journalist for each settler. This is a reality that also we have to try to emphasize, to deal with it, and to see how we can make our words—our work—reach outside.
> It is very clear to everybody [that it is] for the benefit of the Israeli authorities to erase any kind of popular resistance, any kind

of poplar movements or civil society. Because of all the propaganda outside, nobody considered that there is a civil society in Palestine. It is very rare to find people who say, "Yes, there is a civil society." And it is our role to emphasize this point. I think the most practical thing that we can do is to go out to the field. We, the Palestinians. I am fed up with the statements; I am fed up with theories; I am fed up, and there are possibilities to practice. It needs the time, the effort, and the people. I think if we believe in what we are doing, so we should do it! We should just go out and practice it. And that's the power of it.

"Our rights exist as long as we practice them," declared Abu Keshek. "The moment we stop practicing our rights, we lose them."

Conclusion

Barriers to the success of the nonviolent movement comprise both factors external to the movement and weaknesses within the movement itself. Activists on both sides reported marginalization as being a major external constraint—significantly more so within Israeli, as opposed to Palestinian, society. Not surprisingly, those nonviolent organizations whose activities were humanitarian or educational enjoyed wider acceptance in both communities than those whose activities were perceived as purely political.

Additional external constraints on nonviolent organizing include the fact that Israelis continue to benefit from the occupation (Israel's "colonialist character"); the increasingly stringent restrictions on Palestinians' movement; the absence of effective, visionary Palestinian leadership; the mainstream media's domination by the Israeli narrative, and the consequent tendency to ignore the abuses suffered daily by Palestinians (not to mention nonviolent efforts by either "side") in favour of sensationalistic portrayals of bloody (Palestinian) attacks; and the violence of patriarchal aspects of Palestinian culture.

Among the internal weaknesses identified were the absence of a coherent, proactive Palestinian strategy of resistance to the occupation and for achieving independence and of effective "leadership for nonviolence"; lack of coordination among nonviolent organizations; as well as relatively ineffective use of the media. Ways of "awakening compassion" within the Israeli mainstream for the Palestinians and a sense of shared destiny were also seen to be lacking.

What, then, can be done? The chapter concluded by examining ways in which nonviolent organizations and their supporters might address these constraints and challenges, or already were doing so: building inter-organizational coordination and developing a Palestinian national strategy; spreading ideas about nonviolence more widely, utilizing Palestinian, rather than imported, models; and employing mediators to help deal with difficult intergroup dynamics between the two sides. The importance of the Palestinian and Israeli movements' filling complementary, interlocking roles in the struggle was mentioned. Increased focus on efforts inside Israel—in educating the public and raising their awareness of the abuses suffered by the Palestinians; promoting increased participation in NVDA and noncooperation inside the borders of the state; and broadening the movement by recruiting more diverse participants, including the mainstream—was strongly advocated. Further suggestions included a return to First Intifada tactics, reframing of the conflict in civil and human rights terms, increased organizing of women and other specific sectors of the society, improved media coverage so as to "get the word out" more effectively and to combat dehumanization of the Palestinians by the media. Israelis' going and experiencing Palestinian reality first hand was also widely felt to be an important means both of strengthening the movement and of decreasing its marginalization in Israeli society.

We shall now turn our attention to nonviolent strategies that have proven successful in the past, with a view to learning from and building on these past successes, as well as identifying recent trends in Palestinian nonviolence.

NOTES

1 After the assassination of then Prime Minister Yitzhak Rabin in Kings of Israel Square (*Kikar Malchei Yisrael*), Tel Aviv's major venue for large demonstrations, the square was renamed after him.

2 Avraham Burg, son of one of the founders of the right-wing National Religious Party, was speaker of the Knesset 1999–2003 as well as being a former chairman of the Jewish Agency for Israel. In September 2003, he famously wrote an article (which appeared in English translation/adaptation in *The Guardian*) stating that "the end of the Zionist enterprise is already on our doorstep" and calling upon Israel to shed its illusions and realize that it must choose between racist oppression and democracy. See www.guardian.co.uk/world/2003/sep/15/comment.

3 See Chapter 1, Note 1.

4 Human rights groups in the study cited were the Association for Civil Rights in Israel (ACRI), B'tselem, Hamoked, Physicians for Human Rights, and the Committee against Torture, as well as RHR.

5 Reference is to the five hundred or so Israeli military personnel or graduating high school students who had signed one or another declaration refusing to serve as of October 2003. The most recent figure I have been able to find (from 2004?) is over 1,600.

6 Meaning there is no real difference between the occupied territories and Israeli proper in terms of the struggle to preserve the "Jewish homeland."

7 The reference is to the shooting of 29 Muslim worshipers at the Ibrahimi Mosque in Hebron in 2004 by Dr Baruch Goldstein from the nearby Kiryat Arba settlement.

8 Rabbi Moshe Levinger, his wife Miriam, and their followers were the vanguard of Israeli settlers inside the city of Hebron in 1979.

9 A 3-minute clip of this television news broadcast is shown in the award-winning documentary *Bil'in Habibti* (Bil'in my Love).

10 I interviewed Elias Rishmawi in January 2006 as well as September 2003, with greater focus on details of the Beit Sahour tax strike in the later interview.

11 This strategy is described in more detail in the Holy Land Trust section of Chapter 3.

12 "Beyond '67"—i.e., in the territories occupied in the 1967 war.

13 Although these comments were made by Jeff Halper at the North American Friends of Sabeel conference in Seattle in February 2004, I have heard/read similar comments of his as recently as his January 2009 presentations in Vancouver (see Kaufman-Lacusta 2009).

14 Yossi Beilin (a Labour MK at the time) was one of the architects of the Oslo Accords as well as lead Israeli negotiator in drafting the 2003 Geneva Accord, to which Benvenisti is referring above.

15 For listings of some such Palestinian media outlets, see "Useful Websites."

16 Chapter 9. Also, see Halper 2008 for details.

7

Learning from the Past, Building for the Future

———

One year after the internationals from ISM came, there is more interest in the wall.

Abed el-Karim Dalbeh (The Freedom Center, Tulkarm, operated by the Democratic Front for the Liberation of Palestine [DFLP])

We've had all sorts of small victories along the way. The most important thing is the shift in Israeli society towards a two-state solution, and we can take credit for that, period. And I also take pride in the fact that it was the Israeli and Palestinian NGOs that turned [the wall] into an issue on the international agenda. When people say we're ineffective, I try to hold onto those small successes.

Gila Svirsky ([Israeli] Coalition of Women for Peace)

Yanoun was the story of people who nearly gave in to the pressure of the settlers, and abandoned the village; and they came back (not all of them, but it is still now a living village). Without the involvement of Ta'ayush, especially, and other groups there, it could have been one more place which is lost.

Adam Keller (Gush Shalom)

This important section of Israeli society—I mean the soldiers—they were tools of the occupation: they used violence, they used to kill, they used to destroy, they arrested many of the Palestinians; we know that. But they [i.e., those Israeli soldiers who are now members of Combatants for Peace] reached a point when they told themselves, "Stop what you are doing. We are criminals now, from the humanity side." They help us a lot as Palestinians, and also they help themselves as human beings. We are going very slowly, and we must work very hard, but I hope at the end that it's not a long distance: maybe three, four, five years, and we will succeed.

Wael Salame (Palestinian member of Combatants for Peace)

I think what is effective is not going to the army.

Uri Ya'akobi (signatory to the Israeli High School Seniors' Letter)

In the last couple of years, the nonviolent civil resistance has become more organized. The other thing is, the size of the Israeli [involvement] is becoming larger, and that is also a great point. And also, that the internationals are coming. They really are our messengers in their countries, because we don't trust the media. ... [T]hose people—the internationals and the Israelis and the Palestinians—became the voice of the voiceless, and it's really a great thing. So there are lot of things that have changed for the better or developed in a good way in this struggle.

Mustafa Shawkat Samha (village activist)

[295]

Successful Nonviolent Strategies: What Has Worked and Why?

Despite its relative marginality and other impediments to its success, the nonviolent movement has chalked up some notable victories over the years. And even if these have been relatively small when compared to the magnitude of the task, they provide a good entry point for a foray into some speculation regarding the potential for nonviolent struggle in the future. We shall begin with another look at the classic example of a successful instance of sustained nonviolent resistance during the First Intifada—the Beit Sahour tax strike, which was described earlier in this book by Elias Rishmawi—and about which Rishmawi remarked in January 2006, "Why we held to nonviolence then was because we could do that in a highly efficient way. It turns out that this kind of resistance was very effective in terms of driving the occupation forces crazy and driving them to really losing control of the occupied territories."

Israeli and International Participation: A Successful Strategy

Elias Rishmawi and the Beit Sahour tax strikers were perhaps the first Palestinians to realize the importance of cultivating support from amongst the ranks of "the enemy" through initiating dialogue with Israelis. The bonds that developed between the Beit Sahourians and their Israeli supporters as a result of their ongoing dialogue activities and joint actions, created, said Rishmawi, "a strong power with which we were able to do miracles with nonviolent resistance." More specifically, he pointed out that the Beit Sahourian's proactive approach to challenging the military tax system was "influential on all those concerned: Palestinians, Israelis, the Palestinian Authority, the Israeli authorities, and the international community." In our September 2003 interview, Rishmawi mused:

> I think we wanted to prove something in those days: that as humans we can do something, that we have brains and we are not less than anyone else, and we can resist occupation in nonviolence and make a breakthrough from within the system itself; and we did it. We did it! These were times of pride and dignity, and there was an overwhelming feeling during those years. It really was fantastic!

Although the strength and unity of the Beit Sahourians were undoubtedly the key factors in sustaining the protracted strike, and it was they who bore the brunt of the tremendous repression that was unleashed against the town, they were not alone: "At the same time," said Rishmawi, "we did have this communication with our Israeli counterparts, and they were supporting us all the way in this." Despite her more recent doubts regarding the effectiveness of grassroots activism as opposed to political involvement, Israeli participant Judith Green also reminisced in glowing terms about the days of the First Intifada, when what had begun as living-room meetings with a few folks from Beit Sahour who had come to West Jerusalem in search of dialogue partners gave rise to months of risky and often clandestine acts of solidarity.

> It happened that the first couple of activities that we had then had to be done a bit secretly, in terms of avoiding the army. Although there weren't roadblocks and things, there were restrictions on what Israeli Jews and Palestinians could do together at the time: how many people could meet together, where, when, if you slept there, if you didn't sleep there; and we had to circumvent all kinds of things like that. And we did it successfully, which really gave the group a lot of solidarity, I think: taking risks, planning things together. We also found we had a very good reception at the time by the community of Beit Sahour; and on the Israeli side, lots of people were willing to and interested in taking part, even if the activities were somewhat adventurous in nature. Because in contrast to now, I'll say, the atmosphere then—although there was obviously a certain level of violence involved in the First Intifada—was a lower level of violence. Eventually, as we all know, there were hundreds of people who were injured and killed, but somehow the nature of it was more diffuse. There were a lot of different things going on, and the whole impression wasn't one of violence.
>
> Also, I think that people in Israel realized pretty quickly (maybe this was partly due to some of the NGO work) that it was really a popular movement, that it wasn't being directed by outside forces. At that time, the PLO [leadership], of course, was outside of Israel. So, I think it was easier for Israelis then to deal with what they could see were local Palestinians, the people who were actually living here. Since the Oslo Agreements, I think the way Israelis understand the Palestinian demands, needs, experiences, and all that, has been very much complicated by the return of PLO personnel from abroad, to the detriment, I think, of the whole issue. I think it was easier for Israelis to deal with, to understand, to be empathetic with the fact that the local Palestinian population was living in limbo, that for thirty years nothing had been decided.

Of course the situation in 1988 seems like heaven compared to what it is now in 2003. But still, the fact that the people weren't being represented, that they had no vote, that they had no civil rights, and this and that [meant that] a wider branch of the Israeli political spectrum could accept that there's a problem here and we have to find out what it is these people who are uprising want, what their message is, and if we can talk to them. And in those first few years, between 1988 and 1993, we really had a lot of success (we and many other groups that were all created in that very fertile period) in opening up [Israeli] people's ears and hearts to things. Also, the Palestinians weren't being quite as beaten on the head as they are now. The level of people's experience—I can't say it was acceptable; it's never acceptable when anybody is shot or imprisoned without reason—but it wasn't as violent, as totally traumatic as it is now, so people were able to listen better, and we had considerable success.

In the context of the present Intifada, the stories of the long-term joint struggle in Bil'in and of smaller-scale campaigns in other villages resisting the wall readily come to mind as examples of how participation by Israelis, internationals, or both, has provided much-needed support for indigenous nonviolent action. In the opinion of International Solidarity Movement (ISM) coordinator Saif Abu Keshek, on top of "the organizational side, the involvement of the Palestinian people, the involvement of society, and lots of effort and energy being put into the First Intifada," "Israel wasn't prepared. They didn't know how to [suppress] the people, how to stop them. All of these elements played a role in the success of the First Intifada." In the Second (Al-Aqsa) Intifada, however, he feels that Israel "played a very tricky game": counting on the assumption that nobody was paying much attention to the Palestinian cause globally, and "So suppressing the Intifada or suppressing a popular movement and destroying it easily could be done by causing as much death as possible," without fear of the sort of outcry such actions might arouse elsewhere.

In my opinion this explains why so many [Palestinian] people were killed during the first years of the Second Intifada: 2001, 2002, 2003. Those years witnessed lots of death, and I think Israel wants an end to the popular resistance, because for Israel, having a civil [resistance] movement in Palestine is a big problem. And then if no civil [resistance] movement existed, if all the Palestinian resistance is only a people who are shooting from time to time—[the Israelis] can justify all policies they want to commit against the Palestinian people—starting from entering houses and destroying houses, reaching to practical ethnic cleansing. Nobody will stand against such a process at a time when Israel is able to justify it.

But, concluded Abu Keshek: "Proudly, I say Israel failed to destroy the civil [resistance] movement in Palestine. The presence of internationals from the beginning [of the Al-Aqsa Intifada], which was a response to the failure of the official international community, gave lots of opportunities and lots of support for Palestinians to start moving."

Palestinian Center for Rapprochement (PCR) director, George N. Rishmawi, described further benefits of involving internationals and Israelis in the Palestinian struggle.

When people feel that their pain is being recognized and people know about it and they might do something with regard to it, they will not feel that they are left alone and helpless. I think one of the reasons for the suicide attacks comes from the fact that the Palestinian suffering is being ignored and belittled and the resistance is being viewed as terrorism, while the Israeli aggression and occupation is viewed as self defence. This is very frustrating. But when people see internationals coming, Americans and British in particular—because, you know, Britain was occupying Palestine and now America is the main supporter of Israel—then people feel that there is a chance, that it's not all Americans supporting Israel or not all the English people supporting Israel. Even more, when they know that Jews are coming.[1] "So, not all Jews are supporting Israel." You know the stereotype that we Palestinians have about Jews—an average Palestinian does not even say "Israelis," they say "Jews"—which puts all the Jews in the world in the same category, that they are against the Palestinians. And I think Jews who do not accept that have a big responsibility to show that they are not with the occupation, that they are not supporting the occupation.

PCR and ISM co-founder Ghassan Andoni indicated another important outcome of the latter's strategy of recruiting participants from around the world, when he lauded the ISM model of placing "the kid from Boston in Balata." This, stated Andoni, "not only attracts the circle of activists, but even attracts media and community attention and brings a better chance for more positive reporting about Palestine in the American press." As Huwaida Arraf put it, "Every person who comes to join the ISM has a community around them."

Otherwise Israel and Palestine seem so far away. We do need to wake up the international community. That's what we are trying to do, and I think we've hit on one of the ways to do it. If nothing else, the International Solidarity Movement has made people feel that there are people out there that care enough to come. We have no financial backing or anything like that, but I think it's very effective because, in the end, I do think that people power can overcome. We have been under attack a lot, but I think in the end, we'll overcome; we're not letting these attacks stop us, and I think that's important. We can't really stop those negative articles that are written about us and Israeli government attempts to equate us with terrorists, saying that we harbour terrorists and all of these things; but when they're called to task on it, they can't prove anything. And that's important, and we just have to invest a little more energy in making sure people understand that and in getting more publicity, more information out there about what we're doing. It's difficult, but I think we have been effective in, at least, interesting people who otherwise would not be interested and would not care.

Equally important, this "outside" presence has often made it possible for Palestinians to carry on with their lives a little more normally by lessening their vulnerability to harassment by the Israeli military and neighbouring settlers. Said Tequ'a mayor, S'leiman Abu Muferreh, "The presence of the internationals with the ISM helped us a lot. It prevented the settlers from attacking again, and that gave us a little time for harvesting. Otherwise we would not be able to reach the fields." And Israeli activist Liad Kantorowicz described a project in the village of el-Khader, coordinated by the PCR in Beit Sahour, whereby Israelis were able to help the villagers overcome some of the limitations placed on them by the occupation authorities, who were making it difficult for them to reach the fields to pick their crops, as well as forbidding them to haul their produce to market.

They are only allowed to go to the fields on foot and to pick as much as they can, and even if they were able to go into the field and pick a lot more, they are not allowed to drive on the roads, which are settler roads, to deliver [their produce]. So one of the actions that we were engaging in is helping people get to their fields safely, without being turned back by the Israeli military, and getting Israelis to come to the fields and help the Palestinians deliver the foods to various Palestinian markets, like in East Jerusalem and Bethlehem, so that they can somewhat sustain the economy. And also working with them to see if they can get permits to drive on the roads.

For a number of years, beginning as far back as 2000,[2] Israeli and international participation in the annual olive harvest in the West Bank has served a similar function; in fact, sometimes the ongoing presence of outside activists has been the decisive factor enabling villagers to return to homes they had abandoned to escape settler violence.[3] And, as Neta Golan has pointed out, the presence of Israelis is all the more important now: when internationals are so much easier to deport than previously, an Israeli presence makes a real difference. Adam Keller told me about one such intervention, which had taken place just a few days before our October 2003 interview when, in a latter-day reprise of the "illegal" meetings between Israelis and PLO functionaries in Romania in 1986 described earlier by Reuven Kaminer (of which Keller had been a part, though not one of the four who were arrested) and in Hungary in 1987, Adam Keller and other members and supporters of Gush Shalom decided to visit Yasser Arafat's headquarters, the *Muqata'a* in Ramallah, on the evening of October 4, 2003. There had been a suicide bombing in Haifa earlier that day, and it was feared that the Palestinian president was at risk of a possible deportation attempt (some even feared assassination) by the Israeli authorities. Speaking less than two weeks later, Keller told me that, "At least from the reactions that we heard, we felt that our presence did make some difference."

> For example, Ehud Yatom, a Knesset member from the Likud, spoke in the morning [and said] that after the suicide bombing in Haifa, he had expected that now, at last, the deportation of Arafat would be implemented. And then he said, "I stayed up the whole night and every hour I listened to the news, expecting to hear that Arafat had been deported, and I feel very disappointed that this did not happen. And these leftists were there to give him a human shield, and this is really very terrible—that is a terrible rift in our society." That I heard at seven in the morning, after we had spent that night there. Of course, I don't delude myself that our presence there was the only reason, or even the main reason; I think that the veto by Bush was the main reason the army didn't go there. But still, we were an additional complication, one more hurdle in the way, which was making it more difficult to take such a decision, and I felt quite satisfied with it.

Women's Special Contribution

Ronnee Jaeger, one of the couple of hundred Israeli women of Machsom/ Checkpoint Watch (at the time of our September 2003 interview—by April of 2006, the nearest approximation was 400),[4] stated emphatically: "I think our presence absolutely cuts down the violence."

> The things that are documented by B'tselem, by the Committee Against Torture, they don't happen while we're there. I know that. On the other hand, it's getting harder. I think that our presence keeps a lot of worse things from happening, though increasingly, terrible things *are* happening while we're at the checkpoint. It's important to be there and to document it, but I don't want to document it only for future history. It's documented both for Israelis and the outside world. We do things in both languages. We try very hard to get people to come. Every now and then we get a little note on our website, so we know people are reading it. We just had a meeting with UN personnel who felt that our information is really important for them. They use it all the time. And B'tselem, Physicians for Human Rights—everybody uses it.

Both their gender and the fact that most are "middle aged" gives the women of Machsom Watch an advantage in encounters with the (mostly quite young) Israeli soldiers manning the checkpoints:

> We've kept it as women-only, which makes the soldiers feel much less threatened, and we began with mostly women my age, so we look like, as we say in Hebrew, *dodot tovot* (good aunties). I think I look like a lot of their grandmothers, and I think that that's a help.

And of course, as Israelis, they can sometimes win an argument with a soldier.

> Because of Israel's "sweeping arrests," hardly any Palestinian hasn't been arrested, and then that makes him a problem. We found out that there were permits that people needed to get through. And for a long time, we simply would have arguments with the soldiers about whether the soldiers decided whether a certain permit was a forgery. "How do you know? What makes you such an expert that you know? Does this person look like a person who's dangerous…" We'd go through this, and then they'd usually let them through.

"We always tell [the soldiers] that they have to be accountable to us as citizens," fellow Machsom Watcher, Maya Rosenfeld, had told me. "They don't think so, but still our presence there forces them, in a sense, to communicate in one way or another with us—which would not have been the case with a Palestinian group."

> The military orders oblige the soldiers at the checkpoint to allow humanitarian cases in, for example. This always raises the question of what is a humanitarian case. This is being raised every single time. I have heard many a soldier tell me that a humanitarian case is someone who's half dead: If a Palestinian is so sick that he cannot take care of himself, then this is a humanitarian case, and he may be okayed. But we try to make them aware of the fact that a humanitarian case is *anyone* who wants to see a doctor, [that] it would be grounds for us to file a complaint when we've seen soldiers that prevented people from going through for medical reasons. We always attack them in those grey areas where, at least in principle, they should act according to certain regulations which we know. And when they do not follow these regulations, we are there to say "this and that happened." Or, for example, that we've seen them beat someone or use abusive language. These are always grounds to file a complaint.

"The question," states Rosenfeld, "is what happens to these complaints"—do they bring about any change? Even though it's often impossible to know, "it's very good to do," she says.

In an article about Israeli women's nonviolence published on the internet in mid-2003, Gila Svirsky described actions by some of the nine groups constituting the Coalition of Women for Peace, of which she was a cofounder.[5]

> Some of these involved civil disobedience, such as lying down on the street to block the entrance to the Israeli Ministry of Defense, as a way to protest 'closure' in the territories. Subsequent actions, often in cooperation with mixed-gender peace organizations, involved other nonviolent but illegal acts—the rebuilding of demolished homes or the removal of blockades and filling in of trenches intended to enforce the closure. In other actions, individual women stood in front of army bulldozers or chained themselves to olive trees in an effort to prevent further destruction of Palestinian homes and property. Some of these actions ended in arrests.

This coalition of women's peace organizations has also staged mass actions of nonviolence that are legal. A year and a half ago [December 2001], 5,000 Israeli and Palestinian women marched together from the Israeli to the Palestinian side of Jerusalem under the twin banners, "The Occupation is Killing Us All" and "We Refuse to be Enemies." This June [2003], Israeli women staged a mass "lie-in" in Tel Aviv, with 1,000 women wearing black, stretched out on the pavement as a sign of mourning for the victims of the occupation.

Some of the member organizations of the Coalition engage in other forms of nonviolent resistance. The presence at checkpoints of the women in Machsom Watch is often enough to prevent particularly cruel harassment of Palestinians. Recently these women prevented a soldier from firing at a child by deflecting his gun, leading to their arrest for "interfering with the IDF". The organization New Profile supports conscientious objection to army service, and last year launched a "Women Refuse" campaign. What do they refuse? "To raise our children for war, to ignore war crimes committed in our name, to support the occupation, to continue our normal lives while another nation is suffering because of us." This is a profound use of nonviolence—an attempt to change the militaristic culture of Israeli society and to instil the values of nonviolence in Israeli children.

The most successful case in Israel of the use of nonviolence in the service of peace is the Four Mothers Movement. This group, founded in 1997 by four women whose sons were serving in the Israeli army, sought to mobilize the Israeli public to demand that Israel withdraw its troops from Lebanon, based on the argument that Israel's prolonged presence there serves no security purpose, but jeopardizes the lives of soldiers. ... The Four Mothers Movement never used civil disobedience, but held small demonstrations and vigils that highlighted the sincerity of their plea as law-abiding women, not politicians. Their status as mothers who had sons serving in combat units gave them the right, in the eyes of the public, to challenge Israeli policy in Lebanon. ... The deaths of Israeli soldiers were on the increase in Lebanon, and the message of the Four Mothers fell on attentive ears, feeding public dismay over the seemingly endless body bags. Within 3 years of the start of the movement, the Israeli army withdrew from Lebanon.

The women's peace movement in Israel has used nonviolence in varied and creative ways. While the most dramatic actions have had civil disobedience and risk-taking at the core, a large array of lawful actions has also been used, and no less effectively. ... [T]he strategy of nonviolence clearly provides a greater moral strength and persuasiveness than violent strategies. The practice of nonviolence has also been empowering to those who feel otherwise helpless, and results seem to confirm its effectiveness.

The Complementary Roles of Activist Organizations and the Media

Amira Hass, addressing the April 2007 joint struggle conference in Bil'in, stressed the interconnected roles played by the media and concerned journalists, on the one hand, and activist groups, on the other, in achieving even small successes.

> One cannot work without the other. Their pressure and my pressure, or that of other journalists who work like myself, have to be seen together; they are not separate. A few weeks ago I had an off-the-record talk with a former Israeli officer—a very high officer—and I asked if it's only our imagination that, when we publish something about a case of somebody—like a person who needs an operation and they don't get a permit to go to Israel or to Amman to be operated on—if it's just by coincidence that, when we publish it in an Israeli paper, in the Israeli media, that suddenly all the security problems have been erased and the person gets the permit. He told me, "No way, this is not a coincidence."

Hass made the point, however, that despite "all the successes of the media together with the hard labour of anti-occupation groups," real structural change has not resulted.

> So many Israelis are fighting against the new manifestations of the Israeli occupation, and we have not stopped the wall. We have not stopped the confiscation of land. We have not stopped the separation between Gaza and the West Bank and other forms of separation. So there is an enormous gap between all the efforts that we put in and the real result. And the real result is that we're not facing only a regime of occupation. It is an occupation—a colonialist system, an apartheid system—but it is also at the same time, strangely enough, a democracy for Jews. It is a democracy for Jews, because I'm standing here and I can say whatever I want, I can write whatever I want, people in Israel can protest however much they want in whatever arena, and nothing happens to them. We can publish whatever we want and we can tell the truth as much as we want. And yet, the impact is so limited.
>
> I don't want to discourage us now, especially not here in Bil'in, which has been the example—as Budrus has been—for a wonderful

struggle, such a long struggle. But still, we have to face the reality that when we finish this conference, when we go home, our impact on changing this reality is very limited.

Nonetheless, Hass went on to describe and analyze two dramatic exceptions to her caveat: "two struggles that succeeded a bit more than changing in a limited personal way."

One struggle was when, at the end of 1995, the Israeli Ministry of the Interior under Labour—it *was* Labour—started to cancel or to revoke the residency status of Palestinians in East Jerusalem by the thousands. It was done without any warning. People realized all of a sudden that for different reasons their residency rights in Jerusalem had been revoked. A campaign was started against this policy, and after two or three years, the Israeli Ministry of the Interior had to backtrack. I remember that in 1999 I queried the ministry and got the reply that about 8,000 identity cards of Jerusalemites—that is, their right of residency—had been restored to them.

Another struggle which brought about some sort of change in Israeli policy was [around the issue of] demolition of houses in Jerusalem and also in the West Bank. This campaign was headed by the Israeli Committee against House Demolitions. It involved a lot of acts of civil disobedience, rebuilding houses which had been demolished for lack of a building permit. And it too was successful, because for some time after this, the authorities had to suspend this policy. The same person that told me about the media told me that here there was a clear order from higher up to stop the demolition of houses.

Now, if we analyze these campaigns, we see the similarities. Both were run jointly by Palestinians, Israelis and internationals, both inside and outside the country. Both used a combination of legal means [i.e., the law courts],[6] popular grassroots activities, and the media. They could reach the media because people made themselves visible. The media—and especially the media in our democracy-for-Jews—is Jewish, so it is affected by the interests and the mentality of the ruling class, which is Jewish people. This places Jewish-Israeli journalists in a paradoxical position, because the fundamental role of the media is to monitor power, and we are *at* the centre of power but we also have to *monitor* the centre of power. So the people's movement has to be visible in order to make it into the media.

"Imported" Ideas of Classical Nonviolence Enhance Local Initiatives

Another opportunity to share memories of the 1980s presented itself to me when I interviewed Sami Awad at the Holy Land Trust. Although many had scoffed at his uncle Mubarak Awad when the U.S.-trained psychologist returned home to Palestine advocating nonviolent resistance to the occupation, in retrospect it seems that there were those who took his ideas seriously, even then. For instance, when I met with Sami Awad in September 2003, I told him of having gone to see his uncle Mubarak on a visit to Jerusalem in February 1988, hoping to discuss the possibility of involving Canadians in an act of nonviolent resistance at Canada Park,[7] something the elder Awad had been working on with a group of West Bank Palestinians just prior to the outbreak of the First Intifada. This project never came to fruition, since the Intifada directed energies elsewhere. But at the time of my visit, Awad had just returned from Gaza, where he had gone to urge the Intifada leadership to replace the full-day commercial strikes currently in place with half-day strikes so they could continue in the long term—on the Gandhian model. They subsequently did so. "That's why he was deported," remarked nephew Sami, "He was seen by the Israelis as a very effective threat to them."

"You know," said Sami Awad, holding up a small book entitled *Non-Violent Resistance: A Strategy for the Occupied Territories*, "this little booklet that he wrote in '84, three or four years before the Intifada, is talking about nonviolence in the occupied territories." He pointed to a list of 121 Ways to Resist the Occupation, adapted for the booklet from Gene Sharp's original 198 nonviolent techniques[8] and told me, "Many of these ways were adopted and used by the people."

> That's when the eyes of the Israeli government opened and they said, "Well, maybe he has something to do with this [uprising]." He was involved with the local communities and meetings and things like that. He was not the one who said "Let's do it!" but when it was happening, he was very involved with the leadership. You know, it's incredible. His involvement, for the time he was here, has resulted in—I can't even say a number—but at least ten organizations that have spun off of his philosophy of teaching nonviolence and democracy.

Sometimes, Just Plain Chutzpah is What's Needed!

Ghassan Andoni described the successful nonviolent occupation of an Israeli military base in late 2000, not long after the outbreak of the Al-Aqsa Intifada.

On December 28 we gathered some internationals, a few hundred Palestinians, and an Israeli group, and we actually marched [in] and took over an Israeli military camp east of Beit Sahour. The soldiers were taken by surprise, and some of us went up to the soldiers' tower, raised the Palestinian flag, and asked the soldiers to leave the site because their existence there was useless, but harmful to everybody: "You are not here to protect anybody. There are no settlers around, there are no roads the Israelis use, and you are only shelling and bombarding civilian homes and destroying their lives. If you move from here, everybody will be happy, including Israelis." Of course we didn't expect them to leave, but we occupied the place for about three hours and then left. They started gathering and preparing their guns and threatening, but we ignored them and continued inside there and left after a few hours, when we were ready to leave.

The army was really embarrassed by this. Media in Israel attacked the army for allowing this to happen. The army wanted to defend itself by declaring that we never entered the sovereignty of the camp, which led us to publish the pictures, which embarrassed them again. So they started saying, "Well, we were planning to move the camp two hundred metres to the east, blah, blah, blah," and we said, "Fine, give us back the land, if that's your plan." And, in fact, they did: they actually moved it and covered it with like an artificial mountain of dirt and rocks, so that it looks like a castle now, and that encouraged us. We saw that it was symbolic, but we felt that there was power in such symbolic actions.

Creative Actions Bring Increased Media Coverage

Creativity in campaigns and even in isolated actions, such as the audacious one described above, is an important factor in keeping the media interested. Even something as simple as a soccer game between Palestinian villagers and international volunteers can provide enough of a sense of novelty to draw in the international media, as George N. Rishmawi recounted.

Interest by the media in the nonviolent actions sometimes is up and sometimes it's down, and sometimes we have to be very creative in the actions so that the media will be interested. August, 2001, was the most successful media campaign. CNN came to cover a football [i.e., soccer] game that we organized—a football game! That was a football game on the playground that people were not allowed access to near el-Khader village, and the soldiers were on the opposite hill, and anybody who went to the football field, they would just shoot at them. So we organized a football game between the villagers there and the internationals. How simple it was, but it was symbolic at the same time and defying that soldiers were shooting at everyone. [The media] covered that and, of course, they covered all the other actions. We were on the first page of the *International Herald Tribune*; we were on CNN also several times.

Of course, in the beginning of the [Israeli military] incursions in April [2002], we got lots of media attention. The internationals who entered the Church of the Nativity also brought lots of media attention. This kind of thing is important, and Palestinians see it on TV; now many Palestinians have satellite dishes and they watch the mass media, like CNN and BBC, and Arab media—al-Jazeera and all of that. When the internationals were there and people started talking about that all the time, they started to feel that there is an importance to the presence of the internationals there in Palestine, so they can expose what the Israeli army's doing to the whole world. Many Palestinians believe that the main reason that Israel has a free hand is that people in the world do not know what is really happening in Palestine, what Israel is doing to the Palestinians, because the media do not report everything.

The Importance of Adaptability and Persistence

Stating that "all our actions have not been so useful politically," Issa Souf, brother of Nawaf Souf and a veteran of years of joint Israeli-Palestinian nonviolent actions in and around Haris village, displayed a valuable openness to change strategy when necessary.

We tried many times to open [access to] the villages, to take the blocks away from the entrances to the villages; but we haven't succeeded any time because if we succeed to move the blocks or the soil from the entrance or the street, in the same minute the bulldozers come and put it [back] again. And maybe we lose someone from that action, because the soldiers come and are shooting and arresting people, and this happened many times. Many times they arrested Neta [Golan] and many of her international friends, and they stayed at the police station for a long time. And some of them cannot come back because the Israeli military don't allow them to.

So when we felt that these actions were not useful, we stopped them. We stopped these actions and activities and limited [our activities] to helping the suffering families from the Palestinian people—like those who lost their jobs, who lost their olive trees, who have a killed son or wounded or a bad case. And all of these cases are humanitarian cases. It's not because of terrorism or anything, just feelings of humanity and human rights that we feel inside us. We were giving these families food, because no one from these families has income to continue their lives, and many of them have lost their jobs because no one can leave the village or the city. These were good actions for the Palestinians, for us, and for the Jews.

Souf went on to describe how the influence of the nonviolent activism in Haris spread beyond the village, beginning with ISM and the International Women's Peace Service (IWPS), both of which got their start in Haris.

Many activities in all the West Bank started after us, and that means we have opened many eyes to this [nonviolent] way by our struggles against the occupation. [W]hen we had a good action in the West Bank, many, many other people were thinking and searching for a way to continue their struggle peacefully, so when they heard about it on the TV or in the newspapers, they started making other relationships with other groups in the world or from Israel and continued in these actions, and now there's a big movement in Palestine of international people and also of Israeli peace groups.

One of the Israeli groups (in this case both Jewish- and Palestinian-Israeli) that Issa and Nawaf Souf and other activists in Haris have long cooperated with is Ta'ayush. Through its reliable hands-on work, Ta'ayush has done more than bring humanitarian aid in to those pauperized by the occupation. It has, importantly, built trust and made a strong political statement. Yossi Wolfson, commenting in October 2003 on "a very big growth in real nonviolent direct action" since 2000, praised the group: "Ta'ayush did a lot of great work in just being very persistent. If they are stopped at a road block, they will get off the bus and walk. It's not about demonstrations and being taken to prison and so on; it's about bringing assistance to a village and also olive harvesting. They just do it, and they will not let themselves be stopped."

In July of 2002, Ta'ayush activists Leena Delasheh and Noa Nativ, at their public presentation in Vancouver, BC, gave some examples of the group's nonviolent resistance activities. Said Delasheh:

> The Israeli army decided at one point that they would barricade the entrance to the village of Issawiya with a road block; a village five minutes from the Hebrew University, a part of the Jerusalem municipal territory. And the army did not give the village any reason at all for closing the village. No explanation. The citizen's questions were not answered; the police didn't even bother answering them. So we decided to work together, Palestinians from the village of Issawiya and Ta'ayush, to dismantle the roadblock. And we came, hundreds, and we began working side by side, Palestinians and Jews, to dismantle the barricade. The other part of the group were holding hands and blocking the police from preventing the work from going on. And the police, of course, were not gentle with us, to say the least. They used brutal force and caused many injuries. Some of our activists went to the hospital; one old lady got a head injury from a sound grenade that hit her on the head. And the police used teargas and they arrested three of our activists; and we went together—Palestinians from Issawiya and Ta'ayush activists—to the police station and waited outside for hours until the police released all of the people who were taken into custody.

At the same presentation, Noa Nativ spoke about Ta'ayush's effective support for the South Hebron Hills cave dwellers who have faced repeated expulsions and destruction of property since at least as far back as 1995.

> In the summer of 2001 we organized a convoy to the South Hebron area two months after another expulsion had taken place, and again, the residents were allowed to return. We came there a few hundred people, saw the place, spoke with the people. It was all very nice, until two days later they were expelled again, and our activists arrived immediately, spent the night with them until the court gave the order that they were not to be expelled again until further discussion, as it always does—and as the Israeli army always ignores after a while, though it's useful for several months at a time—and ever since, we've been in close contact with them.

Effective Personal Nonviolence: An Israeli, a Palestinian and an "International" Tell Their Stories

Israeli military refusal (the refusenik movement) in general is treated in more detail in the next section, but Yesh Gvul activist Peretz Kidron also shared this story of how he dealt with an attempt to compromise his personal "not in the occupied territories" stance.

> The one good story I have is: I turned up for duty, and I said, "I'm not serving in the occupied territories." So they said, "Okay." I was very surprised. Then they said, "We're going off to a firing range." So I said, "Interesting. Where is that?" They said, "Beit El" [a West Bank settlement housing a military headquarters]. So I said, "Beit El—I'm sorry, I'm not going." And this officer came over, and he was *so* offended. He said, "We understand that you refuse. We've accepted all that; and now, all we're asking you to do is get on the bus, go there, fire off a couple of clips at a target, then get on the bus and come back. Can't you possibly do it just this once?" Now, the unit would assemble at a police station in Abu Ghosh [a Palestinian village inside Israel]. We were just outside Abu Ghosh. [The officer] was wearing a yarmulke [skull-cap signifying that he was an observant Jew]. I said, "You know, I'll do it, but on one condition: you and I are going down into the village and we're going to share a *steak lavan* (white steak; i.e., pork), just this once." He turned pale and walked away. And then they didn't know what to do, because they needed me. So I did a month's duty without having fired a single shot, which is totally against regulations, because you're not allowed to hold a weapon unless you've had some kind of practice.

Nafez Assaily recounted examples of personal interactions with the Israeli authorities where he was able to apply his understanding of nonviolence to good effect.

> I have a house in Hebron near [the settlement of] Giv'at Harsina. They surrounded the settlement with a fence, and they built a new fence to make a distance between the old fence and the new fence, and the bulldozer began to work on my land. So I went to the bulldozer and began to take pictures. The man got out and asked why I was filming him. I said, "I'm not interested in you. I'm interested in what your bulldozer is doing. I have the right to film because this is my land, and you didn't ask my permission. I understand that you do your work to get money, and you have a family to feed, and this is your *parnassa* [livelihood (*Heb.*)]. I told him, "I have nothing against you, but the settlers who sent you, they didn't ask permission from me to dig on my land, so they have to ask permission. Then my answer will be yes or no, but digging on my land without my permission is illegal. I understand their

need for security, but they didn't respect my property." Now since two months, they stopped digging. They built a fence on the neighbours' [property], but near my land they didn't do anything. I assume two things: Because I turned it from a political into a civil issue, that "You dig on my land without my permission, and this is not [legal]," maybe they are waiting to find something legal for this. Or they are waiting for the Israeli army to support them with a military bulldozer and do the work. So this I consider a kind of victory.

Assaily also described coming upon soldiers who were harassing Palestinians on their way to work in Hebron, claiming it was an illegal assembly because of the numbers.

I had negotiations with the army about it, until the army found their senses that it was nonsense, just people who wanted to go into Hebron to do their work. And the people passed. It wasn't planned. Another thing was that I did communicate with them in an effective way with nonviolence. First of all, I showed them that I understand their work. Second, I showed them that I understand that they have orders. And also, at the same time, I showed them that the people need to pass for their work and for their *parnassa*. It works sometimes, and sometimes it doesn't work. But I'm speaking about the times it worked.

Marylene Schultz is a French national originally from the Alsace region. She has a Jerusalem I.D. and has lived and worked in the West Bank for some forty years, since before many of her fellow activists were born. She has initiated a number of nonviolent vigils and actions of her own, as well as taking part in quite a few Israeli anti-occupation activities; and when travel for Palestinians was freer, Schultz often brought teenage girls from the West Bank group home where she worked along with her to the Women in Black vigils in Jerusalem, where she is a regular participant. She described an encounter with soldiers at Qalandiya checkpoint, between Ramallah and Jerusalem.

We tried to say to the soldiers, "Please put down your gun when there are children." My [Hebrew-speaking] friend spoke a lot with the soldiers. Once we were there and there were some female students trying to go home to Tulkarm, because their university was closed. And when the students were coming, [my friend] stopped to talk to the soldier, and the soldier answered and answered and answered, and all the students passed. And once, when we had a sign offering to help carry people's loads—in English and Arabic—a soldier asked me, "Why don't you have your paper in Hebrew?" I said, "There are no Israelis who have to carry something here—unless you want me to carry your gun, and I will throw it very far." He said, "I would like to do the same."

Military Refusal: In a Class by Itself

One of the principal categories into which Gene Sharp divides his list of 198 nonviolent tactics is noncooperation. In the military context, this may include refusal to carry out unjust orders or even to serve at all. Israeli military refusers are, by and large "selective" in their refusal, declining service in occupied territory, but carrying out other military duties assigned to them. Some, like the signatories of the High School Seniors' Letter (*Michtav haShministim*), refuse all military service for the duration of the occupation. A very small minority are out-and-out pacifists. The common denominator among Israeli refuseniks is their unwillingness to cooperate with the repressive regime: a very powerful method of resistance. In fact, the very existence of an Israeli movement of refusal to serve in an occupying army is widely regarded as being of key importance in hastening the end of the occupation. As Yesh Gvul's Peretz Kidron points out, "If you can convert soldiers to make this whole army of occupation thing insecure and make it controversial—make people think about why it is—this is the most effective way of campaigning against the occupation."

New Profile
Although the antimilitarist organization New Profile may not employ nonviolent action in the usual sense of the word, it is impossible to ignore the group's vital role in the Israeli military refusal movement. Speaking in late 2003, Rela Mazali described "a very broad-based, mostly unorganized draft resistance movement in Israel today."

About a half of eighteen-year-olds who are candidates for conscription in Israel—and that excludes automatically most of the Palestinian citizens of Israel—either don't enlist at all or drop out quite early on, so that mandatory military duty is being completed by only a half of the candidates. This has not yet registered in public consciousness. People still talk about "our people's army," still talk about "everybody" going. But in fact, many of the young people, for various reasons—not all of them to do with the conflict, necessarily—are saying, "I'm dropping out of this game; it's not mine. I'm not playing it. I don't buy into the politicians' deployment of the military. I don't trust them. I just want to go ahead with my life and do what I think."

So, this is a very large de facto movement. A small part of it, and a very important part of it, and a very brave part of it, are declared refusers who come out openly and say, "We will not be part of this military" or "We will not be part of its actions beyond the Green Line." There's a spectrum of different ways of formulating this strategy, from the pilots, on the one hand, who have recently said, "We are not going to bomb places where there are innocent [civilians]," but who don't object to serving, to flying, to bombing places where they don't think there's innocent [civilians], etc.; through Courage to Refuse, who accept military service, but don't want to serve beyond the Green Line and don't want to commit war crimes; through Yesh G'vul, who are a different "shade"; and all the way to the high school seniors (*Shministim*) and many members of New Profile, who are against serving altogether in an occupying army, and some of whom are also pacifists, both men and women.

Conscientious Objection: For Women Only

Actually, Mazali explained, partly as a result of pressure exerted by Knesset Members on behalf of New Profile several years before, as well as pressure from the Israeli High Court of Justice, "we got a response from [then Defence Minister Ehud Barak] stating that pacifists were recognized by the army," which "has stated, as it were, that it does recognize pacifists." "But," she continued, "in fact the conscience committees hardly exempt any pacifists at all." On the other hand, "there's a legal provision allowing women to be exempted from the military on grounds of conscience," although this is not well known, "so that a young girl who feels that she doesn't want to enlist on grounds of conscience often doesn't know she's legally entitled." New Profile provides guidance to female draftees who want to claim C.O. status, to "help them find their way through that maze."

That's part of what we do. Men have no provision explicit in the law for conscientious objection, no legal recognition of their right to freedom of conscience. In Israel, there's no such thing in law. This discrimination is rooted in sexism. Men are the "real soldiers," and girls are the kind-of "toy soldiers" or "imitation soldiers." They're not the real thing, so who cares anyway if they do serve or don't serve? It's not such a big deal.

I don't need to tell you that today the occupation is more brutal and rampant and unleashed in its criminal cruelty than it's ever been. And that's saying a lot, because it was cruel before, too. So, in that sense, things are getting worse and worse. On the other hand, looking mainly at Israeli-Jewish society, I can see more and more symptoms of this society's getting fed up with the effects of militarization. The big, broad-based, undeclared refusal movement is one symptom, but there are others. And we have a role in that, although we're just one catalyst within a whole complex of different factors that are operating there. For instance, six years ago, when the first young man we actually accompanied from his first declaration of pacifism through the whole process of going repeatedly to the military, and eventually to the High Court of Justice, and just a couple of months ago getting finally exempted after more than five years—that's Yinon Hiller—when we began accompanying him and, among other things, looking for legal counsel, we had a really hard time finding a lawyer. Today, some of the very law firms that we originally approached are out there at the forefront of this struggle on the behalf of the refusers, including the Association for Civil Rights in Israel and including well-known law firms that work on human rights. So they've moved considerably, and they are now very publicly associated with the legal struggle concerning refusal and draft resistance. Now that's an accomplishment, and we definitely had a very specific role in that, in pushing some of these firms and organizations, in posing the questions to them, and not taking "no" for an answer.

And then in this past year, there has been—this is a funny "accomplishment"—the highest number ever of young men resisting conscription in prison at one time. And literally all of them, in one way or another, have been involved with us, have been supported by us. I'm not saying that it's all our work. I mean they're their own people, they grew up in the families they grew up in, et cetera, but definitely we had a lot of input here. And we also are among the groups that are making this known, that are getting the word out there. So that's a very clear and direct effect of our work. We're pretty well-known by word-of-mouth as a network to which people can turn when they need information about these issues.

New Profile is also the first organization to deal systematically with women's draft resistance and conscientious objection. "There were a few individuals, like Toma Ŝik, whom you may have heard of—but never any organization."[9]

> We do that. We provide them with very orderly information, with support; we accompany them through the process once they've made their decisions. And the whole issue of bringing women's draft resistance into visibility, into public knowledge, is quite new. And that is the work of New Profile—and, of course, of the wonderful young women who are doing this, some of whom are members of New Profile and some of whom aren't. And that's fine. Each of them chooses her own course. Each of the girls has to go before a committee that is often quite aggressive and humiliating: it's a committee of men, most of them military. But today, at least, many girls do that, and if they're insistent enough, most of them are exempted.

Yesh Gvul: There is a Border! There is a Limit!

Peretz Kidron is a long-time member of the first Israeli refuser organization, Yesh Gvul, and editor of the compilation of refuser statements, *Refusenik: Israel's Soldiers of Conscience* (Kidron 2004). He spoke about Yesh Gvul's beginnings in "a sort of mutual assistance, solidarity, nothing more."

> But that was very important, because until then, people had been refusing on an individual basis, and they'd had very little significance beyond as a statement of conscience by the individual. Why refusal? Well, because certainly you can't fight a war without an army. But the same holds true of an occupation. There's no occupation without an army of occupation, and there's no army of occupation without soldiers. It's as simple as that. If you can convert soldiers to make this whole army of occupation thing insecure and make it controversial; make people think about why it is. This was the most effective way of campaigning against the occupation.
>
> It's a very effective technique, because it hits a particularly sensitive place in the power structure, because it hits at the army. And it has enormous potential because the army never know where it's going to end. Today they're twenty, and each one of those has ten, fifteen, fifty friends, colleagues. You know, from their point of view, it's a rotten apple, where they never know when the whole barrel is going to go. So that's the power of it. I was involved in all

kinds of groups, in all kinds of protests. But I felt that general protests against the occupation had very little effect, whereas dealing with the issue of refusal is the very guts of the whole military thing, and that's the point. I was still serving as a reservist when I first began with Yesh Gvul, but I continued even when I ended my reserve service, because I still consider it the most effective bunch to work with, and it hits closest to the jugular of the regime that we oppose.

I think it is a very effective, very important sphere of activity. I think it's probably the most important, because it has such enormous impact. It kind of spurs people's conscience, particularly at a time like this when there are lots of people who say, "Yes, we agree with you, but what the hell, what's the point?" And they prefer to stay home, and why bother? And, you know, the refuseniks won't leave them alone. How can you sit at home when this guy's gone to prison? So in that sense, it kind of steps on people's tails and gets them active. So I think we have a very good effect on the broader peace movement.

And then there's, of course, the fact that the refusenik issue has a direct effect on policy making. The policy makers have to consider the possibility that maybe the army won't march. There were several examples [of this effect on policy]: there was the [1982] Lebanon War, in which, according to [then army commander] Moshe Levy, one of the reasons for the army recommending an end to the fighting in central and northern Lebanon was that they said, in his words, "refusals were running in the hundreds, and we were afraid they would run into the thousands and tens of thousands." Interesting, because *we* didn't know about the hundreds. We only knew of a hundred and sixty-eight people who went to prison. Maybe there were a few hundred more [i.e., who refused but didn't go to prison]: maybe that was what he was referring to. Anyway, the army never gives out exact figures.

The army initially says, "Oh, we get a hundred percent reporting for duty," and then they don't give any more statistics. Then you hear that when they want a hundred soldiers, they have to send out two hundred notices, because there are always a hundred who are [getting out of serving] one way or another. So that's a kind of diffuse dissatisfaction, but not real opposition. Usually for every open refusenik there's ten or twenty grey [i.e., people who avoid service without refusing outright]. I don't think that the grey refusal has the same kind of effect on the army, even though it's much bigger. It doesn't have the same kind of effect, because it's not that the army has a physical shortage of manpower. It's just the deterrent effect of the potential: "One guy just refused; I wonder how many buddies he has." And that, for the army command, is very scary. And then there was what Netanyahu said when he came back from the Wye Plantation talks. He said, "We have to show that we're working for peace, because if we don't, next time there's a war, half the army won't show up to fight."

Although Yesh Gvul doesn't generally work with Palestinians directly,[10] Kidron maintains that "On the political level, I think that we are—in all humility—enormously important to the Palestinians."

> You say "Yesh Gvul," and, you know, *chapeau* [makes as if to tip his hat respectfully]. While the five *Shministim* were in prison, they wrote an open letter to the Palestinians demanding an end to attacks on civilians, and this was published in the Palestinian press. And I can't think of anybody else, any other Israeli whatever his credentials, who could have got that message through in that kind of way and have it listened to. I don't know what effect it had, but at least it got through. And I don't think any other organization, including peace groups, would have been able to do it, because [refusal to serve] has aroused a terrific amount of respect on the Palestinian side.

Shministim: High School Seniors Say "No!"

Sitting on the grass across the road from the army base where he was under "open detention" for his part in that year's High school Seniors' Letter, Matan Kaminer pointed out that, although conscription is not an issue for the bulk of Israel's Palestinian citizens, it is for the Druze community in Israel.

> There are Druze refuseniks; many of them are treated much more harshly by the army, as are Russian refuseniks. I think that the Druze refusal is very important. I'm happy always to hear about new Druze refuseniks, because, first of all, it requires more courage than it does from us, because they're treated more harshly. Second of all, I think if that community gets into refusing, it will be a very important development.[11]

Although "[refusal] alienates a lot of people," said Kaminer, "I think it's effective."

I don't think it's much more effective than, say, any other anti-occupation work that's being done, but it's part of the process. The strength of refusal is that it's a direct action, even by the fact of it's being a non-action: It's noncooperation; it's disobedience. The occupation can't exist if it's not supported by Israeli society, whether that is by the soldiers themselves, whether that is by the community that sends them, whether that is by our tax sheqels; and refusal is a big part of ending that. It highlights the part that Israelis have to play in ending the occupation. It says, "We are not going to be there, we're not going to be a part of that..."

The refusal movement is not just a movement of young people about to enlist; it's also—in the past, more dominantly—a movement of older people who are in the reserves. Older men, specifically. [Their numbers had] kind of fallen during the last while, but since our letter came out two years ago, it's become more dominant again. There was the officers' and combat soldiers' letter, which came out after our letter, which had about five hundred signatories and included all sorts of combat soldiers and officers who were refusing to go to the territories. This year there was a letter signed by twenty-seven air force pilots, of whom the majority are retired; there are nine who are still on active reserve duty, which means they do a flight every week or so. It's very *active* reserve duty, and they've refused to be part of the assassination flights in the territories. I think all nine have been thrown out of the air force in the past few weeks. That's the latest development in the refusal issue. On that plane, it's effective.

The Importance of Not Being There—and of Explaining Why

The effectiveness of refusal on the "Israeli consensus" is more ambiguous, says Kaminer. "The mainstream consensus in Israel is that you go through the army. Everybody does it."

It's not something that you argue about, even if you disagree. Some people on the left say that you can change things from within. That is, if you are a more humane soldier at the roadblock, then you can change things, you can make life easier on the Palestinians. That's one approach. I can't completely deny that it might be effective in some specific quarters, but basically, I think the most important thing is not being there. It's not only not being there, but saying clearly why you're not there and that you're willing to face the consequences for not being there, even though we don't think that we're criminals or that we need to be put in jail. It alienates a lot of people, especially those who have a mainstream way of thinking. "You're not taking part of the national burden. What right do you have to criticize if you're not part of it? Why don't you leave the country altogether?" People say that, but I think they basically understand our point of view.

A lot of people tell me, "I don't agree with you, but I respect your commitment to your beliefs and your willingness to accept the consequences." That changes something in people's thought. Even if they don't agree with you, they have to think about it. They have to see refusal as one more approach that they have to deal with. Even if they don't agree with it, they have to explain to themselves why they don't agree with it and why they're not willing to do that. That's significant, especially for people who are on the left, and who do see and agree that Palestinians have rights and that the Palestinian state is something that needs to happen for us and for them. When they're faced with our decision, I think that it makes it more difficult for them to serve. They have to think about it twice.

Whenever anybody asks me—and I get asked this question a lot—"What are you doing here at the base? Why are you dressed the way you are? Why do you have to do this or that?" I say I'm under detention. "Why are you under detention?" "I refused to join the army." "Why did you refuse to join the army?" "Because of the occupation." Then we start talking about the occupation. The more people I meet, the more people I talk about it with. That's the first topic of conversation with anybody that I meet. It gets a bit tiring, but I think it's effective in that way, because it makes people have to think.

I think most young people in Israel, and in the West generally, are uninformed, and, more than that, they're disinformed by the media and by the educational system. I think fighting that is a priority, getting the word out on everything from the occupation to social injustice to the war in Iraq and so on. It's a constant struggle because the other side has a lot more resources than we do. But the fight's not over yet.

Combatants for Peace: Not an Oxymoron

When Elik Elhanan, one of the founders of Combatants for Peace, completed his compulsory service in the Israeli army—not long after the death of his younger sister in a suicide bombing, and with a growing sense of disillusionment with military solutions—he left Israel as well, "with a very clear idea in my head that there is no one to talk to, there's nothing to talk about because nobody cares about anything. Everyone was dreaming of a 'new Middle East'; nobody wanted to see what was going on the ground. And I said, 'The hell with it.' I'm not going to die or kill for these people. I'm out of there." Then he came back.

The big change, the really radical change, was that I decided not only to come back, but to engage myself in political activity, to become a political activist. I come from a background of political activists, and I always had a very negative opinion about all of that. But I did my undergraduate studies in France, and over there I got acquainted with—basically—a notion that doesn't exist any more in Israel, and that is of a politicized society that is politically involved. And I came to realize that there is a possibility to change things like that, and that even if the system is fucked up, there are still ways to work: around it, underneath it, behind it, you can still do things and bring about change.

I think, like in most other places, the society in Israel is much more intelligent than the leaders give it credit for, and people are willing to listen and are willing to talk and are willing to hear. And I think that the same is true, also, on the Palestinian side. Because over there, what has been going on in the last seven years [i.e., since 2000] is not a popular struggle, by no means. It's not a popular struggle. And engaging people and moving people towards some more positive action—political positive action—I think this can bring a lot to the Palestinian society, as a society. For us, as Israeli peace activists, it's very important, because the question we are confronted with constantly is, "Where is the Palestinian peace [movement]?" And I can say, "here." And often you hear the question—we heard it hundreds of times in hundreds of meetings—"You are nice guys, but other people that are not ...?" And we can tell them, "Listen, we are not nice guys. This guy is a terrorist; I am a war criminal. We are not nice, by no means. We made a change, everyone can make that change."

Like, nobody would listen to "Nice Guys for Peace," but "Combatants for Peace"—the fact that I was an officer in a[n Israeli] Special Forces unit—these words have more weight. As somebody who stabbed soldiers and spent ten-to-fifteen years in prison because of that, [a Palestinian Combatant's] words have more weight. And we want to use this weight to really promote popular debate. I don't think that we will create the critical mass that will change things, but we want to create debate; we want to integrate those ideas in the discourse that exists today in Israel/Palestine. We hope to reach enough people so that our voice will be heard also outside the marginal left, and we think that, really, the combatants are the people that can carry this voice over. And we want to engage as many combatants as possible from both sides in this activity.

Not "Nice Guys" but Not Radicals Either

Elhanan is also active in the refusenik group Courage to Refuse, and he points to that group's "normal, mainstream, middle-class" profile (like that of the Israeli members of Combatants for Peace) as giving these groups an advantage over the earlier, more "radical," refusenik organizations in terms of potential impact on the broader Israeli public. When the Courage to Refuse statement (originally called the Combatants' Letter) was published in January 2002, he says, "All of a sudden, people who were not radical left wingers, but normal, mainstream, middle-class Israelis made that statement, and people joined and it grew incredibly." Although he thinks highly of the Anarchists Against the Wall, Elhanan explained that he feels that "with their funny hairdos and with their piercing everything and with their gender and anti-meat issues, and all that—with all due respect, and I really do mean respect—the message somehow doesn't get across."

> They're getting a very good reputation, but by people who know them. For example, our [Palestinian] friends, the first time that they saw them, they were completely shocked. The next time, they were their best friends, and you see how they're treated in Bil'in. But when an up-and-coming politician has to decide if he's going to bet on these guys or on those guys, the ones with the piercings and gender issues, I think, will lose. We [Combatants for Peace] present something that is much more appealing to the mainstream, which is, at the same time, much more difficult to digest. Because they are anarchists, we know where to put them. But where do you put the officer from [the elite unit] Sayeret Matkal who is standing together with the Palestinians? So in a way, it's something that opens a door, but is much more challenging.
>
> You know, back in the day, Yeshayahu Leibowitz[12] said that if five hundred officers and soldiers will refuse, then the earth will shake here. In Courage to Refuse, there were six hundred and thirty, and the earth—well, it moved a bit. What we're aiming for [in Combatants for Peace] is basically the same notion, but with five hundred Israeli combatants and five hundred Palestinian combatants, we can hopefully reach an impact. I think that we'll probably need more, but if we can create a group that will be large enough and

popular enough... In the last year we did more than seventy activities inside the Israeli community—mostly meetings, lectures, house meetings, meeting in schools, universities; actually, now we're going to a pre-military school—and we see the reactions.

Sitting in his office near the a-Ram checkpoint between Jerusalem and Ramallah, Palestinian ex-fighter Wael Salame emphasized another aspect of Combatants for Peace that makes it unique.

> It's not like the other organizations that are working for peace on both sides, Israeli and Palestinian partners. We are very different: we were fighting each other before. This is the background for us. And also we have a clear message for the whole world—and there is agreement between both sides—what we are looking for first of all is to end the Israeli occupation of the Palestinian territories, to have a Palestinian independent state in the Eastern part of Jerusalem and the occupied territories.
>
> And this is the same message that we are fighting for since 1974, when our leader Yasser Arafat was in the Security Council in the States, and he raised the olive branch and the gun. We are looking and we are fighting for the same points. But what is different or what has changed is the way. What we are looking to do now is to reach these points in a nonviolent way. We are just sitting and talking to each other from both sides. Because violence will bring more violence. Blood will bring more blood, and this circle doesn't stop.

Salame is hoping to help forge a nonviolent way towards a solution—the end to the Israeli occupation—cognizant of the price in blood paid for "the fighting way that didn't bring any solution." "The problem is," he says, "all the power is focused in Israeli society and international society and the American leadership, and we have to fight inside the international media to clarify who's the liar, who's the killer, who's the occupier, who's the victim." Besides confronting the media and their own communities, members of Combatants for Peace venture, along with their partners from "the other side," onto each other's turf.

> For example, we are talking in a lecture on the Israeli side, somewhere in a high school or in a house meeting, and the soldier who refuses now, our partner from our organization, he starts to talk about what he did when he served in the Palestinian territories, the crimes that he did—in front of his people. And I follow him to explain

what I paid for this kind of terrorism. At the minimum, he changed maybe two or three, sometimes ten or twenty persons: he changed their mind and he opened their mind to think about there's another nation beside [them], there's another people living behind these borders. This helps us. Many of them, before they send their kids to serve in the Israeli army, he tells them, "Just, you have to think. There is a human being you are going to fight—with no guns, with nothing. They are fighting to liberate themselves, to liberate their land, and there is an occupation. We are a tool of the occupation." This helps us.

Also, we on the Palestinian side are starting to talk about violent and nonviolent ways: where we are going to win and where lose. For example, if there is any Palestinian activity inside the civilian society [i.e., attacks against Israeli civilians], how much we pay for that when the Israelis attack [in response]. It's not very hard to convince the Palestinian people, because we have chosen this way for a long time. [Whether] we are fighting with the violent or nonviolent way, we are going to reach the same point, to end the occupation. And we give as an example an international example (for example, India and also South Africa) and explain that to the people. Directly, they agree with you.

But, said Salame, Israeli military activity and the building of "facts on the ground" (i.e., settlements and bypass roads, the wall) "make our way very difficult," adding, "I have to talk with the Israeli families."

They have to know when they send their kids to serve with the occupation, they have to accept one thing: maybe they will get their sons back as a dead body or injured; and the other Palestinians, they have to defend themselves and liberate their lands. Ours is a nonviolent way, but for the others, I am not going to push them to change their way. And this is their right—to fight like other peoples. I have to defend, but in a different way.

"We are looking for new members to join us," said Salame. "We don't need to be ashamed to say that we want many Palestinians and Israelis to come over to the nonviolent struggle."

I think that that is the basis for a solution, and that's our strength. And I think that, in the end, it is most legitimate and most legal to call upon people not to commit crimes—be they crimes committed by Israeli soldiers or be they crimes committed by Palestinian fighters.

I am not at all embarrassed to say this. I think that this is something that we must call for, and we hope that many, many people will join us. We know that our potential to grow is very great because there is a huge number of former Palestinian prisoners who today are not violent and are interested in joining this struggle and there is a huge number of Israelis who are not serving in the army, either because they have refused publicly or because they simply stopped serving and don't wish to go, and all of these people are candidates for the organization, including women. We are definitely calling upon people to join us. It's very important.

Discussing Important Trends in Palestinian Nonviolence

Time and time again—when asked what they thought were the most important developments in the nonviolent struggle over the preceding two years—Palestinian interviewees, theoreticians and grassroots activists alike (among those I spoke to on my December 2005 to January 2006 trip) tended to place the rise in Jewish and, more specifically, Israeli, participation high on their lists. This was the case despite the fact that some, although acknowledging the value of this trend in specific instances, argued for a different focus for Israeli activists' energies: the transformation of their own society from within.[13] Other frequently lauded developments were the presence of international activists, the recent increase in Palestinians' understanding, appreciation, and application of active nonviolence, and the increased international (including Israeli) awareness of the situation in Palestine—with emphasis on the role of the nonviolent movement in these developments. ISM and Biddu village activist Mansour Mansour touched on all the above points.

> The whole change that came with the Hague International Court decision [on the illegality of the separation wall] didn't come from nothing. It came out of the work of the Palestinian popular resistance, the Palestinian grassroots people who were resisting nonviolently and who succeeded to show that to the international community. It also came from the international activists who came through the International Solidarity Movement and who showed their solidarity with the people. They brought these efforts and new way of resistance of the Palestinian nonviolent resistance to the awareness of the media here in Palestine, and at the same time,

there was a kind of slow increase in the Western and European countries of a kind of awareness of the Palestinian situation—that our people are fighting for our rights, we're resisting in order to get our freedom, and we are not attacking the Israeli state. We are only resisting soldiers who are present in our land; we are not going to Tel Aviv to attack. And the attacks done by Palestinians are a result of continuous Israeli military occupation, and what has been done by Palestinians is just in retaliation for Israeli assassinations and attacks. So this is one [aspect] of the change. There is also another change that has been declared by the big countries like the United States, England, or Europe: they admit that the Palestinians should have an independent state side-by-side with the Israeli state. And this is another big change.

Mansour also remarked on the "many reports, many filmed reports or articles in Israeli newspapers talking about the resistance and the right of people to have their land, and that the wall is illegal, and issues like that," which are, he says, undermining Israel's propaganda efforts. Another very important change, he said, is increased media coverage of nonviolence.

People have started concentrating more on nonviolent resistance, to show it to the international community through the media. We were doing nonviolent resistance since 1936, but it wasn't shown in the media, it wasn't addressed well in the media. Now people start working hard to address this issue and to talk about this issue.

Rising Jewish and Israeli Participation
Lastly, Mansour cited the importance of "having a live presence inside Israeli society supporting our resistance and who work very hard."

We have succeeded as Palestinians to find the core, the point inside the Israeli community where they can support us in our demonstrations. And they are in our demonstrations, they've been with us, they participate, they support. And they come here not only in words, but they come here with their bodies. And this is a very important change in the Palestinian nonviolent struggle. This change is very, very critical and important to our fight.

Like Mansour, Dr Eyad Sarraj regarded Israeli participation in the Palestinian struggle as vitally important. Although the Gaza psychiatrist cited "the death of Rachel Corrie and the way her story was seen all over the world"—as evidence that not only Palestinians, but also other "people can really sacrifice their life for this struggle"—as the single most important event impacting on the Palestinian nonviolent struggle, he felt that the most important development in the nonviolent movement was "the establishment of the International Solidarity [Movement] and the campaign against the wall—which, in one way or the other, was shared by so many people, including Israelis. What was most important for me to see," stated Sarraj, "was the Israeli and Jewish involvement in the struggle against the occupation, against the wall."

Increasing Palestinian Appreciation of Active Nonviolence

An encouraging trend observed by nonviolence trainer Husam Jubran was an increased understanding by Palestinians of the meaning of active nonviolence.

> I remember two years ago, when I started to go around the West Bank visiting villages and cities, speaking about nonviolence, it was difficult to use the term, to say *la'unf.* The moment I said that, people were suspicious, sceptical. But through our work and showing that nonviolence is an active form of resistance, there is more readiness to accept, and I feel that it has more respect. That is, when I go now to speak about it, I think people respect what we say and what we do, unlike two years ago. This, for me, I think, is the major development. And also, on the national level, I think there is more readiness among people to adopt active forms of nonviolence.

Pacifist lawyer Jonathan Kuttab, too, spoke of seeing greater acceptance of the term "nonviolence" among Palestinians.

> One of the most important things to remember is that until relatively recently, most Palestinians did not use the term nonviolence, did not self-consciously go about strategizing in a nonviolent fashion, but that the vast majority of Palestinians have, for a long, long time instinctively followed a path of nonviolence.

Kuttab enthusiastically described his observations regarding the current village-centred resistance to the wall.

I definitely do see a new change, a new group of Palestinian leaders—and Palestinian people in the villages resisting the wall, and not just young people—young and old. Again, they are not doing anything new! They've always done that. People stood in front of bulldozers long before Mubarak Awad came and was talking about that. But now they are using the words, they are using the terms, they are not afraid, they are deliberately saying, "We are being nonviolent; we are deliberately not using violence, because it does not help us. We are the people of this village. We are not just a few young people with guns. In fact, we'll keep those totally tucked away. We don't want them to appear on the scene anywhere." In fact, the Israelis have to interject agents provocateurs and send in their disguised security forces pretending to be Arabs to walk among the demonstrators and throw stones and start violence, in order to justify the army's retaliation. And it's the villagers who are saying, "Who are you? We don't know you. Stay away! We are the people of this village, and this is neither the time nor the place to be throwing stones." Even throwing stones is being avoided by those villages resisting the wall, because they begin to understand how even small steps of violence like throwing stones can be the trigger and the justification for massive Israeli retaliation.

Another aspect of this trend is the increased participation by local people in nonviolent actions, as reflected in the comment by ISM organizer Saif Abu Keshek that, "We developed from the level where we had a hundred internationals and forty or fifty Palestinians in a demonstration to a level where the majority who are participating are Palestinians."

After the summer of 2003, we started to feel the real change. I participated in demonstrations in Jenin, Tulkarm, and Nablus where we had thousands of Palestinian people out in the street together with a couple hundred internationals. That's very important. Now we have this Friday demonstration in Bil'in where we have hundreds of Palestinians and a few internationals. At the last demonstration that we had, we were discussing the level of risk we were willing to take—people inside ISM, including Palestinians and internationals. We had two internationals who were willing to take a frontline position and be arrestables, and we had seven Palestinians from the ISM group alone. That doesn't include the people of the community, the people of Bil'in who are participating. All seven [Palestinian] ISM organizers were arrestables. I think it is very important to notice such a development. It is very important to emphasize it and to give it the right space and effort to support.

I think we are witnessing a very important development in the nonviolent movement of Palestine.

In the wake of the December 2005 conference, and already planning for ISM's Freedom Summer 2006 campaign, Abu Keshek declared: "We came, we discussed, we talked about nonviolent resistance in Palestine. Let us practice it! That is my call."

Mohammed Abu-Nimer—a scholar in the field of Peace and Conflict Resolution and a frequent writer on nonviolence in Islam, as well as in the Israel/Palestine context[14]—remarked at the presence (in the post-conference march to the wall now separating Bethlehem and Jerusalem, in which he and I had participated just prior to our interview on 30 December 2005) of "religious Muslim leaders who joined us in the protest and were very clear about their message, [Sheikh Tayseer Tameemi] the highest religious authority in Palestine marching with us in support of nonviolent resistance, and he was in the front line negotiating with the soldiers." Said Abu-Nimer, "That's, I think, a major change." Abu-Nimer also mentioned the recent "re-emergence of the Palestinian nonviolent resistance groups" as well as the presence in the Palestinian Authority of "elements" with an appreciation for the power of nonviolence.

> I think in this Intifada—the Intifada that started in 2000—there were some sparks of nonviolent resistance [early on], and then it got very militarized by the different political factions. And I think what happened later—what we're seeing in last two years or so—is the re-emergence of the Palestinian nonviolent resistance groups, and many of these are active in the different villages. A [further] measure of change, I think, is the fact that the there is a Palestinian National Authority, and there are elements in that authority who know, understand, and appreciate the fact that nonviolent resistance could be powerful. Unfortunately, we haven't capitalized yet on their potential, and I think that's another change that has been taking place, absolutely, and I think that's something that needs to be recognized.

Joint Resistance to the Wall
Riad Malki, too, cited the grassroots resistance to the wall in the villages— with its high level of participation by Israelis and internationals—as being a crucial development.

I believe this is what we want to happen. Internationals are supporting us; we have Israelis joining us; and when we meet, it's very clear that the Israeli army, with its own superiority, is reduced to using only the minimum force of superiority against us. They cannot use their tanks, they cannot use their F16s, they cannot use their missiles. They have to use their soldiers. And soldiers, when they see this, some of them might become hesitant to go and attack women and children and others simply because these people are resisting, especially when they see there are Israelis and internationals there. I believe that what's happening in these places is excellent. I would love to see it spread all over, everywhere.

Conclusion

A strategy widely regarded as successful by the activists I interviewed was the participation by Israelis and/or internationals in Palestinian-led nonviolent actions and campaigns (e.g., Rapprochement–Jerusalem's solidarity with the Beit Sahour tax strikers, the International Solidarity Movement's protective presence from early in the Al-Aqsa Intifada). In addition to benefits already mentioned in earlier chapters, this strategy was described as facilitating some semblance of normal life for Palestinians— enabling farmers to harvest crops unmolested and possibly helping prevent the deportation or worse of Palestinian leaders.

Israeli women's organizations, notably the ten that make up the Coalition of Women for Peace, have used a number of successful strategies, ranging from dramatic use of civil disobedience to campaigns challenging the militarism of Israeli society and, of course, the impressive work of Machsom Watch, whose members use not just their being female and Israeli—but also the fact that as mainly middle-aged Jewish women, they look like the soldiers' mothers and grandmothers—to good advantage in confronting and attempting to ameliorate human rights violations at checkpoints inside the West Bank as well as those dividing the West Bank from Israel, violations which they document and publicize to Israeli legislators and the media at large. Journalist Amira Hass describes the complementary roles played by the media and activist groups such as Machsom Watch and ICAHD in bringing about some encouraging victories (e.g., the reversal of a 1995 policy of revoking residency rights of Jerusalem Palestinians and a dramatic slow-down in house demolitions—even if real structural change has yet to occur. "Imported" approaches to nonviolence, such as those introduced by Mubarak Awad, have enhanced local initiatives; and creativity and audacity of actions—whether by groups or individuals—contribute to their success (and sometimes their successful media coverage).

Military refusal, an important form of nonviolent noncooperation, is in a class by itself. Small numbers of outright "refuseniks" notwithstanding, it has been reported that "mandatory military duty is being completed by only a half of the candidates." The anti-militarist group New Profile does important work in support of draft resistance, and is the only organization to support women draft resisters. Peretz Kidron, from the oldest refusenik organization, Yesh Gvul, extols refusal as "the most effective way of campaigning against the occupation," since "There's no occupation without an army of occupation, and there's no army of occupation without soldiers," and gives the example of the then army commander attributing the end to fighting in parts of Lebanon during the 1982 Israeli invasion to his perception that "refusals were running in the hundreds, and we were afraid they would run into the thousands and tens of thousands."

Young refusenik Matan Kaminer praises the courage of Druze refusers; for him personally, the most important thing is "not being there" and "saying clearly why you're not there and that you're willing to face the consequences," since hearing this makes people think about the occupation and perhaps question their own military service.

For Elik Elhanan and Wael Salame, both ex-fighters and members of Combatants for Peace, bringing—in Elhanan's words—"war criminals" and "terrorists" to speak to high school and college students, ordinary people in both communities and telling them "We made a change, everyone can make that change" is highly effective. "No one would listen to 'Nice Guys for Peace' ..." On the other hand, Elhanan values their "normal, mainstream, middle-class" image in helping them to be heard outside the "marginal left."

The picture of important trends in the Palestinian nonviolent movement—particularly as painted of the two years between my first two interview trips—was a generally hopeful one, with the practice and appreciation of nonviolence observed to be increasing within Palestinian society. In what Mohammed Abu-Nimer refers to as "the re-emergence of the Palestinian nonviolent resistance groups" after the militarized period following the beginning of the Al-Aqsa Intifada, a broader cross-section of Palestinians is participating in nonviolent actions and, in contrast with the past, they are now actually calling what they do "nonviolence" (*la'unf*, in Arabic). Another recent development has been participation by Muslim religious leaders (including Sheikh Tayseer Tameemi, the highest religious authority in Palestine at the time) in marches supporting nonviolent resistance, and increased support for nonviolence, as well, amongst certain "elements" of the Palestinian Authority. The importance of greater involvement by internationals in general, and the establishment of the International Solidarity Movement, in particular—especially "Israeli and Jewish involvement in the struggle" (Eyad Sarraj) were frequently cited as a positive trend, and Riad Malki characterized the resistance to the wall by grassroots villagers often joined by Israelis and internationals as a crucial development, concluding "I would love to see it spread all over, everywhere."

We shall now have a look at where these trends may take us, as activists share their thoughts about and hopes for the future prospects of the Palestinian nonviolent movement (Chapter 8) and finally, their visions for the future of the region (Chapter 9).

NOTES

1 At the time of our interview (October 2003), Huwaida Arraf estimated that approximately twenty to twenty-five percent of ISM volunteers were Jewish and forty percent American. Current figures are not available, since following a 2003 raid on the ISM offices, they have, "done [their] best not to keep records." (Neta Golan, email correspondence, May 2009)

2 Rabbis for Human Rights were among the first to bring Israelis and internationals to join Palestinians in harvesting olives as a deterrent to settler harassment soon after the outbreak of the Al-Aqsa Intifada. A mainly Israeli Olive Harvest Coalition was formed in 2002, and by 2006 included, among others, Gush Shalom, ICAHD, Yesh Gvul, Combatants for Peace, Machsom Watch, Coalition of Women for Peace, RHR, and Ta'ayush. See also Ya'akov Manor in Chapter 1.

3 Yanoun is a small Palestinian village from which most of the inhabitants fled during 2002 due to harassment by settlers from nearby Itamar—gradually returning only once assured of an ongoing presence of members of Israeli and international organizations. Participating organizations have included Ta'ayush, Ecumenical Accompaniment Programme in Palestine and Israel (EAPPI), International Women's Peace Service, and Rabbis for Human Rights. For

recent reports from EAPPI volunteers in Yanoun, see the "Reports" section at www.eappi.org/en.

4   Figure of 400 from "Machsom Watch at IDF Checkpoints: No one will be able to say, 'I didn't know.'" by Yonatan Preminger in *Challenge*, March–April 2006 as posted on www.machsomwatch.org.

5   Gila Svirsky, "Nonviolence in the Israeli Women's Peace Movement," August 31, 2003. © Arabic Media Internet Network. Quoted with permission. Complete article currently (April 2009) accessible at http://groups.yahoo.com/group/GSN/message/22207.The Coalition of Women for Peace (formerly "for a Just Peace"— name shortened to accommodate a former website URL, coalitionofwomen4peace) now comprises ten women's organizations, the newest addition being Bat Tzafon (Daughter of the North) for Peace and Equality, made up of Jewish and Arab women from Northern Israel. The other nine are: Bat Shalom, The Fifth Mother, Machsom Watch, Noga Feminist Journal, NELED, Women in Black, New Profile, TANDI, and WILPF-Israel. I encourage readers to learn more about these groups (especially those not covered here) on the Coalition website (www.coalitionofwomen.org) and to check out www.whoprofits.org, the Coalition's website that lists companies—Israeli or other—that profit from the occupation.

6   "legal means": Hass later clarified (in the QA session) that this referred to using the court system for appeals and law suits against the authorities, in addition to other activities "including acts of popular and civil disobedience, which some may label as illegal." Hass stated that "if people are confined only to what is defined as legal by the authorities, then we would have stayed—I guess—in slavery."

7   Canada Park is built on the site of three (Keller [1987: pp. 115, 129] says four) West Bank villages emptied in 1967 for the straightening of the Tel Aviv to Jerusalem Highway. *Memory of the Cactus* is an excellent documentary incorporating newsreel footage and photos of the military takeover and expulsion of the populations of Imwas, Yalu, and Beit Nuba; survivor reminiscences; and testimony by present-day activists, including Israeli "revisionist" historian Ilan Pappe. See trailer at: http://www.youtube.com/watch?v=tdbiEtbYQoA.

8   For the list of 198 nonviolent tactics see, *inter alia*, Sharp 1973. An article adapted from Mubarak Awad's booklet, reprinted in the *Journal of Palestine Studies*, vol. 13, no. 4 (Summer, 1984), pp. 22–36, was apparently cited as evidence of incitement and used against him in his 1987/8 deportation hearings.

9   Toma Šik (17 August 1939 – 13 July 2004) himself refused to serve in the Israeli military, and for some thirty years counselled Israeli youth who were considering refusal. He was a fervent esperantist and active in War Resisters International and Amnesty International, as well as PINV and Gush Shalom. He was tragically run down and killed by a tractor while walking at night near the remote Hungarian farm where he was involved in establishing an "egalitarian agricultural commune."

10 Although Yesh Gvul's "target audience" has always been almost exclusively Israeli youth, the group did have one joint activity with Palestinians, a statement issued during the Beit Sahour tax strike. As Kidron tells it: "Someone said, 'Beit Sahour. Tax revolt. Nonviolent civil disobedience.' So we went off to Beit Sahour: we visited them and [made] declarations of support, and we issued a joint statement. The statement is in the book [Kidron 2004] and I have a plaque that was given to us by the mayor of Beit Sahour."

11 Although, as mentioned in Chapter 1 (see note 11), Israeli Druze are conscripted, there is a significant movement of refusal. A report from "Refworld" states that "The Arab Druze Initiative, an organization of conscientious objectors to military service, estimated in April 2006 that the number of Druze youth refusing military service had climbed to 40 per cent, despite the threat of arrest. With increasing tensions among Druze and state-backed Jewish settlers in the north, some Druze warn that their community's willingness to serve the state will further decline." See http://www.unhcr.org/refworld/topic,463af2212,469f18732,49749d05c,0.html (accessed 4 May 2009).

12 Yeshayahu Leibowitz (1903–1994) was a widely respected Israeli scholar and philosopher with controversial political views. Among other things, he publically espoused military refusal and caused an uproar some thirty years ago by referring to settlers as "Judeonazis."

13 For example, Muhammad Jaradat. See especially Chapter 4: Dynamics of Power between Palestinian and Israeli Activists.

14 See especially Abu-Nimer 2006.

8

THINKING ABOUT THE FUTURE
OF PALESTINIAN NONVIOLENT STRUGGLE

———

We have to support the Palestinians to be sumud. That's really our job, to support the Palestinians in their struggle, because I think that the strength of the Palestinians—their steadfastness—in the end will prevail. I think our message to the Palestinians should be that "you're not as isolated as you feel you are. I can see, behind a wall, that you really feel a sense of isolation and despondency. But we're here for you. We're working hard for you, and I think we're succeeding."

Jeff Halper (Bil'in, April 2007)

In the foregoing chapters we have reviewed numerous examples of nonviolent actions and campaigns, some of which have yielded tangible results. We have also seen some encouraging trends. But the many shortcomings and failings of this not-yet-fully-formed movement have also been apparent, and a list of things that must be changed in order to increase its effectiveness was not hard to come by, nor were suggestions for effecting such changes. After meeting and hearing from so many dedicated nonviolent activists—and especially following the heady experience of the nonviolence-centred conferences in Bethlehem in December of 2005 and Bil'in in April of 2007, I was especially interested in my interviewees' thoughts regarding the future prospects for the success of the Palestinian nonviolent movement. These contributions make up the first section of this chapter.[1] A number of those whom I interviewed around the time of the Bethlehem conference (or whose conference presentations I recorded) expressed ideas and hopes regarding the development and future role of the movement, and the chapter will end with their words.

Future Prospects for Nonviolent Struggle against the Occupation

Light at the End of the Tunnel
I found widespread optimism regarding the future of Palestinian nonvi-

olence amongst those I interviewed on my December 2005/ January 2006 and April 2007 visits. Although reluctant to go so far as to say she was optimistic, Wi'am activist Lucy (whom I interviewed in January 2006) told me she thought that most Palestinians want peace and that "you will find all people thinking about nonviolence." When I mentioned to her that Dr Mustafa Barghouthi, who previously had avoided the term, was now using it publicly, she concurred.

> Yes, because the people started [saying]: "Oh, stop it! We have to be clear, to clarify what nonviolence means and which way we have to use it, and this is what we do believe as Palestinians." I am neither optimistic nor pessimistic. I don't want to be optimistic and then be shocked, and I'm not pessimistic, because I want to have the light. Also I like this [saying]: Instead of cursing the darkness you have to light a candle. And this is what we are following. Let's see the light at the end of the tunnel and work for that.

Optimism for the Future of Palestinian Nonviolence

A few days after my conversation with Lucy, I asked anthropologist Kathy Kamphoefner whether she was optimistic about the future of the nonviolent struggle in Palestine. "Oh, absolutely," she responded, focussing—as had Palestinians like Jonathan Kuttab, Husam Jubran, and Lucy—on the new acceptance of the term "nonviolence."

> One of the things that's changed is that you can say the term "nonviolence" and people understand it better. It used to be, when you said "nonviolence," people thought of it as something passive, or accommodation. The actions against the wall by the popular committees, I believe, are what's changed it. People have become aware of how active they are, and so that's shifted the way people think about nonviolence on the Palestinian side. It's very important because, as you and I know, nonviolence is not passive and never was passive. But part of the problem is with the name: it's "non" something, so what does it mean? I've done nonviolence training in Russia and in China and the U.S. and here, and in all those places, that's been a problem. It's a persistent myth about nonviolence. So the action itself is correcting that misperception, which is enormously helpful. I think more and more people are becoming attracted to nonviolence, either as a tool or as a principle.

A Palestine-wide conference to develop nonviolent strategies to end the occupation, organized by Holy Land Trust and Panorama, in partnership with the American Friends Service Committee (AFSC), was held in Ramallah in April of 2005.[2] At that time, trainer Husam Jubran was quoted on the AFSC website as remarking: "A year ago nonviolence was seen as submissive, as a way for Israel and the West to pacify the Palestinian people. Now, much progress has been made and many see nonviolence as an active tool to resist and end the occupation." Jubran had been optimistic, too, when I interviewed him just prior to the Palestinian elections of January 2006, and had expressed hope that the outcome would "generate a movement to resist the occupation on a national level using massive demonstrations and nonviolent activities." A year later, I asked how he felt, given the Hamas victory and the ensuing factional strife. "To be honest with you," he replied:

> I am still optimistic about the future of the nonviolent movement and believe there is a good chance to see more activities that are nonviolent. I think the internal clashes will strengthen our ideas about nonviolence and the need to use it on all different levels, whether we are fighting the occupation or addressing our internal issues. What happened may only delay the emergence of such a movement but will never mange to kill or prevent it.

Hamas Involvement in Nonviolence

"Let me here remind you of two incidents that took place during the past year and before the clashes started," continued Jubran, pointing out that these two examples of nonviolence were particularly significant since they were carried out by Hamas supporters.

> First, the nonviolent action of Beit Hanoun women who helped militants hiding inside a mosque to escape capture.[3] Second, the top-of-roofs stand where hundreds of Palestinians protected houses threatened to be bombed by the Israeli air force using their bodies and succeeded to prevent them from doing so. [These] were good signs of a revival of the use of nonviolent activities.

Elik Elhanan, an Israeli member of Combatants for Peace whom I interviewed in April 2007, also mentioned Hamas in the context of nonviolent resistance. On December 23, 2006, said Elhanan, a march protesting construction of a settlement road through agricultural land belonging to Palestinian villages north of Hebron took place with the participation, despite inclement weather, of some two hundred Palestinians, Israelis, and internationals.

> Hamas organized this. At the end there was a podium, and on the podium you had like six or seven Israeli organizations that spoke, you had international organizations, and all the Palestinian organizations from the Communist Party to the Islamic Jihad, that were present together. So you see how it's changing. I really do believe that this thing is picking up on a low or medium level, and I do think that this is the way to change. And I really do think that Israelis have a lot to contribute there, and we, as Combatants for Peace, even more so.

Israeli Activists Largely Supportive

Although there were some sceptics among my Israeli interviewees, most were wholeheartedly supportive of Palestinian nonviolence, with some sharing the opinion expressed by Jaffa-based Israeli activist Elana Wesley that, "for the Palestinians, it's the only way that they have a chance of achieving anything." Said Wesley, "I think that the message slowly, very slowly, gets through to a lot more Israelis over a period of time. I don't mean for it to sound like a huge number, but the number of Israelis who are questioning things that they have not questioned previously, I think, is definitely on the increase." And Physicians for Human Rights member Hannah Knaz—despite feeling that it was the small percentage of violent incidents during the First Intifada, rather than the overwhelming preponderance of nonviolent actions, which had brought international attention to the Palestinian struggle—told me in January 2006: "The time has come for nonviolent resistance. I think the Palestinians have gotten to a place where they can use it, and this can also bring attention to their struggle."

Additional Causes for Optimism

When I interviewed Panorama Center-Ramallah's Riad Malki, also in January, he expressed satisfaction with progress in the nonviolence program that Panorama and Holy Land Trust were working on in partnership with Quaker Service–Jerusalem (AFSC).

We believe that this commitment of ours, and persistence over the years, has really produced very concrete, effective results. Obviously, it took more [time] than what we expected, but we should really underline here that we were working against the tide. Because at a certain time in our history, it was very difficult for people to understand and perceive and even to listen to these ideas, when the whole situation—the prevailing conditions—were supporting other ideas. But now, it is extremely important.

Mohammed Abu-Nimer cited the presence at the December 2005 Celebrating Nonviolent Resistance conference in Bethlehem of Palestinians "from many strata of the society, who believe in this type of work" as evidence of a growing culture of peace.

I think that what the Palestinian groups are doing in terms of nonviolent resistance is investment in the culture of peace in the Palestinian community, and it will also affect the Israeli public. I think we're doing a kind of economic investment, that this is our new stock market in that sense, and it will be very helpful for us to nurture it more and more. I'm very happy with it and I'm very optimistic, regardless of what will happen with the occupation or political movements.

Referring specifically to recent developments and prospects for the future, Abu-Nimer added, "I think in the last two years, the spark of over ten organizations who do nonviolent direct action or nonviolent indirect action—of education, of spreading consciousness about this—I think is an incredible opportunity for the Palestinian nonviolent resistance."

The Contribution of International Participation
The ISM's Saif Abu Keshek, responding to a comment from the floor during the Bethlehem conference regarding the difficulty of efficient and productive nonviolent resistance in the face of Israeli repression, expressed his belief that with the participation of internationals, "There is still a huge possibility for the nonviolent resistance in Palestine to make a very strong change," adding that, "I think this kind of movement can be very efficient and very productive in a time that we find thousands of activists who are working in the nonviolent field coming to Palestine, defying the orders of the Israeli authorities."

[341]

Planning in Anticipation of Complete Separation

Although Abu Keshek was, he told me, always optimistic ("one of the main strategies in nonviolent direct action"), he was as yet unsure of the movement's future political and logistical situation in light of the anticipated "total separation" between Palestinians and Israelis that would be brought about by completion of the wall.

> The most confusing question for me as an organizer in the nonviolent direct action movement in Palestine is: "What can we do in the next step after separation?" Now we are able to reach the construction sites; we are able to protest; we are able to go out to the street; we are able to block soldiers; we are able to enter occupied houses; we are able to go to checkpoints, to organize demonstrations. We are able to do all this stuff. Israel is going to finish the wall. Israel is going to impose total separation between people and their land. [The Israeli military] won't need to enter the territories any more. They won't need military operations. But there will still be problems. People still will want to move from one place to another, people will want to cross this wall, people will want to [pass through] gates. What will our strategies be? What should our strategies be? How can we function? And I'm looking very, very deeply at this point and [being] very thoughtful about it because I think we need now to start planning.

After describing what steps he regarded as necessary to build an effective nonviolent movement,[4] Abu Keshek concluded, "I think there is a big future for a nonviolent movement in Palestine."

> I think it is actually the movement that can [bring about] a very strategic change in the conflict. And the elements that I just explained are very essential to ensure, not only the continuity of such a movement, but also the success of the movement itself. So, yes, there is a very good future; I am very optimistic about it. It needs of lots of work and effort.

Palestinians and Israelis Marching Together

Even though some Palestinian activists I spoke to felt that Palestinian nonviolent actions were generally best pursued without "outside" participation, we have seen that this sentiment was not widespread in this interview sample. Veteran Beit Sahour activist Elias Rishmawi, for example, envisioned the future of the nonviolent movement in distinctly "joint" terms, based on a shared desire to redress the wrongs done to the Palestinian community.

> What I see is people of good will and good intentions on both sides trying to do something together. At some point it gives a meaning that what is being done wrong—what the Palestinians are resisting— is also being received by a sector of the Israeli community as wrong, and they are ready to resist it as well.

Referring to the wall as "a bad and evil thing," Rishmawi maintained that "the wall has been erected in order to impose political realities on the ground" and "no Israeli leadership can persuade any person that this wall has been erected for security reasons."

> As such, in my opinion, it is the responsibility of the Israeli people—even before the Palestinian people—to resist wrong decisions made by any Israeli government, because this is going to affect the future of the area. And if the injustice continues, then resistance will continue. One of the things that I'm really happy to see is that Palestinians and Israelis are marching together against evil things like the wall. Whether this is going to be a core for a Palestinian-Israeli coalition, I think it's premature to say. I hope it will be one day, because, listen: we are here together, and I think our destiny as Palestinians and Israelis is more or less the same. The world, with globalization, is becoming like a small village. If the whole world is becoming a small village, then the whole Middle East is what? Israel/Palestine is what? We are talking here about a small land and a small population. We need to come up with a certain vision that will help both of us to think that without having peace, justice, and equality, there will be no solution.

An Important Role for "Third Parties"

Riad Malki, too, stressed the importance of "third parties"—Israelis included—and their role in the future of Palestinian nonviolent resistance.

> When we look toward the future, we see that there is great opportunity; there is a great opening that we have to take, that we have to utilize to the maximum. And always, when we say this, we should always believe that the role of the "third party" is extremely important. We could not on our own, as Palestinians,

achieve all these objectives of ours without the involvement of a third party: I'm referring to the people in the international community, both Israelis and non-Israelis. We should not exclude the Israeli people from having an important role as a third party in promoting nonviolent resistance in Palestine and in guaranteeing successes for this approach. And also at the same time, it's very clear that the non-Israeli third parties—the Americans, Europeans, etc.—can provide the type of support that the Palestinian activists need. They can make people in their own countries knowledgeable about the type of activism the Palestinians are really doing, and this might create further interest in the whole nonviolent Palestinian movement. This is extremely important, because you need the support, the involvement, the participation, the encouragement, the solidarity of the international movement.

Highlighting the vital role that Israeli activists, specifically, could play in the future success of nonviolence in Palestine, Malki concluded his interview with a call for more joint actions, and the mobilization of the Israeli public in a nonviolent effort that "could turn the history of the two peoples upside down. ... make people start to see the future through different eyes."

We need always to highlight the important role that the Israeli activists could really play in order to make such a movement successful: their participation in the "on field" activities; their participation in sit-ins, in demonstrations within Israeli society and streets is vital; their writing the articles in different newspapers is vital; their participation in different public meetings in different places within Israel itself is vital. This is important in order for the Israeli public at large to know that there is another way for Palestinians to resist the occupation, and resisting the occupation could be done through nonviolence—meaning that we are not targeting human lives: what we are trying here is to save human lives by working together.

"I believe that the majority of Israelis want to see an end to the occupation," Malki stated, "and if the Palestinians will approach them by saying, 'Let's work together to end the occupation through nonviolent forms of resistance,' I believe we can mobilize the majority of the Israeli public in this regard." This, in turn, would draw more Palestinians into the movement as well as "attract[ing] the attention of the world leaders, who could really put further pressure on the leaders of both peoples in order to really see a political solution to the conflict itself."

> I believe everything starts from there, and I believe everything ends there. So it's very important where we can talk about creating a new fabric of human relationships through these activities, because there is no limit to it and there are no boundaries, and there are no walls or barriers that will prevent an Israeli from coming and joining, there will be no reason why not to work together to end the occupation—as long as we are really doing it in a nonviolent way.
>
> I would love to see Europeans, Americans, Israelis participating in each and every village and town where there is a reason to resist the Israeli occupation. I would love to see that, because the moment we start really working together, the moment we destroy the walls that separate us, and the moment that we can find ourselves working together on common issues and common agendas—we will become partners with the same objectives rather than enemies. This is extremely important, and that's why I believe what's happening in Bil'in, what's happening in Aboud and other places, is extremely, extremely important. It could turn the history of the two peoples upside down. It could change the whole reality on the ground. It could really develop new human relationships between the peoples and the individuals. It could make people start to see the future through different eyes. And I believe this is the great opportunity. I would really love to see it multiply everywhere. I would like to see more Israelis involved; I would like to see more Israelis coming in—because I believe this is the beginning of the end, and this is really the right path that the Palestinians have to take.

Hope Empowers Resistance, Resistance Breeds Hope

"The most important thing that we realize about the future is that there is always hope," declared ISM activist Mansour Mansour.

> If I didn't think about the future, I wouldn't resist. If I didn't have hope, I wouldn't be here at this conference, which we also consider to be a way of nonviolent resistance. So we always have hope that peace will come through those people, like us, like the internationals who come to support us, and like the Israeli peace activists who are coming to support us also to resist. The most important thing that we are working on very hard is to have a more positive future. There is always hope wherever we continue resisting. And this is what we will try to do always. We will continue resisting; we'll gain

the fruit of our resistance; and in the future, we are sure that there is somebody who will taste the taste of freedom.

Exposing the "Evil of the Occupation" with Nonviolence

And perhaps prophetically, Jonathan Kuttab told me in December 2005:

> I think the Israelis will continue to work very hard to prevent the Palestinians from ever accepting any cease fire, from ever accepting any *tahdi'a,* any quieting down, even when Hamas itself wants to move away from violence and to move towards elections, they will try and prevent them from joining the elections. They will try to push them towards violence with more targeted bombings, by selecting really painful targets that almost call for revenge and retaliation, to steal them away from the path of nonviolence.
>
> I think nonviolence is the greatest threat to the continued Israeli occupation, and therefore Israel will try its best to provoke Palestinian radicals and militants into continuing with the military operations which most Palestinians see are not an option, are not really helpful at all. If Palestinians can manage, however, to avoid these provocations and to exercise almost inhuman restraint and self-discipline, I think that they stand a very good chance of exposing, through very painful sacrifices, the evil of the occupation— to the point where it will be no longer sustainable.

Ideas and Hopes for the Future of the Palestinian Nonviolent Movement

Learning from the First Intifada

Walid Salem (of Panorama's Jerusalem office) based his comments upon his understanding of the effectiveness of the (largely nonviolent) First Intifada, from which he had gleaned some very specific suggestions for the promotion of nonviolence in the Israeli-Palestinian context. In a presentation that he delivered during one of the many workshop sessions at the Bethlehem conference, Salem proposed four major changes in approach "in order to promote nonviolence ethically and also as a tool to lead us to a two-state solution with Israel and Palestine."

> One is to move from the notion of human rights to the notion of citizens' rights. It is not enough for Palestinians to continue speaking

about the rights of Jews in this land as human rights, rights of human beings. If the Palestinians continue speaking about it that way, it will mean the Jews' rights for worship in the holy places, and that's all, but not the right of nationhood and statehood. So we should move from the issue of just thinking about the rights of the other as human rights to thinking about the rights of the other as citizens' rights, including statehood and national rights. The same is needed from the Israelis: to recognize the Palestinians not only as human beings, but moreover, as a nation and also as citizens, including the right of the Palestinian refugees to be citizens in their state.

The second issue is to move from transferring the pain to transforming the pain. Suicide bombings and terrorist acts inside Israel, these are ways to transfer the pain, but they are not ways to transform the pain. You are not transforming it into something positive; you are transferring the pain from one generation to another, from one act to another act. Terrorist acts are acts of revenge, they are not acts that lead to liberation and statehood; therefore, they are acts that transfer pain and do not transform it. We need to transform pain and not transfer it.

The third issue is to move from elitism to participation, so the people will become the centre of gravity, not the elites, not the leaders. Nonviolence in Palestine has a problem that everything is in the hands of the leadership, and the leadership, at the same time, doesn't have a strategy. Therefore, this deprives the people of their strategy and their action according to that strategy.

And fourth is a move for the average people, the average human beings, the average citizens, from "carelessness" to responsibility. A move to be responsible citizens. There are a lot of Palestinians who did not act as responsible citizens. We need this move also, in order to promote nonviolence.

The Importance of Experience-Based Strategy

Speaking from his experience as a coordinator of grassroots nonviolent campaigns "on the ground," International Solidarity Movement (ISM) activist Saif Abu Keshek stressed the importance of developing a strategy based on experience and not from "learning theories" or "looking at analysis and experiences of nonviolent direct action and looking at how we can implement it in Palestinian society."

Now it is time to start with a very clear strategy. We need to learn a lot. It is not that we lack knowledge, but we need to strengthen our experience, to strengthen our knowledge, to be able to deal with the future. We need to strengthen the solidarity movements outside. We need to make connections between these movements; we need to establish networks; we need to globalize the Palestinian nonviolent resistance. All this involvement of foreign governments and foreign authorities in the Palestinian-Israeli situation has made the people of these [countries] involved, too. And so we need to look for ways of how we can ensure the continuous [presence] of as many people as possible on an international level.

Civil Resistance Requires Credible, Capable Leadership

When I met with Amneh Badran in October 2005, she outlined her ideas for effective resistance to the occupation, using the term "civil resistance" to indicate unarmed/non-militarized forms of struggle.

> I would look again to organize civil resistance. Secondly, getting international support and making pressure on Israel should be another priority, so I'm one of those who support sanctions, boycott, divestment on Israel: economic boycott of Israeli products. It will take some time, for example, to make civil disobedience in areas like Jerusalem, but noncooperation, economic boycott [could be implemented immediately].

The sort of civil disobedience she had in mind, she said, was "active resistance against checkpoints, against the wall."

> I think if there would be 2,000 through a checkpoint, the Israelis might shoot, and some people might be killed, some people might be injured, but eventually the checkpoints will not stand forever. Two thousand unarmed people at every checkpoint. But this needs a leadership with credibility, a leadership that can lead.

Dr Eyad Sarraj, too, spoke (over the phone to Beit Sahour from his Gaza office in January 2006) of the need for credible leaders who espouse nonviolence and bemoaned the fact that, whereas "the message is quite powerful, unfortunately the messengers—so far—from the Palestinian side, are not as powerful."

> You need credible leaders who can move the masses, who really are well-respected and well-perceived by the people, quite popular, to

start such a movement. I once encouraged Ahmad Yassin, the leader of Hamas, to start a nonviolent movement against Israel, against the occupation. Marwan Barghouthi was once a potential leader. Unfortunately, he fell into the trap of nationalism and violence and so on. So you need something totally different. Mustafa Barghouthi is a very good potential leader, if only he were not a politician. If one believes in nonviolence, I think it needs to be completely devoid from political ambitions.

A contrasting view regarding leadership was expressed by nonviolence theoretician Gene Sharp, who cautioned participants in his Bethlehem conference workshop to beware of dependency on a single charismatic leader, a tendency he regards as dangerous. "What is needed," said Sharp, "is to spread the know-how of how masses of people can act; then, [if] they kill or jail a particular person, it doesn't make a lot of difference to the movement. Even in India, they anticipated leaders being jailed by the dozens. In one case, I was told, I think it was in Bombay, they had a list of successor persons: thirty-three or thirty-four replacements."

Appreciate and Support Local Leadership

Along the same lines, conference presenter Mohammed Abu-Nimer—who has written elsewhere about the long history of Palestinian nonviolence (e.g., Abu-Nimer 2006)—emphasized the importance of appreciating the many local leaders "who are doing wonderful work" and who should be given "more space"; for instance, through opportunities to speak at conferences such as this ("We had about twenty-five of them. We had four of them who spoke to the entire plenary"), as well as other means of disseminating information about their work.

> There's pressure to have the next Gandhi, the next Abdul Ghaffar Khan, or the next Martin Luther King—or whoever—and I think that's a mistaken strategy. I think there are plenty of local leaders. There are plenty of charismatic leaders; they're doing, actually, lots of wonderful work. As I said, in the village of Budrus and the village of Bil'in, or many other places, there are groups with local leadership. I think it is a mistake [by] the international and even local groups who continue to say that we need one leader to do that. I think we ought to be careful in what we wish in that sense.

Abu-Nimer continued, referring to the leadership of the popular committees in the villages resisting the wall: "There is a need to appreciate the local leadership who are doing wonderful work in that area."

> That's another segment of the Palestinian resistance movement and campaign, and they've been successful in Budrus, they've been successful in Beit Suriq and other villages, and I think they need to take their proper place in the Palestinian national resistance movement. I think that it's essential to appreciate, highlight, and support that by linking them more with the people and with other organizations. I think they need to be more visible and more recognized, both internationally and, I think, locally.

Making the Movement More Inclusive and Effective

On the topic of "how to make the movement more inclusive and more effective," Abu-Nimer elaborated:

> There is a very strong presence of the Palestinian nonviolence groups here [at the conference]. And what we're looking for is a more coordinated strategy among these groups from the different factions, from the different political groups, and also support from the international community for something like this. I think a second need is to engage the Palestinian National Authority in genuinely supporting the NGOs or the movement for nonviolence, supporting it more than it is right now—in the sense of ministers and the president [putting] their political weight behind that movement and supporting it in many other ways, rather than being sometimes an obstacle or just paying lip service to the nonviolent resistance.
>
> The third thing is to work with many of the local NGOs in terms of common agenda, rather than being driven by donor agendas—overcoming the "culture of proposals." I mean many of the organizations are really, in my view, being hurt by this competition over proposals from the donors; and to some extent, sometimes that [is] dictating the type of activities that they do. And in my view, it's the responsibility of the donors to encourage this type of coordination, as well as the local organizations who are working towards this. There are some genuine organizations that are moving—and their activities are moving—regardless of what the donors want, but I think it's very essential for the international support not to dictate the type of activities and the type of agenda for the nonviolent movement.

And the fourth thing is to engage the religious leaders and religious Muslim and Christian groups who operate out of religion. I think as long as we have a secularized nonviolent resistance movement, we are limited in the amount of reaching out to the groups and the people. With the movement reaching out and working more closely with these resources of Islamic nonviolence and Christian nonviolence, I think we would be in a much better position in terms of reaching out.

Lastly, Abu-Nimer called for more encouragement for and coordination with Israeli nonviolent activists and pointed out the need for Palestinians to expand their nonviolent resistance to target issues of violence within their own society.

Our nonviolent resistance movement in Palestine will always be limited in its impact if our colleagues inside Israel do not engage in an active direct nonviolent resistance like we do. If the bulk of the Israeli peace movement continues to be limited to a camp clustered around Peace Now, with its mainstream Zionist ideology, the effect of our work will be very limited. So what we of the nonviolent resistance in Palestine need to do is to extend our hand and help or coordinate with the Israeli nonviolent resistance groups that are beginning to emerge in that society.

And finally, the last point here is how do we deal with our own internal cultural violence? We suffer from small arms, we suffer from insecurity in our homes. And that's not only because of the occupation; that's because of many reasons that I have listed here. And we need to expand our nonviolent resistance from facing only the occupation to facing domestic violence, abuse of children, and all of these problems that plague our society. I said what I had in my heart.

Nonviolent Resistance Organizations and Movement-Building

Addressing a plenary session of the Celebrating Nonviolent Resistance conference, Ghassan Andoni shared his conception of the role to be played by organizations such as the Palestinian Center for Rapprochement (PCR) and ISM—with their commitment to actively engaging in nonviolent resistance—in building a broader nonviolent movement.

In order to introduce a collective change towards a new struggling path [i.e., nonviolence], believers in nonviolent resistance have the duty to stand at the forefront of the struggle and integrate in the community resistance. Only by doing so are peacemakers entitled to a legitimate voice. Inasmuch as we believe that in a democracy we have the duty to convince a majority of our stance before it can become approved policy, the same efforts need to be invested in convincing resisting nations that peacemaking is not only ethical but also effective.

Going even further, Andoni threw out a challenge to the international peace and justice movements (which he characterized as being "centered in fairly stable and prosperous societies" and hypocritical in their "conditional recognition of justice") in which he stressed the importance of pursuing a strategy of "offensive nonviolent engagement," with nonviolent direct action (NVDA) at its core.

> Many of us can easily be trapped into blaming the victim, mostly in statements that reflect conditional recognition of justice: "If Palestinians are super-loving human beings, then they deserve respect." You all have [respect], and you are not [super-loving]. Allow me to say this is hypocritical. I believe justice is the truth, and the truth cannot be conditional or subjected to point of view. I would not slight reality by stating that probably the majority of people working for peace and justice would feel uncomfortable with offensive peacemaking work and would like to keep it at the level of preaching, training, and mediation. Engagement in conflict with nonviolent means doesn't stand at the core of peace and justice work. And this is true because the world peace and justice organizations are centred in fairly stable and prosperous societies that have mostly looked at crisis regions with either the eye of a sympathizer or that of a potential mediator.
>
> Active peacemaking in crisis regions cannot but be controversial, because it challenges much of the longstanding traditions in the international peace camp. It requires taking sides, as opposed to preserving objectivity. It requires engagement in the conflict, as opposed to work bridging the gap and mediating. And more importantly, it requires readiness to take considerable risk. In summary, it pushes peacemaking to new frontiers that many are hesitant to cross. Direct nonviolent action stands at the core of offensive nonviolent engagement methods. It is, in the simplest terms, a call for attempting to dismantle injustice. In a crisis region, attempting to dismantle injustice requires the physical obstruction of the oppressive machinery, including the most powerful one—I mean the army. This is horrifying. This is dangerous and could have drastic consequences.

If we are able to approve offensive peacemaking work as a legitimate tool in crisis areas, then—and as a matter of principle—we all need to stand in support of the ones who decided to do it. I believe that people in the peace [movement] have the moral obligation not to turn their backs on the ones who decided to stand in the front lines of the conflict.

We need to admit that the world of peace organizations also suffers from hypocrisy. We want a more just and peaceful world, but we are willing to place limits on ourselves and only work through the legal means that the same ones who inflict injustice have designed for us. Ladies and gentlemen, in the case of military occupation, abiding by the occupation's laws is admitting that we have nothing to do in this area.

While expressing "deep appreciation to the many great people who stood in support" of NVDA efforts such as the Beit Sahour tax strike and actions in which ISM is currently involved, Andoni posed searching questions regarding the nature of peacemaking.

A few, especially academics in nonviolence, advise us to not [engage in] peacemaking when the region is dominated with a high level of violence, saying that we should first focus efforts on lowering the level of violence inflicted *by the oppressed side*. Is it true that peacemaking is a mere management of violence? What if resistance fades away and injustice remains? Are we advocating slavery? My own experience has taught me—and I'm not a scholar and I have never studied nonviolence—that nonviolence is most needed when violence dominates conflicts.

Many were critical of us when we decided to avoid teaching and preaching and [instead] adopted a strategy of active positive engagement. Ours was attempting to positively influence the conflict through engagement and through becoming part of it, through gaining more recognition for nonviolence, and through attracting more involvement in a civil-based resistance. If you examine the record during both the First and Second Intifadas, it clearly proves that statements of condemning and condoling or expressing sorrow were fruitless, while positive engagement did have an impact and did not pass unnoticed.

Recognizing Palestinians' right to resist the occupation by other means than nonviolence came as we recognized that beside our moral stance, we need to define a legitimate reference to our work, and the only one acceptable to us was international law and UN resolutions. Taking a stand contrary to accepted international standards would have reflected a tendency [on our part] to impose new standards on others, something that is unthinkable from our side. Whether during the First or the Second Intifada, we could hear peace organizations clapping in support, but we could at the same time hear their hands pushing to preserve a distance from us. If one-tenth of the support provided for training, workshops, conferences, and meetings were allocated to support real grassroots work on the ground, to the people who are really fighting injustice, I believe we could have achieved more and would have said that we stand on more solid ground.

Conclusion

When it came down to activists' articulation of their thoughts regarding the future prospects for nonviolent struggle against the occupation, the general tone in late 2005 to 2007 was optimistic. A major cause for this optimism was the increased acceptance and growing understanding within Palestinian society of the term nonviolence, with many now acknowledging "nonviolence as an active tool to resist and end the occupation" and not as "a way for Israel and the West to pacify the Palestinian people," as had been the widespread perception in the recent past. Other encouraging observations included the involvement of Hamas-affiliated groups in nonviolent actions, a supportive attitude amongst Israeli activists, and progress in the development and presentation of nonviolence programming—including both the December 2005 Bethlehem conference (where "many strata of society" were represented) and the pan-Palestinian nonviolence conference in Ramallah earlier in the year.

The growing level of "third party" (international and Israeli) participation in the nonviolent struggle was cited by several interviewees as a factor strengthening the movement. Lastly, Jonathan Kuttab—referring to nonviolence as "the greatest threat to the continued Israeli occupation"—warned that Israel will, for that reason, persist in trying to provoke Palestinian militants to execute "military operations," unhelpful as these are, and he predicted that if Palestinians succeeded in resisting these provocations, there would be a "very good chance of exposing ... the evil of the occupation—to the point where it will be no longer sustainable."

Ideas and hopes for the future of the Palestinian nonviolent movement included several that come under the rubric of heeding the lessons of the (largely nonviolent) First Intifada: returning to broad popular participation, finding ways to "transform the pain" [suffered] into something positive instead of "transferring" it to others (through violence against civilians), and in particular, shifting the focus from human rights for both Palestinians and Israelis to citizens' rights, "including statehood and national rights."

Saif Abu Keshek extolled the development of experience-based strategy, rather than basing strategy on learned theory, and advised networking with solidarity movements worldwide; and more than one activist pointed out the nonviolent movement's requirement for credible, capable leadership—something that has been a recurring theme in this book—though in this case with the caveat, voiced by Gene Sharp, to beware of dependence on a single leader and, rather, "to spread the know-how of how masses of people can act." In a similar vein, Mohammed Abu-Nimer counselled resistance to pressure to find "the next Gandhi, the next Abdul Ghaffar Khan, or the next Martin Luther King," and instead "to appreciate the local leadership who are doing wonderful work." Abu-Nimer offered several other suggestions for strengthening the Palestinian nonviolent movement, including increasing its inclusiveness, especially by reaching out to Muslim and Christian religious communities; getting the PA to "[put] their political weight behind the movement"; and increasing coordination with and support for Israeli nonviolent activists. He criticized the "culture of proposals" and called on local NGOs to set their own agendas rather than letting them be dictated by funding bodies abroad. He also reiterated the need to target violence within Palestinian society as well as that from without.

Finally, Ghassan Andoni spoke about the important role in building the nonviolent resistance movement played by activism-oriented organizations such as PCR and the ISM with a commitment to active nonviolent engagement in the struggle ("with direct nonviolent action ... at the core")—including "attempting to dismantle injustice ... [by] the physical obstruction of the oppressive machinery, including ... the army"), controversial as this may be. Not mincing his words in confronting those who advocate an approach to peacemaking based on "lowering the level of violence inflicted *by the oppressed side*," Andoni challenged them to instead "support real grassroots work on the ground ... the people who are really fighting injustice."

NOTES

1 See also Riad Malki's discussion of marginalization in Chapter 6.
2 See Chapter 3 and Pierce 2005 for details about the conference and the program leading up to it.
3 "A group of 1,500 unarmed women performed a nonviolent protest in an effort to free their men, who were imprisoned inside the mosque. Two of these women were shot dead, and 20 were injured." (from www.jerusalemites.org/Testimonies/7.htm) See also www.justworldnews.org/archives/002206.html.
4 See Chapter 6.

9
LOOKING AHEAD

I, as a Palestinian, believe in "two states for two peoples." But there are many people who believe in one state. We will first of all stop the barrier, end the occupation; afterwards, whatever the two peoples choose, we're for it.

Nazih Shalabi (Mas'ha peace camp organizer)

Oh, if I had my wish, it would be I think a very virile, very active, very wonderful place. There are so many potential possibilities for cooperation, for building on all levels: on the economic level mainly. And through cooperation there could be so much done.

Zahra Khalidi (Palestine-Israel Journal)

I don't care if we have a chrysanthemum on the flag or a piece of seashell. It doesn't matter what. I don't feel that for the sake of a piece of cloth I need to die or to kill or to suffer... Somebody once said that there is no flag that is big enough to hide the shame of the murder of innocent people.

Yonatan Shapira (Pilots' Letter/Combatants for Peace)

I'd like very much for the Israelis to say 'thank you' to us and to say 'sorry.' Thank you, because they took our lands, and sorry because they made us refugees. Since the Israelis never say thank you and never say sorry, we have to take the thankfulness from them and [their] say[ing] sorry to us by means of nonviolence. This is how I see the future.

Nafez Assaily (Library on Wheels for Nonviolence and Peace)

Of course, what I would like to see is just to have our rights like the Israelis, at least like the settlers. What I would like to see is to have a gymnasium here in the city and to have a football team for the Palestinians and to have theatres. And I would like to have a government, maybe to have a Palestinian currency. This is what I would like to see, just to be like the other peoples in the world, to be independent.

T.M. (student nonviolent activist, Hebron)

I always said that my ideal solution would be a bi-national democratic state, and it always looked like a long shot that doesn't look very feasible for either side. I'm not sure any more what my vision is. You know, if we could have two decent states living in some kind of a cooperative state, probably a confederation would be ideal. The United States of Palestine-Israel would probably be my ideal vision.

Veronika Cohen (Israelis by Choice, Rapprochement-Jerusalem, et al.)

Some day, because we started this [nonviolent] way of struggling, for sure we will have our independence, we will have our freedom, we will have our rights. We will follow India, we will follow Yugoslavia and the other countries who struggle in this way, and we will keep more people alive if we continue in our way, and we will never give up this way. We will continue, and we will win, because justice will win.

Mustafa Shawkat Samha (Village activist/ISM)

In the distant future, the people, each on his side, will reach a state where they will understand that we are all human beings, where whoever caused suffering to another will apologize for it, when it will be possible to live together. But what we need to do now is to bring this period of life of suffering, this period of life of bloodshed, to an end. Everyone knows that in the end people sit down to talk, and there is a solution this way or that, so why let all this blood be spilt? And why let all this suffering continue? And why let this sea of hatred grow and grow in the hearts of our children, in the minds of our children? Why not implant love—implant humanness—in our children? That's how I look to the future.

Nawaf Souf (Haris village activist/Ta'ayush and ISM)

Our vision and most of the Palestinians' vision, as well as mine, is a two-state solution: an Israel co-existing side-by-side with a Palestinian state with full rights—national and human—a fully viable state, with all the borders well-defined; not a state with parts of it being isolated from one another, with a lot of cantons and Bantustans. That would not help the growth of the state and it would also not help the peaceful existence in the future.

Fu'ad Giacaman (Arab Educational Institute, Bethlehem)

A Fundamental Change of Focus

In looking towards the future, perhaps the heftiest serving of "food for thought" was provided by those who called for a fundamental change of focus. Jeff Halper, for example, posited the need for a radical reframing both of the conflict itself and of movement goals; and Judith Green went so far as to suggest that work through NGOs, however well-meaning, may no longer be an effective approach.

Reframing: Providing an Alternative Way to View the Conflict
As Halper told the April 2007 Bil'in conference, for instance, requirements for the success of the nonviolent movement (and, by extension, of the entire struggle for a just solution in Israel/Palestine) go beyond

development of more sophisticated strategies and improvement in leadership—as important as these may be. What we need is "a paradigm shift in the lingo we use." We need, he said, to "reframe the conflict."

> In the Israeli framing—which is very powerful; it makes sense to people—we're this "little country defending ourselves against terrorists." We have to reframe it. We have to step back and show that Israel is the strong power, to show that it's an occupying power, and to show that the occupation is proactive: it is not defensive. And if we can begin to make that shift, then I think you begin to break through. I think it's crucial, because it's not just a matter of giving alternative information. You've got to give people an alternative way to see the conflict, or else they don't know what to do with your alternative information.
>
> One way in which we reframe it—which works better in Europe than in the States—is by adopting the language of human rights. I think human rights language is very powerful. And if you begin to talk about self-determination, if you begin to talk about universal human rights, I think that says something.
>
> One of the keys is to show that Israel is the strong party. What Israel has succeeded in doing is casting itself as the victim. And if Israel is the victim, then it has no responsibility. You can't hold a victim responsible. A victim is a victim. So we can begin to show that Israel is a proactive occupying power. One of the issues we're trying to stress is the whole arms issue. You know, Israel is the third largest arms exporter in the world, number three only to Russia and the United States. If we can begin to show these other aspects of Israel—how strong Israel is, the fact that the occupation is proactive (Israel did not build 300 settlements for security reasons; the wall is not a security barrier, it's a political border for expansion): if you can reframe, I think this is crucial for what we're trying to do.

Challenging the notion that Israel is a democracy, Halper described it instead as an ethnocracy: "a country that belongs to one particular people that is privileged over everybody else."

> I think we have to start to use the term ethnocracy, because as long as [Israel] is seen as a democracy that's simply defending its own citizens, and so on, it distorts everything. The point is, we have to say there's an occupation, there's an oppression of the Palestinian people; that it isn't a matter of terrorism, it's a matter of a proactive Israeli claim to the entire country. Israel wants to establish an ethnocracy on this whole country.

Stating that "In my opinion, I don't think Israel can remain a Jewish state at all, because you can't have an ethnically pure state in the twenty-first century," Halper cautioned that Israel is headed for either ethnic cleansing or apartheid unless it undergoes a radical restructuring as was done in South Africa, transforming it "from being an ethnocracy of white Europeans to being a country of all its citizens."

> That, in the end, is what has to happen here. The struggle actually goes beyond the occupation. Occupation is only an expression of a much deeper problem, and that is an attempt on the part of Israel to create an ethnically pure state in this whole region; and it can only do that, not by separating from Palestinians, but by confining Palestinians to little prison islands. Israel claims the whole "Land of Israel" from the Mediterranean to the Jordan River, so what it ideally wants to do is to transfer the Arabs out of the Land of Israel into Arab countries; but if it can't do that, then at least to have apartheid.

Labelling the Israeli form of apartheid *nishul* (literally displacement or dispossession), Halper warned that Israel could create a Bantustan-type arrangement that it could "sell as a two-state solution." He called for an international anti-apartheid campaign to challenge such a development and reminded his audience that "the key is to bring people here and to have them see the realities on the ground," especially legislators and other influential people.[1]

Political Power Rather than Activism

On a somewhat pessimistic note, Judith Green—speaking from the perspective of her many years of experience as a part of Rapprochement-Jerusalem and, before that, as an activist in Israelis by Choice, as well as out of her sense of disappointment with the more violent character of the Al-Aqsa Intifada—advised today's Israeli activists to redirect their energies altogether.

> I guess I'm most appreciating the very basic level where you're able to hold some school-kid's hand and walk across the street with him—and maybe even that doesn't always prevent him from being shot. On that individual level, obviously, every good deed that you do is significant. I don't mean at all to say that's not the case. But

I'm talking about political change, not doing good deeds. In the long run, you can see very clearly that the power is not with the local groups, the power is on the top. And I think one of the lessons of all the work that we did in the nineties was that you can't really ignore power centres and political authority. It's very nice to have grassroots activities and NGOs and extra-parliamentary groups, but I think a problem in Israel—and I wouldn't say this is the same in Palestine, but in Israel—is that so many good people put all their energies into NGOs and extra-parliamentary activity and totally neglected the political parties. That's one of the reasons we're stuck with what we've got now. If we had put as much effort and time into, maybe, strengthening the political parties that we could have supported, and if, in the end, whatever the party might have been had twenty seats instead of six or something, that would make a difference; it would make a lot more difference than if some new NGO was formed or some NGOs changed their strategy to this or that, which really, in the long run makes very little difference.

I'm really kind of sorry in a way that we, like most of the people in the world, don't look for political power and are sarcastic and dismissive of political parties because they're not "pure". And they're not. You know, there're all kinds of problems in political parties, but it makes a big difference who's in the Knesset, and who's the prime minister, and who's the president of the United States. And in the end, they're the ones who are doing this tremendous harm here, and we have no way of stopping them, in my opinion, without changing the political spectrum, without getting elected.

If young people ask what should we have done differently, or what should we do now (like I'm an old advisor or something), I really would say to them to look for professions where you get power—because money also is an important issue in power and in support of political parties—and not to be so idealistic that you really end up just wasting your time, in a sense. Because it's not an intellectual game, it's a power game, and it's a life-and-death game. Maybe people realize now that without political power and without moneyed people behind the political power, your ideology, whatever it is, is not going to be effective.

Visions of a Shared Future

To my amazement, a plurality of those who responded to my question, "What is your vision for the future of this region?" (more than twenty of the fifty-odd interviewees who expressed a preference for one sort of political solution or another)—Israeli and Palestinian, nominal one- and two-staters alike, when pressed as to what they would really like to see, and not necessarily what they thought was feasible—spoke in often idyllic terms of some form of regional federation or confederation or even of a more internationalist (or nation-less) arrangement. Another surprise was the number of interviewees who proposed two states as either a compromise dictated by practicality or a step on the way to an ultimate vision of a single democratic state (four) or of a broader regional confederation or global society (nine)—for a total of thirteen—nearly equal to the number for whom a two-state solution was the preferred final outcome (fourteen). And virtually every one (as well as the nine who indicated no preferred political paradigm) spoke, sometimes quite lyrically, of the qualities they hoped would reign in their envisioned society—be it one state, two states, federation, or other.

A total of nine of the Palestinians who shared their visions with me did not specify a preference for a particular political solution, but—whatever their personal preferences may actually have been—chose to speak instead about the hoped-for qualities (freedom, justice, equal rights, neighbourliness, love ...) of the society they envisioned. Nonviolence trainer Husam Jubran, for instance, did not cite a political configuration for his "hope to have a good future" when he told me: "I wish we could live in a time where there would be no conflict, and people in all the Middle East could move freely everywhere in the Middle East, that we could go to Jordan, Egypt, Syria, Israel without any fear or facing any problems—the same with Israelis, the same with Jordanians, the same with Egyptians." Jubran qualified his upbeat vision, however: "But under current circumstances, I don't think this is a practical or true vision. I think it's more an ideal vision"—sadly a conclusion shared by many. Below are the "ideal visions" of a small sampling of interviewees, beginning with those who spoke primarily about the quality of that future, rather than the quantity of states.

Sami Awad spoke both for himself and for Holy Land Trust when he stated that, "My vision is that every single person who lives in this land has an equal right. Very simple."

> As an organization, we have made it very clear that we don't promote one sort of political solution over another: two-state

solution, one-state solution, or a bi-national solution, or a confederation, or a secular state. That's not what we're here to do. We're here to give the people the tools to empower themselves to be able to speak and act to achieve their rights. And what I tell Israelis is that I want to have the same rights you have—exactly—not any more and not any less. And that's what our vision is. For people to have freedom of expression, freedom to choose their leaders, freedom of assembly, freedom of media, to travel, to work, to provide for their families. Everybody wants that, and that's what our mission is here. That's what we hope to see will be the future. There isn't any person better than the other; there isn't one group of people that's better than the other. And these are barriers that exist in this conflict, and we have to break these, and nonviolence is the way. I believe that.

Similarly, Abdel Hadi Hantash (Palestinian Land Defence Committee cartographer and friend of Christian Peacemaker Teams, Hebron), extolled living as good neighbours, with mutual respect.

I hope to reach the peace, and I hope, when we finish our problem here, to work with many peace groups in the world. I am ready to help them, but I think that we have a long time to wait. When I say that I am a Muslim Peacemaker Team, for me there is no difference between you [he knows I'm Jewish] and Greg [of CPT] and me and anyone. We try to live together, to be friends, to visit me and to visit you. The good life is to be good neighbours, to be good friends, to live together, to respect me and to respect you; not to hate me and to hate you. This is the life.

Two-State Solution

A fair number expressed a clear preference for a two-state solution. Mohammed, an ISM activist from Qalqilya, was among those who emphasized how tired the Palestinians were of all the killing and how much they would prefer "just to live together without problems, without fighting each other" once both peoples reached the stage of realizing that "we are two nations and we have to live beside each other." This was a view echoed by S'leiman Abu Muferreh, mayor of Tequ'a village:

I'm looking for an independent Palestinian state, getting rid of occupation of the '67 areas, according to the [UN] resolutions.

And that means an Israeli state nearby—two neighbour states. This is what I hope can happen. And another important thing is: we are looking for living in freedom, peace, and justice. And when we say that, I don't think at any time it means hurting others.

Suheil Salman (PARC – Tulkarm) meanwhile envisioned two states in the context of a "new world" of peace and true democracy:

> First, for our nation to live in peace, to have an independent state, [where] our people can grow food for their children, have safety, and enough [to eat], and so on, and we hope all the world will be at peace. This is what is called a new world. Also occupation will be ended in all the world, not only here. Unreal democracy will be finished, and the nations of the world will take their rule in their hands.

Jamal Dar'awi, secretary of the Popular Committee against Settlements in a Bethlehem-area village, spoke through an interpreter. Even so, it was clear from his tone of voice and manner that early in our exchange he was sticking to the "party line," but by the time we got to the question about vision, he had warmed to the subject and was, I think, speaking from the heart.

> First of all, I do hope that stability and peace will prevail in the whole region. What I really do hope is that the Israelis will withdraw from the [post-war] 1967 boundaries to their state. And I do really also hope that we will live in peace with our neighbours the Israelis, with good relations, very nice relations with our neighbours. And why not also even initiate personal relationships, also trade and commerce and everything, and there might be some personal friendships from somebody Tel Aviv and one in Hebron. So we would like to initiate such relationships.
>
> We are people who would like to reach the point where we live under a state in spite of the wish of the Israeli occupation. Whether they accept it or not, we want to reach the point that we live in a democratic state of our own people. Sure, we do believe that the path to peace is not always full of flowers, and there might be lots of thorns along the path, but we look to the outcome.

Said Galia Golan (veteran Peace Now activist), "My vision is two states living side by side with the degree of cooperation that's possible."

Whatever is possible would be great. And I also say, if it winds up being a 'cold peace,' that's fine with me, too. If we can't get anything better than that, that's better than what we've got now. I do want to end the occupation. I want to end control over people, ruling over another people. I want to see an end to the conflict. Whatever there is afterwards, I don't care if they have a democracy or if they have a dictatorship; that's their business to decide their future. I think it's presumptuous for countries to go around saying, "you should have a free [market] economy, you should have a balanced—" You know, in the Roadmap it says that the Palestinians should have a written constitution. They didn't notice the *we* [Israelis] don't have one! It annoys me. They take this theory, which I think is false anyway, that democracies don't fight democracies, and therefore you can't have peace unless it's a democracy. I mean, that's nonsense! So I don't have a vision of what they should do afterwards.

It'd be lovely if we could get over the hatred and the pain that we've had of this conflict. It would be lovely if we could have coexistence, if we could have open borders, if we could have cooperation. It would be lovely, but I don't intend to give up the State of Israel. I'm not in favour of one state. I don't think we should all just live together and forget about nationalism. I don't think that either population is ready for that. The Palestinians want their own state. Put them as a minority in some other state, and I don't think they'd be happy with that. And we certainly wouldn't be happy with [being a minority].

Two States as a Necessary Starting Point, But Not the Ultimate Goal

Palestinian stateswoman Hanan Ashrawi, while envisioning an eventual regional solution with more porous borders, was among those who felt that two states were the prerequisite for a broader, regional, solution.

> I still believe we need to have a two-state solution, at least on the way towards solving the regional problem. Because the bi-national state will emerge as a de facto outcome of the refusal to accept the liberation of the Palestinians. But ultimately, it seems to me the whole region is due, long overdue, for a genuine liberation.

When I asked if she had in mind something like a federation, she replied, "Yes—in the sense that people have to transcend outmoded forms—whether of conflict or of boundaries or of self-definition—and to redefine ourselves and our relationships in ways that are more human and constructive."

Amos Gvirtz, too, felt that two states were a necessary starting point, to be followed by what he called a "European process" leading to a federation or confederation, and ultimately: "I would like to see a global society living in equality, where differences of nations or religions only make it more interesting, but are not used as a cause for conflict."

> But this is unrealistic. In our case, since we do have two national movements where one nation is rebuilding itself as a nation (this is the Israelis, the Jews) and one of them is creating themselves as a nation [the Palestinians], and since they are in this historical process of creating themselves as a nation, I don't believe we can take that from them. But my vision is to see what I call a European Process: peace in the Middle East, a process towards a common market of the Middle East that will bring us in the process towards a kind of confederation or federation in the future. This is my vision for what I believe can be realistic. It should start as a two-state solution. Each nation should practice its nationality, and when they get fed up with this nationality and will start to look at their needs of existence, they will go for a common market and the process towards confederation or federation. This is for me a vision of many years.

"I don't believe in states ... I believe in humanity," asserted Gaza psychologist Dr Eyad Sarraj, the roar of F16s passing overhead audible over the phone line as I interviewed him "long distance" from Beit Sahour, West Bank in January of 2006.

> You know, I mean I don't believe in states being built on religion or [ethnicity], or whatever. And I don't believe in borders. We are in the twenty-first century. I think that the age of computer technology has so advanced while people's territorial instincts have not advanced as much. For the sake of pragmatism and for the sake of reality and for the sake of understanding that Jews have struggled for a long time to establish their own state and they're still going through the nationalistic stage—and the same goes for the Palestinians, because they never had their own state—I can accommodate the idea of having two national states, but eventually I hope that the two states will merge in one, and even that state will merge in the Middle East.

When I asked Rabbi Jeremy Milgrom about his vision of the future in October 2003, he was one of those who posited a two-state solution as a station on the way to an ideal of Jewish-Palestinian partnership in a single state. His comments in April 2007, however, reflected his sense of the deteriorating political situation in the region—and his growing opposition to a Geneva-Accord-type solution.

> Politically, I think the most helpful thing would be if the Palestinian Authority disbanded, if the Palestinians boycotted the attempt of Israel to maintain the façade that there is some kind of solution under Israeli domination. Then the world says, "This is corrupt, this is impossible, and we have to do something different." In the meanwhile, international agencies would step in and guarantee the rights that Israel is barely allowing. The world believes that Israeli politicians are capable of the peace process. They clearly aren't. I think the settlements are a huge obstacle, and that the settlements are preventing any reasonable small Palestinian state from being established.

Noting that "most people would be astonished to discover that Israel has not only refused to acknowledge and allow the return of a single Palestinian into Israel, but it even does not allow Palestinians to come to the West Bank and, I presume, Gaza also," Rabbi Milgrom added: "I think that a Palestinian state which would not insist on the right of return is betraying the Palestinian people; and I think, therefore, that the ability of Palestinians to be manipulated into some great concession like that on the right of return is detrimental to the Palestinian people, and therefore that in itself would be a reason for the Palestinian Authority to be disqualified."

Federation, Confederation, and Beyond

ICAHD's Jeff Halper, too, no longer views the two-state solution as a viable option. When I interviewed him in Jerusalem in October 2003, Halper explained how a "two stage" solution—with two separate states as the first stage—might lead, ultimately, to a Middle East economic union reaching beyond Israel/Palestine to neighbouring states to encompass Lebanon, Syria, Jordan, and maybe Egypt.

This kind of union would allow for regional development. And this, I think, would also relate to the refugee issue because, like in Europe, a union would disconnect residency from citizenship. In other words, say you had a Palestinian state. It couldn't really deal with the issue of refugees by itself. It's too small; they want to come back to Israel. But if, like in Europe, they're also citizens of the Middle East Union, they can go live and work wherever they want to. You could have refugees coming back to Israel, but they would come back as Palestinians, just like the Greek workers today are going to Italy because the economy's better. The same would be true here. The Palestinians would remain here, and at the same time the settlers could stay where they are, because they're Israelis; and Israelis wouldn't vote for the Palestinian parliament, so they'd lose all their controlling aspects.

And what will happen if there's a regional approach is that Israel/Palestine will be the strongest [component] economically, and you're going to get an influx of workers from Jordan and from Syria. But if those workers came in as Jordanian and Syrian citizens but also as citizens of the Middle East Union, they could move here and work here and live here without threatening either Palestine or Israel from the point of view of influx of big populations—because they wouldn't vote [here]; they'd be citizens of their own countries.

Hence, such a confederative solution would address Palestinian concerns regarding their right of return to parts of Palestine controlled by Israel, while also allaying Israeli-Jewish apprehensions that Israel would "lose its Jewish character." In response to a question from the floor at the February 2004 Sabeel conference, Halper expanded on the latter point.

I'm saying that there's a very vibrant Israeli culture, Israeli institutions, Israeli economy that will continue to exist, so that even if the State of Israel evolves into something else—whether it's one state or a confederation or a country of all its citizens, or whatever—in a sense, it'll still have a very strong Israeli-Jewish or "Israeli-Israeli" component to it. And that's only good. I think Israel would flourish in conditions of peace and real integration into the region, in which I don't think you need a state. Today, of course, with the conflict, that's a hard message to sell to Israelis. But what we have to know when we're strategizing is where we're going, and what's going to be in the next ten, twenty, or thirty years, and to try to give people hope—certainly a vision of what's possible—and then we can begin to build a strategy.

After speaking about Gush Shalom's version of a two-state solution, with the slogan "Two peoples, two states, one future," Gush spokesman, Adam Keller, went on to elaborate his personal preference for the long-term: "for Israel to become a real integrated part of the Middle East."

I would like to see a Middle East confederation or federation more-or-less on the model of the European Union—which is not perfect; but for us, the European Union is the practical demonstration of the fact that what seemed to be very, very deep-seated nationalisms and hatreds could be laid to rest. Certainly in 1939, if someone would have predicted that France and Germany would get to the relationship that they now have, that they would have the same currency and they would be the chief partners in a Europe-wide federation, they would have been considered a very wild, utopian dreamer. So that's what we aim for.

Now, what will happen is, I suspect, a little bit less beautiful, because it is very rare that visionary dissidents get to actually implement what they dream. But there is a certain moment where the ideas that the dissidents have been propounding out of moral principles and out of a "pure vision" of a better society are taken up by the mainstream of society because the mainstream of society perceives these ideas—or some version of these ideas—to be in their interest; and then they are taken up by mainstream politicians, who come, out of quite egoistic and realpolitik considerations, to decide that this is what is going to benefit their careers. And then the politicians are implementing it—or some version of it—and the version of it which has gone through this process is often not exactly the same that the dissidents had dreamed about.

So the vision that I hope for, which I would like to see, is that we would have in the Middle East something like the European Union. To be realistic, I think it is very likely that we will have something else: we will have between Israel and Palestine something like the relations between the United States and Mexico. Because if you take the United States and Mexico, you have a first-world country side-by-side with a third-world country. But you have more than that: Mexico is much more poor than the United States, and the Mexicans know that the land on the other side of the border was taken away from them by force. There is a Mexican community living on the other side of the border which is not exactly equal citizens. And still, with all this, it has been nearly one hundred years since there was any kind of armed action between the United States and Mexico (if you consider Pancho Villa's raid in 1916). So if Israel and Palestine get to that point, it will not be enough for me, but it will certainly be a big improvement over the present situation.

For Meron Benvenisti, "some kind of confederation of Israeli and Palestinian cantons" is the solution that would best speak to the condition of the Palestinian citizens of Israel.

> They are my neighbours; I have to think about them. A solution that does not take them into consideration is not a solution at all. Even if you had a Palestinian state, their problem is not resolved. There are more than a million of them, and they are going to create such terrible problems for Israel very soon, when they become twenty-five percent of the population. And people will say, "Now go to the Palestinian state." Their perception of what they are is not to go to the Palestinian state: they are attached to their land. So they are going to be the victims. They are going to pay for that.
>
> You can't say, "Have a Palestinian state, and this is the end of the conflict," like [Geneva Accord co-author, Yossi] Beilin. You can't declare an end to a conflict. That declaration itself is hubris; that is the extreme arrogance. So I believe to be less arrogant and to accept the situation and *not* the principle that twenty years ago was a slogan—an important perception based on equality—two states for two peoples. Now, after thirty-five years or fifty-five years or a hundred years, it has turned into, I believe, something that is not very progressive.

When I asked Benvenisti about his stance on the Palestinian right of return to this envisioned confederation, he replied that while he objected to "'The Right of Return' as if it is an absolute right," he stressed that he recognizes "the fact that they belong. Yes," he stated, "I find them sons and daughters of this land and I find no difficulty in acknowledging it." And, like Nafez Assaily, he emphasized the symbolic value of apology—or, in Benvenisti's case, "a declaration of culpability."

> That, I think, is more important—the symbolic aspect of that is extremely important: that [the Palestinians] must be told openly, "Yes, we regret; we are sorry—for *our* share." I wrote it in the book [Benvenisti 2000], and that's still my opinion.

The Palestinians, too, should "acknowledge their part in what came to pass, because they also share some responsibility," said Benvenisti, citing a European precedent for such an exchange of apologies.

I find the example of Czechoslovakia and Germany very illuminating, because both sides are responsible, and both sides [apologized]: The Germans said, "We are sorry for Hitler," and the Czechs said, "We are sorry for the expulsion [of the ethnic Germans from Silesia and Sudetenland]." Each said it in the parliament of the other, and I thought that was a very courageous thing on both sides and a good example. To formulate that kind of declaration is one step forward.

One State

Of those who mentioned one state, whether as their ideal or as second choice after something broader, most made a point of stipulating that the state they envisioned should be democratic and egalitarian. Samah a-Tout (Project Hope, Nablus), for example, expressed a preference for a world without borders: "I would like to see all the people living in peace, thinking about the others as humans, as brothers and sisters, not as anything else. One world, actually. I don't agree with countries, even. But if there is a country, it must be one country. One democratic country is a really great solution."

Not surprisingly, Ziad Abbas, the only refugee-camp-dweller I interviewed, regards the right of return as key to Middle East peace. Sceptical that this is coming anytime soon, he cherishes "a simple dream, not far from Martin Luther King's dream, just to feel equal like everyone."

> I believe the key to peace in the Middle East, the whole Middle East, is the right of return. Some people say the key to peace in the Middle East is Jerusalem, because it's the Holy City, etc. Maybe Jerusalem is a Holy City, but for me the key to peace in the Middle East is the right of return: no right of return, no peace in the Middle East. And when we speak about the right of return, it doesn't mean we want to destroy Israel or we want to kick them into the sea. Just that we want to live equal with them. If they recognize our right to return back, then we can negotiate how to build the cities, the villages. I want to go back to my roots, which are in Zakaryya Village, which is fifty-five kilometres from here [inside Israeli proper].
>
> Since I was a youngster, I heard all the time, "Peace, peace, peace. Peace is coming. The peace plan, etc." But in the content, nothing happened around me as a human being. I don't see any content. So I'm dreaming to see a future to feel equal like everyone. I don't want to control others or confiscate the rights of others. At

the same time, I don't want to see anyone confiscate my rights as a human being, as a refugee, as a Palestinian. I need just to feel equal like everyone, to travel where I want, to live where I want. And I want to feel my freedom; I want to be free. Really, really what we are looking for is we want to feel free as human beings, not something more than this. I want to feel my dignity. I want to feel that others respect me as a human being. They don't deal with animals like they deal with us now in the checkpoints. What we are dreaming now is a simple dream. It's not far from Martin Luther King's dream, just to feel equal like everyone. And that's all.

Abbas stressed the inadequacy of a two-state solution from the refugee point of view.

When the people speak about two states, an Israeli state and a Palestinian state, for us as refugees, what's this? What's two states? What about two-thirds of the Palestinian people? Where will they go? Two million or five million refugees, where will they go? My sister is living in Syria, and she has been living there almost since 1967, and she still feels she is living there temporarily. And my nephews and nieces, despite being born and growing up there, they are dreaming and they are struggling to return to their homeland.

Many times we took the children [from the Ibdaa Center in Dheisheh where Abbas is director] to visit their original villages of 1948 [i.e., their villages of origin inside Israel]. We found out that the land belonging to thirteen villages has become the American Independence Park. It's just a forest where the Israelis can have fresh air and a barbecue and have a nice time. And the original people, including the new generation, are living in refugee camps. If you think about it, where is the justice? We have a space where we can return back;[2] we are not speaking about "we want to kick them out and we want to replace them." The ideal solution is to live in one state, in which each one has his own practices, rights, and lives equal to everyone.

Refugee rights activist Muhammad Jaradat characterized Israel as it is currently constituted (i.e., a quasi-European state with favouritism towards Jews embedded in the legal system) as "the main source of the conflict in the region," before elaborating his vision for a more inclusive future.

There should not be laws based on blood transmission. Israel has to transform all its laws, based on international human rights, international values, and then there will not be a problem. If we get rid of the Israeli system as a racist system with discriminatory laws, then I think it will not be a problem for a Qatari person from the Gulf to come to live [here] and not a problem for a Jew to go to live [there]. You know, the culture of the region is a hospitable culture; it tolerates differences. And you know, Jews in the Arab world were active and positive citizens. Palestinians were composed of Judaism, Christianity, and Muslim, and the Druze and the secular people. We had no problem until the Zionists came. Now, if we succeed in taking these discriminatory laws away, and Israel normalizes itself as a normal state—not an abnormal state and not threatening the peaceful existence of the region and blocking the development of the region—I do believe the whole Arab world will unite, and there will be one market, one residency, and one vote.

The duty of the Israeli activists is to dismantle the roots of the discriminatory laws. There could be a Palestinian and Israeli citizenship law which allows people who have connection to this piece of land to be able to live and reside in it like normal people like they are friends. You cannot say the Jews have the right to return but Palestinians or Arabs who have connections here have no right. This is where it becomes discriminatory. Now, if you have both of them, *ahalan wa'sahalan*! I wish—and this is a dream, you know—to see the whole region united in one market, in one currency, in one law that respects human dignity. And this is a long struggle that we have to go through.

Though not a refugee himself, Muhammad Jaradat, in his role as coordinator of BADIL's Refugee Campaign Unit, is thoroughly acquainted with refugee issues. He called for a United Nations commission to deal with the rights of refugees, Palestinian and Jewish, alike.

I don't care much about how many dunams of land or how many acres of land we will get or not get. I care if my people will get their rights, will enjoy their rights of return, restitution, and compensation. These are the three things. Why should the Israeli Jew from Germany have the right of restitution, return to Germany to get all the compensation for the losses, all this, and me, as a Palestinian who's been looted and had my land stolen, has to give up?

Jews that were displaced from Arab countries, Jaradat suggested, "can be given the free choice like the Palestinian refugees: to return, restitution or residential rights, or stay in Israel, or leave to another country. Like a Palestinian should be given the choice."

I do recognize that these people are Iraqi Jews or Moroccan Jews or Yemenite Jews, and they have left property there. If they haven't sold it legally (as well, if there's a Palestinian who sold his land, it's a different issue), they have the full right to take it back and be compensated for the use of their property and for their suffering. That's a thing that we Palestinians will support them in. I am with them. They have to receive restitution. I will fight for their rights also, in Egypt, Iraq, Morocco.

Ya'akov Manor (Israeli independent activist) made a distinction between a single bi-national state and the "state of all its citizens" that he hopes will be achieved some time in the future.

Okay, the dream, dream, dream is a single state of all its citizens. A democratic, civil state of all its citizens. This is my dream, and not a bi-national state in which each nationality has autonomy. I don't have a problem with each group maintaining its ethnicity and culture. It's even right and proper; no one should have to give this up. My parents came from Greece, and I love to eat—I just plain love to eat—but if I love Greek food, am I going to give that up? No. So the same with people who are Palestinian. They won't give up their symbols, their culture. That's just fine. Their religion. I've no problem with that.

Manor cautions, however, that were a single state to be attempted too soon, "Israel would become the ruling society."

The economic and planning power would be in Israel's hands, and we would essentially create a kind of awful inequality, transforming the two or three million Palestinians living in the region to slaves: "drawers of water and hewers of wood." And I don't want that under any circumstances.

For that reason, says Manor, a single state must be preceded by "some sort of joint political entity like a confederation or federation—depending on which is suitable—which might also include Jordan and perhaps also Syria. And then, after many years of cooperation in the realms of the economy, security, ecology, the distribution and exploitation of resources, etc., etc., it would be possible to think about one state."

Present Needs First, Visions of the Future Later

And finally, a few of the Israelis I interviewed found the idea of articulating a vision of the future inappropriate, given the pressing need for addressing ongoing abuses, although—as in the case of the Palestinians we met earlier in this section who eschewed talk of political solutions in favour of qualitative descriptions of their envisioned future— this didn't stop them from remaining hopeful. Among these were psychotherapist Yitzhak Mendelsohn (wounded in a West Jerusalem attack by a Palestinian gunman in 1994), historian Reuven Kaminer, and Bustan's Devorah Brous. Mendelsohn looked towards joint action to promote healing.

> I would love to see shared projects that take care of the damage to both sides. I think that the repair should be done by common initiatives, where Palestinians and Israelis will have the shared responsibility for repair, regardless of asymmetry in the responsibility for the damage. Here the asymmetry works in favour of the Palestinians. There is much more repair to be done there, so we will do more repairs there. But the consciousness of the Palestinians that they are responsible for repairing the other side, that's the thing that is my vision, and I think that it is possible. But the only way to arrive at this point is when Palestinians will say, "Yes, we also created damage"—different ones, with different proportions; not with Apaches and F-16s, it's true. We are not doing an accounting of the damage; there's damage here, there's damage there. Both sides have damage we have to repair, and where there's much more damage, we repair more; where there's less damage, we repair less, but we repair together.

Kaminer, on the other hand, was adamant: "I don't need visions of the future! I'm also very unhappy about the argument of one state, two state. I don't need a vision of the future! I have to stop what's going on now!"

> The possibility of a change in the near future is a two-state solution. That possibility can oscillate, and it depends on the crises in American foreign policy; it doesn't matter what I want. But my hope for the future is to wake up some morning and to say that we're getting rid of the occupation step by step. Because what's going on is horrendous. People can't live! People are choked, and they can't move from place to place, and they can't make a living. It's horrible.

And Brous, while not rejecting out of hand a vision for the future, also stressed the importance of first of all providing for the basic needs of the Palestinian population. "People need water to drink. People need medical supplies in the hospitals. They need the ability to [get] to the hospitals. I don't really think it's the time for us to bring people together to focus solely and entirely on reconciliation and on doing that kind of work—it isn't really suitable for this stage of this protracted conflict." In the context of her long-term hopes for a bi-national state, she described the groundwork that must, in her view, come first.

> My vision is to strengthen the civil society that's working for peace and justice and human rights and true democracy—which is not ethnocracy—which is beginning to happen right now, where the Israelis are working among the Israelis, sometimes in [cooperation] with Palestinians, sometimes independently; where the Palestinians are working independently and sometimes in [cooperation] with us—to strengthen a voice against a continued state of conflict and war where violence is the language that's dominant in the region, where violence is the tool that is the most effective and the most efficient at expressing dissent. I think that we're trying to build something where there are bridges between Israelis and Palestinians, to shift the focus of our society from some kind of narrow nationalism, on either side—or some maximalist claim to all of the land, for Greater Palestine or for Greater Israel—but to shift it towards a place where the peoples of the nations that are working together to effect social change will actually have a more significant voice here.
>
> I think that it's valuable to have a place where Palestinians and Israelis work independently, where we don't feel the need to promote co-existence and "peace" right now. I don't think anyone knows what the word "peace" means anymore. I don't think that that's something that needs to forcibly meld us together, or weld us together, I should say. But rather, a common set of principles—justice and human rights and equal distribution of our limited, dwindling resources on this land—that's something that's a strong enough motivator to bring us together.
>
> Basically, the idea of returning to the 1967 line is an archaic formulation. This line is no longer visible; this Green Line is no longer green. You can't find it on the maps, especially with the construction of this wall and all of the land confiscation and the absolute brutal destruction of the line. So for groups to talk about the return to the '67 borders and the ending of the occupation, I feel, is short-sighted. What's happening in the West Bank and Gaza, in many ways, is also being reflected inside Israel. So that's

why it's absolutely not enough to stick with this idea that we need to return to '67 borders. Ending the occupation is a brilliant goal, and we need to start there, but it's not enough. We need to go much further than that.

Conclusion

Looking towards the future, Jeff Halper and Judith Green both propose rethinking how we approach the conflict itself and the goals of the movement. Halper posits the need to "reframe" the conflict: The depiction of Israel as an innocent democracy and a victim of terrorism that is simply defending itself must be replaced, he argues, with a more accurate perception of the occupation as a pro-active policy by an ethnocracy that is the strong party in the conflict and is engaged in ethnic cleansing. He calls for an international anti-apartheid campaign aimed at Israel, to forestall the development of "a Bantustan-like arrangement" that Israel could "sell as a two-state solution." Green, disillusioned by the disappointing level of achievement by grassroots activism and extra-parliamentary NGOs, advises young Israeli activists to turn their energies instead to gaining political power through elected office.

Of the interviewees who shared their personal visions for the future of Israel/Palestine, a surprising number favoured something beyond the usual "one-state, two-state" refrain. Of the fifty-plus who expressed a political preference, for example, more than twenty mentioned some form of federation or confederation as their ultimate vision, while thirteen of those who stated their preference for a two-state solution viewed this as either a stepping stone to another solution (mainly either one state or confederation) or as a compromise dictated by necessity, almost as many as the fourteen who preferred two states outright. Although responses regarding preference for a single-state solution were more complicated to interpret precisely, one form or another of this solution was mentioned significantly more often as either first choice directly (between eight and ten respondents, depending on how choices are counted) or ultimate aim (between four and seven) than as a step on the way to something broader (six or seven). Another surprise for me was that nine Palestinian respondents eschewed expression of any political preference, speaking instead of the sort of society they envisioned, with qualities such as equal rights, freedom—"freedom of expression, freedom to choose their leaders, freedom of assembly, freedom of media, to travel, to work, to provide for their families." "Equal rights"—as Sami Awad put it, mutual respect and neighbourly relations (Abdel Hadi Hantash), and replacement of hatred and bloodshed by love (Nawaf Souf). A few of my Israeli interviewees deferred thoughts of a vision for the future of the region, finding the need to address present abuses far too pressing for such an exercise. Instead, they spoke in terms of such shorter-term initiatives as "shared projects that take care of the damage to both sides" (Yitzhak Mendelsohn); meeting Palestinians' need for "water to drink ... medical supplies ... ability to [get] to the hospitals" (Dvora Brous), or simply staying focussed on "getting rid of the occupation step by step" (Reuven Kaminer).

Stressing that much groundwork remains to be done within both societies in order to achieve her long-term goal of a bi-national state, Brous moved beyond politics to declare the need to strive for "a common set of principles—justice and human rights and equal distribution of our limited, dwindling resources on this land." "Ending the occupation is a brilliant goal," stated Brous, "and we need to start there, but it's not enough. We need to go much further than that."

Overall, I found the visions of a common future that the activists I interviewed shared with me—many reaching out beyond the boundaries of Israel and Palestine—a refreshing and hope-inspiring antidote to the despair that threatens to descend when one is confronted with the day-to-day reality in the region. Despair, as I recall hearing someone (I think it was Simha Flapan, founding editor of *New Outlook* magazine) once say, is the greatest enemy of peace. And to echo Mansour Mansour, "The most important thing that we realize about the future is that there is always hope."

* * *

This concludes the interview (and conference presentation)-based portion of *Refusing to be Enemies*. I have endeavoured to keep commentary to a minimum and to let the interviewees do most of the "talking." In Part IV, Analysis, we will hear from four activist-thinkers, three of whom were also interviewees. Jeff Halper's piece—drawing examples from the text to illustrate his thesis regarding the necessary components of nonviolent strategy—is flanked by essays by two Palestinian proponents of nonviolence: Ghassan Andoni—activist in the Beit Sahour tax strike of 1988–93, initiator of dialogue with Israeli activists during the First Intifada, and cofounder of the ISM—gives a historical overview of Palestinian nonviolence and asks "Can nonviolence work?" and Jonathan Kuttab, pacifist and lawyer (and incurable optimist), argues "that nonviolence is more effective and suitable for resistance, precisely by the Palestinian people at this time of their history and under the current conditions." Starhawk—a Jewish-American peace and justice activist and writer, who has been in Palestine with the International Solidarity Movement on four occasions—provides a comparison of the challenges faced by Palestinian nonviolent activists with those encountered by their U.S. counterparts. In the Conclusions and Epilogue, I focus on present and potential future roles for Israeli activists in Palestinian/Israeli joint struggle.

NOTES

1 For a more thorough discussion of Israeli apartheid/*nishul* (dispossession), reframing, and related issues, as well as other concepts referred to in Jeff Halper's segments of the present book, please see Halper 2008 as well as "Israel-Palestine: Apartheid or Confederation?" (http://icahdusa.org/2007/85). Halper also spoke about many of these points during his January 2009 Canadian tour (see Roth 2009 and "Strategic Organizing for the Middle East: Thinking outside the box with Jerusalem-based activist Jeff Halper," http://archive.peacemagazine.org/v25n3p08.htm – a corrected version of my article which appeared in the July–Sept. 2009 print-edition of *Peace Magazine*).
2 Ali Abunimah quotes geographer Salman Abu-Sitta: "90 percent of [former Palestinian] village sites are still vacant today." (Abunimah 2006, p. 120 and associated notes)

PART IV

—

ANALYSIS

10

PALESTINIAN NONVIOLENCE: A HISTORICAL PERSPECTIVE

Ghassan Andoni

Nonviolence in Historical Context

Palestine embodies a century of resistance, and within this heritage there is one type of resistance that is particularly worthy of examination: namely nonviolence, or, as it has been more commonly known in Palestine, civil-based resistance. Civil-based resistance has been and still is one of the major components of the Palestinians' struggle for return and independence. The general strike of 1936, which lasted for six months (and is considered the longest general strike in modern history), is only one indicator of how early in their struggle Palestinians began to employ civil-based resistance.

Following the 1948 war (and the resulting *Nakba* or catastrophe) and until the early 1960s, the few Palestinians who managed to escape forced evacuation and remain inside the nascent Jewish state were placed under martial law. The ones who lived in or fled to the West Bank came under Jordanian administration, the ones who lived in or fled to the Gaza Strip came under Egyptian administration, and the remaining Palestinians who fled to other Arab countries lived in refugee camps under the regimes of those countries. During this period, most Palestinians became politically inactive or joined the various national Arab parties, believing that Arab unity was a necessary step towards regaining their rights in Palestine.

The Rise of Armed Struggle in the Palestinian Diaspora

The mid-1960s witnessed the revival of Palestinian nationalism, which became even stronger following the defeat of several Arab armies in the 1967 war. This period witnessed the birth of the modern Palestinian revolution in the refugee camps of the diaspora. It is no wonder that the revolution became romanticized around the idea of regaining the lost paradise (Palestine) by conducting a military struggle against Israel.

Born of the diaspora, and emerging after a shameful defeat of major Arab states, the modern Palestinian revolution developed around the concept of popular armed resistance. Similar to many liberation movements, the Palestinian liberation movements set up bases in the Arab countries bordering Israel and launched cross-border guerrilla warfare.

As the existence of Palestinian refugee camps was forced upon the Arab host countries, and as guerrilla warfare gave rise to Israeli retaliation against these countries, a conflict of interest developed between the Palestinian liberation movements and Arab host regimes. Around this time, most of the efforts of the Palestinian liberation movements operating under the umbrella of the Palestinian Liberation Organization (PLO) were devoted to defending their right to use the territories of Arab countries to fight against Israel. Consequently, these conflicts of interest eventually developed into civil war between the PLO and its allies, on the one hand, and Arab regimes in both Jordan and Lebanon, on the other (in 1970 and between 1975 and 1990, respectively).

This entire era was characterized by the struggle to defend the Palestinians' right to conduct guerrilla warfare, and armed struggle became sacred in the eyes of most Palestinians, a fact which greatly influenced the future of the Palestinian liberation movements.

The Prevalence of Nonviolent, Civil-Based Resistance in the Occupied Territories

Meanwhile, the Palestinians who lived under Israeli military occupation in the West Bank and the Gaza Strip adopted more diverse means of struggle, primarily focusing on civil-based resistance. In addition to becoming more politically active, these Palestinians began establishing the infrastructure for a Palestinian civil society that would be as independent as possible of the Israeli occupation authorities. Hundreds of non-governmental organizations in the fields of human rights, health, environment, education, and preservation of cultural heritage were established, in addition to national universities and trade unions. In addition, many civil society groups such as student unions and women's rights groups were also established, forming the community base for a

Palestinian national movement with a unique character, while remaining linked to the PLO.

The First Intifada (1987) represented the first encounter between the Israeli occupation and the Palestinian national liberation movement inside the occupied Palestinian territories. During the First Intifada, resistance stopped being limited to elitist guerrilla groups and became a popular resistance in which almost all sectors of the community took part in one form or another. Protests, massive marches, picketing, civil disobedience, tax revolts, and defiance of all occupation orders were combined with the creation of popular committees and a local leadership who became the popular authority in place of the occupation's "civil administration." The confused occupation authorities felt they had totally lost control, and therefore escalated their oppressive measures against entire communities to a level never before witnessed.

Despite the fact that small groups of young people hurled stones at soldiers and settlers any time they entered Palestinian communities and that small, armed militant groups emerged in a few localities, the First Intifada was, on the whole, a massive civil-based nonviolent resistance.

The first Gulf War shook the region like an earthquake, bringing an end to the three-year-old Intifada. Such a tragic end made it impossible to judge the success of the Intifada. One thing is obvious, and that is that were it not for the Intifada, there would not have been a Palestinian delegation at the Madrid peace conference.

Palestinian and Israeli activists worked together for the first time during the First Intifada. Dialogue groups aimed at creating a better understanding of the other side, as well as joint Palestinian-Israel anti-occupation activities, became common practice in many Palestinian communities.

The diplomatic process begun at the Madrid conference ultimately produced the Oslo Accords, in accordance with which the PLO returned to the Palestinian territories. This was understood by most Palestinians as a step towards the creation of an independent Palestinian state. However, what was supposed to be a peacemaking process combined with a gradual state-building process was smashed under the boots of settlers and Israeli right wingers. The burial of the assassinated Israeli prime minister, Yitzhak Rabin, signaled for all practical purposes the burial of the peace process itself.

Palestinian and Joint Nonviolence since the Year 2000

With the disastrous failure of the Camp David talks in the summer of 2000 began the bloodiest crisis ever between Israel and the Palestinians since the occupation began. Despite the incredible level of violence deployed against the Palestinians, civil-based nonviolent resistance emerged in a number of Palestinian communities. Nonviolent direct actions—initiated by Palestinian, Israeli radical, and international activists who joined forces in the International Solidarity Movement (ISM)—became widespread throughout most of Palestine from Rafah in the south of the Gaza Strip to Jenin in the far north of the West Bank. In addition, many Palestinian communities initiated their own nonviolent resistance against the Israeli occupation, especially after Israel decided to build an 800-kilometre-long wall cutting deep into the West Bank, which—in combination with the huge network of military checkpoints—isolates farmers from their fields and Palestinian communities from one another. While the village of Bil'in stands out as an example of such resistance, similar initiatives emerged in dozens of other localities such as Budrus, Jayyous, al-Walajah, and Tel al-Rumeida.

On thorough examination of civil-based resistance in Palestine within the context of the hundred-year-old Palestinian resistance, and comparison of Palestinian civil-based resistance with other examples, such as those of India, South Africa, and the U.S. Civil Rights Movement, some characteristics become obvious.

The Uniqueness of the Palestinian Experience of Nonviolence

In India, civil disobedience and noncooperation succeeded in convincing the British occupier that it was impossible to rule more than 300 million Indians with a mere 100,000 troops. The examples of India and Palestine are similar in the sense that both peoples were seeking to end a foreign occupation. The British occupier, however, did not establish colonies in India and did not attempt to push Indians away and replace them with British citizens. In fact, India was a clear example of the failure of a tiny military minority to continue to rule over a vast majority. The case in Palestine is different in that the occupied and the occupier are almost equal in number and the Israeli occupation is a colonial one, with both Palestine and Israel asserting national claims to the same piece of land.

The South African example is more similar to the Palestinian one in the sense that a minority of colonial whites had settled in the country and were ruling over the black majority through a complicated apartheid system. Yet, in South Africa, the demand for "one man one vote" was an effective slogan in the struggle to end the Apartheid regime. In the case of Palestine, the one man one vote formula is considered by Israelis to threaten an end to their dream for a Jewish state in Palestine, and thus is not a feasible solution, at least for the foreseeable future. In addition, in order for both sides to coexist in South Africa, it was sufficient to revise laws and reform the legal system. In the Palestinian case, however, the issue is far from being exclusively internal. Both Israelis and Palestinians envision it as a national conflict, where the struggle is focused on land and resources and the lost residency rights of Palestinian refugees.

Finally, the U.S. Civil Rights Movement was a struggle to delegitimize discrimination. In Palestine the struggle is a national one, and the discrimination stems from Israel's desire to take over land and resources and to rule over another nation. Indeed, the Palestinian case is probably more similar to that of the native Americans than to the civil rights struggle.

Palestinian Resistance: a "Generational" Phenomenon

One cannot help but notice that Palestinian resistance comes in waves that resemble a sort of "generational" pattern. Prior to 1948, Palestinians revolted in the early 1930s and then around the end of the British Mandate, 1947–48. The modern Palestinian revolution dates from 1965, and from then up to 1982, the Palestinian liberation organizations were almost fully engaged in civil wars, trying to protect their right to use Arab territories as a base for their fight against Israel. In 1987, a new generation of Palestinians in the occupied territories took the lead and launched the First Intifada. In the year 2000, the next Palestinian generation took the lead in launching the Second Intifada (Al-Aqsa Intifada).

Looking at each wave of resistance, one cannot but notice that each had its own character and that there existed practically no degree of continuity or of experience passed from one generation to the next. In the 1930s the resistance was mostly civil-based, in the 1940s it was mainly guerrilla warfare. In the 1960s it was primarily an armed struggle, in the 1980s it was again mainly nonviolent civil-based resistance. In the year 2000 it was once again largely guerrilla warfare.

One might conclude that very little of what is learned about resistance by each generation of Palestinians is passed on to the next, and that each generation brings its own experience and potential onto the battlefield. In other words, each generation brings its own surprises into the conflict. For example, the generation that started the Second Intifada were children during the First Intifada. Much of what they experienced or witnessed of Israeli brutality characterizes their behaviour and methods of resistance during the current crisis. It may be possible to understand this phenomenon as a defense mechanism that ensures the continuity of resistance even if the previous generation was defeated on the battlefield.

It is also obvious that each generation of Palestinians is influenced by cultural changes taking place in the society in which they live. Early generations were influenced by the village culture, and for them the land was most sacred. The 1960s generation was influenced by the refugee camp culture, and for them return to the lost paradise (the homes from which they had been ejected in the part of Palestine that became Israel) was most sacred. The First Intifada generation was influenced by the rise of secular nationalism and civil society values, whereas the Second Intifada generation is influenced by the rise of Islamic culture in the 1990s.

Palestinian-Israeli Relations at the Grass Roots

Joint work between Palestinian activists in the First Intifada and Israeli peace activists was based on assumptions that need to be examined more carefully.

What drew Palestinians to such work was the hope of gaining allies from the enemy side by the exercise of political moderation (i.e., separating opposition to the Israeli occupation of the Palestinian territories seized in the 1967 war from the issue of the existence of the Israeli state itself). The unification of forces against the occupation was seen by most Palestinian activists as a legitimate cause, with many precedents in the history of national liberation struggles. Yet, both sides were incapable of avoiding clashes over issues like Jerusalem and refugee rights, such that it was not possible at any time to agree on what would constitute a just solution. This is precisely why such joint efforts were impossible to revive during the Second Intifada, which erupted as a response to the failure to deal with the issue of Jerusalem and the rights of Palestinian refugees.

The objective for most Israeli left-wing activists during the First Intifada was to help create a Palestinian peace movement similar to the Israeli Peace Now movement. Trying to impose parallel responsibilities onto an unparallel situation was simply fruitless, and much of the joint work done on the grassroots level collapsed at the sight of the first Palestinian standing on a rooftop and waving at Iraqi missiles launched towards Tel Aviv.[1]

Both assumptions—that gaining allies from the enemy side was possible and that a Palestinian "Peace Now" could be established—failed the test of reality due to the absence of agreement on the meaning of justice in the context of the Palestinian-Israeli conflict.

What was needed to efficiently combat the prevailing situation was, from my point of view, an active Palestinian civil-based resistance and an active Israeli anti-occupation movement—without the imposition of organizational alignment or of parallel responsibilities.

This new formula, which has been deployed during the Second Intifada, has proved capable of attracting members of a few radical anti-Zionist groups to work together with Palestinian and International activists but has not brought about the participation of the mainstream Israeli "peace movement."

We can only refuse to be enemies when we can arrive at a joint definition of what justice means in the context of the Palestinian-Israeli conflict. Pragmatic steps to influence the conflict in a positive way are always possible and do not oblige either side to "cross over to the enemy."

A fundamental question, implicit in this article, is: Can nonviolence work in Palestine? This is difficult to answer. So far, civil-based resistance has proven to be useful and is likely to positively influence the course of events of the ongoing crisis. But can it really work? Can it truly bring about an end to the occupation and a just solution for the Palestinians?

Ultimately this depends on many factors, including how Zionist Israel wants to be, how unbiased the media can be, how powerful the anti-occupation movement in Israel is, how massive civil-based resistance in Palestine can be, and the degree to which lost Palestinian rights are restored.

NOTE

1 During the 1991 Gulf War, it was reported that Palestinians were sighted cheering-on missiles aimed at Israeli cities, dancing and shouting *Allah hu akbar!* (God is great).

11

TOWARDS A STRATEGIC NONVIOLENCE

Jeff Halper

Progressive civil society has a great many achievements under its belt, and many, if not most of them, are the fruits of nonviolent struggles. The modern history of nonviolence begins, perhaps, with one of its greatest victories: the abolition of the trans-Atlantic slave trade in 1807. Since then there have been thousands of instances of nonviolent resistance, from individual acts to national struggles—some well-known, others less so, the vast majority probably forgotten or remembered only in local tradition.

It is well to keep this in mind. Nonviolence is a multi-faceted philosophy and approach to political and social change, but it *is* political. In the globalized reality in which we live, where people power is often dwarfed by heavily militarized regimes supplied with weaponry, privatized armies, and motives to use them by their corporate allies, many groups struggling for nonviolent change have tended to define themselves as activist rather than political. That is, viewing themselves as small, marginal, powerless groups often at odds with their own societies, they have in effect given up trying to affect governmental or trans-governmental policy; instead, they settle for mere protest, for documentation of political wrong-doing, and for forms of advocacy which might be more or less effective, but lack the strategic dynamism of people who believe they can actually influence policy and overthrow or reform political regimes.

What I would like to distil from Maxine Kaufman-Lacusta's work is a conception of *strategic* nonviolence which, as part of wider struggles for social justice, *believes* it can "win" and therefore invests thought in how to do so. The task of nonviolent groups and movements is to effectively insert themselves into the political process, whether as part of a movement's leadership or as smaller groups on the side able to influence events through strategic interventions. How to move from the micro to the macro and back again, how to connect grassroots actions that appear as stand-alone or merely spontaneous acts to wider political processes, is the task before us.

Precisely because grassroots resistance is the essence of popular struggle against oppression, the often problematic relationship between activism and strategic campaigning, different in detail in every struggle yet constantly present, should be thoroughly discussed and acted upon. Activism on all levels is absolutely essential for any struggle, and particularly for a nonviolent one, since it aspires to transform society even after political liberation has been achieved. A movement based on the grass roots lends credibility to political leaders while also constraining them by making the will of the people manifest. But activism by its nature is tactical and reflexive; it needs to be connected with larger, ongoing campaigns in a wider movement for liberation. Activists arise from, and often represent, the people, but they only fuel the engine; the actual engine of change is an organized movement.

The interviews with activists in Palestine/Israel found in Maxine's book contain a great many insights generated by courageous and creative people through their experiences "on the ground." By their nature they tend to be action-oriented, yet the issues they are dealing with cover organizational and political considerations along a broad spectrum. Immediate "lower-level" problems, for example, revolve around what to protest, what and how to message, and how to organize, while "middle-level" concerns have to do with how to cooperate across barriers of power, national conflict, class, and culture, how to sustain actions, and how to build a movement—all within the "higher" aims of ending the occupation, achieving a just peace and, in general, playing a role in the global struggle of making the world a better place to live. How to engage in struggle on all these levels against powerful, oppressive, and often violent state, corporate and other international forces, often including religions and hostile ideologies, is difficult enough. Activists, committed but usually part-time, under-resourced, and often young, do not always have the time and energy to immerse themselves in the literature of resistance or even spend hours brainstorming and doing the office-based "infrastructural" work (planning, networking, applying for funds, administering, reporting, developing materials, etc., etc.). They, indeed, learn "on the job" and have to figure things out for themselves, often in the real-time of immediate struggle. But to add to all this a commitment to nonviolence, the added task of pursuing the struggle with, as it were, one hand tied behind your back, makes it all the more difficult.

This book—and hopefully this chapter, which tries to place the nonviolent struggle-in-action into some kind of a conceptual framework—represents a valuable resource for peace- and justice-makers precisely because it comes from "the ground" up. Rather than starting from scratch, activists in other places labouring on other issues can dip into the experiences and reflections of the dozens of individuals whose voices are woven into this book so as to apply them to their own situations. In fact, Maxine's approach to these activists, giving them voice and the space to unfold their thoughts while gently, unobtrusively directing the conversation and, when appropriate, adding a comment linking them to what others have said, conveys a kind of an ongoing conversation to which activists can avail themselves without getting bogged down in distant theory or long expositions of only tangential relevance. Indeed, it is a conversation we activists in Palestine/Israel are having without being aware of it, so we, too, are the beneficiaries of Maxine's service to us: helping us articulate our approaches to nonviolent direct action and sharing them in the absence of a structured opportunity to do so. This chapter takes her effort a step further and attempts to summarize and organize into a coherent, concise discussion—including an attempt at identifying underlying issues and strategies—ideas, opinions, and approaches which nevertheless need to be structured if only for the sake of accessibility.

Tactical vs. Philosophical Nonviolence

This is a book describing nonviolent actions, tactics, and strategies of grassroots resisters—Palestinian, Israeli, and international—to Israel's repressive occupation, although it touches on wider structural sources of violence and oppression deriving from Israel's prevailing ideology, institutions, and policies, as well. It is fair to say, I think, that most of the practitioners represented here follow a nonviolent path as an accepted course of action, some because the very idea of engaging in violent resistance is reflexively unacceptable. As Galia Golan, a leader of Peace

Now, put it: "We don't use violence, but we're not ideologically nonviolent." Says Yonatan Pollak of Anarchists Against the Wall: "It's not that I don't think that the Palestinians have a right to shoot at soldiers if they invade their cities; under international conventions that's legitimate. I just think that it's tactically unwise." And Peretz Kidron: "Yesh Gvul [an organization of reserve soldiers who refuse to serve in the occupied territories] makes use of the powerful tactic of nonviolent noncooperation 'selectively.' We're not pacifists, and I could imagine a situation in which we would say, 'No, this is a time to go into the army and pick up a gun.'"

When pressed, most Palestinian activists also articulated what might be called tactical nonviolence: the adoption of nonviolence for a myriad of practical reasons. "Having internationals actively involved," says ISM leader Huwaida Arraf, "reduced the level of violence used against Palestinians." Furthermore, she adds, nonviolence is certainly a central element of the Palestinian struggle: "...if a Palestinian father is not marching in the streets, he's trying to figure out a way around the checkpoint so he can feed his children; or a student is studying at home instead of being out there in the street or doing a sit-in or something somewhere... And that is a rich part of the resistance that I think needs to be recognized."

Riad Malki, a veteran Palestinian leader and, as of this writing, foreign minister of the Palestinian Authority, expressed the Palestinian commitment to nonviolence in blunt terms: "Any person that understands very well the balance of powers—or imbalance of powers, the lack of symmetry between the two sides—can immediately understand and can even anticipate what kind of outcome could be if the Palestinians opt for using violence and the armed struggle as a way to solve their own conflict."

Of the organizations surveyed in this book, a number stand out in the centrality of a principled adherence to nonviolence as a philosophy of life and resistance. In no particular order, the groups in which philosophical nonviolence informs all actions are the Hope Flowers School of el-Khader; the al-Watan Center for Civic Education, Conflict Resolution, and Nonviolence in Hebron; the Center for Rapprochement Between People (PCR) in Beit Sahour; the Holy Land Trust and the Wi'am Palestinian Conflict Resolution Center in Bethlehem; Palestinians and Israelis for Nonviolence (PINV, the local affiliate of the

International Fellowship of Reconciliation); the Palestinian Center for the Study of Nonviolence (PCSNV) in Jerusalem; and Panorama—all, interestingly enough, exclusively Palestinian organizations, with the exception of PINV. Their commitment to nonviolence goes beyond using it as merely a tactic: they seek to disseminate it throughout society.

Yet here, at the very outset of the discussion, among people who claim to follow a nonviolent struggle for a variety of reasons—moral, tactical, or philosophical, or some combination of these—we encounter a carefully couched yet significant difference in Palestinian and Israeli approaches. Being part of the stronger, oppressing society, less afraid of retribution on the part of the Israeli authorities and freer to speak out against their government's policies, one might expect Israeli activists to embrace a more philosophical nonviolence. But a reticence to adopt nonviolent tactics across the board, stemming, it appears, from an unwillingness to step out of Israeli society or "alienate" themselves from it can be detected. Thus Gila Svirsky, a long-time leader of Israeli women's organizations, comments: "I am a believer in nonviolence and civil disobedience as an effective strategy, but not by Israelis doing it on the Palestinian side... I have come to realize that Israelis doing that activity radiates to the Israeli public that we are 'on the Palestinian side,' that we do not care about Israeli security and Israeli well-being, that all we care about is Palestinian security and well-being... When I think logically and rationally about what works, what works more is working on the Israeli side to educate Israelis."

Six Elements of Effective Organizing and Struggle

In reviewing the interviews that make up *Refusing to be Enemies*, what emerges are a number of elements which would seem to be essential for an effective strategy of resistance, movement-building, and advocacy, elements necessary both to sustain a resistance movement and to insert it into the political process. For purposes of discussion, I arrange them into six key categories: (1) trust building and coordination of positions; (2) groundedness, the need to "be there" with the people; (3) development of a political analysis deriving from realities "on the ground"; (4) reframing the oppressor's narrative; (5) developing an effective strategy and program of advocacy; and (6) providing leadership. I will integrate views culled from the book's interviews to illustrate each point. My aim is to organize the often free-ranging discussion held with the many activists into a more focused and analytical and, hopefully, more useful form.

1) Trust Building and Coordination of Positions

Peacemaking across inequities of power is not easy—nor is it symmetrical. And, indeed, Chapter 4, "Joint Struggles and the Issues of Normalization and Power," opens with a list of pertinent questions reflecting this fundamental issue:

> How do activists engaged in nonviolent resistance to the occupation—coming from a wide variety of organizations, both Palestinian and Israeli—view joint activism? What do truly joint organizations look like? What do interviewees see as the pros and cons of working together, whether as individuals in joint organizations or in joint endeavours involving uni-national organizations from both communities? Do they think that activists from the two communities should form joint organizations to engage in this struggle? Should Palestinian and Israeli groups work together—with varying degrees of cooperation, coordination, and joint action—while maintaining their autonomy as organizations? Is joint action effective? And what do they feel about the dynamics at play in joint endeavours (whether joint organizations or less formal formations) and the roles of the two "sides"?

To begin with, the "both sides" discourse so evident in mainstream Israeli political discussion, intended to blur the power differences and create a false symmetry between the occupier and the oppressed, is conspicuously lacking among Israeli peace organizations; even the more "moderate" ones like Peace Now recognize that the power differential inherent in the occupation places disproportionate responsibility on Israel. Trust building, the absolute starting point of joint work across chasms of power between groups belonging to antagonistic parties, is thus primarily an Israeli responsibility. Amos Gvirtz, one of the founders of ICAHD, refuses to use Highway 443 between Tel Aviv and Jerusalem, which passes through the occupied territories, and insists on bringing his passport whenever he visits the Palestinian territories. Sometimes trust building requires a great degree of sensitivity and reflection on the part of Israelis. We are part of the occupying people, after all, and we do not fear reprisals when we go home. No one is going to demolish our homes. In meetings with Palestinians, for example, we tend to speak first, the most, and in the loudest, most authoritative voices.

There are also cultural differences which should be recalled here. Kathy Kamphoefner, an anthropologist working with the Christian Peacemaker Teams, contrasts the direct Israeli communication style (which she describes with the Arabic term *dughri*, used also by Israelis) with the Palestinians' more circuitous *musayara* approach. How such subtle micro-dynamics affect the relations between Israeli and Palestine groups is not greatly appreciated, I believe, and not much discussed—although several Israeli activists did mention their concern with "reproducing the occupation."

More substantive differences of analysis, opinion, and priorities, which arise in any political setting, are compounded when, again, they involve members of two "sides" to a conflict. These differences affect the partners' very ability to work together. The experience of the Jerusalem Link is a case in point. In this project of Palestinian and Israeli women, which has survived over a decade and a half, differences between the Israeli and Palestinian members over the right of return—indeed, on its very centrality to a political solution—offer an insight into this source of tension. In Amneh Badran's view as a Palestinian, "Israeli peace groups, the majority, are seeking a compromise based on self-interest, and they are not seeking a solution based on principles."

And, in fact, there is one major disparity between the sides' agendas that impacts on the issue of trust. Many Israeli groups see cooperation with Palestinians as only half of their agenda; influencing Israeli public opinion, even government policy, constitutes the other half. This makes sense, since ending the occupation is a goal common to all Israeli peace organizations, and most think it important to work within Israeli society (how much energy to invest inside Israel as opposed to generating international pressure on Israel is a question raised primarily by the more "radical" groups). Thus they tend to couch their positions, statements, and actions in terms which do not alienate them from the Israeli mainstream, and hence depart in tone and content from their positions and priorities. Gila Svirsky expresses this view clearly when she says, "We felt very strongly, as women, that [there had to be] this organic vision of peace: it's not only about withdrawing our troops, it's also about transforming Israeli society." According to Galia Golan, "We consider ourselves in Peace Now a political movement, where first and foremost we're trying to influence policy, and that means also influencing public opinion, and then it's always a question of how that can best be done."

The question is: Is this just a tactic of Israeli peace groups to remain within the parameters of Israeli debate, thereby affecting it, or do their views genuinely differ in fundamental ways from their Palestinian partners'? The confusion is a source of constant tension. "The Jerusalem Link speaks about dismantling all settlements—and the wall," says Badran. "Of course, we [Palestinians] don't agree [with the Israelis] on how we describe it. I would say 'apartheid wall'; [the Israeli women] would say 'separation barrier.' I would say 'two-state solution, Palestine and Israel'; and they would say 'two-state solution, Palestine and Israel, and both countries have a right in the land.'" All this suggests that an ongoing process of clarification regarding positions and principles, accompanied by transparency, is necessary if activists of the oppressor and oppressed societies are to continue working together. This happens infrequently at best between certain Israeli Jewish and Palestinian organizations.

Even the nature of the relationship between activists across the chasm of the occupation is disputed. Muhammad Jaradat of BADIL believes that a working relationship is essential—"If we do not have a strong Israeli community of resistance to the militarized society, to the racist regime in Israel," he says, "we will not make a big change"—yet, he contends, "There is a difference between solidarity and joint work." Although Jaradat rejects the concept of "solidarity" as an appropriate role for Israelis—he lauded that of "joint work," the latter involving activists with "one foot" in their own societies, which for Israelis means striving to dismantle the racism and militarism of their own society, of which the occupation, in Jaradat's view, is but one symptom.

This seems to be a view shared by many Palestinian organizations (especially of the left), and is also generally accepted by left Israeli peace groups. It does not reflect the view or wishes of the mainstream Zionist peace organizations, probably because, as in the debate over the right of return, it requires Israeli organizations to subordinate their polity's views and policies to those of the Palestinians, which they are unwilling to do. Galia Golan of Peace Now flatly states "...when we do things with Palestinians, it's with the purpose in mind of trying to prove there's a partner (for peace negotiations)... When we're trying to stop the building of settlements, we never do them jointly with Palestinians. What we're trying to do on the settlements is we're addressing the Israeli public, we're addressing the Israeli government... We consider the settlements *our* problem..."

Golan seems to be thinking in terms of two separate peace movements, one Palestinian, the other Israeli, so that the Israelis—with their desire not to alienate their own society and often with an explicitly Zionist agenda that cannot be accepted by their Palestinian partners—can retain control over how their message is conveyed. When "joint" actions are conceived or joint organizations proposed in this context, the Palestinians view them as attempts to "normalize" relations in terms acceptable to Israelis, but without adopting a political program which Palestinians would consider as leading to a just resolution of the conflict. If "joint" resistance activities are pursued, Ghassan Andoni of the ISM argues, this should only take place if these activities are led by the Palestinians. He adds: "You don't need two peace movements to arrive at peace. You need an active Palestinian resistance supported by an active Israeli peace or anti-occupation movement. If you have those two, peace will become tangible. But if you have two peace movements, peace will run far away."

By late 2000, following the initial silence of most Israeli groups in the face of Israel's disproportionately violent response at the time of the outbreak of the Al-Aqsa Intifada, relations between erstwhile Palestinian and Israeli "partner" organizations had deteriorated to the point where PNGO, the Palestinian NGO Network, convened an emergency session of its General Assembly on October 22, which issued a statement calling on all Palestinian NGOs "to stop all normalization with Israel, particularly any projects between Palestinian and Israeli organizations, unless they are based on a common political stance of rejecting the occupation and recognizing international legitimacy, including the international resolutions pertaining to the inalienable rights of the Palestinian people" and specifically naming projects conducted in the framework of the EU's "People to People" program, the Peres Institute for Peace, and the "Joint Projects Program" funded by the American Agency for International Development (USAID). Of note, explicitly excluded from this prohibition were "solidarity projects launched by Israeli human rights organizations and … cooperation with Israeli institutions which support the Palestinian right to freedom and statehood and a comprehensive, just and durable peace that meets Palestinian national rights" (see also Chapter 4, Endnote 12).

2) Groundedness, the Need to "Be There" with the People

Groundedness, simply "being there" with and for the oppressed, is perhaps the most common element uniting the activists that Maxine interviewed; indeed, it defines the essence of activism. Groundedness defines a particular relationship with those with whom we are working, and it is especially important since we, activists who are overwhelmingly middle-class and educated, are placed in a position to "represent" oppressed people who sometimes lack our analytical language and access to the media and political decision makers. Andoni clearly sees activism as a means of encouraging mass participation:

> The ISM in the long run saves lives of both Palestinians and Israelis. It is the model of resistance that complements Palestinian resistance and actually presents to the Palestinians another idea, which is civil-based resistance, hoping that Palestinians would finally go in line with this, and this would allow for a more massive Israeli peace movement to stand in support. And when that happens, I can tell you, peace—a just peace—becomes a realistic option in the Middle East.

Ta'ayush, a joint movement of Jewish and Palestinian Israelis, is organized on similar grounds. Says Leena Delasheh:

> [I]n Ta'ayush, we try to bring an alternative. We try to let people know the other side. We try to bring people together. We bring hundreds of Israelis to the occupied territories. We get people to meet, we get people to speak, we get people to see for themselves the situation that brings other people to despair.

In the occupied territories, of course, Israelis and Palestinians occupy a very different political space. Israelis (Israeli Jews, in particular) are privileged. We will not be shot (at least not deliberately), we may be detained for a few hours but we will not be charged, and if we are occasionally charged, we will be given community service or a fine rather than jail time. "Palestinians," says Maya Rosenfeld of Machsom Watch,

> cannot—as we [Israeli activists] can—take advantage of the fact that we are Israeli citizens. We are not welcome at the checkpoints—on the contrary—but there is not much that can be done about this. We are there, and the fact that we are there has an impact, and the soldiers—we always tell them that they have to be accountable to us as citizens; they don't think so, but still our presence there forces them, in a sense, to communicate in one way or another with us. If we were Palestinian, that would not have been possible.

Although Palestinian civil society has been NGO-ified, and many people of the grassroots express dismay, anger and alienation from the very organizations which exist and are funded to represent and serve them, this criticism is not aimed at the Palestinian groups surveyed in this book, precisely because they are seen as "being there" for the people. The Israeli organizations mentioned here, as well, have managed to maintain a working relationship with their Palestinian partners ("dialogue" groups excepted) despite the tensions generated in the Second Intifada, obstacles to shared work placed in front of them by the Israeli authorities (such as a ban on Israelis entering Palestinian cities and on West Bank and Gazan residents entering Israel, including Jerusalem), and the constraints of "normalization"—again, because they have "been there" for the Palestinians throughout. Indeed, the very range of activities reviewed in this book attests to the vibrancy of Palestinian and Israeli resistance, all of it nonviolent. Discussions of nonviolence often dwell on the need to express love and concern for the oppressor and to combat demonization. Interestingly, this is hardly mentioned, if at all, by the people interviewed here. This is evidence, I would suggest, of the success of both communities in maintaining "normal" working and even personal relationships through an extremely violent period and over the chasms of power and alienation. A central slogan of the Israeli peace movement, "we refuse to be enemies," reflects this insistence on preserving close relations. To be sure, Israeli groups must endeavour to counter the tendency, in their own society and among so-called "pro-Israeli" supporters abroad, to demonize Palestinians—demonization often directed against the most militantly nonviolent organizations such as the ISM and ICAHD—but the lack of concern over "loving" each other indicates a healthy relationship of solidarity, trust, and daily joint endeavours which make such declarations superfluous.

3) Development of a Political Analysis Deriving from Realities "On the Ground"

Another element of strategic nonviolence is the necessity for *a grounded analysis that takes a critical stance.* I have in mind something very different from academic analysis or professional reports, of which there are many: instead, an analysis arising out of political realities "on the ground," which is both current and leads directly to action, be it in the form of resistance, demonstrations, press conferences, or campaigns and other kinds of strategic activism aimed at putting an end to the source of oppression. A critical position is rooted in the realities "on the ground" and derives its authority from "being there." Gene Sharp, who comes closest to being a theorist of nonviolence, describes it in this way:

> [I]f a planned action is really going to contribute to achieving the goal… we need to understand the situation, your situation, in depth; and that includes consideration of people's insights and capacities. [We also] need to understand our opponents in depth, not superficially, not by what they've done in recent years, only: Where do they come from, and what have been their sufferings. And I think this is not yet understood or appreciated among most Palestinians… [W]e need to understand nonviolent struggle in depth. We must not only learn from our own experience; we should be wise enough to learn from the experience of other peoples in other countries over decades and sometimes centuries, of how they have struggled for their own liberation against all kinds of forces. [And] if we accept in principle nonviolent struggle, we must learn how to develop and plan strategies to use our actions most effectively. And I must confess that when I was here in the eighties, it was very hard to find Palestinians who understood strategic thinking; I think that has improved significantly since I was last here.

Not every activist, of course, is interested in or capable of producing a grounded analysis, but without it the origins of the conflict cannot be grasped or effective strategies and actions developed. Indeed, the grounded and unsparingly honest question behind any critical analysis is: What *the hell* is going on here? It is a question upon which all effective resistance and advocacy is predicated.

Unfortunately, Maxine has chosen not to pursue the issue of analysis in the interview portion of this book. It would appear, however, that a nonviolent approach to resisting oppression and resolving this conflict is fundamentally tactical by nature, being more concerned with the message of nonviolence than with its effectiveness as a tool for change. This may simply be because a nonviolent approach to resistance and political change has, in the eyes of its practitioners, more to do with campaigns and practical matters than analysis. That said, it is also apparent that Palestinians and Israelis are coming from different places. For the Palestinians the issues are clear; indeed, if I have any criticism of their advocacy—and perhaps this relates to Sharp's comment about a lack of "strategic thinking" among the Palestinians—it is that their presentations of the conflict often tend to consist solely of a litany of injustices they have suffered rather than balancing them with a plan of action, believing, it seems, that once the injustice is known, getting international law and the international community to kick in is merely a technical matter which should not even require "advocacy."

Israelis have to undergo a journey in order to arrive at a critical understanding of the conflict—in space, actually entering into the occupied territories, and in experience, allowing themselves to be exposed to the horrors of the occupation. Merely "discovering" the realities of the occupation is the first step of this process. Describing the experiences of women taking part in Machsom Watch activities, for example, Maya Rosenfeld says that: "As time went on, we understood the much deeper implications of the closure policy, and our perception of our work changed. For example, on our tags we used to have just 'Checkpoint Watch' written, and now we also had 'Women for Human Rights.'"

Most difficult for Israelis, perhaps, is taking that "leap" beyond the us-and-them formulation, getting to a point where they can genuinely see the conflict from the Palestinian point of view and integrate it into their own positions even if it contradicts Zionist aspirations, prevailing public opinion, and fundamental elements of Israeli policy, as well their own closely held opinions. A shift to a critical position is not one that every Israeli peace activist is willing to make.

A critical stance does not imply, in terms of Israeli activists, adopting Palestinian perspectives holus-bolus, but rather reframing their own Israeli conception of the conflict in ways that reflect Palestinian views—or at least do not contradict or minimize them—yet also present alternative Israeli positions which help their own society break out of its dead-end, us-or-them, either-or framings. Michel (Mikado) Warschawski of the AIC, one of the most veteran practitioners of Israeli–Palestinian solidarity and joint struggle, is one who does understand the negative impact that misunderstanding and misrepresentation, arising from a lack of critical awareness, has on work across power differentials. In his view, "the place of Israeli activists… is not and cannot be and should not be symmetrical with that of the Palestinians. The Palestinians are those who are conducting their struggle in their own … ways …and the essence of our role is … to aid them to the maximum in the success of their struggle, including by explaining this struggle … so that there will be better acquaintance with the true, living Palestinian reality, and not the fantasized one. Really to place ourselves, in a fundamental way, as a kind of helping force." He describes how this delicate process worked itself out through the grounded activities of the Palestinian–Israeli Committee Against the Iron Fist:

> The most important success in my eyes was how we learned, in the course of working together, to take into account and to base our activity on, not only an understanding of what was effective for our own constituency, but also what was effective and possible from the point of view of the other. [...]
>
> In the course of working together on this committee, there quickly developed a "common minimum," if we can call it that, which improved as time went on. That is, participants developed an ability—without giving up their respective uniqueness—to respect not only the political needs of the other side, but also its fundamental point of view, its ethical boundaries; something which could only be done on a basis of complete trust. [...]
>
> And because we were who we were, there was first of all a degree of trust which would be hard to find in the Peace Now-ish crowd. This trust was the outcome of our respect for the Palestinians. Firstly, we told them, "You set the limits, because you are the ones who are demonstrating under occupation." In this case this meant: "If you say that demonstrating without flags is out of the question, and the police say no, and you don't want to demonstrate, fine; if you say okay, we're willing to do without flags on this or that condition,

we will be your spokespersons in negotiations with the police, because it's no problem for us and for you it is," not out of obsequiousness towards the Palestinians, but to compensate in some measure for the absence of symmetry in Israeli–Palestinian relations. Secondly, we said, "We will not monitor your behaviour during demonstrations. Each side will monitor itself. I don't see myself as mediating between the police and the demonstrators. If the police say take down a sign, you take down your own sign. We depend on you. We know that this is the agreement which we made with the police, we made it together. It's your responsibility." We have complete trust, and this trust was created in the course of our work.

4) Reframing the Oppressor's Narrative

One great advantage an occupying power such as Israel has over its victims is the ability, inherent in a state's capacity to control language and mobilize the media, to overwhelm the voice of the oppressed with its own self-serving framing. Israel's framing of the conflict can be conveyed within a single compelling sound-bite: Israel is a small Western democracy besieged by Arab terrorism. Period. It is a framing which contains all the necessary buzz words—Western, democracy, terrorism, and Arab—while effectively implanting the image of Israel as the victim. It is also noteworthy for what it omits: occupation, Israel's overwhelming political and military superiority, and the pro-active nature of its occupation policies as reflected in particular in its settlement enterprise.

ICAHD has worked assiduously to formulate and disseminate counter-framings which highlight the case we want to make (see, for example, Chapter 9)— "that Israel is the strong power, . . . that it's an occupying power, and . . . that the occupation is proactive"—while exposing the falsity and injustice upon which the Israeli claims are based. If done right, an effective reframing creates support for the oppressed, whose voice is seldom heard in a coherent manner, and delegitimizes the claims of the oppressor.

New Profile has taken as its main mission the demilitarization, or "civil-ization," of Israeli society. This requires fundamental reframing. Says Rela Mazali:

> We think that Israeli society is a war society, a war culture that is perpetrating wars, not experiencing wars that are imposed on it

from the outside; that the reasons are not external, maybe never were, but definitely haven't been for several decades now; and that it's up to us to become aware of this and to stop it. We think that part of the reason why Israelis haven't done this up until now is that they're caught in these militarized mindsets, behaviour patterns, political structures that are very militarized; and the whole of our education system and our culture are all very deeply militarized in a way that is not always immediately obvious—and we're working to try and change that.

ISM has as a strategic goal, "to challenge the misinformation that was out there—that the beginning of the Intifada was all the Palestinians' fault and all Arafat's fault for rejecting Camp David and resorting to violence," says Huwaida Arraf. It counters the prevailing media message that "Palestinians can't live with Jews, and their intent was and had always been to destroy the Jewish state" with an alternative discourse based not on Palestinians vs. Israelis or Arabs vs. Jews, but on freedom vs. occupation.

Neither the Palestinians nor the Israeli peace movement have formulated such reframings, placing us at a distinct disadvantage in putting our views before the international public. An awareness that we should be reaching target audiences has resulted in only a partial reframing. Rev. Naim Ateek characterizes Sabeel's principal strategy as educating and waking up fellow Christians. Sabeel has developed a kind of reframing. Rev. Ateek speaks of "a loving God of justice, compassion, and inclusion" in contrast to the Zionist ideology in which a tribal, exclusivist, territorially based God "gives" the Land of Israel solely to Jews. Rev. Ateek also reminds Christian audiences abroad that Palestinian Christians exist, are targeted by and suffer from occupation policies, and are in need of their support. Examples of this are his two books on Palestinian liberation theology (Ateek 1989 and 2008) and his essays, some of which can be viewed at www.christianzionism.org, website of the organization Challenging Christian Zionism, which offers an "alternative biblical view" to evangelical Christians in particular.

Mirroring Ateek's efforts, Rabbi Arik Ascherman says that a prime goal of Rabbis for Human Rights is to "introduce into people's intellectual universe an alternative way of understanding Torah" to counterpoise the "very volatile brand of extreme nationalism and extreme particularism" that has become increasingly dominant in the [Israeli-Jewish] religious ethos with "true, authentic Judaism." So, says Rabbi Ascherman, "we try to introduce to people's intellectual universe an equally authentic, equally textually based, equally Jewish-humanistic understanding of the Jewish tradition."

Some groups, lacking explicit reframings, hope that simply exposure to the occupation will change views—a kind of low-level, experiential reframing which, by its nature, can only reach small groups of local people with a diffuse "message." "The humanitarian aid [of Ta'ayush convoys] is not the main reason we come there," says Leena Delasheh. "We come there to bring Israelis to the place, to show them what is actually happening, what the occupation is doing, to bring people to protest the occupation, and to bring people together." Noa Nativ sees Ta'ayush activities as helping Palestinians reframe as well. The convoys, she says, are intended "not to reach just the Jewish public, but also the Palestinian public, because a lot of the Palestinians in the occupied territories, all they get to see of Israeli society is the settlers and the army, and this is not representative of Israeli society, and we do want to give them also a bit of hope about the people who do want peace in Jewish society." And Israeli journalist Amira Hass, speaking at the April 2007 Conference on Nonviolent Popular Joint Struggle held in the West Bank village of Bil'in, argued that Machsom Watch "challenge[s] the Israeli male monopoly over the security discourse."

If it is true that nonviolence has played a crucial role in many, if not most, of the major struggles against authoritarian rule in the past decades, then why does it seem a kind of after-thought, a desirable part, perhaps, of the resistance to Israeli occupation, but seldom more than a fallback position when other forms, such as armed resistance, have been proven too costly or even impossible? Few of those interviewed in Maxine's book *defined* their actions by nonviolence; instead, they followed it for purely pragmatic and tactical reasons. It seems to me that the proponents of nonviolence—not merely as a theory or value but as a genuinely effective way to pursue liberation—have got to be more up-front, more explicit, even more assertive as to why a nonviolent approach is better than the others.

This is especially urgent after 9/11, when the terms of discourse changed radically. We often hearken back to Gandhi, Martin Luther King, Lech Walesa, and Bishop Tutu, but in those days decolonization and struggles against authoritarian and racist regimes carried with them a certain legitimacy. Today the highly militarized states of the West, locked in resource wars that have generated such terms as the "clash of civilizations," have aggressively used language and laws to delegitimize "dissident" movements and individuals. "Rebels" such as Che or even figures of the American "Revolution" once had a certain caché. The current discourse lumps all anti-hegemonic forces under a single rubric—"terrorists" or "insurgents"—for which there is zero tolerance and no legitimacy. The burden has shifted to us to just as aggressively reframe the discourse.

Zero tolerance in language as well as policies and actions can nip nonviolent movements in the bud, since dissidents or liberation fighters have been conflated by those who control the media with forces subversive to capitalist and Western hegemony. If we are to match the efforts of governments, corporations, and publics (such as the Israeli Jewish public) who are effectively manipulated by their opinion-makers, we must also organize better and frame our campaigns better. Reframing, including sharp, compelling, and succinct presentations of why nonviolence is so important and strategic, is needed. "In spite of all the effort we are making," says Jamal Dar'awi of the Popular Committee against Settlements, Bethlehem area, "I do confess that we are still not doing sufficient work to convey our message to the world, and we should be stronger in conveying that message."

Hope Flowers School's Ibrahim Issa goes one step further, calling for a *Palestinian* framing and model of nonviolence, something that would help the Palestinian public to grasp, accept, and internalize what otherwise might be considered a foreign conception. Pointing out that "nonviolent philosophy is very much related to culture," Issa cautions against attempting to apply an Indian model to Palestine. And rather than "waiting for Americans or Europeans to do the nonviolence work," he runs programs for local Palestinians, who "know more about the little details of their culture than others" to learn, themselves, "to do the nonviolence."

5) Developing an Effective Strategy and Program of Advocacy
Civil society has been shown to possess considerable power (someone called us "the second superpower"). And, indeed, we have some significant victories under our belt—the anti-apartheid struggle, the struggles against

authoritarian regimes in Eastern Europe, Iran, and the Philippines, just to name a few. We also have new instruments at our disposal: a rich language of human rights, which is steadily entering the public consciousness; an ever-growing corpus of international law; legal instruments such as the International Court of Justice and the International Criminal Court, through which to pursue our campaigns; access to wide sections of the global public through the Internet; the ability to organize at the grass roots globally through World Social Forums and at other venues.

The lack of a nonviolent framing aside, what seems to be missing in the struggle to liberate Palestine, however, is an effective set of campaigns—as opposed to a large number of disjointed actions—both on the ground and internationally (although the BDS [Boycott, Divestment, and Sanctions] campaign has gained considerable momentum, mainly after the interviews for this book were completed). Huwaida Arraf, long a truly strategic thinker as well as activist, lays this out clearly.

> But there's also being realistic and recognizing the state of Palestinian politics and Palestinian society today: There's no strategy for the resistance; there's no strategy for getting to where we need to go for our independence. We don't have a strategy for achieving it.
>
> The Palestinian leadership thinks that strategy needs to be negotiations. I'm not opposed to negotiations, but I recognize that the Israeli government is led by the Zionist ideology, and we cannot expect that Israel is just going to give us this land because it's right, because it's just, because we're human beings. That's not going to happen. The Israeli government—the Zionists in this area—have had a long-term strategy, and they're implementing it very slowly, and the Palestinian community does not have a strategy for reaching their independence. So, whereas I'm not opposed to negotiation, I don't think we can negotiate in the absence of a very strong backing: an active resistance and a nonviolent resistance.

Her concerns are echoed by Sami Awad.

> We [Palestinians] don't have a strategy now. All Palestinian organizations, working together or separately—what we currently have is sporadic activities that take place. So for example, a road is blocked; we go and remove it. The wall is being built; we go and protest it. The Israeli army imposes curfew; we defy the curfew and go on the streets. Now these are all very dangerous and very courageous activities, but they're all just reacting to what the Israeli

military's doing. A strategy means we set up the plan of action of what we want and be proactive in this matter.

The question before all of us activists is: are our actions actually contributing to an end to occupation, and if they are not, what is missing that would make them more effective? Grounded activism, as important as it is, is insufficient. Martin Luther King worked with political forces to pass the Voting Rights Law in 1964, without which his actions on the ground would not have succeeded. Governments may be the only parties that have the authority to broker a peace settlement, but they will not do so unless prodded by us, the people. Our main target population, then, is civil society. How to mobilize civil society is a complex and difficult task, but we need to believe that we can influence events, we need to see ourselves as actors, not merely as gadflies. As I say earlier in this book:

> One of the problems is that events on the ground happen so fast that you're just organizing about one thing, and it all-of-a-sudden becomes irrelevant and you're in a whole different situation. . . . It's very important to organize against the wall, but at the same time, events are moving much faster than that. The problem we have in the Israeli peace movement—and I think a problem facing the Palestinians—is that we don't have a program to sell. We still have to say "End the Occupation," but you have to bring into the discussion human rights and international law . . .

As to concrete suggestions for effective campaigns of advocacy, the conversation stopped well short. A few commonsense pieces of a strategy emerged: Ibrahim Issa mentioned a Hebrew-language Palestinian TV station, Mustafa Barghouthi talked of "our duty as Palestinians to give the world the right narrative about Palestine" by better organizing Palestinian PR, and Saif Abu Keshek of the ISM spoke of the films they are producing. Others noted tactics that had seemed to work in the past: the importance of Israeli solidarity in supporting Palestinian resistance in places like Beit Sahour during the tax revolt of the First Intifada and in Bili'in, and in publicizing their actions; the ISM's strategy of recruiting participants from around the world (called the "kid from Boston in Balata" strategy); occasional mass actions called by the Israeli Coalition of Women for Peace together with Palestinian women's organizations; the many, frequent, and varied activities of all the various Israeli and Palestinian groups, supported here and abroad by internationals. Indeed, says Sami Awad, many of Gene Sharp's suggestions contained in his 1984 booklet *Non-Violent Resistance: A Strategy for the Occupied Territories* were in fact adopted.

But does all this activity equal an effective strategy? Far from it. They are, at best, grounded, localized activities. Nowhere among the interviews was a coherent strategy articulated, certainly not towards international civil society or governments. Since this question was not asked of the interviewees, we cannot know—at least from this book—what their thinking is on this important matter.

Which brings me to a truly radical, counter-intuitive thought: Maybe we don't need to organize any more than we are. Maybe we don't have to coordinate more than we do. Maybe we just need to persist, to continue our actions "on the ground" in the knowledge that by highlighting the injustices underlying the occupation we are providing enough information and visual opposition for the media and diplomats. In the absence of a strategy, perhaps the very ability to insert ourselves directly into political processes—our stubborn protests, from Bil'in through rebuilding demolished Palestinian homes to sailing boats into besieged Gaza to monitoring checkpoints, organizing grassroots resistance, bringing diplomats, journalists, and the public into the occupied territories, and all the rest—perhaps this is enough. Public opinion in the world is shifting in our direction; even Bush's support was not enough to nail down apartheid in the "Annapolis process"; a new American administration seems aware that the issue is not going to go away—partly because of us, as well as grassroots Palestinian resistance—and the media is becoming more critical. Just maybe we are succeeding more than we realize. The BDS campaign, spreading day by day and in which many of us are involved, gives us all the strength to continue. I would still like more strategizing on our part, but that seems unlikely.

6) Providing Leadership

A final element of strategic nonviolence involves the complex and delicate issue of *leadership*. On one level this is an element over which there is little disagreement. Leadership means developing the ability to "read" the political map and, out of an understanding of how political power works, formulating a strategy of what must be done to effectively resist injustice and, with others, embarking on effective actions. On other levels, however, it is such a difficult facet of strategic campaigning that it has virtually been eliminated in terms of the Israel–Palestine conflict—to its detriment, I believe.

Leadership today has been devalued and delegitimized, often, ironically, in the name of non-hierarchal ways of planning and carrying out actions. Groups become paralyzed—in particular, attempts to form coalitions—because many activists do not want to sanction leadership, either their own or certainly that of other partner organizations. This reluctance to follow leaders is fully understandable, of course, within a nonviolent framework that values all voices and forms of participation. Yet in order to rise to effective political actions and become more than merely vehicles of protest, nonviolent groups must develop appropriate models of leadership which are both effective and conform to progressive principles.

Another issue affecting leadership has to do, again, with working relationships across the power divide. Ghassan Andoni, for example, insists that the principle of Palestinian leadership in joint activities is fundamental. Andoni clearly defined the roles that he envisions for Palestinians and Israelis, respectively, in the overall struggle against the occupation when he stated, as quoted above: "You don't need two peace movements to arrive at peace. You need an active Palestinian resistance supported by an active Israeli peace or anti-occupation movement." I tend to agree with this, at least in Palestine/Israel. We at ICAHD have always had a policy of coordinating every action with our Palestinian partners—and viewing ourselves as the junior partners. As I stated earlier in this book, "Everything we do is coordinated with the Palestinians, and that's given us a lot of credibility over the years"—has made us credible partners and has made it clear that we are neither being patronizing nor have we come to tell the Palestinians what to do. "I think our decision on how to work with Palestinians has played a key role in our ability to succeed and to develop the relationships that we have developed."

I agree less when it comes to international advocacy. True, this is the Palestinians' struggle and only they can determine what the solution to the conflict should be, but non-Palestinian activists abroad trying to influence their own peoples and influence their own governments receive precious little guidance or support from Palestinians in Palestine. Nor do Palestinians even engage in international advocacy in a systematic way—except perhaps in the case of BDS. This places non-Palestinian advocates in a difficult situation: Palestinians claim, and rightly so, the leadership of their struggle and, with the constraints of "normalization," seem at times not to cooperate fully even with Israeli groups who are genuine political partners. Yet they do not take the lead in building an international movement of liberation (again, with the recent exception of BDS).

Riad Malki and Sami Awad speak of developing grassroots leadership, which is indeed crucial. Awad mentions "core groups" of young nonviolent activists being trained in various Palestinian cities, the members of which "are very committed to nonviolence, are committed to liberation, [and] to working with their community as well... That's what nonviolence is to us. It's not just weapons to resist the occupation; it is how to build the community for the future, how to resolve internal problems, how to unify the different factions and different ideas that you have in your community, which is a very big problem for us today." But a Palestinian leadership must take the initiative on *all* the fronts of the struggle, or develop new ways to empower their Israeli and international supporters.

A Final Word

Reading the interviews in this book, one cannot but be impressed with the range and depth of thought of all the activist-interviewees, not to mention Maxine's skill in eliciting the responses she did and weaving them into a coherent narrative. Perhaps a main value of the book, however, would be to point out gaps in the development of a strategy of nonviolent resistance and advocacy which should be addressed. If we look at the six elements of a strategy outlined here, from the most local-based to the most global, it is clear that far more of the strategic thinking and the planning of actions takes place at the local end than the international. How to connect those levels, and what roles to assign the various actors, would seem a key responsibility of a Palestinian leadership.

It is also not clear to what degree nonviolence is considered a strategic element of the work of the Palestinians and Israelis interviewed here. It *informs* what they do, of course, and it reflects their common values, but its strategic function seems limited to protecting Palestinian resisters and imparting values of nonviolence to the wider population. A "big" question should be asked and addressed: What would a genuine campaign of strategic nonviolence look like which would be waged both on the ground and internationally, involving all the actors in a coordinated way? It seems to me that *Refusing to be Enemies* provides a useful and inspiring summary of the first stage of the project, but should be used to point the way forward, so that a nonviolent Palestinian struggle for liberation can itself provide a model for other oppressed people.

12

PALESTINIAN NONVIOLENCE:
A PACIFIST PALESTINIAN PERSPECTIVE*

Jonathan Kuttab

Nonviolence by Any Other Name...

There are a number of things that must be kept in mind when studying Palestinian nonviolence. One of the most important things to remember is that until relatively recently, most Palestinians did not use the term nonviolence, and did not self-consciously go about strategizing in a nonviolent fashion, but that the vast majority of Palestinians have, for a long, long time, instinctively followed a path of nonviolence. Historically, the vast majority of Palestinian nationalist activism and Palestinian resistance has been nonviolent. This is very much contrary to the image that is seen in the West, which represents the Palestinian as a terrorist or, at best, as a "liberation fighter" with a gun in his hand, fighting for freedom to liberate his land. The reality of course is that the vast majority of the Palestinian people have never participated in armed struggle except through songs, slogans and rhetoric. This is really part of the problem, because Palestinians have perfected the language of armed struggle, but not the actual *practice* of armed struggle, while all the time practicing nonviolence without calling it by that name, without following the proper path of nonviolence, and without claiming that what they are doing is nonviolent resistance.

---

* This chapter, with minor edits, is excerpted from an interview conducted during the Celebrating Nonviolent Resistance Conference in Bethlehem, on 28 December 2005.

Sumud and Belief in "International Legitimacy"

Palestinians have felt that the occupation and the Israeli onslaught against them were directly connected to robbing them of their land, robbing them of their identity, and evicting them from their land. They therefore followed a policy which they referred to as *sumud*—steadfastness—to try and hang on to their land, resisting the confiscations; to try and stay on their land, resisting forced evictions and deportations and what they saw as ethnic cleansing; and a fierce affirmation of their identity, with the words Palestine and Palestinian, which were denied to them by the occupation, which spoke of them as faceless Arabs. Instead of "the Arabs," they insisted on "the Palestinians"; they insisted on their flag; they insisted on their identity; they insisted on their right to choose their own leaders at a time when the entire world was demonizing the PLO and demonizing Yasser Arafat. They said, "No, we have the right to choose our leaders, good or bad."

It may well be that the choice was bad. It may well be that the Palestinian Authority and the PLO have proven themselves to be very poor leaders for the Palestinians. But the Palestinians hung on to the concept that they would decide who their leaders were, and not the world; not the Jordanians; not Israel. Nobody could speak for them; they are not under trusteeship. In a sense, that was a nonviolent struggle. There was a continued and perhaps naïve belief that somehow the justice of their cause, that history, that God, that public opinion will somehow vindicate them. This is why they have so much faith in the United Nations. They have more resolutions in the United Nations than anybody else, and yet they still continue to believe in international legitimacy, that international law somehow will ultimately prevail. If that's not nonviolence, I don't know what is. And this has been instinctive; this has been pervasive; this has been throughout all sectors of society.

Armed Struggle Never Widespread, Despite Pervasive Rhetoric

Even when so-called "armed struggle" was at its height, it was never practiced by more than a few thousand young people, especially in the occupied territories, where weapons were almost impossible to come by.

Yet people continued to persist in their resistance to the occupation, their resistance to the attempts to dissolve their rights: their right of return, for example, and their right to sovereignty, statehood, and their identity. Throughout, this resistance was consistently nonviolent, although it was never declared as such.

We can blame the international press for this, we can blame the Israelis; but perhaps a large part of the blame falls on us. We have not used the language and the rhetoric of nonviolence. We have all-too-easily adopted the language of armed struggle and armed resistance to the point that when the PLO abandoned the armed struggle, many people felt that they had abandoned *all* struggle. When the leadership from outside came in as the Palestinian National Authority (PNA), having given up the armed struggle against the occupation, they in effect gave up all struggle. And the local people, who had been struggling all these years—largely nonviolently—felt abandoned by their leadership, who were no longer practicing *any* form of resistance or any form of struggle. This is why the marches, the strikes, the boycotts—all of which are classic, traditional, popular forms of nonviolent struggle, which have prevailed throughout the Palestinian movement—were never given prominence, but only the armed struggle, and recently, of course, the suicide bombings, which are—probably even in terms of armed struggle— very bad, very ineffective, very counterproductive, and very illegal and very immoral. Yet the language, the image, the rhetoric of that violence continued to be given recognition and prominence, while the genuine nonviolent resistance was almost ignored, even though it was the prevailing method that people used for resistance.

The Value of Nonviolence Increasingly Recognized

I think a couple of developments have changed Palestinians' perceptions of nonviolence. One of these was during the First Intifada, when Mubarak Awad and the Palestinian Center for the Study of Nonviolence began, for the first time, using the language of nonviolence and began fighting the image in the Palestinian community that nonviolence means abandonment of struggle. Basically, they said that nonviolence is a very powerful, positive, affirmative, assertive method of struggle, which requires as much, in fact much more, dedication, organization, resources, and sacrifice than armed struggle; that, in fact, those who are practicing nonviolence are not abandoning the cause, they are only reinvigorating it and naming it with its proper name.

Mubarak was quickly deported, but many of his ideas, and the literature that he wrote or that he had translated into Arabic—the works of Gene Sharp, for example—became widespread throughout the Palestinian community, became read by the intellectuals, and became remembered and found their effect throughout the First Intifada, which was by and large a deliberately popular mass movement of nonviolence. Yes, there was stone throwing, which was almost more symbolic than an effective method of creating injury to the other side. But yet, there was the confrontation of the massive military might by a largely unarmed civilian population, and there were some creative methods of non-violence. Gene Sharp, who methodically lists all the different methods of nonviolence used throughout history and across the world, noted, for example, the occasion when Palestinians insisted, as a method of resistance, that they would not run on Israeli time, but they would follow their own clock and would change from summer to winter time at a different time than the Israelis. This was a classical form of nonviolent resistance that had never been practiced before. I don't know anybody else who has practiced it since. But it was a very deliberate, a very creative form of nonviolent resistance.

So, with the First Intifada there came a great recognition of the value of nonviolence. I think the second important turning point was during the Second Intifada. During the Second Intifada, after a period of quiet, Palestinians resorted to weapons again, this time in the presence of the Palestinian National Authority, which had its armed police force. This time they had access to light arms, largely coming from Gaza and smuggled in; and they started to extensively use the method of suicide bombings, which had rarely been used before in the Palestinian struggle, and which were extremely deadly and created a lot of casualties—among both Israelis and, with the massive Israeli retaliation, Palestinians.

At some point during the Second Intifada, the Palestinian people, including Palestinian military armed groups, suddenly realized that armed resistance is both ineffective against the vastly superior Israeli might, and also counterproductive, because it hurt rather than helped the Palestinian cause; it speeded up, rather than hindered, the gobbling

[up] of Palestinian property and the expansion of settlements; it slowed down, rather than speeded up, the coming of Palestinian sovereignty and statehood; it somehow legitimized, rather than delegitimized, the corrupt and inefficient Palestinian National Authority; and at its very height, it showed that inflicting high casualties on the enemy does not advance your cause. This was a very, very difficult lesson for the Palestinians to learn: that somehow their success is inversely proportional to the amount of casualties that they inflict on the Israelis but directly proportional to the amount of suffering and sacrifices they incur, particularly among civilians, the innocent, and children.

This is not something that is easy for people to understand, because most armed groups intend to inflict injury on the other side. And yet, any rational analyst of the current situation quickly realized that Palestinians are better off if they suffer more, and they're worse off if they inflict casualties on the Israelis, particularly civilians. So many people, without necessarily buying into the philosophy and the spiritual dimensions of nonviolence, began to realize that we seem to be making a mistake. Because every time that we try to inflict injury on the other side, we are hurt more; but every time injury is inflicted on us, we seem to garner more support, more sympathy, more solidarity, better internal cohesiveness, and to approach our goals—our national goals—rather than deviate from them. So I have heard many of my friends who are dedicated to armed struggle telling me "This is not working. This is not working. Maybe you and Mubarak Awad were right after all, because the most we can inflict is a suicide bombing that will kill thirty, forty, fifty Israelis. But when we do that, we lose, we don't gain. It seems that it reinforces and strengthens Israeli society and its oppressiveness of us and weakens our own society in its resistance to the occupation."

After 9/11, with the international consensus of condemning terrorism and fighting it, it became clear that Palestinians desperately needed to distance themselves from terrorism, even to the point of giving up and abandoning legitimate armed struggle against military targets. This was not easy for Palestinians to articulate, to stand up and say "we are opposed to these things" with any serious conviction; and yet, it is very much the prevailing opinion among Palestinians, not just officials, but ordinary people, including cadres of Fatah and other groups. Even Hamas is reaching the point of saying, "What are we achieving through these activities? We need to be much more careful;

we need to be much more selective with our targets. We need to avoid civilian targets. And maybe we need to reconsider armed struggle as a strategy. Maybe there are other methods that will accomplish for us our national goals."

It is no accident that a conference like this has been greeted with great favour by all sectors of Palestinian society, including Hamas. When in the past, before he was deported, Mubarak Awad used to talk about nonviolence, he was mocked, he was laughed at, he was ridiculed; sometimes, he was even accused of treason, of playing into the hands of the Israelis, of being more interested in public opinion than in liberating the homeland. Now it is the opposite. You can go anywhere in Palestine, and Mubarak Awad is a hero. People are looking up to him. They see that his methods really work, that he must have something in mind. And the more the Israelis show zero tolerance for violence, the more Palestinians begin to see, "Well, maybe this is what works. Maybe this is what is needed." Add to that the anarchy and the failure of the Palestinian Authority to use its weapons as police, as security forces, to provide Palestinians with personal security; instead, we saw anarchy, we saw personal vendettas, corruption, and thuggery. This made Palestinians also reconsider: Where does the gun stand? Is the gun as glamorous as we once thought, or is it more important to have a proper civil society, proper organizations, proper procedures, and proper democracy—for elections to choose leadership, rather than whoever has the gun throwing their weight around. All of this has helped reduce the popular glamour of the gun and the weapons.

I think these are real changes that have occurred in Palestinian society, making nonviolence a much more viable option for people to talk about, not just to practice. As we have seen, Palestinians have always been practicing nonviolence; they just haven't recognized it, they haven't used the word nonviolence, they haven't openly critiqued armed struggle. It used to be that it was almost an article of faith that Palestinians believe in armed struggle and that the gun is the path to liberation and victory. Now people are more sanguine about it and are more willing to speak openly and deliberately in favour of nonviolent resistance.

Conclusion

Most Palestinians are not, like myself, pacifists. I am a lawyer—I recognize that we cannot and we should not say that somehow Palestinians have no legitimate, legal right of armed resistance, any more than an Israeli would say that Israel has no right to defend itself. Unless one is willing to be that radical—and I don't hear anybody being that radical—one cannot deny, morally or legally, the right of the Palestinians to pick up arms to defend themselves. But I would strongly argue that nonviolence is more effective and suitable for resistance, precisely by the Palestinian people at this time of their history and under the current conditions. Under these conditions, to try to outviolence the Israelis is crazy! You know the example that is used? If you have somebody who is a sumo wrestler, who is much heavier and more powerful than you, then to try to wrestle him would be stupid. If you have to challenge him, challenge him to a chess game, maybe, or to a ping-pong tournament, where at least you may stand a chance, where his tremendously powerful [physique] is not to his advantage, but maybe to your advantage.

So to try to outviolence the Israelis, again, is totally ludicrous. We would need not only to have much more fire power, but also we would need to have, perhaps, some weapons of mass destruction under our belts, as Israel does. We would need to have some chemical, some biological, some nuclear—God forbid!—and this is not what we want; this is not what we need. So when I discuss these issues with my Palestinian friends, I don't follow the spiritual path to nonviolence. I say, "Forget it!" Granting your legal right to armed struggle: Is this effective? Will this work? Is this the best thing to do at this time? Granting your legal right to armed struggle: Is it wise? Is it useful? Is it in your interest? And the answer to all these questions is no! If anything, it is counterproductive. Even if you were to use it legitimately and properly, only against military targets and only in self-defence, it is still not the best method for you to proceed.

13

THE UNIQUE CHALLENGES OF PALESTINIAN NONVIOLENCE

Starhawk

The Palestinian struggle for self-determination has always been waged with a diversity of tactics, from civil resistance to armed struggle. The world's attention has mostly focused on rocket strikes and suicide bombings, while the broad-based nonviolent movement only rarely breaks through to the global media. Nonviolence as a strategy faces some unique challenges in the Palestinian context, and to illuminate these I will make some comparisons with other nonviolent movements for social change that I have been part of.

I am not Palestinian, and I cannot speak for Palestinians, nor will I attempt to describe the whole broad range of nonviolent resistance in the Palestinian struggle. Others can do that more effectively. I *can* speak of my own experience as a volunteer with the International Solidarity Movement (ISM), between 2002 and 2004. Since that time, I have not been allowed back into the country by the Israeli authorities because of my connection to the ISM. My knowledge of subsequent events is second-hand, but I do get constant reports from volunteers there and maintain a close connection to the struggle.

I am also Jewish, and grew up in the mainstream, pro-Zionist American Jewish community, raised to love and support Israel without question. I have a personal understanding of what it means to question the myths that have formed one's basic beliefs and worldview, and allow in a glimpse of the harsh realities they conceal.

In addition, I have been an activist since my high school days during the Vietnam War. In the early 1980s, I participated in my first organized nonviolent direct action, a blockade at the Diablo Canyon nuclear power plant in central California. I went on to become a nonviolence trainer and organizer in many campaigns, against nuclear weapons and U.S. military intervention in Central America, and for a wide spectrum of environmental and social justice issues.

In writing this article, I have drawn on that experience—especially in the antinuclear movement of the 1980s and the global justice movement of the late 1990s and early 21st century, because they have had some direct influence on the forms of organizing practiced by the ISM and other groups offering direct support to the Palestinian nonviolent resistance movement. I will also make reference to the Civil Rights Movement in the United States in the 1960s, as it, too, is a powerful example of effective nonviolence.

Withdrawing Consent to be Controlled

One of the insights that underlie a strategy of civil resistance is that institutions based on power-over and control always rest on some level of consent. No system of control can stand if it has to physically enforce every one of its decrees. Imagine if an armed police officer had to stand at every crossroads to enforce the rule to stop at a red light! No country could afford it.

Systems of control require us to mostly police ourselves. We stop at the red light because we know this is a law that works to everyone's benefit, making the streets safer for us as well as others. But we also police ourselves in many subtle ways, obeying laws and decrees that are not to our benefit. Nonviolent direct action is one method of actively withdrawing that consent, refusing obedience, and thereby shaking the foundations of control.

So, in the U.S. Civil Rights Movement, Rosa Parks withdrew her consent from segregation, refusing to police herself and meekly sit at the back of the bus. Her arrest sparked a boycott of the bus company, during which the larger African-American community of Montgomery, Alabama, withdrew its compliance and refused to ride the buses. This hurt the company economically, and the public attention the boycott gained hurt it socially and politically.

How Nonviolent Direct Action Works

Nonviolent direct action works in four basic ways. First, by directly interfering with a wrong or injustice, we raise the social, political and economic costs incurred by the holders of power. We can directly challenge unjust laws or institutions: hammering on the nose cones of missiles or sitting in at a segregated lunch counter.

Second, nonviolence can work by changing the hearts and minds of the oppressors, by humanizing the oppressed and making it harder psychologically for the agents of control to use extreme force and violence. Power holders always depend on lower-level enforcers to carry out their decrees. Politicians don't stand at the checkpoints they authorize: soldiers do. The true interests of those enforcers are often closer to those of the oppressed, and if they can be encouraged to question their allegiance to the structures of power, empires fall. One of the most dramatic examples of this was the fall of Slobodan Milosevic in Serbia in 2000: Otpor!, a youth and student movement with a strategy of nonviolent direct action that culminated in an uprising against the dictator, succeeded partly because the police refused to interfere.

Third, a nonviolent direct action campaign seeks to mobilize broader public support for change. It dramatizes the violence inherent in the system and makes injustice visible. So, for example, the Civil Rights Movement of the 1960s dramatized the inherent violence of segregation. No one visibly sees the pain of a child told to drink at a separate water fountain or relegated to an inferior school. But when southern sheriffs were shown on TV setting vicious dogs on crowds or spraying them with fire hoses, the violence became visible and public outrage was mobilized. Third parties, including the federal government, were forced to intervene.

To mobilize public opinion, we also need to understand the stories or narratives that support the status quo and to find effective ways of challenging them. Facts are important—but facts don't counter myths or deeply held beliefs. Facts can always be denied, dismissed, contested, or reframed to fit a belief. And facts must be heard if they are to have an effect. The drama of an action can focus attention on an issue and give people a reason to pay attention to facts. A counter-story, a narrative that hits us on an emotional as well as a rational level, can shift people's beliefs.

Finally, a nonviolent direct action campaign empowers those who take part in it. It calls on us to make hard moral and strategic decisions, to find our courage, and to act from our deepest strength. It gives us a means of taking action which can embody our highest values of love and compassion. Instead of seeing ourselves as passive victims, we become active agents of change.

Examples of Successful Nonviolent Direct Action

Nonviolent direct action is a tool, not a strategy. It does some things well, but it is not the only tool for contesting power, and it is not the appropriate tool in every situation. To build a house, a carpenter needs saws, hammers, drills, and levels. Many tools are also needed to make change, and successful campaigns use a multiplicity of approaches— legal marches, rallies, petitions, public education, lawsuits, and media strategies as well as direct action.

Major nonviolent campaigns in the United States—such as that undertaken by the Abalone Alliance against the Diablo Canyon nuclear power plant in the early 1980s and the blockade against the November 1999 meeting of the World Trade Organization in Seattle[1]—made use of a whole range of nonviolent tactics and strategies and, thus, whether they achieved their immediate goals or not, they contributed significantly to building the movement.

My own initiation into nonviolent direct action came at the 1981 blockade against the Diablo Canyon nuclear power plant. During months of preparation, we met in small groups called "affinity groups," which made all major decisions about the action by consensus. At the blockade itself, we sat at the front gate of the plant or hiked into the back country to disrupt the security zone, got arrested, and spent days in a makeshift jail set up in an old warehouse, where we planned a similar campaign against nuclear weapons.

Although the Diablo Canyon nuclear plant did eventually go online, the scale of the opposition and the delays and expense incurred discouraged the utility company, Pacific Gas and Electric, from going ahead with plans to build fifty others in California, and Diablo Canyon was pretty much the last nuclear plant to be built in the United States. But perhaps the greatest success of this campaign was the empowerment that participants came away with. More than 1900 participants were arrested in two intense weeks of actions. In jail, we held workshops on related issues, celebrations, and talent shows, and began organizing a movement to counter nuclear weapons. The style of organizing and decision-making we learned at Diablo became core to the building of many later movements, including the global justice movement.

In the case of the WTO mobilization, the Seattle blockade and the larger movement it sparked also succeeded on all four fronts. We did successfully stop the meeting, at least for a day, and enormously raised the economic and political costs of its going forth. The blockade also shifted the public dialogue, from an unquestioning acceptance of the virtues of free trade, to at least a sense that something was deeply wrong. The prevailing narrative was: "Free trade will bring prosperity to all. Take the bureaucrats away, let the entrepreneurs have their head, unfettered by pesky regulations and rules, and we will create so much wealth that everyone will benefit." But the fierceness of resistance called that myth into question. As longtime activist and politician Tom Hayden said in the midst of it, "A week ago, nobody knew what the WTO was. Now—they still don't know what it is but they know it means tear gas."

The WTO blockade and the broader global justice movement also succeeded in empowering participants to organize, to create hundreds of mobilizations, and to bring their skills into other movements and situations. Many of the internationals joining the ISM came out of a background in global justice actions. In the United States, after hurricane Katrina devastated New Orleans, many activists used their mobilization skills in grassroots relief efforts. Others have turned to community organizing and building of alternatives.

The Challenges Facing the Palestinian Nonviolence Movement

I will not attempt here to give a history of the Palestinian nonviolence movement—others have done that effectively.[2] Instead, I would like to look at the challenges the movement faces in the four areas outlined above, and to look at some of the similarities with and differences from other campaigns.

First, one of the key strategic goals for internationals in Palestine has been to open up political space for Palestinians themselves to organize and act, for the movement in Palestine faces far greater violence and reprisals from the Israelis than the campaigns described above. In the antinuclear movement, we suffered sometimes rough arrests and jail terms, but very few beatings or instances of severe repression. The global justice movement has faced assaults, arrests, dogs, horses, tear gas, pepper spray, and rubber bullets, and activists have lost their lives, especially in the global South. The Civil Rights Movement faced beatings, dogs, and fire hoses, and suffered church bombings and the murders of activists.

But this degree of violence is the daily reality in Palestine. Palestinians who take action are at risk of being shot by real bullets, shelled, placed in "administrative detention" for months at a time without trial, and having their families targeted and their homes demolished. The presence of internationals generally lessens the likelihood that the Israeli military or settler vigilantes will respond with lethal force. But that is not always the case, and internationals have lost their lives in the struggle or suffered grievous injury.

In addition, Palestinians face a struggle that goes on and on without foreseeable end. Seattle lasted a week; Diablo Canyon two weeks. Of course, there were many months of preparation and planning, but the intense phase of action was short and discreet. But in Palestine, the action is never over. There is no truly safe ground to retreat to. Any home is subject to search, and any town subject to siege and closure. The situation rarely gets better, and most people do not expect the immediate future to be any brighter. The stress is unending, and that takes a toll on everyone.

Overall, international support has made some space for Palestinians to engage in active nonviolent resistance, and that has brought some small victories. The route of the separation wall has been pushed back in some areas to preserve Palestinian land. Countless times, intervention at checkpoints or an international witness in a camp or town under siege has allowed people to get to work or go home from the fields or get medical care. Internationals delivered supplies under fire when the Church of the Nativity was under siege in Bethlehem in 2002. The international presence, that same year, in the compound with Arafat may have prevented the Israeli military from attacking. In the Palestinian context, where the reality is often so bleak that any thread of hope can feel like a lifeline, the impact of small successes can be greatly magnified.

The nonviolence movement has changed the hearts and minds of some Israelis. Moreover, it has provided a way in which Israelis who support justice for Palestinians can cross the line and themselves participate directly in the struggle. Groups like Rabbis for Human Rights, Anarchists Against the Wall, Women in Black, Kvisah Schorah (Black Laundry), and many others have joined in peace camps or demonstrated against the wall side by side with Palestinians. Friendships and alliances have been built—and in the context of the extreme separation of the last few years, that alone is a victory.

The movement has also empowered its Palestinian participants. It gives ordinary people a means of taking some action against the forces that hold an iron grip on everyday life, without the huge moral and personal price of engaging in armed struggle. It offers a number of ways in which people can do something to challenge the occupation and act in service of their own goals and self-determination. The most deeply traumatizing aspect of violence is the helplessness and powerlessness it instills. Anything that counters that helps in maintaining mental health and resilience, and survival. And for Palestinians, survival itself is a form of resistance.

Perhaps the greatest challenge the Palestinian movement faces is that of changing the prevailing narrative, in which Israel is always the victim and Palestinians are inevitably hate-filled terrorists. Particularly in the United States, where the grip of the pro-Israel lobby is so strong on media and politicians, it is difficult to get media coverage for nonviolent Palestinian actions and even more difficult to get a hearing for anything but the prevailing story.

Raised as I was with the American Jewish story about Israel, I know its power and its appeal. The story goes like this: "We were oppressed for two thousand years, we had nowhere we could truly be safe and call home, we were victims of genocide by the Nazis—but at last, after two thousand years, we have returned home and built our own state. Israel is the restitution for the losses of the Holocaust and the millennia of persecution we've suffered."

It is not hard to understand why that story would have such a deep hold on the hearts and emotions of my family and teachers in the 1950s, in the wake of the Holocaust. It is a little harder to understand why it would appeal to a new generation today, like many of the most fanatic settlers, who grew up in the United States without suffering much discrimination themselves—but it offers a sense both of belonging and entitlement, a combination hard to resist especially when combined with a good justification for feeling sorry for yourself. Who doesn't, at times?

The story, of course, leaves the Palestinians out. Indeed, the Palestinians, just by existing, spoil the story completely.

The first defense against any challenge to the story is simply denial. There are no Palestinians—there never was a Palestine—there is no partner. The second line of defense is "Okay, Palestinians exist, but they're bad. They're dangerous fanatics, they hate us, they are trained from birth to kill us, they don't love their children, they aren't human like us."

Countering the story is difficult. Here's one example. In the spring of 2008 we attempted to put out a call through an environmental list serve for teachers for a project in the West Bank. In the call, we mentioned that the area is often under siege from the Israeli military, that travel is difficult because of the checkpoints, that people are losing their lands, their livelihoods, and their crops to the separation wall. We were told that our post was "political," and that there was "corruption on both sides." And yet the post simply described some of the realities of life in the West Bank. Merely to describe them is to lay oneself open to charges of being anti-Israeli, and by extension, anti-Semitic, because if we name them and tell the truth, Israel begins to look more like an oppressor and less like a shining example of democracy and refuge.

But no past suffering exempts a people from responsibility for the consequences of their actions and policies. Many Israelis and many Jews recognize that our real security and wellbeing depend on recognizing reality and on struggling for justice for all people.

Our own eyewitness accounts are the most powerful counter to the prevailing narrative. As internationals, our other key strategic task is to go home and tell our own stories. We must speak about the tragedies and injustices that we have seen. But powerful, too, are the moments of humor and joy and connection. I can speak from personal experience of what it is like to sit with a family while soldiers search their house and destroy most of their possessions. I can also speak from personal experience about the Palestinian family that laughed every time I showed up and made me belly-dance with their fifteen-year-old cousin. I have huddled with the children in a house on the Rafah border as tanks shot bullets into the walls. I have also seen the glow of pride on an old woman's face as she filled my hands with oranges from her own tree. All of that is important to tell, for all of it asserts the existence, the humanity, and the ultimate dignity of the Palestinian people.

So let me end by telling a bit of my own story.

As I said, I was raised on the prevailing story about Israel, and although I have been a progressive activist all my adult life, I found myself avoiding the issue of Israel and Palestine as it felt too painful to confront. I first visited Israel on a Hebrew High School Ulpan trip in 1966, when I was fifteen. My next trip was not until the late 1990s, when I went to do work in women's spirituality with Israeli women. Although I expressed a weak desire to visit the West Bank, my friends discouraged the idea and I didn't press it. I returned a year or two later, and connected with peace groups but not with Palestinians. I remember feeling that the situation was intractable: too many fanatics and too much violence on both sides. That was a view that was comforting, as it alleviated any need for me to take responsibility or to recognize the enormous power differential between the Israeli occupiers and the Palestinians.

But in the next year or two, I began reading reports of the work Neta Golan was doing, staying in Palestinian villages as a witness to deter settler violence. I began emailing back and forth with her. She encouraged me to come to Palestine, but I had many other issues I was involved in and many responsibilities.

However, in April 2002, the Israeli military invaded Jenin after a suicide bomber attacked a Passover Seder in Israel. An army bulldozer operator went on a rampage and flattened hundreds of homes in the refugee camp. Another friend of mine, who was in the country, sent back an anguished eye-witness description of what it was like to be in the camp several days later, searching for bodies and pleading for international help.

Her story broke through all my denial and excuses. I knew I had to go. I had only a short window of time that June when I could make the trip, but I went, and met up with Neta.

While I was assisting her with a nonviolence training session in Jerusalem, we got word that the Balata refugee camp was under siege. We gathered our group, found a driver to take us up into the mountains, and hiked into the city of Nablus, where the refugee camp is located.

Walking down into the silent, empty city under curfew, I remember feeling terrified, not so much of the tanks and the possible repercussions, but of the strangeness, of the Other. I no longer believed the myths of my childhood, but I did believe that the Palestinians had no reason to like me or welcome my presence.

But as we walked, people began poking heads out of windows, or leaning out of doorways to wave and smile. Some handed us sunflower seeds to chew on.

We walked down, down through the city and, as dusk began to fall, came to the entrance of Balata camp. A tank stationed there shot at us as we tried to enter—we plastered ourselves against a wall and decided to take another way in.

As we stood in the gloom and the gathering dark, worried because our contact was on the other side of the camp and because being out after dark was extremely dangerous—I looked around and thought, "This is the one place on earth I was never supposed to be. Me—a nice Jewish girl in a Palestinian refugee camp? How did I get here?" I had a sense of having entered a forbidden zone, of having trespassed over a line I was never supposed to cross.

And then a window opened above us, and a woman beckoned us in. Within minutes, we were inside a house, sheltered by a family who wanted internationals to be present. For the Israelis had rounded up and arrested all of the men from the camp—but this family had managed to hide their son, who was traumatized and mentally ill from being beaten and arrested.

The electricity was off, so we ate by candlelight—pita, hummus, cucumbers, and salad. Within an hour, we were all sent out to nearby homes. I stayed with a woman and her three young children. We slept on mats on the floor, and something in me transformed. I had entered the heart of the forbidden zone, and had found welcome. I had faced my own fears—not so much of the tanks, but of the Other, and found human beings more like me than different.

There's a saying from the Upanishads: "Who sees all beings in their own self, and their own self in all beings, loses all fear." I did not go to Palestine for a personal growth experience—and for Palestinians, the situation is one of constant, sustained assault, not transformation. And yet, to my surprise, being there was the most profoundly transformational experience of my life.

Wherever I have been since, whatever I have faced, I have never again felt fear in the same way as before.

The world situation and the situation in Palestine are changing day by day. Whatever the shifts may bring, the nonviolence movement has a powerful role to play in securing the rights of the Palestinian people.

Although it faces great challenges, it also draws on great strengths. As Martin Luther King said, "I believe the universe is on the side of justice." Ultimately, only justice can bring about true peace and security, and the nonviolence movement can hasten the day when justice will prevail.

NOTES

1 Giugni 2004, p. 45; "The Abalone Alliance Story," http://www.energy-net.org/01NUKE/AA.HTM; "The Real Battle in Seattle," http://www.realbattleinseattle.org/taxonomy/term/17.
2 Inter alia: Salem 2005a; King 2007; AFSC 2005.

14
CONCLUSIONS

I would like to wrap up with a summary of my overall conclusions regarding involvement of Israelis in joint struggle against the occupation and with some comments on noncooperation by Israelis with government policies as an important part of this joint struggle. (Needless to say, most of the caveats below apply to participation by internationals as well as to that of Israelis.)

To be both valuable and valued, joint struggle must go beyond solidarity to include a shared sense of common cause. We have seen, moreover, that:

- "on-the-ground" joint struggle can take the form of joint organizations, but more often seems to work best in the form of loose coalitions;
- a sense of "good relations" must not be allowed to dull Israeli participants' recognition that ending the occupation (and the racism and militarism underpinning it) is their battle every bit as much as that of the Palestinians;
- effective joint struggle requires Israeli participants' sensitivity to the inherent imbalance of power in their relationship with the Palestinians, and an understanding of their supporting and subsidiary role as Israelis; and
- Israeli participants in joint struggle must be aware of and guard against the danger of allowing promised satisfaction of their own agendas to compromise the interests of their Palestinian partners— whether as an outcome of the abovementioned imbalance of power or because of greater willingness on the part of the establishment to deal with fellow Israelis than with Palestinians.

In addition to Israeli participation "on the ground" in Palestinian nonviolent resistance to the occupation, work inside Israel is also an important part of joint struggle and can take a variety of forms, including:

- sharing accurate information about the situation in the occupied territories—by those engaged in joint struggle there;
- combating racism and militarism within the borders of the state, including discriminatory laws;
- noncooperation with institutions of the occupation from within Israel. Although a tradition of noncooperation by Israelis exists, there is much room for expansion. Israelis can learn from successful campaigns of noncooperation elsewhere and from their own and the Palestinians' history and experience.

Here I would like to expand on the specific area of noncooperation with the institutions of the occupation by Israelis—before proceeding to an epilogue looking towards the possible future expansion of this approach—and to observe that there has indeed been, in addition to the long history of participation by small numbers of Israelis in Palestinian-led nonviolent actions inside the occupied territories, a similarly small proportion of Israelis who have, over the years, withdrawn their cooperation from some aspect of Israeli policy. A partial list includes:

- those who, in the 1960s to 1980s, forged ties with Palestinians against the "national consensus" (Warschawski 2005) and persisted in doing so even after the 1986 passage of a law (repealed in 1993) that criminalized such contact (Chapter 2);
- those who, during the First Intifada, persisted in entering Beit Sahour and other places under curfew, to bring food and people—to express solidarity, to show a readiness to challenge their own military; or, earlier, who went to Birzeit and Bethlehem universities and faced IDF teargas along with their Palestinian colleagues (Chapters 2, 5; Warschawski 2005; Nunn 1993);
- those who have refused and refuse now to serve—either altogether as long as the occupation continues, or in the occupied territories (or Lebanon), or simply refuse to follow orders that they find contrary to their consciences (such as Yesh Gvul, the *Shministim*, Sayeret Matkal, Pilots' Letter signatories, Combatants for Peace, Breaking the Silence);
- Combatants for Peace, made up of Israeli refuseniks and Palestinian former fighters who have foresworn violence for the sake of working together "to terminate the occupation and stop all forms of violence,"

are also part of yet another category of noncooperation: those who regularly meet and work with "the enemy" to forge a shared future. Others include the Bereaved Parents Circle, Ta'ayush, and Windows–Channels for Communication; and[1]

the fact that joint struggle in the occupied territories, itself, may be considered a form of noncooperation (especially when this necessitates Israelis' entrance into "Area A," which is complicated by a sporadically enforced law prohibiting entry by Israeli citizens to areas under the jurisdiction of the Palestinian Authority). As Israeli investigative journalist Amira Hass pointed out, "the common struggle of Israelis and Palestinians" challenges Israeli efforts aimed at keeping Israelis and Palestinians apart (by such means as the wall, checkpoints, laws restricting movement) when their intent is to pursue joint activity against the occupation (Kaufman-Lacusta 2008)—though dialogue is regarded as "kosher"—and the fact that they stymie attempts by the Israeli authorities "to create an unbridgeable distance between the two peoples" may indeed be (as Hass contends) the main success of such joint efforts (Chapter 4).

Although there are, as yet, relatively few Israeli groups or individuals actively pursuing noncooperation specifically inside the borders of Israel proper, readers will recall a number of additional examples from earlier in this book; e.g., Gila Svirsky's description (quoted in Chapter 7) of New Profile's 2002 "Women Refuse" campaign, in which the participants refused: "To raise our children for war, to ignore war crimes committed in our name, to support the occupation, to continue our normal lives while another nation is suffering because of us." This Svirsky described as "a profound use of nonviolence—an attempt to change the militaristic culture of Israeli society and to instil the values of nonviolence in Israeli children."

Similarly, Israeli pacifist-activist-nonviolent theorist Amos Gvirtz gave a number of examples of how Israelis, whether acting alone or as part of an organized group, can (and, in some instances already do, to some extent) implement "withdrawal of popular and institutional co-operation," in describing (Chapter 2) forms of noncooperation embodied in what he refers to as "preventive nonviolence." These included, along with military refusal, boycotting of goods from settlements in the occupied territories, refusal "to work there or to be involved in anything that legitimizes the settlements, the occupation—refusing to make a tour in the Golan."[2]

Conclusion

Noncooperation by Israelis within the "borders" of the state, complementing their involvement in joint struggle in the occupied territories, has—thus far, with the notable exception of refusal to serve militarily in the occupied territories—been confined to relatively isolated instances. Yet it is, I believe, a major area of activism that needs to be greatly expanded and extended if the nonviolent struggle to end the occupation is to succeed and lead to a just, viable, and enduring peace. Indeed, in my opinion, what is needed—in addition to support for Israeli refuseniks and reinforcement of the growing movement of joint struggle exemplified by Bil'in and its sister villages—is a complementary *movement* of Israeli nonviolent action, especially multiple forms of noncooperation, inside Israel.

NOTES

1 "Windows–Channels for Communication [*Halonot* in Hebrew, *Shababik* in Arabic] is a non-profit organization made up of Jews and Palestinians from Israel and Palestinians from the Occupied Palestinian Territories (OPT). Established in 1991, Windows promotes acquaintance and understanding between people from both nations in order to empower participants to work together towards positive change." (from www.win-peace.org, accessed 14 October 2009) Ongoing projects include a tri-identity-group children's magazine produced by joint Youth Editorial Boards of 12- to 15-year-olds and a video group for older youth, school programs and friendship centres in both Israel and the occupied territories, as well as distribution of humanitarian aid and promotion of the occupied territories' economy through the sale of Palestinian olive oil at their friendship centre in Tel Aviv.

2 Gvirtz reserves the term "active nonviolence" for actions by the oppressed to redress injustice; e.g., the Palestinians, the Indians under Gandhi, the Southern blacks under Martin Luther King. For the Israelis, he says: "When we demand from our government to stop doing things that are unjust, that are done by violence, that provoke violence, our demands are in the [realm] of preventive nonviolence."

15

EPILOGUE

As I write this epilogue in October 2009, seven years have passed since Ghassan Andoni and I sat together briefly in the home of Seattle-based Middle-East justice activists Ed Mast and Linda Bevis to discuss cooperating on this book project, and six since the first of my trips to the region with this book as the focus. On one level, the situation there has only worsened: the "peace process" is moribund—if it ever existed in any meaningful way—the wall has grown to encase much of the West Bank, and settlement construction continues apace, as do land confiscations and house demolitions. Gaza has been under an escalating state of siege for nearly four years, with the horrendous bombing raids of January 2009's "Operation Cast Lead" still a fresh memory. And on and on.

Despite the bleakness of the situation, however, I take considerable hope from reports of persistent and spreading campaigns of nonviolent resistance in Bil'in and other villages impacted by the wall and from the increasing coverage this is beginning to garner even in the mainstream media (publication of Mohammed Khatib's article "Palestine's Peaceful Struggle" on *The Nation* website on 11 September 2009 being but one example – see Chapter 5). A 13 September 2009 visit to the Anarchists Against the Wall website, www.Awalls.org, came up with reports of anti-wall demonstrations in recent weeks by villagers and Israelis, sometimes with international supporters, in Deir Qaddis and Kharbata, Nil'in, Biddu, Ma'asarah, and at the Azun–Atme checkpoint, as well as in Bil'in.

To get a sense of the spread of the so-called "Bil'in Model" of nonviolent joint struggle to areas of the West Bank relatively far from the well-known village, I spoke to Samer Jaber, an organizer from the village of el-Khader (on the road between Bethlehem and Hebron) in November 2007, some six months after returning from the last of the three visits I'd made to Palestine and Israel primarily to collect interview material for this book. He told me that he sees Bil'in as part of a chain stretching back at least as far as earlier campaigns in Budrus, Deir Qaddis, and Mas'ha. "We see it as one of the successful models in the chain—the long chain, the long series," said Jaber, "and we have a different experience [than] in the North [of the West Bank]." As such, he warned, the significance of the "Bil'in model" should neither be minimized nor exaggerated. Although he characterized the Bil'in experience as "one of the most important experiences" and described "good contact with Bil'in and different leaders," Jaber cautioned that the aim is "first of all to transfer the principles of the experience, not to make a copy." He went on to describe some of the distinguishing characteristics of the Bethlehem district. Notably, in contrast to Bil'in—a village of a few thousand residents, all Muslim, in a district where villages are spread out—around Bethlehem, a heterogeneous population of around 200,000 is distributed among several villages in a relatively small area. This allows them to rotate the demonstrations from village to village and "to deal with Bethlehem as one united organic body." This is advantageous on two levels: the fallout from demonstrations (harassment by the military, for example) isn't focused on one village, so people suffer less, and there is more opportunity to learn from each other's experience. "So," says Jaber, "Bil'in plays a good role, but we can't copy this experience."

Jaber also stressed the necessity of developing relationships "that [are] built on trust and honest, and being with the people, working with the people," and being open to the fact that "the regular people can teach us and give us new experiences that are unique," while at the same time remaining "independent, even from the Palestinian Authority." Lamenting the Palestinian leadership's lack of political vision over the preceding seven years (i.e., since the fall of 2000...), he spoke of the importance, as well, of being "independent of the missing vision and [to] create from the grassroots level another vision," "in the long run—and not in the short run—one state for the whole population."

In this light, Jaber's take on relations with Israeli activists was telling and epitomized his commitment to an egalitarian joint struggle that steers clear of normalization.

> I believe deeply in joint struggle and not normalization. Normalization for me means peace under occupation—just we stay silent under Israelis and this occupation—while joint struggle means that we join together to understand, to plan, and to lead together. I have some friends from the Anarchists [Against the Wall]. They said, "We are ready to do whatever you ask us." I told them, "I will not, never, ever ask you to do something." He said, "What do you want?" I said, "What I want [is] that we want together to do

something." So we plan together; we do everything together. This is the joint struggle.[1]

Israeli Anarchist Kobi Snitz, whom I interviewed in Vancouver in April 2008, also balked at reference to "the Bil'in model." While readily acknowledging the Bil'in people's unusual degree of perseverance, and their creativity, he pointed out that, "As you well know, there's been lots of Palestinian nonviolent resistance; even [jointly] with Israelis, there's been a lot. And the Bil'in people would be the first to admit it." So Anarchists Against the Wall has ongoing relationships with Bil'in and some other villages, Snitz told me, but they also go wherever else they may be invited.

> It almost never happens that we're invited and we can't find people to go, even if it's a handful. I think we've managed to get there just about every time that we've been invited. Sometimes we're not [invited]; sometimes they don't need us. We're happy just to get the call and we show up. If they feel that there's more that's needed, that we need to plan more or to consult with us, then we're happy to do that.

Joint Struggle in the Occupied Territories—Not Everyone's Cup of Tea

But what of the vast majority of Israelis—even of Israelis strongly opposed to the occupation and its abuses—who are not or do not feel able to actually physically participate in joint struggle side-by-side with Palestinians engaged in nonviolent resistance? How can they advance the struggle for a just peace?

Palestinian lawyer/pacifist/nonviolent organizer Jonathan Kuttab told me (5 November 2007) that what is needed in his view—and has yet to take place—is for "Israeli Jews with a conscience" to "make a clean break with some of the accepted, applied, respected positions in the broader Israeli society." "They need to become radical," said Kuttab, "and they need to make a much more serious and thoroughgoing critique of Israeli society and to act upon it."

For example: to be willing to talk about boycotts, divestment, sanctions, cut-off of aid; to openly call for things that the peace movement never called for before because it sounded like a betrayal of Israel and of Israeli society. Now for them to really work for peace with any integrity, they need to do that, and many of them are not, I think, willing to do that or haven't made that decision, and that's why they are silent. That's why you don't hear from them; that's why you don't see them. They are there, but for them to stand up and be counted requires them to be much more radical than they have been so far. They almost can no longer think of themselves as Israelis in the old fashion.

"In the old times," Kuttab recalled, "people of the peace movement used to think of themselves as the 'true Israel,' as real Israelis, as the real holders of the vision—the spirit—of Zionism. They can't do that anymore."

Because the spirit of Zionism and the heart of what Israel is or has become is no longer something that they can live with or be consistent with what they consider to be the true and genuine humanitarian justice, international law, decency, humanity, etc. The racism that has been endemic, institutional, integral, at the very heart of Israeli society and institutions and laws now is no longer being sufficiently camouflaged. It is now out in the open, and they need to contend with it, and they don't like it. Many of them simply have left the country because it's no longer comfortable. Others are quiet. They feel paralyzed because what they really need to do, they may not be willing to do.

On the one hand, says Kuttab, "[These Israelis] have enough conscience and enough decency and humanity to say, "this is not me. This is not something I like; this is not something I want to happen in my name." On the other, he adds, however: "I'm saying something much deeper [than what action they should take]; I'm saying, 'Who are you? Part of who you are is no longer possible.'"

Perhaps Jonathan Kuttab is right—that a radical break with Israeli and Zionist norms is required before "Israeli Jews with a conscience" will be able to "really work for peace with any integrity." I do think that this is, in fact, a break that has been made by many of those who actually join in Palestinian nonviolent resistance actions, in Bil'in and elsewhere. On the other hand, recognizing that the number of Israelis willing to go that far is limited, and acknowledging the importance of Israelis' working for the transformation of their own society from within so as to extirpate the militaristic and racist roots of the occupation (cf. New Profile, Muhammad Jaradat, et al.), I am left with the question of what additional steps those who still cling to their Israeli (or even Zionist) identity (as well as those who do not) can take on their own side of the border—that will contribute significantly to the strengthening of the joint struggle against the occupation. And what comes to mind is an increase in acts of noncooperation.[2]

Nonviolent Noncooperation—Concept and Practice

Anyone who has been a teacher or parent of a teenager, or of a two-year-old for that matter, has experienced the coercive force of noncooperation—the power of the less powerful to totally hamstring the more powerful simply by saying "NO." Nonviolence theorist Gene Sharp has repeatedly pointed out the power of widespread nonviolent noncooperation as a strategy for weakening the hold of an oppressive regime. In *The Methods of Nonviolent Action*, part two of his 1973 three-volume compendium, *The Politics of Nonviolent Action* (Sharp 1973), fully 103 of his well-known list of 198 methods of nonviolent struggle are listed in the category of noncooperation. These include various forms of social noncooperation (such as boycotts of social affairs or ostracism of persons or groups, total personal noncooperation—going limp during arrest and imprisonment ..., collective disappearance), economic noncooperation (including 26 forms of economic boycott and 23 forms of strike), and political noncooperation (which includes several forms each of rejection of authority, citizens' noncooperation with government, what he calls citizens' alternatives to obedience—ranging from slow compliance through refusal to disperse and noncooperation with conscription, to civil disobedience of 'illegitimate laws'—and culminates with actions by government personnel and by domestic and international actions by governments). In *From Dictatorship to Democracy: A Conceptual Framework for Liberation*, Sharp's more recent practical guide to the use of nonviolence in opposing oppressive regimes (which has thus far been translated into 21 languages and used in popular struggles in various parts of the world), he stresses the key role played by noncooperation with the regime and withdrawal of legitimacy from it (Sharp 1993/2002).[3]

I would contend that much of the power of nonviolence for change lies in this aspect, this "the power of saying no"—as illustrated by Sharp and others who recount instances from around the world. Examples from the Palestinian struggle abound as well, and some are mentioned elsewhere in this book; e.g., the six-month general strike of 1936, the great variety of strikes and boycotts and clandestine solidarity/joint work of the First Intifada and today, in *sumud* itself, and most recently in the burgeoning movement for worldwide "BDS" (Boycott, Divestment, and Sanctions) aimed at terminating the Israeli occupation.

An Important Role for Israelis in the "Great Chain of Nonviolence"

As Sharp states, "Withdrawal of popular and institutional cooperation ... diminishes, and may sever, the availability of the sources of power on which all rulers depend" (Sharp 1993/2002). It seems to me that in the present struggle, given the factors mentioned above, Israelis (especially but not exclusively Jewish-Israelis) are uniquely situated to carry out this powerful form of resistance from within the borders of the state—in areas increasingly inaccessible to Palestinians from the territories—and that intensification in this form of action inside Israel would be both valuable in and of itself and complementary to the equally vital work of joint struggle side-by-side with Palestinians on the "other" side of the border. Support for this position comes from Norwegian sociologist and professor of Peace and Conflict Studies, Johan Galtung.[4]

In discussing the conditions under which nonviolence is most likely to be effective, Galtung notes that between friends, "gentle forms of nonviolence may be more than sufficiently persuasive ... [N]o action such as noncooperation may be needed. ... Self and Other see each other as extensions of themselves. Coming to terms with each other is to come to terms with themselves." Between foes, however, for nonviolence to work, "[m]ore has to be done to evoke ... images of a cooperative future. Action, even very direct action of noncooperation and civil disobedience, may be needed in order to make very clear which structural relations are absolutely intolerable ..." (Galtung 1989 p. 14).

After introducing the complicating factor of dehumanization of the foe (something we have unquestionably seen in Palestine/Israel)—whether for religious or historical reasons[5]—Galtung concludes that, "It is not obvious that nonviolence against an oppressor is primarily the task of those who are oppressed. They certainly have not only the right but also in a sense a duty to resist. But if their resistance is an invitation to even more brutal oppression the question can very legitimately be asked, What are the alternatives?" (p. 20).

Galtung, of course, dismisses the option of resorting to violence and proposes instead "nonviolence, to destroy the oppressive structure, *but by others than the victims themselves* [emphasis mine, MKL]; *for* them, *on behalf* of them, partly also *of* them, but not primarily *by* them." This follows from his earlier statement and question: "The whole theory of nonviolence is based on the idea of Self recognizing the human being in the Other, appealing to that human being not only for compassion with one's own plight, but also for self-interest in a better future, to be enjoyed together. But what if a process of dehumanization has taken place ... ruling out the Other as a human partner?" (p. 14).

The end of the Vietnam War, for example, he states, "was brought about to a large extent by nonviolence. But this was not the nonviolence of the Vietnamese people ... It was brought about by people closer to Washington posing the credible threat of making the country ungovernable" (p. 19). Thus:

> It is when one's own people ... start reacting the same way, nonviolently sending the forceful signal that "we are not tolerating this any longer," that chords of responsiveness are being touched... Nonviolence ... is supposed to work by "stirring sluggish consciences," making the oppressor aware of the amount of suffering he has brought upon the oppressed. But if the oppressed are not seen at all or are seen as dangerous, capable of inflicting suffering on oneself, this no longer works. If, in addition, they are dehumanized ... the situation becomes even worse. There is little or no resonance since there is no common humanity ... to play on. (pp. 19, 20)

Galtung postulates, therefore, that the appropriate primary nonviolent activists should be:

> Those whose active or passive cooperation with the oppressor is needed for the oppressor to oppress. And/or those who are sufficiently close to the oppressors to be seen by them as human beings, and to touch the human nerve in them, if not in sympathy with the victims, at least in response to the demands put upon them by the intervening/interceding group.[6] (pp. 20, 21)

Hence, just as it required the intervention of the "Aryan" wives of German Jews imprisoned during WWII to bring about their release—and not anything the imprisoned Jews themselves might have done—(pp. 22, 23) and just as the fact that Gandhi and his "educated, urbane" followers, "speaking English better than the oppressors ... with a history of what the British would recognize as 'civilization' at least three times as long as what the Britons could muster" and his supporters inside Britain together humanized the struggle of the Indian masses for the British (p. 21) and white participation in the U.S. Civil Rights Movement "brought the black people's condition closer to the whites' hearts..." (p. 25), so too in the case of Palestine/Israel.

> [T]he concrete issue brought up here is who should fight nonviolently. And the answer given is, *not only the Palestinians, but also the Israelis* [emphasis mine, MKL]—and everybody else for that matter, against the hard nucleus of those in favour of occupying somebody else's land and even expanding farther...[7] (p. 24)

In light of the function of members of the oppressor society in humanizing the nonviolent struggle of the oppressed in the eyes of the oppressor—thereby constituting a vital link in what he terms the "Great Chain of Nonviolence"[8]—Galtung advocates both "massive participation of Israeli Jews and Arabs [sic] alongside the Palestinians ... in nonviolent actions"; i.e., joint struggle (which he refers to as "the Self in the Other") and nonviolent activism "by Jews inside Israel who would find the goal of peace between Jews and Arabs by far superior to continued Zionist expansion in the search of 'secure borders'..." ("the Other in the Self") and with sympathizers all over the world (pp. 54, 55; 68, 69). I view Galtung's concept of the "Great Chain of Nonviolence" as reinforcing the conclusions derived from my reading of the responses of the activists interviewed for this book regarding the importance of these twin aspects of joint struggle.

As pointed out earlier (Conclusions), the number of Israelis who have, over the years, practiced some form of noncooperation with government policies, has been small. Nonetheless, it seems to me that for many Israelis who, unlike the Anarchists Against the Wall, are hesitant to join Palestinians in nonviolent actions in the occupied territories, it might be more "comfortable" to participate in/expand acts of nonviolent noncooperation at home, the majority of which are not so extreme as to put them at risk of long terms of imprisonment. For others—those who are willing to tackle more challenging forms of noncooperation[9]—developing and carrying out such strategies might constitute a logical addition to their work with joint struggle (Kaufman-Lacusta 2008).

Boycott, Divestment, and Sanctions—Israelis' Role in the International Campaign

Support for Boycott, Divestment, and Sanctions (BDS) was an action recommended by several of the activists interviewed for this book, and was dubbed by some (e.g., Mohammed Khatib of Bil'in—Chapter 5) as the most important activity in which Israelis, not to mention internationals, could engage in in terms of putting effective pressure on Israel to end the occupation. Kobi Snitz, too, told me that "the most effective work Israelis can do is BDS support,"[10] and Palestinian political and cultural analyst Omar Barghouti (a prominent figure in the Palestinian BDS movement who spoke at the April 2007 Bil'in Conference on Nonviolent Popular Joint Struggle) made the point that in July 2005, when more than 170 Palestinian civil society organizations in occupied Palestine, in Israel, and in the refugee diaspora called for BDS against the Israeli occupation, "a crucial feature of the call, which people sometimes forget, is its direct appeal to conscientious Israelis to support it."[11]

That this would constitute a form of noncooperation with Israeli policies is obvious; how Israelis might participate is perhaps less so. Referring to queries by those who wonder how Israelis could boycott their own economy, Snitz remarked, "We [Israelis] would be supporting international BDS efforts, not boycotting the corner store." Elsewhere Snitz and a co-author described a number of functions for Israeli boycott supporters, including "research into the corporations and institutions supporting and legitimizing Israel's apartheid system" and "[t]ranslation of BDS resources and news from other languages to Hebrew." As well, "organized Jewish-Israeli endorsement for the [BDS] campaign" helps "counter the crude characterization of Israel's critics as anti-Semites" and "the charge that progressive Israelis, or the Israeli left, do not support BDS."[12]

A major role that Israeli supporters of BDS see for themselves is that of issuing their own calls for international BDS, in consultation and coordination with the Palestinian initiators of the campaign. A website called BOYCOTT, Supporting the Palestinian BDS Call from Within, for example, prominently displayed one such call, which read in part:

> Reiterating the Palestinian call, we urge civil society institutions as well as concerned citizens around the world to find inspiration in the strength and effectiveness of the anti-apartheid movement of the 1980s:
>
> - Integrate BDS in every struggle for justice and human rights by adopting wide, context-sensitive and sustainable boycotts of Israeli products, companies, academic and cultural institutions, and sports groups, similar to the actions taken against apartheid South Africa;
> - Ensure that national and multinational corporations are held accountable and sanctioned accordingly for profiteering from Israel's occupation and other Israeli violations of human rights and international law;
> - Work towards cancelling and blocking free trade and other preferential agreements with Israel;
> - Pressure governments to impose a direct and indirect arms embargo on Israel, which will guarantee end-user compliance with international law and human rights principles.

(This was followed by the signatures of 37 Israelis, including Kobi Snitz and a number of other prominent academics, when accessed on September 22, 2009 at www.boycottisrael.info/content/boycott-stands-dr-neve-gordon-bds-and-against-oppression).

In fact, at the time of writing (October 2009), Israeli voices are increasingly being heard along with those of Palestinian activists and other representatives of Palestinian civil society calling for BDS, among them historian Ilan Pappe and the late Tanya Reinhardt (both of whom left Israel in the wake of harassment for their political stands—on BDS and related issues), Jeff Halper (see pp. 118–19 and Chapter 11) and, more recently, Neve Gordon (amid calls for his dismissal from the post of Senior Lecturer in Politics and Government at Ben Gurion University).

Israeli Noncooperation—Additional Room for Expansion[13]
In addition to participation in BDS campaigns, some possible forms that Israeli noncooperation might take include:

- picketing and conducting boycotts of companies involved in construction of the wall and settlements, and other companies and institutions that profit from the occupation;
- leafleting workers in these enterprises, encouraging withdrawal of their services from settlement and wall-related construction and settlement-based industry;
- ostracism of settlers (e.g., like that practiced by the Danes during WWII against German soldiers occupying their country);
- boycott of and nonparticipation in sporting events in which settlers participate;
- avoidance of frivolous travel to the occupied territories, such as skiing in the Golan (as mentioned above by Amos Gvirtz);
- refusal to use "Israeli-only" roads when travelling in the occupied territories (e.g., to join a demonstration);
- following the example of the military refusers by withholding cooperation with other discriminatory provisions, such as administration of the permit system; exclusive Israeli provision of water, electricity, phone service; other vulnerable points in the "matrix of control" as described by Jeff Halper (Halper 2008; "Dismantling the Matrix of Control," September 11, 2009 on www.merip.org/mero/ mero091109.html; *inter alia*).

The initiation or intensification of actions such as these would pose little or no risk to participants (with the possible exception of the last mentioned) and, taken together, they could constitute a major source of pressure on the Israeli occupation authorities—from within.

We have seen throughout this book that, as Palestinian nonviolent resistance to the occupation becomes more widespread, increasing numbers of Israelis are drawn to participate in some form of joint struggle. It is my hope that this participation will continue to expand and will increasingly include both joint struggles within Palestine itself and the perhaps less rewarding on a visceral level, but equally vital, struggles to weaken the roots of the oppression on the other side of the border, inside Israel. To that end, I suggest, there is much to be learned—both from the history of the struggle in Palestine and from the experience of the world-wide nonviolence community—which might serve to facilitate the development of new and more effective strategies for an Israeli movement reaching beyond the currently prevalent tactics of "protest and persuasion" and occasional "nonviolent intervention" (e.g., direct action) to embrace a conscious strategy employing the powerful tactics of mass noncooperation.

NOTES

1 Kobi Snitz responded with surprise to Jaber's comment, explaining that, since it is the Palestinians who must face the consequences, "We mean that the tough calls should be made by the Palestinians. That is, I think, what we mean by, 'You tell us what to do.'"

2 This page (443) and the first two paragraphs of page 144 are based on my 2008 article in PIJ (Kaufman-Lacusta 2008).

3 Similar statements, as well as detailed examples, can be found in Sharp's other writings; e.g., *The Politics of Nonviolent Action*, cited above, and the pamphlet *There are Realistic Alternatives*, Boston: The Albert Einstein Institution, 2003.

4 Johan Galtung is a founder of the discipline of Peace and Conflict Studies, as well as founder of the International Peace Research Institute in Oslo, the International Peace Research Association, and the *Journal of Peace Research*, *inter alia*, and since 2004 has been a member of the Advisory Council of the Committee for a Democratic UN. He is credited with the formulation of the concepts of structural and cultural violence and of negative vs. positive peace.

5 "The conditions of dehumanization are probably found more readily in religion and history; in doctrines of theology and in great traumas suffered by a nation in its course through history. ... That people inflicting traumas on others are seen as nonhuman goes without saying; the victims may need this image in order to express and explain their own calamity. But the other way also holds. The victims may be seen as nonhuman by those inflicting the traumas in order to justify their own cruelty, and for fear of becoming the objects of a counter-trauma, revenge ..." (Galtung 1989, p. 15)

6 It should be pointed out that Galtung is fully aware of the drawbacks, as well as the advantages, of this approach. His review, in the same book, of several "successful" nonviolent struggles introduces a sobering note, as he shows that outcomes have been anything but unqualifiedly positive in terms of the original goals of the struggle, and cautions—in terms echoing Palestinian concerns regarding normalization—to beware of pitfalls such as "collusion at the top" leading, even unwittingly, to more benefit for the "in between" interveners than for the people on whose behalf they are struggling. Jeff Halper makes a similar point (Chapter 4), and Kobi Snitz, as well, has written ("Teargas and Tea: Problems of Principled Opposition within the Israeli Movement against the Wall and the Dilemma of Privileges," on *A-Infos: a multi-lingual news service by, for, and about anarchists* [www.ainfos.ca/ainfos336/ainfos38304.html, posted 18 February 2009, accessed 14 October 2009]): "The privileged position of Israelis means they have greater access to the media, the ability to move much more freely and face much less legal and physical risk, etc. This tends to increase

the influence Israelis have on decisions about the struggle which affect their Palestinian counterparts considerably more. ... That is to say that, in a sense, the privilege is extended in the struggle as well. ... The value or even justification of joint political action should be weighed with this in mind."

7　For Johan Galtung's ideas of steps necessary for a nonviolent outcome in Palestine/Israel—surprisingly a propos considering he was writing early in the First Intifada—as well as his suggestions for specific forms of nonviolent action by Israelis and internationals, see Galtung 1989.

8　Re the "Great Chain of Nonviolence" and dehumanization of the oppressed: "The long-term approach would bè to struggle against the sources of dehumanization, bridging all gaps within and between societies. But the short-term approach would be to mobilize the in-between groups, have them act out their political conscience and consciousness on behalf of those too far down and away to have an effective voice. And then build social and human ties to solidify that political cooperation, in both directions, with the oppressors and with the oppressed..." (Galtung 1989, p. 32)

9　A few of the many resources for examples of successful campaigns of non-cooperation include AFSC 2005, Sharp 1973 and 93/2002, Palestine Monitor 2007, Kennedy, R. Scott and Mubarak E. Awad 1985, and websites such as www.warresisters.org, www.lysistrataproject.org, www.trainingforchange.org, and www.starhawk.org.

10　Like many others, Snitz also feels draft resistance is similarly strong and effective.

11　Omar Barghouti continued: "To be in effective solidarity with Palestine today is to actively support some form of BDS. This is what the overwhelming majority of Palestinian civil society is calling for. Boycott, divestment, and sanctions, however, do not come in 'one size that fits all.' If the basic premise that Israel needs to be pressured is accepted, then various forms of boycott, divestment, and sanctions can be adapted according to the specific context in each country." More recently, in an article on the Counterpunch website dated October 21, 2008 ("Countering the Critics: The Boycott and Palestinian Groups"), Barghouti stated even more explicitly: "[T]the only true fighters for peace in Israel are those who support our three fundamental rights: the right of return for Palestinian refugees; full equality for the Palestinian citizens of Israel; and ending the occupation and colonial rule. Those are our true partners. They ALL support various forms of BDS [...] On the other hand, groups that, for tactical reasons, support only a subset of BDS, or a targeted boycott of specific products or organizations in Israel or supporting Israel, are also our partners, of course. Boycott is not a one-size-fits-all type of process. It must be customized to suit a particular context to be most effective. What is important to agree on, though, is why we are boycotting and towards what ends." (Accessed September 17, 2009 from www.counterpunch.org/barghouti10212008.html)

12　"Israeli Citizens for a Boycott of Israel" by Roee Harush and Kobi Snitz in *Al-Majdal* Issue No. 38 [Summer 2008], accessed September 22, 2009 at www.badil.org/al-majdal/2008/summer/articles12.htm.

13　The sentiments and list that follow are based on those first published in Kaufman-Lacusta 2008.

16

AFTERWORD

In January of 2010, the hardcover edition of this book already bound for the print shop, I returned briefly to Palestine and Israel to gather some firsthand impressions, with the aim of tracing developments in three specific areas that I'd examined in the epilogue to the hardcover edition. The three, which I planned to focus on in a revised epilogue or (as I soon decided) an afterword to the paperback edition, were: the present status of the Palestinian-initiated and -led campaign for boycott, divestment, and sanctions (BDS); the state of joint struggle, both on the Bil'in model and otherwise; and lastly, nonviolent noncooperation by Israelis inside Israel—was it becoming a more significant part of the spectrum of resistance to the occupation than it had been when I did the last of the interviews for the hardcover edition (mostly 2007 and before)? I spoke to ten activists on my January trip—all but two of whom (Hisham Jamjoum and Aliyah Strauss) appear in earlier chapters of this book—one (Rev. Naim Ateek) a month later at a conference in the US, and one (Omar Barghouti, whom I had quoted in the book but not yet interviewed) in April via email.

What I heard gave me pause. On the one hand, there were reports of impressive strides in the BDS campaign. On the other hand, though mixed, responses regarding joint struggle in the West Bank were dominated by depressing accounts of stagnation in that arena and, as to noncooperation inside Israel, the response was disappointingly meagre: nothing new seemed to be happening. I began to question whether my sense that the time had come for the latter form of resistance had been premature, or whether I might have been "barking up the wrong tree" altogether. Happily, more recent events have shed a more positive light on both of the latter two areas, as well as providing confirmation for the growing success of the BDS campaign.

The Campaign for Boycott, Divestment, and Sanctions

Boycott is not a form of punishment, but it is meant to add pressure on Israel until it respects human rights and international law and ends its military occupation of Palestine.

George N. Rishmawi (Palestinian Center for Rapprochement between People)

BDS appears to be thriving. An August 19 *Electronic Intifada* article posted on www.PACBI.org and accessed on September 2 reports that throughout the West Bank, "Palestinians have galvanized around campaigns to promote locally-made products and locally-harvested food instead of a myriad of items made in illegal settlement colonies on occupied Palestinian land in the West Bank," while the Palestinian Authority (PA) has been distributing lists of settlement products. George N. Rishmawi, writing that same day, reported that the recent boycott of settlement products launched by the PA (reinforcing existing local community initiatives) had resulted in the exodus of some factories from the settlements to avoid it. Meanwhile, a September 2 visit to the principal BDS website (www.bdsmovement.net) turned up accounts of a boycott of Israeli goods by the Olympia, WA (USA) (hometown of Rachel Corrie) Food Coop, exclusion of additional Israeli companies from the Norwegian government pension fund, a demonstration at the port of Vancouver, BC (Canada) aimed at preventing the unloading of an Israeli-owned freighter, and demands by 6,000 Irish shoppers that their supermarket stop stocking Israeli goods.

Despite some disagreement regarding what particular "flavour" of BDS was preferable, all of my January 2010 interviewees supported some form of BDS and agreed that the campaign was making great strides. And BDS movement leader Omar Barghouti (in his April 2010 email interview) reaffirmed his remarks, cited earlier in this book (see p. 451, note 11), that "Boycott is not a one-size-fits-all type of process. It must be customized to suit a particular context to be most effective. What is important to agree on, though, is why we are boycotting and towards what ends." Defining the parameters of this flexibility, Barghouti explained:

Context-sensitivity is a key principle of the BDS movement that the Palestinian BDS National Committee (BNC) takes to heart.

BDS is not an ideology or run by a political party; it is a wide movement that brings together groups and individuals of diverse ideological and political backgrounds that converge on their utmost respect for international law and the morally consistent application of human rights.

Emphasizing the key importance of recognizing the Palestinian-led nature of the campaign and the fact that "[s]olidarity with the oppressed primarily means understanding and recognizing what the oppressed need and want to achieve freedom, justice and self determination. Imposing objectives and frameworks on the oppressed is usually indicative of a colonial attitude, whether recognized as such or not," he made it clear that, since "the Palestinian Civil Society Call for BDS is *the* reference for the global BDS movement, . . . the principles, the rights, upon which the movement is based are the same [everywhere]." "What differs from location to location according to the political and organizational context," he explained, "is the specific target of the BDS campaign in that location."

> Some allies in BDS campaigns in the West are not fully on board with the BDS Call itself. However, they are active in specific BDS campaigns, and they refrain from contradicting or opposing the BDS Call itself. We consider them allies in the movement, but not full strategic partners. The latter need to agree with us, in the BNC, on our principles and goals, [i.e., "the right of return for Palestinian refugees; full equality for the Palestinian citizens of Israel; and ending the occupation and colonial rule"(ibid)], regardless of what action or campaign they undertake to help us get there. As I've jokingly said in my talks, even if a partner adopts the BDS Call and then decides to launch a campaign targeting Israeli tomatoes only, we'll be very happy with them as strategic partners. E.g. Code Pink,[1] is a good example of that. They've endorsed the BDS Call and chose to focus their creative energies on boycotting Ahava, the Israeli cosmetics company that manufactures in the OPT. Many campaigns in Europe have also a narrow focus in their BDS targets, and that's perfectly fine.

"Where we have problems," concluded Barghouti, "is when any group tries to appropriate the right to set the movement's goals and/or parameters instead of the Palestinians."

Among the Israelis who expressed unconditional support for the Palestinian Call to BDS was the AIC's Michel Warschawski, who regards it as "perhaps one of the most important things that has happened in the past ten years in the struggle for the implementation of the rights of the Palestinian people."

> This is a quantum leap, because we are passing from a situation wherein we denounce the occupation and condemn the oppression to a situation of [being on the] offensive, an offensive whose goal is to exact a price from the State of Israel (not from Israeli society) so long as it continues to violate all international laws, all the UN resolutions, and to behave like a nation of hooligans. And there is a strong voice in the world saying that what's needed is sanctions, what's needed is to punish and to bring pressure to bear on a state that is not conducting itself in accordance with the [international] law.

In that connection, says Warschawski, "I always try to say BDS plus Hague."

> That is to say, an important part of "S" is accountability [used English word here – MKL] before international law of people who are suspected of war crimes or crimes against humanity. The call for [their being brought before the] International Court, the call to take the Goldstone Report seriously, especially his recommendations at the end regarding the necessity of taking legal action against those suspected of war crimes is, in my view, an integral and even central part of the BDS campaign.

ICAHD coordinator, Jeff Halper, also emphasized the importance of the BDS campaign, including its extension into the realm of legal challenges. "BDS is really, I think, a tremendously growing movement," he stated. "I think it's achieved critical mass in the last couple of years." Halper's particular take on BDS in some ways goes even further than does the Palestinian Call in terms of breadth of focus. He explains: I'm more for BDS-SL, myself. I think BDS is important—boycott, divestment, and sanctions—but there's two other pieces of that. One ["S"] is solidarity. And there, for example, I think a tremendous initiative is when local communities twin with Palestinian ones. . . ." pointing out that even if such a proposal is voted down in the end, "That's a tremendously consciousness-raising thing."

"L" [legal] refers to challenging the practices of the occupation in international courts, "which Israel really fears."

> We've been trying the Israeli courts for all these years, and obviously we've exhausted that remedy, so now we're poised to go to the international courts. Some groups have gone after military people, and we're trying to prepare a case now about house demolitions for the international courts. Other people have worked on other issues, including the Goldstone Report, of course, and things like that. So in other words, I see this all as one package: BDS-SL. And I think that's really giving a focus to the international community that's very strong.

ICAHD endorses the 2005 Palestinian Call for BDS, specifically, including it's conditions of "end of the occupation, equal rights for Palestinians, and the right of return."

> The idea in the very beginning was, let's try to boycott or divest from companies that were profiting from the occupation, whether Israeli or not. Actually, Gush Shalom was one of the first that started a boycott of settlement products. And then it developed into divesting from companies that profit from the occupation. And some of us thought at that early stage that that was a good focus, because we're focusing on the occupation. But then, over the years, Israel's behaviour has been outrageous, and certainly issues like Gaza bring up wider issues of human rights, and there's arms issues that can't be confined to the occupied territories. So it became harder and harder to separate the occupation from Israel in general. We're in favour of all the boycotts across the board.

The Israel section of WILPF, the Women's International League for Peace and Freedom, has also voted to support BDS. A new interviewee on my January 2010 trip was long-time WILPF activist Aliyah Strauss, who told me: "We had a discussion, we voted. It was not an easy discussion, but we have come out in favour." Although at time of writing (August 27, 2010), they hadn't yet determined whether to endorse the official Call—right of return and all (a discussion of this subject is pending), their statement is strong, and includes, as well, the call for a cultural and sports boycott of Israel. "Our rationale," stated Strauss, "is until it hurts the Israelis, they're not going to pay attention." Also active in the Coalition of Women for Peace, Strauss pointed out, "In some way we're all profiting from the occupation."

The largest project of the Coalition is the whoprofits.org campaign, and what they say is that the economies of the settlements and Israel are so intertwined that, even if we don't buy Ahava hand cream or Bagel and Bagel snacks [both produced in the occupied territories], we just can't get away from it. So you do your best.

As to recent progress of the BDS campaign amongst the Palestinian population and internationally, both Hisham Jamjoum of ISM and George N. Rishmawi of PCR cited the recent endorsement by the PA of a Palestine-wide boycott of settlement products, as well as the importance of its growth in other regions of the world, notably in parts of Europe such as the UK and Sweden. Rishmawi described BDS as "definitely one of the most important methods that can really get people around the world to be part of the attempts to end the Israeli military occupation of Palestine." Of course, he added, in contrast to the limited availability of non-Israeli products in Palestine, "in the U.S. and in Europe, there are so many options, and I think that makes it a lot easier." Citing studies that indicate that the Palestinian market makes up only a very small percentage of the Israeli economy ("Some people say about four percent only"), Rishmawi stressed the importance of international boycott and divestment. Moreover, he reminded me, "the Call for [boycott] includes not only Israeli products but any products that contribute directly to maintaining the occupation."

Like Barghouti, Rishmawi expressed support for selectively targeted boycotts, especially in cases where a boycott of all Israeli products might be interpreted as an attack on Israel rather than on the occupation. Noting that the campaign had been gaining momentum in the previous year or two, he commented:

> I think that after the war in Gaza there was some increase; people became more aware of Israel. I can see that this movement is growing, maybe slowly, but growing. And it's good that churches are getting on board. But they are still worried about what the repercussions could be, so there is a need for more advocacy work on the church level as well because churches can really be effective; they can reach people.

"You know," added Rishmawi, "there was a [U.S.] Congress resolution to support the boycott of South African apartheid, at a certain point. So also, if we can get lobbying on that level, I think that can help very much, and it will encourage people."

Current State of Joint Struggle

It's really interesting that the army is moving so much against it, and arresting leaders, and really trying to stop it and crush it, because I think they are fearful that it will spread. Unfortunately, it has not spread fast enough, because I think if it does, it will make a difference.

Rev. Naim Ateek (Sabeel, Ecumenical Liberation Theology Center) on joint struggle in the villages along the route of the wall

When I asked them in January, there was general agreement amongst my interviewees that the joint struggle against land confiscation for construction of the wall in the villages was thriving and even spreading. Nevertheless, there was an undertone of reduced participation by Israelis in anti-occupation activism and a sense of the decreased overall importance of the Israeli left's contribution to the struggle to end the occupation. The most daunting comments about the present state of joint struggle came from Jeff Halper and Michel Warschawski (Mikado). And although both agreed that on the whole, the size and effectiveness of the Israeli "peace movement" had diminished dramatically in recent years, their interpretations of the situation were diametrically opposed.

"Joint struggle isn't doing very well," Jeff Halper told me. Citing as an example the fact that Israeli organizations hadn't been invited to participate in the major Gaza solidarity demonstration at Erez Checkpoint on December 31, 2009, he described what he saw as a troubling trend, perhaps understandable, but problematic, nonetheless. "The Palestinians are retreating from involvement with Israeli groups," he said, "and I think with Jewish groups and Jews abroad, under the rubric of normalization."

> I think there's a real danger here that the Palestinians are going to isolate themselves, they're going to cut themselves off from really important allies, and at the same time, they're going to be seen as being narrow. I think there's a real question here: Is the process of

excluding more and more Israeli groups, for example, contributing to ending the occupation or not, and if it isn't, then it could be politically correct, and it could be what some Palestinians want to do to keep the movement pure or whatever, but I think it's counterproductive.

"Israeli groups are feeling less and less welcome," Halper told me.

For example, when Stop the Wall or some of the other Palestinian groups talk about Bil'in, they never acknowledge the Anarchists, they never acknowledge the Israelis that are there. There's an irony here—I think it's too bad—and that is that we work with all kinds of Palestinians, especially on the ground, but it's the intellectuals and the leadership that's getting to be the most aloof and stand-offish and doesn't want to deal with Israelis. The grassroots are fine. I think we've been there for them, and there's this trust and so on, but it doesn't extend to the intellectuals. And the ones who should be in some way reaching out and helping to form broader alliances—mobilizing civil society—are pulling back.

"In other words," he continued, "there's getting to be more and more of a delegitimization of the Israeli narrative, of everything Israeli: everything Israeli is colonial, is not legitimate, and so on. It doesn't bode well for joint struggle."

When I asked Mikado (Michel Warschawski) about the sense that Israeli participation in Palestinian-led actions was recently being downplayed or even ignored, his response was unsympathetic. There was a new trend, he said, "in what remains of the left—the more radical left, let's say, since the rest has simply collapsed and disappeared—a new-old trend of being insulted and moaning that 'the Palestinians don't pay attention to me; the Palestinians aren't mentioning me.'" He explained, "The Palestinians gave importance to the opposition and dissidence inside Israel exactly in proportion to what it was."

When we were big and strong and effective—like during the first Lebanon War and like during the First Intifada—the Palestinians knew how important this was and knew to value it; they knew this was a serious ally that was helping them reach their objectives and their rights. Now that we have become a much more marginal element, of course the Palestinians will refer to it less. Israeli-Palestinian partnership—not to mention Israeli-Palestinian brotherhood—is built by virtue of the place we fill on their agenda. If we don't fill any place, or a marginal place, they'll say, "Good for you, that's very nice, but we have other priorities; leave us alone. There are a few thousand activists, whose actions we value, but they're not the most important [thing] on our agenda." When we were 400,000, this *was* the most important [thing] on the agenda. We need to stop being insulted and viewing the whole world and the Palestinian struggle in our own navels.

Even so, Mikado wasn't totally pessimistic. That these forces would again be significant, he had no doubt.

We were a force, we weren't a force, we became a force, we returned to being a non-force. I'm not frightened by this. We shouldn't be frightened by this, and especially not be insulted when the Palestinians don't look in our direction so much, when this direction is pretty empty relative to what it was. We *will* be strong; we *will* move Israeli society; we *will* move Israeli politics—because in the past, we succeeded in moving Israeli politics; we succeeded in building a movement that compelled Israel to get out of Lebanon; we succeeded in building a movement that, in the end, compelled [Israel] to recognize the PLO and to open negotiations with it and to begin a process that seemed like a process [leading to] the end of the occupation. Today we've returned to what we were in the seventies, let us say: a protest movement, not a movement that influences, and the [Palestinians'] way of relating to us is proportional to the strength and the effectiveness that we exhibit in the Palestinians' struggle for their rights.

Despite this, however, "There are Palestinians who understand that the matter of Israeli-Palestinian partnership is far more than a matter of expedience—of how much we help them, how much we aid them in the achievement of their objectives."

There is a minority that is aware that, essentially, what we are building in [the course of] joint struggle today either prepares the ground—or doesn't, depending on how meaningful or how marginal it is—for what the connection between the two peoples can be once the conflict is behind them. But this is a minority, even among activists, who think about "what will our connection with the Jews be?" [The majority] want to rid themselves of the occupation, don't want to see settlements, want the right of return.

We [Israelis] also need to understand that we're not the centre of the universe for them.

Explaining the dramatic overall decrease of participation by Jewish Israelis in the Palestinian struggle—and even in actions organized by Palestinian citizens of Israel and vice versa—that he has observed over the past two or three years, Warschawski lamented "the triumph of the policy of separation—the triumph of the wall policy—even amongst the activist camp" and the virtual absence of "the Jewish-Arab dimension, not to mention the Israeli-Palestinian dimension or the Israeli-Arab on the level of all of Palestine, which ten years ago was central. Today," he says, "it's not there at all."

> First and foremost, it was the weakening of the movement in Israel that diminished its importance in the eyes of the Palestinians. The second thing was the triumph of the wall philosophy. That is to say, we have internalized the wall. When you ask me what the central task of the Alternative Information Center is today, in 2010, my answer is to keep the small cracks in the wall open. Really to keep [them open] with our elbows and to say "pass through!" It's still possible to pass through, to bring information across, to bring people across, to bring activism, to bring partnership / cooperation—but it has shrunk to a minimum.

"Hence," he adds, "the importance of Bil'in, the importance of those actions that are *very* important even if they touch just a few hundred people or, at best, a few thousand and not the tens of thousands that it was possible to speak about in the period when you were writing the book—when it was truly a matter of tens of thousands." "Where is everybody?" Warschawski asked, rhetorically. "Both societies, even at the level of activists, have pretty well closed in on themselves. That's what I mean by the triumph of the wall philosophy. It has succeeded. Now, I don't think that even this is irreversible," he concluded, "but we are in a new era in this context."

Although like Halper, Adam Keller, too, regarded the exclusion of Israeli organizations from the December 31, 2009 Gaza solidarity demo at Erez checkpoint as exemplifying a current trend on the part of Palestinians to marginalize the Israeli Jewish groups, he didn't feel that this had had a significant impact on the joint struggle in the villages along the route of the wall.

There is the pattern which developed in Bil'in, especially, and Ni'ilin is already now very much involved, and now, in fact, Sheikh Jarrah[2] is very much taken up with it—there is quite a good pattern of Jews and Arabs from Israel, and local Palestinians, and Palestinians from other places, and internationals all working together.

Like Jeff Halper, Keller felt that the problem lay "more where intellectuals and political campaigners—Palestinian and pro-Palestinian—formulate a comprehensive policy," but that "on the grassroots level, where the leadership of a village or a neighborhood is faced with a concrete threat (the wall, settler encroachment, etc.), [they] are very happy with Israelis coming to help." Keller, for example, spoke of the healthy power dynamic he has observed in Bil'in, with planning meetings usually being held in English (a neutral language in this case) and participants sitting in mixed groups.

> You see an empty chair and you sit there. And also the discussion: the Israelis propose this, and the Palestinians propose [that]. It is the people who are involved in the struggle and they make suggestions and sometimes argue—and you have Israelis and Palestinians on both sides of the argument. That, I think, is a very important development.

Rev. Naim Ateek, too, enthusiastically affirmed the importance of the joint struggle in Bil'in and other villages impacted by the wall, even as he expressed "great disappointment that we have failed to see it becoming a national movement." "[T]hat kind of activity needs to become more national and needs to affect more villages and towns throughout the area—and I keep hoping that it can be done," he said.

By contrast, ISM's Hisham Jamjoum described Israeli participation that is growing both in terms of numbers and acceptability by Palestinians.

> And they grew more and more, and you can see [Israeli activists] even in Nabi Salah now. It's near Birzeit. It's a new place, new location for nonviolent actions now. And also they reach even the Nablus area. Before, they couldn't go; now they reach the Nablus area, because the Palestinians understand that there are really Israelis who want to support them. In the beginning there was concern about the Israelis, because they considered all Israelis as Israeli army or Israeli security or from the government, but now they understand the Israeli people who are supporting them.

On the other hand, though, Jamjoum was adamant that, "We can't say it's a joint struggle."

> It's our struggle, but [Israelis and internationals] are supporting us. Absolutely, it's a Palestinian struggle. It's our struggle and our land and our issue. We can't say Israeli struggle, but they are supporting and in solidarity with us—supporting us strongly and supporting us in the best way ever. As Palestinians we appreciate that, and we understand that, and we love them all; we really love them all. But we say it is a Palestinian struggle.

Nonetheless, Jamjoum concluded our interview with a strong statement of support for participation by Israelis and internationals in the Palestinian nonviolent resistance effort.

> Believe me, Palestinians plus Israelis plus internationals can do a lot, here inside Palestine, inside Israel, and everywhere in the world. So that's why I'm working all the time together. That's why I appreciate and I love everyone working with us, [whether] Israeli or Palestinian or international.

George N. Rishmawi, too, applauded Israeli participation in Palestinian-led actions, and felt it to be important, although, like Mikado, he regarded it as "very minimal."

He pointed out that "joint struggle is always dependent on the acceptance by a certain community to have Israelis involved there," but as a journalist with a focus on nonviolent activism, he was sceptical regarding the contention that Israelis are becoming less welcome and that their presence isn't being reported even when they are present.

> I think when they are there, people will be willing to mention them, because people feel it's good when you write, especially for a Western audience, that Israelis are a part of the nonviolent activities. As you know, in media reporting, it is very important to say who is against this wall or the occupation in general, and I believe it's good always, when there are Israelis, that they should be mentioned. Anyway, it's good also for the fairness and honesty of the report. I don't get the impression that when they are there that they are ignored in terms of reporting. Because if people did not want to say that they were there, they would simply just tell them, don't come. Maybe they would be a little hesitant the first time, or shy to

tell them don't come, but at a certain point, they would get that message clear.

Rejection of "Israel-centric" Struggle

Omar Barghouti's comments, I believe, shed some light on what, I expect, may underlie Hisham Jamjoum's "disclaimer" regarding the term "joint struggle", as well as perhaps accounting for at least some of the reluctance encountered by Halper and Keller regarding Israeli organizations' (and that of their representatives, as opposed to individuals) participation in Palestinian-led actions. Firstly, Barghouti described a tendency that he has observed whereby "[a] few Israeli and international activists have a tendency to make the struggle Israel-centric, arguing that *ending the occupation is good for Israel, above everything else, as if that should be the overriding concern* [emphasis Barghouti's, MKL] for anyone seeking justice and human rights." Said Barghouti, "We totally reject that view."

> This is not a symmetric struggle where "both sides" are in conflict or progressives from "both sides" are partnering to better their mutual destiny. This is a case of occupation, colonization and apartheid by one side over the other. The struggle is, therefore one for freedom, justice and self determination for the oppressed, above everything else. Only by ending oppression can there be any substantial potential for coexistence based on full equality, not a master-slave type of coexistence, that many in the peace industry advocate.

Barghouti's second point focused on the concept of normalization in Palestinian-Israeli relations as defined by the BNC—the leadership of the Palestinian Call for BDS—and on the two conditions set out by the BNC "without [fulfilment of] which relations between a Palestinian side and an Israeli side would be regarded as constituting normalization"—based on the definition of normalization as "relations and projects that give the false impression of normalcy despite the continuation of colonial oppression."

> The two conditions are: 1- The Israeli side must recognize the internationally sanctioned and inalienable rights of the Palestinian

people, including the right to self determination; 2- The project itself, regardless what its nature may be (cultural, academic, environmental, medical, etc.) must have as its main objective resisting the occupation and/or apartheid. A joint artistic project, say, that ignores the oppressive colonial reality and calls for people from "both sides" to engage in some artistic endeavour, as if art were "above politics," is indeed cynically politicizing art and presenting a deceptive image of normal relations despite oppression.

Quite aside from the question whether or not a given project is worthwhile pursuing or whether Israeli involvement is welcome or even helpful in a given case, "A joint project that satisfies condition (1) above and condemns the occupation, on the other hand, and advocates for its end is not normalization," he concluded. "Nothing in the boycott criteria opposes such projects."

The Spread of Joint Struggle – and Persecution of Nonviolent Leadership

I asked Neta Golan whether she thought that the kind of joint project, partnership, cooperation—whatever we want to call it—that we see in Bi'in and similar places was spreading? Was it being adopted more broadly? Like fellow-ISMer Jamjoum, she answered in the affirmative.

The short answer is yes. The long answer is that it's at the stage right now of building the framework [for] a national proactive strategy as opposed to a localized reactive strategy (see www. popularstruggle.org). It's still in the preliminary stages but it's growing. Israel knows that it's growing, hence it's arresting the leadership that exists and trying to make it clear that organizing such demonstrations—what they call "incitement to disturb the public order"—is a crime punishable by over a year in jail. Popular Committee members and leading Palestinian activists from the Bil'in and Ni'ilin committees are being charged with incitement. Adib Abu Rahmeh has been in jail for almost a year now. What they want Abdullah Abu Rahmeh for is organizing demonstrations. But incitement is the common charge, and that's what the secret service is asking the kids [i.e., young boys picked up during night raids] when they interrogate them: "Who organizes the demonstrations?"

Like Adam Keller and Rev. Naim Ateek (and George N. Rishmawi, below), Golan regards this persecution of the nonviolent leadership as a "good sign." Said she, "It means we're on the right track, and they acknowledge it, and they're trying to stop us; and they don't have a chance."

Noncooperation

In Jan/Feb 2010, my questions regarding nonviolent noncooperation by Israelis inside Israel yielded, on the whole, disappointing responses. In response to the first (regarding noncooperation action currently taking place inside the borders of the state), most respondents could not think of much beyond what had already been on the agenda in 2007 and before; i.e., the admirable but small numbers of Israelis engaged in refusal to serve in the IDF (either selectively, in the occupied territories, or altogether until the occupation ends) and the even smaller numbers involved in the "civil-ization" activities of organizations such as New Profile and in the beginnings of support for BDS (Boycott from Within, of which Neta Golan is a part, for example), and, of course, the women of Machsom Watch and the challenge their actions present to the separation policy and to what Mikado described as the "wall mentality". The second question (as to what additional forms noncooperation by Israelis inside Israel might take and, especially, whether there might be attempts to somehow disrupt the Israeli occupation regime's mechanisms of oppression) understandably gave rise largely to responses like "I can't tell them what to do" on the part of Palestinians. Rev. Naim Ateek, for instance, expressed appreciation for "the good number of Israeli organizations that have emerged in the last few years," and the "great work" they're doing, but told me that he'd like to see more of them shifting their focus "to put pressure inside Israel itself, rather than only thinking about what they can do on the West Bank."

> I cannot tell them what to do, but I think if you bring them together—because of their knowledge of what can be done, what cannot be done; what can be effective, what cannot be effective—you can bring them together to work out a strategy that can be effective within Israel itself.

At this point, though, most Israeli activists tended not to have many ideas beyond some very small-scale actions. Jeff Halper, for example, cited as examples of Israeli noncooperation with the occupation regime (the still very small) Boycott from Within, as well as the very act of travelling to Ramallah, Bethlehem, Bil'in—illegal for Israeli citizens—"just those few things that might be the kernels of something." Said he, "You can't really say there's major movement today of noncooperation. I mean we're doing it de facto. We're not declaring that we're going; we're not making it a campaign, which I think at some point we should."

The idea of Israeli citizens making their "illegal" entrance to the West Bank into a publicly announced challenge of the law against this, "so [other] Israelis know about it," appealed to George N. Rishmawi, too.

> For example, if Israelis try to come here and challenge the Israeli military order not to come here, that's one thing that can be obvious; and when they come to Bil'in and other places, that's a clear challenge of the Israeli military order not to go to Palestinian areas. But it has to be public, also.

"Refusing to serve in the army is one important thing," added Rishmawi. And though, in general, he, like Rev. Ateek, felt that Israelis were the ones to consult about possible additional forms of noncooperation ("They know the structure and they know what they can do in this"), he went on to reflect on why, on the whole, this kind of activity is relatively rare.

> Unfortunately, everything that Palestinians are involved in has to do with security. For example, how Israelis would think about not enforcing a certain procedure or law: if it had to do with Palestinians, then they're risking a security issue, so they will be hesitant. They cannot violate it unless they would be really willing to go and do civil disobedience and to refuse to abide by certain laws.

Aliyah Strauss is a long-time participant in Machsom Watch—a group that clearly does challenge this law. Not only are they facilitating Palestinians' crossing of the "border" between Palestinian- and Israeli-administered areas, now, more often than not, the checkpoints they monitor are located wholly inside the West Bank (see especially pp. 107–109). Apart from that very important form of activism, the other noncooperation that came Strauss's mind was her personal participation in the boycott of products from the settlements. And Rachel Benshitrit told me:

> My own way of not cooperating is not cooperating with the separation policy. So I try to actively connect with Palestinians and cooperate and even do business together, trying to connect more between the people and trying to create opportunities for people to get to see each other on the same level, not as occupier and occupy-ee, or whatever the word is.

Benshitrit stressed the importance of "educating and changing the atmosphere in the street in all communities, to reintroduce hope that there is a partner [for peace] and that somehow there must be a way that we can trust each other in order to reach some kind of solution." And that, of course, is where the work of New Profile (the Movement for the Civil-ization of Israeli Society) comes in. As Adam Keller told me, aside from refusal to serve in the army and support for BDS, "I can't say that these things [i.e., acts of noncooperation by Israelis] are very, very deeply flourishing. They are there, though." Citing a recent speech by Nurit Peled-Elhanan (mother of Elik Elhanan of Combatants for Peace, qv) "where she was very much emphasizing this that the only thing—or the main thing—which we can do is to refuse [i.e., reject] the brainwashing which is being done to our children in the schools," Keller stated, "I think that the question of the education and struggling about the education is an important aspect of this noncooperation." New Profile's members, he added:

> are very much working on this aspect of trying to influence the curriculum in the schools, For example, opposing very much the tendency to have more and more officers going into the school and explaining to the children how wonderful it is to go to the army and what heroic things the soldiers are doing. Or opposing nationalistic elements in the school curriculum. . .

And, added Beate Zilversmidt, "There are quite a lot of individual parents who don't allow their children to take part in visiting events and locations which are identified with settlers."

George N. Rishmawi, too, affirmed the importance of New Profile's work, agreeing that this was a form of noncooperation which, although "it will take some time, prepares for a new peace loving generation step by step."

> New Profile is trying to eliminate the militarism in the Israeli society, and that's not an easy job. I think it's very important. But you see what they are now facing from the government: Every now and then they are summoned for questioning and things like that. Their office was raided. This shows that they are doing the right thing.

Another group that was often mentioned in this context was Israeli Anarchists Against the Wall. Michel Warschawski was effusive in his praise for them and for the other young members of what he refers to as the "Seattle generation", who form the vanguard of Israeli activists in Bil'in and other villages resisting the wall. When it came to the question of widespread Israeli noncooperation, however, Warschawski was surprisingly reticent. "There's no mass movement against the occupation at all, so clearly there's not a mass movement of nonviolent noncooperation," he told me, while applauding the originality of this younger generation of activists and dismissing his own "generation and a bit younger, the Lebanon War generation, shall we say" as "already ossified in a way, in our methods." As to noncooperation by Israelis inside the Green Line, he responded: "It may be that I don't talk about it out of ossification, out of the fact that my terms of reference were crystallized in the course of very many years." When I spoke to him again briefly in early August, he was no more optimistic, saying that he saw no essential change, "other than the fact that [the situation] keeps getting worse."

Amos Gvirtz, on the other hand, who had earlier enumerated a number of methods of personal noncooperation (see especially p. 58), now cited both the Gush Shalom boycott of settlement products and ICAHD's rebuilding of Palestinian homes demolished by the Israeli occupation forces and cultivation of land slated for confiscation (or already confiscated) for the construction of settlements.

> There's planting on confiscated land, and there's working on land in order that they won't confiscate it. Because, you know, they have a technique—that if a person hasn't worked his land for three years, [it becomes classified as fallow] they can take it. So then, by virtue

of your going and, say, gathering olives, you prove that he is indeed using his land, and so there is no basis for taking it [from the Palestinian farmer] on the grounds that he hasn't cultivated it.

Noncooperation by Israelis with oppressive occupation policies, yes, but again, not inside the state itself. So, what about the possibility of the creation of "traffic jams" by bureaucrats within the apparatus, I asked. "To refuse [to cooperate in those situations] could be a nice dream; I don't believe that it will happen," replied Gvirtz. Describing his observation of police actions demolishing Bedouin homes in Israel's Negev as "in my eyes, sometimes more severe than what's happening in the territories," he lamented:

> I haven't heard of a single instance of refusal. This drives me crazy. I don't understand it! It's beyond my comprehension: a man whose day's work [includes] demolishing people's homes on top of their heads. It astonishes me anew each time. So I don't expect anything from them anymore. They don't give a damn. There is a lot of racism in this, and it's always presented to them that [the Bedouin] are violating the law, and [the police] are enforcing the law. I don't expect anything of them. Nothing. They wouldn't have gone to work there if they had a conscience. No, I don't expect anything.

"Israelis not buying products produced by Israelis in the territories, not going there to serve [in the military]: to me, that's preventive nonviolence and that's very important," said Gvirtz. "But to expect that those whose work is [to enforce the oppressive policies] would refuse—if only! I don't see it."

Conclusion

BDS has seen unprecedented growth after the war of aggression on Gaza and the flotilla attack. People of conscience round the world seem to have crossed a threshold, resorting to pressure . . . to end Israel's impunity and western collusion in maintaining its status as a state above the law.

Omar Barghouti "Beseiging Israel's siege" in
The Guardian, 12 August 2010

Being persecuted is like being handed an official certificate stating, "On behalf of the government, I hereby confirm that your activities are regarded with alarm as a real threat and that we can no longer afford to ignore you."

Adam Keller (Gush Shalom)

Adam Keller—ever the optimistic voice—wrote in mid-August, 2010 (personal email correspondence), regarding the developments of the preceding six months or so:

1   Both BDS and the Free Gaza Movement have become much stronger and more prominent after the Gaza Flotilla raid in May. A conspicuous example is the Pixies cancelling a Tel Aviv perform-ance due to the raid, after earlier resisting all kinds of pressures. This got enormous media attention in Israel, because they have many Israeli fans and because it underlined the increasing isolation of Israel.

2   The Palestinian Authority quite belatedly but very energetically taking up a boycott campaign—of the settlements only. . . . This makes it a far more serious and threatening thing for Israeli industrialists based in the settlements, and some of them are in the process of moving out (or pretending to—we have hard work determining which is which).

3   The Sheikh Jarrah campaign is gaining momentum and the support of (relatively) mainstream people, much more than anything else. This is in my view because the injustice is so blatant. . . In Sheikh Jarrah . . . people wanted to live quietly in their homes and were evicted at night and settlers taking their place on the basis of a title deed showing that before 1948 it was Jewish owned land—while Palestinian title deeds from before 1948 are invalid in Israeli law—a blatant and obvious racist double standard. So, many people who would not come to Bil'in or the Gaza border do come every week to demos in Sheikh Jarrah.

4   Due to all the above, there is a growing counter-attack from the government and the extreme right. In a way, a compliment. After years when they said the Israeli Left is dead, now they find we are alive and kicking and a real threat. . . .

Keller isn't the only one to recently articulate a sense that the Israeli Left might in fact be again becoming a real force for the Israeli authorities to contend with. An article (by Gershom Gorenberg, 8 August 2010) entitled "The Rebirth of the Israeli Peace Movement" (www.prospect.org/cs/articles?article=the_rebirth_of_the_israeli_peace_movement) begins, "After being comatose for a decade, the Israeli left may be regaining consciousness—woken by the injustice of Sheikh Jarrah." And developments—some quite exciting—in the unfolding BDS campaign and more generally in nonviolent resistance can be followed on a number of websites that have been cited earlier, as well as on www.ramallahquakers.org/newsletter/newsletter.php. For me, though, one of the most heartening recent trends has to do with the apparent beginnings of growing non-cooperation with Israeli policies from inside the state.

When I mentioned to Omar Barghouti that I hadn't heard much in terms of growth in noncooperation inside Israel from my January interviewees, he wasn't surprised, explaining that "[a]t first, the colonial society bands together against perceived external threats of isolation that can lead to a pariah status."

> The prospects for the struggle from within to challenge the structures of colonialism and apartheid seem at that stage improbable if not altogether dreamy, . . . [But] when the struggle inside associated with the struggle from outside start producing sustainable pressure that considerably raise the price of oppression, this seemingly invincible or garrison-oriented unity starts to crack.

Thus,

> When Israel's oppression is met with a substantial resistance, . . . particularly in the form of sustainable BDS campaigns leading to comprehensive UN sanctions, as was the case in South Africa, the BDS movement inside Israel will gain considerable momentum and ordinary, apolitical Israelis will start re-thinking whether they want to continue "living by the sword," as Sharon put it, as a world pariah in a state that is shunned, loathed and widely boycotted by international civil society. Then the quest for normalcy, for a peaceful and economically viable life, under severe and daunting pressure from within and without, will lead many of those Israelis to withdraw their support to Israeli apartheid and occupation and, later, to even actively join movements that aim to end both. Collapse of the multi-tiered Israeli system of oppression then becomes a

matter of time. Again, we've seen it all before in South Africa, despite the obvious differences.

As Neta Golan stated, describing her involvement in Boycott from Within (Israelis supporting the Palestinian Call for BDS within Israeli society), "[C]onvincing the Israeli public to give up the benefits of oppression *is* impossible" and so "we must create a situation where oppression is no longer beneficial."

And indeed, there does seem to be change in the air

I was preparing to write what promised to be a rather disappointed and even pessimistic afterword, a spate of articles about "disobedient Israelis" hit the Israeli press and the Internet. In May, writer and long-time activist Ilana Hammerman "smuggled" three young Palestinian women into Israel and took them to the beach. She described this "day out" in an article in the daily *Ha'aretz* and now faces possible prosecution. In July, eleven more Israeli women joined Hammerman, and now, says an August 23 article by Nazareth-based writer, Jonathan Cook, inspired by Hammerman's example, "nearly 600 Israelis have signed up for a campaign of civil disobedience, vowing to risk jail to smuggle Palestinian women and children into Israel for a brief taste of life outside the occupied West Bank." One of them stated, "We want to overturn this immoral law that gives rights to Jews to move freely around while keeping Palestinians imprisoned in their towns and villages." And Hammerman is quoted as stating that "her immediate goal was to kick-start a discussion among Israelis about the legality and morality of Israel's laws and challenge the public's 'blind obedience' to authority." www.opednews.com/articles/Israelis-Risk-Jail-To-Smug-by-Jonathan-Cook-100823-397.html

And just a couple of days ago, as I struggled to meet my deadline for this afterword, my attention was called to a statement that "[m]ore than 150 Israeli academics say they will no longer lecture or work in Jewish settlements in the West Bank" (http://www.bbc.co.uk/news/world-middle-east-11141774). The academics, stated the BBC online article, had referred to "[l]egitimatisation and acceptance of the settler enterprise" as being critically damaging to chances of peace between Israel and the

Palestinians and said that their action was in support of the 53 Israeli actors, writers, and directors who, the previous week, had declared their refusal to perform at a new cultural centre soon slated to open in the settlement city of Ariel. The article goes on to state that yet another letter, this one from a number of well-known Israeli writers and artists, is expected soon.

Could this signal the beginning of the end "of the multi-tiered Israeli system of oppression" that Barghouti describes? Have the "Israeli Jews with a conscience" that Jonathan Kuttab referred to (p. 441) begun, at last, to "make a clean break with . . .. broader Israeli society" and to act upon their "more thoroughgoing critique of Israeli society," as he proposed back in 2007? Could this, indeed, be the beginning of the "movement of Israeli nonviolent action, especially multiple forms of noncooperation, inside Israel" that I allude to in my Conclusions as a necessary complement to joint struggle in the occupied territories in the achievement of "a just, viable, and enduring peace" in the region? As Adam Keller says at the close of his August 2010 note, "Well, we will see what comes next – it will certainly not be boring."

NOTES

1 A US organization much involved in bringing delegations to Gaza and campaigning for an end to the Israeli siege there.
2 An East Jerusalem neighbourhood where weekly joint demonstrations in support of the Palestinian inhabitants threatened with eviction by settlers claiming prior Jewish title to their homes have been going on since January 2010, growing both in size and breadth of participation.

WORKS CITED

Abunimah, Ali. 2006. *One Country: A Bold Proposal to End the Israeli-Palestinian Impasse.* New York: Metropolitan Books.

Abu-Nimer, Mohammed. 2006. "Nonviolent Action in Israel and Palestine: A Growing Force" in *Bridging the Divide: Peacebuilding in Israeli-Palestinian Conflict,* ed. Edy Kaufman, Walid Salem, and Juliette Verhoeven, pp. 135–169. Boulder and London: Lynne Reiner Publishers.

AFSC Middle East Resource series Middle East Task Force. 2005. "Palestinian Nonviolent Resistance to Occupation Since 1967." Part of series, *Faces of Hope: A Campaign Supporting Nonviolent Resistance and Refusal in Israel and Palestine.* As of November 2009, this and other *Faces of Hope* resources can be found at http://www.afsc.org/israel-palestine/ht/display/ContentDetails/i/18841/pid/13380#facesofhope, or go directly to this PDF at http://www.afsc.org/israelpalestine/ht/a/GetDocumentAction/id/44976.

Ateek, Naim Stifan. 1989. *Justice and Only Justice: a Palestinian Theology of Liberation.* Maryknoll, NY: Orbis Books.

———. 2008. *A Palestinian Christian Cry for Reconciliation.* Maryknoll, NY: Orbis Books.

Audeh, Ida. 2007. "A Village Mobilized: Lessons from Budrus" on *The Electronic Intifada* (http://electronicintifada.net/v2/article7005.shtml as of April 2009).

Awad, Mubarak E. 1984. "Nonviolent Resistance as a Strategy for the Occupied Territories" in *Journal of Palestine Studies,* Vol. 13, No. 4:22–36.

Barghouti, Omar. 2008. "Countering the Critics: The Boycott and Palestinian Groups" on *CounterPunch* (http://www.counterpunch.org/barghouti10212008.html as of November 2009).

Benvenisti, Meron. 2000. *Sacred Landscape: The Buried History of the Holy Land since 1948.* Trans. Maxine Kaufman-Lacusta. Berkeley: University of California Press.

Burnat, Iyad. 2009. "Support Bil'in's Struggle" on www.bilin-ffj.org (accessible at http://www.bilin-ffj.org/index.php?option=com_ content&task=view&id=212 &Itemid=1 as of November 2009).

Eldar, Akiva. 2005. "There's a system for turning Palestinian property into Israel's state land" in *Ha'aretz*, December 27, 2005 (© *Ha'aretz*, 2005 – accessible at http://www.haaretz.com/hasen/pages/ShArt. jhtml?itemNo=662729).

Flapan, Simha, ed. 1979. *When Enemies Dare to Talk: An Israeli-Palestinian Debate (5/6 September 1978) Organized by New Outlook*. London: Croom Helm.

Galtung, Johan. 1989. *Nonviolence and Israel/Palestine*. Honolulu: University of Hawaii Institute for Peace.

Giugni, Marco. 2004. *Social Protest and Policy Change: Ecology, Antinuclear and Peace Movements in Comparative Perspective*. Lanham, MD: Rowman and Littlefield.

Halper, Jeff. 2008. *An Israeli in Palestine: Resisting Dispossession, Redeeming Israel*. London: Pluto Press.

Hass, Amira. 1999. *Drinking the Sea at Gaza: Days and Nights in a Land under Siege*. Trans. Elana Wesley and Maxine Kaufman-Lacusta. New York: Metropolitan Books.

——. 2003. *Reporting from Ramallah: An Israeli Journalist in an Occupied Land*. Ed. and Trans. Rachel Leah Jones. Los Angeles, CA, and New York: Semiotext (e); Cambridge, MA: Distributed by MIT Press.

Izenberg, Dan. 2009. "New Bil'in barrier route reduces Modi'in Illit expansion" in *The Jerusalem Post*, April 26, 2009 (accessed from www.palsolidarity.org on May 5, 2009).

——. 2009a. "Bil'in villagers appeal Canadian court" in *Jerusalem Post*, October 21, 2009 (accessed from www.international.jpost.com on November 6, 2009).

Kaufman-Lacusta, Maxine. 2008. "The Potential for Joint Struggle: An Examination of Present and Future Participation by Israelis in Palestinian Non-Violent Resistance to the Occupation" in *Palestine-Israel Journal of Politics, Economics and Culture*, Vol. 15, No. 4/ Vol. 16, No. 1:137–145.

——. 2009. "Strategic Organizing for the Middle East: 'Thinking outside the box' with Jerusalem-based activist Jeff Halper." *Peace Magazine*, Vol. 25, No. 3:8–10. (Please read corrected version at http://archive. peacemagazine.org/v25n3p08.htm instead of the print version.)

Keller, Adam. 1987. *Terrible Days: Social Divisions and Political Paradoxes in Israel.* Amstelveen, Netherlands: Cypres.

Kennedy, R. Scott and Mubarak E. Awad. 1985. *Nonviolent Struggle in the Middle East: The Druze of Golan: A Case of Nonviolent Resistance* and *Nonviolent Resistance: A Strategy for Occupied Territories.* Philadelphia: New Society Publishers in cooperation with Resource Centre for Nonviolence, Santa Cruz, USA.

Keshet, Yehudit Kirstein. 2006. *Checkpoint Watch: Testimonies from Occupied Palestine.* London and New York: Zed Books.

Khatib, Mohammed. 2007. "Bil'in will continue to struggle against the wall and settlements" on *ZNet*, Sept. 20, 2007, www.zcommunications. org/znet/viewArticle/14425.

——. 2009. "Palestine's Peaceful Struggle" web exclusive available from *The Nation* at http://www.thenation.com/doc/20090928/khatib.

Kidron, Peretz, ed. 2004. *Refusenik: Israel's Soldiers of Conscience.* London: Zed Books.

King, Mary Elizabeth. 2007. *A Quiet Revolution: The First Palestinian Intifada and Nonviolent Resistance.* New York: Nation Books.

Lendman, Stephen. 2007. "Unrecognized" Palestinians," accessed April 2009 at www.icahd.org/eng/news.asp?menu=5&submenu=1&item=482.

Nunn, Maxine Kaufman. 1993. *Creative Resistance: Anecdotes of Nonviolent Action by Israeli-based Groups.* Jerusalem: Alternative Information Center (1993 English, 1994 Hebrew).

Pierce, Paul. 2005. "Faces of Hope: Palestinian Nonviolence Conferences Focus on Ending Israeli Occupation" in *Among Friends*, no. 98, p. 5 (PDF accessible at www.fwccemes.org/documents/files/among-friends-98.pdf).

Reinhart, Tanya. 2002. *Israel/Palestine: How to End the War of 1948.* New York: Seven Stories Press.

Roth, Martha. 2009. Interview with Jeff Halper. *Outlook: Canada's Progressive Jewish Magazine*, Vol. 47, No. 2:15–17.

Salem, Walid. 2005. "The Anti-Normalization Discourse in the Context of Israeli Palestinian Peace" in *Palestine-Israel Journal of Politics, Economics and Culture*, Vol. 12, No. 1:100–09.

——. 2005a. "Palestinian Non-Violence and Human Security from Below: Palestinian Citizens Protection Strategies in the First and Second Intifada." Quoted with permission. For published version, see *The Viability of Human Security from Concept to Practice*, ed.

Monica den Boer and Jaap de Wilde. Amsterdam: Free University of Amsterdam Press and University of Chicago Press.

Sandercock, Josie, Radhika Sainath, et al. 2004. *Peace Under Fire: Israel/Palestine and the International Solidarity Movement*. London and New York: Verso.

Sharp, Gene. 1973. *The Politics of Nonviolent Action* (3 volumes). Boston: Porter Sargent.

——. 1989. "The Intifada and Nonviolent Struggle" in *The Journal of Palestine Studies*, Vol. 19, No. 1:3–13, as reproduced in the program of the Celebrating Nonviolent Resistance Conference, Bethlehem, December 27–30, 2005.

——. 1993/2002. *From Dictatorship to Democracy: A Conceptual Framework for Liberation*. Boston: The Albert Einstein Institution (2002) [first U.S. edition of Bangkok: Committee for the Restoration of Democracy in Burma (1993)].

Shulman, David. 2007. *Dark Hope: Working for Peace in Israel and Palestine*. Chicago: University of Chicago Press.

Stohlman, Nancy and Laurieann Aladin, eds. 2003. *Live from Palestine: International and Palestinian Direct Action Against the Israeli Occupation*. Cambridge, MA: South End Press.

Warschawski, Michel. 2005. *On the Border*. Trans. Levi Laub. Cambridge, MA: South End Press.

——. 2006. "Some Reflections on the Bil'in Generation" in *News from Within*, Vol. XXII, No. 3 (accessible at www.alternativenews.org).

Zaru, Jean. 2008. *Occupied with Nonviolence: A Palestinian Women Speaks*. Minneapolis: Fortress Press.

USEFUL WEBSITES

Albert Einstein Institution – www.aeinstein.org

Alternative Information Center (AIC Jerusalem / Beit Sahour) – www. alternativenews.org

Alternative Tourism Group – www.patg.org

al-Watan Center for Civic Education, Conflict Resolution, and Non-violence (Hebron) – www.alwatan.org

Anarchists Against the Wall (AATW) – www.awalls.org (includes extensive background on joint struggle, particularly as directed against the wall)

Applied Research Institute – Jerusalem (ARIJ, located in Bethlehem) – www.arij.org

Arab Educational Institute – Bethlehem (AEI) – www.aeicenter.org

Association for Civil Rights in Israel (ACRI) – www.acri.org.il

BADIL – Resource Center for Palestinian Residency and Refugee Rights – www.badil.org

Bat Shalom (Israeli component of the Jerusalem Link) – www. batshalom.org

Bereaved Families' Forum (aka Parents Circle) – www.theparentscircle.com

Bil'in – www.bilin-ffj.org (official website of Friends of Freedom and Justice–Bil'in) and www.bilin-village.org (includes contact information for both the village and Israeli and international organizations involved in joint struggle in Bil'in)

B'tselem – The Israeli Information Center for Human Rights in the Occupied Territories – www.btselem.org

Bustan Sustainable Community Action for Land and People (formerly Bustan l'Shalom/l'Salaam) – www.bustan.org

Checkpoint Watch – see Machsom Watch

Christian Peacemaker Teams (CPT) – www.cpt.org

Coalition of Women for [a Just] Peace – www.coalitionofwomen.org (includes links to its 10 constituent organizations, including Women in Black, New Profile, and Machsom Watch). www.whoprofits.org is the Coalition's listing of companies—both Israeli and other—that profit from the occupation.

Combatants for Peace – www.combatantsforpeace.org
Compassionate Listening – www.compassionatelistening.org
Ecumenical Accompaniment Programme in Palestine and Israel (EAPPI)
    – www.EAPPI.org/en
Electronic Intifada – http://electronicintifada.net
Faculty for Israeli-Palestinian Peace (FFIPP) – www.ffipp.org
Free Gaza Movement – http://freegaza.org/
Friends of Freedom and Justice–Bil'in – www.bilin-ffj.org (see also Bil'in)
Gaza Community Mental Health Program (GCMHP) – www.gcmhp.net
Grassroots Palestinian Anti-Apartheid Wall Campaign – www.
    stopthewall.org
Gush Shalom – www.gush-shalom.org
Ha'aretz newspaper – www.haaretz.com ("home" to a number of
    progressive journalists, including Amira Hass, Gid'on Levi, Meron
    Benvenisti, Akiva Eldar, Meron Rappaport...)
HaMoked: Center for the Defence of the Individual, East Jerusalem –
    www.hamoked.org.il
Holy Land Trust (HLT) – www.holylandtrust.org
Hope Flowers School – www.hopeflowersschool.org
Ibdaa Cultural Center (Dheisheh Refugee Camp) – www.ibdaa194.org
International Fellowship of Reconciliation (IFOR) – www.ifor.org
International Middle East Media Center (IMEMC) – www.imemc.org
    (a project of PCR), IMEMC is a joint initiative of Palestinian
    and international journalists, providing non-partisan reporting in
    English and Spanish (and Arabic via PNN, qv), print and audio, its
    cooperation with PNN providing more comprehensive coverage
    for both services. Includes extensive coverage of nonviolent actions.
International Solidarity Movement (ISM) – www.palsolidarity.org
International Women's Peace Service (IWPS) – www.iwps-pal.org
Israeli Committee Against House Demolitions (ICAHD) – www.icahd.org
Jahalin Bedouin info site – www.jahalin.net
Jerusalem Center for Social and Economic Rights (JCSER) – www.jcser.org
Jerusalem Center for Women (Palestinian component of the Jerusalem
    Link) – www.j-c-w.org
JUSTVISION: Supporting Israeli and Palestinian non-violent civic
    peace builders through media and education – www.Justvision.org
Library on Wheels for Nonviolence and Peace (LOWNP) – www.
    lownp.com

Machsom Watch – www.machsomwatch.org

MIFTAH – The Palestinian Initiative for the Promotion of Global Dialogue and Democracy – www.miftah.org

New Profile – Movement for the Civil-ization of Israeli Society – www.newprofile.org

Nonviolence International – www.nonviolenceinternational.net

Nonviolent Communication – www.cnvc.org

Ometz LeSarev (Courage to Refuse) – www.seruv.org.il

Occupation Magazine – News, summaries and commentary by people opposing the occupation – www.kibush.co.il (sources include *The Other Israel, IMEMC, Gush Shalom, Counterpunch,* inter alia, as well as journalists from a wide range of Israeli, Palestinian, and international publications)

Palestine-Israel Journal of Politics, Economics and Culture – www.pij.org

Palestine Monitor – www.palestinemonitor.org. Nonviolence-related materials (as of November 2009) include a feature on Israeli conscientious objectors and a short video about Bil'in nonviolent activist and photographer, Rani Burnat (son of Wajee Burnat), crippled by a bullet in the neck during a nonviolent demonstration in 2000.

Palestine News Network (PNN) – www.pnn.ps. English, French, and Arabic news. Coverage by independent Palestinian journalists, PNN prominently features a link to PRESSENZA, an international press agency specializing in news about Peace and Nonviolence.

Palestinian Agricultural Relief Committee (PARC) – www.pal-arc.org

Palestinian Center for Policy and Survey Research – www.pcpsr.org

Palestinian Center for Rapprochement between People (PCR) – www.pcr.ps

Palestinian Center for the Study of Nonviolence (PCSN) – see Holy Land Trust

Palestinian Environmental NGOs Network Friends of the Earth— Palestine (PENGON) – www.pengon.org (includes a Stop the Wall campaign)

Palestinian Medical Relief Society (PMRS) – www. pmrs.ps

Palestinian Non-Governmental Organizations' Network (PNGO) – www.pngo.net

Panorama, the Palestinian Center for the Dissemination of Democracy & Community Development – www.panoramacenter.org

Physicians for Human Rights (PHR-Israel) – www.phr.org.il

Popular Struggle Coordination Committee – www.popularstruggle.org

Public Committee Against Torture in Israel (PCATI) – www.stoptorture.org.il

Rabbis for Human Rights (RHR) – www.rhr.israel.net

Rachel Corrie Foundation – rachelcorriefoundation.org

Sabeel Ecumenical Liberation Theology Center – www.sabeel.org (with links to international Friends of… groups)

Seeds of Peace – www.seedsofpeace.org

Siraj Center for Holy Land Studies – www.sirajcenter.org

Ta'ayush (Palestinian- and Jewish-Israelis opposing occupation and racism) – www.taayush.org

The Other Israel – http://otherisrael.home.igc.org. Also http://toibillboard.info and http://adam-keller2.blogspot.com ("Crazy Country," Adam Keller's recently-launched personal blog)

Union of Palestinian Medical Relief Committees (now Palestinian Medical Relief Society – PMRS) – www.pmrs.ps

Wi'am Palestinian Conflict Resolution Center – www.alaslah.org

Windows–Channels for Communication – www.win-peace.org (aka Windows for Peace, *Shababik, Halonot*). Joint organization of Jews and Palestinians from Israel and Palestinians from the occupied territories, working mainly through media-related educational programs.

Women in Black – see Coalition of Women for [a Just] Peace

Yesh Gvul (Israeli refusenik organization) – www.yeshgvul.org

Zochrot (Israeli group promoting awareness of the *Nakba*) – www.nakbainhebrew.org and www.zochrot.org

INDEX

Abbas, Ziad, 17–18, 282, 371–2

Aboud. *See under* nonviolent resistance to the wall

Abu Dis, 140, 207, 213–14, 235

Abu-Heikal, Feryal (Tel Rumeida, Hebron), 225, 238n11

Abu Keshek, Saif
  difficulty of anticipating the effects of total separation, 342
  do-it-yourself documentation to supplement media, 291–2, 410
  equal importance of Israeli participation in anti-occupation actions and inside Israel, 171
  importance of basing strategy on experience, 347, 355
  importance of international participation in nonviolent resistance, 28, 341
  mass participation by local people as an important trend, 329–30
  motivation for joining the ISM, 28
  need to globalize Palestinian nonviolence/world-wide networking, 348, 355
  optimism regarding the future of the nonviolent movement in Palestine, 342
  relative ease of suppressing the Second Intifada by force, 298–9
  similarity of Israeli and Palestinian cultures and "healthful dynamic" between them, 182

Abu Muferreh, S'leiman (T'qu'a village), 81, 251, 290, 363–4

Abu-Nimer, Mohammed
  factors within Palestinian society impeding nonviolence, 271–2
  importance of appreciating and publicizing work of local nonviolent leaders, 349–50, 355
  important trends in Palestinian nonviolence, 330–1
  need to tackle violence in own society, 351, 355

program for a more effective and inclusive nonviolent movement, 350–1, 355
  spread of Palestinian nonviolent action 2003–2005, 340

Abu Rahmeh, Bassem, 230, 236, 237n11, 239n22

Abu-Sitta, Salman, 379n2

Abu Zayyad, Ziad, 159

Action Committee for the Jahalin Tribe (ACJT), 138–40, 185
  See also Jahalin *under* Bedouin; Mazar'a, S'leiman; Milgrom, Rabbi Jeremy

active nonviolence, 83, 88, 106, 328, 332
  See also activism, nonviolent; nonviolence; nonviolent resistance; Palestinian nonviolence; *nonviolent activism of individual organizations/locations*

activism, nonviolent
  anti-wall (*see* nonviolent resistance to the wall)
  as empowering to participants, 425–6, 429
  First-Intifada-era (*see under* Intifada, First; Palestinian nonviolence; *names of individual groups*)
  by Jews inside Israel, 446
  joint (*see* joint activism)
  and strategic campaigning, 392–3
  present day Israeli, persistence of in Bil'in, 168

activists/activist groups
  deciding to become, 20–7
  independent (*see* Manor, Ya'akov; Milgrom, Rabbi Jeremy; Tamimi, Manar)
  international, as educating home constituencies about Palestinian nonviolence, 344
  Israeli
    anti-Zionist working with Palestinians and internationals, 389
    bringing home message of Palestinian nonviolence, 144
    influencing policy, 391
    noncooperation by with Israeli policies as a way of strengthening joint struggle, 443, 444–6

as occupiers, 175, 397
role of within Israeli society, 153, 166,
170, 186, 373, 398, 443
administrative detention, 64n4, 195, 199, 428
of Beit Sahour tax strikers, 194, 198–9
of Committee Against the Iron Fist activists,
48s
of Jad Isaac, 44
of Muhammad Jaradat, 38n8
affinity groups, 426
agents provocateurs, 190n19, 238n16, 329
Aimour, Sabrin, 10
Al-Aqsa brigade, 15
Al-Aqsa Intifada. *See* Intifada, Second
Alternative Information Center (AIC), 11, 13,
45, 61, 77, 139
appreciation of, 161, 282
American Friends Service Committee (AFSC)
partnership with HLT and Panorama, 89,
338, 341
QIARs, Kathy Kamphoefner and Paul
Pierce as, 167, 198n17
American Independence Park, 372
Amit, Zalman, account of a Bil'in
demonstration, 221–2
Anarchists Against the Wall, Israeli, 71, 284,
323, 439
Bil'in, presence in, 168, 205, 206, 214,
219, 226, 286
as visible Israeli presence, 206
See also Pollak, Yonatan; Snitz, Kobi
Andoni, Ghassan, 102, 152, 379, 383–9, 439
his adoption of nonviolence, 14
armed struggle, the rise of in the Palestinian
diaspora in the mid-sixties, 383–4
on building and broadening Palestinian
civil-based resistance, 103, 351–2
dialogue and joint activism, role of in, 198
commitment of ISM and PCR to nonviolent
"positive engagement" in conflict, 74,
353, 355
on communication with Israelis and
internationals, 15
differing roles of Palestinian and Israeli
movements, 173, 279
"generational" character of Palestinian
resistance, 387–8
historical background to Palestinian
nonviolence, introduction, 383
ISM and PCR policy re Israeli participation,
173

ISM as saving lives of both Palestinians and
Israelis, 74
on joint activism, emergence of widespread
post-2000, 386
nature of peacemaking, 353, 355
on "offensive nonviolent engagement"
centred on NVDA, 352–4, 355
prevalence of nonviolent, civil-based
resistance in the occupied territories,
pre-First Intifada period, 384–5
questions regarding marginalization of
nonviolent organizations, 246
quoted by Halper, 399, 400, 412
on role of international pressure, 103
solidarity activists need to fully engage in
the struggle, 103, 286
on the uniqueness of the Palestinian
struggle, 386–7
annexation, 64n1, 134, 233, 280
Annexation Wall, 64n1
anti-occupation movement, need for active
Israeli, 103, 173, 279, 285, 389, 399,
412
"anti-peace law," 63
Ansar III. *See* Ketziot prison camp
apathy, Israeli, 280, 281
Applied Research Institute–Jerusalem
(ARIJ – Bethlehem), 43, 73, 94–95
apartheid
Israeli, 224, 232, 291, 305, 360, 377, 411,
447
South African, 280, 387, 408, 448
wall, 64, 91, 138, 187, 192, 202, 203, 398
(*see also* Annexation Wall; separation/
security barrier; separation wall; wall)
Arab Educational Institute (AEI), 254
Arab unity, 383
Arabasi, Sheikh Tayseer, 182
Arafat, Yasser, 128, 265, 324
blamed for Second Intifada, 104, 406
demonization of, 416
international and Israeli protective presence
with in besieged *Muqata'a*, 184, 301,
428
armed struggle/armed resistance by
Palestinians, 10, 61, 325, 407
as "article of faith," 420
glamour of reduced by PA misuse of its
weapons, 420
in "mixture of activities" (along with
nonviolence), 56, 254

distinction between legitimate and
illegitimate violence, 262
effectiveness of refusal, 317
extent of support for refusal movement in
Israel, 260–1
importance of Yesh Gvul as a "mutual
support" network for refusers, 317
impracticality of nonviolence for
Palestinians, 75
personal motivations for joining Yesh Gvul,
317
pitfalls of ideology, 117
refusal as the most effective way to campaign
against the occupation, 317, 332
political significance of Israeli refusal for
Palestinians, 319
story of personal nonviolence, 312
Yesh Gvul and "selective" refusal, 75, 394
King, Martin Luther, 52, 93, 347, 371, 372,
407
pressure to find a Palestinian, 349, 355
and primacy of justice, 433
studied in Bil'in, 230
and Voting Rights Law of 1964, 410
Knaz, Hannah, 113, 340
Knesset members, Israeli, 20, 48, 110, 144,
214, 301, 315, 361
Kollek, Teddy, 41
Kuttab, Jonathan, 379
armed struggle
negative consequences for Palestinians of,
418–19
reduction in Second Intifada prevalence
of post-9/11, 419–20
emergence of outspokenly nonviolent
village resistance, 328–9
impossibility of "out-violencing" the
Israelis, 421
increasing Palestinian use of the language of
nonviolence, 328
nonviolence as greatest threat to the
occupation, 346
nonviolence as "more effective and suitable
for [Palestinian] resistance," 421
Palestinian faith in ultimate international
recognition of the rightness of their
cause, 416
Palestinian nonviolence historically
overshadowed by rhetoric of armed
struggle, 415, 416–17
prediction of increasing Israeli efforts to

provoke Palestinians to violence, 346
on realization of counterproductiveness of
armed struggle in Second Intifada,
418–19
silence/paralysis of "Israeli Jews with a
conscience" on uncomfortable issues,
442
sumud as a form of nonviolent resistance,
416
value of active nonviolence as first widely
appreciated by the Palestinians during
the First Intifada, 417–18
on working for peace with integrity:
requirements for "Israeli Jews with a
conscience," 441–2

Labour Party, 125, 306
land
as sacred, 388
claims to the, 262, 386
land, confiscation of Palestinian
in Bil'in, 210, 212, 213, 223
figures and dates, 229
in Budrus, 208
continuing, 254, 305, 439
increased during Oslo period, 8, 264
inside Jerusalem, 40
in Mas'ha, 203
obliterating the Green Line, 376
Protests against, 97
in Budrus saved 95% of land slated for
confiscation, 209
(*see also under* Bil'in)
sumud and, 416
Law of Return, Israeli, 27, 38n14
leadership
Awad, Mubarak—involvement of with First
Intifada, 307
defined (Halper), 411–12
delegitimization of in nonviolent movement,
412
lack of strong Palestinian national, 273,
292 (*see also under* Palestinian
Authority)
lack of vision of Palestinian national, 266
lack of will of Israeli, 264
need for credible, for nonviolence, 266,
274, 348–9, 355
need to develop new models of, 412
Palestinian, development of local for

in Deir Qaddis, 439
in Jayyous, 55, 386
    first to resist on a large scale, 203, 235,
        237n3
    international solidarity, 386
in el-Khader, 237n3, 439–41
in Kharbata, 439
in Ma'asarah, 439
in Mas'ha, 55, 238n11, 439
    and AATW, 206
    background, 203
    joint peace camp, 203–4, 235, 237n3
in Ni'ilin, 237, 439, 237n3
praised by Malki, 331
praised by Warschawski, 192
in Tel al-Rumeida, 386
Tulkarm women's demonstration, 179–81
in al-Walajah, 386
nonviolent struggle, 391
    allows possibility of joint action, 59
    conditions for success of, 52–5
    faith-based, 5
    less widespread during Al-Aqsa Intifada, 73
    Palestinian as model for other oppressed
        people, 414
    practitioners of, changes attitude towards,
        60, 70
nonviolence training
    Awad, Sami on, 89
    in Beit Sahour attended by PPU activists,
        99
    European/North American style, attempt to
        introduce, 139
    Jubran on, 15, 93–4
    by Kamphoefner abroad, 338
    by PCR and ISM, 15
    by PINV, 133
    political and social issues dealt with during,
        94
    Starhawk and, 423, 431
    Svirsky participation in training for
        nonviolence trainers, 190n22
normalization, 91
    as "peace under occupation," 440
    dangers of, 155, 186, 399
    definition and discussion of, 153–5, 187n1
    joint struggle and, 155, 163, 440–1
    Palestinian Authority directive on, 159,
        189n13
    PNGO (The Palestinian Non-
        Governmental Organizations

Network) ban on, 101, 135, 157,
    188–9n12, 399–400
Arraf on, 155
and PCR, 101, 156
strategies for avoiding normalization in
    joint activism, 157–63, 164, 435
"being there," 401
challenging the occupation, jointly,
    155–7, 158, 160
challenging to Israel's separation policy,
    162–3
Israeli participants gain understanding
    of situation, making sure that,
    157–8
moving from dialogue to direct action,
    155, 156
Palestinian leadership in joint endeavours/
    supporting role of Israelis, 399, 435
prioritizing the struggle against the
    occupation, 163, 435
protecting the shared environment: a
    "needs-driven [joint] project" 157
sensitivity to disparities of power, 435
sharing the risks with Palestinians as
    "partners in struggle," 163
spreading the word that Palestinians
    and Israelis really can live together,
    importance of, 158–9
Nusseibeh, Sari, 48

objectivity, 352
observers, European at Rafah crossing, 268
occupation, 20, 159, 305, 321, 389
    Checkpoint Watch confronting, 109
    dependence on army of occupation, 317
    dependence on support of Israeli society,
        320
    end to
        calls for, 189n12, 114, 127, 324, 357,
            363, 364
        not enough, 376–7, 378
    joint struggle as the only way to destroy,
        162
    militaristic and racist roots of, 153, 443
    nonviolence as greatest threat to, 346
    nonviolent resistance to (see also civil
        disobedience; civil resistance;
        demonstrations/protests/marches;
        ISM; nonviolence; nonviolent
        noncooperation; nonviolent resistance

power differential between Palestinian and
Israeli activists: considerations of in
joint activism
avoiding reproduction/replication of the
oppressive relationship, 165–8, 176
overview, 165–6, 186–7, 397
clear communication, importance of in
context of, 178–9
cultural styles and
differences in, 397
impact of, 166
power imbalance in joint activism, redressing
the, 171–7
importance of Palestinian leadership, 169,
173–4
Israelis are junior partners, 175–7
important to consult with local communities
re inclusion of Israelis, 173–4
Israelis and internationals cannot assume
welcome, 173, 174
must await invitation, 177
Palestinians are hosts and must be
recognized as such, 172–3, 174–5
recognize and respect Palestinians'
vulnerability to consequences, 176,
177
power, responsible use of, 225, 279
powerlessness, sense of as most traumatizing
effect of violence, 429
pragmatic nonviolence, 51–57, 64, 93, 125
pressure on Israeli occupation authorities
from within the state, 449 (see also
nonviolent noncooperation and under
activists/activist groups: Israeli)
international (see international pressure)
principled nonviolence. See Gandhian
nonviolence
prison, education in, 426. See also under
education
prisoners, Palestinian ex-
as nonviolent activists (see also Andoni,
Ghassan; Jaradat, Muhammad; Jedda,
Ali; Salame, Wael; Souf, Nawaf)
as potential members of Combatants for
Peace, 326
Project Hope (Nablus), 250
See also a-Tout, Samah
protective presence
Internationals as, 59, 428, 432 (see also
CPT; EAPPI; ISM; IWPS; third
parties)

Israelis as, 59 (see also under Golan, Neta;
ICAHD; Israeli participation/presence,
benefits of; olive harvest; Rabbis for
Human Rights)
training to be, 139
Profile 21. See Khenin, Ido
Public Committee Against Torture in Israel
(PCATI), 302

Qalandiya checkpoint, 184, 313
Qalqilya, "Mohammed from…" (ISM
activist), 363
Quaker International Affairs Representatives,
167, 190n17
American Friends Service Committee
(AFSC) partnership with HLT and
Panorama, 340
Quakers, 166
and "preventive nonviolence," 58
See also Kamphoefner, Cathy; Pierce, Paul;
Zaru, Jean
Quebec Superior Court, Bil'in suit and

Rabbis for Human Rights (RHR), 30, 85,
127, 146, 156, 161, 284
basic mandates and activities of, 110–12
and the Jahalin, 140, 185
junior partner role in actions in the occupied territories, acceptance of, 176–7
1993 Speaker of the Knesset's Prize, 249
and olive harvest, 111, 249, 333n2
al-Watan activities, participation in 98
See also Ascherman, Rabbi Arik
Rabin, Yitzhak, 128, 261
assassination of, 264, 294n1, 385
breaking-bones policy, 113
forced to disclose occupied territories
budget, 195–6
racism
international—valuing internationals' lives
above Palestinians', 106
Israeli, 435, 436, 442
duty of Israeli activists to contend
with/dismantle, 153, 166, 170, 186,
373, 442
and roots of occupation in militarism,
153, 443
Ta'ayush challenging inside the state, 120
towards Mizrahi ("Oriental") Jews, 123

violence
  abhorrence/rejection of, 36, 324, 393
  dominance of in the region, 376
  inherent of oppressive system: dramatization
      of by nonviolent direct action campaign,
      425
  futility of mutual, 253, 270, 324
  Israeli (*see* Israeli violence *and under* army,
      Israeli; settlers, Israeli; soldiers, Israeli)
  of Israeli society vs. classic Jewish attitudes,
      30
  of the occupation, 77, 81, 268
  of the oppressed side, hypocrisy of
      international peace and justice
      community towards, 352–3, 355
  of the Second Intifada (*see* Malki, Riad;
      Salem, Walid)
  Palestinian (*see* Palestinian use of violence;
      suicide bombings)
vision
  for future (*see also* confederation/federation;
      one-state solution; two-state solution)
    non-political qualities, 361–2, 377–8
    overview and stats, 361–2, 377
  need for, 343
  PA lack of, 266, 440

Wadi Naar checkpoint, 109
wall, the, 7, 325, 439
  built to impose political realities, 343
  as catalyst for joint activism, 202
  cutting into West Bank, 386
  defined, 64n1
  and Israel's security, 359
  and the law (*see* victories, legal [of
      nonviolent action])
  nonviolent resistance to the (*see* nonviolent
      resistance to the wall)
  obliterating the Green Line, 376
  as political border for expansion, 359
  position of Coalition of Women for Peace
      on, 115
  and settlement construction, 222
  success in getting it onto the international
      agenda, 295
  tours of the, 205, 237n8
  See also Annexation Wall; apartheid wall;
      separation/security barrier; separation
      wall *and under* West Bank
war
  crimes/criminals, 295, 314, 322, 324–5

in Lebanon (*see under* Lebanon)
  of 1948, 383
  of 1967, 383
  on terror, myth of, 159
Warschawski, Michel (Mikado), 64, 77, 139
  attitude towards nonviolence, 61–2, 227
  Committee Against the Iron Fist, 45–9,
      404–5
  condemnation of killing of civilians, 61
  First Intifada as example of mass popular
      struggle, 62
  importance of international participation,
      227
  importance of mass rather than avant-garde
      activism, 61
  learning from Bil'in, 227
  need for strategy in Bil'in struggle, 228
  participation in nonviolent initiatives by,
      61
  praise for Bil'in-style joint activism, 192,
      226–7
  supporting role of Israeli activists, 184, 186,
      404
al-Watan Center for Civic Education, Conflict
      Resolution and Nonviolence
      (Hebron), 11, 98–9, 394
  activities frustrated by Israeli authorities,
      98, 99, 147
  combating mutual stereotypes, 257
  connections with Israeli and U.S.
      nonviolence organizations, 98
  conservatism of local community, 98, 256,
      257
  harassment of participants, 98, 258
  participation in programs, 258
  See also Hashlamoun, Nayef
water
  Israeli control of, 449
  joint work in managing, 94
  lack of drinkable in Gaza, 268
  scarcity of, 182–3, 376, 378
  settlers breaking pipes, 24
Weitzman, Ezer, 129n6
Wesley, Elana, 205, 225–6, 340
West Bank, 125, 153, 331, 367, 430
  internal closure policy in, 107–9, 128n4
  Israeli activism in, 158, 168, 171
  number of settlers in, 268
  olive harvest in, 301
  reoccupation of towns and cities of in
      2002, 108